Limits of
Adjustment
in Africa

Titles on Development & Economics

Adjusting Privatization
Case Studies from Developing Countries
CHRISTOPHER ADAM, WILLIAM CAVENDISH & PERCY S. MISTRY

*The Impact of Structural Adjustment
on the Population of Africa*
ADERANTI ADEPOJU (ED.)

Structural Adjustment & Agriculture
Theory & Practice in Africa & Latin America
SIMON COMMANDER (ED.)

Structural Adjustment & the African Farmer
ALEX DUNCAN & JOHN HOWELL (EDS)

Structural Adjustment & Beyond in Sub-Saharan Africa
Research & Policy Issues
ROLPH VAN DER HOEVEN & FRED VAN DER KRAAIJ (EDS)

Negotiating Structural Adjustment in Africa
WILLEM VAN DER GEEST (ED.)

Limits of Adjustment in Africa
The Effects of Economic Liberalization, 1986-94
POUL ENGBERG-PEDERSEN, PETER GIBBON,
PHIL RAIKES & LARS UDSHOLT (EDS)

Service Provision Under Stress in East Africa
JOSEPH SEMBOJA & OLE THERKILDSEN (EDS)

Debt-Conversion Schemes in Africa
Lessons from the Experience of Developing Countries
AFRICAN CENTRE FOR MONETARY STUDIES

Instruments of Economic Policy in Africa
AFRICAN CENTRE FOR MONETARY STUDIES

Limits of Adjustment in Africa

THE EFFECTS OF ECONOMIC LIBERALIZATION, 1986-94

EDITED BY
POUL ENGBERG-PEDERSEN
PETER GIBBON • PHIL RAIKES
& LARS UDSHOLT

Centre for Development Research
Copenhagen
in association with
JAMES CURREY
Oxford
HEINEMANN
Portsmouth (N.H.)

Centre for Development Research
Gammel Kongevej 5
DK-1610 Copenhagen V
Denmark

in association with

James Currey Ltd
73 Botley Road
Oxford OX2 0BS
England

Heinemann;
A Division of Reed Publishing (USA) Inc
361 Hanover Street, Portsmouth
New Hampshire 03801-3912
USA

1 2 3 4 5 00 99 98 97 96

British Library Cataloguing in Publication Data
Limits of adjustment in Africa:
the effects of economic liberalization, 1986-94
1. Structural adjustment (Economic policy) – Africa
2. Africa – Economic policy
I. Engberg-Pedersen, Poul
338.9'6

ISBN 0–85255–152–5 Paper (James Currey)
ISBN 0–85255–153–3 Cloth (James Currey)

**Library in Congress Cataloging-in -Publication Data
applied for**

ISBN 0–435–07403–2 Cloth (Heinemann)

Typeset in Times by the Centre for Development Research, Copenhagen
Printed in Great Britain by Villiers Publications, London N3

Contents

Preface

Structural adjustment consists of reforms aimed at stabilizing developing countries' external and internal balances and promoting their growth by devaluation, producer price increases, trade liberalization, privatization and supporting institutional changes. Its adoption has usually (but not always) occurred in a context of economic crisis and on the basis of promises of resources from donors, led by the two foremost international financial institutions, the International Monetary Fund and the World Bank. The latter are also largely responsible for the design of adjustment programmes.

Over the last decade well over half the countries in Sub-Saharan Africa have embarked upon such reform programmes, which were heralded with grand claims to promote 'accelerated' (1981) or 'sustainable' (1989) development. But little of the kind has occurred. Only a few countries have returned to even the low growth path of the 1960s and 1970s. Instead there has been a general contraction in per capita growth. There is even little evidence of stabilization in the main pre-adjustment economic imbalances. The social picture today is also hardly more encouraging than it was at the outset of the current period of policy reform. While the proportion of poor people has perhaps not increased in those countries where there has been per capita economic growth, it has certainly increased on the continent as a whole. There is fairly strong evidence that the adjustment period has everywhere seen a further deterioration in the position of the worst-off groups - amongst whom women are disproportionately represented. Meanwhile, because population has increased at levels ahead of growth there has been increasing pressure on resources of all kinds, from land and water to state-provided services and human labour. As these resources become spread more thinly, people turn to new ones of lower quality - poorer land, cheaper inputs, less well-capitalized informal economic activities, child labour, lower quality medicines, and so on. The result is a significantly increased level of overall vulnerability to recession, famine and disease.

Many factors are responsible for this, from deepening world-wide economic recession and adverse international terms of trade to civil strife and AIDS. According to some critics of adjustment, not only have the reform programmes had meagre results, but they have themselves contributed to the growing crisis.

It was in this context that in March 1994, when debating the country's new *Strategy for Danish Development Policy towards the Year 2000*, the Danish Parliament encouraged the Government to launch an independent analysis of the effects of structural adjustment programmes in Africa. In September 1994 the Ministries of Foreign and Economic Affairs requested the Centre for Development Research, Copenhagen, to carry out this study, on the basis of a thorough review of adjustment outcomes across a number of sectors in Sub-Saharan Africa generally and in five countries (Burkina Faso, Ghana, Tanzania, Uganda and Zimbabwe) in particular. The current volume comprises the outcome of these studies.

The studies presented here provide a comprehensive overview of developments across all the main economic and social sectors in the countries examined and in Sub-Saharan Africa more generally. In particular, attention is focused on macroeconomic changes, developments in agriculture, industry, education and health, and on cross-cutting issues such as informal activities, aid relations, governance, public sector reform, gender, environment and poverty. The studies have been carried out on the basis of access to the broadest possible array of published and unpublished materials. The latter include reports and evaluations by the international financial institutions and the principal bilateral donors, of normally restricted circulation. This has made it possible for the analyses presented not only to be unusually comprehensive, but also for them to take account of the most recent trends.

The main conclusions of the study are drawn together and presented in the first, multiply authored contribution. This contribution is written in a more popular style than the others, as a direct intervention in the Danish development debate. As a result, it also comes minus the academic 'dress uniform' of footnotes and references found in the country studies. Its main findings will not be rehearsed in toto, but one central observation may be signalled here. This is that insofar as there has been a common adjustment experience, it is one of a steady and accelerating undermining of the conditions of operation of Africa's key post-independence economic and administrative structures - public enterprises, marketing boards, input supply schemes, and state institutions of various kinds. These structures and institutions, themselves largely the creation of an earlier development assistance paradigm, were already in serious decline and - arguably - were never really sustainable in the first place. However, the notion dear to the designers of adjustment, that a hastening of their demise would lead to a spontaneous growth of effective 'free market' alternatives, has been exposed as a sad example of ideological naivety. Under certain highly specific conditions there has indeed been an expansion of productive private enterprise, but in general the private sector has found it more profitable to pick over the carcass of the old structures than to invent new ones. The result is that the policy dilemma remains, while the capacity to resolve it has been further eroded. Hence, the vulnerability of African societies has increased.

While it is important to make such generalizations, it is also necessary to acknowledge their limitations. The studies presented here have been written against the background of a complex methodological debate about how to assess the effects of adjustment. This debate is directly referred to both in the first contribution to the volume and the last, Knud Erik Svendsen's conspectus of the recent literature on adjustment. On the basis of an acknowledgement of the practical difficulties associated with other approaches, the authors have adopted what is basically a 'before and after comparison' methodology. But in the process they also recognize that this methodology precludes claims being made about direct causality. The relation outlined above, for example, does not imply that things would have been much different without adjustment, or that only adjustment contributed to it, or that adjustment has not had certain possibly countervailing effects as well.

It is nonetheless worth underlining that, even in a less methodologically guarded form, the central generalization noted above would probably be accepted by a broad range of independent observers. Indeed, apart from public pronouncements of the international financial institutions, there are by now few contributions which try to make a case that adjustment has been successful outside of a few specific cases such as that of Uganda - described in this volume by E. A. Brett. In circles previously identified with strong claims for adjustment, a wish to draw a veil over the whole episode may even be noted. But progress towards both sustainable development and sustainable aid relations will only be possible if it is acknowledged that it is important to be at least as frank about the experiences of the 1980s and 1990s as the authors of adjustment were about those of the 1960s and 1970s.

The Editors, Copenhagen

Acknowledgements

Many individuals inside and outside the Centre for Development Research have contributed to the production of these studies. J Carlsen (Denconsult) assisted in the drafting of the first, multiply authored contribution. Background sectoral survey and issue papers for both it and the country studies were prepared by P Bennell, P Engberg-Pedersen, P Gibbon, K Havnevik, P O Pedersen, G Singleton, K E Svendsen, L Udsholt, J Winpenny and E Cromwell, and M Wort. S Folke, A Olukoshi, F Tarp and O Therkildsen acted as discussants at workshops when these and the country surveys were presented. The main burden of administrative, secretarial and bibliographic assistance at CDR was provided by R Egendal, A Hammerlund, K Nielsen and (above all) K M Ohlsen.

**Structural Adjustment in Africa:
A Survey of the Experience**

**Poul Engberg-Pedersen, Peter Gibbon,
Phil Raikes & Lars Udsholt**

Centre for Development Research

1. Development Problems and Adjustment in Sub-Saharan Africa

1.1 What is Structural Adjustment?

The term structural adjustment is normally used in one of two closely linked senses. One implies a shift in economic *policies* from an interventionist stance, which permits and sometimes encourages state intervention in the economy, towards a neo-liberal position which aims to minimize it, letting the market allocate resources wherever possible. In this sense, it is a Third World version of policies which have dominated international economic discussion for the past 15 years. But it also stands for the *mechanisms* which have been used since about 1980 to persuade Third World countries, often very reluctantly, to follow such policy prescriptions. These mechanisms, and their coordination through the international financial institutions (IFIs), are examined in Chapter 2.

Structural adjustment lending dates from about 1980 for a number of reasons, all connected to changes in the world economy occurring around that time. The first OPEC oil price-rise of late 1973 led to recycling of accumulated 'petro-dollars', and sparked off a major monetary boom from 1974 to 1979. This led to an enormous expansion of lending to Third World countries and an increase in their indebtedness, concealed until 1979 by high inflation and low real interest rates. Between 1979 and 1981, with conservative parties gaining power in several major countries, reducing inflation was promoted to first economic priority. It was achieved by deflationary policies which reduced levels of economic activity, employment, demand and thereby prices of Third World export products. Nominal interest rates were increased and, with sharply reduced inflation, real interest rates increased by ten to fifteen times - with a similar increase in indebtedness.

The debt crisis was born, and a growing number of African countries found themselves in desperate need of foreign exchange to continue their development programmes or even to import necessities. A demand was created for quick-releasing flexible 'programme' lending, and its urgency increased the scope for imposing conditionality. The major shift in economic thinking meant that this would be used to try to push through a dramatic change in the economic policies of recipient countries.

1.1.1 What is 'Structural' about Structural Adjustment?

Structural adjustment involves measures to reduce the spending and direct economic involvement by the state, to move towards market allocation of resources and provide an 'enabling environment' for private enterprise. What is 'structural' about this? The point is worth pursuing, since the notions of structure as used by the IFIs and their critics are almost diametrically opposed. To show this simply, one can outline what each side sees as major structural problems.

For most concerned with development processes other than the IFIs, structural problems tend to refer to economic and social imbalances seen to obstruct development. The export bias of colonial economies and its distortion of transport networks could be seen as such a problem. So could the fact of an input-output table full of blank spaces, or the (lack of) policies which have kept some areas undeveloped sources of out-migration. Development is seen, at least in part, as a matter of overcoming these structural imbalances. Since their effects include distorting markets, state intervention is suggested to improve structure and so provide the optimal conditions for private sector participation.

For the IFIs, the main - or only - structural problem is market distortion, usually as a result of state intervention in the economy. In the African case this means assuming that the root cause of Africa's current ills lies not in its history of colonialism and its form of integration into the world economy, but in the policies which have aimed to offset these imbalances, with their unintended effects in the form of excessive state intervention in the economy and especially parastatal monopolies.

1.1.2   Stabilization and Adjustment

Some authors emphasize a distinction between 'stabilization' and 'structural adjustment'. The former is generally associated with the IMF and concerned with measures to improve macroeconomic balance and stability (reducing public expenditure and foreign trade deficits, raising the rate of interest, moving to market valuation of foreign exchange). In this formulation 'structural adjustment' is the responsibility of the World Bank and refers to longer-term measures like civil service reform, investment in human capital and the provision of an enabling environment for private enterprise. Stabilization is seen as a precondition for adjustment.

This fits with the normal sequence of negotiation, in which a working agreement with the IMF is usually (but not always) a precondition for negotiating a World Bank loan. In reality, both IMF and World Bank tend to impose whole lists of conditions, some of them overlapping, so that the distinction breaks down. Moreover it is misleading, if taken to imply that 'stabilization' requires only adjustments within the existing structure. Both the IMF and the World Bank have in mind a reorientation of development policies, from state-led growth to the 'neo-classical' model, in which the state's main function is to provide the conditions for market - and private enterprise - led growth. In recent years it has also become apparent that strict sequencing with stabilization first and structural adjustment later can well be counterproductive to the achievement of IFI goals. Imposing 'stabilization-type' conditions without reforming the institutions supposed to carry them out has had significant negative effects.

1.2   Structural Adjustment in Africa

1.2.1   Why Africa?

On average, the economic growth of African countries has been slower over the past thirty years than that of comparable developing countries elsewhere. Data problems make comparisons highly dubious, and sources disagree widely over the figures, but most agree that in general there has been negligible overall growth in per capita incomes since the early 1960s. Slow growth up to the mid-1970s was followed by decline for the following decade. Other economic measures tell a similar story. Deficits on foreign trade and in government budgets grew steadily, while the proportion of investment paid for by local saving declined. This was reflected in a massive increase in foreign debt and the proportion of exports needed for debt-service, implying a vicious cycle of increasing dependency on external donor funding. In most African countries, a decline in the provision of social services started well before structural adjustment and has continued through it.

The 'development' process has probably been more extensively and heavily state-controlled in Africa than in most other parts of the Third World, though this says as much about the small size of the private business sector as about the size of the state. For some neo-liberals the size and character of the state sector are exogenous variables, determined by the rent-seeking behaviour of the local elite; that is, the elite choose a system involving heavy control because this allows them to extract rent by working its control to personal advantage. This is certainly one factor, but it is certainly no coincidence that organized corruption tends to accelerate in periods (as from 1975 onwards) when public sector real wages are falling. It is far from certain that rent-seeking is even the most important factor. At least as important is that, from the first, the notion of development applied to Africa was interventionist-modernizing in its inspiration. It looked to the state as the dynamic factor coordinating and initiating development. Whatever its merits or demerits there can be no doubt that a 'modernizing' consensus dominated the professional formation of development policy both before and after independence.

1.2.2   Sub-Saharan Africa at Independence
At independence, most African countries lacked even the minimal levels of skills and infrastructure needed to develop their national economies and societies. Colonial regimes had concentrated on development of export-crop production, except where there were minerals to exploit. Agriculture was by far the largest sector and peasant agriculture accounted for most of that. Up to half of total GDP was estimated to come from subsistence agriculture, with 70 percent and upwards of the population getting their incomes from agriculture. Where there were white settlers, they commonly dominated export and domestic markets, receiving most of any credit, investment and infrastructure, and pressuring colonial states to limit competition from African peasants. Otherwise peasant export-crop production was prioritized. Industrial sectors were small, disarticulated and largely foreign-owned. Road and rail construction reflected the needs of settlers and exporters of agricultural or mineral products. African education beyond primary level was minimal, as was job experience in anything but the lowest-level unskilled jobs.

1.2.3   From Independence to Structural Adjustment
Not surprisingly, most African states increased state spending hugely in the years after independence, on education and infrastructure, on the development of (export) agriculture to pay for expanded imports, and on industrial investment. Many aimed to attract foreign private investors, especially for industrial development. But most found them less interested in investing their own funds than in loan-funded joint ventures where donor and African states guaranteed the loan and the latter also guaranteed the market by imposing protection. Thus, much state economic intervention arose less from efforts to supplant private business than from the conditions imposed by business for its involvement.

One can divide the period from the early 1960s to the present into three broad phases. *From independence to about 1973* was a period of standard interventionist development policies in a relatively calm international setting. Terms of trade for many export crops were declining, but from historically high levels. Worldwide levels of inflation were negligible. African economic growth rates were higher than they have been since, but at the time were considered unimpressive, and gave rise to pressures for more dynamic activity, especially as populations were finding the fruits of independence more meagre than expected. This accelerated three linked trends: rising investment as a proportion of GDP; more rapid expansion of imports than exports; and faster expansion of government spending than revenue. In many African countries, by 1973 the resulting government and balance-of-payments deficits seemed likely to halt the increase in investment.

The second period *from 1973 to 1979-82* could be considered one of state consumption gone wild. Its main feature was a worldwide monetary boom, arising from petro-dollar recycling. This was associated with a burst of donor spending in many African countries, which blew away the emerging macroeconomic constraints and set in motion an investment (or project) boom. This led to overheating in many economies, since the increase in funding went far beyond what local institutions could handle, operate or maintain. Expanded investment increased incomes and demand. Imports of capital and intermediate goods for investments pre-empted increasingly scarce foreign exchange (because of both terms-of-trade losses and stagnation in agricultural export production). The macroeconomic effects included further expansion of public expenditure and foreign trade deficits, and increased foreign indebtedness.

These in turn aggravated a number of structural tendencies. Except for settler-colonies, most African countries had minimal non-agricultural private sectors at independence, usually dominated by non-Africans. Post-independence development continued this tendency. In the agricultural sector modernizing peasant production relied heavily on the state and on interventions in the marketing process. During the period up to the mid-1970s, a standardized form of project emerged for agriculture, encouraging the use of purchased inputs by supplying them at (cross-) subsidized rates and with cheap credit, through monopoly marketing boards which collected the debts and crossed the subsidies.

The flood of new aid projects for agriculture, manufacturing and infrastructure all increased the size, complications and cross-cutting of these systems which exaggerated all their faults and had a seriously negative impact on agricultural production. The costs of the organizations set up to operate subsidy-modernization systems rose faster than the benefits and showed themselves in reduced producer prices. This both reduced overall deliveries and shifted production away from export crops (which had to be sold to the monopolies unless they could be smuggled out) towards food crops, for which the state control of marketing had never been effective.

In manufacturing, investment in the late 1970s was focused in parastatals because most investment was by donors who chose them as partners. According to the then accepted infant-industry argument - and often because it was a condition of foreign investment - most manufacturing investments in Sub-Saharan Africa, private or parastatal, required heavy protection, often by crude non-tariff means which lent themselves to corruption.

The availability of donor funds also accelerated expansion of economic and social infrastructure and services, with similar effects on efficiency, or rather its absence. More generally, employment in the public sector expanded very rapidly, partly due to political pressures to find jobs for the increasing number of young people emerging from higher education during the 1970s. This imposed a steady upward pressure on the overall public wage bill despite rapidly falling real wages, aggravating operational problems by crowding out other components of recurrent spending.

All these problems redoubled in a *third phase in the early 1980s*: worldwide retrenchment, declining terms of trade, tight money and massively increased debt. As foreign exchange became increasingly scarce it was rationed and often reserved for projects, further squeezing already inadequate supplies of consumer goods and providing further scope for illegal profiteering. The foreign-exchange shortage was aggravated by significant reductions in foreign aid, sometimes as a result of disagreement about conditionality. Capacity utilization in local manufacturing dropped to very low levels and consumer goods became increasingly unavailable, further aggravating the disincentive effects on export agricultural production and so the general situation.

1.2.4   Africa under Structural Adjustment
The bulk of this Report concerns processes occurring under structural adjustment in Sub-Saharan Africa. In almost every case, structural adjustment agreements have started with major devaluations of heavily over-valued currencies. They have also invariably included a number of other stabilization conditions, centring on reduction in public expenditure deficits and controlling the monetary and credit supply, with the intention of reducing inflation and releasing funds for productive and/or private investment. While some programmes advised increases in the proportion going to social services, this was invariably over-ridden by general budgetary stringency - and by increasing proportions allocated to debt-service. Where trade was confined to parastatal monopolies, programmes included conditions for deregulation and privatization, increasing in scope and urgency over time - and with variable success. Liberalization of non-agricultural trade and minor crops normally came first, with significant positive effects on agricultural production through improved access to basic consumer necessities. Export crops and major food crops took longer. Civil service reform and wholesale privatization are still in their infancy.

1.3   Problems in Assessing Structural Adjustment
The discussion of structural adjustment takes place across a major intellectual divide. The attitude of any observer to structural adjustment will be strongly affected by the degree to which he or she accepts the neo-liberal market paradigm as a satisfactory explanation for the current situation in Africa and set of prescriptions for its future development. This does not, of course, mean that only rigid extreme positions are possible. Most people find themselves accepting some aspects of the market paradigm and structural adjustment, but rejecting others. Critiques of adjustment tend to take one or more of three forms.

1. The most common criticism among concerned members of the general public is that structural adjustment has made poor people still poorer, and especially has led to massive deterioration of social services. The most common IFI responses are: a) that

this is not the case; that increases in income among poor people from market freeing and informal activity have made them better-off; and b) that this takes no account of what would have happened without structural adjustment - and so by implication without the funds which were withheld until agreements were reached.

2. The neo-liberal paradigm is simplistic and misleading in important respects. The notion of a free market in Africa or anywhere else is a misleading chimera and a more solid basis for African development would involve acknowledging a significant though limited role for the state, with all its faults.

3. The paradigm is basically correct, if over-simplified, but it needs to be applied with far more finesse and knowledge of/sensitivity to local circumstances. An intermediate position distinguishes between the short-run adequacy of stabilization and adjustment conditionality, and its inadequacy as a framework for long-term growth.

The commonest current neo-liberal response is to accept that the IFIs were not fully prepared for the structural problems of imposing structural adjustment. But any short-comings in results are mainly attributed to failure to implement structural adjustment conditionality and notably to encourage private investment. Rather than counselling sensitivity, the concern is often for harder conditionality around programmes to privatize parastatals more rapidly.

These positions reflect differences going far beyond structural adjustment and could not be settled by reference to the evidence, even if it was far better than it is. The following paragraphs indicate some of the problems of evidence.

1.   External factors

It is obvious that both internal and external factors have played a part in generating the current situation, but it is extremely hard to sift out and assess the specific effects of structural adjustment from those of other processes or pressures. Something may have occurred or changed during the period of implementation of an adjustment programme, but it is difficult to tell whether or not it resulted from adjustment - or from what part of it. For most African countries, agriculture accounts for up to or even over a half of GDP. Its growth is evidently vital to GDP growth figures. Yet the major single factor affecting short-term changes in production is the weather. When countries are dominated by agriculture, a bad harvest shifts the whole economy downwards. A drought can seriously disrupt both policy and all economic and social life. In the final analysis, it makes little sense to try to weigh the percentage effects of different internal and external factors. It makes far more sense to try to trace their interaction in processes developing over time.

The state of international markets and terms of trade might be considered another external factor, though this is only partly true. Many, if not most, of Africa's export crops face inelastic demand, so that a given change in output leads to a relatively large price change. Anything which increases aggregate output significantly will therefore significantly reduce prices. The effect of adjustment on expanding export production has not been very successful in Africa, but elsewhere in the world it has - and has therefore contributed to falling prices. Just how much of the' massive fall in (say) cocoa prices comes from successful adjustment programmes around the world is impossible to say, but it is probably not small. Whatever their cause, terms-of-trade declines offset part of the short-term positive effects of devaluation and exaggerate the negative ones (more expensive imports, higher debt). Africa's terms-of-trade losses in the 1980s exceeded total net aid inflows.

2.   *Funds versus conditions*
In almost every case, the signing of a structural adjustment agreement unlocks the door to a major increase in foreign funds. To what extent is this responsible for measured positive effects like increased exports, GDP growth or capacity utilization in industry? Since the increases in funding have often been very substantial (often well over the value of domestic exports) one would suppose their effects to have been considerable, especially when directed specifically at (say) increasing the capacity of industries by providing spare parts or raw materials.

3.   *Implementation versus 'slippage'*
Often, structural adjustment programmes have included so many open-ended conditions that even with the best of wills they could hardly be implemented in full. But most governments do considerably less than that, especially where conditions hit entrenched interests or threaten the demise of valued institutions. So any outcome observed will be a result partly of policies or changes implemented and partly those which have not (in addition to other factors). The more detailed sections of this Report, and in particular the five country studies, show that complex patterns of policy change are involved in most adjustment processes, and that these not infrequently have unintended effects.

4.   *'Before and after' versus 'With and without'*
Much energy is used on debating the merits or demerits of these two types of comparison. This is not an important issue when considering one country, especially single processes within it, where the history of the process must be part of the analysis. But for comparisons across 'Africa' or 'Sub-Saharan Africa' such considerations do become important.

How can one use 'before and after' measures, when all countries started on structural adjustment at different times and implemented programmes at different paces and sequences? One cannot. For many purposes, the only figures available for comparisons are between the early 1980s and later 1980s. Since most countries started on adjustment from mid-1980s onwards, this may have some (but obviously not full) explanatory power.

The issue of 'with and without' should be simpler. In practice this method usually involves cross-section comparisons of countries identified as 'good adjusters' and 'mediocre' and 'bad' adjusters. It is associated with problems of inconsistent classification. The IFIs' lists of 'good' and 'bad' are seldom the same, underlining that even this year's model adjuster can fall seriously short next year. Other problems are that the IFI selection of good and bad adjusters often seems tilted towards showing the most favourable possible results from adjustment, and that non-adjusters are often countries ravaged by civil war, which have no recognizable economic policies at all.

5.   *Measurement issues*
GDP growth figures are heavily dependent on agricultural sector growth which is dependent on the weather. Many of the figures for agricultural production are little better than informed guesswork and by no means capable of bearing an analysis of fractions of a percent growth which often hangs on them. Chapter 3 and some country

reports show that there is some evidence of 'optimistic estimation' of post-structural adjustment production increases by IFI and national sources, though specially the former. This is not the only area of shaky statistics; they pervade every area of most African economies.

6.   *Balance and stability*
Among the aims to be achieved by structural adjustment, the notions of stability and balance are always prominent, which might lead one to believe that they are objectively measurable. They are not. No country ever maintains a precise balance between imports and exports, or between government revenue and spending. For most African countries the issue is invariably one of getting deficits down to 'stable' or 'sustainable' or 'acceptable' levels, which in turn means to levels acceptable to the IFIs and other donors, and on the basis of which they will continue to provide new loans and/or reschedule existing debts. A country can be considered more 'balanced' and 'stable' after structural adjustment than before, even though debt as a proportion of GDP, debt-service as a proportion of exports and the public spending deficit are all larger than before. This is not just hypothetical. It is the case with Tanzania and some other 'adjusters'.

7.   *Intended and unintended effects*
Neo-liberals see the major structural problem facing Africa as state control of the economy and market distortion arising from the development policies of the pre-adjustment period. Are adjustment programmes likely to generate similar unintended effects of their own? From some evidence in this Report, the answer would seem to be yes. Many of these seem similar to those of statist development. There is, for example, evidence that the sheer mass of conditions imposed under some agreements leads to overloading of capacity. The general assumption that liberalization will reduce opportunities for corruption and rent-seeking is not always correct. Plenty of examples can be found where the sequencing or other aspects of adjustment presented opportunities for aggravated corruption. Investment promotion and foreign-exchange allocation seem to have given particularly good opportunities for ill-gotten gain, partly because they have not removed the scope for selective use of various interventions.

1.4   Features of the Five Case-Study Countries
The case-study countries were chosen for this study as major recipients of Danish assistance and otherwise as wide a variety of countries as possible. They have in common that the IFIs consider most of them to be among the most successful implementers of structural adjustment, and those which have benefitted most from it. Ghana is generally presented as the single most successful adjuster, often closely followed by Uganda and/or Tanzania. Zimbabwe and Burkina Faso started on structural adjustment much later than the others.

1.4.1   Burkina Faso
Before independence Upper Volta was a province of French West Africa, in which its position was as provider of migrant labour and cattle on the hoof to the larger economies of Senegal and Côte d'Ivoire and exporter of cotton on the world market.

Given its small size (now 10 million), unfavourable location and lack of access to investment capital, this continued after independence. It was less affected than most by the investment boom of the 1970s; not only its economic structure but also its public expenditure and foreign deficits remained largely unchanged. Indebtedness was still minor in the early 1980s.

In 1983, a young officers' coup brought to power Captain Thomas Sankara, who changed the country's name to Burkina Faso and shifted the direction of development towards the rural areas, improved social services, popular mobilization for the building of infrastructure, active promotion of environmental conservation and the rights of women, and price controls. A number of state and party institutions were set up to direct this process. Policies also included a home-grown 'structural adjustment', in the sense of greater austerity in public spending. On the basis of this, according to the World Bank, 'Burkina saw several years of growth, fuelled by high public investment, good weather and increased agricultural production in onchocerciasis-freed areas, but nonetheless faced economic crisis as the economic foundations of the policies pursued were weak.'

The economic gaps were not large, and it was a political rather than economic crisis which brought in adjustment. Increasing opposition by the urban and educated population to various 'levelling' measures, including an attempt to freeze teachers' salaries, lay behind a new coup in 1987. Captain Blaise Compaoré took power, and signalled a shift towards accommodation with the West and the IFIs. IFI and other aid funds, which had been severely reduced, were restored, notably for the 20 percent increase in public spending which unfreezing teachers' salaries involved. Negotiations were entered for an adjustment programme, which was agreed in 1991 and followed by IMF funding. Since the 1987 shift, Burkina Faso has been seen by the IFIs as a 'model pupil' in its fulfilment of structural adjustment conditions. The exception to this has been devaluation. Burkina Faso's currency is the CFA Franc, which is tied to the French Franc, and can thus only be devalued by common group and French agreement. It was only devalued in January 1994.

1.4.2   Ghana

Prior to independence in 1956, Ghana (Gold Coast) was the most advanced of British colonies in tropical Africa. It was the world's major producer of cocoa, and with no white settlers to impede their advance, African access to education and jobs in the civil service was far in advance of most other colonies. It was a 'middle-income country'.

After independence, under the leadership of Kwame Nkrumah, Ghana became a leading 'radical' country, with an ambitious agenda of social(ist) change and construction. This involved levels of investment and taxation which proved unsustainable and increased corruption and inefficiency. Western donors were appeased when Nkrumah was replaced in a military coup, but standards of economic management declined further under different phases of military rule with civilian interludes, provoking a junior officers' coup under Flight Lieutenant Jerry Rawlings in 1979. By this time, two decades of financial laxity and mismanagement had led to macroeconomic chaos. Exchange-rate overvaluation and high export-taxation led to rapidly declining exports (cocoa, timber, gold) from the mid-1970s, while external factors plus a large public spending deficit increased the rate of inflation to an average 80 percent per annum. In 1983, a major drought was superimposed on all this, pushing Ghana's economy to its lowest point yet.

Decisive action was needed, and after debate over whether to move to the left or the path represented by structural adjustment, Rawlings and his advisers took the latter, mainly for pragmatic reasons concerning access to funds. Ghana's Economic Reconstruction Programme (ERP) has by now been through three phases. The first was primarily concerned with macroeconomic and fiscal stabilization, and is generally seen as among the most successful of such exercises. It increased revenue collection significantly, allowing both increased expenditure and a smaller deficit. Massive devaluation brought previously smuggled exports back home and increased their levels. The second phase of ERP concerned itself with more detailed and sectoral issues, while the third has focused heavily on privatizing the remains of the state and parastatal sector.

1.4.3 Tanzania

The area which is now Tanzania was first colonized by Germans and became a League of Nations mandated territory under Britain after 1918, which limited the extent of further white settlement. Tanzania has a large semi-arid central part and all high potential areas spread around its borders. This continues to hamper competitiveness by raising costs of transport and communication. For six years after independence in 1961 Tanzania followed a standard modernization approach to development with an emphasis on agricultural production for exports, and private foreign investment for industry and infrastructure. Average growth rates of agriculture and GDP were high by present standards, but at the time considered as unsatisfactory. Agricultural policy was seen to have failed as were attempts to raise foreign funding. Political cracks began to appear as it emerged that the fruits of independence were unequally distributed.

President Nyerere announced the Arusha Declaration in 1967, introducing a move towards socialism and self-reliance, and nationalization of the economy's rather low 'commanding heights'. Paradoxically, this led to a rapid increase in the availability of foreign funding as firms, unwilling to risk their own funds, found it profitable and risk-free to enter construction and management agreements, financed by loans guaranteed by both Tanzania and their home states. Another major trend of this period was the policy of *ujamaa vijijini*, which grew into a programme for the forced resettlement of the mass of the rural population in 'development villages'. More and more goods were confined to sale through state or parastatal agencies. This had led to high rates of investment, under heavy state control even before 1974-75. The monetary boom multiplied all these trends, especially since the then President of the World Bank had singled out Tanzania's post-Arusha policies as an inspiring example of how to develop Africa.

Trying to do too much too quickly took a major toll on efficiency, as expanded investment and activity in all sectors of the economy severely overstrained capacity, and notably the morale of state and parastatal workers, whose real wages were falling. After 1980, Tanzania, as a well-known example of 'socialist' development, was a particular target for the IFIs, which imposed a severe 'lending hiatus' from 1980 to 1985, bringing the country to heel. In 1986, the first adjustment programme was signed and the flow of donor funds rapidly climbed back to previous levels. Already from 1985, agricultural production had started to increase and this continued after 1986. By the early 1990s, much of Tanzania's state-controlled system had been dismantled, with trade deconfined, foreign exchange liberalized, monopolies over agricultural marketing removed and much of the parastatal manufacturing sector privatized or waiting to be. This has led to praise for Tanzania from the IFIs for 'resolution'.

1.4.4   Uganda
Colonial Uganda was little affected by white settlement, allowing more space at an earlier period for African economic advance, though much of it limited to hereditary chiefs. Uganda has plenty of fertile agricultural land and an unusually reliable rainfall pattern, so prospects of agricultural and industrial growth were considered to be good. But the divide-and-rule policies of the colonial administration aggravated religious and ethnic conflicts in a country characterized by great regional inequalities. The first Obote Government became embroiled in these conflicts, and in 1966 suspended the democratic process, using the army against former traditional rulers and elected local governments. In 1971 the army, under General Amin, deposed Obote and initiated a reign of terror and economic mismanagement which reduced the country to near ruin. The economy was also hit by his expulsion of Asians and expropriation of their property.

Amin was overthrown in 1979, but the situation remained tense through several changes of government, deteriorating towards civil war in 1982-86. In 1986, the present National Resistance Movement (NRM) Government took power, though it took some years before its rule was consolidated over most of the country. The economy was in ruins and macroeconomic control almost totally absent. Restoration of order and stability was evidently a precondition for any other advance, and this needed both a coherent strategy and foreign funds. In 1987, after a brief attempt to 'go it alone', the NRM accepted a standard structural adjustment programme, the Economic Recovery Programme (ERP), though with reluctance and no great commitment to its goals. Between 1987 and 1991, when a new ERP was initiated, two clear wings emerged, with the Minister of Finance supporting a policy of going slow and obstructing liberalization where possible. His sacking in that year indicated a shift in favour of adjustment by President Museveni. This was followed by a more positive attitude to implementation of liberalization, privatization and civil service reform, which has pushed Uganda into the ranks of 'good adjusters' in recent years. There can be no doubt of the enormous improvement in most aspects of the Uganda economy since 1986, nor of the role of deregulation in it. But what proportion of the improvement comes from adjustment, how much from increased foreign funding, and how much from post-war recovery, is hard to tell.

1.4.5   Zimbabwe
Zimbabwe differs from the other case-study countries in having remained a settler colony up to 1980 and in still having an economy (and agricultural sector) dominated by large, mostly white-owned firms and farms. The late date of independence, and the fact that Rhodesia was under sanctions (however ineffective), meant that Zimbabwe missed the boom of 1975-79 and was thus not seriously indebted in 1980. But it was recovering from ten years of bitter civil war under a settlement which severely limited the scope for transferring land to Africans by allowing only free-market sales. In the event, however, after an initial burst of land transfers, the ZANU-PF Government lost interest in this issue and transferred far less than would have been possible.

At independence in 1980 the Zimbabwean Government had one of the strongest and most diversified economies in Africa, partly as a result of the sanctions intended to bring the illegal Rhodesian regime down. These formed a protective barrier behind which the settler regime developed a reasonably efficient and well integrated modern agricultural, industrial and service sector. It also depended on internal economic controls, particularly over foreign exchange. This development was largely confined to whites. Both agricultural production and per capita GDP fell between 1973 and 1980. The African communal lands were excluded from agro-services, most infrastructure and social services.

The early 1980s saw the lowering of barriers to African crop sales to the parastatals which, together with extension of their buying networks, took the African contribution to official maize sales from 1 percent to almost 50 percent and for cotton yet higher. The costs of this, the expansion of social services to Africans, plus other controls led to complaints from the private sector represented by the Confederation of Zimbabwe Industries about 'crowding out' private borrowing and excessive (tax and other) costs on private business. The World Bank managed to enlist the CZI in a rather cautious call for trade liberalization, in return for specified benefits like increased funds for credit to private industry.

The Zimbabwe Government introduced its own structural adjustment programme in 1990, including easing of price controls, abolition of most minimum wage legislation, a shift of public spending away from social services and measures intended to make credit and/or foreign exchange more easily available to private investors. The intention had been to produce a programme which would satisfy the IFIs and lead to a structural adjustment credit. This did not happen, and in 1991, the Government produced another, more tightly specified programme, which included reduction in parastatal subsidies, extension of the Open General Import Licence, further tariffication of protection, and a 25 percent cut in (non-educational) civil service employment. This was accepted, with some delay (and probably further tightening of conditions) by the IFIs and loans were extended. It is very hard to assess the effects of structural adjustment in Zimbabwe, not just because it is so recent, but because its first year of operation coincided with the worst drought of the century, throwing out demand targets and shifting parts of the economy onto an emergency basis. Nonetheless, the achievements to date seem modest in view of the significant costs to be endured by the poorer sections of the population.

2.   Adjustment, Aid Relations and Governance

2.1   Introduction

The advent of structural adjustment in 1980 represented a revolution in aid relations, although the bulk of aid remained tied to donor-specific projects. The two main changes which occurred have been an extension of *aid conditionality* based on balance-of-payments support, and an introduction of *aid coordination* modalities.

Aid conditionality means that the granting of aid is tied to whether recipient countries adopt, or promise to adopt, certain recommended policies. At first only the granting of new short-term balance-of-payments aid was linked to policy conditionality, but over time most new programme and project aid became so linked. The policy conditions to which the granting of aid was linked initially concerned only macroeconomic matters but were soon extended into attempts to restructure the state-market relation. The structural adjustment agenda emerged in a period in which market-based solutions to economic reform were gaining international credibility, and the opportunity to test them in Africa was provided by growing economic crisis and aid dependency in most countries.

Aid coordination is the other side of the coin to aid conditionality. In a situation where there are multiple donors for particular countries, and where their total aid flows are significantly greater than those of the main institutions sponsoring structural adjustment (the World Bank and the IMF), then aid conditionality can only have a chance of working if other donors link their release of funds to decisions made by the World Bank and the IMF.

For this reason, the latter institutions have played a major role in enhancing mechanisms of aid coordination which give the enforcement of conditionality a central role. The main mechanism is the annual Consultative Group (CG) meeting for each recipient country, chaired by the World Bank and attended by representatives of recipient governments and the main multilateral and bilateral donors. Some CG meetings (e.g., those for Kenya in 1991 and Malawi in 1992) have taken aid coordination as far as suspending all new aid commitments to those countries pending the implementation of further policy changes.

A third issue which will be considered in this section is that of *governance*. Africa's economic performance in the 1980s did not significantly improve, and it became evident that there was a considerable gap in most countries between reforms which had been promised and those which were actually delivered. Donor attention increasingly turned to questions of the representativeness of African governments, the degree of accountability and openness in their political and economic management processes, the extent to which the latter were influenced by informed public discussion, and the extent of corruption in them. Increasing attention was also paid to issues of social pluralism, human rights and military expenditure.

These issues came to form the basis for a donor 'governance' agenda, which now shares an importance only slightly less than that of economic reform. The problems it raises are at least as profound.

2.2   Evolution of the Reform Packages

The IMF and the World Bank have been the two main organizations behind structural adjustment from the outset. Before the dawn of structural adjustment, a clear division of labour existed between them. The IMF provided short-term balance-of-payments support to countries requiring it, and exercised some conditionality in this connection. This almost always referred to the international value of the currency of the recipient government, corresponding to the Fund's view that making the latter more competitive was the single most effective way to restore macroeconomic stability. Although it always prided itself on being able to offer a broad range of policy advice, the World Bank meanwhile concentrated on lending for large-scale development projects without strings and usually on soft terms. The main change introduced by adjustment was the movement of the World Bank into the sphere of macroeconomic policy-based conditional lending monopolized at the time by the IMF. Its main instrument was quick-disbursing balance-of-payments support in forms broadly similar to those already provided by the IMF. There has been a continuous subsequent confusion about the precise roles of the two organizations.

The IMF was involved from the outset of the adjustment process in Tanzania, Ghana, and Uganda but only later in Zimbabwe and Burkina Faso. This difference in time reflects a perception amongst recipients that the IMF remains more conservative and restrictive than the World Bank in both its policy and lending conditions and that therefore agreements with it are best avoided unless there is no alternative. Zimbabwe and Burkina Faso entered into negotiations with the international financial institutions from positions of relative strength and were hence able - at first anyway - to deal exclusively with the World Bank. However, it is also clear that what recipients perceive as the deficiencies of the IMF, many other donors and private creditors perceive as its strengths. Agreements with the IMF are seen by most creditors as the best guarantee available that their loans will be repaid. While losing its policy-setting monopoly, the IMF's key role has become that its presence is the toughest seal of approval available for continuation of disbursements of all kinds, while its absence casts doubt on the 'reliability' of a government as a partner.

The country studies show that since the beginning of the adjustment process the IMF has broadly continued to concentrate on balance-of-payments support in return for exchange-rate, government expenditure and fiscal and monetary policy reforms. However, this has not excluded an interest in other issues, from agricultural producer prices to trade liberalization and restoration of private property rights. Over time IMF lending packages have become longer-term and many of them are now on concessional terms. These ways of operating were ones adopted by the World Bank in 1980-81 to distinguish its own balance-of-payments support from the Fund's, while agricultural prices, trade liberalization and property law have been mainstream Bank concerns for a decade. This has further increased the confusion about their respective roles. Within its non-disputed core issue areas the IMF's interests have meanwhile changed somewhat over time since the early 1980s and are now concentrated on the central issue of government deficits. Within this there has been a move from highlighting the negative role of consumer subsidies and (*sotto voce*) social spending to drawing attention to the negative role of subsidies/loans to parastatals.

The country studies indicate that there is little administrative rationale to justify the expensive co-existence of the IMF and the World Bank, whose numerous missions and separate negotiating procedures are a burden on the few economic managers and policy-makers in core government ministries and central banks in African countries. The IMF's lead role in guaranteeing the presence of 'correct' economic policies is also questionable in light of the increasing emphasis on national ownership of economic and structural reforms.

All the countries in the study have had agreements with the World Bank. Uganda's, Zimbabwe's and Ghana's agreements with the Bank coincided with the adoption of reform programmes, but Tanzania's and Burkina Faso's followed attempts at 'home-grown' programmes of varying lengths and comprehensiveness. For three of the four anglophone countries under consideration in this study a common pattern of World Bank-supported programme evolution occurred. This comprised the following stages:

Stage 1: *Stabilization/agricultural price reform/some external trade liberalization.* This stage of reform combined an emphasis on restoring key macroeconomic balances with the central concern of 'getting prices right', enunciated in the original (1981) World Bank credo on Africa's problems. The latter proposed the use of devaluation to shift rewards to export-crop producers, thus providing a platform for 'accelerated growth'.

Stage 2: *Internal trade liberalization/investment promotion/social dimensions of adjust-ment.* This stage of reform reflects a general change of emphasis by the Bank in the late 1980s, when it acknowledged that 'prices were only part of the picture'. The delivery of effective services to producers, and a more active policy relation to the entire supply side were also necessary. African governments should now concentrate on the provision of an 'enabling environment' for the private sector. Around the same time the World Bank began to promote specific sector-based adjustment loans (SECALs) in which sector rehabilitation was traded for sector deregulation.

Stage 3: *Public sector reform, beginning with the banking sector and civil service, and social expenditure rationalization.* This stage of reform reflects a change of emphasis in the early to mid-1990s. For an 'enabling environment' to come about, there is a need for a radical shrinkage in the role of the state. This should enable the state more effec-tively to concentrate on what should be its mainstream activity: 'human resource development'. This in turn requires greater planning and prioritization of government spending.

Stages 2 and 3 were never conceived of as replacements for Stage 1, but rather additions to it. Because of this, there has been a continuous broadening of the reform agenda. Many African countries acquired adjustment programmes only in the mid-1980s or later, and hence went through these stages in a very rapid progression. Nevertheless there has been an overall movement from a period of clearly macroeconomic reform to one of macroeconomic and more general institutional reform.

This development has been accompanied by an explicit concern with the 'sequencing' of reforms. Some supporters of adjustment now argue that it might have been better to start the whole process with dismantling the public sector, since 'market-rational' actors would then have been in place to respond to supply-side signals. On a less grandiose scale it is now commonly accepted that it would have been more sensible if internal trade liberalization had preceded real devaluation, and if the latter had preceded external trade liberalization more systematically.

The overall change in emphasis tends to be ascribed by the IFIs to a 'learning process': it was only when initial reforms failed to be implemented or failed to generate the anticipated results that other more intractable problems were highlighted, and donors reacted accordingly by placing the latter's resolution on the agenda. An alternative way of reading the same process is that many IFI assumptions about economic and social actors in recipient countries were naive and ideologically biased. Subsequently, there has been less of a learning process than a combination of ad hoc rectifications and a series of uncoordinated and ill thought-out plunges into new areas which remain poorly understood. The changes also indicate divergences of opinion within the World Bank itself.

Behind the differences in emphasis, the central assumption has remained unchanged since 1980, however: governments should minimize their involvement in the economy, which the private sector can take care of much better. The latest trend in the Bank is to drop explicit reference to structural adjustment. Some have claimed that this means that the policies referred to under this name are now no longer being pursued by the IFIs. While there is certainly genuine debate about these issues, the move may also have a tactical aspect. A senior World Bank official recently explained that because recipient governments have become sceptical of the reform agenda as a whole it was easier to 'mobilize consensus' around its key components if these were presented as separate elements.

There have also been changes in emphasis about the nature of the instruments or techniques which the IFIs have recommended as best practice in carrying out particular reforms. In the early days there were different fashions for how to manage *devaluation*, before settling on the setting of exchange rates by auctioning foreign exchange received from balance-of-payments support. On *budgetary stabilization* there was an early emphasis on increased revenue generation as well as expenditure cuts. The former became de-emphasized during the 'enabling environment' phase but has now strongly reappeared. In recent years, there are even signs of 'second thoughts' with respect to removal of all protectionist barriers as the obvious route to *trade liberalization*. An acknowledgement of the usefulness of selective protection is emerging in some World Bank documents, although still not in practical policy.

2.3   Aid Conditionality and Coordination

Two main areas of discussion have emerged around conditionality: can it be morally and politically justified? And is it effective as a means of inducing change?

Morally and politically, opponents of *conditionality* have argued that the introduction of conditionality turns aid from a gift into a contract-based bargain. However, the contract is oppressive, since it is entered into by parties with totally different positions of strength. In the process the national sovereignty of the recipient is abrogated and a 'second imperialism' introduced. Supporters of conditionality, on the other hand, have argued that he who pays the piper should call the tune, and that in any case most African governments are insufficiently representative to justify claims to genuine sovereignty.

While the critique of conditionality is far from watertight, neither of these replies stands up to examination. African populations also pay the piper, while some of those now calling the tune - most obviously the IMF - at present make no net contributions at all. Likewise, while it may be true that many African governments are unrepresentative of their citizens, the implication of conditionality is the clearly unjustified one that donors are somehow themselves more representative. In any case, governments enjoying genuine legitimacy have been equally subject to conditionality.

It is also hard to justify conditionality as it has been practised. Recipient implementation records are often quite poor and there is now widespread agreement that lack of ownership of policies by recipient governments is a major problem. Difficulties in getting conditionality to work as planned are implicitly recognized in actual donor practice. 'Contractually', recipients are supposed to implement a series of policy changes prior to receiving initial funds and further changes according to an agreed timetable, thereby triggering the release of later instalments or 'tranches'. However non-implementation, particularly towards the end of timetables, is usually forgiven, and non-implemented measures postponed, diluted or forgotten entirely.

As far as policy-related *aid coordination* is concerned, the World Bank achieved increasing hegemony in relation to other donors from the mid-1980s. Despite the latter's often rather different orientations a common consensus on the need for more orthodox macroeconomic management was forged and subsequently extended to questions of price reform, the 'enabling environment', 'governance' and human resource development. The World Bank has retained control of this process by a combination of launching bids for expert status on all development policy issues of major current concern; promoting a consistent neo-classical interpretation of them with an associated market-based solution; and supplementing this with an add-on, social compensatory package of some form (usually funded by those bilaterals most concerned about the issue). However, its hegemony is only partly a result of this approach. The lack of systematic challenges to the Bank from within the donor community (apart from a few international NGOs) also follows from other donors' lack of comparable research and analytic capacity as well as their disillusion with pre-conditionality aid modalities.

In recent years bilateral donors have felt that they have a greater input to World Bank decision-making, through a second major aid coordination mechanism, the 'Special Programme for Africa' (SPA). This has developed from being a body focusing on mobilizing higher levels of donor funding to a participatory forum for broad inter-donor exchanges on development policy issues. Significantly, however, it excludes recipient country governments from the policy dialogue.

Any discussion of aid relations needs to proceed from the starting-point that the type of aid which is central to structural adjustment - (supposedly) quick-disbursing balance-of-payments support - represents no more than a quarter of all aid, and no more than a third even of the World Bank's. The great bulk of aid remains in project forms, and in contrast to balance-of-payments support the coordination of the latter remains seriously flawed.

Theoretically, recipient country governments and more specifically their Ministries of Finance and Planning should draw up development priorities and, after consultation with line ministries, seek funding from donors. The recurrent costs of implementing these development priorities should be raised locally and their management be undertaken by relevant line ministries. This does not happen. Recipient countries' development budgets tend to be driven by donors, each of whom has its own pet sector (and countries/regions). Most projects are complex to manage and many donors prefer to do this themselves rather than to allow recipients to do so. There are more projects than there are recurrent funds to support staffing and maintenance for them. Donors tend to insist on donor- and even project-specific planning, implementation and review procedures. They often find their own ways to get line ministries to establish them without core ministries being involved. These tendencies become increasingly pronounced as the number of donors (governmental and NGO) proliferate and as they all seek a presence at all levels of social and economic life. The results are that:

- line ministries become increasingly tied up with managing donor projects and disarticulated from core ministries;
- more and more local capacity is occupied by aid administration rather than policy development and prioritizing;
- major parts of development expenditure are outside the central budget and central control; and
- there is an increasing disparity between the level of resources which can be raised locally and those required to reproduce development activity.

Structural adjustment programmes have always involved implementing a large number of policies which otherwise might not have been considered. With the expansion of these programmes there has been a steady expansion of conditions: some recipient governments adopt Policy Framework Papers committing them to 50-100 separate reforms. This obviously makes further demands on already severely overstretched capacity. Growing recognition of these problems has led to increasing donor interest in the principles of 'strategic aid management', strategic dialogue on development priorities and effective overall aid coordination. But so far there has been little evident progress on any of these fronts, or even much sign of their recognition as an over-riding priority.

2.4   Ownership, Accountability and Transparency

The country studies suggest two main conclusions on the issue of *public ownership of adjustment*. There is virtually no broad public ownership of adjustment in any of the countries considered, but there is also very little effective or systematic opposition to it. Adjustment programmes (popularly known usually by their acronyms, such as 'ESAP' or 'ERP', or in the Burkina Faso case simply as 'Americans'!) mostly tend to be accepted as a fact of life by the general public. Where there has been a sharp decline in the economic situation, as in Zimbabwe, they tend to be blamed for everything, including the weather. Where the economic situation has improved they attract less blame, but little outright praise. This situation is by no means exceptional in the history of African economic policy-making. Apart from some massively popular expropriations of foreign-owned property (Tanzania 1967, Uganda 1972, etc.), little if any macro-economic policy-making has ever been widely owned.

This reflects the generally undemocratic traditions of most African governments, and the corresponding lack of capacity to handle thoroughgoing debate. In the case of structural adjustment - especially in its early phases - this has been compounded by fears on the part of national leaderships and the IFIs that programmes would be stalled or governments overthrown if the full content of agreements became public knowledge. These tendencies have restricted the formation of a popular base for adjustment policies, even amongst those groups who benefit from them.

Simultaneously, there has been surprisingly little effective systematic opposition to adjustment, except on issues of privatization and higher education reform. Privatization does raise issues of sovereignty and workers' rights, but popular concerns have instead mainly focused on inter-racial issues relating to the extension or resurrection of the dominant role in the private sector of Europeans in Zimbabwe, Asians in Tanzania and Uganda, Lebanese in Ghana, etc. The general absence of systematic opposition tends to reflect the fact that most negative effects of adjustment have impacted in a diffuse way, or have been partly deferred (the evident absence of large-scale retrenchments in most of the countries studied), and that almost without exception emergent opposition parties have their roots in the same political elite who were involved in approving programmes in the past and who remain anxious not to fall out badly with the IFIs.

Regarding *government ownership*, while adjustment was not strictly speaking imposed it was normally accepted as a 'second-best' option to a continuation of the status quo (usually some form of statism), albeit with slightly revised incentive systems. Gaining access to further donor funds, as opposed to their policy 'expertise', was the primary recipient government motivation for initial agreements in all cases. Indeed, being trapped within an aid dependency situation there was often very little serious alternative.

In Burkina Faso and Zimbabwe, recipient governments contributed directly or indirectly to dialogue about the content of the programme. Elsewhere this opportunity apparently did not arise. Subsequent government contributions to programme design have remained extremely limited. Even the most rudimentary forms of dialogue have remained restricted to very narrow circles of senior ministers and officials, and often seem to relate more to issues of pace rather than content. Potential opponents and sceptics seem to be screened out of the dialogue except where they occupy such senior positions (e.g. Minister of Finance) that this is impossible.

Despite increasing verbal emphasis on the desirability of broadening ownership, the IFIs have until very recently been highly cautious even in their efforts to promote widened ownership within governments. The main focus has been on winning over un-decided or sceptical powerful key figures, particularly the President, by moral and material incentives of various kinds. A secondary focus has been to isolate and neutralize significant explicit opponents. Nonetheless, over the last five years, more weight has been placed upon encouraging private fora internal to the recipient country elite, such as government-organized seminars and Presidential Commissions. The latter have been particularly common in East Africa, where there is a tradition of them. These may delay desired reforms or (in the case of the Tanzanian Land Commission) come up with what were at the time the 'wrong' recommendations, but their legitimizing and consensus-forming functions with respect to the elite are now widely canvassed. On the other hand, the IFIs have been anxious to avoid a proliferation of types of consultation which threaten to slow down implementation. Insistence on the desirability of speed in implementation has if anything increased over the years.

The World Bank has recently started to argue that the level of recipient 'ownership' should itself be used as a criterion for allocating aid. To some this appears a welcome move away from reliance on imposition and conditionality. Yet, it is associated with an emphasis that conditions should be 'agreed' rather than done away with. The disparity in resources between the parties entering such agreements of course remains, making it inevitable that they will be constrained.

No discussion of these issues should neglect the question of 'reverse leverage'. As already noted, donors, including the IFIs, often recognize that 'ownership' is weak or absent and that implementation of certain measures is likely to be at best painfully slow, yet they persist not only with dialogue but also with actual disbursements. For some recipient countries (although none included in this study) the debt situation is so potentially threatening to public and private Western creditors that there is extremely strong pressure to bring them under some supervision by the IFIs even if the short-term results are unlikely to be spectacular. In other cases, notably Ghana but increasingly

Uganda and to a lesser extent Tanzania, the IFIs themselves have such strong stakes in the confirmation of possible 'success stories' that they are inclined to overlook slippage and misdemeanours which would be punished elsewhere.

Few recipient governments have clear traditions of or procedures and mechanisms for the formulation and implementation of far-reaching changes in policy. In addition there has been a general loss of capacity to carry out many basic functions effectively, arising from falling real resource levels, collapsing salaries, and declining professionalism. The typical solution of the IFIs to lack of capacity has been to repeat the bad practice of much project aid of substituting themselves (or their consultants) for recipient country senior planning and technical staff and/or to try to concentrate 'promising' local senior planning/technical staff in new units dedicated essentially to implementing donor agendas. When adequately resourced, these dedicated units are apparently effective in bringing about some short-term changes but their longer-term benefits are questionable. Moreover some of them (notably in the case of Social Dimensions of Adjustment initiatives) have also been located outside the control of recipient country Ministries of Finance, even though donors have been simultaneously pressing the latter to centralize control over spending. The alternative strategy of broadly-based promotion of improvements in civil service pay, professionalism, analytical capacity, coordination and initiative has so far been implicitly rejected as too slow and costly. As the Ghana country study shows, the insulation of 'change-makers' has sometimes also been supported by leading politicians as well as the IFIs, since the former distrust the civil service for their own reasons.

Hence while African governments would almost certainly not have carried out many reforms which they have done if it had been up to them alone, the use of conditionality has probably strengthened pre-existing tendencies of non-accountability and non-transparency, further overstretched an already diminishing state capacity, and insulated the reform process from the supposed object of reform. On the other hand, any programmes which would be wholeheartedly owned by broader constituencies almost certainly would not conform to the current preferences of the IFIs. If donors want policies locally designed and owned they will generally have to accept at least some quite different policies.

2.5   Governance Issues

A general relation has already been suggested between adjustment, as it has been introduced so far, and non-transparency and non-accountability. On the other hand, most adjusting countries already had broadly non-transparent and non-accountable forms of decision-making prior to adjustment, and there are no strong reasons to suppose that these would have become more open. Turning to more general aspects of governance, a few words will be said about military expenditure and pluralism and human rights. The issue of corruption is addressed in Section 3.4 on informal economic activities.

Military expenditure and its reduction entered the donor agenda around 1990-91, with the end of the Cold War (and hopes of a 'peace dividend') and increased IFI emphasis on social sector rehabilitation. From the mid-1970s to the mid-1980s, military expenditure seems to have declined in real terms in Africa as a whole, except in countries involved in prolonged civil wars. Since then, it seems to have risen again, though somewhat limited by post-1990 scrutiny. Of the countries in this study, only

Tanzania has figures stretching from the early 1980s, which show a decline from 13 percent to 7.6 percent of total budget by the early 1990s. Others have figures only for the 1990s. In Uganda, where civil war ceased in 1986, military expenditure fell as a proportion of the total budget from 15 percent to 9 percent. Zimbabwe (15-13 percent) and Burkina Faso (14-12 percent) showed smaller reductions. Since Uganda, Tanzania and Zimbabwe have all experienced a winding down of major military commitments in this period, it would be wrong to ascribe responsibility for the trend firmly to structural adjustment.

Pluralism and human rights: Here a distinction will be drawn between social pluralism (the presence of non-state actors in the public sphere) on the one hand and political pluralism and human rights on the other. A restricted definition of human rights as political rights will be used here, as human rights in the sense of access to social and economic assets is discussed elsewhere in this Report.

Regarding *social pluralism*, most African countries saw an extension of non-state actors in the field of social provision during the crisis years which generally preceded adjustment. In particular, as state capacity declined, local elites began supplementing or providing local social services via self-help organizations, home town associations and so on. This tendency was strengthened by the steady increase in the share of overall aid passing through international NGOs in the 1980s. Since the late 1980s channelling higher shares of aid through NGOs has become official policy both of bilaterals and of the World Bank itself. However, while this has served to institutionalize a plural social presence it has also provided incentives for governments to 'divest' certain of their branches to the NGO 'sector', thereby generating the phenomenon of government-organized NGOs. Otherwise there does not seem to be much broadening of the nature, as opposed to the number, of non-state actors during the adjustment period.

Africa had a very poor record on both *political pluralism* and *human rights* prior to the adjustment period, but this period has seen considerable improvements in both. Of the countries examined in this study only one (Zimbabwe) was formally politically pluralistic at the beginning of its adjustment process, but three of the other four became so during it. Neither in Zimbabwe nor in the three referred to (Tanzania, Burkina Faso and Ghana) does the resulting pluralism have very deep roots, however, especially in the political party sense. It is ironic that of the countries reviewed only the remaining one (Uganda) is engaging in a process of formulating a new constitution with input from elected representatives. Much more practically important than multi-party systems has been the emergence of certain public fora, most notably independent newspapers, in which current questions can be debated with an unprecedented degree of freedom.

There is no evidence of a positive causal link between any of these changes and adjustment, however. Political pluralization and improvements in the observance of human rights have either largely been responses by ruling elites to perceived pressure from donors for democratization (a pressure which arose in 1990 but subsided again shortly afterwards), or have actually arisen as a result of pressure from organized opponents of adjustment (Ghana amongst the countries studied here, and Nigeria and Zambia from outside this group). Likewise the only clear link between adjustment and human rights issues is that in some countries (Zimbabwe, Ghana prior to 1987) organized opponents of adjustment have had their human rights infringed.

3. The Effects of Structural Adjustment on Key Aspects of Development in Sub-Saharan Africa

3.1 Macroeconomic and Structural Issues

3.1.1 Macroeconomic Policy

The aspects of structural adjustment discussed in this section are fiscal and monetary, exchange-rate and foreign trade policies. These are the areas of structural adjustment which were initiated first and probably most systematically.

1. *Fiscal and monetary policy*

Fiscal policies address the balance between public revenue and spending. Under structural adjustment, major concerns have been to reduce the deficits of government and parastatal corporations characteristic of the late 1970s and early 1980s, thus reducing public borrowing and hence the rate of inflation. Besides creating generally more stable economic conditions this is intended to benefit the private sector by reducing levels of taxation and making official credit cheaper and more available. Monetary policies share the goal of maintaining low inflation rates and adequate real interest rates by regulating the supply of money and credit.

Fiscal deficits were almost always reduced in the first years of adjustment programmes in Sub-Saharan Africa, only to rise again later. Many countries, including all five studied here, attempted reductions (in part at least) by restructuring their revenue base, with very varied outcomes. On the expenditure side, cutting central government budgets has proved easier than attaining reductions in overall spending. Parastatal deficits have usually failed to decline and in some countries have sharply increased, partly because a significant means of cutting state budgets has been to make parastatals fully internalize the costs of their operations, so moving deficits from the state budget to the parastatals and their creditors.

Meanwhile, reductions in government spending have not equally affected all expenditure headings. Despite frequent recommendations for increased spending, allocations of funds to social services have often tended to decline, while those to debt-service rise. Within recurrent expenditure the proportion going to the major fixed element (wages and salaries) has increased despite huge reductions in real wage levels. Shares of expenditure on complementary inputs (e.g. transport, school-books, medicines, tools) and on repair and maintenance have correspondingly declined.

In those countries where overall fiscal discipline has been relaxed during the 1990s, generally this has been a consequence of a combination of rising debt-service charges, pressures to restore some of the losses in civil service real wages, and problems of revenue collection. Some of these factors appear incorrigible, and in the absence of sustained growth will continue to generate budget deficits. Table 3.1, which sums up post-independence economic development in Sub-Saharan Africa, indicates that average deficits have almost doubled on the continent as a whole during the adjustment period.

Monetary policies in the early 1990s were found by the World Bank to be fair or better according to three indicators: revenue from printing money ('seigniorage'), the rate of inflation, and the real rate of interest; but these policies have come under pressure because of fiscal problems. Financial sector policies have aimed at contracting credit to the public sector, while enhancing the role of market mechanisms in allocating credit, but these policies have been slow in implementation.

Table 3.1 Trends in Sub-Saharan Africa's Economic Performance, Structure and Macroeconomic Balances, 1965-92

Indicator	Economic Performance Indicators (average annual change in percent)							
	1965-73		1973-80		1980-87		1987-92	
	SSA Total	Excl. Nigeria	SSA Total	Excl. Nigeria	SSA Total	Excl. Nigeria	SSA Total	Excl. Nigeria
GNP per Capita	2.9	1.2	0.1	-0.7	-2.8	-1.2	-2.0	-0.4
Agriculture	2.2	1.9	-0.3	0.7	1.3	1.8	1.8	1.1
Industry	13.8	-	4.3	1.8	-1.2	3.4	2.4	1.6
Export	15.1	5.7	0.2	2.0	-1.3	1.7	3.5[a]	3.4[a]
Import	3.7	3.4	7.6	2.9	-5.8	-1.5	0.8[a]	2.0[a]

Indicator	Structural Economic Change and Macroeconomic Balances							
	1965		1980		1987		1992	
	SSA Total	Excl. Nigeria	SSA Total	Excl. Nigeria	SSA Total	Excl. Nigeria	SSA Total	Excl. Nigeria
Agriculture (percent of GDP)	43	40	30	34	34	35	30	29
Industry (percent of GDP)	18	20	33	25	28	24	25	23
Gross Domestic Investm. (percent of GDP)	14	15	20	20	16	16	17	17
Gross Domestic Savings (percent of GDP)	14	15	22	15	13	11	12	10
Government Consumption (percent of GDP)	10	12	13	16	16	17	14	16
Govern. deficit incl. grants (percent of GDP)			6.8	4.7	5.5	4.7	8.4	8.4
External Balance (percent of GDP)			(1.5)	(7.0)	(4.2)	(5.1)	(3.7)	(6.1)
Net ODA (percent of GDP)			3.6	6.6	8.0	9.6	11.3	14.0
Total Debt Service as percent of Exports			11.6		27.5		25.7	
Terms of Trade (1987 = 100)			154	128	100	100	80	79

[a]   1986-92.
Source: World Bank Tables.

2.   *Exchange-rate policy*

Prior to adjustment, exchange rates were fixed by national governments, who also organized foreign-exchange allocation on an administrative basis. One result was a clear over-valuation of most African currencies. Under adjustment the objective has been to enhance the international competitiveness of local production vis-à-vis foreign production in local as well as in foreign markets, via more competitive exchange rates and the gradual liberalization of foreign-exchange markets. The theory is that exchange rates could be made both more realistic and stable by the introduction of 'near-market' allocative mechanisms. In practice these mostly involve auctioning donor balance-of-payments support to local banks and forex bureaux. Outside those countries whose currencies were part of the CFA mechanism (who did not devalue until January 1994) nominal exchange rates have fallen continuously. Only where balance-of-payments support has not been absorbed promptly have exchange rates stabilized or appreciated.

3.   *Foreign trade policy*

Strategies of import substitution in much of Africa in the 1970s resulted in foreign trade policies aimed at protecting local industries through high tariff rates and import controls, sometimes in the form of a licenze system. Parastatals which were inefficient and selected powerful private businessmen were favoured by this system, as well as the genuine infant industries it was designed to protect.

Trade policies under structural adjustment have taken the following forms: 1) a gradual move from a general system of import control towards open general licensing and a slowly decreasing 'negative' list of items requiring an import licence; 2) a gradual move from non-tariff to tariff controls, and a subsequent reduction in effective rates of tariff protection; and 3) the introduction of various forms of export incentives. Donors provided much of the funding for imports under open general licence arrangements, in exchange for these policy reforms. Because of problems which will be indicated elsewhere in this Report, attention has increasingly turned back to the third of these instruments.

3.1.2   Macroeconomic Effects of Structural Adjustment

1. The effect of the external environment and changes in the inflow of foreign aid

Of the factors working alongside policy changes to produce macroeconomic outcomes in Sub-Saharan Africa, probably the most important are changes in the flow of external finance (official and private transfers net of debt repayments) and changes in international terms of trade. Barter terms of trade have deteriorated rapidly for most Sub-Saharan African countries in the adjustment period (see Table 3.1). The reduction in local purchasing power has sometimes but not always been offset by increasing net transfers. In some African countries the real net increase in resources has been drastically reduced by servicing of old debt contracted in the pre-adjustment period.

The five countries studied were all negatively affected by decreasing terms of trade in the adjustment period, although less severely than some mineral and oil exporting countries. In Burkina Faso and Zimbabwe, aid flows associated with adjustment were insufficient to offset the combined negative effects of changes in terms of trade and debt-service, but in Tanzania the aid boom associated with adjustment more than offset the combined negative effects of a moderate decline in terms of trade and a very serious debt-service burden. Countries which have not adjusted have been deprived of much concessional aid, and this must account for a large share of their apparently greater difficulties.

2. Effects on 'market signals'

An important assumption of the IFIs was that the policies described above would not merely 'administratively' ensure stability and growth, but would send clear and attractive market signals to private actors. Hence a very important immediate aim was to 'get right' the inflation rate, interest rates, real import costs and real export returns.

Inflation.

As a result of contractive fiscal and monetary policies inflationary pressures have generally been controlled, in spite of the inflation imported via the heavy devaluation of local currencies. The record of the five case countries differs, however. In the initial period, inflation rates were most effectively reduced in the countries with the most rapid inflation in the early 1980s - Uganda and Ghana. In Burkina Faso and Tanzania inflation was controlled in the same period. However, the situation seems to have changed slightly in the 1990s. Due to increasing budget deficits (particularly in Ghana and Tanzania), the effect on food prices of drought (Zimbabwe in 1991-92) and increases in the share of total tax accounted for by sales taxes, inflation increased in all five countries in 1992 and 1993.

Real interest rates.

Historically there have been two quite separate credit systems in most African countries: an official one with low or negative interest rates but reserved mainly for parastatals and 'insiders'; and an unofficial one with very high positive interest rates. A major policy aim was to unify these credit markets, implying higher real interest rates for state enterprises and lower ones for ('non-insider') private borrowers. In fact the credit system has proved recalcitrant to reform. Officially approved borrowers have continued to enjoy low real interest rates in most countries, at least until very recently. On the other hand, in countries like Zimbabwe where the system has always been nearer IFI-set objectives, restrictive monetary policies have overshadowed events. Steep increases in interest have occurred for all borrowers, with an apparently depressive economic effect.

Cost of and access to foreign exchange; real returns to exports.

The general aim of devaluation was to reward exporters and penalize importers. The reward of exporters has run into two problems. Firstly, the terms of trade for many important African commodities have continued to fall sharply, wiping out local currency gains to producers. Secondly, exporters of agricultural products are mostly not themselves the direct recipients of foreign-exchange earnings. Until recently these passed mainly through marketing authorities, who frequently retained disproportionate shares of the increased earnings. For those foreign-exchange buyers privileged by the pre-adjustment system of allocation, structural adjustment has meant a drastic increase in the local cost of imports. But the elimination of the government-controlled system has not resulted in really market-based allocation. On the one hand the total forex available is increased by donor balance-of-payments support, and on the other the fact that credit allocation has not been deregulated results in continued discrimination against the genuinely private sector (i.e. those elements lacking in political or personal influence). Without access to credit it is difficult for small-scale entrepreneurs to raise the sufficient amounts of local currency required to bid in the foreign-exchange auction through banks and forex bureaux.

3. Medium-term macroeconomic outcomes
The IFIs assumed that through reforms to the regulative system and through improved market signals along the lines described, economic stability would be accompanied by enhanced economic performance and improved levels of savings and investment. This section focuses upon export performance, savings and investment and growth in GDP.

Export performance.
Measured by value of exports in fixed prices this has generally remained weak. According to the World Bank, between 1986 and 1992, the median rate of export growth for Sub-Saharan Africa was 3.5 percent per year compared with 9.2 percent in other developing countries. Although this was an improvement on the period 1973-87 (see Table 3.1), it is disappointing in view of the large devaluations. In three of the countries studied, international values of exports increased between the last three years for which figures were available before 1991 and the first three years after. In Uganda they fell, while in Zimbabwe they remained broadly the same. Of the countries where export values increased, only in the case of Burkina Faso was this increase higher than 3.3 percent. In Zimbabwe and Tanzania exports marginally increased as a share of GDP; in Ghana and Uganda they fell while in Burkina Faso they remained the same. By contrast there has been a clear and unambiguous trend in imports in all the countries examined. Their relation to export earnings has become increasingly tenuous, although the real value of imports per capita declined by some 30 percent during 1980-87 alone for Sub-Saharan Africa.

Savings and investment behaviour.
Any stabilization of fiscal balance and inflation would be expected to have a direct effect on savings and investment behaviour - particularly in the private sector. However, data from Sub-Saharan Africa generally do not suggest favourable changes. Savings rates continued their downward trend since 1980, while investment shows no sign of real recovery (see Table 3.1).

Among the five case-study countries, Ghana, Tanzania and Uganda had relatively large increases in gross investment between 1981-86 and 1987-91 (Ghana from 6.3 percent to 15.1 percent; Tanzania from 18.3 percent to 26.9 percent; and Uganda from 7.8 percent to 11.1 percent). Since 1991 investment has continued to increase in Uganda and Tanzania but has tailed off in Ghana. In Zimbabwe there has been a sharp increase in private investment, but one heavily offset by a collapse in public investment. Data on savings are also contradictory: Uganda exhibits a strong increase, albeit from a very low base, while there is no clear trend in Burkina Faso. Savings have declined sharply since 1991 in Zimbabwe and Ghana while Tanzania apparently exhibits a consistent trend of net dissavings. The latter figures are consistent with consumption (or at least private consumption) accounting for an increasing proportion of GDP.

Changes in GDP.
Generally speaking most adjusting countries in Africa have experienced a limited

expansion in the overall size of their economies during the adjustment phase. Once population growth is taken into account these levels of growth disappear or are seen to be more marginal. It also seems to be the case that growth has tailed off in the 1990s, with industrial growth in particular contracting (see Table 3.1). The countries examined adopted adjustment in different periods and against different backgrounds.

Upon adjustment three of them - Ghana, Tanzania and Uganda - showed an immediate rapid improvement in growth, of around 3 percent per annum each. Prior to adjustment though, Ghana and Tanzania were experiencing particularly acute economic crisis while Uganda was engulfed in civil war. Since 1991 growth has stagnated or slowed down in all three, although in Uganda and Ghana it still exceeds population growth. Growth in Burkina Faso dropped from an average of 5.8 percent in the pre-adjustment years of 1986-90 to 3.2 percent in 1991-93, while in Zimbabwe (whose growth in 1986-90 averaged 3.8 percent) the economy actually contracted in size. There appears to be a close relation between increases in growth and increases in aid volumes, which expanded very considerably in the three most successful performers examined here (Ghana, Uganda, Tanzania).

4. Medium- and long-term effects of structural adjustment
Structural transformation.
According to the advocates of adjustment, the latter implies a degree of structural transformation, i.e. a relative growth in those economic sectors producing exports and/or able to substitute for imports. The still weak export performance of the case-study countries has already been noted. Related to this has been an apparent reinforcement of the basic shape of most recipient economies. Although the share of agriculture in GDP in Africa as a whole has apparently fallen (see Table 3.1), the more successful performers examined here have actually seen agriculture increasing its share of GDP. Nor does the relative size and strength of the private sector seem to have changed. Many important reforms, of course, have not been implemented, but even if they were to be their suitability to promote long-term, sustainable growth remains unclear.

Increased debt burdens.
Relatively large increases in investments for rehabilitation and expansion of economic infrastructure (roads, water and power supply, telecommunications, etc.) have been undertaken by adjusting countries in order to promote production of tradeables. These investments have mostly been financed by foreign capital in the form of grants and loans. In Sub-Saharan Africa (excluding Nigeria) aid increased from an average of 7 percent of GDP in 1980 to 14 percent in 1992. Despite the fact that a large proportion of the capital inflows has been in the form of grants, and that debt rescheduling has been part of structural adjustment, the debt-service burden had by 1993 reached extremely high levels (30 percent plus of export values) in all the countries examined. Debt/export ratios reached 300 percent plus in Uganda and Tanzania and 200 percent plus in Ghana, i.e. clearly unsustainable positions.

3.1.3 Conclusion
Some aspects of macroeconomic stability were initially achieved, notably reduction in government deficits and inflation, but it seems that these have not been sustained. Other aspects of stabilization, notably in the trade balance and the balance between local

revenue and expenditure, have either been artificially plugged by increased aid volumes or are further away than before adjustment. Growth has recovered in some places, but not spectacularly, and also seems to be faltering. Exports have not taken off and although private sector activity has been deregulated, conditions for its operation remain otherwise largely unchanged. There are few signs of long-term private investment.

Some of this reflects non-implementation of the adjustment agenda but much of it reflects the agenda's own inadequacies. International conditions have been very adverse and increased aid levels have barely compensated for this. In many cases aid does not seem to have been used productively and there is little sign of a long-term transformation toward sustainable recovery.

3.2   Agriculture under Structural Adjustment

3.2.1   Main Features of African Agriculture

1.   Peasant agriculture in tropical Africa is overwhelmingly a matter of small peasant farms, which produce most agricultural output, and provide income for most of the population. Much production is aimed directly at household (subsistence) needs, but all households are also involved with markets. Many cannot survive from own-farm agriculture, so family members also engage in wage-labour, petty trading and other activities to earn a living and spread risk. Risk-spreading also involves cultivating a network of kinship and other relations, to provide security in time of need, or improved access to resources. These tend to be strongly patriarchal, marked by patron-client linkages, and linking into local political structures. This reflects a structure in which men own or control most land and other resources, while women do most of the work, specially but not only in food-crop production. While it is convenient to refer to the household as the basic productive unit, this can be misleading, since many households function as only partly linked sub-units. Most rural African societies are not egalitarian, and would not be characterized by perfect competition in the absence of state intervention.

2. Production techniques in farming over much of tropical Africa are in transition from long-fallowing or shifting cultivation, to permanent cultivation on one fixed farm - under pressure of population increase and the expansion of cash-crop farming. In some areas of high rainfall and population pressure, complex methods of soil regeneration have been developed locally. However, researchers, extension agents and policy-makers tend to think in terms of *replacing* 'traditional agriculture' (a term which implies lack of change) with a modern agriculture based on use of inputs and machinery, rather than *integrating* relevant aspects of both.

3. Migration. Another contribution to increased pressure on land has been movement into marginal areas of low and unreliable rainfall, usually previously grazed by pastoralists. This involves both social conflicts and the need to adjust farming techniques to new and difficult circumstances. With continued population growth and differentiation, further adoption of cash crops, and often declining prices for them, poorer households in both types of areas face sharpening crisis.

4. Variation. African conditions are far more varied than those of (say) western Europe. Climate varies from humid tropics to desert or cold highland. Soils vary from very rich to almost worthless. Cultivation takes place from sea level to 4000 metres, and varies from extensive grazing or shifting cultivation to irrigated multi-cropping. Farm size varies from tens of thousands of hectares down to the normal fraction of a hectare. There is also much variety in size and type of farming within the peasant sector. Most households produce crops and livestock, for own use and for local markets, sometimes also producing small amounts of export crops. During 1975-85, many smaller peasant farmers were encouraged to produce for national maize markets by donor projects involving subsidies on transport, inputs and credit. Elimination of the subsidies under structural adjustment has tended to reverse this. Large production units account for more marketed output than land area. Zimbabwe's agriculture is still dominated by a few thousand very large, mostly white-owned farms and ranches. Large (ex)-settler farms are important in Kenya and Côte d'Ivoire. Tanzania, Ghana and Uganda have smaller private large farm sectors, dominated by businessmen, civil servants, politicians and foreign companies. Many countries also have a parastatal farming/ranching sector, though most of these are currently being closed down or sold off under IFI pressures. Another type of large unit involves contract farming, in which a private or parastatal company organizes a group of small producers, providing inputs, controlling crop-growth and buying the produce, according to strict time and quality controls. This has been used especially for products for which quality is important, those which need immediate processing, and those whose price is high enough to pay the high costs of supervision and administration involved.

3.2.2   Major Policy Trends prior to Structural Adjustment

From before independence up to the mid-1980s, African governments, their external advisers and donors all saw the state as the most important dynamizing factor for peasant agriculture. Policy was dominated by agricultural modernization theory, which sees increasing productivity as coming almost solely from increased use of purchased inputs and mechanized equipment. Since African cultivators were seen to be 'resistant to change' it was up to the state to 'develop' them. Its research stations generated or imported innovations. Its agricultural extension service spread the information and 'persuaded' peasants to use them. It was taken for granted that, given the costs of distributing small amounts, inputs and credit would have to be subsidized. Credit to small peasants without property titles could only be secured through a 'crop-mortgage', and repaid by 'deduction-at-source' (by the purchasing agency). So efforts to modernize peasant agriculture were increasingly coordinated in projects which made inputs and machinery available at subsidized prices and on cheap credit and featured a monopoly over purchase. Thus most of the elements of parastatal marketing, criticized by the IFIs, were deliberately introduced as necessary components of modernization policy.

We have heard much over the past 15 years about general problems of state monopolies, but far less about the enormous variations in efficiency and honesty between institutions and time-periods, or their close relation to the requirements of agricultural development policy. Maintaining accounting control gets more difficult the greater the number of activities and cross-subsidies involved. More problems arise with arbitrary political interventions, as for example when senior politicians or state officials order parastatals or co-operatives to provide inputs or credit to individuals, schemes or villages, despite previous failure to pay or repay. Worst of all, things go totally awry during periods of grandiose political 'transformation', when resources are deployed especially wastefully. Similar problems arise with large bursts of donor aid.

For much of tropical Africa, this happened in 1974-79. With a steady increase in state spending since independence, many countries faced serious budget and foreign-exchange constraints by 1973. In that year, the Sahel reached the final year of a multi-year drought, and many countries of eastern Africa were suffering food shortages, just as aid inflows were peaking. These events pushed the issue of food security to centre stage. While the proportion of aid going to agriculture fell, the absolute amount rose. Countries were awash with projects and programmes to attack food insecurity and poverty by spreading modern agriculture to small peasants. Large amounts of money chasing limited project opportunities led to wasteful spending. The shift of focus to food crops actually reduced levels of production, especially for export crops, while increasing indebtedness at all levels.

Local states expanded their parastatal monopolies to (try to) accommodate the increase in aid. But parastatals' shape and size was every bit as much decided by donors and their consultants, who usually designed the programmes and always had the final say as to whether they would be funded.

3.2.3   Structural Adjustment and Agriculture

The period 1979-81 saw a sharp turn in IFI and other donor policies, placing the blame on the very institutions whose growth they had supported throughout the previous decade. One can (very roughly) distinguish two phases of agricultural adjustment, the first covering most of the 1980s (both before and after adoption from about the mid-1980s on). The second dates from about 1990. The prescriptions in the first phase included devaluation, cuts in general state expenditure and tighter control over parastatals, to increase producer prices for export crops and thus exports. The second phase shifted from specific measures to institutional changes, which meant closing or privatizing what remained of the state marketing sector. This has increasingly, and largely unintentionally, undercut the whole agricultural modernization model.

Both phases reduced investment in agriculture, by squeezing the budgets of Ministries of Agriculture and parastatals. They also reduced the scope for donor or state intervention, by eliminating the subsidies underlying most policy initiatives. But this only occurred with a lag, even after the conclusion of structural adjustment agreements. Most development spending was based on donor funds, and structural adjustment increased their availability. Moreover, one response of governments required to make budgetary cuts was to cut allocations of funds without annulling the activities they were meant to fund - for example subventions to parastatals or co-operatives to cover subsidies or other loss-making activities. This was true of grain marketing in the early 1990s in Zimbabwe, and in Tanzania during the late 1980s/early 1990s, where a large fertilizer subsidy was 'funded' by allowing parastatal deficits and bank borrowing to increase. The obvious effect of this has been to increase parastatal overdrafts with hidden state expenditures. Given this, the widespread claim by the IFIs that governments are doing fine on structural adjustment but are dragged down by inefficient parastatals seems disingenuous.

Within this general framework, there have been differences between export and food crops. In the first phase of adjustment, focused on increasing export-crop production, most energies were directed at restructuring and reducing the margins of export parastatals, like COCOBOD, the Ghanaian parastatal board controlling cocoa, or Tanzania's coffee, cotton and cashewnut authorities. In Ghana, devaluation and increased producer prices did increase production (and bring home informal exports via neighbouring countries). In Tanzania, IFI-induced interest-rate increases (together with falling terms of trade without removing parastatal monopolies) contributed to an increase in marketing margins of export-crop parastatals and to a fall in real producer prices in spite of devaluation. This and similar cases partly account for the shift of emphasis since 1990: from tighter control of parastatals, to their privatization.

This has encountered resistance, not only, as World Bank reports usually present it, because it hits personal interests (which of course it does), but for policy reasons. How can cheap inputs and credit be provided, or markets for small peasants in less accessible areas, by a weak and largely uninterested private sector? Nonetheless, by the mid-1990s, a large proportion of export-crop marketing had been divested or no longer monopolized. In Uganda and Tanzania, at least so far, this has been associated with increases in producer prices. In Kenya the reverse is the case.

Food-crop marketing was monopolized later than export crops in most countries, and far less effectively. In Uganda and Ghana control was always negligible. In Tanzania and Kenya, state monopolies controlled much less than half the trade, even in maize and wheat. More generally, donor projects to develop peasant maize production invariably depended on parastatal agencies. In Zimbabwe the Grain Marketing Board was the institution which successfully brought small peasants into the national maize market, from which they had previously been excluded, and purchased most of the crop other than subsistence needs. Burkina Faso seems nearer to Zimbabwe than the others.

The response of the IFIs to all countries has been (almost) identical: get rid of the subsidies and then the parastatal agency, even if this excludes significant numbers of peasants from a major source of income - often one which they had specifically been encouraged to take up only a few years earlier. Besides Zimbabwe, this has been the experience of smallholders in Tanzania's Southern Highlands, Zambia's Northern Province and maize producers in Ghana. Perhaps as a result of French influence, Burkina Faso is the exception, whose grain monopoly is not (yet) slated for privatization.

3.2.4 Production Policy under Structural Adjustment

Statements in adjustment plans that investment in agriculture should be expanded have usually been over-ridden by budgetary cuts. Statements about improving the supply of inputs or credit normally turn out to mean closing down existing state-controlled (subsidized) programmes to allow prices and interest rates to rise enough to attract the private sector. Sectoral adjustment programmes contain the same predictable features: removal of most remaining state intervention in marketing and of subsidies, liberalization, and, paradoxically, introduction of the World Bank's 'Training & Visit' (T&V) extension system, which is expensive, top-down and entirely within the pre-adjustment paradigm.

T&V concentrates heavily on input use and especially fertilizer use on hybrid maize. But devaluation has increased fertilizer and other input prices enormously and this, together with removal of subsidies, has had a large and negative impact on input use and maize production. The positive side of this is that it has persuaded some governments and donors of the benefits of a low-input approach to developing peasant agriculture. The negative side is that few have got beyond such vague phrases, that still fewer have even started on the mass of research needed, and are discouraged from doing so, while the World Bank still pushes T&V.

Policy statements also stress a shift to small peasant farmers and the need for low-external-input policies. But in Ghana, where expenditure on research has increased under structural adjustment, this has not been coordinated with smallholder farmers or local researchers. There is no more evidence of such a shift elsewhere. This is not surprising. The whole training and job experience of state extension personnel inclines them to look upwards to what their superiors want rather than out towards the farmers. Moreover the labour requirements of a policy of using research to improve existing small-farming methods, would be massive - and unthinkable under current budgetary stringency unless organized in a completely different way.

3.2.5   Input Use Levels under Structural Adjustment

Use of purchased inputs is low in African peasant agriculture, for reasons which are in dispute between neo-liberals and agricultural modernizers. The former argue that state monopoly marketing and input distributing agencies have distorted markets and reduced output prices, so reducing returns to inputs and demand. Modernizers point out that adoption of inputs has basically been the result of state/donor projects, often run through parastatals/cooperatives, and involving subsidies. This has been a very expensive way of increasing input use, and has hugely increased the liquidity and other problems of state monopolies. It is argued by the IFIs that private traders will rapidly adapt to this trade if the circumstances are right, but historical examples are not encouraging. The only known cases where private business has introduced input use without a major state input or subsidy, is in 'contract-farming' type schemes for, say, tea, sugar or tobacco (and most of these have been subsidized). These are even more costly than modernization through extension and subsidy, and thus affect correspondingly fewer people.

The current situation is that devaluation has enormously increased relative prices of inputs and made most current extension advice economically unviable (especially for fertilizer). Where data are available, as in Ghana and Kenya, input use has clearly fallen sharply. If this was associated with more precise levels of application, better integrated into general husbandry improvement, this might not necessarily be bad. But most extension personnel are still retailing advice from the 1960s and 1970s, which is now irrelevant.

3.2.6   Trends in Production and Marketed Output

IFI sources all claim an increase in agricultural production under structural adjustment, and their figures show this unequivocally. FAO figures paint a much less clear picture. Its 1994 *Production Yearbook* shows an index of total agricultural production from 1980 to 1992. African growth rates were identical for the two 7-year periods 1979/81-1986 and 1986-93. 24 percent of 37 sampled countries did better in 1986-93, 22 percent did much the same and 54 percent did worse. As shown in Table 3.2 the main difference between the two periods is that variation between countries increased. More did well, but more did really poorly in the second period. With population growing at around 3 percent, over 70 percent of countries would have registered a per capita decline.

Table 3.2 Growth in Agricultural Production in 37 Countries in Africa

Average annual Growth, Percentages	Percent (rounded) of total number of countries	
	1979/81-1986	1986-1993
Over 6	-	3
5-6	5	3
4-5	3	8
3-4	16	16
2-3	30	14
1-2	27	16
0-1	8	16
less than 0	11	24

Source: FAO, *Production Yearbook 1994.*

Table 3.3 shows figures from two sources for the countries studied here which are generally thought to be well above average in implementing adjustment and agricultural growth. Taking FAO figures, only Ghana and Uganda increased growth rates in the second period; with World Bank figures, only Uganda and Tanzania. In general, for 29 countries two-thirds of World Bank estimates were over twice or less than half those from FAO.

Table 3.3 Different Estimates of Agricultural Growth, percent per annum. Agriculture in GDP, constant prices

Case country	FAO 1979-86	FAO 1987-93	WB 1988-92	Country data 1988-93
Burkina Faso	6	3.3	0.8	..
Ghana	4	4	1.6	1.25
Tanzania	2	0	5.0	1.6/4.5[a]
Uganda	2	4.7	3.3	3.8
Zimbabwe	3.5	0.5	-2.1	3.3

[a]   Agriculture GDP at 1976 prices, Tanzania Government/World Bank, 1994.

In *Tanzania* an increase in agricultural growth, starting with Tanzania's own structural adjustment programme (1984-85), continued under the World Bank-supported programme from 1986. This is quite modest in relation to the import-support funds poured in and improvements in the weather, and is certainly not an 'agricultural boom' as asserted in one World Bank publication. Adjustment failed to increase producer prices for export crops up to 1989, resulting in very limited growth in (measured) output and sales. Most of the increase in production came from domestic crops and the 'non-measured' sector. Buoyant maize production is as likely to be a result of a fertilizer subsidy, which the IFIs failed to eliminate until 1992, as of structural adjustment policies. Freeing markets does seem to have stimulated increases in production, but their size can only be guessed at.

In *Uganda* a recent World Bank report has also claimed an 'agricultural boom'. This seems exaggerated although all sources agree on growth of over 4 percent per annum since 1987-88, with higher growth in monetary than subsistence agriculture. Production of the two main traditional export crops coffee and cotton has stagnated in volume terms, while the value of coffee exports had fallen by 1993 to about one third of the level of the early 1980s, as a result of terms-of-trade deterioration. Tea and tobacco production and exports have both grown rapidly.

In *Ghana* where the focus in the first adjustment programme was on cocoa, devaluation did increase production from 1984 on, but the effect peaked in the late 1980s. FAO figures show average exports for 1991-93 as being 96 percent of the level in 1979-81. Domestic crop production increased in 1984, but was largely a bounce-back from a very poor previous year. This pushed prices down, after which production stagnated until 1991. Since then it has grown quite rapidly according to FAO.

Zimbabwe: Devaluation provided price incentives for increased tobacco exports, which in the early 1990s were double their 1979-81 level, though most of the growth came before structural adjustment in the 1990s. Cotton production grew to 1988 and has stagnated since then. Peasant producers with limited alternative options seem likely to be the losers. Maize production has varied and is hard to analyze, with a major drought in the first year of structural adjustment. Recent communal area deliveries account for about 60 percent of the total, but the infrastructure sustaining this is being dismantled.

Burkina Faso: The overall value of agricultural production grew rapidly during 1984-86, then remained at that level until 1990, before moving up to another plateau, some 30 percent higher. From the timing, structural adjustment may in the last three years have contributed to this. Devaluation in 1994 seems to have benefitted both cotton and livestock producers.

Long-term trends: Arriving at conclusive judgements about these trends is of course very difficult, not only because declining terms of trade for most of Africa's export products have severely reduced the nominal price increases expected to derive from devaluation. Weather is perhaps the most important single factor determining inter-annual fluctuations in agricultural production and renders many short-term assessments of structural adjustment unreliable. The long-term outlook for most of Africa's major export crops is no better than that for the short term: continued stagnation or further decline. There may be unworked opportunities for 'non-traditional' (niche) exports, but all the signs are that increasing desperation to expand exports, coupled with low elasticity of demand, will reduce the revenues to be earned here too, when it does not simply open markets for large-scale, low-cost producers, mostly outside tropical Africa. With no reason to expect improvement in exchange rates, costs of imported inputs and machinery are likely to remain high. This leaves the small-scale producers of rural Africa to intensify their agriculture without mechanization or high input levels. This can be achieved technically, by improved organization of the available resources. Whether it will happen is another matter. Its main precondition is a large increase in research, much more closely integrated into existing patterns of farming, to develop their strong points with well-aimed innovations, rather than discard them for a model of 'modern farming' no longer relevant or economically viable.

While the way forward must involve low-external-input agriculture, this is not a panacea. It is by no means an easy option, since by sparing on purchased inputs, it requires more and more skilled labour to be expended. Beyond that, what those skills are precisely has yet to be established in most cases - and it is something which needs to be established in conjunction with peasant farmers, taking account of the specifics of where they live, its climate, soils, and social structures, labour availability etc. It is not an easy option in research terms either. One or two simple fertilizer recommendations for a country the size of Tanzania will no longer do (they never did). But all of this involves an enormous increase in the labour expended in the field and the question how it is to be mobilized and paid for under present circumstances remains entirely unanswered.

3.3 Industry

3.3.1 Industrial Development in Africa

Of all sectors, industry shows the divide between state interventionist and neo-classical thinking most clearly. For state interventionists the small size and especially the disarticulation of Africa's industrial sectors have been seen as a clear hindrance to development, reducing economic options and increasing dependence on imports. Since it was obvious that new factories, operating on the small scale dictated by most African domestic markets, would not be internationally competitive, protection was almost invariably a feature. Besides the theoretical argument, based on 'infant industries', this was usually politically necessary. Domestic manufacturing firms normally had the political strength to demand protection, while prospective foreign partners were unlikely to invest without assured markets.

The major problem with this line of thinking has been that enthusiasm for the claimed general benefits from industrial investment too easily excluded close scrutiny of the specific costs and benefits. Thus, investments were often approved, despite the fact that the goods produced were more expensive and of poorer quality than imported ones. For consumers this can mean a narrower choice at higher prices, i.e. a reduction in real incomes. Further negative effects arise if the inferior items produced are of strategic economic importance (water pumps, fertilizers, agricultural and other tools). Such problems have been not infrequent in African industrialization.

For neo-liberals 'consumer choice', expressed through the market, should be supreme. Questions of economic structure disappear from view. Specific costs and benefits are the only criteria and the focus for industrialization is the development of internationally competitive industries aimed at the world market. Few tropical African countries have the infrastructure and other conditions for their successful operation, though. From this follows the conditionality applied by the IFIs to the broken-down and highly protected manufacturing sectors (often dominated by parastatals) found in pre-adjustment Africa: reduce or eliminate producer subsidies, raise interest rates, and impose financial discipline on parastatals (often as a prelude to privatization or liquidation), set up incentive schemes for private enterprise and improve its access to foreign exchange, and reduce lending to the public sector to make more available to the private.

Industrial structures: For most purposes industries can be divided into three standard categories, large, medium and small/micro. The latter are discussed in Section 3.4. Given the size of Sub-Saharan African economies and markets, *large-scale firms,* whether public, private or joint-venture, necessarily operate non-competitively since their output typically suffices for all or most of the local market. In almost all cases, there are significant political and economic barriers to entry, and those who have surmounted them almost invariably wield or have access to influence. Ownership is divided between a small minority of local Africans, a larger group of local foreigners (white or Asian for example), foreign private business, parastatal agencies, and joint ventures between two or more of the above. In all the countries studied (except Zimbabwe) parastatal and joint enterprises predominate. This size group, and notably parastatals with donor connections, has been the major focus of donor import support and rehabilitation programmes during adjustment.

Medium-sized firms, typically employing 5-50 employees, also operate in regulated formal markets, often with high protection against imported commodities. Generally, being smaller and less politically influential, they will be more subject to the vagaries of protection policy (sudden elimination for example, to benefit a politically powerful importer) and less favoured by incentive schemes. They do, however, often attract the interest and funds of donor 'small-scale industry' projects.

Industrial development in Sub-Saharan Africa started under colonialism with some agricultural and food processing, largely for settler demand, together with engineering and construction largely determined by state (and railway) needs. Both the rate and scope of investment increased after independence, when most countries aimed at partial import substitution, starting with the 'easy options', but sometimes taking intersectoral linkages and requirements into account. An expansion of industrial investment really took off in the 1970s, both as a result of the lending boom, and because of the expansion of a new form of investment designed for states engaged in giving aid or engaging in export promotion. This was the donor- or recipient state-backed loan, normally to a parastatal (often a new one), accompanied by a supply and management contract to a donor firm. In the process recipient governments contracted both risks and debts.

Patterns of industrial development, so far as they represented anything other than what donors were willing to offer, stressed both export enhancement (agricultural and mineral processing) and import substitution. The latter was supported by protection and import confinement. Few of the resulting industries were ever internationally competitive, although many depended heavily on imported inputs. With the forex shortages and collapsing domestic demand of the pre-adjustment 1980s, large numbers scarcely functioned at all. However, in the case of larger markets like Zimbabwe, which avoided this crisis, or Kenya where loans were forthcoming, largely private industrial sectors continued to function more or less as before.

3.3.2   Industrial Development under Structural Adjustment

Assessing the impact of adjustment on industry in Sub-Saharan Africa involves all the measurement problems listed in Chapter 1. In comparing the five countries studied here, further complications arise. Zimbabwe has a large and complex industrial sector, built up under the UDI regime. Currently it accounts for nearly a quarter of GDP and employs 20 percent of the labour force. In Burkina Faso, manufacturing employs less than 10,000 people, or only 1 percent of the labour force. In Ghana, Tanzania and Uganda, it accounts for 14 percent, 8 percent and 5 percent of GDP respectively - in all cases below the mid-1970s level.

Zimbabwe and Burkina Faso only started on adjustment programmes in 1991. Manufacturing growth in Burkina Faso has been lower since adjustment than before it started. In Zimbabwe, it has actually contracted. Part of the decline can be attributed to the adjustment process, and its sequencing. The other three countries have longer adjustment histories, but otherwise different backgrounds. Tanzania was seeing its ambitious plans for basic industrialization founder on inefficiencies, corruption and a desperate shortage of foreign exchange dictated by the IFI 'lending hiatus'. All three faced problems of revitalizing parastatal industrial sectors that were largely broken down. Similarly, the content of adjustment programmes for industry has varied, depending on starting position. Zimbabwe's relatively large, sophisticated and well-organized private business sector was active in mediating and presenting its own interests during the negotiations. For most of the others, adjustment, with its connotations of austerity, redundancy and privatization or liquidation, was at best grudgingly accepted. Many parastatal managers were understandably reluctant to do more to assist in their own demise than what was necessary to get the foreign funds which might postpone this fate.

The changes induced by adjustment can be grouped under different policy headings. Periodization is more difficult as sequences varied:

Foreign exchange: Adjustment almost always started with a major devaluation, which increased the prices of imported inputs and the need for foreign exchange. Especially for enterprises started with donor support, the latter was supplied in the form of commodity import-support grants, debited to the enterprise. This was gradually supplemented, then replaced by Open General Licensing systems which allocate donated foreign exchange essentially on the basis of a queuing system. This improved access to spare parts and raw materials for those firms (mostly parastatal or joint venture) which could get credit to buy foreign exchange. Capacity utilization of such companies then increased significantly in the short run. More recently, problems with OGL systems have led to a change to foreign-exchange auctions, still of mainly donated exchange. All this has meant a shift in constraint from forex to local credit with which to pay for it.

Credit and investment promotion: Starting from the assumption that subsidized credit to parastatals was crowding out lending to the private sector, adjustment has concentrated in raising interest levels to market rates and directing more of it towards the private sector. Donors have also begun to redirect their industrial assistance towards private or semi-private firms, offering tax and duty incentives for private investment.

Foreign trade and protection: Adjustment has simultaneously involved reducing protection levels and moving away from non-tariff protection (like quotas) and imports confinement. The next step is to reduce the tariffs. The idea is that this both reduces costs of imported inputs and improves competitiveness through increasing incentives for efficiency. However, it may also expose producers to dumping etc. by foreign competitors.

3.3.3   Effects of Structural Adjustment on Industrial Development

Table 3.4 shows World Bank industrial data since 1980. The figures are consistent with national data for three of the five countries. But national data show rather higher growth in Ghana (index for 1992: 135), and for Burkina Faso a completely different trend, peaking in 1989. The impact to date of adjustment on industries in the five countries has been very varied.

Table 3.4 Manufacturing GDP at Factor Cost (1987 prices, Index, 1980 = 100)

Country	1980	1981	1982	1983	1984	1985	1986	1987	1988	1989	1990	1991	1992
Burkina F	100	91	102	102	102	103	97	114	108	117	126	130	138
Ghana	100	81	64	57	65	80	89	99	103	104	109	111	115
Tanzania	100	89	84	79	79	79	74	79	84	89	89	100	100
Uganda	100	89	84	47	47	37	37	42	53	58	63	68	74
Zimbabwe	100	106	106	106	100	111	117	117	122	128	138	138	128

Notes: Shaded areas are pre-adjustment years.
Source: *World Bank Tables*, 1994.

The most positive and consistent outcome is for Uganda, where production has at least doubled from 1986 to the present, by an average 9 percent per annum. In Ghana and Tanzania, the initial effect was very positive, as import support relieved constraints, but since then, especially in Tanzania, it seems to have slowed. In Zimbabwe, the decline since adjustment (and drought) has been very severe.

Table 3.5 Annual Average Growth Rates of Manufacturing Output 1980-93

Country	1980-85	1985-93	1991	1992	1993
Burkina Faso	1.4	4.7	3.2	6.8	1.0
Ghana	-5.5	4.3	1.1	2.7	2.3
Tanzania	-4.7	4.3	12.0	1.9	2.1
Uganda	-	8.0	12.7	3.6	3.7
Zimbabwe	0.9	3.1	2.8	-9.5	-8.3

Source: World Bank, *Trends in Developing Economies*, 1994.

Table 3.5 shows rates of growth for different periods. These were higher in the late than in the early 1980s, both in the three countries which had started adjustment, and in Zimbabwe and Burkina Faso, which had not. The decline in rates of growth in Ghana and Tanzania during the 1990s reflects closure or running-down of parastatal enterprises prior to sale or liquidation, increased cost and difficulty of access to credit, and increasing difficulties in competing with imports as protection is removed. In Ghana, 120 factories are reported to have closed during 1988-92, though there is no information on whether new firms have started up to replace them. In Tanzania, much parastatal manufacturing is to be scrapped or sold, the latter seemingly hampered among other things by lack of potential buyers. In Uganda such problems seem to have been less serious.

Enterprise surveys in Ghana and Tanzania allow pre- to post-adjustment comparisons, although the results are inconclusive. Of 131 enterprises surveyed in Tanzania 1986-1992 production increased in 60 percent, decreased in 30 percent, and was unchanged in 10 percent. In Ghana, a survey of 168 firms in the food, metal, wood and textile branches reported positive sales growth in real terms for only about one third of the sample, between 1988 and 1991.

Data on capacity utilization are scarce. For Uganda, it is said to have risen steadily since the start of adjustment/the end of the civil war but it is unclear by how much. In Ghana, utilization doubled from 18 percent in 1984 to around 40 percent in 1989, and then to some 60 percent in 1992, a very significant increase. In Tanzania, by contrast, one study shows a fall from 38 percent in 1982-84 to about 29 percent in 1986-89, rising to 37 percent for 1990-91. Later studies find a decline thereafter. Decline in production on the scale experienced by Zimbabwe from 1992 must clearly have reduced capacity utilization.

Branch impacts. The impact of adjustment on different branches has been quite uneven within and between countries, making general conclusions hard to draw. The findings of a study in Ghana seem generally plausible: industries faring well after adjustment tended to have a strong local resource base, access to cheap inputs, or natural protection. But data from elsewhere show that leather and textiles, both based on local raw materials, have generally fared badly. It also seems likely that heavily import-dependent industries have fared worse, being more vulnerable to devaluation, but no data showing this have been encountered. Besides adjustment-related factors like increased utility charges, dearer inputs and credit and more exposure to competition, other factors which dampen the growth of manufacturing output in all the countries studied are continuations of pre-adjustment problems. These include inefficient banking systems, poor infrastructure and overmanning. In Ghana, Tanzania, Uganda and Zimbabwe governments have been lobbied hard by local entrepreneurs for increases in overall levels of protection, but to little effect.

Investments. Adjustment has not usually led to significant increases in private investment, with the exception of Zimbabwe. Recent research indicates a continuation in 1989-94 of an already well-established pattern of disinvestment by British companies with equity involvements in anglophone Africa. A major reason seems to have been the effects of local devaluations on internationally denominated earnings. All five countries have legislated new investment codes that substantially remove previous controls on domestic and foreign investment. Investment centres have also been established to promote and facilitate the investment process. These produce regular reports of dramatic increases in the number and value of investments approved but, in practice, only a tiny fraction ever become operational. The success of adjustment in industry depends heavily on the emergence of private investors to take over from the state, but in most cases, the incentive system remains badly skewed against this.

Table 3.6 Manufactured Exports Pre- and Post-Adjustment

	Burkina Faso	Ghana	Tanzania	Uganda	Zimbabwe
Value (US$ million)					
Pre-adjustment	15.7	5.1	43.9	1.2	428.7
Most recent	17.3	10.4	61.9	0.5	387.9
Percent change	10.2	103.9	41.0	-58.3	-9.5
Share in total exports					
Pre-adjustment	12.1	0.7	14.4	0.3	30.8
Most recent	12.1	1.1	15.7	0.3	31.3
Percent change	0	0.4	1.3	0	0.5

Notes: 'Pre' adjustment value estimates are averages for the three years immediately prior to the start of adjustment programmes. The 'most recent' figures are for 1990-92 for Ghana, Tanzania and Uganda, and 1991 and 1992 for Burkina Faso and Zimbabwe.
Source: IMF, *Statistical Yearbooks.*

Productivity. Reliable data on the development of productivity are generally not available. In Tanzania, average value-added per employee (in constant 1976 prices) was slightly higher (5.2 percent) during 1988-90 than in the three years immediately prior to the start of the adjustment programme. With real wages in the manufacturing sector falling by half during the same period, this implies a massive drop in physical productivity, but the World Bank claims that efficiency in the industrial sector has improved.

Exports. Table 3.6 shows changes in the value of manufactured exports from the case-study countries during the adjustment process and demonstrates that the new incentives created by adjustment policies have not yet resulted in significant increases. Indeed, in Uganda and Zimbabwe, the value of manufactured exports has declined. The World Bank asserts that the export drive in Tanzania has tripled manufactured exports between 1984 and 1990, but this is not supported by IMF trade statistics. The share of manufactured goods in total exports has remained virtually unchanged in all five case-study countries.

3.4 The Informal 'Sector' and Informal Economic Activities

3.4.1   Informal Economic Activities prior to Structural Adjustment
A lot of claims are made about growth of the 'informal sector' in relation to structural adjustment. Most such claims are of doubtful validity, because of lack of data and

because of inconsistent uses of the notion itself. Here the term will be used simply to mean economic activities that are unregistered and exist outside state regulations. This usage covers *small-scale or micro-enterprises*, which comprise by far the largest number of informal enterprises. Most of the turnover of informal economic activity is probably derived from *the informal activities of incorporated enterprises*, often quite large by local standards, as well as those of smaller, partially formal enterprises. By this is meant activity based on 'informal' access to and distribution of state-allocated resources; favourable loans for investment; relief from or avoidance of taxes or duties; the 'blind eye' of police or customs; or spin-offs from parastatal corruption. Even if demonstrated, growth in the level of informal activities cannot simply be said to imply either the growth of small business or a move towards freedom of markets.

Many African colonies, particularly those dominated by settlers, discouraged the growth of *small-scale enterprises*, both artisanal and trading, with licensing and credit-restriction policies. Both rural and urban populations were to be served by the formal sector, which was often granted monopoly status. An active informal sector serving Africans emerged anyway, but its overall level of activity remained much smaller than it would have been. After independence, with (some) reduction of barriers to entry and rapid growth of urban populations, the main dynamic of their growth seems to have been growing money incomes, rural and urban. A lasting division of labour emerged within the sector with clear gender-based specializations: trade in foodstuffs, beer-brewing and basketry amongst women; other trade, repairs, manufacturing and mining amongst men.

With the onset of economic crisis in many African countries from the late 1970s onwards, small-scale enterprises seem to have grown more rapidly, and most governments gave up systematic efforts to control the process. This time, their basic dynamic seems to have been shortages of imported and formally produced goods and services, combined with rising unemployment, declining real wages, and the collapse of state systems. This stimulated certain forms of artisanal production, as well as informal trading in crops, forest products, minerals, and game trophies.

Operating conditions for small-scale productive enterprises in Africa generally remained quite poor in this period. Although increasingly tolerated, operators enjoyed little legal security and usually had problems gaining access to credit. A still more serious problem has been an absence of markets for and skills in making high labour-input manufactured goods, of the type which have allowed some small-scale enterprises in Asia and Latin America to make a successful transition to medium-sized status.

Informal aspects of formal sector activity have also been present in Africa since the colonial period, but their growth also started to accelerate and become more noticeable with increasing shortages of formally produced goods and services (and foreign exchange); falling formal sector incomes/official agricultural prices; and declines in the effectiveness of sanctions. In the immediate pre-adjustment period the most important activities were probably informal access to licences, permits and credit; illicit sale of public property or confined goods; illicit acquisition of private monopolies to distribute or purchase otherwise confined goods; smuggling, plunder of reserved natural resources; and undeclared provision of services for hard currency.

3.4.2   Structural Adjustment, Aid and Informal Economic Activities
Structural adjustment policies generally have not directly addressed *small-scale enterprises*. Indirectly, they are seen as evidence of market orientation, and much of the

thrust of liberalization has been to admit them to the formal economy. Simultaneously, there has been a major expansion, among bilateral donors and NGOs, of what may be called 'micro enterprise developmentalism', in which support to small-scale enterprise, usually in the form of credit, is seen as an instrument for overcoming poverty and even organizing the poor (especially women). However, given the size of the sector relative to the resources available, such efforts are bound to be largely gestural and limited in their impact, even if they set local accumulation processes in motion.

As far as *informal aspects of formal activity* are concerned, there is a general faith that a combination of more open markets and civil service reform will lead to the formalization or elimination of the worst excesses, but little in the way of specific policies.

Trends in adjusting countries.
Small-scale enterprises. Where reliable figures are available there has been at least a continuation and possibly an acceleration in the growth of activity and employment in small-scale enterprises, in urban and rural areas, in the latter case to an extent that some commentators are now referring to 'de-peasantization'. In urban areas meanwhile it is now accepted that small-scale enterprises account for the overwhelming bulk of employment.

Adjustment outcomes vary considerably between and within countries. There seems to have been some revival of the earlier 'income' dynamic of small-scale enterprise growth in areas where adjustment and increases in aid receipts have been associated with growth and based on demand from those sections of the population whose incomes have risen. But with increased formal unemployment and major real income reductions for many, even in 'successful adjusters', increasing numbers of poor and downwardly mobile people have been also forced into small-scale activities, concentrated in those areas where barriers to entry (and rates of return) are lowest. This expansion has been especially evident amongst women, where it remains concentrated in the branches listed above.

Evidence is sketchy, but the general picture shows a tiny minority of enterprises which are evolving economically and a mass which only provide what one commentator has called 'involutive self-employment'. Where, as in Zimbabwe, there has been no growth in incomes or consumption, increased entry and competition have very considerably reduced operators' returns - especially in branches where women predominate. In a number of countries there appears to have been a change in the distribution of small-scale enterprises by branches. Prior to adjustment, the more dynamic branches were those producing substitutes for unavailable formal goods. With trade liberalization these goods are again available, and the dynamism has now shifted to informal trade (local and international) in relatively high-valued imported goods.

Informal activities by formal enterprises. There is no evidence of the predicted (by proponents of adjustment) decline in these types of activities, if anything the reverse. Firstly, wage-compressive 'civil service reform' has made it more rather than less likely that state employees would be pushed into informal activities. Secondly, the pre-privatization limbo that most public enterprises are in encourages the plunder of their remaining resources. Thirdly, and most importantly, far from reducing the number of rent-commanding niches - and the rents that can be extracted from them - the type of deregulation of economic activities which has occurred under adjustment has tended simply to shift their location.

Illicit foreign-exchange transactions and smuggling once commanded the major premiums. With trade liberalization and increased donor import support, it now seems that the major gains and the locus of illicit dealings have shifted to 'working' the formal system, whether by avoiding payment in local currency for official foreign-exchange purchases, obtaining official exemptions from duties and taxes on legally imported goods, or benefitting from new private sector incentive programmes previously reserved for state agencies.

3.5   Public Sector Reform

3.5.1   The State of the Reform Agenda

Adjustment until recently aimed at a reduced state and public sector in four respects:

- Removal of central planning and control through the release of markets and enhanced private sector development.
- Reduction of government budget deficits through removal of subsidies, privatization of public enterprises and transfer of public services to private institutions.
- Modernization of the public sector through increased wage differentiation, decentralization and civil service reform (based on reduction of numbers and functions).
- Liberalization of government-controlled regulation over prices and allocation of foreign exchange and essential commodities.

So far, structural adjustment has had significant effects only through liberalization. Adjustment has removed some of the instruments of the state (market control and subsidies), but has had little effect on the size and structure of the public sector, including the number and functions of parastatals. Modernization has largely failed, since (correctly) it has been seen by politicians and public employees as primarily a vehicle for cuts.

At the same time, the functions and capacity of the state are - once again - seen also by the IFIs as the key to the development of African societies. The World Bank is currently leading donors in adopting a new longer-term approach to public sector reform. The advocates of adjustment now distinguish between a) what is possible to achieve under adjustment and b) what requires longer-term interventions not based on the policy-conditionality type of adjustment lending:

a)   Completing the original agenda plus rationalizing revenue and expenditure management and creating a rolling investment plan.

b)   Building consensus on social development; upgrading the quality of the civil service via career streams and promotion systems based on merit; strengthening budget and investment management; building policy analysis and regulatory capacity; enhancing accountability at all levels; building a transparent legal framework.

Both the restated and current objectives and their sequencing are questionable. The likelihood of failure is high when donors promote cutting down and privatization without a clear set of nationally determined objectives on the intended relations between state, market and civil society, and without effective strategies and instruments to reach these objectives. This has produced a negative starting-point for future public sector reform: the existing overall capacity of the public sector has been reduced, and government commitment to the design and implementation of future reforms is low.

3.5.2   Privatization of Public Enterprises and Services

Structural adjustment has encouraged privatization of public enterprises and services in two ways. Firstly, under the heading of public enterprise reform, efforts have been made to have parastatals dismantled (particularly in the case of marketing and input supply boards), commercialized (through performance contracts with public utilities), liquidated (through closures), exposed to competition (by private companies), and divested (sale of public assets). Exposure to competition has been particularly evident in the financial sector. Privatization has been relatively rare. Burkina Faso, Tanzania, Uganda and Zimbabwe all divested less than 10 percent of their public enterprises during 1986-92. According to The World Bank's *Adjustment in Africa* report (page 103):

> The available data on the public enterprise sector are sparse and disappointing, showing no significant reduction in the number of enterprises, little improvement in their financial performance, unacceptable returns on government investment, and inability to meet the demand for cost-effective, efficient provision of public services. Divestiture is proceeding slowly among small and medium-sized firms and scarcely at all among large enterprises. ... Performance contracts and other attempts to boost the efficiency of enterprises remaining under state ownership have failed.

Loss-making and ineffective public enterprises constitute an unsustainable burden on public budgets and national credit markets. Hence, the reform objectives were valid. However, adjustment has to a large extent contributed to the malaise, rather than curing it. When governments remove subsidies without wanting the consumers and users of public services to be hurt, public enterprises are forced to internalize the unavoidable deficits. Many public enterprises have at the same time been hit by increased costs of imported inputs and direct competition from imports. In all the countries studied, parastatal debts have increased dramatically during adjustment. As a result, a majority cannot be sold off in anything resembling their current shape, while across-the-board liquidation remains politically unacceptable.

The second form of privatization concerns the strong appearance of non-governmental providers of public services, particularly in health, inputs and credit but also in fields such as local security and conflict resolution. With the exception of agricultural inputs, this change has come about by default rather than by design, as service users have been forced to look for alternative providers. There are growing concerns about the equity implications of the consumption of such services which are heavily fee-based. Meanwhile, government providers of health and education services seem to be entering a vicious circle of declining service quality and increasing reliance on user charges. Frustrated users will not pay user fees unless quality services are provided first.

Currently, donors are promoting attempts to enhance private sector participation in new aspects of public infrastructure services. Privatization of operations and maintenance is attempted, even if the presence of private capacity (in terms of skills, resources and willingness to invest) is far from certain. The lack of attention to the question of private capacity to take over from the public sector is a general weakness of the privatization measures promoted by structural adjustment programmes.

3.5.3   Managing Public Income and Expenditure

Donor efforts to reduce unsustainable budget deficits are discussed generally in Section 3.1. A combination of lack of returns to these efforts and the new priority of safeguarding expenditure on human resource development has led to the recent adoption of two instruments: initiating public expenditure reviews; and conditionalities on the allocation of government budgets. These instruments have so far had six major deficiencies:

- They have addressed budgets rather than actual expenditure patterns, despite the consistently huge differences between budgets and expenditure.
- They have been unrelated to the revenue side, which has contributed to the difference between budgets and expenditure.
- There has been excessive attention to mechanisms of budgeting and expenditure monitoring rather than priorities of resource allocation between sectors, types of expenditure, levels of government, etc.
- They have dealt with government budgets that are totally inadequate relative to the needs for government expenditure on public services: enforced reallocation gives few results when available resources are extremely low and cannot even finance the operation and maintenance of existing facilities.
- They have only to a very limited extent addressed one of the major causes of the lack of transparency and priority-setting in public resource allocation, viz. the project-specific demands for donor-specific procedures of financial management.
- The public expenditure reviews have been undertaken by international consultants flying in and out of capitals, which has done little to increase the ownership of government expenditure management by the government itself.

As a result, these new efforts have yet to produce significant changes in resource allocation by substance, purpose and level of government. They have hardly influenced the rather chaotic carving up of government expenditure, which is instead the result of a combination of historical convention and donor demands for adherence to 'their' procedures of budgeting, procurement, implementation, accounting and auditing for individual projects. The donor-provided institutional development assistance in this field may have improved the capacity of governments to track project-specific expenditure, but it has not addressed the project-specificity of expenditure as such.

3.5.4   Civil Service Reform

Civil service reform was not part of the initial adjustment agenda, but from 1986 to 1988, many adjustment programmes started to focus on civil service retrenchment and wage bill curtailment, and the broader agenda which included staff censuses, functional reviews of line ministries, training and personnel management systems. During 1989-94, civil service reform was increasingly linked up with issues of good governance (mainly accountability and rule of law). At the same time, a recognition of the long-term nature of institutional reform led to a delinking of civil service reform from adjustment lending through greater reliance on separate technical assistance loans and administrative adjustment programmes. During 1980-1994, the World Bank signed seven structural adjustment loans and eight technical assistance loans with the five countries studied here, which included one or more of the following civil service reform components: retrenchment of public employees; censuses aimed partly at elimination of ghost workers; improved computer management; modern incentive structures; staff training; and organizational change.[1]

Even with these rather narrow objectives, the achievements have been limited. Basically, the size (in terms of number of public employees and share of GDP), structure (in terms of levels of government and types of institutions) and even functions (in terms of both regulation and service delivery) of African governments have remained much the same. The wage bill in the public sector has been an explicit target in adjustment programmes. Among adjusting countries, some have seen a decrease and some an increase in the share of wages and salaries in public expenditure and in GDP. Similarly, the number of civil service personnel actually increased by more than 5 percent in Tanzania during 1985-92, while it decreased by 5 percent or more in Ghana and Uganda.[2] The reduction targets agreed between governments and the IFIs have been achieved mainly through elimination of ghost workers and lay-offs among low-paid temporary workers and local government staff. The fiscal benefits were limited, due to the low salaries of most retrenchees and the scale of severance payments to some.

Significantly, the real wages of civil servants have been allowed to decline dramatically during the period of adjustment, which undermines the capacity of the public sector to lead and carry out adjustment and other reforms of society. In Ghana, even after significant increases in the early 1990s the level of real wages only reached some 50 percent of the 1977 level. In Zimbabwe, real wages of civil servants were reduced by two thirds between 1980 and 1993, a steeper fall than in any other sector. In Tanzania, a public expenditure review estimated in 1989 that over the preceding decade and a half pay had fallen by 80 percent in real terms. An increase in the salaries of certain grades was stated to be desirable (it was said that the minimum:maximum pay differential within the service of 1:10 was a performance disincentive to managers and professionals), but no mechanisms were suggested for effecting it.

3.5.5   Perspectives on Public Sector Reform: Building National Capacity

Structural adjustment has achieved little in terms of shifting public sector institutions towards a new role vis-à-vis both the market and civil society, or even in terms of

---

[1] Capacity Building and Implementation Division, Technical Department, Africa Region, World Bank: 'Interlinkages Between Structural Adjustment Loans and Civil Service Reform in Sub-Saharan Africa', SPA Working Group on Civil Service Reform, working draft, September 1994, Annex 2.

[2] Mamadou Dia: 'A Governance Approach to Civil Service Reform in Sub-Saharan Africa', World Bank Technical Paper Number 225, Africa Technical Department Series, Washington, 1993.

creating the environment for a qualified debate on such shifts. The implicit assumption in most adjustment programmes that capacity exists in the private sector to take over the functions of the state, including effective delivery of public services, is far from being generally valid, despite the appearance of many new actors in service delivery. In fact, structural adjustment has had negative effects on state capacity and effectiveness and on the motivation and professionalization of public sector employees due to salary freezes, retrenchments, debatable but unimplemented privatizations, and removal of subsidies for provision of services. Meanwhile, related administrative reform and technical assistance programmes have only just started to build capacity in the leadership of the civil service. The effects are still limited, due to the weakness of current capacity-building conceptions, the resistance of those in power and many intended 'beneficiaries', and the continuing failure to halt the declining real wages of civil servants.

The weakness of current capacity building conceptions is nowhere more evident than in their central assumption that the disappointing results of past support to civil service reform are due to the 'patrimonial character of the state', which is supposedly seen in: lack of accountability and rule of law; patrimonial pay and incentive systems; a disabling regulatory burden on private sector development; distorted resource mobilization; bureaucratic budget management; recruitment based on subjective criteria; public employment managed as a welfare system; pay levels unrelated to productivity; and loyalty of officials to the person of the ruler rather than to the state.

From this follows a top-down 'governance approach to civil service reform', which distinguishes among African countries by putting them on a 'high', 'low' and 'in-between' scale of patrimonialism and mechanistically prescribes more or less thoroughgoing Westernization as a solution. Accordingly, problem cases should be offered full-scale administrative sector adjustment programmes, whereas the 'least patrimonial' only require free-standing technical assistance loans aimed at institutional development (Mamadou Dia, *op cit.*). The administrative sector adjustments in question imply the highly prescriptive 'off-the-shelf, instant remedy' approach, which characterized the first generation of adjustment programmes in the early 1980s. An adoption of such programmes that is being favourably considered by donors in the SPA Working Group on Civil Service Reform would have the consequence of narrowing the way in which three fundamental issues are approached:

- Questions of good governance are limited to management issues: effective service delivery; budgetary accountability; and an efficient judiciary.
- Questions of national ownership are focused on government commitment to the implementation of reform packages agreed with external partners.
- Questions of political liberalization and the political role of civil society are restricted to an emphasis on achieving consensus as a prerequisite for development.

Political liberalization in its present form does not necessarily lead to improved legitimacy of the state and current government; nor is it likely to lead to broadly-based consensus on the direction of societal development or the need for macroeconomic and structural reforms. On the contrary, genuine liberalization - to the extent that it happens - will unavoidably lead to the articulation of conflicting interests and to more transparent struggles over government policies and resources. Hence, the challenge of national capacity building during times of political liberalization can only be met through the promotion of a reform agenda, which can accommodate and make use of organized conflicting interests. An 'enabling environment' is needed not just for private economic interests, but also for different political interests and social groups to participate in policy-making and in the subsequent use of policies.

Public enterprise reform must be completely redesigned. Privatization is not a viable option, when public enterprises are bankrupt, and there are no private buyers. Liquidation is not an option, when the services provided are essential for economic development. Replacing government subsidies and deficit-financing only by government guarantees for credits in the private financial market precludes financial sector reform and hampers credit-financed private sector development.

Civil service reform must be rethought and redesigned with a starting-point in the need for user-based accountability. The current modernization approach, which implies transfer of a Western model of insulated and autonomous bureaucracy to the state machinery in Africa, leads to frustration and to manipulation by the strong at the top of African bureaucracies and in donor agencies. Civil service reform must be made more appropriate with a combined starting-point in: a) bottom-up real-life demands for the services and decisions of the public sector, which differ not only between countries but also between sectors and levels of government in individual countries; and b) the historical and cultural specificity of relations between power and people and between state and civil society in individual countries. This approach to public sector reform is not yet even in its infancy.

Meanwhile, civil society institutions must not be overburdened with tasks and resources, as a consequence of disillusionment with the public sector. Non-government service providers depend on financing from two sources: user fees and donor funds. The former source has limited financial potential, and the latter increases aid dependency. Delegation of resource mobilization and retention rights to public bodies with local accountability is the only way to make sustainable the delivery of public services. Such accountable local bodies are also needed to solve local conflicts and to guarantee the rights of groups and individuals to meet their own development requirements.

In the past, *capacity building* was equated with training, organizational restructuring and blue-print advice provided by resident long-term expatriate experts. More weight is needed on the following instruments to build capacity in the public sector:

- Organization of regular workshops and seminars that involve all relevant organizations in exchange of views on sector- or area-specific problems and possible approaches to their solution; this is well suited for donor financing.
- Analysis of development scenarios leading to policy and strategy options; these analyses should increasingly be made by national researchers, but this may see donors in an active role in cooperation with national institutions as long as the analyses are being used in national policy- and decision-making.
- Provision of flexible financing, tied to the performance of national and local institutions in reaching the overall goals established for them; again this may see donor involvement through flexible aid.
- Support for staff development, including performance-based compensation, without simply duplicating the management theories that still have not proven themselves in Northern bureaucracies.
- Use of advisers and consultants for catalytical tasks, preferably of the 'short-term recurrent intervention' type, which allows national and local institutions sufficient time to absorb the advice given - and to disregard much of it.

Box 3.1: Retrenchments in Tanzania and Zimbabwe

World Bank and IMF agendas on civil service reform in *Tanzania* have been identical to those elsewhere in Africa. The civil service is said to be overstaffed, underpaid, poorly equipped, and suffering from poor morale, low motivation, widespread absenteeism and corruption. The Bank and the IMF have concentrated on reducing numbers, seen as a precondition of any significant wage increase. The first serious attempt to address these issues was a ghost worker census in 1988. This was poorly designed and concluded that almost a third of all those registered as in civil service employment were ghost workers. Later this number was reduced to 16,000, and these were eliminated from the payroll. A World Bank Public Expenditure Review was conducted in 1989, concluding, on the basis of unexplicit reasoning, that the civil service was overstaffed by 50,000 in relation to its current functions. UNDP was brought in to identify which posts should be abolished and concluded that the actual level of overstaffing was 27,000.

Here the matter appears to have rested until 1992-93 when the World Bank succeeded in getting the number 50,000 reinstated and a timetable agreed whereby 10,000 would be retrenched in 1992-93 and 20,000 more in each of the following two years. A retrenchment package was also simultaneously agreed. It is unclear how many retrenchments have actually occurred under this agreement. According to the *Daily News* (10 March 1993) 2,123 retrenchments were carried out in 1992-93. Other sources put the figure at 3,000, but the Tanzania government Civil Service Reform Programme Action Plan, produced for the 1994 Consultative Group meeting, stated that there had been 10,292 retrenchments by mid-1994. Personnel in health and education were exempted from the exercise on the grounds that they were in 'short supply'. In fact, in education at least, their numbers have continued to grow, even though the education infrastructure is in a state of collapse.

The 1994 Public Expenditure Review, also carried out with little Tanzania government input, took a still more critical tone. Civil service numbers were said to have increased substantially in all areas, to a total of 355,000. The Tanzanian government therefore had to consider not just the adjustment of its staffing levels to its agreed range of functions but also the immediate pruning of these functions themselves. The Review now stated that the 'real feasible' size of the civil service was only 225,000. It was therefore necessary to carry out 40,000 retrenchments per annum for the next three years, and that previously exempted grades be included in the target groups. It seems extremely unlikely that much will come of this proposal. Reasons have been found to avoid implementing even the later stages of the 1992-93 to 1994-95 retrenchment plan.
(*Source:* Tanzania Country Study).

A central feature of *Zimbabwe's* economic reform programme was the announcement that there would be 'a reduction of 25 percent of the number of civil servants (excluding education) over the next 4 years'. Why the figure of 25 percent was chosen is a mystery and no attempt to justify it has ever been made. Later the announcement was modified in two ways. Firstly, health sector state employment was also exempted from the cuts. This meant that the 25 percent figure would apply to 'core' civil service employment of roughly 93,500 (1989 figure, up from 71,100 in 1980). Secondly, instead of applying to civil service numbers, the cuts were said to be being applied to civil service posts. However, nobody seems to have counted how many civil service posts there were in 1989-90. Again on an arbitrary basis it was assumed that there were 92,000 posts at this time. There are reasons to believe that the figure was very much higher.

The object of the exercise now became to reduce the 'number of posts' by 25,000 by 1994-95. Over time this target has been reduced to 23,000. A timetable was produced indicating that 12,000 posts would be eliminated by June 1993, a further 7,000 by June 1994 and 3,000 by June 1995, and UNDP assistance was received to identify the posts in question. The confusion marking the birth of this exercise has continued throughout its life. In October 1992 the World Bank stated that 8,472 posts had already been abolished. The Consultative Group meeting in early 1993 was given a figure of 7,204. By June 1993 this had climbed to 9,700 in one document, 10,044 in another and 13,000 in a third. Over a year later, towards the end of 1994, a figure of 11,000 was given. What is certain is that the number of civil servants retrenched is considerably below all those cited in this paragraph. According to the January 1994 Policy Framework Paper for 1994-96, there had been 4,896 actual civil service retrenchments at this time. IMF figures on employment in public administration show a fall to 89,600 by June 1993 (equivalent to 3,900 net retrenchments).
(*Source:* Zimbabwe Country Study).

These modest instruments of capacity building can be used with or without aid. They do not imply donor withdrawal from the corridors of the public sector in Sub-Saharan Africa. But they are built on a priority for national capacity and sovereignty, and do not fall prey to simplistic visions of attacking patrimonialism.

3.6   Social Services: Health and Education

3.6.1   Introduction

In most African countries the economic crisis preceding structural adjustment implied significant reductions in health and education budgets. This had serious consequences for the quantity and quality of government social service provisions at all levels. In debates on the impact of adjustment on social sectors critics have expressed fears that stabilization attempts, focused on reducing government expenditures and balancing budgets, have led to further cuts in government provision of social services. Declining service quality, staff reductions and the introduction of user fees have been blamed for declines in school enrolment and health clinic attendance, especially for poor people in rural areas. Partly in an effort to address these criticisms, the IFIs approached overall social sector reforms in the late 1980s. Their main argument has been that while overall spending levels are indeed low, the effects of this are exaggerated by the distortion of African government spending toward tertiary levels of provision (universities and hospitals in the capital).

This Section points to several notable features of health and education during structural adjustment. First, the share of social sector expenditures in government budgets shows a decline for education while no clear trend is evident in health. But population growth and the limited size of available resources have implied that already low per capita expenditure figures have declined further in many countries. Second, a range of social indicators show improvements during the 1980s despite economic crisis and structural adjustment. This trend is probably the result of both the long-term effects of pre-adjustment social sector investments (such as primary education and basic health care), the introduction of certain low-cost health programmes (e.g. immunization campaigns and oral rehydration therapy), and the increase in private and externally funded social services. Third, while data are still patchy, a growing body of evidence points to user fees for primary services as being both cost-ineffective and socially imbalanced.

3.6.2   The Effects of Structural Adjustment on Health and Education

At the level of sector budgets it is hard to substantiate claims about drastic reductions in the share of education and health sector expenditures in overall budgeted expenditure, although the story might be different if the definition of the latter includes debt-service. The opposite also holds true, though: lack of changes in the share of education and health programmes in total government expenditures relates more to built-in inertia in how public expenditures are distributed than to priorities influenced by adjustment lending. To the extent that economic reforms have led to a general increase in aid inflows one may conclude that adjustment programmes have assisted governments in maintaining social sector financing at levels that would otherwise not have been sustainable.

While economic policy reforms during the 1980s did not touch directly upon overall social sector spending levels, adjustment programmes did include measures aimed at rationalizing government expenditure in the health and education sectors. These measures include attempts to influence staffing levels, to increase the share of non-wage recurrent expenditures, and to introduce cost recovery measures.

1.   Staff retrenchment and salary costs

Adjustment conditionality has often sought to contain staff levels in health and education institutions, often by laying off support staff and untrained health and education personnel, or (as in Ghana and Burkina Faso) increasing teachers' working hours. However, actual retrenchments have so far been limited and in some cases (including Zimbabwe and Tanzania) employment was actually increased. On the other hand, real wages have declined everywhere, leading to an exodus of more highly qualified workers.

2.   Cost recovery

In a number of cases, adjustment programmes have introduced cost recovery measures to supplement central government recurrent expenditures. However, the breakdown of government services had often led to a system of cost recovery prior to structural adjustment, cf. Box 3.2. This happened via the introduction of local 'registration fees', 'under the counter' payments within the framework of government institutions and/or by leaving private sector services as the only available option.

Box 3.2   User Fees for Social Services

In Tanzania user fees for primary education were introduced in 1984-85 prior to structural adjustment, but charges in public health were only launched by 1992.

In Zimbabwe user fees were increased and systematized for health services in 1991-92, aimed at raising 5percent of total health expenditures by 1993, growing to a targeted 8percent in 1995. However, preliminary studies show highly uneven levying practices. In education, user charges were introduced in 1991-92 and covered roughly 3 percent of total sector expenditure in 1992-93.

In Uganda, private expenditures in both health and education outweigh government spending. Approximately two thirds of total health expenditures and as much as three quarters of spending for primary education are privately (i.e. household) financed.

Ghana levied user fees throughout the adjustment period, mainly in the health sector but increasingly in education, too. Recent dialogue between the government and the World Bank has actually aimed at containing them, since district councils had increasingly come to view pupils in primary schools as easily targetable tax payers.

Burkina Faso does not have experience with user fees in education and health, but 90 percent of all drugs sold are privately supplied.

Source: Country Studies.

Three issues have been debated in the context of cost recovery. First, whether the administrative costs of instituting and collecting user charges would outweigh the actual revenue collected through the charges; second, whether fees would imply reduced school enrolment and health clinic attendance; and third, whether funds collected to finance national revolving funds (e.g. for text books or medicine) would remain available for such purposes rather than being absorbed in central or local government general revenue.

Mechanisms to collect user fees and/or issue exceptions for them have proven unwieldy and bureaucratic. There is a substantial risk that resources generated in this manner remain with central government or are used for private purposes. The Tanzania country study shows how preconditions specified by cost recovery designers prior to the implementation of health user charges had still not been put in place after a period of two years. The Zimbabwe study finds that since incomes from cost recovery have only reached 2.7-3.5 percent of expenditure in education, its net benefits are socially and administratively questionable.

Data on the impact of user fees on access to social services are patchy. Where reliable time series data are available for places where services were previously genuinely free, as in Zimbabwe, they show declines in school attendance (although perhaps not of the order anticipated by critics) and postponement of treatment in health services. However, here and elsewhere they also show a preparedness to pay for social services, closely related to quality and availability of supporting materials.

3.   Social sector conditionalities

Since around 1991, adjustment conditionality has sought to protect or expand government funding for *primary* education and *primary* health care by means of intra- and/or inter-sectoral reallocations. Among the countries studied this approach was used in the Burkina Faso public expenditure review (PER) 1992, in Uganda PERs 1991-94, in Uganda adjustment credits, in Ghana's education sector reform programme and in the Tanzania PERs. The emphasis has been on budget allocations rather than on sector policy reforms.

Several public expenditure reviews have concluded that the (re-)establishment of budgetary and financial management capacity in finance ministries and in the ministries of health and education takes substantially longer than initially envisaged. This relates to the highly diversified expenditure pattern of primary education and primary health care in particular. Hence, there has been little impact of these conditionalities. Spending on tertiary services is in absolute terms already so low that its reallocation to primary sectors would have limited results. There seems to be some confusion about which vehicles are most appropriate to induce changes of the kind envisaged.

In the late 1980s, the World Bank gave more emphasis to sector adjustment lending at the expense of general programme lending. However, this has only to a limited extent been applied to social sector reforms. In its 1992 operational directive on adjustment lending the Bank noted that 'adjustment lending is usually not the most appropriate instrument for supporting reforms in the social and infrastructure sectors.' In the countries studied only two examples appear of World Bank support for policy-based lending for social sector reform: Ghana's education sector adjustment reform that has been under implementation since 1986, and Burkina Faso's human resources adjustment programme.

3.6.3   Trends in Government Budget Allocations for Health and Education

Trends in government expenditure for social sector programmes are often used as a measure of how governments prioritize human resource development during periods of economic crisis. The level and trend in education and health spending are often equated with the extent to which poor people benefit from government budget allocations.

However, such data are seldom reliable, and there is frequently substantial variation between budgeted figures and actual expenditures. Weak reporting systems have faced substantial difficulties in monitoring both the array of donor-funded projects in the social sectors and the magnitude of private expenditures in this field.

In the 1980s in Africa as a whole, education registered a drop in its share of total government expenditure while there is no clear trend for health. Of the countries studied, Ghana increased expenditure on health and education during the decade, while Uganda decreased it, relatively at least. Tanzania is reported to have increased the share of health and education expenditures in total government expenditures in the first phase of adjustment, but to have failed to maintain this progress in the 1990s. Since adopting adjustment, Zimbabwe has seen the social sector share of expenditure decline. Average per capita consumption figures in both health and education repeat this trend: a decline for Uganda, an increase in Ghana and a temporary one in Tanzania. Figures for the early 1990s show declining per capita expenditures in Zimbabwe and Tanzania. For Africa as a whole the general trend is one of declining per capita expenditures within the social sectors during both the 1980s and the 1990s.

Most African countries have seen investments in the social sectors relying still more on donor funding: government contributions are often as low as 10-20 percent of total capital expenditures. Domestically generated resources for health and education are mainly spent on recurrent expenditures with wages receiving the larger share. In recent years there has been a decrease in funding for non-wage recurrent expenditure in health and education. In this context, the severe lack of e.g. basic medicine and text books has most often resulted in declining quality and low productivity in government social service provision.

The budgetary trends outlined above have had different implications for government social service provision at various levels. While African governments have generally maintained a dominant position at tertiary levels, there has been de facto privatization of substantial parts of primary health services and secondary education. The extent to which the chief role is played here by missions, local and international NGOs, private entrepreneurs, etc. varies greatly among countries. Uganda represents an extreme version of this privatization; in Zimbabwe on the other hand, government provision of health and education services was still being significantly increased immediately prior to adjustment.

While various aspects of economic policies have been subject to intense debate during the last decade, general questions of social sector policy and capacity have only been touched upon incidentally, if at all. Economic crisis and adjustment in Africa have also led to declining institutional capacity to tackle broader issues related to social sector reform.

3.6.4   Trends in Health and Education Outcomes

Central to any analysis of the social impact of adjustment must be trends in social indicators such as nutrition, literacy and mortality. However, data are neither consistent nor reliable. The causality between economic policy reforms, budget priorities, social sector programme implementation, and actual trends in outcome cannot be firmly established.

Nutrition data show mixed performance during the 1980s: increasing calorie availability, increases in absolute levels of child malnutrition and possibly an increase in the number of underfed people. Infant and child mortality rates show marked declines during the 1980s, while life expectancy and vaccination rates both generally rose. Literacy rates and primary enrolment ratios show improvements in the course of the decade. Enrolment data for Burkina Faso show strong improvement. Tanzania has registered the largest drop among the countries with available data, and although some growth has probably been experienced in recent years levels are still far below those achieved in the early 1980s.

3.6.5   Conclusion

The impact of continuing economic crisis in Africa has left donors and governments alike struggling to identify ways and means to increase the coverage of social sector services, improve efficiency and enhance quality. Adjustment conditionality today most often includes measures to protect general social sector spending and/or to refocus expenditures on primary provision. However, the short- to medium-term perspective of adjustment programmes has proven not to be a constructive framework for designing and implementing institutionally complex and resource-intensive social sector policy reforms and investment programmes.

User fees for social services have in many cases been introduced formally or informally prior to adjustment by government, local institutions and/or social sector personnel at field levels. Still, adjustment programmes have not made efforts to contain or reduce user charges, and in some cases the IFIs have made programme lending conditional on the introduction of cost recovery measures. Available data highlight how such payments for basic education or primary health care may reinforce inequities by severely restricting poor people's access to essential services.

3.7   Poverty and Equity during Structural Adjustment in Africa

3.7.1   Introduction

The impact of adjustment programmes on poverty and equity has been intensely debated for more than a decade. Critics of World Bank and IMF programmes have focused on the negative impact of measures such as devaluation, abolition of subsidies, introduction of user fees for social services and lay-offs of government employees. The Bretton Woods institutions have responded that the various adjustment measures serve to promote economic growth, which in turn is argued to be the best available means to reduce poverty in Africa. Furthermore, proponents of adjustment have contended that the majority of apparently welfare-oriented government programmes and expenditures, including social sector spending, were anyway biased against the interest of the poor.

The contemporary literature points to three important new issues. First, rural areas have witnessed increasing differentiation as a result of adjustment-induced changes in agricultural pricing and marketing. This has improved conditions for some agricultural producers but has reduced the income opportunities of others. Second, contrary to conventional wisdom the rural/urban gap may have increased during the course of adjustment, to the disadvantage of rural areas. This is due inter alia to the immediate effects in urban areas of increased inflows of aid and imported consumer goods, problems related to agricultural liberalization, and lower than expected levels of public sector retrenchment. Finally, although African governments and international agencies emphasize the difficult plight of the poorest population groups, the experience with targeted assistance to particularly weak and vulnerable groups is so far largely negative.

3.7.2   The Nature of Poverty in Africa

Poverty in Sub-Saharan Africa is deeper than in other developing regions in the sense that the poor's average incomes are much lower in Africa than in other developing regions. Numbers of poor people are estimated, even by the World Bank, to have remained constant or slightly increased during the latter part of the 1980s. However, national data sets are often incomplete and employ different methodological approaches to the measurement of poverty. In the early 1990s reliable income distribution data were available for only 6 percent of the continent's population (comparable figures for Asia and Latin America are 95 percent and 55 percent respectively). This hampers inter-country comparisons, with regard to the characteristics of poverty and to the effects of adjustment on poverty indicators.

The multi-dimensional nature of poverty is increasingly acknowledged. It is necessary to consider several issues in addition to the absence of a sufficient monetary income. These include lack of employment opportunities, lack of access to social services and to economic assets such as land and credit, food insecurity and mal-nutrition, lack of proper shelter, physical isolation in inaccessible rural areas, and vulnerability to external shocks, disease etc. On this basis, the evidence suggests that poverty in Sub-Saharan Africa is overwhelmingly a rural phenomenon, both in income terms and with regard to access to social services. Significantly higher proportions of the population in rural areas fall below the national income-based poverty line than in urban areas. Available income data for Ghana, Uganda and Tanzania point to 80-90 percent of poor households being located in rural areas, while 44-60 percent of rural households are categorized as poor. The rural/urban gap is also significant in regard to access to safe water, education and health services.

3.7.3   The Changing Emphasis of Structural Adjustment on Poverty and Equity

The explicit objectives of structural adjustment on social issues have developed through three phases: during the first phase, *1980-1986*, poverty and equity issues were most often not addressed during the design and implementation of the reform measures. Stabilization was seen as a necessary precondition for restoring growth. Social sector expenditures were often identified as contributing to government deficits and hence creating inflationary pressures in the economy. Only occasionally a reference was made that economic growth would in turn be decisive for efforts to reduce poverty.

Following widespread international concern about the poverty implications of adjustment, articulated mainly by UNICEF, growing attention was paid to social aspects of the adjustment programmes during *1987-1992*. Institutionally, the World Bank came to dominate these efforts, while the IMF remained largely mute. From 1987, the Bank president's reports to the Board recommending the approval of an adjustment credit have been required to include an assessment of the social impact of the programme (usually ½-1 page). More importantly, the World Bank, UNDP and the African Development Bank began collaborating on the Social Dimensions of Adjustment in Africa programme (SDA), see Box 3.3. This period was characterized by four trends.

First, the basic macroeconomic design of adjustment programmes remained unaltered. Second, work was initiated to establish a general framework for analyzing the social impact of adjustment, including a series of household surveys. Still, only occasionally did individual adjustment operations refer to specific poverty indicators. Of 32 IDA-financed 'poverty oriented structural and sectoral adjustment loans' (the Bank's own definition) only 11 included indicators to monitor poverty issues, and only four set specific targets for any of the indicators (these figures refer to all countries receiving concessional loans, not only those in Sub-Saharan Africa). Third, beginning with the 'Programme to mitigate the social costs of adjustment' in Ghana, a number of social action programmes were being designed as add-ons to adjustment programmes. Fourth, a number of adjustment programmes began to focus on budget allocations to the social sectors.

From approximately *1992*, the SDA programme as such was abandoned for a number of reasons. Still, a number of the social action programmes, priority surveys, etc. were still being implemented within World Bank country operations. Current programmes are supposed to reflect the Bank's 1991 'Poverty reduction strategy', cf. Box 3.4.

Box 3.3 The SDA Programme: High Ambitions - Poor Performance

In 1987, the World Bank initiated a 'Social Dimensions of Adjustment in Africa' (SDA) programme in collaboration with UNDP and the African Development Bank. It was meant to provide a swift response to the criticism made by UNICEF and others that adjustment did not consider the negative social impact of economic reforms. The main element of the programme was the promotion of 'social action programmes'. These provided the World Bank, African governments and donor organizations with visible examples of efforts to mitigate the alleged negative effect of adjustment. More than half of total SDA funding was allocated to such activities, although they have remained of little financial significance compared to the overall magnitude of adjustment lending. In the period 1988-93 the World Bank committed US$4 bn for adjustment programmes, while social action programmes initiated in the SDA framework received a meagre US$141 million.

All of the four anglophone countries studied here have had such a programme. In Burkina Faso a number of individual projects rather than a programme were put in place. The SDA programme has explicitly aimed not only at reaching the poor but also enhancing the political sustainability of the adjustment process. Social action programmes have targeted special measures on vulnerable and vocal though not necessarily particularly poor groups of the population.

Key problems in design and implementation have related to lack of administrative capacity since targeted programmes are highly demanding in the identification of 'worthy' target groups. Not surprisingly, poor people often live in locations where government services are weak or non-existent. Other barriers have included political and administrative hesitation if not resistance from African governments as well as from the Bretton Woods institutions to involve NGOs, trade unions and community-based organizations in the design and implementation of such programmes.

3.7.4   Assessing the Link between Adjustment and Poverty
Three aspects of this question will be taken up: the impact of general economic measures on poverty reduction; the social impact of agricultural reforms; and the position of particularly poor and vulnerable groups during adjustment, including the experiences from social action programmes.

Box 3.4 Adjustment Programmes and the World Bank's Poverty Reduction Strategy

In 1991, the Bank adopted a poverty reduction strategy with three elements: promotion of labour-intensive growth, since the poor's most abundant resource is labour; increased investments in human-resources, notably primary education and primary health care to increase the poor's income-earning opportunities; and provision of social safety nets to protect vulnerable groups during adjustment.

Inside and outside the Bank it has been debated whether the first leg of the strategy implies anything more than liberalising markets. Generally, most observers argue that this has so far not been the case. Moreover, 'flexible labour markets' remain conspicuous by their absence, and specific interventions to improve access to credit for both rural smallholders and urban informal sectors remain largely absent. Recent trends in adjustment lending point to increasing attention being paid to social sector expenditures (see above), but in the Africa region there are no clear links between protecting and enhancing sector budgets and the wider issue of sector policy reforms. Finally, the Bank seems reluctant to promote the setting up of social safety nets in the Africa region on the basis of poor performance of the SDA programme and in light of the 'weak institutional framework' and the high proportion of the absolutely poor in the total population.

---

1.   Adjustment, growth and poverty

Assessments of the impact of adjustment reforms generally on poverty reduction in Sub-Saharan Africa are hampered by an absence of time series data on poverty and the varied implications of different elements of the adjustment agenda. To the extent that adjustment has succeeded in restoring basic macroeconomic balances, halting inflation and increasing the inflows of concessional finance, this is assumed to be at least neutral, if not positive for the position of poor people. Subsidy removal and trade and exchange-rate reforms as pursued under structural adjustment seldom further harm the poor, as the pre-adjustment policy regimes in these areas were normally ineffective in allowing the poor access to cheap foreign exchange or officially priced imports. Parallel markets had adjusted to the new price levels prior to structural adjustment. Zimbabwe and Burkina Faso are exceptions to this trend; in these two countries subsidies and official exchange rates were applied for a wider variety of consumer goods.

With regard to recent trends in poverty a distinction may be made between *structural* and *conjunctural* poverty. The latter refers to the impact of economic recession on the welfare of different groups of the population, whereas structural aspects of poverty relate to more basic questions of social organization, resource endowment, etc. Conjunctural poverty seems in several African countries to play a greater role in urban areas as the population here has been most affected by decreases in formal sector employment and (more important) sharp drops in formal sector real wages, withdrawal of subsidies and deterioration in social services. Conversely, structural features of poverty are of immense importance in many rural areas. Decisive features in this context include inequalities in access to land, implements and labour.

Some evidence points to a growing rural/urban gap under adjustment. It suggests increasing differentiation in rural areas where the poorest may have been further marginalized, thereby skewing the potentially positive impact of price reforms. Conversely, urban areas often seem to have benefitted most from the increase in aid inflows and imported goods. These developments may have brought about a boom in the construction sector and in demand for informally provided services. On the other hand, conditions for more (mainly women) operators in the lower echelons in informal trade have worsened due to intensified competition.

2.   *The social impact of agricultural reforms*

The general thrust of structural adjustment to shift terms of trade in favour of agricultural export crops should benefit rural populations. As already noted, reservations are in order with regard to impacts on the incomes of poor people. These concern the skewing of benefits toward better-off households, questions of intra-household gender inequality and the imperfect nature of rural markets for wage labour.

The World Bank is still far from taking on board agricultural policy reform measures designed to address such questions. Thus, the most recent adjustment credit to Uganda is presented as a 'poverty-focused operation' since it involves general policy measures to stimulate coffee and cotton production and due to its focus on protecting the social sectors. Such claims can only be substantiated by both more specific data and more fine-tuned policies. There is still a long way to go before the emerging understanding of poverty as a multi-dimensional feature is translated into the design and implementation of general economic reforms aimed at reducing poverty.

3.   *The position of the poorest population groups*

There seems to be agreement that the poorest population groups have not benefitted from structural adjustment; on the contrary they are probably in a more vulnerable position. Limited or no assets make it difficult to take advantage of new incentives, and lack of education generally implies less information on new possibilities. Meanwhile, social action programmes have invariably passed those groups by. Nor is there much sign of change on the horizon. The experience of social action programmes and (adjustment-related) declines in administrative capacity appear to have led donors to conclude that targeted interventions aimed at specific poor and vulnerable groups are generally not sustainable in Africa.

In several countries, the World Bank has supported the establishment of a 'social fund' that often operates independently of central government institutions and on the basis of specific project applications to be presented by local NGOs, communities and private contractors. This 'demand-driven' approach may avoid some of the problems of earlier interventions, but it is questionable whether the poorest population groups stand to benefit from this approach, and whether it is institutionally and financially sustainable.

Conclusions: The most positive interpretation which can be made of the adjustment/poverty relation is that the results have been mixed, and that the poorest have not benefitted at all. This serves to underline the necessity of reform programmes to tackle poverty in a more substantive manner. Furthermore, it highlights the long-term nature of the efforts required for high and sustained growth in order to generate resources to deal with the problem.

3.8   Adjustment and Gender

3.8.1   Pre-adjustment Trends

While situations varied from country to country, and while evidence is patchy in many regards, there is little doubt that gender has been a fundamental basis of differentiation in post-independence Africa. There is also some evidence that gender differentiation has expanded and deepened with the advance of commodity production. The main forms of gender differentiation comprise economic, household and social roles, statuses and incomes, and access to resources/entitlements of various kinds. But access to services and resources such as agricultural training and extension, credit, health and education has also been highly differentiated, reinforcing inequalities further.

Gender differentiation in agriculture is particularly important in Africa. This differentiation has included rights and ownership over land, labour, implements and income. Regarding land rights it seems that in most parts of Africa women have enjoyed customary rights to cultivate and harvest a part of household plots and have been able to continue to assert and sometimes transmit these rights in the case of the death of their spouse. However, where customary arrangements have given way to private property there has been a strong tendency for continuation and transmission rights to disappear. Regarding production roles in agriculture, with some major exceptions (e.g. parts of Ghana and Nigeria), women have been identified with the production of subsistence rather than cash crops and livestock keeping and are further identified with responsibility for transplanting, weeding and harvesting as opposed to land preparation. Meanwhile, it appears that despite male control over most income, there are fixed gender-specific financial responsibilities which must be met and which are also skewed against women.

Increased commodification affects many of these inequalities. The commercialization of peasant food-crop production which has been a widespread feature of the later post-independence period has been variously reported as leading to women's loss of rights over disposal of produce from their plots and/or to men charging their spouses rent in exchange for the continuation of their disposal rights.

In the pre-adjustment period continuous but slow growth occurred in most African countries in women's participation in the formal economy, particularly in the education and health branches of the public sector. The proportion of women in paid formal employment remained low or very low in most cases, however. A much greater expansion occurred, apparently beginning in the 1970s, in women's participation in the informal economy. Indeed the enormous growth in the latter in the period of crisis which preceded adjustment seems to have been mainly driven by women seeking to compensate for general contraction in real household incomes. By the onset of adjustment women formed a majority of informal sector participants in most African countries. Although the informal sector was virtually the only place where women entrepreneurs were likely to be found, it was also marked by strong internal gender differentiation, with women concentrated in those branches combining low capital requirements with work tasks conventionally regarded as part of women's household roles.

3.8.2   Explicit and Implicit Adjustment Objectives on Gender

From the outset structural adjustment programmes have been gender-blind. Even with the attempts of the last few years to address issues of social and economic inequality, women have only been targeted as part of wider groups (the poor, the rural poor and so on). Although this deficiency is now acknowledged by the World Bank, its most recent general publication on adjustment makes only one specific reference to gender.

Sustained criticisms have been made of the effects of adjustment's gender blindness on the general validity of its macroeconomics. The argument is that in ignoring the gendered nature of the agricultural division of labour and rural household income distribution, adjustment's designers have severely over-estimated the possibility of increasing peasant cash-crop production via producer price rises. Most of the labour that must re-allocate from 'non-tradeables' is female, but this labour is not allocated through the market. It therefore appears to be locked into the sub-sector where it already has typically low earnings. In other words, women are concentrated in activities that according to adjustment need to decline, but their mobility to do so is severely constrained. It has further been argued that adjustment is in fact likely actually to *increase* female labour immobility in important respects, through the intensification of women's domestic care duties as public service provisions are rationalized or withdrawn. This is quite aside from questions about who in gender terms reaps any benefits arising from agricultural adjustment.

A separate line of criticism of the macroeconomics of adjustment has been that, in ignoring structural constraints in general, it assumes a higher level of supply responsiveness than is empirically warranted. Hence studies which seem to confirm peasant women's labour immobility may also in fact be observing other elements of lack of supply response. The main area where gender is an *implicit* object of adjustment is education, where stress is laid on protecting or improving girls' primary education, and deregulation of informal trade, which has high concentrations of women participants (see below).

3.8.3   Current Trends and Their Attributability

Women as agricultural producers: The discussion on women as agricultural producers/labourers under adjustment has tended to revolve around the theme described above, together with the linked one of who (in gender terms) attracts the benefits of adjustment when and where these exist and/or the disadvantages where these predominate. Adjustment has not been associated with an agricultural boom. Empirical studies which enable an assessment of the relation of women's labour mobility or immobility to this trend are scarce. One from Tanzania indicates that patriarchal relations could be consistent with mobility as well as immobility, however. Here an apparently successful expansion in cotton production has been associated with a transfer of women's (unpaid) labour from food crop production to porterage. A recent study from another country (Côte d'Ivoire) appears to indicate that female labour immobility there has proved secondary in importance to other structural constraints on producing cash crops.

Recent empirical work has thrown little light on the issue of who in gender terms has captured the benefits of agricultural adjustment. There are indications of women's access to resources deteriorating in various ways. In Ghana, an adjustment-related extension of cocoa farming further into forest areas removed access to certain traditional forest products (e.g. honey) on whose trade women were dependent for income. Evidence from Tanzania appears to show that women's (and some men's) access to land is declining as a partly adjustment-related informal land privatization took hold.

The other side of the adjustment objective of promoting export-crop production has been a systematic withdrawal of the subsidies and services to food-crop production characteristic of most African countries in the 1970s and early 1980s. This is the branch of agriculture in which women have traditionally been concentrated, but as producers they always benefitted less than men from subsidies and services. Still, the latter's withdrawal may still disadvantage women most. In Malawi, for example, evidence shows that women's use of inputs declines much faster than men's in such a situation.

Women as formal sector employees: It is frequently stated on the basis of evidence from Asian and Caribbean countries undergoing adjustment, that in so far as adjustment is associated with declines in formal sector employment levels and real wages, these affect women employees in particular. On the other hand, where adjustment improves conditions for, and leads to, the expansion of export-oriented industries, these are generally ones with high concentrations of female labour.

Some evidence was supplied by the country studies on this issue. A generally surprising finding was that there had actually been far less labour shedding than anticipated in any of the countries concerned. Only in Zimbabwe were even limited data available to assess the gender implications of the retrenchments which had occurred. This suggested that women were not being disproportionately shed from the public service. On the other hand they were significantly under-represented on the retraining programmes organized under the generally ineffectual Social Dimensions of Adjustment initiative. Furthermore, the branch of formal sector manufacturing which was expected to 'kick-start export-led recovery' (the predominantly female textiles industry) was actually the one most comprehensively hit by trade liberalization in all the countries considered.

Data on wages for Zimbabwe meanwhile showed that the other major concentration of women's private sector employment, domestic service, witnessed a fall in incomes whose severity was matched only by agricultural labour's. At the same time there was a notable increase in the numbers of women engaged in informal manufacturing activities, still concentrated, however, in the most low-technology and low-profit areas.

Women as traders: Strong evidence exists from all the case-study countries of a continued expansion of women's participation in informal trade during the adjustment period. In Zimbabwe such participation only really became pronounced during adjustment itself. It seems that the earlier sharp fall in total urban household income has been arrested during the adjustment period in Tanzania, Uganda and Ghana. In part this seems likely to have been the result of even greater economic activism than hitherto, with virtually all family members joining the informal sector. All the same it seems that the *individual* incomes of women informal sector traders, who are mostly concentrated in the lower ranks of food, fruit and vegetable trading, have probably dropped, since it is in these areas that competition has been most intense (in some countries real prices of these goods have also fallen). Individual women-trader incomes have fallen even in nominal terms in Zimbabwe.

One positive development for informal sector operators in African countries has been a relaxation in the level and forms of regulation of the sector, which previously imposed high costs (time and financial) on participants. This deregulation appears to be partly adjustment-inspired but also a function of problems of state capacity and a recognition by politicians that, in phases where the sector represents the single fastest source of employment growth, such regulation would be increasingly politically counter-productive.

There is evidence of the entry of some women to certain high-profit branches of informal trade such as international trading of high-value items, which in the context of trade liberalization has recently become legitimized and has apparently expanded. However, it is almost entirely better-off women who are involved and it is still unclear whether women will be able to enter the high-value branches of domestic trade (e.g. purchase of export crops) opening up for private operators in a number of countries.

Women as home managers and consumers of social services: The period has every-where seen either no significant improvement or a continued fall in the affordability, availability and quality of social services, and therefore no improvement in women's related home management burdens. However, with the exception of Zimbabwe the general picture was very discouraging on all these fronts prior to adjustment. At the same time certain of the coping strategies which women have had to adopt as a result of the withdrawal of subsidies have had a direct effect in increasing the amount of time spent of domestic duties. In Zimbabwe for example, obtaining 'straight-run' maize meal instead of the previously subsidized roller meal variety may involve several separate operations rather than simply a visit to a shop. But in countries with pre-adjustment histories of shortages like Tanzania, increased availability of consumption items generally (albeit at high prices) has reduced women's time allocation to shopping.

There has been much concern about trends in women's health and educational statuses under crisis and adjustment. On health status, time series data are so patchy that extracting gender-related trends even about particular countries is impossible. On education the evidence is clear that there has been no significant improvement in women's relative status, although it is less clear whether there has been a deterioration (data from Tanzania and Zimbabwe point in different directions). The failure to improve women's access to education is of particular concern, given the verbal priority it has received in all quarters.

Given its previously parlous and skewed state, the real reduction in social support to women in many parts of Africa has perhaps been exaggerated; on the other hand there is evidence that adjustment has intensified women's household management problems on the income side in some places at least, and not improved them sufficiently in others, to the extent that women are still being pushed in very large numbers into insecure and only marginally remunerative forms of informal employment. Meanwhile there may be new opportunities for some women with greater initial resources. However, the latter opportunities have not opened to them as women. While the World Bank acknowledges this in increasingly explicit ways, little or no change on the ground has followed as a result.

3.9   The Environment

Many of Africa's current environmental problems arise from pressure on land and other resources, arising from population increase and expansion of commercial cultivation. These are long-term issues dating from long before structural adjustment, though the current situation is affected by it.

Studies of the impact of adjustment on *peasant agricultural techniques* are inconclusive. Reducing subsidies and devaluation increase input prices and reduce input use, especially of fertilizer. It should also increase producer prices for products, through devaluation for exports and cost reduction for all crops. Some see this as environmen-tally positive, since reducing wasteful use of fertilizer means less groundwater pollution.

Opponents point out that groundwater pollution is not a major problem, given the low levels of fertilizer use. But reduced yields imply that more land (and often more marginal land) must be taken into cultivation to provide for household needs. If not, 'intensification' without soil regeneration occurs, which reduces sustainability and/or increases soil erosion. No general conclusion is possible; the outcome varies by crop and other external circumstance.

Another issue recently raised concerns *'erosive'* (maize, cotton, tobacco) and *'non-erosive'* (tree) crops. The argument goes that, by increasing relative export-crop prices, tree crops (coffee, tea, cocoa) are encouraged at the expense of the 'erosive' ones. This argument has little merit. Export tree crops are not substitutes for the 'erosive' annuals. They grow at different altitudes and climates. Expanding tea production more often involves cutting forest than switching from maize, and it makes little sense to think of moving away from Africa's major food crop. In any case, it is more relevant to consider erosive and non-erosive ways of growing crops than crops themselves.

Soil erosion is a long-term African problem, partly the result of geomorphological processes under way for millions of years, but also arising from inappropriate land use, some of which results from increased pressure on land, forcing reductions in fallow periods, and hence in soil regeneration. If adjustment works as intended, increased producer prices will lead to increased agricultural production, while increased input prices mean limited fertilizer use. This seems to imply more land cultivated or soil deterioration. This is not necessarily the case, since appropriate low external input farming would make far better use of lower input levels.

A similar example is the expansion of *fuelwood* use with increasing population, largely without feasible alternatives in the rural areas. This leads to increasing denudation around population concentrations, and ever longer distances travelled by women to collect firewood. Adjustment may affect this by encouraging the commercial captivation of wood for this other purpose, but the likely outcomes are again unclear. Urban fuelwood use is more directly affected by adjustment, since devaluation increases the price of alternative fuels like electricity and kerosene and so increases the demand for firewood and charcoal.

Other environmental problems, like *deforestation* resulting from logging, animal species loss through *poaching* and *pollution by industrial or mineral production*, derive simply from commercial decisions and are in theory more amenable to regulation. While often ineffective before structural adjustment, capacity for regulation has been weakened by budgetary cuts and by the general reduction in regulation and control, aimed at encouraging private sector activities.

One export whose extent has increased rapidly over the past decade is timber, and this seems likely to eliminate Africa's remaining tropical high forest in the next few years. If structural adjustment is to claim the credit for increased non-traditional exports, it must also accept responsibility for aspects like this, as well as for accelerated loss of animal species and aggravated pollution including mercury poisoning arising from increased mineral production.

4. Beyond Structural Adjustment: National Capacity and International Support

4.1 Summary of the Experience

4.1.1 The Inevitability of Adjustment

Some form of adjustment was necessary to address the economic imbalances faced by most Sub-Saharan African countries in the early 1980s. It is always preferable to reach an orderly, policy-based improvement of macroeconomic developments, rather than to reach such 'balances' through a complete breakdown of the formal economy and the public sector. Without an organized attempt to address the problems, such a breakdown could have been a real risk if private banks and donors had reacted individually to the mounting debts and the weak local resource mobilization, e.g. for operation and maintenance. Non-project funds from the international financial institutions (IFIs) had to be used to support the balance of payments and the public budgets of Sub-Saharan African countries.

There are three other positive features about the history of structural adjustment in Africa. Firstly, a combination of increased aid inflows, devaluation and removal of restrictions on private trade relieved constraints on the import of much needed inputs and goods and provided incentives for a stabilization of export earnings in a period of sharply declining terms of trade. Secondly, the attempt to address institutional structures, in addition to macroeconomic factors, implied a recognition of some of the underlying causes of the economic problems. There *was* excessive and inefficient state control of many aspects of local, national and international markets. Thirdly, it was appropriate that the World Bank through non-project adjustment lending supplemented the IMF's standard stabilization package aimed at external and public deficits and debts. The Bank's adjustment agenda was modified repeatedly over the period, as a result of greater realism about what policy-based adjustment lending can achieve in Africa. In view of the costs of adjustment, this cannot be called simply a constructive learning process, but it does show a capacity in the IFIs to respond to external pressure and lessons learned. There is now also greater willingness to discuss Africa's long-term development requirements (although the weakness of strategy displays the crudeness of simplistic adjustment models).

The move from stabilization to deregulation and gradually to other institutional issues was accompanied by a move from the IMF to the World Bank in the driver's seat. The issues of external debts, budget deficits and other imbalances, which are traditional IMF targets, also became addressed through the World Bank-led consultative group mechanisms. As time passed, the division of labour between the two organizations became increasingly blurred. It may be questioned whether it is reasonable and cost-effective for the world community to demand from the weak African governments that they deal with both Bretton Woods institutions on almost identical issues.

The mid-1990s have seen a mood of consensus dominating deliberations on macroeconomic and structural reforms, at least among multilateral and bilateral donors and core ministries of African governments. This takes the form of statements such as: it is time to move beyond structural adjustment towards comprehensive economic, social and political reform and development, which is owned by both government and civil society in Africa. While few would disagree with this, it is important not to forget that such statements are also admissions of a degree of failure of the whole process, economically and politically.

4.1.2   Gaps and Weaknesses in Structural Adjustment

Recognition and analysis of gaps and weaknesses in the adjustment process are the only way to move towards a more honest dialogue, acknowledging the continued differences in power and resources between donors and recipients - and in fact the increasing aid dependency, which is also a result of 15 years of structural adjustment in Africa.

Pointing to the deficiencies of adjustment immediately brings up the debate about whether these are caused by adjustment or by non-implementation of the adjustment package. Clearly, non-implementation of many institutional adjustment measures has restricted the impact of the full programme. For example, agreed targets on privatization of public enterprises and a reduction (typically 25 percent) of the number of public employees have seldom been met. But it is not certain that full implementation would have removed the gaps and weaknesses summarized below. The view that 'more of the same type of structural adjustment will save the day' certainly does not hold.

1.   Limited effects on growth - Increased vulnerability

Structural adjustment has not resulted in major improvements in GDP growth in any Sub-Saharan African country. At best, some countries may be on the way back to the growth rates of the 1960s and 1970s - wholly inadequate in relation to the levels of poverty and unmet basic needs of a population that has grown by more than 50 percent during the adjustment period. Moreover, structural adjustment has not affected the economic composition of GDP, including the balance between consumption, savings and investment. Different sectors have retained their pre-adjustment shares in most regards, with the exception that informal activities have grown in employment terms.

Most fundamentally, despite their central position in the programmes, export values have hardly shifted. Export promotion may have been successful in terms of volume, but faced with declining international terms of trade, it has left African economies with an even greater transformation problem in future. In some commodity markets, structural adjustment has compounded the problems, as traditional African exporters compete with each other. Despite a widening trade gap, plugged only by aid, real imports per capita have been halved during the adjustment period. Structural adjustment has not addressed the key questions: What contribution can Africa make to the future world economy and the international division of labour? And how in the process can Africa escape from its current ensnarement in ever-increasing vulnerability?

2.   Pushes in the wrong direction

Structural adjustment has also pushed Africa in wrong directions. Three aspects are of particular significance: Firstly, government capacity has decreased as financial cuts have not been counter-balanced by timely capacity building. Secondly, aid dependency has increased for both governments and NGOs, for development and recurrent expenditure, and for imports. Thirdly, African societies have become accustomed to operating under an external 'policy command' which discourages national dialogues on societal reform.

3.   Errors of design - Sequencing
The sequencing of adjustment reforms has been problematic in at least five respects: increases in producer prices before removal of major bottlenecks in infrastructure; liberalization of financial markets and increases in real rates of interest before necessary changes in the real economy, in particular some kind of parastatal reform; liberalization of foreign trade without effective export promotion policies and incentives; deregulation of national markets without measures to promote an effective and competitive private sector; and introduction of cost recovery in public services before measures to ensure availability of inputs and effective services in a transitional period.

These sequencing problems reflect an exaggerated faith in immediate and strong supply response from the private sector. A related design error concerns the assumption that institutions can be changed overnight. Predictably, it has taken a long time for both public and private institutions (and society in general) to adapt to change.

More generally, donors discuss one 'sequencing issue', which is really something else. The link between political liberalization and national consensus building on the one hand and government commitment to economic reforms on the other is inappropriately seen as a matter of timing. It is assumed that liberalization will automatically lead to consensus in favour of policies already being followed. Some donors seem to believe that in this way they can avoid controversies, conditionalities, and non-implementation of reforms.

4.   Negative effects
Structural adjustment has in a few fields had negative effects, which must not be forgotten. Although the overall effect on poverty may not be negative, as opposed to the earlier view of many critical voices, access to markets and to government and parastatal services has become less regular and more costly for the poorest people particularly in remote areas, and equity has almost certainly suffered as those without assets, including many women-headed households, are unable to take advantage of new opportunities.

Despite the financial, political and intellectual resources invested in structural adjustment since the early 1980s, African countries face increased uncertainty in the mid-1990s. This is due to a mixture of: national and international developments outside the reach of adjustment programmes (including drought, population growth, AIDS, and falling international terms of trade); simplistic assumptions behind and too high IFI expectations about the potential effects of adjustment; the above-listed weaknesses in adjustment design; and non-implementation of important aspects of structural adjustment as designed and agreed between the parties.

It makes no sense to assign 'shares of the blame' to these different factors. Instead two facts must be taken as the starting-point: there is a need for comprehensive reforms aimed at broad-based development; and there is a need for continued aid and an active role by the donor community. These requirements are discussed below.

4.2   Elements of Long-term Development in Sub-Saharan Africa
Obviously, this Report cannot and should not attempt to outline a long-term development strategy for Sub-Saharan Africa. On the other hand, it is impossible to examine the current attempt in many circles to move 'beyond structural adjustment' without a

starting-point in the development requirements that must be on the top of the reform agenda in Africa. This Section presents a few essential elements of development in Sub-Saharan Africa.

4.2.1 National Capacity

Throughout, this Report has criticized weaknesses in donor understanding of national capacity issues. To come to grips with this issue, it must be approached not just as a technical but also as a political one. On the one hand, the damage done to capacity by stabilization was underestimated, while on the other the increased aid flows meant an absolute increase in demands on the capacity which remained. Once this problem wasperceived, it was more often than not deepened by efforts to implement adjustment independently of existing government structures.

National capacity is a question of ensuring that citizens and their institutions can enhance the skills and resources needed to define and implement their own development aspirations on the basis of national goals and priorities that are established through democratic processes. Hence, national capacity has economic, political and social components and refers to the levels of skills and resources of both individuals and institutions. In the present context of defining national capacity as a starting-point for the reform of society, the following *public institutions* are particularly important: the education system; the civil service; institutions of policy analysis and debate; all forms of democratic fora; and the suppliers of economic and social services. The capacity of the private sector also needs addressing. Building capacity is primarily the task of African societies themselves. However, it requires international support in the form of aid, partly out of solidarity partly to offset the negative effects of global market forces and the trade and financial policies of industrial countries. The role of international support is assessed in Section 4.3.

4.2.2 Agricultural Development

Under adjustment, most of the assumptions of the classical modernization approach have been retained, while the institutions which supported it have been undermined or abolished and its economic base removed by devaluation and subsidy elimination. Market changes and new incentives have had some positive effect on food production, but little on export revenues, while the equity effects of adjustment are most likely negative. Massive price increases have reduced fertilizer and other input use which, given increased population pressure, implies that sustainable intensification must be achieved by better use of fewer inputs. This will involve what is loosely known as low-external-input agriculture - but this must on no account be seen as a panacea or easy solution. On the contrary, maintaining or increasing fertility with lower input use is likely to involve more work for both peasant farmers and extension services. The latter must start out from what exists and attempt to improve on it. This could include experiments with cost recovery in extension, which could have a dramatic effect on the quality of advice.

4.2.3 Poverty Reduction

Where adjustment has brought about growth, the proportion of poor people has probably fallen. But there are many situations where adjustment has not brought about growth. Even where growth has occurred those who were most poor have not benefitted from it. Poverty has been addressed by the IFIs only in response to external pressure for them to do so.

Reform programmes must take into account the need to protect and extend poor people's access to resources such as land and credit. Moreover, for the increased investments in social infrastructure to pay off, three issues need to receive more attention. Firstly, social sector reforms must base themselves on the involvement of local communities during the design and implementation of primary service delivery in order for basic education and primary health care programmes to respond adequately to poor people's needs. Secondly, resources must be allocated and capacity must be enhanced in central and local government institutions providing health and education, to increase efficiency and quality in social service delivery. Thirdly, central government user charges for primary services must be contained and in most cases phased out, while 'community-based user charges' should be accepted only when institutional mechanisms are in place to ensure that they are effectively controlled by beneficiaries.

Social safety nets must be reconsidered since existing measures, such as social action programmes and funds, are institutionally complex and/or fail to deliver assistance to poor people. Beneficiaries have often been less deprived population groups with political visibility and influence. Interventions to support particularly vulnerable groups must take their starting-point in sustaining existing community coping mechanisms, rather than creating new complex institutions.

4.2.4   Gender

Structural adjustment was predicted by many critics to lead to accelerated gender inequity, because men tend to be far more associated than women with the production of 'tradeables', whose production adjustment was specifically addressed to promoting. However, a decisive shift toward production of tradeables has yet to materialize. Still, there is evidence that in so far as there are benefits for producers associated with adjustment these tend to be monopolized by men, and that where there are disadvantages these tend to fall heaviest on women. This is simply due to the uneven distribution of social power between men and women in Africa; in most situations women are unable to resist men's usurpation of their resources, whether these are in the form of cash, labour, farm inputs or land. Adjustment and aid-based development policy are hardly the appropriate vehicle for dealing with this fundamental issue. Still, there is a case for targeted support to certain measures which might promote its long-term resolution, like schemes to protect women from loss of more tangible sorts of assets, to assist their political self-organization, and perhaps to establish gender quotas in the allocation of public goods and services.

Access to affordable and effective social services as well as subsidies have in the past cheapened the share of household reproduction costs traditionally allocated to women. Retaining some forms of subsidy would require a less dogmatic approach to development generally, as well as an increased revenue effort. But a commitment in this direction would be more meaningful than the vague exhortations in favour of NGO-led 'micro-enterprise development' or increasing the proportion of girls receiving primary education without reference to the modalities for such a move, which currently comprise the only two strings on the IFI 'gender awareness' bow.

4.2.5   African Debts and Exports

Out of 32 severely indebted low-income countries (SILIC) 25 are in Africa south of the Sahara. 18 African countries have both debt-service/export ratios exceeding 25 percent *and* debt/export ratios exceeding 300 percent. Uganda and Tanzania are both placed in this category. It is generally estimated that debt/export ratios above 200 percent and debt-service/exports ratios beyond 15 percent are not sustainable.

Africa's external debt and structural adjustment have been interlinked since the early 1980s. Satisfactory debt-service by African governments has been a precondition for receiving adjustment lending. Furthermore, eligibility for rescheduling and debt cancellation has been conditional on African governments agreeing to World Bank and IMF initiated structural adjustment programmes.

Since the 1980s, debt owed to official creditors has increased its share of Africa's total debts. By 1993 it was estimated that African debts to multilateral creditors, export credit agencies and aid agencies amounted to 62 percent (half of which relates to multilateral institutions) of the total debt burden of US$169 bn. Until about 1988, debt rescheduling for African low-income countries was considered a viable option. It was expected that temporary relief from current debt-service obligations combined with the expected growth effect of adjustment programmes would enable African governments to meet future debt obligations.

Since 1988 it has been agreed that rescheduling would have to be supplemented with cancellation of debt services falling due within a certain period. Although 23 countries benefitted from these more concessional terms in the period 1988-July 1994, the total sum of actual debt relief amounted to only US$2.5 bn (the figures include 5 non-African countries). Only in December 1994 did creditor governments accept the discounting of bilateral debt to reduce future debt-service obligations to sustainable levels. But it is still unclear what proportion of the debt will benefit from the new terms, and whether beneficiaries will still be required to show the same degree of 'satisfactory' adjustment performance as has been the case so far. The first test cases in the Paris Club (among them Uganda) show that the new debt-reduction terms only reduced debt stock by a meagre 2.5-3 percent in one case, while in two other cases only debt-service reductions were achieved, not debt-stock reductions.

The World Bank has recently noted that export growth cannot solve the SILICs' debt crisis. The majority of these countries would require sustained export growth rates during the next five-year period of no less than 15 percent annually to bring the debt/export ratio below the critical threshold of 200 percent. Recent experience of actual export performance points to exports growing at an average annual rate of around 3 percent. Thus, actions to reduce significantly the African debt overhang are urgently required and must aim at substantial reductions in the total stock of debt. Without such debt reduction it is not realistic to expect public and private investments, important for development, to expand.

Perhaps the most difficult long-term development issue to tackle is Africa's export expansion. Africa's share in the world market has dropped significantly since the beginning of the 1970s, and real imports per capita are at a low level. So far efforts to increase raw material exports have shown some results but have also increased the downward pressure on the prices of these products, where competition from other developing countries is serious. The evident answer is to diversify exports and to reduce imports through more efficient and broad-based production. But Africa is late in this process which cannot be handled by the ongoing international market liberalization. It requires special arrangements: support to industrial development, external finance for export promotion, selective credit programmes, etc.

4.3   International Support

The active adjustment efforts of the IFIs since the early 1980s, increasingly supported by bilateral donors, have raised very serious questions about African state integrity and influence on vital policy issues. Conditionality-based structural adjustment implied external determination of economic policy, coupled with external financing of recurrent expenditure often in the form of 'rehabilitation'. This is clearly unsustainable for both partners to the aid relationship, donor and recipient. 'A sense of ownership' is now being seen as necessary to ensure the implementation of reforms. 'National sovereignty' is again being heralded, though perhaps more in relation to social and institutional development than on macroeconomic issues.

However, such sovereignty is severely constrained by aid dependency. Unfortunately, the most likely current alternative to aid dependency is not independent sustained development but aid starvation. The striking aid fatigue in North America and much of Europe, which has resulted in falling aid allocations, makes the challenge to international cooperation serious indeed. Ironically, even conditionality may become a victim of reduced aid allocations and, in particular, of the tendency to reduce policy-based lending relative to project aid. For the World Bank, adjustment lending declined from 29 percent of the total in 1989 to only 12 percent in 1994.

The task is to establish an equitable aid contract, which acknowledges the legitimate development aspirations and priorities of Africans and makes full use of their capacities. But why aid, when the public demands of African leaders increasingly concern trade concessions and debt cancellation? In the present context, it suffices to say that both a halt to the free fall in Africa's international terms of trade and a reduction of African countries' debt to bilateral and multilateral institutions are essential preconditions for sustainable development. However, among international relations only aid has - because it is a political contract - the potential to address the elements of long-term development outlined above. Additional resources from higher export prices and lower debt-servicing are necessary but not sufficient in themselves. Hence, five elements of an equitable aid contract are presented below as a provisional framework for discussion.

1.   Respecting and building national capacity
A first step must be to halt the donor-inflicted *undermining of national capacity*. Adjustment programmes have contributed to this through financial cuts and ideological attacks on the public sector. But the real culprit is donor insistence on the use of donor- and project-specific procedures in all stages of the project and programme cycles. Donors must reduce their presence - through advisers, consultants and short-term missions - in the corridors of government institutions at all levels of society, in particular in the offices of national decision-makers, who are left with little time for their own problem assessment, reflection, priority-setting, planning, implementation support and performance monitoring.

An effective alternative is well-known, and there is no insurmountable excuse for not changing aid procedures in this direction. It requires discipline from donors who must: support the integration of their aid programmes into the recipient's institutions and procedures, including through un-tied procurement; adhere to national priorities, as expressed in policies and plans; ensure longer-term predictability and transparency in aid flows; and minimize their insistence on donor- and project-specific planning, implementation and review procedures.

Accepting home-grown priorities is difficult for donors. However, it does not preclude policy dialogue between the parties and even donor conditionality. The point is that bilateral and multilateral donors must ensure maximum integration, once there is agreement on objectives. The next step must be for both parties to ensure that the involved national and local institutions have the required resources and capacity for policy implementation. A few essential, but currently underutilized instruments for capacity building were presented in Section 3.5 on public sector reform.

2.   Supporting programmes based on dialogue on policies and strategies
This starting-point requires support for programmes based on genuine dialogue on policies and strategies. Such a framework has been outlined in numerous contexts in recent years. The following list is based on a World Bank paper on future aid to Africa:

1. Most donor-recipient dialogues must focus on national policies, programmes and practices that are *sector-wide* in scope. *Area-wide, multi-sector* programmes may also be supported if there are clear national policies and practices of delegation to local bodies.
2. Sectoral policies and programmes must be *prepared by local stakeholders*. Local ownership must be built in from the beginning, through active participation of local stakeholders in programme preparation.
3. Programme support must *comprise all significant donors active in the sector*. Aid effectiveness cannot be enhanced unless all donors, and the recipient government, buy into a more coordinated approach.
4. The approach should involve *common implementation arrangements*, to comply with the suggestions made about respect and support for national capacity. Programme design needs to begin from an assessment of existing institutional capacity, and donors must be willing to accept smaller programmes and lower rates of funding commitments in order to achieve eventually larger and faster sustainable development impacts.

It should be added that the World Bank is itself still quite far from living up to such requirements at country level. The strategy for Danish development cooperation, adopted in 1994, could fit into such an organization of development cooperation, but it would require change in country-level operations, especially with respect to common implementation arrangements.

3.   Providing adequate resources
Despite strong efforts to assist Africa, e.g. through the Special Programme for Africa (SPA), the inflow of external resources has barely compensated for debt payments and losses on terms of trade. This squeeze has negative effects not only on foreign direct investment, where Sub-Saharan Africa has little to expect, but also on local private investment. The economic situation may now be somewhat more stable in some African countries, but it is fragile. The emphasis on national capacity and sector programmes

has significant implications for the future forms of aid transfers:

1. *Capacity building* requires flexible and transparent funding on a grant basis, with a multi-year donor commitment. It requires a combination of technical and financial assistance, where the flow of both forms is tied in with the needs of the recipient institution and in particular its capacity to use the funds effectively.
2. *Sector programmes* (or area-specific programmes) are a useful mechanism for large-scale financial assistance, including indirectly balance-of-payments support. They must be supported under a multi-year plan, which regulates the size of transfers according to the changing balance between needs and achievements.
3. *Balance-of-payments support*, *contingency funds* and *emergency relief* will still be needed on a short-term basis. However, the aim must be to limit these relative to funding for long-term development cooperation (based on dialogue) under capacity building and sector programme assistance.

4.   Reorienting conditionality to capacity and performance

The use of conditionality by the IMF and the World Bank increased rapidly in the second half of the 1980s and into the early 1990s. As the conditionalities, partly promoted by bilateral donors, extended into political, institutional and social fields, non-implementation became the order of the day. At the same time, the scope for sanctions by the donors in response to conditionalities not being met was reduced, partly because donors needed success stories to reflect their insistence on the adjustment model. A major problem with the adjustment-related conditionality has been its starting-point in short-term measures, on the assumption that stabilization could be achieved independently of structural change. Furthermore, conditionality is biased towards cuts, deregulation and dismantlement, i.e. 'negative' interventions, on the assumption that these will lead to a supply response through the release of market forces.

Whether conditionality is justifiable or not, it is time to 'reverse the order' so that existing capacity and the requirements of long-term development are taken as the starting-point for decisions about using conditionality. Very provisionally, this can be seen as suggesting four steps:

Firstly, each African country should have a set of *long-term development objectives* covering the desired shape of society, including the role to be played by public and private sectors, civil society and different social groups. Respect for this would delegitimize external insistence on *one* development paradigm. On the other hand, it does not necessarily require 'national consensus', though equity and social integration must be guaranteed. A *national policy framework* must incorporate strategies linking short- and medium-term measures to long-term objectives. Hence, it requires *policy coherence* on the side of African governments.

Secondly, the development objectives and the policy framework should be translated into *national priorities, plans and programmes*, to which donors can relate, and whose implementation can be monitored. Rather than a return to defunct five-year plans, a system of medium-term rolling development programmes is required with budget estimates tied to sector strategies, programmes and projects. Again, policy coherence is called for, not policy orthodoxy.

Thirdly, the *capacity* of society at large and, in particular, of national and local institutions to implement the above policies and programmes must be assessed and agreed to between donor and recipient *prior to* any large-scale commitment of donor funds. Capacity includes resources (e.g. the scope for national and local resource mobilization), structure (effective institutions) and competence (people with skills). If capacity is deemed critically insufficient in these respects, donor resources must be phased into the required capacity building, which should be supported separately.

Fourthly, aid funds must be released for both capacity building and implementation. Conditionality should be tied to *performance* in implementing the agreed programme. This requires ex-post monitoring and a sufficiently long time perspective to give national and local institutions the space for capacity building and implementation. A difficult balance must be struck between sanctions on poor performance on the one hand and long-term donor commitment to capacity building on the other.

Obviously, these suggestions require further reflection, particularly in these regards:

1. Is conditionality related to policy coherence and performance more acceptable to African governments than the adjustment-related conditionality which is based on policy orthodoxy and short-term prescriptions?
2. Conditionality related to policy coherence is insufficient to avoid cases of economic mismanagement on the one hand and of human rights violation on the other. What additional measures are required beyond such conditionality?
3. Would poor performance under policy coherence and capacity-related conditionality lead to donor selectivity between countries (i.e. reallocation of aid to 'better performers') or mainly between sectors within individual recipient countries?

5. *Reforming aid coordination and the roles of individual donors*

The four elements of a reformed aid relation presented above are practical efforts both to make aid more effective and to put African institutions in the driver's seat. A final precondition is that aid coordination is reformed and that different types of donors find more effective roles for themselves, involving change along the following lines:

• From externally driven aid coordination, led by the World Bank (occasionally UNDP) and organized outside Africa in Consultative Groups and the SPA working groups in donor capitals, whose membership is restricted to donors;
• To nationally driven aid management, led by core and line ministries of the recipient government and organized as part of the regular policy-making, priority-setting, planning, programming and budgeting procedures of African institutions.

Such a change would have to be implemented gradually in line with the building of capacity to implement development cooperation in the steps described above. As capacity building and sector programme support are operationalized, capacity will gradually become available at country level to take over from Consultative Group meetings. Furthermore, there is still a need for international fora for deliberations on development in and aid to Africa. The significance of the SPA working groups must be recognized: they serve to improve the quality of donor approaches in essential fields such as poverty alleviation and public sector reform; they could minimize the burden on African governments by weeding out extreme preferences and pet approaches by individual donors; and they could make overall aid more effective by forcing individual donors to find an optimum position in a transparent and accountable division of responsibility.

As regards the multilateral donors, one encounters a paradox. On the one hand, there is much to be said, in terms of cost-effective use of the significant resources of each donor, for a return to the originally intended division of labour, with the IMF in a limited role in relation to short-term financial imbalances, and the World Bank with a broader development role. On the other hand, there are risks in this division of responsibility between the Bank and the Fund. It took time for the IFIs and other donors to begin to realize that a comprehensive approach was needed. But some still work according to a division of labour premised on a framework of a rolling agenda of short-term stabilization of macro balances and liberalization of markets, followed by medium-term adjustment (structural reforms such as deregulation and privatization), and finally by 'development' (investments, civil service reform, etc.).

The only solution to this paradox seems to be to organize a single macroeconomic and institutional dialogue between African governments and all donors, including IMF and the World Bank. In terms of issue coverage and membership, this mechanism could resemble the current Consultative Group mechanism. In terms of location and leadership (in and by developing countries) the change towards nationally driven aid management would have to be gradual, in response to improved capacity in national institutions.

This raises a significant question: Should each African government remain 'on its own' in the dialogue with a multitude of donors? Here, two things must be considered. On the one hand, cooperation among African governments must be encouraged as a counter-balance to the numerous donor coordination mechanisms. On the other hand, all parties to development cooperation should strive to ensure that dialogue directly emanates from democratic decision-making bodies in individual African countries.

Two more issues need to be raised in the current discussion of a more equitable aid contract between donor institutions and African societies.

The accountability of the IFIs: The governments of developing countries and international NGOs have correctly pointed to the inadequate accountability of the IMF and the World Bank. Accountability is primarily a question of ensuring policy coherence also within the IFIs, viz. in the form of correspondence between the numerous progressive and accommodating statements and the practice of programme and project lending. There are three ways to achieve such accountability:

1. Placing the IFIs under the policy direction of economic bodies in the UN. This is the least effective approach. It would lead to greater inefficiencies in the overall aid system. The democratic bodies of the UN lack capacity to establish clear priorities and effective policies for the IFIs. Closer links between the Development Committee of the IMF/the World Bank on the one hand and the UN's Economic and Social Council (ECOSOC) on the other would lead to lip service and useless compromise rather than to coordination and transparency.
2. Making maximum use of the existing governing bodies of the IFIs. Under the catchword of 'active multilateralism', Denmark has - laudably - prepared itself for critical monitoring of and influence on the policies of all multilateral institutions, including the IFIs. There are two simple requirements here. Firstly, countries like Denmark must exercise their ownership of the IFIs, to push them in less orthodox directions. Secondly, these 'like-minded countries' must consistently support the capacity of the least developed countries to influence IFI policies.
3. Exposing the policies and programmes of IFIs to qualified public debate in recipient countries. Two flaws demonstrate clearly the need for greater IFI accountability at

country level. Firstly, structural adjustment programmes took on excessive importance because they were both formulated and received as 'grand designs' for societal change. Secondly, discussions on the World Bank's country assistance strategies do not seek active involvement of recipient countries, apart from a narrow range of top civil servants.

The accountability of the IFIs *must* be improved, but this can and should primarily take place at the level of individual developing countries. The emphasis on national policy coherence and capacity and on policy and strategy dialogue is the best approach to force the IFIs to be accountable to the users of their resources and advice. Bilateral donors, providing the funds for the World Bank, could and should play essential roles in constantly monitoring the effectiveness of the IFIs. It is inappropriate that the weak UN agencies are more exposed than the strong IFIs to scrutiny and demands by donor countries. The need for transparency and accountability is at least as great in the IFIs.

The comparative advantage of the IFIs: Questions were raised above on the duplication of efforts between the IMF and the World Bank. More fundamentally, the present Report has argued for a starting-point in African policy coherence and a transfer of policy-making to the institutions of African countries. This implies a reduction in the hegemony of the IFIs in the field of development policy-making. Provided both African governments and bilateral donors live up to their policy analysis role, a real question is raised about the future role of the World Bank and the IMF.

2

Country Studies

Burkina Faso
1983-94

Mike Speirs

Danagro Adviser AS

Introduction

In contrast to many other Sub-Saharan African countries, there were no structural adjustment loan agreements in the 1980s between the government of Burkina Faso and the international financial institutions (the International Monetary Fund and the World Bank). Nevertheless, there is a history:

> ... when Captain Thomas Sankara took over in Upper Volta (now Burkina Faso) in 1983, he initiated a process which bore a lot of resemblance to the policies advocated by the World Bank concerning the size and modes of intervention of the public sector. Drastic budget reductions, cuts in pay and numbers employed in public administration, a general reduction of deficits, an upward shift in agricultural producer prices, tight control upon parastatal operations - and the demand that they meet financial equilibrium - and an appeal to private sector investors to engage in new productive investment are examples of such public policy reforms. Roughly speaking, something like three-quarters of the World Bank's recommendations were met by Sankara without any World Bank intervention (Fontaine, 1987: 17).

According to this view, the only conditionalities imposed on the economy were those of a revolutionary, military government, intent on 'inventing a new future' for the people of this ex-French colony located on the southern fringes of the Sahara desert. However, these conditionalities were significant. Fontaine (*ibid.*: 17) also commented that:

> If one had to measure the 'degree' of involvement of the state in the economy through indicators such as the public budget or deficit expressed as a percentage of GNP, the volume of subsidies to parastatals, or, in orthodox neo-classical fashion, the extent of price distortion from a 'rational' norm, one would conclude that Burkina witnessed a disinvolvement of the state - and should pass the test of 'economic liberalisation'. I suppose, however, that very few people would maintain this position, if only because of the development of *Comités de Défense de la Révolution* throughout the country.

The excesses of the CDRs (revolutionary defence committees) were a major contributory factor in the downfall of the *Conseil National de la Révolution* (CNR) led by Sankara. In October 1987 the radical policies of the CNR were 'rectified' through a military coup which bought the present president, Blaise Campaoré, to power at the head of the *Front Populaire*. In 1989, negotiations began with the World Bank, and consultants prepared an economic memorandum (World Bank, 1989) which was the first step towards the structural adjustment programme (SAP) agreed in March 1991. The first SAL (adjustment loan) was approved by the executive directors of the World Bank in June 1991, two days after a referendum had approved a new constitution in Burkina Faso, thereby completing the transition from military rule to an *état de droit* ('lawful' state).[1] Since 1993 the IMF has also provided loans through the enhanced

---

[1] The timing of the approval of the first SAL (World Bank, 1991) is also significant, particularly in the context of land reform and the revision of 'revolutionary' land ownership legislation (see sections 2.1 and 4.1, below).

structural adjustment facility (ESAF).

Subsequently, according to some assessments of the first two years of the structural adjustment programme (1991-93), the government of Burkina Faso has performed as an exemplary pupil in the tricky business of macroeconomic reform in the context of extreme poverty. Nonetheless, difficulties have been encountered and opposition to certain adjustment measures has been vocal, particularly amongst university students and the trade unions in Ouagadougou. For the vast majority, the 80-90 percent of the total population who inhabit the rural areas, it is difficult to ascertain the extent to which the SAL, the ESAF agreements and the sectoral adjustment programmes have affected their incomes, welfare and daily lives.

The purpose of this review is to attempt such an assessment. In addition to a survey of the standard macroeconomic indicators used to determine success or failure in implementing a structural adjustment programme, this paper includes consideration of a number of important processes and factors in the Burkina Faso case.[2] In this analysis, the historical background to the agreements with the IMF and the World Bank in the early 1990s is of particular significance.

Although the SAL, the use of the ESAF of the IMF, and the sectoral adjustment programmes (to support reforms in agriculture, transport, health, education and public institutions) have entailed important changes in development strategies, the public sector and government institutions which are affected by the attached policy conditionalities represent only a small part of the overall economic canvas. The activities of farmers (including pastoralists and agro-pastoralists), traders, private sector *entrepreneurs* and small business people in the informal sector account for a large share of overall income and weath in the country. The extent to which the policies of the CNR (1983-87), the *Front Populaire* (1987-91) and the government led by Blaise Campaoré (elected in May 1992[3]) have been able to determine the contours of economic policy has been intimately linked to a series of power struggles: between these military and democratic governments and 'the people'; between different governments and the donor community (notably France and the Bretton Woods institutions) and between the countries of the sub-region through various inter-governmental organizations, of which the central West African bank (BCEAO) plays a particularly important role.

Some of these conflicts came to a head in the arguments associated with the devaluation of the CFA Franc in January 1994. In contrast to Ghana and Nigeria, whose currencies steadily lost their value during the 1980s through successive devaluations in connection with SAPs, the CFA Franc used in Burkina Faso (issued by the *Banque Central des Etats de l'Afrique de l'Ouest*) was maintained at the same fixed parity with

---

[2] The background paper prepared by Bassolet and Ouédraogo (1994) forms the basis of the assessment of macroeconomic trends in Burkina Faso, notably in the period 1991-93. I am indebted to these authors and to several other colleagues at the *Centre d'Etudes, de Documentation et de Recherche Economique et Sociale* (CEDRES) of the University of Ouagadougou, for numerous analytical insights and for their collaboration in my previous research into agrarian change in Burkina Faso in the 1980s (Speirs, 1991a). Thanks are also due to Peter Gibbon, Lars Engberg-Pedersen, Hans-Otto Sano and Knud Erik Svendsen for comments on earlier drafts.

[3] The presidential elections gave Campaoré a new seven-year mandate in December 1991, as described in section 2.4 (below). Otayek (1992) gives a detailed analysis of the contradictions which arose during the democratization process in Burkina Faso from 1987 to 1991, as 'Marxism retreated from Africa'.

the French Franc from 1948 until the long expected devaluation in 1994.[4] This event has profound implications in terms of economic cooperation and regional integration in West Africa, as well as in terms of improving the competitive advantages of the Burkinabè economy.

With the devaluation of the CFA Franc, Burkina Faso entered a third phase of structural adjustment. Starting with *auto-ajustement* during the revolution (1983-97), the country has also undergone 'internal adjustment' with the backing of the Bretton Woods institutions since 1991, and then 'external adjustment' together with the other Franc zone members. But the results of these different packages and reforms are limited. Rainfall and world cotton prices continue to exert decisive influences on economic performance. Although there does appear to have been some increase in private sector investment, dependence on foreign aid transfers for investment in production and in social services has also increased.

Prior to the devaluation, the impact of the SAP was largely felt in terms of import expansion, linked to the disbursement of aid in connection with sectoral adjustment programmes. But both the government budget deficit and the current account deficit increased, emphasizing the failure to augment taxation revenue and exports (both of which stagnated during the 'internal' SAP period). The extent to which an altered exchange rate can provide a stimulus for sustainable growth will depend on a range of variables; not least on the outcome of further struggles over access to, and control over resources, particularly in the rural areas where the search for appropriate and equitable land tenure arrangements continues. The impact of further public investment in human resource development (notably improved education) and private investment (creating employment opportunities in manufacturing) will also be significant.

1. Structural Development Issues in Burkina Faso Prior to Adjustment

In the absence of any structural adjustment loan agreements in Burkina Faso during the 1980s, first the CNR government led by Captain Thomas Sankara, and initially the government of the *Front Populaire*, tried to go it alone with economic reform programmes. The contrast with revolutionary Ghana under the PNDC government led by Flight Lieutenant Jerry Rawlings in the 1980s is instructive in this context. In spite

---

[4] The value of the CFA Franc was halved relative to the French Franc, while maintaining a fixed exchange rate. *The Economist* (15 January 1994) commented on this devaluation with the headline: 'France retreats from its empire'. A summary of exchange rates 1985-94 is provided below:

Exchange rates: Average annual rates of F.CFA per US$ and per French Franc

	1985	86	87	88	89	90	91	92	93	94
F.CFA/US$	449	346	301	298	319	272	282	265	287	605
F.CFA/FF	50	50	50	50	50	50	50	50	50	100

Source: IMF and BCEAO data

of the anti-imperialist rhetoric of the PNDC, Rawlings negotiated with the World Bank and the IMF to obtain structural adjustment loans, and largely accepted the conditionalities imposed. He survived the 1980s, but Sankara was eliminated in a rectification of the revolution which led to the new economic policies of the Front Populaire and ultimately to the SAP in 1991. Sankara and Rawlings were close comrades in arms and at one point even proposed forming a federation between Burkina Faso and Ghana.

The distinctive feature of the period from 1983 to 1987 (and to a lesser extent from 1987 to 1991) in Burkina Faso was the concerted effort to channel resources into tackling the major rural development problems of the country through an investment strategy based on an initial *programme populaire du développement* (PPD, 1984-85) and then a five-year popular development plan (1986-90). Although the results of these efforts were mixed, the main aim was to implement economic development strategies which would benefit the rural masses (Martin, 1986). In terms of policy statements at least, introducing a 'rural bias' was seen as the key to developing agriculture and stimulating economic growth.

This represented a sharp contrast to the period from independence (in 1960) to 1983, during which successive governments were characterized largely by their incompetence and inability to deal with the structural constraints of the economy. Corruption (misuse of funds, etc.) was rife and Upper Volta remained firmly fixed in a pattern of dependence on aid (including food aid) and on migrants' remittances. The latter factor has had a considerable impact on the balance of payments since independence; it is estimated that around two million Burkinabè work as (often seasonal) labourers on the plantations, in the factories and in the informal sector of the relatively well developed coastal countries in West Africa, notably Côte d'Ivoire. This migration started during the colonial period, when Upper Volta became a surplus labour reserve for agricultural development programmes in other regions of *Afrique Occidental Française* (notably the cocoa plantations in Côte d'Ivoire, and the large-scale irrigation scheme known as the *Office du Niger* in Mali).

The population growth rate accelerated in the 1970s, and averaged around 3 percent per annum in the 1980s. It is estimated that the total population of Burkina Faso reached 9.5 million in 1992 (World Bank, 1994b: Annex 3).[5] However, the population is unevenly distributed, with the highest density in the central and northern *plateau Mossi*. Migration from this severely eroded and degraded land towards the cotton producing areas of the south and west as well as to the main towns has accelerated, and the annual urban growth rate is estimated at over 8 percent (Laclavère *et al.*, 1993: 28-29).

In terms of economic performance in the period prior to the *révolution démocratique et populaire* (RDP, August 1983), the introduction of intensive cotton growing linked to the establishment of cotton ginning facilities in the west of the country (in collaboration with the *Compagnie Française de Développement des Textiles* and with some World Bank funds) was the major innovation. Otherwise, largely subsistence food-crop cultivation and livestock herding were the main sources of income in the rural areas. A few manufacturing industries were set up (notably breweries) and a sugar cane plantation was established near Banfora in the south-west. According to the World Bank (1989) economic memorandum, per capita GNP grew at an average annual rate

---

[5] Laclavère *et al.* (1993: 26) quote estimates suggesting that the total population will be around 18 million in the year 2015. A new census will be organised in 1995.

of 1.2 percent in the period from 1965 to 1984.

In 1989 the World Bank estimated the growth rates of value added in the different sectors of the Burkinabè economy as indicated in Table 1. As is the case in many Sub-Saharan African countries, all data pertaining to economic performance should be treated with great caution. There are considerable difficulties associated with the collection of data and the estimation of gross domestic product (GDP), government budgets, growth rates, exports and imports and so on. Indeed, a part of the adjustment strategy proposed for the period 1994-96 concerns improving the statistical base in Burkina Faso, in order to be able to carry out and monitor the 'ambitious program of reforms' (World Bank, 1994a: 15).

Table 1   Sectoral Distribution of GDP and Growth of Value - Added, 1965-87

	Sectoral distribution of GDP (percent)		Percentage growth of value added (in constant 1979 prices)	
	1965	1985	1977-82	1982-87
Primary (agriculture, livestock, forestry)	53	45	2.2	5.4
Secondary (mining, manufacturing)	20	18	3.8	3.8
Tertiary (commercial, transport, services)	27	37	4.1	3.8

Source: World Bank, 1989.

More recent estimates reported by the UNDP (1994) and the World Bank (1994c) indicate that the percentage of GDP derived from primary production (crop cultivation, livestock and forestry) has not declined significantly since 1985. Similarly, around 37 percent of GDP was derived from the tertiary sector in 1992. Recent growth rates in the different sectors have varied, as described and analyzed below (section 3).

The slow growth of the economy from 1960 to 1983 has been studied by a number of observers, notably in a review of 'dependent development' by Ouali (1986). The main trends were summarized by Savadogo and Wetta (1992: 54), who argued that:

> Remoteness, the dominance of Côte d'Ivoire and Senegal in former French West Africa and the constraints imposed by membership in the West African Monetary Union (UMOA) made industrialisation based on import substitution an unfeasible development strategy. In view of the limited importance of known mineral deposits, a strategy focused on mining was also not appropriate, and because of the narrowness of the domestic market it was not possible to concentrate on a 'self-reliant' approach. Because of these limitations, Burkina's development in the 1960s and 1970s was led by the export of cattle and cheap labour to neighbouring coastal economies and of a few cash crops such as groundnuts and cotton to Western Europe.

As Bassolet and Ouédraogo (1994: 2) have observed, the relatively healthy external payments balance in Burkina Faso in this period was largely due to foreign aid and migrants' transfers. The current account and trade balance were in deficit throughout the 1970s, but a cautious borrowing policy kept public debt at a level 'trivial in absolute terms and in relation to GDP and exports' (Savadogo and Wetta, 1992: 55). A significant debt ratio first emerged in the mid-1980s (see section 3.3, below).

Given the lack of investment in developing industrial and manufacturing capacity, the low overall growth rates recorded in the 1960s and 1970s were largely due to poor performance in the agricultural sector. Drought was one major factor, but the slow rate of increase in domestic food production and steadily increasing quantities of wheat and rice imports also contributed to the deteriorating balance between food supply and demand (see section 4.2, below). Thus: 'except for cotton farming, agriculture in early 1980s still faced the same structural problems of poor soil fertility, backward technologies, low use of fertiliser and other modern inputs [...] that it had confronted 20 years earlier' (*ibid.*: 56). Similarly, human capital development in the form of investment in improved health and education services was minimal, although infant mortality rates had dropped and primary school enrolment rates had increased to 27 percent in 1983 (*ibid.*: 57).[6]

The rise in oil prices and inflation rates at the end of the 1970s, and increases in the import bill (including food imports), as well as the downward trend in the world market prices of export commodities, had a negative impact on the balance of payments and the budget deficit. Savadogo and Wetta (*ibid.*: 58) concluded:

> The current account deficit (after transfers) which had averaged 5-6 percent of GDP in the late 1970s, reached 8 percent in 1982. Less acute, but still measurable was the deterioration in the budget deficit, which rose by 2 percentage points relative to GDP between the late 1970s and 1982, and the inflation rate, which climbed from an average of 6.5 percent in 1965-80 to 11-12 percent in 1981-82. Adjustment was therefore unavoidable.

In the following examination of attempts to confront the structural constraints limiting economic growth in Burkina Faso, the period from 1983 to 1987 is treated as illustrative of 'self-imposed adjustment' (*auto ajustement*). This term was coined by Savadogo and Wetta (1992), and seems to accurately describe the strategy adopted by the *Conseil National de la Révolution*, as Fontaine (1987) also observed. But the implications of rejecting any approaches to the Bretton Woods institutions for obtaining additional financial resources to support the adjustment process were considerable. This raises the interesting question, which has been much debated in Burkina Faso and elsewhere, concerning the extent to which a resource-deficient Sahelian economy is capable of 'self-adjustment.'[7]

---

[6] The *Human Development Report* (UNDP, 1994), where Burkina Faso ranks as number 172 of the 173 countries for which data are compared, indicates significant differences in the school enrolment rates for boys and girls (see also section 6.2, below).

[7] See, for example, the papers by Savadogo and Larivière (1993), Speirs (1991b) and Tallet (1989), the review by Devey and Lingane (1993) and the study by Zabré (1994), as well as the comments on the CNR period in the World Bank (1989 & 1994b) reports. Zabré's book about economic development in Burkina Faso is provocatively subtitled *une tradition d'ajustement structurel*. Zabré was *Ministre du Plan* in the Front Populaire government; he resigned in 1991 during the negotiations with the World Bank.

2. History and Objectives of Structural Adjustment in Burkina Faso

2.1   Evolution of Dialogue, 1983-91

Apart from the termination of loans for cotton production and processing and the approval of loans to improve agricultural research and services, as well as an agreement with the World Bank-funded *Programme Engrais (fertilizer scheme)* which involved the phasing out of fertilizer subsidies during the 1980s, the CNR government conducted no formal negotiations with the World Bank and the IMF.[8] In this context, the retrospective comments in a recent report (by the same Bank) on aid to Burkina Faso are worth quoting in full:

> 1991, as a watershed year for the adoption of comprehensive reforms, takes on all the more significance when viewed in a historical perspective, in which the Sankara years [...] occupy a special place. The Sankara regime had a marked impact on Burkina's recent history and economic developments. With bold and egalitarian objectives, the regime nonetheless undermined the economic base of Burkina Faso and its efforts proved unsustainable. The regime's political orientation was inspired by central planning and a Marxist-Leninist ideology, distrustful of external intervention, in particular of the Bretton Woods Institutions. The private sector was discouraged by confiscatory measures and political interference in the management of enterprises. Domestic and internal [is this a misprint?, M.S.] trade were increasingly controlled. In 1984, the government launched a development program aimed at mobilising rural and urban people to construct public infrastructure. In the social sectors, the government sought to improve the education and health status of the population by aggressive vaccination and literacy campaigns, and launched the construction of a large number of health centres and schools. The authorities actively promoted environmental conservation and the role of women. Burkina saw several years of growth, fuelled by high public investment, good weather, and increased agricultural production in onchocerciasis-freed areas, but nonetheless faced economic crisis as the economic foundations of the policies pursued were weak (World Bank, 1994b: 2).

In this description, the vaccination and literacy campaigns are called 'aggressive', not 'comprehensive' or 'urgently needed'. UNICEF gave them full marks! But it was a pity that 'egalitarian objectives' were incompatible with the 'economic foundations' of policies in Burkina Faso. No doubt this is often the case, since poverty does not allow much room for manoeuvre, and the radical stance of the CNR government on questions of income distribution, public expenditure and investment in rural infrastructure were

---

[8] The discussion in this section is based largely on the observations by Bassolet and Ouédraogo (1994) and by Savadogo and Wetta (1992). The effect of removing fertilizer subsidies was assessed in a recent joint evaluation of fertilizer deliveries (programme aid) to Burkina Faso (DANIDA/DGIS, 1994), as well as in the study by Sanon *et al.* (1993) which compared rates of fertilizer use on cereal and cotton crops (see section 4.2, below).

controversial.

Much has been written about the political struggles which engulfed Sankara and the CNR government. Several observers have investigated why different groups, including foreign investors, the aid community and NGOs, other French-backed governments in West Africa, and different sections of the indigenous population (women, the young, the unions, peasant farmers, the military, and so on) approved or disapproved of the CNR strategy.[9] Suffice to say that the economic results of this period were perhaps not as meagre as some have suggested, although the political costs were high.

Savadogo and Wetta (1992: 58-69) offer an alternative interpretation of the same period, stressing the growth-orientated policies pursued in agriculture and mining, as well as the importance attached to human resource development (education and training). Here again the political costs were significant. Indeed, the breakdown of the dialogue with the trade unions, in particular with the teachers' union following the dismissal of 1400 teachers in connection with a strike in 1984 (protesting against the wage freeze in the public sector), was instrumental in the fall of the CNR government in 1987.

It is ironic to note that one of the main reasons for entering into negotiations with the World Bank on a structural adjustment programme in 1989 was the budgetary cost of reinstating these teachers, which the *Front Populaire* agreed to do in 1988 (Otayek, 1992: 84). Increased public sector expenditure requires increased public sector revenue and hence increased taxation, as recommended in the SAP and in the ESAF arrangements, as well as reduced expenditure on 'non-productive' sectors (such as the military). The total public sector wage bill jumped by over 20 percent with the re-employment of the teachers, from F.CFA 42.3 bn in 1987 to F.CFA 51.5 bn in 1988 (IMF, 1993c, Annexe Table 16).

The dialogue with other key actors on the domestic scene was also fraught with tension. As Savadogo and Wetta (1992: 69) point out, although the 'distribution of benefits had been radically altered within the country', at the same time 'people's tribunals had effectively reduced the traditional power of the rural chiefs and were exerting strong control over the civil service.' The 'democratic' nature of the 'popular and democratic revolution' in 1983 became increasingly obscure.[10] Discontent was particularly obvious in the urban areas and the coup d'état led by Blaise Campaoré against his erstwhile friend and fellow soldier on 15 October 1987 was not unexpected.

The roles played by the French Government and by key political figures in Côte d'Ivoire in backing the coup have never been fully clarified. However, given that the anti-imperialist rhetoric of the Sankara Government clearly placed the French in the

---

[9] Another historical aside: Savonnet-Guyot (1986: 180) observed that after the coup in 1983, '*le capitaine Sankara s'employant à rassurer tout le monde, les commerçants se disent favorables à la Révolution si on respecte la libre enterprise, les hiérarchies religieuses si on reconnait leur pouvoir spirituel, les chefferies coutumières si la tradition est maintenue, les syndicats si leur pouvour est respecté par les CDR'*. On the conflicts between the government and business people, see Labazée (1988), for a study of the struggles with the powerful trade unions, see Kabeya-Muase (1989), and for a survey of internal contradictions in the CNR government, see Otayek (1988).

[10] The monument to the *Discours d'Orientation Politique* (the major political statement) delivered by Sankara on 2 October 1983, still stands in the middle of a roundabout in Ouagadougou. The document itself is a fascinating historical review of exploitation by different 'enemies of the people' in Burkina Faso. See, inter alia, the study by Martin (1986).

'imperialist camp', and that the ban on imports of fruit and vegetables from Côte d'Ivoire (introduced in 1987 in an attempt to encourage import substitution) was a direct confrontation with a powerful neighbour, it is likely that the removal of this unruly captain was fairly high on the regional political agenda. On the other hand, many foreign NGOs and some aid agencies appeared to support the political and economic strategy of the CNR government (Sharp, 1990). The Americans were particularly sceptical, and the USAID programme in the country was terminated following speeches at the United Nations by Sankara in favour of the PLO and other liberation movements.

Creating a 'democratic opening' became a major priority for the *Front Populaire* (Otayek, 1992: 84-91). Space does not permit a detailed review of the debates which took place in the period from 1987 to 1991 when the agreement with the World Bank on the conditions of a first SAL was reached. However, it is important to stress the gradual thawing of the political climate in the capital, as a number of well-known political actors returned to the stage. At the same time, Campaoré manoeuvred skilfully with the various opposition groups, enabling him to form a party (the ODP-MT) and to draft a constitution for submission to a referendum on 2 June 1991.

But in spite of this democratization, Campaoré is known as a president with a military past. The summary execution of two officers (who were also ministers in the government) suspected of organizing a counter coup in 1989 confirmed doubts about his willingness to pursue democratic means in resolving disputes. The circumstances surrounding this incident, and the assassination of an important opposition leader in December 1991 (just prior to the elections) have yet to be fully explained. Sankara himself was 'rehabilitated' (*in memoriam*) as a national hero in 1992.

Negotiations on economic policy reform were also tense and difficult, both with the unions on the domestic front and with aid donor agencies awaiting the outcome of discussions with the World Bank. In the end, after organizing a national meeting on the economy (on 12 May 1990) which authorized the government to pursue the negotiations with the World Bank, a framework agreement was signed on 5 March 1991. This was followed by a round table session with the donors in Geneva in May, at which the participants approved the strategy while noting that the length of the negotiations (over two years) signified that a 'high quality adjustment programme' had been prepared (Bassolet and Ouédraogo, 1994: 5). The stage was set for a return of the donors following a period at the end of the 1980s in which foreign aid transfers had stagnated (see section 3.2, below).

Meanwhile, as a final act prior to the vote on the new constitution on 2 June 1991, the Council of Ministers of the *Front Populaire* approved a major change in land tenure legislation on 29 May 1991. This was an important item in the conditionalities attached to the first SAL. It is interesting to note that the partial repeal of the revolutionary land ownership law (known as the *Réforme Agraire et Foncière*) introduced by the CNR in 1984 and under which all land belonged to the state, was carried out by an un-elected and un-constitutional government. This happened just seven days before the proposed SAL was submitted to the Executive Board of the World Bank for approval (the loan recommendation was made in a report dated 4 June 1991), and four days before the constitutional referendum.[11]

---

[11] This sequence of events is confirmed by a close reading of the World Bank (1991) report. The consequences of this rushed change in land legislation (allowing private ownership) are examined in more detail below (section 4.1).

2.2   Formal Objectives of the SAP (1991)

According to the country assistance strategy document issued by the World Bank (1994b) and quoted at length above, the CNR regime had 'undermined the economic base of Burkina Faso'. In the report presenting the background to the SAL (World Bank, 1991: 2), it is noted that until 1988 'the economy enjoyed relatively good growth' but that the expansion of 'public consumption and investment spending' as well as the good weather and 'bringing of new land under cultivation' were unsustainable. Unfortunately for the Sahelian governments, control over the climate is not part of their overall development strategy, and the policy instruments to ensure the sustainability of good weather are not yet at their disposal.

However, the public expenditure budget is under the control of the government. Debt arrears had begun to accumulate by the end of the 1980s, the government deficit remained high and the balance-of-payments deficit was also increasing (see section 3, below). Thus, the main thrust of the first structural adjustment agreement concerned controlling public finances. As noted above, this inevitably entailed complex negotiations between the *Front Populaire* government and the World Bank (together with other donors including France) on one level, and with the newly emerging 'democratic forces' on another.

The objectives of the resulting SAL (for which SDR 60 million was available on standard IDA terms) were as follows (Bassolet and Ouédraogo, 1994: 6-7): i) to reform public finances, in order to improve the management of government funds; ii) to restructure the banking sector, by restricting the participation of the state in bank capital to a maximum of 25 percent; iii) to reduce the current account deficit by accelerating the liberalization of trade and by simplifying the procedures for exports; and, iv) to promote the activities of the private sector by creating a favourable business environment (notably through a reform of the labour legislation and by the removal of *rigidités et contraintes administratives*).[12] In addition, various sectoral reforms were proposed, some of which have subsequently become sectoral adjustment programmes financed by the World Bank together with other donors. These include an agricultural sector adjustment programme (PASA), a programme to rehabilitate public enterprises (PASEP), an environmental action plan (PANE), a transport sector adjustment programme (PASEC-T) and a human resource adjustment programme (PASHR). The latter includes measures to reform the health and education services, to encourage family planning and to combat AIDS (see sections 6.2 and 6.3, below).

In introducing the SAL I programme (1991-93), the World Bank (1991: 15) noted that the government had already 'initiated a number of important measures in 1990'. These included freezing the wage bill, implementing a rolling investment programme ('dropping several large and dubious investments') and reducing the scholarships for higher education as well as privatizing, restructuring or liquidating a number of public enterprises (in agro-processing and manufacturing). In addition, the government was identifying receivers for the restructuring of banks to be privatized, was in the process of eliminating price controls on all locally produced goods as well as the controls and taxes on exported goods, and was reducing the controls over imported goods (including the complete elimination of the 'local purchasing requirement').

---

[12] The first SAP was co-financed by the European Community (US$30 m.), the African Development Bank (US$20 m.), Canada (US$13 m.), France (US$17 m.) and Germany (US$12 m.). 53 percent of the IDA loan was un-disbursed as of March 1994 (World Bank, 1994b: Annex 6).

This list reveals the extent to which adjustment was already under way either during the CNR period in which the wage freeze had figured prominently or during the four years of the *Front Populaire* government during which domestic and international trade had been liberalized through the removal of many (but not all) price controls. The prices of some agricultural products (notably cotton and rice) are still fixed by the government, although the agricultural sector adjustment programme (le PASA) aims at complete liberalization. However, coarse grain price controls were abandoned in 1989, partly since they were never really effective (see section 4.2, below).

Given the results of 'self-imposed adjustment', it is not surprising that 'the Burkinabè SAP was unusual in that it appeared to be prescribing relatively "mild" medicine' (Otayek, 1992: 90). Furthermore, given the 'relative soundness of the economy, the SAP had a social dimension' (*ibid.*). Was it pure coincidence that the formal letter requesting the first SAL was signed by the then female Minister of Finance? Or does this reflect the progress towards empowerment of women in Burkina Faso since 1983? At any rate, the gender bias in ensuring that the SAP made provisions for better health and education facilities as well as improved family planning services is worth noting (see also section 6, below).

But at the same time the effort to regain the confidence of private investors through relaxation of controls and restrictions on trade, prices and employment legislation 'meant in effect that the strategy of state capitalism had been abandoned', while redefining the role of the state in the economy was seen as central to the new policy approach (*ibid.*: 91). As the World Bank (1994b: 16) concludes in the country assistance strategy report, future support for adjustment will include 'pressing, encouraging and seeking to contribute to the increasingly intense debate over the role of the state', which will also require 'incentives for productivity increases and diversification in an emerging private sector opposed by old state-supported narrow interests' (*ibid.*: 22). In the meantime, merely keeping the SAL and ESAF agreements 'on track' has proven difficult. The introduction of policy reforms appears relatively easy on paper. But, given the scarcity of financial resources as well as the severity of the constraints affecting Sahelian economies, meeting specific adjustment targets often seems a somewhat illusory process.

2.3   Aid Relations

Policy changes were also reflected in the five-year 'popular development plan' which outlined investment programmes for the period 1991-95 (Burkina Faso, 1990a). According to Bassolet and Ouédraogo (1994: 7), this plan entailed a total sum of over F.CFA 700 bn, to be invested primarily in developing food self-sufficiency, improving the conditions of the *masses paysannes* (by diversifying agricultural production and by agricultural price policies involving transfers to benefit rural communities), and by better conservation of natural resources. Hence it is argued that there was no contradiction between government investment programmes and the SAP. However, in shifting the focus away from the public sector, by emphasizing fiscal and financial balances and by insisting on a reduction in government intervention, the international financial institutions and the donors effectively modified the prospects for implementing the five-year plan as originally put forward.

Nevertheless, with the approval of the overall economic strategy by the World Bank, donors have been in a position to back specific measures as well as the sectoral adjustment programmes. Major bilateral donors operating in Burkina Faso include the Canadian, Danish, Dutch, German, Japanese and Swiss agencies, as well as the *Caisse Française de Développement* (CFD) and the French official aid agency. The European Union maintains a Delegation in Ouagadougou and has committed large sums to development programmes through the Lomé Convention. There are also a host of multilateral organizations (notably UN agencies) and the African and Arab development banks. As noted in the country assistance strategy (World Bank, 1994b: 20): 'the macro-economic and sectoral adjustment programmes have been prepared in close collaboration with the IMF staff and with the assistance from other donors, including France, the European Union, the ILO, the UNDP, the African Development Bank, Norway and Germany.'

Two ESAF arrangements have been approved by the IMF; the first in 1993 for the period 1993-94 (totalling SDR 17.68 million) and the second for the period 1994-95 (in connection with the approval of the Policy Framework Paper).[13] But disbursement delays appear to be a considerable problem in relation to the programmes supported by the Bretton Woods institutions and approved since the SAL I in 1991. Some 80-90 percent of the resources approved under the transport and public sector reform programmes have yet to be spent. Over 100 percent of the US$24 m. allocation for the fourth education programme (which was approved in 1991) was undisbursed as of March 1994 (World Bank, 1994b: annexe 6).

There do not appear to be major differences in approach by the different bilateral aid agencies which operate in Burkina Faso. Most of them have agreed to support and to co-finance different components of the overall adjustment programme (including the sectoral reforms). However, the change of government in France in 1993 was significant in relation to the exchange-rate issue and monetary policy in the UMOA countries.

At this point in the story the acronym jungle takes over. UMOA (or WAMU in English) was the West African Monetary Union, responsible for the issue (through the BCEAO) of the CFA Franc. Economic cooperation between the eight UMOA states has been in the hands of the CEAO (*Communauté Economique de l'Afrique de l'Ouest*), not to be confused with ECOWAS (known as the CEDEAO in French) which includes eighteen West African member countries. In January 1994, WAMU and the CEAO (which never really had an English acronym since it was an exclusively francophone organization) were combined, in connection with the devaluation, to form the UEMOA (*Union Economique et Monétaire Ouest Africaine*). The Nigerians were not pleased, since the prospect of greater integration within the Franc zone represents a counter current to their economic domination of West Africa. The French are ambivalent, and continue to promote economic links with both Lagos and Accra as well as Abidjan and Dakar. Ouagadougou is an isolated outpost near the desert, where French economic and strategic interests are increasingly limited.

The devaluation of the CFA Franc was opposed by the French Government until late 1993, since the special relationship between France and its ex-colonies hinged on the convertibility of the currency and the support given by the French treasury in the form

---

[13] Untangling the details of these different agreements is a bit tricky. The relevant documents are: IMF (1993a, 1993b & 1994) and World Bank (1991 & 1994a). The Policy Framework Paper is particularly interesting, and includes a summary table of all reform measures proposed for 1994-96. The government has also reviewed progress in implementing the adjustment programme (Burkina Faso, 1993d & 1994).

of budgetary transfers. Hence, as liberalism has gained ground in France, efforts to protect the economies of the Franc zone have been undermined. The winds of change are even blowing across 'French West Africa'.

As far as NGOs are concerned, the picture is somewhat different. In the 1980s many international NGOs set up programmes in the rural areas of Burkina Faso, responding to the poverty, famine and underdeveloped infrastructure and social services with everything from water pumps and essential drug supplies to food aid shipments. The CNR government attempted to coordinate the activities of both local and international NGOs, with some success. In general, the stress on rural development and improving agricultural techniques met with approval and support. Nevertheless, as Atampugre (1993: 160-62) points out in an assessment of NGO (Oxfam) support to agro-forestry schemes in Yatenga, certain policy changes (including the privatization of land envisaged as part of the SAP, and mentioned above) may make it more difficult for NGOs to 'target the least advantaged'. The lack of involvement by NGOs in the policy debate associated with the SAP and the sectoral adjustment programmes reflects the diverse and often contradictory stances adopted by these organizations.[14]

2.4   Public Debate on Structural and Sectoral Adjustment

In accordance with the revolutionary ideology, during the CNR period the *Comités de Défense de la Révolution* (CDRs) were supposed to function as organs of mass mobilization and political debate. Drawing up the first popular development plan (PPD) in 1984 was an opportunity to collect the thoughts and ideas of the inhabitants of the 7,000 villages in the country, and to channel their energies into development efforts coordinated (in theory) by the CDRs. But this process went badly astray and by 1986 these 'committees' had in many cases degenerated into repressive groups of (often young) militia, unable to engage in a constructive debate with either the civil service in the towns or the farmers in the villages.[15]

After the coup in 1987 the *Front Populaire* disarmed the CDRs and reformed the movement in connection with a lengthy debate between various factions and communist organizations on the need to establish a single vanguard party (Otayek, 1992: 92-94). In the end a party emerged, following a congress in April 1989. The *Organisation pour la Démocracie Populaire - Mouvement du Travail* (ODP-MT) was initially formed to support the *Front Populaire* government. However, by early 1990 as negotiations with the World Bank got under way, a number of other political parties appeared on the

---

[14] As discussed in the extensive study of NGOs, the state and agricultural development in Africa, Asia and Latin America by Farrington *et al.* (1993). The dynamics of NGO programmes and of 'populism' in West Africa, in the context of confronting environmental problems in developing sustainable agricultural production systems in the Sahel, are thoughtfully assessed by Gubbels (1992).

[15] The study of antagonism and conflict in revolutionary Burkina Faso by Martin (1986) is prefaced with a magnificent photograph showing a group of anxious women and uneasy soldiers nervously participating in *une réunion d'un CDR*. Another example of the role of the CDRs is given in the story of a village land conflict by Fauré (1991). The contradictions of Sankara's modernizing populism in the rural areas were assessed by Tallet (1989: 49), who concluded that: *Sur le plan politique, enfin, la paysannerie n'a jamais constitué un soutien au processus révolutionnaire, et la création de l'Union national des paysans burkinabé devait plus à l'imitation du syndicalisme urbain qu'à l'emergence d'un relais efficace auprès des paysans.* See also the study of populism in development theories and practice by Kitching (1990).

scene. Following the approval of the pluralist constitution in June 1991, Campaoré legalized the formation of political parties of all shades and opinions. This led to a proliferation of different organizations and factions; at the last count there were 74 political parties in Burkina Faso (Bassolet and Ouédraogo, 1994: 10). However, few of these groups represented any major current of organised opposition.

The trade unions have traditionally constituted a powerful force in Burkina Faso despite the limited size of the civil service and the manufacturing sector. Conflicts with the unions led to considerable tension during the CNR period. The issues of salary cuts, 'voluntary' contributions to public works such as the *bataille du rail* in which voluntary labour was used to construct a new railway (as described in section 5.2, below), as well as the price increases for food (and beer), were particularly sensitive. The trade union movement was reorganized after the coup in 1987, and gradually emerged as an effective and vocal opposition to the public sector squeeze proposed through the structural adjustment programme. Students at the university in Ouagadougou also organized strikes and protests against the reductions in scholarships which took effect from 1990. As Bassolet and Ouédraogo (1994: 9) note, the halt in new civil service recruitment, and the change in the practice of approving salary increments from an automatic system to one based on merit, have been (not surprisingly) unpopular amongst the urban public sector employees.

The various tensions came to a head in 1991, after the approval of the new constitution. By this time the first SAP was under implementation, and further budgetary austerity was the order of the day. Some of the newly formed political parties tried to press for a 'national conference' prior to any further parliamentary or presidential elections (Otayek, 1992: 96-98). This call was inspired in large measure by similar exercises in neighbouring countries in 1990 and 1991; notably in Benin, Mali and Niger, where sovereign conferences of all national movements and organizations had assessed the failures of the past (military) governments and drawn up new constitutions authorizing political pluralism.

But divisions and disagreements amongst the opposition leaders in Burkina Faso were skilfully manipulated by Campaoré, who successfully emerged as President elected by universal suffrage in December 1991. Only around 25 percent of the electorate turned out to vote in the presidential election (Otayek, 1992: 98). Then, amidst considerable political agitation, the idea of a national conference was dropped, and the parliamentary elections finally went ahead. The ODP-MT obtained a comfortable majority (78 seats, with only 18 seats going to three main opposition parties) in the *Assemblée des Députés du Peuple* at these elections held in May 1992.

As the IMF (1993b: 1) commented: 'owing to the protracted democratization process that filled the political agenda and absorbed administrative capacity through the first half of 1992, Article IV consultation discussions and negotiations on a follow-up program [to the first SAP] were delayed.' But by early 1993, the new government was in a position to request 'a three year arrangement under the enhanced structural adjustment facility'. However, the 'protracted' process of political debate may continue to absorb resources and time. Building effective democratic institutions in Burkina Faso is not yet complete as Otayek (1992: 100) argued:

> In Burkina, as elsewhere in Africa, the population is waiting for democracy to prove itself superior to authoritarianism, especially by bringing improved economic and social well-being. In other words there can be no democracy without development.

Anything less would be mere 'subsistence democracy', a term coined by an anonymous Burkinabè with few illusions. The policy of adjustment however, despite associated measures for health and education, offers the prospect of deprivation and shortages for the least well-off.

This was written some time before the devaluation of the CFA Franc; the latest adjustment measure in the UEMOA countries in West Africa which has had considerable effects on the living standards of the better-off urban inhabitants, and on the basis of which it is expected that rural incomes will increase (see section 3.4, below). The devaluation also met with organized protests. But in Burkina Faso they were more muted than in some of the other Franc zone countries, since *la paix social* was partly ensured by rapid announcement of wage increases (albeit only 10 percent) and increases in producer prices for rice and cotton. In addition, shortly after the devaluation, the World Bank approved an extra economic recovery credit for Burkina Faso, valued at US$25 m. This allocation was explained as 'front-loaded supplementary financing to bolster support for the aftermath of the devaluation and mitigate its impact on the most vulnerable and politically vocal groups' (World Bank, 1994b: 18).

A final anecdotal observation illustrates the debate about the implications of structural adjustment in Burkina Faso, as seen by a 'man in the street'. During an evaluation of the use of fertilizer supplied to Burkina Faso as programme aid (budgetary support) by the Danish and the Dutch governments in 1993, interviews were organized with private traders dealing in fertilizers in the markets of Ouagadougou and Bobo Dioulasso. When asked (through translation) about the effects of the adjustment programme on his business, one trader looked blank and confused. The interpreter tried again, but it was only when the French expression *ajustement structurel* was translated as 'Americans' (in Mooré, the language of the Mossi people) that the trader understood the question.

2.5   Impact on National Policy-Making, Planning and Governance

Amongst the many difficulties encountered in implementing the SAP, the capacity of the authorities to manage and organize all the different components and keep 'on track' with the different conditionalities has proven a considerable obstacle. In effect, there is little national policy-making aside from the implementation of the agreements. For example, during the round table meetings on the PANE and PASA in Ouagadougou in early 1994, the discussions were dominated by representatives of the donors present.[16] Of course this was the main purpose of the meetings (chaired jointly by the UNDP and the Ministry of Finance and Planning), but it was striking to observe the lack of any detailed critical analysis of the far-reaching measures agreed for the reorganization of the agricultural sector. It was, however, noted that preoccupation with implementing the 50-point agenda of short-term adjustment measures required in the *Lettre de Politique de Développement Agricole* (Burkina Faso, 1993a) tended to take precedence over any efforts which might be deployed to prepare a longer-term agricultural development

---

[16] The PASA (agricultural sector adjustment programme) is assessed in section 4 and the main features of the PANE (environmental action plan) are outlined in section 7 (below).

strategy.

The lengthy negotiations between the government and the World Bank from 1989 to 1991 did offer an opportunity for a number of key figures in the government to gain an insight into Bank procedures and to discuss adjustment conditionalities in some detail. But there are only around 35,000 civil servants in Burkina Faso, and it has been necessary to provide technical assistance and extra support in order to train personnel and managers in the intricacies and new techniques of financial control, value-added tax levying, customs duty (non)collection and so on, as part of the implementation of the adjustment programme. A computerization of the Ministry of Finance and Planning accounting system has also been included in the latest SAP package (World Bank, 1994a: 3-4).

In spite of these difficulties, and the delays in the implementation of many measures due to democratization and other interruptions (such as the failure to increase tax revenue as foreseen), 'performance in maintaining a macro-economic framework consistent with the objectives' of the SAP (supplemented by the ESAF agreements) 'has been satisfactory but uneven' (World Bank, 1994b: 13). But this is largely due to the devaluation of the CFA Franc which has helped, according to the IMF (1994: 5), to transform 'internal' into 'external' adjustment, 'to secure the gains in competitiveness' and 'to enhance Burkina Faso's growth potential'. Otherwise, as indicated in the following section, macroeconomic indicators do not paint a particularly rosy picture in the short term.

Who owns the SAP in Burkina Faso? One way of looking at this issue is through language. The reports and studies distributed (but not publicly available) from the Bretton Woods institutions are drafted in English, which is only read and understood by a maximum of 1 percent of the population. Even French, the official language, is only spoken by around 5-10 percent of the population, mostly those residing in the main towns. Thus, access to information about the process of economic policy-making is limited. On the other hand, despite the high level of illiteracy, 'correct' communication and 'political consciousness' were given a high priority by the CNR government. One legacy of the popular courts which tried those suspected of corruption and abuse of power in the 1980s is that many people listen to the radio which also broadcasts in *langues nationales*.[17]

In a recent assessment of proposals to reform the public sector, Jacob and Nsengiyuma (1994: 17) also consider the issue of economic policy 'ownership' in Burkina Faso and conclude:

> The World Bank should support the resumption of the responsibility for development by the Burkinabè government. The period of structural adjustment [...] can be characterised as a period that leaves the state little room for manoeuvre, making it difficult to set up a real internal debate about which wider objectives to pursue.

In noting that the political choices implicit in the measures proposed in the SAP must be 'internally debated', it is important to stress that many groups, notably women,

---

[17] There are around sixty different *ethnies* in Burkina Faso. Three language groups dominate: *Mooré* (spoken by the 3-4 million Mossi), *Dioula* (widely spoken in the west) and *Foulfoudé* (spoken by the Fulani pastoralists). See also: Laclavère et al (1993: 33-35) and the study of 'state and society' by Savannot-Guyot (1986).

remain marginalized and under-represented. The rural population in general lacks influence over policy-making. This may be particularly serious in the case of the Fulani livestock owners and herders. Is it just coincidence that measures to develop the livestock sector (which accounts for over 10 percent of export earnings and at least 10 percent of GDP) are not specifically mentioned in the Policy Framework Paper (World Bank, 1994a); a document which deals with just about every other facet of Burkinabè life from wages and taxes to labour legislation and school fees?

Despite the ethnic calm which generally prevails in Burkina Faso, differences of opinion do exist on economic policy issues, and these cannot simply be reduced to 'entrenched interests'. Reaching consensus is a lengthy and difficult process, as Helleiner (1994) points out in a discussion of policy disagreements in connection with the implementation of SAPs in Sub-Saharan Africa. After noting that a limited number of government and foreign 'technocrats' have been largely responsible for policy decisions about issues such as currency devaluation or budget allocations in most African countries undergoing adjustment, he concludes:

> While such decision making procedures may have been appropriate, or even necessary, for this kind of decision at the time, they cannot be employed for longer-run and more complex policy changes and investments involving, for example, tax reform, privatizations, institutional change, infrastructure development, and [...] strategies for agriculture, industry, education and health. In these instances, there are far more policy actors and all must be brought in on the decision making (Helleiner, 1994: 7).

Politically, it appears that with the blossoming of the media (private radio stations, numerous newspapers and periodicals) and with an reduction in human rights abuses (the stopping of summary executions of criminals by the police), as well as with a parliament which is gradually finding its feet, a relative stability is emerging. Perhaps the parliamentary basis for 'ownership' of economic policies is stronger. The reduction in military expenditure is another important factor.[18] But the proof of the pudding is in the eating. If economic reform on the basis of le PAS (SAP) is transformed into increasing living standards, everybody will be happy. The evidence of this transformation in terms of growth rates and incomes is mixed.

3.   Effects of Structural Adjustment on Key Development Indicators

3.1   Introduction - Macroeconomic Issues and Growth

In the Policy Framework Paper published by the World Bank in early 1994, it was noted that, 'on the basis of the nationwide consensus' which emerged from the

---

[18] Despite the extensive data in the reports on the Burkinabè economy issued by the Bretton Woods institutions, it is not easy to obtain recent figures for government defence spending. However, in 1991, military expenditure was estimated at 2.2 percent of GDP, a fall from 3.3 percent in 1986 (IMF, 1993c).

presidential and legislative elections in Burkina Faso in 1991 and 1992 (re-establishing 'the rule of law'):

> The government decided in 1993 to accelerate the restructuring of the economy and the reduction of financial imbalances, so as to enhance the competitiveness of domestic production through internal adjustment. [...] The principal targets of the 1993 program, which was supported by resources from the IMF's enhanced structural adjustment facility (ESAF) and a structural adjustment credit from the World Bank, were i) to attain a growth rate of real GDP of about 4 percent per year; ii) to limit inflation (measured by the CPI) to approximately 1 percent; and iii) to contain the external current account deficit (excluding official transfers) at 15-16 percent of GDP (World Bank, 1994a: 1).

This Section reviews the progress towards meeting these objectives, noting in particular the constraints and difficulties which have been encountered in the period down to the end of 1993.[19]

By way of introduction, the problems of measurement and fine tuning of changes in the Burkinabè economy should be stressed. As Tarp (1993: 11) points out, it is necessary to be 'very cautious in the use of data and averages in the African context' of economic crisis. Statistical weaknesses (including inadequate data collection systems) are common and have indeed been accentuated by the 'prolonged nature of the crisis' (*ibid.*: footnote 7). This also suggests a fundamental criticism of adjustment measures as means of promoting growth and development, particularly in countries like Burkina Faso where non-economic constraints are significant.

The World Bank (1994b: 8) implicitly acknowledges this problem in a summary of 'key constraints' affecting growth, which include: 'the extraordinary ecological challenges in this war-zone of land degradation'; the rapid spread of the HIV virus (now estimated to affect 450,000 people); and the difficulties of managing the tension between civil servants (the 'urban elite') who have different 'values and behaviours' from the 'uneducated rural population', and for whom adjustment represents 'an erosion of privileges'. These factors (and others) are difficult to measure in terms of economic indicators. Nevertheless, this list suggests the extent of the difficulties which arise in attempting to transform the Burkinabè economy through adjustment.

Turning to the data available, Table 2 shows different estimates of GDP growth in Burkina Faso from 1983 to 1993. Although the figures for annual rates of growth in output vary from source to source (as shown in the table), the period from 1985 to 1988 was generally characterized by rapid growth, largely as a result of good harvests which were recorded after the disastrous drought years in 1983 and 1984. There was also a gold mining boom towards the end of the 1980s.[20]

---

[19] The impact of the devaluation of the CFA Franc ('external adjustment') on growth prospects is considered in section 3.4 (below).

[20] The average annual growth rate of GDP in the period 1980 to 1992 was estimated at 3.9 percent, considerably higher than many African countries, including neighbouring Côte d'Ivoire (0.0 percent), Mali (2.9 percent) and Niger (-0.7 percent), as indicated by the World Bank (1994c: Table 2).

The estimates also indicate that GDP growth rates were relatively high in 1991; again good rainfall and surplus agricultural production were the main causes of this jump in output (after a bad harvest in 1990-91). Given that over 40 percent of GDP is derived from primary production (notably crop cultivation and animal husbandry), climatic and ecological influences are paramòunt. Nevertheless, the GDP growth data in Table 2 mask a number of important trends in the economic development of the country.

Firstly, as Bassolet and Ouédraogo (1994: 17) point out, the low rates of inflation recorded in the early part of the 1990s (ranging from -0.5 percent in 1990 to 3.6 percent in 1992), were also largely due to the good harvests as food prices fell (see also section 4.2, below). The average annual inflation rate in the period 1980-92 was estimated at 3.5 percent, a fall from the average of 8.6 percent between 1970 and 1980 (World Bank, 1994c). With the fixed CFA Franc exchange rate (until 1994), and stable or falling world prices of key imports, notably fuel, inflation was largely a function of domestic agricultural conditions, and did not figure as a major issue in the SAL I and ESAF negotiations.

Secondly, although mining expanded rapidly at the end of the 1980s as gold reserves were exploited and as zinc and manganese deposits were explored, industrial production stagnated. The difficulties encountered on world cotton markets were an important factor, since cotton ginning and textiles account for a major share of manufacturing in Burkina Faso. Various other agro-processing industries also ran into difficulties at the end of 1980s (see section 5, below). However commercial activities in the service sector picked up in this period, as private *entrepreneurs* began to trade again in the more relaxed (but still uncertain) economic environment after the revolution.

On the other hand, private consumption levels have remained low, and growth has been consistently negative throughout the period from 1989. According to the World Bank (1994b: 6), the Franc zone countries went through a 'severe prolonged recession' in the second half of the 1980s that reduced 'real per capita incomes by some 40 percent'. This 'downward deflationary spiral' impoverished the people and undermined the financial institutions of the region. Since the first SAL in Burkina Faso, real GDP growth has fallen (to the low rates shown in Table 2), largely as a result of 'the downward rigidity of wages and prices', the 'difficulty of making fiscal adjustments' and the decline of world market cotton prices (*ibid.*: 6).[21]

Against this background, devaluation represented one of the few options available for revitalizing the economy. The SAP, as formulated in 1991, was not a sufficient response to the overall economic decline, and the need for 'external adjustment' became increasingly apparent. But before considering the impact of the devaluation in the context of changing trade patterns and balance-of-payments (dis)equilibria, it is useful to summarize some changes in the government budget and in debt, investment and aid transfers. A survey of these indicators shows the limited margin for manoeuvre in the Burkinabè economy, while at the same time illustrating some of the limits of the SAP in the period from 1991 to 1993.

---

[21] The IMF (1994: 2) also notes the decline in real GDP in 1993, 'reflecting primarily a sharp drop in cotton output and a slowdown in manufacturing activity'. The 30 percent fall in cotton production was due to 'farmers' adverse responses to reductions in producer prices, which were compounded by delays in payments from the cotton processing company (SOFITEX)'. See also section 4.3 (below).

Table 2   Estimates of GDP Growth, 1983-93

	83	84	85	86	87	88	89	90	91	92[4]	93[4]
GDP at current prices (bill. F.CFA)	402	418	479	600	608	667	693	703	777	778	797
GDP at 1985 prices (bill. F.CFA)			479	589	597	631	638	652	691	696	
GDP at current prices (US$ m)					2023	2238	2175	2581	2753	2939	2782
GDP per capita (US$)					207	262	248	286	297	308	283
Estimates of GDP growth rate:											
- S&W[1]	1.9	-1.1	8.8	15.4	-1.9	8.9					
- IMF[2]				7.6	1.3	9.6	4.1	1.3	10.5	0.2	-1.0
- WB[3]						5.7	3.3	0.0	6.0	0.7	0.4

Sources: IMF, 1993c; Savadogo & Wetta, 1992; World Bank, 1989 & 1994b.
[1]   Savadogo & Wetta (1992), using the World Tables published by the World Bank in 1990.
[2]   IMF (1993c), using nominal GDP based on data gathered by the BCEAO and the Burkinabè authorities including the INSD (the national statistics institute) as well as staff estimates.
[3]   World Bank (1994b), using real annual growth rate (1985 prices).
[4]   Estimated.

3.2   Government Revenue and Expenditure

As noted above (section 2.2), one of the main objectives of the first SAP as agreed in 1991 was to reform public finances. A number of problems had built up in the transition from military to constitutional government between 1987 and 1991. 'Containing the government budget deficit' (World Bank, 1994b: 4) was considered as a priority. But this has not proven to be an easy task.

Table 3 shows the trends in public revenue and expenditure since 1986.[22] According to Savadogo and Wetta (1992: 61-62), despite a rise in public expenditure under the CNR government, the deterioration in the fiscal balance was first evident in 1986-87. Prior to the SAP agreement in 1991, the authorities 'used treasury resources such as the deposits of public enterprises' as well as the resources of the central bank 'to finance the deficits' (*ibid.*: 62).

In the 1993 review of the economy published by the IMF (1993c: 12) it was noted that between 1986 and 1989, 'budget revenue stagnated at around 12 percent of GDP'. In 1989, the revenue position was improved by extraordinary grants through the 'Dakar initiative'. But in general, the deficits were financed through the accumulation of debt (see Table 4) and through advances to the treasury from the central bank (BCEAO), the savings banks and the price equalization agency (CGP), as well as the national social

---

[22] Unfortunately the revenue and expenditure data presented in the economic memorandum (World Bank, 1989) covering the period 1983-85 are not comparable with the IMF data from 1986.

security fund (CNSS).[23] By the end of 1990, a financing gap of F.CFA 61 bn had emerged, which was met by a further accumulation of arrears and by foreign financial assistance (*ibid.*: 12-13). The SAP was designed to tackle these problems, both in terms of revenue and expenditure. But as Bassolet and Ouédraogo (1994: 13-16) observe, the results of efforts to increase taxation and reduce spending were not spectacular.

Table 3   Public Revenue and Expenditure, 1986-93 (billion CFA Franc)

	86	87	88	89	90	91[a]	92[a]	93[a]
Revenue & grants	**92.9**	**119.5**	**104.6**	**156.1**	**112.9**	**145.5**	**142.3**	**144.0**
Current revenue:	68.5	79.2	78.3	79.8	92.9	107.9	92.9	99.4
- taxes	60.9	65.1	69.7	66.9	76.4	83.2	68.9	72.6
- non-tax	3.8	6.5	8.2	8.4	7.0	24.7	24.0	26.8
- other	3.9	7.6	0.4	4.6	9.5	0.6	0.1	1.4
Grants	24.3	40.3	26.3	76.3	20.0	37.0	49.3	43.2
Expenditure	**131.8**	**146.1**	**140.4**	**133.2**	**145.8**	**164.1**	**163.1**	**181.3**
- current	68.4	71.8	79.9	86.4	106.6	93.2	93.7	120.5
(of which salaries)	*37.2*	*42.3*	*51.5*	*57.1*	*57.5*	*54.5*	*50.9*	*52.2*
- capital	60.1	70.8	60.0	45.1	40.5	70.0	68.5	61.5
Overall surplus or deficit	**-38.9**	**-26.7**	**-35.9**	**23.0**	**-32.9**	**-18.6**	**-20.8**	**-37.2**
Deficit as % of GDP (including grants)	**-6.5**	**-4.4**	**-5.4**	**3.3**	**-4.7**	**-2.4**	**-2.7**	**-4.7**
Deficit as % of GDP (excluding grants)	**-10.5**	**-11.0**	**-9.3**	**-7.7**	**-7.5**	**-7.2**	**-8.8**	**-10.1**

Source: IMF, 1993c: Table 16; 1994: Table 11.
[a]   Estimates.

Despite the introduction of a value added tax, reform of import duty collection arrangements and attempts to raise revenue from the informal sector, total public revenue fell by over 7 percent from 1991 to 1993. According to the SAP targets, it was estimated that revenue would reach over 14 percent of GDP in 1993. But, as recent data indicate, the programme target was not attained, and revenue fell to around 12.7 percent of GDP (IMF, 1994: Table 1). The principal reason was the inability of a weak tax administration to implement effectively the tax reforms, especially the new import tariff

---

[23] The CGP (*Caisse Générale de Péréquation*) plays an important role in raising revenue through the tariffs on rice imports (see section 4.2, below).

regime' (World Bank, 1994b: 4). Import duty exemptions were also approved for certain key agricultural inputs (including fertilizer and pesticides) required to strengthen the performance of the cotton sector.

A further thorough revision of the taxation system was included in the ESAF programmes agreed with the IMF in 1993 and 1994. But the shortfall in government revenue in 1993 (by F.CFA 37 bn, equivalent to around 4.7 percent of GDP) led to new arrears on payments for a total amount of F.CFA 9 bn (IMF, 1994: 3). It is perhaps not out of place to note that tax evasion and fraud appear to have become more common in Burkina Faso since the end of the 1980s. Discipline and social (or moral) control have become weaker, not least in the public sector where employees' disposable incomes have fallen as a result of the wage freeze.

As noted above, restrictions on government spending on salaries and wages have been amongst the more controversial measures in the SAP. The data shown in Table 3 indicate that while capital expenditure on public investment programmes was reduced in 1989 and 1990, the government wage bill increased. Salaries accounted for 61 percent of current government expenditure in 1990 (and over 40 percent of all civil servants are teachers and health workers), but it was aimed to reduce this figure to 50 percent by 1993 (World Bank, 1994b: 5). The figures shown in Table 3 suggest that this target was reached in connection with a reorganization of 'expenditure programming and control' (*ibid.*: 5).

In a review of government budgets during the first SAP period (1991-93), Bassolet and Ouédraogo (1994: 14-15) argue that delays in disbursement of SAL funds affected the overall balance of public finances. Given the problems of meeting fiscal targets and interruptions in the implementation of the SAP due to the political transition, the second tranche of the first SAL was only paid in February 1994 (World Bank, 1994b: 4). The difficulties which arose in transferring the ownership of the four main banks to the private sector also contributed to delays in reaching the targets specified in the original SAL agreement (and the ESAF).

The failure to increase taxation revenue was also one of the main concerns expressed in the ESAF reviews conducted by the IMF (1993b & 1994). But in connection with the revision of adjustment targets following the devaluation of the CFA Franc, it was noted that 'any increase in taxation at this point could be counterproductive, as it would snuff out the nascent economic recovery and further strain the administrative capacity of the tax collection agencies' (IMF, 1994: 12). The government has also been keen to maintain public investment programmes, particularly in health and education, while apparently accepting the need for reductions in capital and current expenditures in 'lower priority sectors'. The IMF (1994: Table 2) estimates that the overall government deficit as a percentage of GDP will remain around -4.5 percent in 1994 (-14.7 percent if grants are not included), as expenditure (notably on imported capital items) increases in the wake of 'external adjustment'.[24]

3.3   Debt, Investment and Foreign Aid

One of the important factors which led to the initiation of negotiations on an adjustment programme with the World Bank in 1989 was the rapid increase in the debt burden

---

[24] Further details of government spending reforms are outlined in section 6 (below), which includes an assessment of the proposals outlined in the Public Expenditure Review conducted by the World Bank (1993).

during the second half of the 1980s. Table 4 shows the extent to which public debt accumulated, although it should be noted that Burkina Faso has relied less heavily on foreign loans than many of the other countries in the Franc zone. Nevertheless, debt-servicing difficulties arose in the early 1990s, resulting in two 'official debt res-chedulings from Paris Club creditors' in 1991 and 1993 (World Bank, 1994b: 10).

Table 4   Total Debt Outstanding, 1984-94 (million US$ and percent of GDP)

	84	85	86	87	88	89	90	91	92	93	94[c]
TDO[a]	432	541	672	865	866	717	834	968	1129	1580	1488
% GDP[b]	41.3	45.4	41.9	46.8	42.5	33.0	32.3	35.2	38.4	56.8	85.6

Source: Savadogo and Wetta, 1992; World Bank, 1994b: Annex 5.
[a]   Total debt outstanding, including public and publicly guaranteed debt, private non-guaranteed debt, IMF credits and short-term capital, in million US$.
[b]   Total debt outstanding as percent of GDP.
[c]   Estimate.

According to an optimistic scenario (see section 3.4, below), 'external adjustment' is expected to lead to an increase in export revenue, but at the same time the debt-service burden has substantially increased, despite the rescheduling agreements and the writing off of some debt by the French Government after the devaluation. With external assistance (including SAL and ESAF disbursements) and further debt relief, the government aims to be able to cover payments obligations and to reduce arrears (as indicated in Table 6). Furthermore, a credit ceiling with the BCEAO has been imposed, and efforts to restructure the banking sector (through a partially completed privatization programme) are also intended to limit government recourse to additional domestic bank credit (IMF, 1994: 13-14).

But the SAL and ESAF arrangements are themselves loans, albeit on favourable conditions, which will lead to an increase in the overall debt burden. By 1994, it was estimated that the total debt outstanding amounted to around US$1,500 m., or about 85 percent of total GDP. Recourse to international credit also has costs.

One criticism which had been levelled against 'self-imposed adjustment' in the 1980s was that the state played a major role in channelling investment into development projects and programmes on the basis of the *programme populaire du développement* and the five-year development plan (1986-90). At the same time, restrictions on the activities of private sector business and traders led to capital flight as many *opérateurs économiques* preferred to invest their profits elsewhere (notably in bank accounts in Abidjan and Lomé). Government intervention through price controls and public investment schemes was considered essential in order to promote economic growth and improved welfare, particularly in the rural areas.[25]

---

[25] Generating domestic savings for investment in infrastructure, agricultural production and human resource development has been a major problem in the Sahel. The amounts of money saved by farmers under conditions which have been characterized as 'complex, diverse and risk prone' (Toulmin, 1991) are relatively

In the context of economic reforms entailing a move towards less state intervention (with the abolition of many price controls and the initiation of a parastatal privatization programme) the government has attempted to encourage greater private investment since the early 1990s. Bassolet and Ouédraogo (1994: 16) estimate that private capital transfers amounted to US$12 m. in 1990 and US$15 m. in 1993, or around 12.5 percent of the total capital supplied to the economy. Nevertheless, the amounts of private capital available for investment have been limited. Gross domestic savings fluctuated from 2.3 to 4.2 percent of GDP in the period from 1988 to 1993, as shown in Table 5.

Table 5   Investment and Savings, 1988-93 (percent of GDP)

	1988	1989	1990	1991	1992	1993
Gross domestic investment	21.6	21.2	19.1	22.7	21.4	21.9
- public fixed investment	10.1	10.1	9.3	8.5	7.0	6.8
- private fixed investment	9.6	11.1	11.2	11.6	14.5	15.3
Gross domestic savings	2.9	3.2	3.3	4.2	2.9	2.3

Source: IMF, 1994: Appendix 2; World Bank, 1994b: Annex 4.

However, the estimates shown in the table suggest that there was some increase in private investment at the beginning of the 1990s. Public fixed investment declined, but in accordance with the provisions of the first SAL, public investment programmes have been approved as part of the overall capital budget (as indicated in Table 3). Furthermore, it is argued that 'with the pickup of economic activity induced by the devaluation', both savings and investment will be boosted (World Bank, 1994b: 7). For the time being this remains an optimistic projection.

Much of the finance available for public investment programmes is in the form of foreign aid transfers. Since 1991, efforts have been made to coordinate the allocation and disbursement of foreign aid in connection with the implementation of the various sectoral adjustment programmes (see sections 4-7, below). However, in the context of macroeconomic reform, it is important to note the extent to which the public sector remains dependent on foreign aid.[26]

Table 6 summarizes the external financing requirements for Burkina Faso, indicating the scale of grant and loan disbursements which have substantially increased since 1991. The data presented in the table clearly illustrate the difficulties which were faced prior to the SAP agreement in 1991. Overall, the financing gap (requirements) is largely covered by external aid (grants and loans) which meets the deficit on the current account balance (see section 3.4, below). There was a distinct increase in grants from aid donors following the SAP agreement in 1991. Similarly, the decline in loans which

---

minimal. Household survival through immediate consumption tends to take priority. See also the studies by Reardon *et al.*, (1992) and Thiombiano *et al.* (1988).

[26] Net per capita 'official development assistance' (aid) disbursements to Burkina Faso amount to around US$44 annually (World Bank, 1991: 10).

had occurred during the period of transition (1987-90) was reversed in 1991. Foreign investment levels remain low, while short-term transfers of capital picked up after the apparent 'flight from Burkina Faso' during the 1980s.

Table 6   External Financing, 1987-94 (million US$)

	1987	1988	1989	1990	1991	1992	1993	1994[f]
Requirement[a]	309.3	330.7	512.5	360.7	594.5	548.3	532.4	537.0
Grants	193.0	201.8	356.7	225.5	299.2	331.7	329.1	280.1
Loans[b]	108.8	88.6	81.8	90.0	145.7	151.5	152.5	206.2
Investment[c]	6.0	1.7	11.3	8.1	0.7	0.0	0.0	1.6
Arrears accum.	22.4	14.8	65.5	49.6	0.0	0.0	24.1	0.0
Debt relief[d]	0.0	0.0	16.6	0.0	135.1	21.5	9.4	26.9
IMF (ESAF)	0.0	0.0	0.0	0.0	8.5	9.1	12.2	24.6
Capital[e]	-20.8	23.8	-19.4	-12.5	5.3	34.5	5.1	0.0

Source: World Bank, 1994b.
[a]   Includes current account deficit, debt amortization, IMF purchases, arrears reduction and changes in reserves (with the BCEAO and the French Treasury).
[b]   Disbursement of the SAP and sectoral adjustment loans administered by the IDA (World Bank).
[c]   Net direct foreign investment.
[d]   Cancellation and rescheduling of debts.
[e]   Net short-term transfers, monetary capital and errors.
[f]   Estimates.

3.4   Trade, Balance of Payments and 'External Adjustment'

Foreign trade in Burkina Faso is largely conducted with the other member states of the UEMOA (principally Côte d'Ivoire) and with the European Union (notably France).[27] Exports consist of agricultural products (mainly cotton) as well as gold, livestock and animal products, and a few manufactured goods (notably tyres). The main imports include food products (of which rice and wheat account for a major share), petroleum products, manufactured equipment and intermediate goods (raw materials for processing industries, as well as fertilizer).

Table 7 indicates some trends in exports and imports since 1986. The figures, which are based on various sources and estimates - many of which are rather unreliable - show that the overall trade balance has deteriorated during this period, reaching a deficit of over F.CFA 105 bn in 1993. In this context it is important to note that smuggling and trade on 'parallel markets' in West Africa are common practices which seriously affect the quality of official data. The informal private sector also plays a significant role in

---

[27] This section is based on the presentation of the trade pattern in the economic review by the IMF (1993c: 22-24) and on data in the paper by Bassolet and Ouédraogo (1994).

the gold trade, which 'may be the principal reason for the declining share of gold in total export revenue' (IMF, 1993c: 22).

Nevertheless, as far as the main exports are concerned, two factors have been particularly important in determining performance. The decline in export earnings from cotton in the early 1990s was largely due to adverse world market conditions. As falling world prices led to cuts in the officially administered producer price in Burkina Faso, many farmers diverted resources from cotton into food-crop cultivation and export volumes subsequently declined. Similarly, the share of livestock and animal products in total exports stagnated in the early 1990s, reflecting the increasing difficulties of market access in the coastal countries of West Africa where cheaper subsidized European imports had captured market shares (see section 4.4, below).

Table 7   Exports, Imports and Trade Balance 1986-93 (billion CFA Franc)

	1986	1987	1988	1989	1990	1991	1992	1993[a)
Export value	**51.5**	**69.1**	**71.5**	**73.3**	**76.3**	**79.3**	**78.5**	**70.5**
- animal products	5.2	5.4	6.5	7.4	7.9	8.2	8.8	8.2
- cotton	12.8	20.5	20.5	24.3	26.5	30.1	27.6	22.2
- gold	10.4	15.8	15.1	14.2	11.8	12.2	11.9	8.2
- other products	22.6	27.4	29.3	27.4	30.1	28.8	30.3	31.3
Imports (fob)	**156.3**	**144.4**	**149.9**	**160.0**	**161.5**	**169.8**	**178.7**	**175.7**
- food prod.	28.7	27.8	30.6	21.0	22.2	26.8	24.1	24.5
- petroleum	15.5	10.1	9.8	13.6	16.8	14.3	15.7	13.9
- equip. goods	52.5	52.0	57.0	64.0	62.4	68.0	76.1	83.6
- raw materials	3.8	3.8	4.4	8.4	8.6	9.1	10.0	
- miscellaneous	55.8	50.7	48.0	53.0	51.5	51.6	52.8	53.7
Trade balance	**-104.8**	**-75.3**	**-78.4**	**-86.7**	**-85.2**	**-90.5**	**-100.2**	**-105.2**

Source: Bassolet and Ouédraogo, 1994: 18; IMF, 1993c: Tables 30 & 31.
[a)   Estimates.

Following a contraction in imports induced by the 'consume Burkinabè' campaign launched by the CNR government in the mid-1980s, the volume of imports has steadily increased. Fluctuations in domestic agricultural production conditions (in the form of good and bad harvests) have a direct effect on imports of food products (and food aid), while the steady increase in imports of equipment, particularly since 1991, reflects the 'increasing availability of external financing for investment' (IMF, 1993c: 23). The SAP agreement with the Bretton Woods institutions in 1991 appears to have encouraged a considerable growth in imports as greater amounts of foreign and private sector finance have become available.

Table 8   Summary Balance of Payments, 1986-93 (billion CFA Franc)

	1986	1987	1988	1989	1990	1991	1992[c]	1993[c]
Trade balance	-101.2	-73.7	-70.7	-86.7	-85.3	-90.4	-100.2	-105.7
Services (net)	-44.8	-49.4	-54.2	-58.9	-56.6	-60.3	-51.3	-56.6
Transfers (net)	137.6	107.8	115.5	161.3	116.2	124.6	121.4	129.4
- private[a]	66.3	49.3	52.3	46.0	43.8	41.6	37.2	34.7
- official[b]	71.3	58.5	63.3	115.3	72.4	83.0	84.2	94.7
Current account (deficit):								
- including off. transfers	-8.4	-15.4	-9.4	15.7	-25.6	-26.2	-30.0	-32.8
- excluding off. transfers	-79.7	-73.8	-72.6	-99.6	-98.0	-109.1	-114.2	-127.5
Capital account	19.3	26.2	19.8	-61.6	21.5	25.0	23.1	24.4
Monetary capital	-4.1	-7.0	0.2	-2.0	1.2	2.0	19.8	14.6
Errors & omissions	3.3		-2.4	6.2	-12.9	6.7		
Overall balance	10.1	3.8	8.2	-41.7	-15.8	7.5	12.9	6.2
Current balance as percent of GDP (incl. off. transfers)	-0.1	-2.5	-1.4	2.3	-3.6	-3.4	-3.8	-4.1
Current balance as percent of GDP (excl. off. transfers)	-13.3	-12.1	-10.9	-14.4	-14.0	-14.1	-14.5	-16.0

Source: IMF, 1993c & 1994, using data provided by BCEAO and staff estimates.
[a]   Including migrants' remittances.
[b]   Including budget support.
[c]   Estimates.

Turning to the overall balance of payments, Table 8 shows the main trends in the period from 1986.[28] Performance on these indicators was satisfactory during the first half of the 1980s, as the current account deficit (including transfers) was reduced to -0.4 percent of GDP in 1984. In the aftermath of the drought as the trade balance deteriorated, the current account deficit rose to -5.9 percent of GDP in 1985 (Savadogo and Wetta, 1992: Table 2.4). However, with improved agricultural output and export performance in the second half of the 1980s, the current account deficit contracted.

The target set in the first SAL agreement was to reduce the current account deficit 'through liberalisation of pricing and external trade regulations' (World Bank, 1991: 16). There is no mention of a specific current account target figure in this agreement, but estimates were made of the external financing required to cover the anticipated deficit.

---

[28] In connection with the debate on data difficulties, it is interesting to note that two indications of the trade balance, obtained from the same source (IMF, 1993c) give different figures!

However, in the ESAF agreement with the IMF it was expected to be able to maintain the current account deficit at 15-16 percent of GDP in 1993. The figures shown in Table 8 suggest that this target was reached, although overall the balance-of-payments position deteriorated from 1991 to 1993. The further decline in private transfers (largely migrants' remittances) to the economy was particularly significant, but, as noted above, the trade balance also deteriorated. All in all, a glance at the balance-of-payments statement suggests that 'internal' (donor-driven) adjustment began to deliver the goods in the form of increased imports, but failed to improve overall economic performance.

Bassolet and Ouédraogo (1994: 20) also present some estimates of the real effective exchange-rate index for Burkina Faso, which declined from 112.9 in 1986 to 130.0 in 1992. This implies a loss of competitiveness due to increasing over-valuation of the CFA Franc in relation to inflation rates in the economies of the main trading partners. The deteriorating terms of trade (due in part to the fall in world cotton prices) were also significant in the early 1990s.

The stage was set for acceptance of the need for 'external adjustment'. Space does not permit an analysis of the lengthy debates which took place during the first few years of the 1990s about the pros and cons of changing the fixed parity of the CFA Franc and the French Franc. Nevertheless, and apparently under considerable pressure from the IMF, the French Government finally agreed to a devaluation in January 1994. This was accepted by the UEMOA governments, and emergency credits were made available to meet the impact of the ensuing, dramatic, price increases.

In contrast to the pre-devaluation period, inflation rates rapidly took off. Dioné (1994: 4) quotes BCEAO estimates of 35 percent price increases in Burkina Faso from January to June 1994. This was somewhat lower than in the more import-dependent economies of the Franc zone such as Senegal and Côte d'Ivoire, where inflation rates in the same period were estimated at around 40 to 43 percent. However, public sector wage increases were limited to around 10 percent in accordance with IMF and World Bank conditions for emergency credit.

In the Policy Framework Paper for Burkina Faso, the World Bank (1994a: 3) set a new target for the external current account deficit of -14.8 percent of GDP in 1996, arguing that:

> The parity change should lead to a major improvement in the competitiveness of the economy, particularly in the tradeable sectors with a high proportion of value added. The increase in prices of exportable goods and services relative to the prices of domestic goods will favour a rapid growth of exports (by 11.5 percent a year on average in volume), mainly gold, cotton, livestock and fruits and vegetables. Similarly, the import substitution sector is expected to benefit from the relative rise in the prices of imported goods.

Furthermore, 'the rise in the price of imports should have entailed a sharp drop in import volume; however, this drop should be largely offset by growing import demand associated with faster economic growth and investment' (*ibid.*: 3). In short, according to this scenario, future adjustment in Burkina Faso will rely on the 'traditional' export sectors of the economy, notably agriculture, where cotton production will remain the dominant 'engine of growth'.

In this context, it is necessary to examine the prospects for improved performance in different sectors of the economy, while noting that the opportunities for export-led growth in Burkina Faso depend on both changes in world commodity markets and on the efforts to resolve increasingly acute supply-side constraints (not least the environmental problems associated with land degradation). As this survey has shown, the macroeconomic reforms of the early 1990s were limited to a package of measures designed to encourage the private sector to invest in productive activities, while attempting to reduce public sector deficits. But although growth in government expenditure was checked, revenue collection failed to increase, and the deficit widened.

By the end of 1993, despite increased aid transfers, both the government budget and the current account balance were deteriorating. Before the major shift in the terms of trade induced by the exchange-rate realignment, the data suggest that the SAP measures had had little impact on overall economic performance in terms of growth (which was stagnating) and exports (which were on the decline). Almost three years of 'internal adjustment' had not transformed the structures of the Burkinabè economy. There is no doubt that in the short term, devaluation of the CFA Franc has improved competitive advantages.[29] But in the longer term other measures will be required to transform poverty into sustainable development.

4.   Agricultural Sector Adjustment

4.1   Origins of the PASA and Natural Resource Management Issues

The government launched an agricultural sector adjustment programme (PASA) in 1992, preceded by several studies of the growth potential and the constraints affecting this key sector of the economy. Negotiations with major donors on the policy reforms began in conjunction with the implementation of the SAP in 1991, but it was not until agreement was reached on the ESAF arrangements in 1993 that the conditions required for introducing further changes in agricultural policies were thought to be met. Formally, the PASA is a loan agreement with the World Bank, the African Development Bank, the European Union and the French Government (the *Caisse Française de Développement*), signed in 1992 on the basis of a policy document for agricultural development (*la Lettre de Politique du Développement Agricole*).[30] This specifies a number of key objectives in the agricultural sector, notably to modernize and diversify production, to enhance food security and to improve natural resource management.

Before outlining the range of measures included in the PASA, it is useful to

---

[29] *The Economist* ('Out of Africa', 14 January 1995) assessed growth in the Franc zone countries one year after the 50 percent change in parity, by observing that although devaluation 'was sorely needed, it alone was never going to deliver vigorous economic growth. [...] Many countries still rely heavily on one commodity, from cotton to cocoa. If, or when, commodity prices drop, the shock will be felt differently across the zone, putting huge strains on the monetary union.'

[30] The measures proposed in the PASA (*Programme d'Ajustement du Secteur Agricole*) are outlined in detail in two documents published by the MARA (*Ministère de l'Agriculture et des Ressources Animales*): Burkina Faso (1992 & 1993a). The World Bank refers to a SECAL (sectoral credit to agriculture), for which a loan of US$28 m. was allocated in 1992 (World Bank, 1994b: Annex 6).

introduce some of the main characteristics of the agricultural sector. Although it is no longer possible to characterize the rural economy of Burkina Faso (and the neigh- bouring countries of the Sahel) as simply 'traditional, subsistence, non-monetarised agriculture', the cultivation of coarse grains (millet and sorghum) continues to provide the main dietary intake of the rural population, while livestock raising (largely in the hands of Fulani pastoralists) is also an important activity. Rainfed crop production in the central and northern areas of Burkina Faso is subject to the vagaries of the weather, and average yields are low. Some irrigation schemes (where rice is the main crop) have been established in the southern and western regions where average rainfall levels are higher. An increase in the irrigated area is also anticipated in connection with two major hydro-electric schemes at Kompienga and Bagré (in the south) which were completed at the beginning of the 1990s (Bassolet and Ouédraogo, 1994: 21).

Cash crops, notably cotton, are also grown in these more fertile and productive areas. Sugar cane, groundnuts, sesame and karité (shea) nuts are also cultivated (or gathered) as cash crops. Maize production is on the increase, as is the cultivation of fruit and vegetables often through small-scale market gardening schemes. Cotton ginning and processing of agricultural produce such as green beans, karité nuts and some fruit, make up the bulk of the agro-industrial output in Burkina Faso. There has been little investment in the processing of animal products, though small dairies, tanneries and an abattoir, as well as a feedlot (near Banfora) have been established.

Researchers have emphasized the dualistic pattern of agricultural development in Burkina Faso (Thiombiano et al., 1988). Although some farmers, particularly in the cotton producing south and west) have been able to intensify agricultural production and increase incomes, many households continue to subsist on food-crop production supplemented by limited sales of animal products and by non-agricultural activities such as migration, handicrafts, small-scale trading and so on. However, as Reardon et al. (1992) observe, off-farm earnings and purchases of grain by rural households have become increasingly important.

In the 1960s and 1970s, as Savadogo and Wetta (1992: 56) point out, despite the provision of aid to 'modernize' agricultural production, to supply inputs and equipment and to improve extension services, the lack of government expenditure on agriculture as well as disincentives in the form of price policies which failed to ensure the adequate remuneration of producers in rural communities, constituted a significant bias against agriculture. Insufficient resources 'trickled down' to the rural areas, and large-scale development schemes did not produce the expected results in terms of raising farmers' incomes. The parastatal grain marketing organization (*Office National des Céréales*) incurred increasing operating deficits, partly as a result of 'cheap food' policies aiming to supply grain to urban consumers at subsidized prices (see section 4.2, below).

Tackling the underdevelopment of the rural economy was a major objective of the CNR government. But the weaknesses of rural infrastructure, agricultural extension and credit services, as well as the increasingly severe environmental problems due to pressure on land, water and pasture resources, were formidable hurdles. The revolu- tionary soldiers seized power in the run-up to another severe drought, and one of the first major tasks was to manage the distribution of emergency relief in the form of food aid. But long-term development strategies were also formulated, and it is in this context that reforms resembling agricultural sector adjustment were first initiated. To some extent it is possible to argue that another of the reasons that the SAP agreement in 1991 was relatively mild in comparison with the conditions imposed on many other African countries, was that an effort to develop a strategy for sustainable agricultural sector growth had already started in the mid-1980s (Speirs, 1991b; Savadogo and Larivière, 1993). But the CNR and early *Front Populaire* governments assigned major roles to state organizations in channelling resources into rural development.

Reform of the extension service entailed the establishment of 12 *Centres Régionaux de Promotion Agro-Pastoral* (CRPAs), which replaced the rural development organizations (ORDs) previously responsible for distributing credit and inputs as well as carrying out crop marketing. The World Bank was involved in funding improvements in agricultural research and in supporting the introduction of better extension methods. But it was focusing attention on land reform and on measures to reduce environmental degradation which laid the basis for an 'alternative' agricultural sector adjustment programme, later formalized in the LPDA.[31]

The *Réforme Agraire et Foncière* (RAF) introduced in 1984 was highly controversial legislation which nationalized all land in Burkina Faso, giving the CDRs the power to determine the allocation of village land. This directly undermined the power of the traditional chiefs (*la chefferie*). As noted above (section 2.1), the change in legislation which was passed just prior to the constitutional referendum in June 1991 did away with this system, providing for private land ownership and setting out procedures for land allocation through local consultative processes.

However, the *mise en application* of the new RAF has been the subject of extensive discussions since 1991, and three national meetings have been organized in an effort to determine the most appropriate combination of 'traditional' and 'modern' legal procedures pertaining to ownership and transfer of land (Burkina Faso, 1993b). 'Does private land ownership lead to better natural resource management in the Sahel?' was the question posed in a study by Faye (1990), who also pointed out that private tenure often increases inequalities in access to common property resources (water, pasture, semi-arid crop land, etc.). The precariousness of access rights for the pastoral communities (transhumant and semi-nomadic herders) to pasture and water resources are particularly difficult to resolve through legislation.

On the basis of efforts initiated in the mid-1980s, a number of donors have supported the introduction of community-based natural resource management programmes. These schemes are designed to encourage the adoption of better and more ecologically sound agricultural production techniques, in order to tackle the increasingly acute need for soil and water conservation, tree planting and anti-erosion measures in connection with efforts to increase productivity and crop yields and to improve animal husbandry. The national community land management programme (PNGT) has become an integral part of the PASA in so far as environmental objectives are concerned.[32]

In addition to the important environmental concerns, the agricultural sector adjustment programme involves 50 specific measures which should be carried out in

---

[31] The CNR government launched a campaign against environmental degradation (desertification) in 1985. *Les trois luttes* concerned restrictions on illegal wood cutting, the indiscriminate grazing of animals on farmland and deliberate burning of vegetation.

[32] The implementation of the *Programme National de Gestion des Terroirs* has been described in various reports (Burkina Faso, 1993c). Studies of soil and water conservation, forestry and environmental protection schemes in Burkina Faso by Atampugre (1993) and Gubbels (1992) as well as the observations on land degradation and natural resource management strategies in the Sahel by Breman and Niangado (1994) and Toulmin (1991) are also interesting.

the period 1993 to 1995. Apart from the RAF, the abolition of price controls and the liberalization of trade in agricultural products (through the dismantling of monopolies) were at the core of the conditions agreed prior to the implementation of the programme. Restructuring of the parastatals involved in cotton and sugar cane production, as well as OFNACER in the cereals market, were also high on the agenda. These are more standard reforms applied to agriculture in 'typical' African SAP packages.

The following sections indicate some of the changes which have been introduced since the beginning of the 1990s. Unfortunately, data on the overall impact of the PASA (and the SAP in general) on agricultural sector incomes and welfare in the rural areas are largely unavailable. Despite the efforts by some researchers at the University of Ouagadougou and elsewhere, information about the extent to which adjustment has led to greater farm output, higher productivity and increasing rural living standards (shifting from an 'urban to a rural bias' in development strategies) is patchy. Nevertheless, implicit in the move to 'external adjustment' through the devaluation of the CFA Franc, was a recognition that economic reform in the public sector alone was not sufficient to generate growth in agriculture particularly through greater exports (Dioné, 1994).

4.2   Cereals Balance Sheet, Food Crops and Fertilizer

Performance in the agricultural economy of Burkina Faso is closely related to cereals production, which accounts for a major share of total output. Table 9 shows the cereals balance sheet drawn up each year in connection with regular monitoring (through the FAO and CILSS) of grain production and markets in the Sahel. It is estimated that average per capita consumption of cereals (millet, sorghum, maize and rice) must be around 190 kg per year in order to obtain sufficient calories for a healthy diet (Thiombiano *et al.*, 1988).

In terms of the food security objectives defined in the LPDA, the cereals balance sheet shows that overall output of millet, sorghum and maize has been adequate to meet demand requirements, at least in the years after the most recent poor harvest in 1990-91. But some areas of the country are structurally deficit, notably the northern (Sahelian) provinces. Imports and food aid account for around 5-10 percent of the total grain consumed in Burkina Faso.

Grain production increased from just over one million tonnes in 1983-84 to over 2 million tonnes in 1988-89. However, according to data presented by Bassolet and Ouédraogo (1994: 24), output of millet, sorghum and maize fell on average by 1-5 percent between 1986 and 1990, but increased by around 18 percent on average from 1991 to 1993. This increase was, as noted above, largely due to adequate rainfall. Estimates of future cereals requirements in relation to the rapidly increasing total population indicate that demand will reach around 2.5 million tonnes by the year 2005 (Burkina Faso, 1992: Annexe, 82). Thus, in order to achieve the food security objective, output must be maintained through more intensive production techniques which lead to yield increases per hectare.[33]

---

[33] As pointed out in the background studies for the sectoral adjustment programme: *Le seul moyen de faire face à cet accroissement de la demande est d'accroître les rendements* (Burkina Faso, 1992: 27). Increasing the productivity of food crop farming in the 'complex, diverse and risk prone' agriculture of the Sahelian

Table 9   Cereals Balance Sheet, 1983-94

	Population (million)	Production (1000 t)[a]	Balance (1000 t)[b]	Consumption (kg/person/year)[c]	Grain imports (1000 t)[d]	Commercial imports (1000t)[e]	Food aid(1000t)[f]
83/84	7.67	1.100	-523	122	115.90	77.70	38.20
84/85	7.87	1.112	-551	120	258.80	172.40	86.40
85/86	8.08	1.587	-186	167	288.80	190.40	98.40
86/87	8.29	1.926	+62	198	145.00	123.10	21.90
87/88	8.47	1.513	-324	152	178.40	164.20	14.20
88/89	8.69	2.101	+133	205	119.59	96.25	23.34
89/90	8.93	1.952	-38	186	124.90	100.30	24.60
90/91	9.17	1.788	-223	166	216.36	126.59	89.77
91/92	9.42	2.454	+220	222	189.23	145.27	43.96
92/93	9.65	2.477	+227	218	139.27	116.60	22.67
93/94	9.99	2.495	+203	212	n.a.	n.a.	n.a.

Source: Burkina Faso, 1988 & 1990b; CILSS & MARA data.
[a]   Net cereals production, including seeds and losses (15 percent).
[b]   Production minus seeds and losses, minus 190 kg/person.
[c]   Total cereals available for consumption estimated as production plus imports and food aid, divided by the total population.
[d]   Total of commercial imports and food aid.
[e]   Including rice, wheat and other cereals.
[f]   Not including other food aid products (such as milk powder and vegetable oil).

The cereals market has also been subject to investigation in connection with the assessment of supply responses to food crop price changes. Official cereals prices were fixed by the government down to 1989. Using World Bank (1989: 76) data, Savadogo and Larivière (1993: 12) argued that an incentive price policy was implemented by the CNR government. Thus, based on 1979 as the index year (100), average grain prices rose to index values of 198 in 1984 and 197 in 1985, falling to 100 in 1986 (after the bumper harvest) and again rising to 115 in 1987 (*ibid.*: 12). But only a marginal share (a maximum of 10 percent) of the total harvest was marketed at these prices through OFNACER (the parastatal marketing board). As data in the study by Bassolet and Ouédraogo (1994: 25) illustrate, coarse grain prices fell by around 2-5 percent from 1986 to 1990. Given surplus production (as indicated in the balance sheet, Table 9), it was impossible to maintain an incentive price policy, and the practice of fixing cereals prices was abandoned in 1989 (apart from rice).

The cereals market in Burkina Faso has always been largely in the hands of a well organized network of private traders. Fluctuations in supply and demand in different regions of the country are met by trade through this network. OFNACER has been

drylands is an important issue (Mortimore, 1995), which was also examined prior to the SAP in the extensive studies which formed the basis of the *Plan Céréalier* (Burkina Faso, 1988 & 1990b).

unable to regulate the market, and is now being liquidated, its functions reduced to managing an emergency *stock de sécurité* (comprising food aid donations). In this context, it is important to note that many households in the deficit areas of the country cooperate in the management of cereals banks, set up (often with the support of NGOs) to ensure supplies of grain during the *soudure* (the hungry season) at reasonable (affordable) prices[34]. In the *Plan Céréalier* (Burkina Faso, 1988 & 1990b) strengthening of this cooperative network was envisaged, using OFNACER to support the operations of the cereals banks. This strategy has been largely undermined by liberalization of grain marketing, although the cereals banks continue to play a vital role for many households in deficit areas.

Grain prices continued to fall by around 11 percent from 1991 to 1993, according to data presented by Bassolet and Ouédraogo (1994: 25). Overall, the agricultural sector adjustment programme does not entail an incentive price policy for food crops. However, rice marketing is an exception to the price liberalization strategy.

In accordance with the SAP agreements, the government has maintained tariffs on imported rice, collected through the *Caisse Générale de Péréquation* (CGP) which transfers the revenue to the treasury, and fixed the purchasing prices paid to farmers on various (cooperative) irrigation schemes. The purchasing price was increased following the devaluation, and efforts are now under way to explore further investment in irrigation. Since rice has become an important commodity in the diet of many households (particularly in the urban areas), import substitution represents a significant alternative to liberalization. Prior to the devaluation of the CFA Franc, the implications of a protected regional cereals market in West Africa were the subject of an extensive debate (Reardon, 1993; Speirs, 1991a). As rice (and wheat) imports have become much more expensive, the prospects for increasing domestic production seem good (FAO/UEMOA, 1994).

The implications of grain price fluctuations in terms of production intensification are significant, particularly given that fertilizer subsidies were progressively reduced during the 1980s, and finally withdrawn in 1987/88 (Sanon *et al.*, 1993). The World Bank was the prime mover in this process, supporting input supply reform through the *Programme Engrais*. While the removal of the subsidy had little effect on fertilizer use in the cotton growing areas, farmers growing cereals have been increasingly unable to afford inputs. Table 10 indicates the trends in NPK and Urea consumption for both cotton and cereal crops, as well as fertilizer prices from the beginning of the 1980s to the early 1990s.

Around 60 percent of the fertilizer used in Burkina Faso is applied to cotton crops grown in the south and west of the country (see section 4.3, below). As the total area sown with cotton (and the number of farmers growing cotton) increased during the 1980s, so the demand for fertilizer also increased, despite the reduction in the level of subsidy. The application of fertilizer on cereals crops declined in the mid-1980s as the subsidy was withdrawn and prices increased. But cheaper imported NPK and Urea after 1987/88 compensated for this decline, as shown in the table (Sanon *et al.*, 1993: 52-56).

However, the purchase of fertilizer for cereals cultivation has subsequently stagnated. In the 1992/93 and 1993/94 crop years, with falling farmgate prices as total grain output increased, many farmers could not afford to purchase fertilizer for use on cereal crops (DANIDA/DGIS, 1994). The consequences in terms of an overall increase in extensive

---

[34] The dynamics of cereals banks have been investigated by Yonli (1993); and some banks are supported by a Danish NGO (Danchurchaid, 1993)

cultivation practices (using more land to grow crops rather than increasing yields per hectare) are serious. On the fragile soils of the central and northern plateau in Burkina Faso, organic inputs (animal manure) can be usefully supplemented with phosphate fertilizer to maintain soil fertility and crop yields. But without any subsidies, and without an effective agricultural credit system (outside the cotton growing areas), most smallholder farmers cannot gain access to the necessary inputs.[35]

Table 10 Estimated Consumption and Prices of Fertilizer, 1980/81-1990/91

	NPK & Urea on cotton (tonnes)	NPK & Urea on cereals (tonnes)	NPK price (F.CFA/tonne)
1980/81	7.371	7.955	94.610
1981/82	7.526	8.438	111.341
1982/83	8.703	10.151	120.082
1983/84	10.002	10.392	122.948
1984/85	11.226	9.971	129.182
1985/86	13.060	8.060	136.930
1986/87	19.063	7.146	147.276
1987/88	22.445	10.153	95.487
1988/89	25.568	13.354	100.137
1989/90	21.732	14.804	110.342
1990/91	23.339	13.104	117.768
1991/92	25.585	13.114	111.697

Source: Sanon *et al.*, 1993; DANIDA/DGIS, 1994.

4.3   Cash Crops and Exports

As noted above (section 4.1), in addition to cotton, the main cash crops in Burkina Faso are groundnuts, fruit and vegetables, *karité* nuts and sesame. Output of these crops has increased steadily over the past decade, despite fluctuations due to adverse weather conditions. For example, according to data presented by Bassolet and Ouédraogo (1994: 24) groundnut production increased by nearly 14 percent in the period 1991-93, and fruit and vegetable output by 4 percent in the same period. Cowpea production also expanded rapidly. Sugar cane production on a plantation near Banfora, which is run by a parastatal (SUSUCO), remained steady at around 30,000 tonnes per year.

However, cotton is the mainstay of the cash-crop economy in Burkina Faso. Table

[35] This issue was explored in a joint Danish and Dutch evaluation of fertilizer deliveries (DANIDA/DGIS, 1994). Amongst the recommendations put forward for consideration by the government, the re-introduction of fertilizer subsidies was stressed on ecological grounds as well as the need to support the production of local phosphate fertilizer (*Burkina Phosphate*).

11 summarizes some of the data pertaining to cotton production and exports during the 1980s and down to the early 1990s. With support from the World Bank and the *Compagnie Française de Développement des Textiles* (CFDT), intensive cotton cultivation was introduced in the 1970s, and rapidly took off in some zones, where a *filière organisée* was established. The supply of inputs and credit as well as the purchase and marketing of the crop were organised by the cotton parastatal (SOFITEX) together with the national agricultural credit bank (CNCA). Many farmers were encouraged to organize in *groupements* (village cooperatives) to obtain seed, inputs and credit (for animal traction equipment, for example) and to market the crop through SOFITEX. Cotton ginning facilities were established in Bobo Dioulasso and several other towns.

Table 11   Cotton Production and Exports, 1983-92

	Cultivated area ('000 ha)	Yield (kg/ha)	Seed production ('000 tonnes)	Ginned cotton production ('000 tonnes)	Exports ('000 tonnes)
83/84	76.7	1,033	79.3	30.1	
84/85	82.3	1,071	88.1	34.3	
85/86	94.6	1,221	115.6	45.9	
86/87	126.7	1,330	169.5	65.4	56.5
87/88	150.0	1,021	158.0	58.6	43.5
88/89	169.4	861	145.8	57.7	39.2
89/90	160.6	968	140.0	62.4	44.4
90/91	166.3	1,139	160.0	77.2	66.6
91/92	185.7	900			

Source: Burkina Faso, 1992: 30; IMF, 1993c: Table 5.

Cotton output declined by around 14 percent from 1991 to 1993 (Bassolet and Ouédraogo, 1994: 24). As noted above (section 3), falling world market prices since the end of the 1980s have seriously affected the cotton economy of Burkina Faso (and the other cotton producing countries in West Africa). The thrust of reform insofar as this key crop is concerned, has been to restructure SOFITEX in an attempt to reduce the operating deficit and accumulated debts (for the payment of inputs supplied to farmers).[36] This also entailed cutting producer prices which are fixed in advance of the cultivation season each year. The result, measurable in terms of maize production in the south and west of the country in the early 1990s, was to encourage a switch from cotton into food crops. But the bottom then fell out of the maize market, and unsold stocks of this cereal have accumulated in the past couple of years.

Following the devaluation, cotton producer prices were increased by 40 percent on

---

[36] Similar arrangements have been agreed to restructure SUSUCO (World Bank, 1994a: 12), although in this case the 'performance contract' is intended to result in privatization, if the 'active search for private investors' yields results.

the basis of a performance contract which had been signed with SOFITEX. As the IMF (1994: 7) pointed out:

> Those farmers who stopped growing cotton during 1993/94 did so not only in reaction to the continuing decline in producer prices but also due to the fact that the reduced prices were not paid in a timely manner by SOFITEX. This would suggest that, in order to maintain farmers' interest in growing cotton, the authorities should ensure that producer prices are effectively paid upon delivery of output.

While it is envisaged that SOFITEX will continue to manage the cotton market, other agricultural parastatals (notably UCOBAM, a fruit and vegetable marketing cooperative) are being privatized according to the conditionalities attached to the SAP. In connection with efforts to diversify agricultural exports (an objective specified in the LPDA), it is proposed that 'the government will facilitate the functioning of the subsector of fruits and vegetables', by 'giving priority to medium-term programs of applied research' (co-financed by the private sector) and by 'formulating regulations aimed at assuring the free play of competition and transparency of the business behaviour' (World Bank, 1994a: 12). With increasingly tough competition on agricultural export markets, there is an urgent need to look closely at the real possibilities for gaining larger shares in fruit and vegetable markets, despite the advantages of reduced prices (in other currencies) following the devaluation. Better West African market integration might be more promising than trying to compete on world markets.

4.4   Livestock Production and Marketing

The Policy Framework Paper (World Bank, 1994a) for the period 1994-96 did not mention any specific measures related to the development of livestock production, rangeland management and improvements in animal husbandry, even in the section dealing with agriculture and natural resource management. Nevertheless, these are important issues in the overall rural economy of the country, and the LPDA includes a number of proposals for the intensification of livestock production and the streamlining of support services (Burkina Faso, 1992: 93-114). In this context it is important to note that there has been an extensive debate about appropriate strategies for livestock development in different agro-ecological zones in the Sahel.[37]

Livestock production systems in Burkina Faso are undergoing rapid change, following the serious losses incurred by pastoralists during the droughts of the 1970s and 1980s. Although it is difficult to generalize, there appears to be a significant trend towards more intensive animal production, integrated within arable farming systems in the southern regions of Burkina Faso. This integration is often initiated through cash-crop production where additional 'labour' is required in the form of animal traction. On the other hand, in the northern, arid, regions of the country where rainfall limits the production of food and cash crops, grazing of cattle, sheep and goats remains a major source of income. In the intermediate zones, various forms of transhumance and agro-pastoralism have emerged, where ensuring access to water and pasture is the key issue.

---

[37] See, inter alia, the studies by Breman and Niangado (1994) and Speirs and Olsen (1992), as well as the papers edited by Scoones (1994).

But the marginalization of pastoralist communities (the Fulani) in the land-tenure debate, and the increasingly violent conflicts related to overgrazing (the destruction of crops and vegetation by animals), are central concerns.

Encouraging the intensification (and *sédentarisation*) of animal production is the main approach put forward in the PASA (Burkina Faso, 1992). However, in certain areas, rangeland management systems of livestock production, implying the mobility of animals in relation to seasonal fluctuations in the supplies of edible vegetation and movement around watering points, may be more appropriate and 'rational' uses of scarce fodder resources. Increasing the use of agricultural by-products (such as cotton stalks and other crop residues) may also provide additional fodder during the dry season.

The devaluation of the CFA Franc, which has provided an opportunity to 're-capture' coastal meat markets, represents an upturn in the fortunes of Sahelian animal production systems. During the 1980s, cheap meat imports from Europe (and Argentina) undermined 'traditional' Sahelian animal product exports to the major coastal markets. Export subsidies available from the EU enabled exporters of frozen beef to capture a significant share of the West African market. However, with the increase in price (in CFA Francs) these imports have now declined, and evidence suggests that Sahelian meat dealers have been quick to adapt to the new conditions (Dioné, 1994: 10).

The establishment of 'modern' export infrastructure for live animals and animal products from the Sahel has been on the investment agenda for some time (Kulibaba and Holtzman, 1990). Improving markets, transport facilities and processing plant (tanneries, abattoirs, etc.) is necessary in order to ensure that Sahelian producers maintain and increase their market shares in the urban areas of the West African coastal countries. Similarly, in some of the bigger towns of the Sahel itself where milk consumption is on the increase, the development of dairies may be part of an import substitution strategy in the wake of the devaluation. Whatever options are adopted in Burkina Faso, it is safe to conclude that the future of livestock production has been enhanced by 'external adjustment', although the ability of producer groups to reap the benefits remains to be seen.

5.   Adjustment in other Sectors

5.1   Industry

Until the end of the 1980s, most of the manufacturing industries in Burkina Faso were publicly owned. A central tenet of adjustment policies as promoted by the Bretton Woods institutions is that such enterprises are inherently inefficient, and that government intervention to encourage the development of manufacturing activities through import substitution leads to unproductive investment and to distortions in the use of domestic resources.[38] Thus, dismantling state-owned and parastatal enterprises goes hand in hand with a policy of market liberalization (reducing tariffs and controls) in the hope of encouraging private (and foreign) investment. Indeed, the slogan *libéral-*

---

[38] Literature dealing with the debate on the appropriate size of the public sector in developing countries is extensive. As Tarp (1993: 17) notes: 'public participation in directly-productive activities in the form of state-owned enterprises, and direct control of the allocation of resources, have been very prevalent features in sub-Saharan Africa. Furthermore, the expansion in government activity in general, and of state-owned enterprises in particular, has been very rapid.'

isation et privatisation is often heard in Burkina Faso and elsewhere in the UEMOA countries.

During the post-independence period, manufacturing capacity in Burkina Faso developed slowly, principally on the basis of processing industries linked to agricultural production (Bassolet and Ouédraogo, 1994: 26). In food processing, companies producing edible oils and soap (SHSB), sugar (SOSUCO) and flour (*Grands Moulins Burkinabè*) were amongst the most important. Tanneries (run by the SBCP) were also government-owned. Together with the breweries (*Brakina* and *Sobbra*, which were partly privately owned), and the cotton processing factories (whose activities were described in section 4.3, above), these constituted the bulk of the manufacturing capacity in the country established prior to the 1980s. Most of these parastatals were located in the south-west, with Bobo Dioulasso as the 'industrial capital' in the centre of the cotton zone.

In addition, a number of construction companies and equipment manufacturing industries developed, including those concerned with tools and agricultural machinery, iron sheeting, tyres and plastics. During the 1980s, bicycle and moped assembly (SIFA) was added to the range of manufacturing activities in Bobo Dioulasso. Fruit processing and fruit juice manufacture was also initiated by another parastatal enterprise (*Savana*). But, as noted in Table 1, in general growth in manufacturing was not spectacular. Using estimates from the end of the 1980s, the IMF (1993c: 6) noted that the manufacturing sector accounted for around 15 percent of GDP, but employed only around 8,000 people, or less than 1 percent of the labour force.

Table 12 Growth in Value Added in Manufacturing, 1986-93

	1985	1986	1987	1988	1989	1990	1991	1992	1993
Value[a]	66.9	86.9	80.9	89.4	92.2	81.0	86.4	76.8	85.8
Percent[b]	n.a.	29.8	-6.9	10.6	3.2	-12.2	6.7	-11.1	11.6

Source: Bassolet and Ouédraogo, 1994: 29.
[a]   Value added in billion CFA Francs.
[b]   Annual change in percent.

Table 12 shows some estimates of the growth in value added in the manufacturing sector from 1985. The rapid growth in value added in 1986 was largely due to major investment in construction in this period (notably the new central market in Ouagadougou). Other construction projects which have required considerable capital investment include the Kompienga and Bagré dams and associated electricity supply networks.[39] The cyclical nature of growth in value added is shown in the table, where low growth in 1990 and 1992 was due to overall demand contraction as the impact of adjustment in the public sector (in the form of wage controls) began to be felt.

The problems faced in developing manufacturing industries in Burkina Faso are numerous. As the IMF (1993c: 6) noted, 'expansion of the industrial sector remains

---

[39] The issue of energy production and supply is considered in section 7.2 (below) in a brief discussion of the environmental problems arising from the substitution of 'modern' sources of energy (gas and electricity) for 'traditional' ones, notably fuelwood (and vice versa, following the devaluation).

constrained by the narrow domestic market, high transportation costs, poor infrastructural facilities and the lack of skilled labour and experienced managers.' But the key constraint was seen in terms of government intervention in the sector. Bassolet and Ouédraogo (1994: 28) have investigated the levels of protection afforded to public sector manufacturing industries prior to the SAP from 1991. The data indicate that while nominal protection rates were high (in terms of the difference between border parity prices and domestic factory gate prices), the operating losses of the industries concerned were also significant. As monopoly enterprises, the government encouraged the banking system to continue to lend to these loss-making companies, which further strained the financial resources available in the public sector.

The SAP agreement in 1991 entailed continuing a programme of privatization of government-owned companies (which began in 1990), as well as reducing tariffs and levels of protection. Thus:

> Price controls on locally produced goods, which had caused a number of companies to suffer financial losses, have been abolished. Moreover, the turnover tax, which unduly raised retail prices and reduced the competitiveness of industry, has now been replaced by a value added tax. Other initiatives include a reform of the investment and labour codes (IMF, 1993c: 6-7).

The effect of these measures on overall manufacturing sector output and employment have not been studied in detail as yet. Although the government has 'decided to fully divest itself of its holdings in industrial and commercial enterprises' (World Bank, 1994: 7), privatization proceeds slowly.[40] This is because private capital is scarce, even though some foreign investors have participated in joint ventures and provided capital to establish and to take over certain enterprises, notably in agro-processing, and bicycle and moped manufacturing industries where French and Japanese capital is involved.

A good deal of economic activity in Burkina Faso takes place in the informal sector. According to Bassolet and Ouédraogo (1994: 30), census data from the mid-1980s showed that over 500,000 people were employed in small informal businesses, where women were particularly well represented. The same authors (*ibid.*: 31) use data from an unspecified source to show that on average from 1985 to 1992, informal production accounted for over 60 percent of secondary sector output and over 55 percent of tertiary sector output (in commercial and transport activities). This involves family-owned businesses such as clothing manufacturers, carpentry and repair workshops, small agro-processing enterprises and retailers. Informal production and processing contributes a major share of value added in the secondary and tertiary sectors of the economy.

In this sense, private business activity has always been alive and well in Burkina Faso.[41] The problem is that informal sector investment levels in manufacturing are low, the capacity to generate employment (at reasonable wages) is limited, and a good

---

[40] The World Bank approved a loan of US$7 m. in 1993 to get a private sector programme under way in connection with rehabilitation of public enterprises (the *Programme d'Ajustement du Secteur des Enterprises Publiques*). Thirteen parastatals were already privatized (or liquidated) by the end of 1993, and the charges for public utilities (electricity, water and telephones) were revised upwards with a view to eliminating subsidies (World Bank, 1994a: 7). See also: Devey and Lingané (1993: 481-482).

[41] See also Labazée (1988) for a historical review of private enterprise in Burkina Faso, and the study by Igué (1993) on the role of women in informal sector production and processing in West Africa.

deal of the profitable activities concern trade and exchange (of imports) rather than production (of domestic goods). Markets are well developed in West Africa, but it remains to be seen whether adjustment policies will be able to transform trade and exchange into productive investment, generating employment and greater income rather than simply profits for a privileged minority.

5.2   Mining

In their discussion of development options in the 1960s and 1970s, Savadogo and Wetta (1992) did not consider that Burkina Faso possessed a significant mining potential. 'Until 1985, the mining of minerals remained insignificant' (IMF, 1993c: 7). Since the discovery of gold at Poura and manganese at Tamboa, as well as zinc and phosphate deposits (at Perkoa and Kodjari), there has been a rapid growth of interest in developing the exploitation of these resources. Gold production has oscillated since the opening of the Poura mine in 1984, but gold exports accounted for around 20 percent of (officially registered) export earnings in certain years (see section 3.4, above). Nevertheless, major difficulties remain and some observers have suggested that the high costs of mining in Burkina Faso, combined with low world mineral prices, militate against the development of viable mining industries.

The story of the manganese deposits at Tamboa (in the extreme north of the country near the Mali/Niger border), provides an interesting example of the issues involved. Numerous studies carried out in the 1970s and early 1980s suggested that extracting the 17 million tonnes of manganese in the area would be unprofitable, given the high cost of transport from this rather isolated area and the uncertain world market for manganese. However, the CNR government decided to enlist voluntary labour in the construction of a railway from Ouagadougou to the north-east. This project became known as *la bataille du rail*, and was highly controversial. By the beginning of the 1990s, the railway line had reached Kaya, some 100 kilometres from Ouagadougou, and trucks were used to bring the first consignments of manganese to the railhead for export.

The Bretton Woods institutions are still doubtful about the viability of this mining programme (IMF, 1993c: 7), but the exchange-rate realignment altered some views:

> As a revitalized mining sector could contribute significantly to export receipts and to tax revenues, the government is seeking to develop it by attracting foreign and domestic private investment. [... in the post-devaluation period] the development of the mining sector will benefit because of lower cost (measured in foreign currency) of exploration, which involves a relatively large share of local labour (World Bank, 1994a: 14).

In addition, as noted above (section 4.2), there is considerable potential to increase the production of local phosphates which could substitute for imported fertilizer. This may be particularly significant in tackling the environmental problems arising through more intensive agricultural production (per hectare). The reorganization and reinforcement of the public institutions involved in mining, proposed in the Policy Framework Paper for the period 1994-96 (World Bank, 1994a: 14), could be a major follow-up to the *Programme Engrais* (fertilizer scheme) also funded by the World Bank in the 1980s, which would entail the development of domestic phosphate mining capacity as a form of import substitution made more profitable by the devaluation of the CFA Franc.

5.3   Transport

Finally, it is important to note that the IMF and the World Bank are also involved in a transport sector adjustment programme in Burkina Faso (known as the PASEC-T). Again, reorientating the sector away from government intervention is the key to the adjustment strategy and at the same time this runs counter to the policy of *désenclavement* ('opening up') of isolated rural areas with public investment in better roads and transport systems, initiated by the CNR government in the mid-1980s. As noted above (section 5.2), the construction of the railway to the north-east was also seen in this light.

Public investment in road construction during the 1980s was significant, and resulted in a doubling of the size of the network (IMF, 1993c: 8). But insufficient resources were used for maintenance and repair. It was concluded that despite the introduction of a national transport company, 'transportation prices are nevertheless high because of poor road conditions, high petroleum prices and vehicle taxation, as well as the steep cost of spare parts' (*ibid.*: 8). Similarly, mounting financial difficulties led to serious disruption in the *Régie des Chemins de Fer Abidjan-Niger* (RAN), the state-owned company which jointly operated the railway from Ouagadougou to Côte d'Ivoire and the coast until splitting into two national companies in 1988.

Both the new Burkinabè railway company (SCFB) and the national bus company (*Régie X9*), as well as the national airline (*Air Burkina*), ran into difficulties at the end of the 1980s, as the bill for transport subsidies grew. Thus: 'to improve transportation services and eliminate the need for subsidies, the government has taken the necessary steps to [...] modernise the operational and financial management of *Air Burkina*, and privatize its railroad (SCFB) and urban transport (*Régie X9*) services' (World Bank, 1994a: 13). In this way it is anticipated that a 'reduction of employment and the clearing of these enterprises' debts and claims, preconditions for their privatisation, will allow them to adapt better to the new conditions of the transportation market in Burkina Faso and the sub-region' (*ibid.*).

For a landlocked country in Sahelian West Africa, transport is a fundamental element of all economic activity, in terms of both domestic commerce and international trade. Transport costs remain high and with fuel costs (in F.CFA) increasing dramatically after the devaluation, it may be anticipated that exports and imports will be affected. However, as the World Bank (1994b) optimistically observes in the country assistance strategy, the government attaches a high priority to regional trade in the context of the UEMOA agreements. According to some observers, this regional dimension, with greater integration of the Sahelian markets in the stronger and more diverse economies of the coastal countries (particularly Côte d'Ivoire, Ghana and Nigeria), may form a focus for development 'beyond adjustment.' (Coussy and Hugon, 1991; Snrech, 1994).

6.   Equity, Poverty and Social Services

6.1   Poverty

Burkina Faso is a poor country. The human development index (HDI) designed by the UNDP (1994) ranks Burkina as the 172nd of 173 countries in terms of combined measures of life expectancy at birth (longevity), years of schooling (knowledge) and income (purchasing power parity dollars per capita). Most recent estimates for similar indicators are shown in Table 13, comparing the data for Burkina Faso with weighted averages for Sub-Saharan Africa as a whole.

In the latest Policy Framework Paper (World Bank, 1994a: 14), it is noted that the 'devaluation and structural reform', while contributing to economic growth in the medium term, 'may entail negative social consequences especially in the urban areas' in the short term. Thus, in the wake of the devaluation and in accordance with the conditions attached to an economic recovery credit (for a total of US$25 m.), the government temporarily re-introduced price controls on certain key commodities ('flour, sugar, kerosene, medicines, cement, school supplies, milk and agricultural inputs').

Subsequently, these controls were withdrawn, with the adoption of 'measures to promote income generating activities and to target distribution of food aid to rural inhabitants in the most disadvantaged regions' (*ibid.*). It is particularly surprising to note that, although there have been cereals surpluses in recent years in Burkina Faso (as mentioned in section 4.2, above), this appears not to have reduced the willingness to use food aid in alleviating poverty.

Table 13   Indicators of Longevity, Education and Income, 1994

	Life expectancy at birth (years)	Primary school enrolment (percent)	Income, GNP per capita (US$)
Burkina Faso	48	31	300
Average SSA[a]	52	66	530

Source: World Bank, 1994b and 1994c.
[a]   Sub-Saharan Africa.

Following extensive involvement in the vaccination and literacy campaigns of the mid-1980s (mentioned in section 2.1, above), UNICEF has gathered data pertaining to the extent of poverty in Burkina Faso, and has funded a number of studies including surveys carried out by teams from the University of Ouagadougou. According to Bassolet and Ouédraogo (1994: 32), these studies entailed determining the criteria on which to assess families in need, the collection of data (from a sample of over 800 urban households) and the development of programmes to support the poorest families in the urban areas (through enhancing 'survival strategies'). In another study, also cited by these authors, which was also carried out by researchers from the University of Ouagadougou, it was estimated that the average annual income of a rural household in the central region was around 80,000 CFA Francs in 1993, of which two thirds was derived from agriculture.[42]

Further studies of poverty in Burkina Faso have been proposed in connection with the design of measures to tackle the 'social impact of adjustment' and to 'define more

---

[42] Compare, inter alia, the studies of household income carried out in the mid-1980s by Reardon *et al.* (1989) which dealt with food consumption in Ouagadougou, and by Reardon *et al.* (1992) covering 'income diversification amongst farm households'. The latter study showed total income levels per household ranging from 23,600 to 45,800 CFA Francs per year in different zones, based on the net value of crop production, plus livestock sales and home consumption, plus transfers and net cash receipts from non-farm sectors.

precisely the most vulnerable segments of the population and their needs' (World Bank, 1994a: 14). But ignoring the results of previous studies seems rather unnecessary. Bassolet and Ouédraogo (1994: 33) are able to report that the level of moderate malnutrition amongst children aged 0 to 4 surveyed in nine provinces in 1987 ranged from less than 30 percent of all children in one province, to between 30 and 50 percent in four other provinces, up to between 50 and 65 percent in four others. 18 percent of birth weights in this study were recorded at less than 2.5 kg.

Since 1988 private household consumption has fallen, as shown in Table 14. Despite the plethora of reports dealing with economic performance under the first SAL and the ESAF arrangements, no data on wage levels and trends are available.[43] However, there is little doubt that poverty is widespread in Burkina Faso.

Table 14   Real Annual per Capita Growth Rates (1985 prices), 1988-94

	1988	1989	1990	1991	1992	1993	1994[a]
GDP	2.9	0.5	-2.8	3.1	-2.2	-2.4	0.3
Total consumption	1.3	-1.9	0.1	0.2	-2.2	-1.3	-12.3
Private consumption	1.9	-2.0	-0.2	-0.2	-2.0	-1.4	-10.8

Source: World Bank, 1994b: Annex 4.
[a]   Eestimates.

For the time being, apart from improving the statistical data base, the Bretton Woods institutions are involved in several poverty alleviation schemes which form part of the strategy to deal with the 'social dimensions of adjustment' (Bassolet and Ouédraogo, 1994: 33). In addition to the distribution of food aid as mentioned, a centre to supply essential drugs has been set up (CAMEG) and programmes to improve food security and to promote women's employment (through a special fund) have been initiated. Furthermore, a public works agency (*Faso Baara*) has been established to generate employment.

In the medium term, it is expected that GDP growth will increase after 'external adjustment', such that more resources will be available to alleviate poverty. On the other hand, measures to ensure an equitable distribution of income are not on the policy agenda, and efforts to increase taxation have not proven a great success (as noted above, section 3.2). In the short term, adjustment in Burkina Faso appears to have had little impact on the extent of poverty. Indeed, the indicators (GNP/capita, HDI, etc.) and surveys suggest that the standard of living for the poorest has gone from bad to worse.

---

[43] There are errors on the scales of the figure (number 6) in the World Bank (1993) Public Expenditure Review, which make it impossible to calculate average wages in the civil service on the basis of the total wage bill (estimated at around 48 billion CFA Francs in 1991). Bassolet and Ouédraogo (1994: 39) quote a figure of 78,300 CFA Francs/year as the *coût salarial moyen* in 1993.

6.2   Education

Some of the controversies surrounding reforms of primary and adult education, as well as the impact of changes in the award of scholarships for higher education during the 1980s, were mentioned in the outline of the history of adjustment in Burkina Faso (section 2.1, above). Measures designed to encourage literacy and greater primary school enrolment were high on the list of priorities under the CNR government, but the approach adopted was not very successful. In particular, cuts in teachers' salaries were very unpopular. This remains a delicate issue in more recent proposals for public expenditure reform (World Bank, 1993).

Despite the focus on literacy campaigns during the 1980s, the standard education indicators show that Burkina Faso lags far behind international levels. In 1992, it was estimated that the adult male literacy rate was around 30 percent, while the female rate was only 10 percent. Around 17 percent of children and young people aged from 6 to 23 were enrolled in formal education, but the mean length of schooling was only 0.2 years (UNDP, 1994: Tables 4 & 5). While 30 percent of boys and 24 percent of girls attended primary school, only 8 percent and 5 percent respectively continued to secondary education. The pupil/teacher ratio in primary schools deteriorated from 44 pupils per teacher in 1970 to 58 per teacher in 1991 (World Bank, 1994: Table 28).

Table 15   Public Expenditure on Education, 1986-91

	1986	1987	1988	1989	1990	1991
Expenditure (billion F.CFA)	13.10	14.85	18.60	16.89	20.46	21.04
- of which, salaries	7.87	8.97	12.63	13.05	13.59	14.25
Percent of total public expenditure	19.00	20.60	23.20	19.50	19.20	22.60
Percent of GDP	2.20	2.40	2.80	2.40	2.90	2.70

Source: IMF, 1993c: Table 19.

Clearly a good deal remains to be done to develop comprehensive primary and secondary education in Burkina Faso. During the 1980s, school construction programmes were initiated in rural areas such that, if a village or community paid for the buildings and equipped the school, the government provided a school teacher. In this way, the total share of government expenditure on education was largely limited to salaries. Table 15 shows the evolution of public expenditure on education in the period from 1986 to 1991, and indicates that spending has remained more or less constant at less than 3 percent of GDP.

The main thrust of the education strategy introduced in connection with the human resource adjustment programme (PASHR) and arising from the public expenditure review (World Bank, 1993), is to limit teachers' pay while encouraging the recruitment of more teachers to work longer hours (double shifts). In addition, further reducing scholarships would 'release resources necessary to improve the quality of university instruction', while 'lowering the average salary paid to teachers' would, it is argued, 'free extra resources to pay operating expenses in primary schools'.[44] This strategy is open

---

[44] As quoted by Jacob and Nsengiyuma (1994: 13). The World Bank (1994b: 13) also observes that: 'Some

to a wide range of criticism.

Some of the issues are raised in a critical review by Jacob and Nsengiyuma (1994: 15) who point out that:

> Measures aimed at increasing the resources allotted to education will have very little effect upon enrolment rates, unless they are accompanied by a parallel augmentation of incomes. In addition, other reasons can be cited [...]: cultural problems, the perception that schooling no longer leads to a guaranteed job in the public' sector, (and) the opportunity costs of sending children to school compared to the gains from agricultural activities undertaken by them (particularly in the case of girls).

In short, the approach proposed to restructure education in Burkina Faso is shortsighted and inadequate. The weaknesses of even a mild SAP become apparent when the sole purpose of sectoral reform appears to be cutting costs, without examining the broader implications in terms of human resource development (including the quality of the education services provided, not simply the number of pupils enrolled). Education costs money, and should be considered as a public good. But this means that extra revenue must be generated, and again difficulties are encountered (as noted in section 3.2, above).

6.3   Health

Despite a steady increase in the allocation of public funds to the health sector (as shown in Table 16), the overall prevalence of disease and malnutrition in Burkina Faso remains a cause of considerable concern. Infant and child mortality rates are high, and it is estimated that only 70 percent of the population has access to some form of health care. Although primary health care centres were set up in many villages during the 1980s and vaccination campaigns were organized, Jacob and Nsengiyuma (1994) argue that too much emphasis was placed on the provision of curative medicine, and not enough attention has been paid to preventive measures. Nonetheless, with over 1 percent of GDP spent on public health services, the government is said to allocate 'more than most other Sub-Saharan African countries and far more than the average low-income Asian country' to this sector (World Bank, 1994b: 13).

There are four main categories of health care provision in Burkina Faso: i) two fully equipped national hospitals in Ouagadougou and Bobo Dioulasso; ii) a series of smaller regional hospitals; iii) medical centres staffed by a doctor with a nurse and midwife; and iv) health and 'social promotion' centres with auxiliary staff (Bassolet and Ouédraogo, 1994: 36). However, according to the World Bank (1994b: 13), there is an excessive concentration of resources in the two main urban centres where two thirds of the midwives, 60 percent of the doctors and 40 percent of the nurses are employed. In addition, 'a significant number of health centres are closed or dysfunctional because of lack of appropriately trained personnel or basic supplies and medicines, leaving traditional healers as the sole option' (*ibid.*). Thus the adjustment programme proposed

---

cost reduction measures, such as the hiring of less costly entry-level teachers, have begun, but much more needs to be done [...] to increase enrolment ratios and quality. [It is also necessary] to engage the University community in a dialogue on achieving its future objectives in a cost effective manner.'

in this sector concerns the re-allocation and decentralization of personnel, improved selection and training of health workers, and increasing access to essential generic drugs.

Table 16 Public Expenditure on Health, 1986-91

	1986	1987	1988	1989	1990	1991
Expenditure (billion F.CFA)	5.09	5.91	7.56	7.67	8.62	9.15
- of which, salaries	4.08	4.64	5.78	6.04	6.18	6.11
Percent of total public expenditure	7.4	8.2	9.4	8.9	8.1	9.8
Percent of GDP	0.8	1.0	1.1	1.1	1.2	1.2

Source: IMF, 1993c: Table 19.

A large section of the latest Policy Framework Paper (World Bank, 1994a: 10-11) was devoted to explaining the measures designed to improve the 'coverage, quality and utilization of primary care services'. The inadequate supply of drugs has been a recurrent issue and a central purchasing agency (CAMEG) was established in the early 1990s. In connection with the devaluation of the CFA Franc, the government was particularly concerned about the prohibitive cost of importing medicines, and it was agreed that the Ministry of Health would receive an allocation for the purchase of an addition to the stock of essential and generic drugs. While the World Bank has actively promoted the role of private business in drug supply (noting that the private sector accounts for 90 percent of all drugs sold), credit to the government for drug purchases was approved:

> To cushion the impact of the recent devaluation [...] this measure will be widely publicised in the media and will not only make drugs accessible to the poor for the first time but also help acquaint the population with these kinds of medicines, encourage the use of health centres, and generate sufficient funds for restocking of essential and generic medicines at the CAMEG (*ibid.*).

Does this mean that the drugs will be sold or distributed free of charge? If they are to be sold, how will this benefit the poor? If they are to be distributed free, how will funds be generated for restocking the CAMEG? Overall, there are serious implications of introducing user charges for health services (as proposed for treatment at the main hospitals) on the welfare of the poorest and most vulnerable sections of the population.

Finally, it is also important to note that a comprehensive family planning strategy has been drawn up by the government in connection with the PASHR (human resource adjustment programme), since: 'the government recognises that rapid population growth entails serious risks of resource degradation, including soil and water in particular, which jeopardizes the quality of life and the feasibility of engaging in agriculture, forestry and animal husbandry' (World Bank, 1994a: 9).[45] Resources will also be

---

[45] A good deal of recent research into these links would contest this oversimplified conclusion. See, inter alia, Mortimore (1995).

allocated to inform the population about the risks of AIDS, and to 'assist communities in caring for the terminally ill' (*ibid.*). The impact of these information activities and the family planning programmes, particularly in the rural areas, has yet to be assessed.

6.4   Public Sector Reform

The adjustment measures introduced in the education and health sectors were largely inspired by the Public Expenditure Review (World Bank, 1993). This exercise entailed comparing the costs of different services in Burkina Faso with those of selected Asian countries, and then proposing cuts and reforms.[46] In their analysis of this process, Jacob and Nsengiyuma (1994) argue that the review failed to take account of the extent of poverty and inequalities in access to services.

However, privatization, the introduction of user charges (for cost recovery in the hospital for example), price increases (after devaluation) and reduced opportunities for public sector employment (except in the education and health services), have successfully 'squeezed' many public sector employees and government staff. As noted above (section 3.1) it appears that an 'erosion of privileges' in the public sector has been effectively carried out, although it is not easy to find out whether the privileges accorded to the military and to top figures in the government have been eroded at the same rate as those on the lower levels of authority. In the medium term, some NGOs and informal sector businesses will benefit from the greater availability of qualified personnel at reduced rates.

In the longer term perhaps increased tax revenues and debt relief will enable the government to think again, and to devise appropriate public sector policies for which resources (human and financial) are available. Until such time as the SAP (in either its 'internal' or 'external' varieties) allows the Burkinabè Government to expand its tax base and initiate redistributive policies, rigorous and selective management of expenditure will be under the control of the Bretton Woods institutions in collaboration with those donors who co-finance specific sectoral adjustment programmes. Jacob and Nsengiyuma (1994) also stress the importance of policy 'ownership' in determining public sector priorities, noting that there is a need to ensure the 'capacity to create an active development policy'. It is unlikely that proposals which focus on 'strengthening the capacity to budget and to monitor the execution of budgets in the ministries responsible for primary education and health' (World Bank, 1993: iii) are sufficient in terms of reducing poverty and developing human resources. The role of the public sector cannot be limited to financial management, but must include the provision of services to the most vulnerable people.

Human resource development particularly concerns women. During the 1980s, there was a good deal of public debate about the role of women in Burkinabè society, and various controversial measures were introduced (notably a ban on prostitution and a move to recruit more women into public services). These discussions culminated in the adoption of a new *code de la famille* (in 1990), in which a proposal to restrict polygamy was particularly hotly disputed. Although it is difficult to determine the ways

---

[46] Although the expenditure review did emphasize the need to increase the numbers of staff in the health and education services (and to reduce military expenditure), this was based on aiming at 'a significant reduction in the average real wage paid' (World Bank, 1993: iii). The devaluation of the CFA Franc has automatically reduced average real wages in Burkina Faso.

in which the SAP has affected women in Burkina Faso since 1991, it is probably safe to conclude that the overall impact has been neutral. Gains in the possibilities of employment in the health and education sectors (or as agricultural extension workers if the ban on civil service recruitment in this sector is lifted), are outweighed by losses in terms of lower incomes and increasing prices of essential goods.

7. Environmental Trends and Issues

7.1 Environmental Action Plan

Since the severe droughts in the Sahel in the 1970s and early 1980s, the need to tackle environmental degradation has been foremost in many proposals for development strategies in the region. The issues are complicated, and there is (as noted above) a tendency to oversimplification in efforts to find answers to the problems of desertification, deforestation, soil erosion and so on. But at the same time, an increasing awareness of the difficulties of developing sustainable agricultural production systems in the harsh conditions of the semi-arid and savanna drylands of Burkina Faso and elsewhere in the Sahel, has encouraged efforts to understand the dynamics of 'complex, diverse and risk-prone' agriculture.

One of the manifestations of this awareness is in the form of environental action plans. However, sceptical observers suspect that little will come of these plans, which have been drawn up by governments (supported by the donors) in a number of West African countries in the past three to four years. Prior to the environmental action plans (drafted with World Bank backing), there were national plans to combat desertification (such as the *Plan National de Lutte Contre la Désertification*, which was backed by UNSO) and tropical forestry action plans (initiated by the FAO). Cynics argue that these plans are simply shopping lists presented to donors for further funding of forestry schemes and environmental protection programmes.

A national environmental action plan (PANE) was prepared in Burkina Faso in the early 1990s. Following extensive consultations with environmental specialists in various ministries, as well as with NGOs and researchers, it was adopted and approved by the government in 1991. Then, after the Rio (UNCED) conference in 1992 it was again revised. Meanwhile, a *cellule* (coordination unit) attached to the Ministry of Environment and Tourism prepared several comprehensive studies of possible environmental protection activities, culminating in the presentation of the PANE at a round table meeting of donors in January 1994 (Burkina Faso, 1993e). By this time, the action plan was considered an integral part of the adjustment process, although the World Bank appears to have limited its support to preparing 'a national program of environmental information management and an environmental skills development program' (World Bank, 1994a).[47]

One of the complications surrounding environmental planning concerns the way in which 'the environment' is often considered as a sector, similar to education, health or

---

[47] The overlap between sections of the PANE (Burkina Faso, 1993c) and the *Programme National de Gestion des Terroirs* (PNGT) is a source of some confusion. The PNGT, funded by the World Bank and other donors, and involving a host of NGOs and implementating agencies such as agricultural research institutions, is designed to improve the management of natural resources in the rural areas (see section 4.1, above).

agriculture. This has led to lengthy institutional and political debates, which tend to detract from the importance of tackling the acute environmental problems in the different sectors of the economy. As far as the Ministry of the Environment and Tourism was concerned, the round table meeting on the PANE at the beginning of 1994 was largely conceived as a means of gaining donor support for a series of forestry and water supply projects which had not otherwise been funded. But at the same time, the parliament has been examining stricter environmental legislation designed to deal with a wider range of issues such as protection measures and pollution control as well as toxic waste disposal and import regulations.

7.2   Forestry and Energy Issues

Traditionally, environmental problems in Burkina Faso have been dealt with by the forestry services. In the classical conception of Sahelian environmental degradation, the disappearance of vegetation, notably trees, has been given the leading role. There is no doubt that deforestation is a serious problem in the region, and the reasons are not hard to find.

It is estimated that the use of wood as domestic fuel accounts for around 90 percent of all energy consumption in Burkina Faso (Bassolet and Ouédraogo, 1994: 42; World Bank, 1994d: 28). Removal of the forest cover has accelerated with the growing demand for woodfuel, given that few substitutes are available, and that requirements have increased rapidly (particularly in the urban areas). Imported hydrocarbons and electric power provide the remaining 10 percent of energy used in Burkina Faso.

Deforestation is also caused by the clearance of land for cropping and by un-controlled grazing of cattle in certain areas of the country. But the demand for woodfuel in conjunction with rapid urban growth rates is one of the most significant factors. Unfortunately, the devaluation of the CFA Franc is likely to have a negative impact on efforts to conserve and replace forest resources in the country.

Already prior to the exchange-rate realignment, it was estimated that fuelwood prices were low in Ouagadougou and other urban centres, relative to the prices per unit of energy produced by other sources (notably imported gas and kerosene). With the devaluation, the prices of these imported energy sources have doubled, which in turn intensifies the demand for cheap substitutes, notably wood. Thus, without compensatory measures 'external adjustment' is likely to lead to further deforestation.[48]

An alternative source of energy, which is also being developed in Burkina Faso, is hydro-electricity. The establishment of a power grid, links to generation capacity in Ghana and Côte d'Ivoire, and the bringing on line of the supplies from the two major dams at Kompienga and Bagré in the south, may provide part of the solution to the energy supply deficit. Appropriate energy pricing policies must form an integral part of a sustainable environmental development strategy. But the key issue of pricing

---

[48] Bassolet and Ouédraogo (1994: 43) also suggest that an increase in the demand for locally produced grain (after the devaluation of the CFA Franc) may encourage further agricultural 'extensification', thereby leading to further depletion of forests and woodlands. However, with the adoption of certain fertilization techniques (as discussed in section 4.2, above), crop yields per hectare could increase. Successful introduction of such techniques may necessitate a serious re-evaluation of fertilizer subsidies, which could compensate for the negative environmental impact of the devaluation.

'traditional' energy sources is largely ignored in the Policy Framework Paper (World Bank, 1994a: 13-14), which focuses only on petroleum imports and further electricity grid linkages.

7.3   Pollution and Pesticides

Finally a few words about pollution and control of dangerous products are in order. As mentioned above (section 7.1) these issues have been included in the proposed environmental legislation which is an important part of policies to achieve sustainable economic growth. In the meantime, in the urban areas there is little effort to reduce air pollution from vehicle emissions, while production processes in manufacturing (textiles, etc.) are unchecked. These problems deserve far greater attention in costing policy reform. Improved regulation of water quality is also important.

A particularly serious issue in this respect concerns the dumping of dangerous pesticides. Like other Sahelian countries, Burkina Faso has been threatened by invasions of grasshoppers and locusts from the desert on several occasions in the past two decades. As a result, the crop protection services have made frequent appeals to the donor community for assistance. In general this help has been readily available, usually in the form of shipments of assorted chemicals which have been sprayed (often from the air) over areas suspected of pest infestation. The indiscriminate use of such pesticides represents a serious threat to the flora and fauna of the Sahel, and has also caused several cases of poisoning. Nevertheless, a large number of donor agencies have participated in this form of 'aid' and stocks of unused chemicals have accumulated.

The devaluation of the CFA Franc may encourage agricultural researchers in the Sahel to intensify the investigation of appropriate, non-toxic, 'integrated', pest management techniques, thereby minimizing the use of costly imports. Cotton cultivation in particular has relied on increasing quantities of chemical pesticides, often applied without sufficient protection and information about the dangerous side-effects. If 'external adjustment' can contribute to the development of farming systems in the Sahel which depend less on the use of 'external inputs' and more on sustainable production techniques ('low-input agriculture'), some of the drawbacks of intensification could be avoided.

8.   Concluding Remarks

In the 12 years since 1983, Burkina Faso has undergone three distinct phases of adjustment packages and processes. During the revolutionary period Sankara's CNR government implemented a development strategy which has been called *auto-ajustement* (Savadogo and Wetta, 1992), imposing the conditionalities associated with military rule in an attempt to encourage improvements in rural living standards and to shift resources into the agricultural sector. This populist revolution was fraught with contradictions, not least in terms of the role ascribed to a streamlined public sector and to the difficulties inherent in reconciling an ambitious political programme with the realities of economic (and ecological) fragility in an impoverished Sahelian country.

Tight controls were introduced on public spending, but private sector *opérateurs économiques*, constrained by the revolutionary zeal of the 'defence committees', did not respond to appeals to mobilize investment resources. Membership of the Franc zone (where monetary policy is controlled by the BCEAO and the French treasury) was also a significant constraint affecting the pursuit of an independent and 'self-reliant' development strategy. By 1987, steady accumulation of debt arrears and growing deficits in public finances (largely as a result of high levels of military expenditure) undermined the CNR government. In the end the political costs of 'self-imposed adjustment' proved too high, as opposition to austerity grew. But it is ironic to observe that much of the groundwork for later public sector reforms (emphasizing better health and education) and for efforts to devise strategies for sustainable agricultural development (through price policies, land reform and natural resource management schemes), was laid in the period from 1983 to 1987, without the backing of the international financial institutions.

State intervention, through controls over trade, marketing and investment, was reduced during the transition, as the *Front Populaire* government moved towards the adoption of a new constitution and the start of 'internal adjustment' in 1991. Public sector reform was at the core of this phase of adjustment, which entailed reallocation of government expenditure accompanied by the introduction of new taxes, by the abolition of most price controls and by the privatization of several state enterprises. In the negotiations between the government and the World Bank on the SAP package (and later with the IMF for ESAF loans) some lessons learnt from the 'popular and democratic revolution' and from adjustment programmes in other sub-Saharan African countries were applied, notably the inclusion of a 'social dimension' stressing further improvements in the provision of health and education services.

However, as economic performance in terms of revenue from exports (of cotton, animal products and gold) faltered, the increasing flows of grants and loans from the Bretton Woods institutions and other donors (in connection with sectoral programmes) could not compensate for the overvalued exchange rate. Imports increased during the first three years of the SAP, but domestic savings and investment levels remained weak. The attempt to raise public revenue through increased taxation was also a failure. While food-crop output increased in the early 1990s, this was not due to incentive policies in agriculture, but to good harvests following high levels of rainfall. Overall, the stagnating GDP growth rate and falling levels of private consumption indicated that living standards were getting worse.

The third phase of the adjustment process in Burkina Faso (and the other UEMOA countries in West Africa) is based on the assumption that 'external adjustment' (devaluation) will shift resources into the production of tradeable goods, thereby leading to greater export revenues (notably from agricultural products). The value of the CFA Franc was halved relative to the French Franc in January 1994. But in the medium and longer term, it is by no means certain that this devaluation will provide the expected stimulus to investment in agriculture and processing. Supply-side constraints in the form of poor infrastructure and the weaknesses of 'human capital', combined with the ecological difficulties associated with developing agriculture in 'complex, diverse and risk-prone' drylands, are significant obstacles.

In the short term, although it is expected that exports of cotton and livestock will increase, real incomes of some sections of the population have been adversely affected by the realignment of the exchange rate. Inflation rates shot up to around 35-40 percent in 1994 and the prices of imported agricultural inputs such as fertilizer doubled. With lower demand, it is anticipated that the rate of inflation will fall considerably; but in the meantime higher prices and reduced incomes also imply greater poverty.[49]

Assessing the results of these different phases of adjustment in Burkina Faso leads to the conclusion that there are two striking factors which seem to determine successes and failures in economic performance. Fluctuations in rainfall exert a decisive influence on the agricultural sector, which in turn affects the overall growth of the economy. Fluctuations in world cotton markets are also rapidly passed on to Burkinabè producers; as prices fell in the early 1990s there was a decline in farmers' incomes and export earnings.

The problem is that these factors, rainfall and world markets, are beyond regulation using the economic policy instruments available through the SAP in Burkina Faso. Trade liberalization and restrictions on government intervention (through ending fertilizer subsidies, for example) also expose producers to the full force of competitive markets. At the same time, with an increasing burden of debt repayment obligations, the margin for manoeuvre in terms of determining public investment priorities is limited. Adjustment seems to have become a 'donor-driven' process, where longer-term economic development objectives are sacrificed in the name of efficiency (cost reduction), and where only imports (or food aid) seem likely to increase.

What is to be done? Getting beyond adjustment, towards a sustainable and equitable growth track in Burkina Faso (and elsewhere in the Sahel), requires new attempts to invent a different future. In examining long-term trends in population (including migration), production systems, the dynamics of market integration and urban growth in West Africa, Snrech (1994) comes up with some useful indications of the main factors and processes in the development of the region. According to this perspective, far greater investment in better education and in the circulation of information, together with productivity increases in informal sector manufacturing and in improved farming techniques, are prerequisites. Furthermore, it is suggested that an important source of growth will be found in diversifying production and processing activities, particularly in the rapidly expanding urban areas, based on building up the capacity of small enterprises to absorb labour and provide employment.

Increasing regional integration, given existing patterns of migration and trade, is also stressed in this *etude des perspectives à long terme en Afrique de l'Ouest* (Snrech, 1994). Stewart (1991) also argues that in order to generate a regional growth process, greater integration (through trade and exchange) would be an important factor in moving from short-term adjustment to long-term development. In loosening the ties which have bound the Franc zone countries to France, the devaluation of the CFA Franc may turn out to be most effective in terms of encouraging commercial links between producers and consumers in Côte d'Ivoire, Ghana, Nigeria and the Sahelian countries; for example through the recapture of the coastal West African meat market from dumped European beef surpluses.

In Burkina Faso, performance in the agricultural sector remains the key to economic

---

[49] Dioné (1994) has attempted a preliminary survey of the distributional effects of 'external adjustment' on incomes in selected rural and urban communities in the Sahel. In describing the effects of an 'orthodox' approach to devaluation, Tarp (1993: 39-41) points out that 'switching' into the production of tradeable goods depends on 'critical price and wage relationships' which are 'the outcome of complex economic and political forces.' He adds: 'If a devaluation raises prices, but nominal wages lag behind, the result is a distributional shift from wage to profit earners. This may easily cause a fall in demand for non-traded goods and an increase in import demand due to differences in the propensity to consume' (*ibid.*: 40).

growth. During the various phases of adjustment, the relationships between numerous determining factors, not only rainfall and cotton prices, have become apparent. The search for appropriate forms of land tenure and the introduction of management schemes to reverse land degradation, as well as the reform of support and extension services, have all figured in the policy debates. But as Gubbels (1992: 92) notes, getting beyond short-term adjustment (as defined in the PASA with its 50-point agenda for reform) will entail exploring a range of 'viable strategies for agrarian change'. This process will take time, and involve further conflicts of access to, and control over, resources (water, land and vegetation). Recognizing the range of approaches to agricultural development thereby broadening the 'options for intensification of production systems in semi-arid zones' (Mortimore, 1995) is also important:

> The contradictions of state interests in African agriculture, their strategies of governance, and the diversity of farmers' responses have meant that the overall effect of state intervention on rural economic life has been intrusive and disruptive, rather than hegemonic. Farmers have not been able to escape the presence of the state, nor have they necessarily wanted to: gaining access to resources and opportunities often means working through as well as around the system. But 'the system' is far from monolithic. Individuals and agencies struggle for influence and resources within the state as well as outside it, and outcomes are not fully determined by any single set of interests (Berry, 1993: 64).

In this spirit, an optimistic conclusion about the prospects for the post-adjustment period in Burkina Faso can be reached. If adaptability and the capacity for negotiation can be maintained, then the (dwindling) financial resources available from the aid donors can be more effectively channelled into strengthening indigenous institutions, rather than enforcing 'external' models of adjustment. With the consolidation of an *état de droit*, the government will be able to play a decisive role in allocating resources and in establishing a legal framework for the resolution of conflicting demands on these resources, as well as the fiscal basis for ensuring a more equitable distribution of income.

References

Atampugre, N. 1993. *Behind the Lines of Stone - the social impact of a soil and water conservation project in the Sahel*. Oxford: Oxfam.

Bassolet, B. & J. Ouédraogo. 1994. 'Programme d'ajustement structurel en Afrique - l'expérience du Burkina Faso'. Draft. CEDRES, Université de Ouagadougou.

Berry, S. 1993. *No Condition is Permanent - the social dynamics of agrarian change in sub-Saharan Africa*. Madison, WI: University of Wisconsin Press.

Breman, H. & O. Niangado. 1994. 'Maintien de la production agricole sahélienne (rapport mi-chemin du projet PSS)'. Rapports Production Soudano-Sahélienne 6. Bamako & Wageningen: IER/AB-DLO.

Burkina Faso. 1988. 'Plan céréalier du Burkina Faso, phase I, diagnostique - bilan et annexes'. Ouagadougou: CILSS

Burkina Faso. 1990a 'Plan Quinquennal, 1991-95 - Secteur agriculture et élevage (avant projet)'. Ouagadougou: MAE.

Burkina Faso. 1990b. 'Plan céréalier du Burkina Faso - le plan d'action'. Ouagadougou: MAE & CILSS.

Burkina Faso. 1992. 'Programme d'ajustement structurel du secteur agricole - Rapport général de synthèse (avec annexes)'. Ouagadougou: MARA.

Burkina Faso. 1993a. 'Lettre de politique de développement agricole (LPDA) - Programme d'ajustement structurel du secteur agricole'. Ouagadougou: MARA.

Burkina Faso. 1993b. 'Troisième séminaire national sur la réorganisation agraire et foncière - rapport général'. Ouagadougou: Ministère des Finances et du Plan.

Burkina Faso. 1993c. 'Les grandes orientations en matière de gestion des terroirs au Burkina Faso'. Ouagadougou: Programme National de Gestion des Terroirs (MARA).

Burkina Faso. 1993d. 'Situation d'exécution du PAS'. Ouagadougou: Secrétariat Technique Permanent du Programme d'Ajustement Structurel, Ministère des Finances et du Plan.

Burkina Faso. 1993e. 'Stratégie du Plan d'Action National pour l'Environnement - document de base (consultation sectorielle sur l'environnement)'. Ouagadougou: Ministère des Finances et du Plan.

Burkina Faso. 1994. 'Instrument automatisé de prévision'. Ouagadougou: Secrétariat Technique Permanent du Programme d'Ajustement Structurel, Ministère des Finances et du Plan.

Coussy, J. & Ph. Hugon (eds.). 1991. *Intégration régionale et ajustement structurel en Afrique sub-Saharienne*. Etudes et Documents. Paris: Ministère de la Coopération et du Développement.

Danchurchaid. 1993. 'Etude des programmes d'appui institutionnel à la gestion des banques de céréales de la FUGN et de la FONADES au Burkina Faso - rapport final (Danagro Adviser)'. Copenhagen: Danchurchaid.

DANIDA. 1994. Report on round table consultations: 'Plan d'Action National pour l'Environnement' (PANE) and 'Programme d'Ajustement du Secteur Agricole' (PASA), Ouagadougou (18-21 January 1994). Copenhagen: Ministry of Foreign Affairs.

DANIDA/DGIS. 1994. Evaluation de l'aide en engrais du Danemark et des Pays-Bas au Burkina Faso - rapport final (Danagro Adviser & Netherlands Economic Institute). Copenhagen and The Hague: Ministère des Affaires Etrangères/Directorat Générale pour la Coopération Internationale.

Devey, M. & Z. Lingane. 1993. 'Dossier - Burkina Faso', *Marchés Tropicaux et Méditerranéens*, 2467.

Dioné, J. 1994. 'Impact de la dévaluation du Franc CFA sur l'agriculture, les échanges et la sécurité alimentaire au Sahel'. Working Paper DT94-03. Bamako: Institut du Sahel (CILSS/PRISAS).

FAO/UEMOA. 1994. 'Etude de l'impact de la dévaluation du FCFA sur la compétitivité des productions rizicoles dans les pays du l'UEMOA'. Rome: Investment Centre FAO/Banque Ouest Africaine de Développement.

Farrington, J. *et al.* 1993. *Reluctant Partners? Non-governmental Organisations, the State and Sustainable Agricultural Development*. London: Routledge.

Fauré, A. 1991. 'La panthère est l'enfant d'un génie - réflexions sur le traitement d'une crise villageoise pendant la révolution burkinabè'. *Politique Africaine*, 44.

Faye, J. 1990. 'Le control privé permet-il une meilleure gestion des ressources naturelles? Paper presented to conference on the future of agriculture in the Sahel (Montpellier), Club du Sahel/CILSS. Paris: OECD.

Fontaine, J-M. 1987. 'Evolving economic policies and disinvolving states - notes in an African context'. *IDS Bulletin*, 18-4.

Gubbels, P. 1992. 'Farmer first research, populist pipedream or practical paradigm? - prospects for indigenous agricultural development in West Africa'. Unpublished MA dissertation, University of East Anglia, Norwich.

Helleiner, G. 1994. 'From adjustment to development in sub-Saharan Africa - conflict, controversy, convergence, consensus?' In G. Cornia & G. Helleiner (eds.): *From Adjustment to Development in Africa*. Basingstoke: Macmillan.

Igué, J. 1993. 'Les femmes et le secteur informel en Afrique de l'Ouest'. Paper presented at UNESXO Regional Workshop on women in the informal sector. Cotonou: UNESCO.

IMF. 1993a. 'Burkina Faso - Document cadre de politique économique et financière pour la période janvier 1993 - décembre 1995'. Washington, DC: IMF.

IMF. 1993b. 'Burkina Faso - Staff report for the 1992 Article IV consultation and request for arrangements under the Enhanced Structural Adjustment Facility'. Washington, DC: African Department & Policy Development and Review Department, IMF.

IMF. 1993c. 'Burkina Faso - recent economic developments'. Washington, DC: African Department, IMF.

IMF. 1994. 'Burkina Faso - Staff report for the 1994 Article IV consultation and midterm review of the second annual arrangement under the Enhanced Structural Adjustment Facility'. Washington, DC: African Department & Policy and Review Department, IMF.

Jacob, J-P. & M-J. Nsengiyuma. 1994. Country desk study - Burkina Faso (Poverty assessment and public expenditure studies for SPA working group). Geneva & Brighton: Institut Universitaire d'Etudes au Développement/Institute of Development Studies.

Kabeya-Muase, C. 1989. 'Un pouvoir de travailleurs peut-il être contre les syndicats?', *Politique Africaine*, 33.

Kitching, G. 1990. *Development and Underdevelopment in Historical Perspective* (2nd edition). London: Routledge.

Konaté, L. & R. Matha Sant'Anna. 1988. 'Ajustement structurel et remuneration des fonctionnaires au Burkina', *CEDRES Etudes*, 24.

Kulibaba, N. & J. Holtzman. 1990. 'Livestock marketing and trade in the Mali/Burkina Faso - Côte d'Ivoire corridor'. (Report by Abt Associates). Washington, DC: USAID.

Labazée, P. 1988. *Enterprises et entrepreneurs du Burkina Faso*. Paris: Karthala.

Laclavère, G. *et al.* 1993. *Atlas du Burkina Faso*. Paris: Editions Jeune Afrique.

Martin, G. 1986. 'Idéologie et praxis dans la révolution populaire du 4 août 1983 au Burkina Faso', *Geneve-Afrique*, 24-1.

Mortimore, M. 1995. 'Population growth, agricultural expansion and natural resource degradation - an oversimplified causality?' Draft paper presented at Danish Sahel Workshop (January), Sønderborg.

Otayek, R. 1988. Burkina Faso - 'Quand le tambour change de rythme, il est indispensable que les dansers changent de pas', *Politique Africaine*, 28.

Otayek, R. 1992. 'The democratic 'rectification' in Burkina Faso'. In A. Hughes (ed.): *Marxism's Retreat from Africa*. London: Frank Cass.

Ouali, K. 1986. 'La dépendance en héritage au Burkina Faso - l'économie avant la révolution', *CEDRES-Etudes*, 16.

Reardon, T. 1993. 'Cereals demand in the Sahel and potential impacts of regional cereals protection', *World Development*, 21-9.

Reardon, T., T. Thiombiano & C. Delgado. 1989. 'L'importance des céréales non-traditionelles dans la consommation des riches et des pauvres à Ouagadougou', *Economie Rurale*, 190.

Reardon, T., C. Delgado & P. Matlon. 1992. 'Determinants and effects of income diversification amongst farm households in Burkina Faso', *Journal of Development Studies*, 28-2.

Sanon, S. *et al.* 1993. 'Impact de la suppression de la subvention des engrais au Burkina Faso'. Etude pour le Ministère de l'Agriculture et des Ressources Animales. Ouagadougou: MARA.

Savadogo, K. & C. Wetta. 1992. 'The impact of self-imposed adjustment - the case of Burkina Faso, 1983-89'. In G. Cornia, R. van der Hoeven & T. Mkandawire (eds.): *Africa's Recovery in the 1990s - from Stagnation and Adjustment to Human Development*. New York: UNICEF/St. Martin's Press.

Savadogo, K. & S. Larivière. 1993. 'Ajustement structurel et performance agricole - quelques leçons de l'expérience d'auto-ajustement au Burkina Faso'. Document 2, Projet d'Etude sur les Systèms et les Politiques Agro-Alimentaires au Burkina Faso. Ouagadougou: CEDRES/LAVAL.

Savonnet-Guyot, C. 1986. *Etat et société au Burkina Faso - essai sur la politique Africaine*. Paris: Karthala.

Scoones, I. (ed.). 1994. *Living with Uncertainty - New Directions in Pastoral Development in Africa*. London: Intermediate Technology Publications.

Sharp, R. 1990. *Burkina Faso - a New Life for the Sahel?* Oxford: Oxfam.

Snrech, S. 1994. *Pour préparer l'avenir de l'Afrique de l'Ouest - une vision à l'horizon 2000* (synthèse de l'étude des perspectives à long terme). Paris/Abidjan: Club du Sahel/CILSS, OCDE & Banque Africaine du Développement.

Speirs, M. 1991a. 'Markets, agriculture and adjustment in the Sahel - the political economy of cereals marketing and agrarian change in Burkina Faso'. Unpublished thesis, Royal Veterinary and Agricultural University, Copenhagen.

Speirs, M. 1991b. 'Agrarian change and the revolution in Burkina Faso'. *African Affairs*, 90-358.

Speirs, M. & O. Olsen. 1992. *Indigenous Integrated Farming Systems in the Sahel*. Technical Paper 179. Washington, DC: World Bank.

Stewart, F. 1991. 'Are adjustment policies in Africa consistent with long-term development needs?', *Development Policy Review*, 9-4.

Tallet, B. 1989. 'Le CNR face au monde rural - le discours à l'épreuve des faits'. *Politique Africaine*, 33.

Tarp, F. 1993. *Stabilization and Structural Adjustment - Macro-economic Frameworks for Analysing the Crisis in Sub-Saharan Africa*. London: Routledge.

Thiombiano, T., S. Soulama & C. Wetta. 1988. *Les systèmes alimentaires au Burkina Faso*. Research series 001. Ouagadougou: CEDRES.

Toulmin, C. 1991. 'Natural resource management at the local level - will this bring food security to the Sahel?', *IDS Bulletin*, 22-3.

UNDP. 1994. *Human Development Report, 1994*. Oxford: UNDP/Oxford University Press.

World Bank. 1989. 'Burkina Faso - memorandum économique'. Report 7594-BUR. Washington, DC: Regional Office for Africa, World Bank.

World Bank. 1991. 'Report and recommendation on a proposed development credit of SDR 60 million to Burkina Faso for a structural adjustment program (SAL I)'. Report P-5562-BUR. Washington, DC: World Bank.

World Bank. 1993. 'Burkina Faso - public expenditure review'. Report 11901-BUR. Washington, DC: World Bank.

World Bank. 1994a. 'Burkina Faso - Policy Framework Paper 1994-96'. Washington, DC: World Bank.

World Bank. 1994b. 'Memorandum on a country assistance strategy of the World Bank group for Burkina Faso'. Report P-13015-BUR. Washington, DC: World Bank.

World Bank. 1994c. *World Development Report, 1994*. Washington, DC and New York: World Bank/Oxford University Press.

World Bank. 1994d. 'Examen des politiques, stratégies et programmes du secteur energétique traditionnel (compte rendu de l'atelier de Ouagadougou)'. Washington, DC: African Technical Department, World Bank.

Yonli, E. 1993. 'Sécurité alimentaire et stratégies paysannes - la dynamique des banques de céréales dans le nord du Plateau Central du Burkina Faso'. In CIRAD (ed.): *Finance et développement rural en Afrique de l'Ouest* (Actes du séminaire d'économie rural, CIRAD/CTA/USAID/Coopération Française). Montpellier: CIRAD.

Zabré, P. 1994. *Les politiques économiques du Burkina Faso - une tradition d'ajustement structurel*. Paris: Karthala.

Ghana
1983-94

Eboe Hutchful

Wayne State University

1. Introduction: Background to Adjustment

From the mid-1970s to the early 1980s a combination of economic mismanagement and internal and external shocks contributed to a deepening crisis in the Ghana economy. Exports declined sharply. Cocoa exports fell from 397,300 metric tonnes in 1975 to 246,500 metric tonnes in 1981. Ghana's share of total world production dropped correspondingly from 24.4 percent in 1974-75 to 15.4 percent in 1980-81. A similar decline occurred for mineral and timber exports. Current account deficits increased from C 70 million in 1976 to C 419 million in 1981, due at least partly to higher energy import costs. In the domestic economy there was similar contraction in industry and agriculture. The local manufacturing index plummeted from 100 in 1977 to 63.3 in 1981. Average capacity utilization was estimated at only 24 percent in 1981. The production of cereals and other agricultural staples also dropped sharply; between 1974 and 1982 the maize crop fell by 54 percent, rice by 80 percent, cassava by 50 percent and yams by 55 percent.

Table 1   Export Production (Volumes) 1975-81 (thousands units)

	1975	1976	1977	1978	1979	1980	1981
Cocoa (tonnes)	397.3	326.7	277.4	268.2	280.8	277.2	246.5
Timber (cubic meters)	623.0	565.0	586.0	591.0	285.0	185.0	222.0
Gold (kg)	16.3	16.5	15.0	12.5	11.1	11.0	10.6
Diamonds (carats)	233.3	228.3	194.7	142.3	122.6	114.9	836.4
Manganese (tonnes)	415.3	361.9	292.4	316.7	253.8	249.9	223.1
Bauxite (tonnes)	325.2	271.6	279.2	327.9	235.3	225.1	181.3

Source: Ghana Government, Quarterly Digest of Statistics, June 1984.

These negative developments could undoubtedly be blamed in part on internal and external shocks, namely rain failures and drought, the rise in petroleum import costs, and other 'imported' inflation. On the other hand, the international climate for Ghana's main exports in much of this period was on the whole much more favourable than in any period since the early 1950s: lower export volumes were more than offset by higher export values so that total export earnings actually rose. The main culprit was rather a series of large fiscal year deficits. Between 1975 and 1981 the total government deficit increased by 690 percent. Expenditure rose by 615 percent in current terms between fiscal year 1975-76 and 1981-82, while revenues increased by only 56 percent. These deficits were covered by heavy borrowing from the central bank with the result that money supply (money in circulation as well as demand deposits held by the banks) expanded by almost 1000 percent between 1975 and 1981. High levels of tax evasion and low tax effort on the part of government meant that in 1981 only about 5 percent of taxable GDP was collected. The effective rate of duty collection by government agencies actually declined from 22 percent in FY 1971-72 to 7.2 percent in 1975-76, against a nominal rate of 45 percent. The Cedi appreciated rapidly; by 1981 Ghana had the most overvalued currency in Africa by a large margin (May, 1985: 13).

Table 2   Index of Mining Production, 1977-81 (1977=100)

	1977	1978	1979	1980	1981
Gold	100	83.6	74.2	73.4	70.8
Diamonds	100	73.1	63.0	59.0	43.0
Manganese	100	108.3	86.8	85.7	76.5
Bauxite	100	117.4	84.3	80.9	65.2
Over-all Index	100	87.1	74.9	73.8	68.2

Source: Ghana Government, *Quarterly Digest of Statistics*, June 1984.

This combination of fiscal deficits and falling domestic and export production led to inflation and falling living standards. The rate of inflation rose to 116.3 percent in 1977, declined gradually to 54 percent in 1979 and 1980 before peaking at 123 percent in 1983. GDP per capita declined by a total of 19.7 percent in 1970-80 (about 2.2 percent per annum) and by 21.2 percent between 1980 and 1983 (or 7.7 percent annually). The index of real wages (1977=100) fell to 44 in 1980, 32 in 1983 and 39 in 1984 (UNICEF, 1987b: 98). In response to sharp reductions in living standards there was large-scale migration of Ghanaian professionals, technicians and skilled workers to neighbouring countries. A pervasive and inefficient system of administrative controls diverted economic activity to a large and thriving parallel market.

Before the adoption of the Economic Recovery Programme (ERP) deepening economic crisis in Ghana had gone hand in hand with a striking absence of systematic policy debate within the country as a whole. Nevertheless after the coup of December 31, 1981 which brought the PNDC to power two main conceptual approaches to economic reform emerged, identified respectively as 'structuralist' and 'monetarist'. 'Structuralists' may very broadly be defined as those who believed that the peculiar structures of the post-colonial Ghanaian economy, in particular its excessive 'openness' and dependence on primary commodity exports, were the cause of the country's past and present crisis. In their view the cause of the economic crisis was primarily external rather than internal. However, 'structuralism' had its variants - nationalist (radical and conservative), socialist, and technocratic - and broad support among a variety of social groups with varying ideological predispositions. While most structuralists advocated state intervention, a large public sector and administrative controls, some (such as J.H. Mensah, the Minister for Finance and Economic Planning in Busia's government) supported the development of a vigorous private sector. Ghana's difficulties with controls were not seen necessarily as failures of controls per se but as the result of governmental incompetence and corruption. Structuralists were particularly critical of devaluation. On the other hand, most structuralists had little to say about monetary and fiscal issues. In the hands of politicians 'structuralist' arguments could also degenerate easily into an excuse to avoid or defer reform.

'Monetarists' on the other hand came to be defined by their attitude to the Ghana crisis rather than by a comprehensive set of ideas. 'Monetarists' were those who advocated IMF-type policy prescriptions for reform. To 'monetarists' the main causes of the economic difficulties were internal and could be located in government deficits and inflation. They advocated monetary restraint, budget balancing, devaluation and trade liberalization to stabilize the economy and to relieve the pressure on the balance of payments. On the whole 'monetarists' were identified with the economic bureaucracy (the Finance Ministry and the Bank of Ghana) and to a lesser degree with domestic business (on the whole, given their import-substitution activities and dependence on imported inputs and tariff protection, many domestic businesses were at least ambivalent about devaluation and liberalization).

I have tried to argue elsewhere that the tension between 'structuralists' and 'monetarists' in the government was temporarily broken with the PNDC's 'Programme for Reconstruction and Development' (December 1982) which carefully attempted to marry structuralist objectives and monetarist approaches. This facilitated negotiation with the IMF and allowed the PNDC to proceed to devaluation and the initiation of the ERP in April 1983. Some degree of repression was subsequently used to consolidate the new programme against remaining opponents (particularly when it became clear that the regime had no intention of honouring the letter of the 'Programme'), but a more important factor in reducing resistance was the easing of the economic situation in 1984-85 and increasing evidence of success of the ERP. While structuralists remained sceptical, from this point on the main debate over the direction of reform turned to matters of precise content. Although there have been several persistent areas of disagreement between the Ghanaian adjustment management team and the Bank and the IMF (underlined by (sometimes) deliberate lapses in implementation (Toye, 1991; Martin, 1992)) many of these have revolved around specific policy and sector issues rather than the underlying thrust of the ERP. They include the future of COCOBOD, the speed and scope of divestiture of the state enterprises, the extent of liberalization of bank credit and interest rates, the desirability and degree of tariff protection for domestic industry, the pace and depth of devaluation in the early period of reform and the decompression of the salary structure. Many of them have also been internal to the Ghana team or between it and specific ministries.

However, some of the disagreements between the Ghanaian and Bank/Fund teams have concerned the general approach and to some degree touch on the limitations in the design of the ERP. In spite of a shared insistence on fiscal discipline the Ghanaians have leaned toward a more 'structuralist' and supply-oriented approach than Bank staff (and for this reason have also insisted on a more 'gradualist' approach). Ironically this 'structuralist' position has been most forcefully articulated by Dr. Abbey, the intellectual leader of the Ghanaian macroeconomic team and the individual in it considered closest to Bank and Fund policy positions. Abbey has been particularly (and, it appears, rightly) critical of the elasticity optimism of the Fund programming model (which assumes that domestic production will respond quickly in the short term to relative price changes both to substitute for imports and to boost exports) and advocated more vigorous intervention both to remove structural rigidities and to restore market forces in the medium rather than short term. In Abbey's view, far from being a showcase for

Fund-Bank prescriptions, Ghana's example 'clearly demonstrates that for the strategy [of adjustment] to be effective some very radical changes will have to take place in the thinking and formulation of adjustment programs by the Bretton Woods institutions' (Abbey, 1989; Abbey, 1991: 523).

In this context the Ghanaian programme raises interesting issues of 'ownership'. Under the ERP, use of conditionality has been lavish (if not always effective), as has been the resort to cross-conditionality. The second Import Reconstruction Credit (RIC II) contained 42 separate 'monitorable targets' (some with several sub-targets); the first and second structural adjustment credits expanded this to 88, and the agricultural sector adjustment credit of 1992 had 40. This is not necessarily as oppressive as it may appear, since many of the conditionalities in the various aid documents referred to the same targets or were repeated or reaffirmed in subsequent documents (a possible indication - as Toye argues - that they were being ignored) and many of them also reflected the view of the Ghanaian authorities. But many as obviously did not. While it is true that the Ghanaian macroeconomic team had a mind of its own, it was operating under severe political, technical, and tactical disadvantages, which forced it to succumb even when it was convinced of the impracticality of the policy prescriptions being proposed. The critical shortage of Ghanaian technical staff also led to high levels of dependence on World Bank and Fund missions and technical personnel. Fund/Bank staff handled a lot of the policy and technical work required by the ERP. This included the Policy Framework Papers, which were prepared annually beginning in 1987 and which had very little Ghanaian input, even though they were supposed to be a tripartite effort; the Human Development Strategy (developed from the UNDP *Human Development Report* and published in 1987); the Accelerated Growth Strategy 1993-2000 (Ghana and the World Bank) as well as the initial design of PAMSCAD. In addition there was heavy reliance on consultants (mainly foreign but some domestic as well) and technical assistance.[1] This ambiguity was also reflected in matters of nomenclature. As Dr. Abbey himself noted, 'there seems to be some argument about whose programme the Ghanaian Economic Recovery Programme is. Some of us in Ghana, of course, think the programme is ours, but frequently it is referred to as the ESAF Program or Ghana SAL I or SAL II' (Abbey, 1991: 524).

Thus, a perception could not be completely avoided that the ERP was to a large degree 'foreign' inspired. Within Ghana itself both protagonists and antagonists of adjustment see the ERP, rightly or wrongly, as at least decisively influenced if not actually designed by the IMF and the Bank. What turned out to be important, however, was what this implied for the perceived legitimacy of the programme. For the business community and those who support the ERP but opposed or distrusted the PNDC one of the key attractions of the programme was precisely the control that it was thought to impose on the government, in terms both of policy and political conduct.[2] For the unions and others critical of the programme, however, it was the agreement with the IMF and the Bank which diverted the PNDC from its original progressive nature. To describe the ERP as 'the IMF and World Bank adjustment programme', as the TUC for instance persisted in doing, was to call into question the very legitimacy of the

---

[1] Partial data on technical assistance are available in the UNDP series *Ghana: Development Cooperation*, UNDP, Accra.

[2] This was acknowledged in interviews with some members of the macroeconomic team in Accra.

programme. Thus for the government, asserting that the ERP was the PNDC's own programme became crucial to recovering its legitimacy.[3]

However, ownership by the government does not imply ownership by the nation or society. One of the key (and undoubtedly most disturbing) issues posed by the ERP has been the very different levels of openness and accountability that characterized the relations between the Ghanaian management team and the donors and the multilaterals on the one hand, and the lack of dialogue and accountability that characterized the domestic posture of the same team, and in general the PNDC, on issues of economic reform. As I have argued elsewhere, the PNDC adopted a deliberate stance of autonomy meant to limit its exposure to and possible constraints emanating from all major social groups (including the bureaucracy), and the success of this strategy was reflected to a large degree in its remarkable ability to maintain a course of rigorous reform. Unfortunately limiting consultation and local input in the design of reform, as well, in general, as limiting public information and participation (beyond supportive 'NGO' types of involvement) was also part of this strategy. Ghanaian research institutes (such as the Institute for Social, Statistical, and Economic Research - ISSER - at the University of Ghana) are only recently coming in from the cold. The cost of this was that while the government was able to persuade the nation that reform was in its interest (and even earn respect on that account), it was unable to attract any great degree of comprehension, enthusiasm, or commitment to reform. Particularly given the magnitude of reform (a scale not anticipated at the beginning of the process by any of the parties) it is fair to say that ordinary Ghanaians have been less empowered than disempowered by the process.

2.   The Adjustment Agenda

Adjustment policy in Ghana has evolved through three phases.
ERP I (1983-86) consisted of a) a stabilization package designed to reduce inflation and achieve external equilibrium, and b) a programme to promote economic growth and export recovery through a realignment of incentives toward productive activity and the rehabilitation of economic and social infrastructure. The main policy initiatives were as follows:

Exchange-Rate Reform: From April 1983 to 1986 the Cedi was devalued through a series of large discrete devaluations from C 2.75 to one US$ to C 160.00 to the US$, in order to bring it closer to the free market rate. The official and free market exchange rates for the Cedi were then unified in three stages at the same time as transactions in foreign exchange were liberalized. The first stage, commencing in September 1986, introduced a second-tier official market covering virtually all international transactions other than cocoa, petroleum, essential drugs and government debt-service payments on debts incurred prior to 1 January 1986. The second-tier rate was determined in weekly

---

[3] For this reason Rawlings has insisted repeatedly that the programme is Ghana's and not the Fund's or the Bank's. As he told one journalist, 'we went in [to the IMF] with our program already prepared'. *Ghanaian Chronicle*, 19-25 April 1993: 1, 12.

auctions at which only the public sector and private importers of non-consumables (though not importers of consumer items under the Special Import Licence), could compete. The second stage, initiated in February 1987, abolished the two-tier system and merged the two markets on the basis of the auction rate. Private foreign-exchange bureaux were licensed in February 1988 to deal in foreign currency and were given the freedom to determine buying and selling rates independently of the auction rate. Access to the auction was progressively expanded and by the end of 1990 included all current account transactions. At the end of 1990 the two markets (the official auction and the bureaux) were merged. At the same time, with a few minor exceptions, all controls on international payments were lifted.

Price Decontrol: Changes in the exchange rate of the Cedi were supported by substantial upward revisions in import and export prices, the abolition of price and distribution controls, and repricing of government goods and services. The list of essential consumer items subject to price control was reduced from 23 to 17 in 1984, then further to eight items and then phased out altogether. The objective of the exchange-rate and price reforms was to 'shift incentives further from trading and rent-seeking activities to production .. to permit producers to obtain a larger share of scarcity rents and to enable them to generate the liquidity necessary for expansion of production'.[4] Major increases in the nominal Cedi prices of exports (particularly cocoa) followed the exchange-rate adjustments.

Monetary and Fiscal Policies: These included strict credit ceilings, increases in interest rates with the objective of reaching positive interest rates, and a set of measures designed to increase tax revenues, broaden the tax base, shrink the budget deficit and reduce reliance on the banking system. These measures included reductions in current expenditures through a discontinuation of public subsidies, repricing of government services, and public sector retrenchment. An important aspect of this exercise was reform of the tax structure to increase revenue mobilization and reduce the tax burden and the reliance on cocoa taxes. Company tax rates were lowered from 55 percent to 45 percent for most sectors and then from 45 to 35 percent for non-financial institutions and 40 percent for financial institutions. Income tax rates were also lowered (from an upper marginal tax of 55 to 25 percent) while extending the taxation net to include previously untaxed allowances and benefits. Import tariffs were also restructured to offer a lower and more uniform pattern of protection and to eliminate concessions on an institutional basis.

Export Sector Rehabilitation Programme: this was designed to rehabilitate the export sectors by relieving supply and input bottlenecks, concentrating initially on cocoa, gold mining, and timber and supported by several IDA credits and bilateral grants. Two of the key ingredients in this programme were the improvement of producer incentives and an export-earning retention scheme that permitted certain exporters to retain a proportion of their foreign-exchange proceeds (45 percent in the case of the Ashanti Goldfields Corporation and 20 percent in the case of the state mining companies). The producer price for cocoa was raised successively from C 12,000 per ton in 1982-83 to C 140,000 in the 1987-88 season and subsequently to C 251,000 per ton and C 308,000

---

[4] *West Africa*, 13 January 1986, p. 78.

per ton in the 1989-90 and 1992-93 seasons respectively (the 1995 price is C 780,000 per metric ton). A key objective was the reform of the State Cocoa Marketing Board (COCOBOD) in order to reduce its operating costs as a share of total cocoa revenue.

Public Sector Investment Programme (PIP): From 1986 the rehabilitation of the economic and social infrastructure was carried forward through a rolling three-year Public Sector Investment Programme, with the objective of removing infrastructural bottlenecks impeding supply response.

Almost 75 percent of the PIP in 1986-88 was funded by external inflows; in 1988-90 external inflows accounted for 69 percent and in 1990-92 62 percent.

ERP II (June 1987-July 1990) inaugurated the adjustment phase proper and was formulated to deepen the ongoing reforms and to attack continuing weaknesses in the economy. It involved a medium-term policy framework aimed at 'establishing a firm foundation for a buoyant, self-reliant, and increasingly integrated economy, and to maintain a viable external payments position over the medium term' (Policy Framework Paper, 1987-90). It had three basic objectives: (a) to achieve an average annual rate of growth of real GDP of the order of 5 percent, thus improving real per capita income by 2 percent. To accomplish this it was planned to increase the domestic savings rate from 10 percent to 15 percent of GDP in 1990 and the investment ratio from 12 percent of GDP in 1986 to 18 percent in 1990; (b) to lower the average annual rate of inflation from 25 percent in 1986 to 8 percent in 1990; and (c) to generate significant overall balance of payments surpluses, averaging about US$110 m. per annum. Starting from 1987 macroeconomic policy was embodied in a Policy Framework Paper which was updated annually.

Under ERP II a number of ambitious structural and institutional reforms were launched. These included reforms in the financial sector, the state enterprises, the education sector, the civil service and PAMSCAD, as well as background work for the Medium-Term Agricultural Development Programme. These structural and sector reforms are discussed below. Macroeconomic actions taken under ERP II included the unification and further liberalization of the exchange rate and international and trade payments system which commenced under ERP I (see above), further reform of personal- and corporate taxes, and final elimination of subsidies on fertilizers and cocoa inputs in 1990. Some of the important policy and institutional measures taken in this period were: legislation to encourage and regulate small-scale mining (following the adoption earlier in 1986 of a new Minerals and Mining Law); a new Banking Law in 1989 and new regulations for establishing and supervising savings and loans companies; the establishment of the Ghana Stock Exchange Company in November 1990, and the passage of a new Investment Code (Benefits to Existing Enterprises), (further amended in 1992) reduced the areas reserved for Ghanaian enterprise from twenty to four, together with initiatives to overhaul and liberalize the legal framework regulating business (with the assistance of the Private Sector Advisory Group set up in 1991); and finally liberalization of the internal marketing of cocoa and the establishment in 1989 of the Export Finance Company Limited to fund the export of non-traditional commodities.

ERP III Since 1993 the official objective has shifted from 'economic recovery' to 'accelerated growth'. The Accelerated Growth Strategy (AGS), published in 1993

(Ghana Government 1993) emphasizes sustainable development and poverty alleviation through private sector development. The AGS aims at a growth rate of 8 percent per annum, reduction of the inflation rate to 5 percent by the year 2000, increases in the domestic savings from 10 to 21 percent and in investment from an estimated 19 percent of GDP in 1993 to 26 percent by the year 2000, and a rise in the tax/GDP ratio from 13 percent to 17-18 percent (based on the introduction of a VAT). The AGS stresses the strengthening of inter-sectoral linkages (in particular through agro-industry), poverty reduction through labour-intensive and high productivity activities, enhanced access of the poor to social services through restructuring of public expenditure and decentralization, further reforms in human resource development (particularly primary education and health), capacity building and public sector management and private sector development. The lending strategy of the World Bank is shifting correspondingly from general adjustment credits to a greater emphasis on sector investment lending.

3.   Macroeconomic Performance under the ERP

The basic macroeconomic situation after just over a decade of adjustment is that, while real GDP has grown encouragingly, savings and investment levels remain worryingly low while the trade and current account balances have significantly worsened. The fiscal balance was apparently stabilized until 1991, but since then two successive deficits have been recorded.

Performance in the fiscal area was generally impressive until 1992. Government revenue as a share of GDP rose from 5.3 percent in 1983 to 14.4 percent in 1986 and averaged 14.5 percent before declining to 12 percent in 1992. With external grants and other inflows revenue rose to over 16 percent of GDP in 1986 and averaged 15.7 percent between 1988 and 1992. In turn this has facilitated a strong recovery of real expenditure, even before taking into account external inflows. Total expenditures rose from about 7 percent of GDP in 1983 and averaged 14 percent between 1987 and 1991 before rising sharply to almost 17 percent in 1992 as a result of the large increase in civil service salaries and other expenditure. At the same time the persistent deficits in the recurrent budget turned into a small surplus from 1986: thereafter the fiscal balance remained in surplus until 1992, when a large deficit (equivalent to almost 5 percent of GDP) was realized. This is impressive given the background of budgetary deficits in African generally, measuring on average about 8 percent of GDP (Roe and Schneider, 1992: 88). As a proportion of GDP public savings increased from 3.8 percent in 1983 to an average of 5.5 percent between 1988 and 1991 (before declining to 0.7 percent in 1992). This has allowed the government to progressively retire first its short-term trade arrears and then its indebtedness to the domestic banking system.

Gross national savings as a proportion of GDP rose from 3.5 percent in 1983 to 13 percent in 1989 and about 12.3 percent in 1991, a sizeable jump but still below earlier achievements. Once more, a decline was registered in 1992 and 1993. Domestic savings net of foreign inflows increased from 3 percent of GDP in 1983 to almost 10 percent in 1989 and averaged 9 percent between 1988 and 1991 before again declining in 1992 and 1993.

Possibly the strongest single feature of the fiscal scene has been the recovery of external official inflows in connection with the ERP. Official grants and long-term concessional loans rose from the equivalent of less than 1 percent of GDP in 1983 to about 10 percent by 1990, facilitating a build-up of gross official reserves and gradual elimination of external payments arrears. Foreign savings made the strongest showing in the overall fiscal picture, reflecting the strongly positive net external inflows from 1987.

Gross national investment as a proportion of GDP rose from a historically low level of 3.7 percent in 1983 to about 16 percent in 1990. This recovery in investment levels has been generated primarily by the public sector, again reflecting the strength of external inflows. Public investment rose from about 1 percent of GDP in 1983 to 8 percent in 1988 and 7 percent by 1990; private investment stabilised at about 4 percent between 1983 and 1987 but expanded to about 9 percent in 1990, before falling again in 1992 and 1993.

Table 3   Selected Economic and Financial Indicators 1983-93

	1983	1986	1987	1988	1989	1990	1991	1992	1993
GDP (billion Cedis at current prices)	184	511	746	1051	1417	2032	2572	3009	3949
					(percent change)				
Real GDP	—	5.2	4.8	5.6	5.1	3.3	5.3	3.9	5.0
GDP Growth by Sector:									
Agriculture	—	3.3	0.0	3.6	4.2	-2.0	4.7	-0.6	2.5
Industry	—	7.6	11.5	7.3	2.6	6.9	3.7	5.8	4.3
Services	—	6.5	9.4	7.8	6.7	7.9	6.3	7.7	7.2
Per capita GDP		2.2	1.8	2.6	2.1	0.3	2.3	0.9	2.0
GDP composition by Sector:					(percent)				
Agriculture	60	48	48.4	47.4	47.1	44.6	44.4	42.5	41.6
Industry	7	—	14.1	14.4	14.0	14.5	14.3	14.0	14.5
Services	34	35	40.2	41.0	41.6	43.5	43.9	45.5	46.4
Consumer Price Index (per cent change)	123	24.6	39.8	31.4	25.2	37.2	18.0	10.1	25.0
Total Consumption (per capita change)	—	3.6	0.7	0.9	1.0	0.2		1.2	
					(percent GDP)				
Gross Savings	3.5	10.2	—	12.5	13.7	10.9	12.3	7.3	5.4
(Domestic Component)	3.0	—	—	9.1	9.5	7.9	9.2	4.1	1.2
Gross Investment	4.0	11.9	—	14.2	15.5	14.4	15.9	12.8	14.8
Public Savings	3.8	—	—	5.6	5.6	4.6	6.1	0.7	3.1
Private Savings	—	—	—	7.3	8.1	6.3	6.2	6.6	2.3
Public Investment	—	7.3	7.9	8.0	7.8	6.8	7.7	8.5	9.9
Private Investment	—	2.4	5.5	6.2	7.7	7.6	8.2	4.3	4.9

	1983	1986	1987	1988	1989	1990	1991	1992	1993
					(percent GDP)				
Revenue and Grants	5.3	14.4	14.9	14.5	15.1	13.2	15.2	12.1	18.0
Expenditure	7.0	14.3	14.3	14.2	14.4	13.0	13.7	16.9	17.6
Fiscal Balance	-1.8	0.1	0.5	0.3	0.7	0.2	1.5	-4.8	-2.5
Broad Money	38	54	53	43	26.9	18	19.9	52.9	53
Bank rate (December)	14.5	20.5	23.5	26.0	26.0	33.0	20.0	30	35
Exports (vol)			7.7	12.1	10.0	7.4	13.8	4.6	17.9
Imports (vol)			12.9	0.3	0.8	7.3	11.9	7.5	5.0
Terms of Trade			-6.9	-9.9	-17.2	-7.5	-0.1	-8.0	10.5
Trade Balance			-109.9	-110.0	-197.8	-308.2	-321.1	-470	-643
Current Account Balance[a]			-101.9	-89.5	-94.9	-215.3	-151.1	-373.2	-545
Capital Account Balance			255.0	217.8	222.4	284.0	391.5	274.0	630.3
Overall Balance			138.5	124.6	127.5	118	170.8	124.3	41.2
Debt Service Ratio Including IMF	46.6	47.1	58.3	68.3	58.1	37.0	29.8	25.8	36.5
Excluding IMF	42.5	37.8	31.8	34.0	32.5	21.6	18.8	18.2	29.7

Sources: IMF (for 1988-1993 data), World Bank and Ghana Government (for all other data).
[a]   Net, including official transfers.

At the root of the post-1991 fiscal problems have been spiralling wage demands and renewed labour militancy. Substantial salary increases to civil servants on the eve of the elections in 1992 raised the wage bill from C 119 bn in 1991 to C 173 bn in 1992. While revenue was falling, higher than anticipated outlays for domestic and external interest-rate payments led to total expenditure exceeding the programme level significantly. The resulting 1992 deficit was financed almost entirely from domestic sources, with the government borrowing C 103 bn from the domestic banking system and C 37 bn from the non-banking sector (net foreign funding of the budget was almost zero). Coupled with strong expansion of credit to the private sector (by 56 percent) broad money grew by 51 percent (against a programmed increase of only 12 percent) and inflation rose from 10 percent in 1991 to 27 percent. The balance-of-payments position also deteriorated sharply with lower earnings from cocoa and timber exports, due to both lower prices and lower than expected export volumes. The 1992 trade gap widened to US$470 m., and further to US$643 m. in 1993. In reaction to these missed targets the World Bank and other donors suspended disbursements, leading to a loss of external inflows of some US$170 m.

1993 programme targets negotiated under an agreement with the IMF called for a turn-around in the overall fiscal balance of over 5 percent of GDP, reduction of growth in money supply to zero (from 53 percent in 1992), lowering of the rate of inflation to 20 percent, increase in gross international reserves to the equivalent of 3.7 months of imports, and finally a real growth rate of 4.4 percent. In line with this the 1993 budget sought to restore macroeconomic stability, with a sharp increase in the petroleum tax and increased impetus to divestiture to generate revenues to finance the expenditure commitments which were responsible for the huge deficit in 1992. In the event, however, most of the programme's benchmarks were not observed, even though the real growth rate for 1993 was exceeded due largely to a good harvest resulting from favourable rains and strong output from the mining sector. The budget recorded an overall deficit of 2.5 percent of GDP, compared with a target surplus of 0.3 percent. Recurrent expenditure exceeded the target by over 2 percent of GDP (largely owing to unbudgeted costs incurred from contributions to ECOMOG, a salary advance to civil servants, and redundancy costs incurred by COCOBOD from the retrenchment of one third of its labour force) while tax collections fell short by a similar magnitude. The current account deficit widened sharply to 9 percent of GDP as against a programme target of 6 percent. Between end-June and end-December 1993 the value of the Cedi fell 34 percent relative to the dollar. The government attempted to contain the resurgence of inflationary pressures by raising the discount rate from 30 percent to 35 percent. In addition a temporary special reserve ratio of 15 percent was imposed on the banks over and above the secondary reserve ratio of 32 percent. Nevertheless broad money grew by 27 percent and the consumer price index more than doubled to 28 percent.

It is not likely that these renewed difficulties with macroeconomic management are a temporary phase. Rather they may prove to be a feature of a change in the political environment. While adjustment in the 1980s had occurred in an authoritarian political context that did not encourage consultation and accountability, the emergence of a more democratic political context since 1992 has encouraged a resurgence of labour militancy, with frequent threats of work stoppage. It is unlikely that this new round of militancy will disappear. Does that mean that Ghana's period of macroeconomic 'stardom' is over? While it is obviously too early at this stage to answer the question, what is clear is that the 'Accelerated Growth Strategy' has been embarked on under difficult circumstances, in relation to which its targets (particularly those on savings and investment) seem clearly ambitious.

This fiscal picture was accompanied initially by strong output recovery in both the domestic and external sectors. However, actual performance varied from sector to sector; it has also involved marked fluctuation and subsequent stagnation or decline in production levels in several sectors. Cocoa production rose from a low point of 159,000 tonnes in 1983-84 to 227,000 tonnes in 1986-87, dipped markedly to 188,000 tonnes in the following year, and recovered again to reach 300,000 tonnes in 1988-89 (see Table 4). The corresponding increases in cocoa exports reflected the coming into production of young trees and a virtual cessation of smuggling (Policy Framework Paper, January 1991). However, since 1989 there has been no further growth. Performance in manufacturing and in the mineral sector has been more consistent. Gold production increased from 10,200 kg in 1983 to 26,100 kg in 1991 and 40,700 kg in 1993, and in terms of export earnings from US$139.8 m. in 1987 to US$304 m. in 1991 and US$495 in 1993, overtaking cocoa as the leading export earner. Overall exports increased by an average of 11 percent by volume and 6 percent by value between 1987 and 1993 (see Table 4). Simultaneously there was a significant recovery of import capacity although much of this has of course been donor-funded. Import volumes more than doubled from a low of US$500 m. in 1983 to more than US$1663 m. in 1993. However, performance has been erratic: value increases in import volumes have fluctuated between 6 percent and 41 percent annually. Overall GDP growth averaged

5.2 percent per annum between 1987 and 1989 (after an initial spurt of 8.6 percent in 1984) but declined slightly to 4.4 percent in 1990-93.

Table 4   Functional Classification of Central Government Expenditure, 1987-93 (in millions of Cedis)

	1987	1988	1989	1990	1991	1992	1993
General Public Services	19,706	31,598	37,919	49,479	41,432	58,540	83,918
Defense	6,659	4,603	6,106	9,006	15,230	23,242	39,491
Public Order and Safety	—	—	—	—	17,155	21,479	30,838
Education	24,430	36,995	47,692	64,638	78,801	118,363	179,234
Health	8,457	12,880	19,853	25,706	28,654	39,450	56,639
Social Security and Welfare	6,554	9,904	14,379	18,389	23,884	34,630	57,752
Economic Services	19,045	25,754	33,124	38,282	54,773	82,691	129,721
Interest on Public Debt	10,587	11,961	18,744	27,316	42,828	61,004	134,778
Other	---	---	---	---	12,594	16,734	27,870
Special Efficiency	3,000	3,007	9,623	7,980	9,320	27,106	50,805
Total Expenditure	102,135	143,899	196,470	254,472	340,262	498,814	813,526
(As percentage of total government expenditure)							
Education	23.8	25.7	24.2	25.4	23.1	23.7	22.0
Health	8.2	9.0	10.1	10.1	8.4	7.9	7.0
Economic Services	18.6	17.9	16.8	15.0	16.1	16.6	15.9
(Agriculture, forestry and fishing)	4.5	3.4	4.6	4.1	3.6	3.9	3.5
Social Security and Welfare	6.4	6.9	7.3	7.2	7.0	6.9	7.0
(In percent of GDP)							
Education	3.3	3.5	3.4	3.2	3.1	3.9	4.5
Health	1.1	1.2	1.4	1.3	1.1	1.3	1.4
Economic Services	2.6	2.4	2.3	1.9	2.1	2.7	3.3
Social Security and Welfare	0.9	O.9	1.0	0.9	0.9	1.2	1.5

Source: IMF.

Although the success of the ERP was undoubtedly a key factor in its political sustainability, other factors intrinsic and extrinsic to the programme should also be borne in mind. First was the fact that in Ghana (unlike some African countries) the crisis had taken years to develop, and could clearly not be blamed on the ERP. In addition, survival strategies were already well entrenched (as was disengagement from the formal sector), shielding most households from the full effect of price changes in the formal sector. Because most consumers were already buying through the parallel market, the upward adjustment of official prices had relatively little effect on inflation and overall real price levels. Even the two shocks that almost threw the ERP off-course in 1983 - the drought and the expulsion of a million Ghanaian illegal immigrants from Nigeria - had a silver lining: the drought diverted blame for rising prices and hardships from the ERP, while the returnees from Nigeria are credited with the strong expansion in cultivated acreage that was to help bring food prices down dramatically in 1984.

Secondly, further reduction in social services and wages was not required in the programme. As Roe and Schneider (1992) have remarked, the Ghana programme has been one of the few in which expenditure on social services (and to some extent wages) actually increased substantially rather than declined. Significant improvements in tax collection and strong external inflows meant that both public savings (at least to 1991) and expenditures went up, as did investment in both economic and social sectors. In spite of redeployment, recurrent expenditure for civil service wages went up significantly (and was in fact the most rapidly growing item in recurrent expenditure).

Third, at the political level there was a widespread consensus among all the important social and political groups that reform was necessary, although there was disagreement as to what form this should take. And although once the ERP was under way it stirred up some opposition, none of the important groups critical of the ERP, such as the trade unions and the left, had a credible policy alternative. Clearly the large volumes of external inflows after years of virtual cessation of aid also played a major role in rallying support to the programme, although the continued dependence on such flows has since become one of the worrisome features of the programme.

Another aspect of the Ghana economy greatly aided the process of stabilization. This was the fact that it had already contracted severely both in terms of public expenditures and real production levels. The large spare capacity that existed throughout the economy meant that relatively large marginal increases in production were possible on the basis on modest improvements in inputs. Even more important was how this shaped the approach to stabilization. The severe contraction suggested that stabilization could not be approached without a strong focus on supply-side issues, in particular the decompression of imports and the rehabilitation of infrastructure.

As already mentioned, while growth has generally been good, certain aspects of the macroeconomic situation raise doubts about the long-term sustainability of economic recovery, and especially concerning Ghana's capacity to move onto a higher growth plane. Savings and investment rates remain low, particularly in the private sector. While the investment ratio had improved appreciably by 1988 (to 14 percent of GDP) it still lagged behind the average for Sub-Saharan Africa (19 percent) and even more for Africa as a whole (20 percent) and was only slightly higher than prevailing levels in the 1970s. It has not moved beyond this level subsequently. In particular foreign private inflows have been negligible, with the qualified exception of the mining sector. Low savings mobilization as well as constraints in the banking sector and strict credit limits have hindered supply response from the private sector.

After initial success in controlling upward price movements (inflation fell from a drought-inspired level of 123 percent in 1983 to only 10 percent in 1985) inflation re-emerged and persisted in excess of target, rising to over 40 percent by mid-1987. It then fell to 10 percent in 1992 before rising again to 25 percent in 1993. Even without wage pressure, inflation has proved difficult to tame owing to the continuing sharp deterioration in the value of the Cedi, recurring poor harvests (as in 1990), higher import (especially petroleum) prices, and rapid growth in broad money as a result of strong external inflows.

Also, while fiscal performance has been generally impressive new elements of fragility have emerged in the revenue base. Overdependence on cocoa has been replaced by overdependence on petroleum tax. As a share of total revenue petroleum tax moved from about 8.4 percent in 1986 to about 22 percent in 1993 while that of cocoa dropped from 17.8 percent in 1986 to about 5.3 percent in 1993. The corporate share of total collected revenue fell from 10.1 percent in 1984 to 8.1 percent in 1993, owing to incentive tax rate reductions, falling profitability margins and narrowed corporate tax base. Tax revenues from imports have risen from 13.3 percent in 1984 to 20.5 percent of total revenues in 1993. Export taxes, however, fell from 21 percent in 1984 to little more than 5 percent of total revenues in 1993 (due largely to the falling fiscal role of cocoa in the economy) (Tsikata and Amuzu, 1993: 5-6, 12; Ghana Government, 1994).

There are also structural problems relating to growth prospects. Beginning from 1986 the price of cocoa plummeted on the world market, declining from £ sterling 2113 per metric ton in 1985 to £ 1567 in 1986 and further to £ 911 in 1989 on the London spot market. It has not significantly recovered since. Nor have the long-term difficulties which this has induced been relieved by changes in the structure of overall output. The shape of the Ghana economy remains much the same in 1994 as it did in 1984 (except for an expansion of the importance of services at the expense of food-crop agriculture) even if it is in much better health. Hence it remains extremely vulnerable. Overall Ghana's terms-of-trade index (1985=100) declined from 103 in 1987 to 71 in 1990 and an estimated 58 in 1993, reflecting falling prices for commodities other than cocoa as well cocoa itself (Table 5).

The 1989 Policy Framework Paper (PFP) correctly identified the constraints to further growth that were emerging in the Ghana economy. These observations were repeated with yet greater urgency in the Policy Framework Paper of 1991:

> In fact, the experience of 1989 and 1990, particularly the intensified inflationary pressures and the impact of the oil price shock, have accentuated the importance of addressing more forcefully in the period ahead a number of structural, institutional and financial problems which continue to confront the Ghana economy.

The measures proposed to deal with the structural problems remain largely ineffective, though. They mainly consist of attempting to provide adequate bank credit to the private sector through mobilizing domestic savings through positive real interest rates and restructuring of distressed banks, while limiting overall monetary expansion to a level consistent with overall macroeconomic stability. It is worth asking whether in this context macroeconomic reform in itself can be expected to elicit a significant or sustainable supply response,[5] and whether more generally there has been an appropriate balance between macroeconomic management on the one hand and attention to issues

---

[5] As indicated earlier, this was one of the main theoretical issues debated between the Ghanaian team and the Fund and Bank.

of the real economy on the other. These are problems not only of policy design but of politics. A structural distance has existed within the Ghana programme between 'adjustment cadres' and enterprise managers (a distance which industrialists have been particularly vocal in complaining about). This has arguably led to excessive focus on macroeconomic aggregates and correspondingly little attention to (or grasp of) sector and enterprise level issues. But the key problem stemmed from basic conflicts within the ERP itself between macroeconomic targets and the objectives of enterprise adjustment.

Table 5   External Trade Indices, 1987-93 (1985=100)

	1987	1988	1989	1990	1991	1992 Est	1993 Est.
Exports							
Price Index	109.7	104.6	87.2	90.0	88.0	83.2	73.9
Percentage change	2.3	-4.7	-16.6	3.3	-2.2	-5.5	-11.1
Volume Index	118.8	133.2	146.6	157.5	179.3	187.6	224.9
Percentage change	7.5	12.1	10.0	7.4	13.8	4.6	19.9
Value Index	130.3	139.3	127.8	141.8	157.8	156.0	166.2
Percentage change	10.0	6.9	-8.2	10.9	11.2	-1.1	6.6
Imports							
Price Index	106.5	112.8	113.6	126.8	124.1	127.5	126.6
Percentage change	10.0	5.8	0.8	11.6	-2.2	2.7	-0.7
Volume Index	130.6	130.9	112.2	141.5	158.3	170.2	203.3
Percentage change	15.8	0.3	14.3	26.1	11.9	7.5	19.4
Value Index	139.1	147.6	127.5	179.5	196.4	217.0	257.4
Percentage change	27.3	6.1	-13.6	40.7	9.4	10.5	18.6
Terms of trade	102.9	92.7	76.7	71.0	70.9	65.2	58.4
Percentage change	-6.9	-9.9	-17.2	-7.5	-0.1	-8.0	-7.7

Sources: Ghanaian Government and IMF staff estimates.

This included the rate of depreciation of the Cedi (which was positive for government revenues but priced foreign exchange almost out of reach of most enterprises),[6] tight credit and high interest rates, withdrawal of subsidies and repricing of public sector services and excessively rapid external trade liberalization. Cumulatively this macroeconomic environment created serious difficulties for producers, and constrained their ability to take advantage of the improved incentive framework.

Even the very success of macroeconomic management led to unanticipated difficulties from the so-called 'Dutch Disease'. Successful adjustment attracted

---

[6] Indeed as I have argued elsewhere (Hutchful, 1995b) in the initial phase of adjustment, revenue considerations rather than international competitiveness were the driving force behind exchange rate policy.

considerable external inflows in the form of grants and concessional loans to support the ERP. This created two problems. First, reserves held by the central bank contributed to very large year-on-year additions to the money supply (see Table 3), much as the budgetary deficits of previous years had done. The second has been increased demand for local goods and services. These two factors together were responsible for the persistently high rates of inflation in the Ghanaian economy in the late 1980s. The increase in money supply posed serious problems of macroeconomic management in view of the limits on money supply imposed by agreements with the multilateral institutions. To contain growth in the money supply the Government imposed strict credit limits and reserve requirements on the commercial banks (Younger, 1992; Kapur *et al.*, 1991; Tsikata and Amuzu, 1991). The credit squeeze which then emerged severely hampered the ability of the private sector to adjust to the new competitive environment. At the same time it discouraged competition and savings mobilization by the commercial banks. The fact that the 'Dutch disease' has occurred in the public domain rather than being channelled to the private sector has also had important economic consequences. As an IMF staff study observed: 'The predominance of public investment and its emphasis on the rehabilitation of the basic economic infrastructure [means that] Ghana's real capital stock in most sectors of the economy has risen only marginally in this period', the exceptions being mining and cocoa (Kapur *et al.*, 1991: 11).

The vision elaborated in the 1993 World Bank report of Ghana emulating an 'East Asian' path of development seems more improbable and misplaced. Until very recently the relevance of East Asian models was almost systematically ignored in Bank discussions on Africa, perhaps following Alderman's observation that a 'significant breakthrough in development economics in the early 1980s was the discovery that Africa is not Asia' (Alderman, 1991: 3). The 1989 text *Sub-Saharan Africa: from Crisis to Sustainable Development*, for instance, almost completely failed to mention the East Asia experience. The latest World Bank report, *Adjustment in Africa*, has, however, forcefully introduced East Asia as the model for Africa to emulate. This model is being seriously explored for the first time in relation to Ghana, the leader in African adjustment efforts. Both the Ghanaian authorities and the Bank are speaking of the possibility of Ghana being on an East Asian growth path (World Bank, 1993a). There are several reasons for the sudden attraction in the East Asian experience, the most important undoubtedly being the fact that it is seen as an antidote to the 'plod-along strategy' (*ibid.*: 89) that has so far characterized Ghana and other adjusting countries in Africa. While in its latest treatment of East Asia the Bank has abandoned (or modified) earlier efforts to treat East Asia as the unfettered triumph of market forces, the many examples of bias and distortion that persist in the World Bank account should give African policy-makers pause for thought.[7]

4.   Agriculture

4.1   Export Agriculture
Policy reforms in the agricultural sector in the first and second phases of adjustment (and the associated conditionalities) initially focused preponderantly on the export

---

[7] For the Bank's latest exegesis see World Bank (1993c). For a response see Fishlow *et al.*, 1994.

sector, and specifically on its rehabilitation and its marketing system. A key focus of ERP I was the improvement of producer incentives (partly accomplished through the large nominal price increases facilitated by devaluation) and reform of the Cocoa Marketing Board (COCOBOD) in order to reduce its operating costs through such avenues as labour retrenchment, divestment of operations outside its core functions, as well as rationalization of its internal organization and cost structures. In the first phase of the ERP COCOBOD was turned into a statutory public corporation and reorganized into operating divisions and wholly owned subsidiaries. Other reforms involved the reduction of employee numbers by 41 percent or 41,000 workers (of which 25,000 were 'ghost workers'). ERP II sought to accelerate these reforms. The conditionalities attached to the IDA credits in support of the structural adjustment programme (SAC I and II) called for a detailed rationalization plan aimed at reducing the operating costs of COCOBOD as a share of total cocoa revenue from 32 percent in 1985-86 to 15 percent in the 1988-89 season, the divestment of 52 cocoa and coffee plantations, identification and elimination of excess labour (COCOBOD employment fell to 42,000 by 1992), rationalization of the cocoa processing plants, progressive withdrawal from road haulage, and the transfer of some of the board's existing functions in production, marketing, transportation, research and extension to the private sector or other state institutions. COCOBOD was required to prepare and implement a rolling three-year corporate plan along these lines (1988-89 and 1989-90) and to sign a performance agreement with government based on this plan. Further conditionalities under the Cocoa Rehabilitation Project (1987-92) called for further privatization of inputs, the elimination of input subsidies and the privatization of the internal purchasing of cocoa.

Although progress was slow several of these targets were substantially accomplished between 1987 and 1991. Further reductions of staff and other reorganizations brought down the labour force of COCOBOD from about 101,000 in 1984 to about 42,000 at the end of 1991. Subsidies were substantially eliminated and a variety of subsidiaries responsible for plantations, a chemical formulation plant and cocoa feeder roads were fully or partly divested. In addition the PBC's monopoly of cocoa haulage was eliminated. These reforms and the streamlining of buying operations and cocoa extension services reduced the operating costs of COCOBOD by roughly one-third after 1987, allowing the official producer price to rise to 51 percent of the fob price by 1992 from only 20 percent in 1983.

While many of these reforms had been contemplated in any event by the PNDC, the call for privatization of the domestic purchasing of cocoa ran into considerable resistance from the Ghanaian authorities for three main reasons. First, a similar liberalization of the internal cocoa trade by the Busia government through the reintroduction of local buying agents (LBAs) had led to a host of malpractices and a drop in quality and was revoked by the Acheampong government in the mid-1970s. Second, Ghanaian officials were not reassured by the example of concurrent attempts to privatize the cocoa sector in Nigeria. In that case considerable disruption was caused when speculative finance entered the sector primarily to gain access to foreign exchange through the export retention scheme, in the process both driving up prices above world market prices and driving down quality. A collapse of the sector eventually occurred when liberalization of the foreign-exchange system precipitated capital flight from the sector. It was assumed that the major difference between Ghana and Nigeria (and the reason why the Nigerian authorities could contemplate such 'reforms' on the basis of minimal preparation) was that unlike Ghana the cocoa sector in Nigeria was virtually moribund and marginal in its contribution to total exports and government revenue. Finally it was considered that the rural credit market was incapable of handling the demands of a fully privatized market (Alderman, 1991: 52), the danger being that buyers might not be able to rely on their own funds but might need as in the past to be propped up by COCOBOD funding.

However, the World Bank insisted that privatization was necessary, since after the initial gains from devaluation further increases from producer incentives could only come from greater market efficiency and reduced reliance by the government on export levies. Hence more radical changes were needed, particularly if the share of export earnings for producers was to rise to the pre-tax levels (between 65 and 90 percent) enjoyed by farmers in competing cocoa-producing countries (World Bank, 1992: 12). Although this is not explicitly stated in the argument, clearly a key reason for this renewed pressure for marketing reform was the fall in world market prices, which had squeezed both producer prices and government revenues, thus making it necessary to minimize marketing losses. Relentless pressure has been brought to bear on both the government and COCOBOD, and in the run-up to negotiating IDA credits to support the Medium-Term Agricultural Development Plan the government moved at last to privatize the cocoa trade. The COCOBOD monopsony was broken in September 1991 and private buyers were allowed to enter the field. However, the terms of private participation were very restrictive, and the fact that COCOBOD itself was to license private traders did not suggest an arms-length approach to liberalizing the market (Gibbon et al., 1993: 21-24). To facilitate the entry of private buyers the number of cocoa buying centres were reduced by one-third and extension centres by two-thirds, and all remaining subsidies on cocoa inputs and cocoa input marketing were eliminated beginning with the 1991 cocoa season. Earlier (June 1991) coffee and sheanut marketing (domestic and external) were liberalized.[8]

The stagnation of cocoa production and exports since 1988-89 has already been remarked on. Behind it lies a story of intensified international competition and falling international prices. This story suggests that excessive emphasis on primary export commodities and cocoa in particular constituted a basic flaw in the recovery strategy. The revival of the Ghanaian cocoa industry occurred in the midst of two major developments. The first was the increasing use by chocolate manufacturers of synthetic and other non-cocoa food substitutes (such as vegetable oil in place of cocoa butter). The second was the emergence of sizable structural surpluses from expanded production by Côte d'Ivoire, Malaysia and Brazil and new producers (such as Indonesia). These factors, combined with low overall consumption growth in the leading importing countries, suggest a decline in cocoa prices which is not cyclical in nature but probably permanent. Both of these dangers could have been anticipated by planners. Ghana's attempt to increase production and exports coincided with similar (and much better organized) efforts by other producers to boost cocoa exports through radical expansion in acreage under high-yielding hybrid varieties, and at a time when it was already apparent that prices were beginning to decline as a result of overproduction. Between 1974-75 and 1988-89 the production of Côte d'Ivoire increased from 242,000 to 850,000 tonnes, that of Brazil from 273,000 to 324,000 tonnes (down from 402,000 in the previous year), and that of Malaysia from 13,000 to 243,000 tonnes. In the same period

---

[8] Progress on these latest reforms remains to be seen. For more extended discussion of cocoa sector conditionality see Toye 1991; Martin 1992; Gibbon et al., 1993.

Indonesia, a new entrant to the market, increased production from 2,000 to 93,000 tonnes (Kofi, 1994: 27). In Côte d'Ivoire the acreage under the hybrid variety (with yields of three times the traditional varieties) expanded from 221,000 hectares in 1977-78 to 544,000 hectares in 1982-83 and 751,000 hectares in 1992-93. In the same time span planted acreage of the hybrid variety in Brazil went up from 109,000 to 305,000 hectares, in Malaysia from 19,000 to 209,000 hectares, and in Indonesia from 24,000 to 190,000 hectares (*ibid.*). On the other hand the adoption of the new varieties in Ghana proceeded much more slowly (from 69,000 to 151,000 hectares - suggesting a ratio of hybrid to traditional varieties of about 1:6 in Ghana as opposed to 1:1.57 in Cote d'Ivoire and 1:1.25 in Brazil, with plantings exclusively of the new variety in Malaysia and Indonesia), ensuring that Ghana would not remains competitive against more aggressive producers. In line with these changes, the world cocoa price by 1992 was less than one-third of its level when the reform process began in 1985. Despite the large increase in local producers' share of the world price, this meant that in dollar equivalent terms at least, they were still no better-off.

Table 6   Cocoa Bean Production, Consumption, and Prices

	Production	Consumption		Producer Price[a]
	(Thousand metric tonnes)	Domestic[b]	Export	(Cedis/metric ton)
1983/84	159	15	148	20,000
1984/85	174	20	162	30,000
1985/86	219	25	193	56,600
1986/87	227	22	205	85,500
1987/88	188	20	168	150,000
1988/89	300	20	281	165,000
1989/90	295	20	275	174,400
1990/91	293	20	242	224,000
1991/92	242	23	254	251,000
1992/93	311	30	281	258,000
1993/94	240	40	200	308,000

Source: IMF.
[a]   Including bonus payments until 1986/87, but excluding bonus payments thereafter.
[b]   Including sales to processing companies, most of whose production is exported.

4.2   Food Agriculture

Several factors underscore the importance of the agricultural sector in Ghana's economy. Agriculture accounts for 46 percent of GDP and 60 percent of exports (although both figures have been declining of late). Agriculture is closely correlated with poverty and is fundamental to the problem of low productivity in the economy. 87 percent of the poor live in the rural areas, and most of these are involved in agriculture to some degree or another. Smallholders are among the most vulnerable in terms of food security (Asenso-Okyere *et al.*, 1993). In addition food prices have contributed disproportionately to the inflationary spiral in the economy, with local food prices consistently outstripping any other commodity in the price index since the 1960s. According to the Ghana Living Standards Survey (GLSS) 68 percent of household consumption expenditure in Ghana goes on food, irrespective of socio-economic status. Nutritional standards have been low throughout Ghana and have yet to recover. Clearly then agricultural growth forms the solution simultaneously to key problems of inflation, poverty, and adequate nutrition in Ghana. The evidence suggests that in several respects agriculture has actually become *more* critical in Ghana's economy, although for perverse reasons. In the late 1970s and 80s agriculture actually accounted for a *growing* proportion of the labour force, reversing previous trends. This is in turn because 'agrarianization' formed a core component in survival strategies and relief of economic stress, as suggested by the speed with which the 'returnees' from Nigeria were absorbed into the rural economy. According to the GLSS, some 58 percent of second jobs in the survey sample were in agriculture. The economic crisis of the late 1970s and 80s, and the return of refugees from Nigeria, were reflected in a rapid expansion of smallholdings. This expansion was also accompanied by a stagnation in agricultural productivity and by considerable fragmentation of agricultural holdings, suggesting marginalization both *within* and *of* the sector. Between 1970 and 1984 there was a four-fold increase in the number of agricultural holdings under 0.8 hectares. At the same time there was a 70 percent decline in the number of holdings above 2.4 hectares (ha.). While farmers with holdings above 2.4 ha. occupied 79 percent of the total cultivable land in 1970, in 1984 this class of farmer occupied only 38.8 percent of the total cultivated area (Sarris and Shams, 1991: 48; World Bank, 1993a: 33 for a somewhat different set of figures). While the reasons for this are probably complex, undoubtedly one of the contributory factors was the explosion of backyard farming during the mid-1970s to early 1980s. This would help to explain the significant increase of smallholdings near urban centres as well as the sharp contraction that occurred in numbers of smallholdings in 1986 as cheap food became available (by this time the 'returnees' from Nigeria would also be exploring other job opportunities outside agriculture). (Ironically another reason may have been migration from the land, suggesting *reduced* dependence on farming for traditional farming households, at the same time as there was *more* self-provisioning by non-farming households through small-scale farming.)

In spite of this, food agriculture received no serious policy attention until around 1990. This first phase of agricultural policy reflected a 'pricist' approach that saw distortion in incentive and regulatory structures, excess taxation and 'rural-urban bias' as primarily responsible for low agricultural production. The major underpinning of policy at this stage was liberalization of input and output markets to bring sector prices more into parity with world markets. Much of this was simply irrelevant to the food-crop sub-sector. As stated earlier food prices had risen steadily since the 1960s and by the 1970s the terms of trade had shifted decisively from cocoa to food agriculture. The problem, as already noted by Killick (1978) with reference to the 1960s and 1970s, was why the supply of food crops failed to respond to these signals. The issue could not have been one of government controls, since unlike some African countries the government in Ghana has never seriously or successfully attempted to control or subsidize domestic food prices, other than through the operation of the agricultural parastatals, which were negligible in terms both of total acreage, production, and distribution. The Ghana Food Distribution Corporation (GFDC), which was responsible for 90 percent of the purchases by parastatals, actually accounted for only 6-8 percent of total food-crop purchases. Lack of financial support and appropriate infrastructure limited its ability to carry out its functions under the Guaranteed Minimum Price (GMP) scheme. Food-crop markets have been controlled overwhelmingly by hundreds of small traders, mostly women, who moved the crop from farm-gate to gathering points and from there to urban markets. Nor was it simply a problem of credit availability. 40 percent of Ghanaian farmers are believed to have received some form of credit, making Ghana's system of rural credit one of the most extensive in Africa, at least until the liberalisation of bank credit in 1991 (see below).

On the other hand, there are many early identifiable structural problems affecting the agricultural sector generally, which were largely ignored. They include a primitive marketing and road system that both adds substantially to final costs (according to Asenso-Okyere *et al.* (1993: 33) about 70 percent of the farm-retail price spread is accounted for by transportation costs) and depresses farmer incomes by limiting their marketing options and bargaining power relative to traders. Input use in Ghana is low even by African standards. In 1988 Ghana used less than 5 kg of plant nutrient per hectare of arable land compared with 6.4 kg for Mali, 21.5 kg in Malawi, and a world average of 98.7 kg. Of 19 developing countries studied by the FAO, Ghana had the lowest levels of fertilizer application. A survey of 1200 farmers showed that in 1989 only 18 percent had used any kind of chemical fertilizer, while 30 percent had never used chemical fertilizers (Asenso-Okyere, 1991: 83). Most agriculture is rain-fed and therefore susceptible to weather conditions; irrigation is both limited and expensive in terms of unit costs. Linkage between research institutes and extension has been non-existent (partly because these functions are controlled by different institutions) and linkages with industry remain low.

Prior to adjustment, despite low local cocoa prices, agriculture was moreover still characterized by policy dualism. This dualism reflected to some extent the strategic interests of the state in the sector, which took the form of maximizing fiscal returns from export crops while either leaving food agriculture to fend for itself, or attempting to displace smallholders with large-scale private commercial or state farming. Nearly 60 percent of research funding went to cocoa during 1975-81 although cocoa accounted for less than a fifth of total agricultural production. In contrast the (food) Crops Institute and its large substation at Nyankpala had the largest professional staff (55) but received only 15 percent of total outlays for agricultural research in this period (Tabor *et al.*, 1993). This trend has persisted under the ERP: in 1986-87 cocoa received 45 percent of research funding but contributed only 17 percent of GDP in the agricultural sector. Moreover, this aspect of dualism was accompanied by overlapping biases in both sub-sectors toward larger farmers and men. Large farmers are more likely to be involved in cocoa and commercial cultivation of food crops and to control access to inputs and credit while smallholders tend to grow less cocoa, consume more of their own product and use fewer inputs. Rural differentiation has taken the form of the exploitation of small peasant farmers by large farmers and food traders alike, who have captured much of the smallholder's potential surplus (Nyanteng, 1978; Sarris and Shams, 1991). The third faultline is the gender differentiation within agriculture which is to some extent a surrogate for the other two since women farmers tend to be primarily smallholders,

Table 7   Production, Acreage, and Yield of Principal Food Crops, 1988-93

	Production (In thousands of metric tons)						Acreage (In thousands of hectares)						Yield (In metric tons per hectare)					
	1988	1989	1990	1991	1992	1993	1988	1989	1990	1991	1992	1993	1988	1989	1990	1991	1992	1993
Cassava	3,300	3,320	2,717	5,702	5,662	5,972	354	415	323	535	552	532	9.32	8.00	8.41	10.66	10.26	11.23
Plantain	1,200	1,040	799	1,178	1,082	1,322	119	164	129	174	157	164	10.08	6.34	6.19	6.77	6.89	8.06
Cocoyams	1,115	1,200	815	1,297	1,202	1,236	141	207	119	203	196	173	7.91	5.80	6.85	6.39	6.13	7.14
Yams	1,200	1,280	887	2,632	2,331	2,720	168	217	142	227	224	207	7.14	5.90	6.18	11.59	10.41	13.14
Maize	751	715	553	932	731	961	540	567	465	610	607	637	1.39	1.26	1.19	1.53	1.20	1.51
Guinea corn	161	215	136	241	259	328	226	286	215	263	307	309	0.71	0.75	0.63	0.92	0.84	1.06
Millet	139	180	75	112	133	198	228	244	124	209	210	204	0.61	0.74	0.60	0.54	0.63	0.97
Rice	95	74	81	151	132	157	52	72	49	95	80	77	1.83	1.03	1.65	1.59	1.65	2.04

Source: Ghana Government, *Quarterly Digest of Statistics.*

tend to specialize in food production and to be less commercialized in their operations, and are less able overall to benefit from credit, extension services and other inputs. As dominant traders in food crops women have attracted none of the attention historically devoted to the cocoa trade. Finally, institutional and policy responsibility for the agricultural sector has been divided between three ministries and the Cocoa Marketing Board (COCOBOD). Agricultural research fell under the Council for Scientific and Industrial Research (CSIR) (which is itself under the Ministry of Industry, Science and Technology), cocoa and coffee come under COCOBOD (which reported to the Office of the Chairman of the Committee of Secretaries) while forestry fell under the Ministry of Lands and Mineral Resources, with rubber and oil palm falling under several agencies (World Bank, 1992a: 10).

The Ghana Agricultural Policy (GAP): Action Plans and Strategies 1986-88 adopted in January 1986 signalled an emerging shift in reform priorities in the agricultural sector and the second phase of agricultural policy. While the GAP repeated many of the usual aims of agricultural policy, it also placed considerable emphasis on the institutional context: strengthening the Ministry of Agriculture and decentralizing operational responsibilities to the regions; improving existing institutions and facilities, such as research, credit and marketing; and ensuring adequate returns to producers to increase efficiency and productivity. This institutional focus reflected a realization during the implementation of the first phase of the ERP that the Ministry of Agriculture and its supporting institutions were ineffective because of past neglect. The aim of agricultural policy 'now became to strengthen the capacity of the public sector to support research and extension services, irrigation and policy planning, and monitoring, evaluation and coordination; and make the investments necessary to expand agricultural production' (Sarris and Shams, 1991: 14).

These objectives were supported through the Agricultural Services Rehabilitation Project (ASRP) in 1987 (with a total IDA credit of US$53.5 m.). The ASRP in turn spawned the Agricultural Productivity Promotion Programme (APPP), funded by USAID and designed to augment the ASRP in the area of extension by improving staff training and mobility. A large proportion of the grant was used to rehabilitate part of the feeder road system in the country.

However, it was not until the adoption of the Medium-Term Agricultural Development Programme (MTADP) - which marked the beginning of the Agricultural Sector Adjustment Programme (ASAP) - that the need for a 'comprehensive and coherent strategy for sectoral development' was recognized. The MTADP sought to define the direction of agricultural policy for the period 1991-2000 and incorporated a programme of policy and institutional reforms and a complementary set of investments believed to be adequate to achieve a higher rate of growth. These reforms ostensibly centre around strengthening the capacity of the private sector to 'support agricultural development'; revitalizing agricultural research and extension services; and increasing the productivity and incomes of the majority of farmers through selective intervention in key areas such as small-scale irrigation, output diversification and increased artisanal production and marketing.

The ASAP is seen by its designers as an opportunity for a renewed and more decisive assault on the remaining vestiges of governmental interference in the sector (World Bank, 1992a: 11). However, the principal emphasis continues to be primarily on liberalizing the market for agricultural products. ASAP conditionalities included: a significant reduction of the role of GFDC through the sale, lease or commercialization of its processing, cold store, milling, storage, transport and catering facilities, and the cessation of domestic buying of grain for price support purposes; the elimination of government control of fertilizer marketing margins, discontinuation of public sector participation in imports of agricultural inputs, and divestiture of the Farmers Agricultural Service Companies (FASCOMS) to force them to operate commercially; the restructuring of the Ghana Cotton Company to increase efficiency and encourage more effective price competition among cotton buyers; and the continuation of policies to liberalize the trade in palm oil (including free exportation of palm oil and elimination of protection to large scale producers). A number of marketing reforms also seem to be preconditions of the ASAP. These included the abolition of the guaranteed minimum price for maize and rice, effective from the 1990 crop season; withdrawal of the state from price determination for cotton and tobacco effective December 1990; freeing of exports of cotton lint and palm oil; liquidation of the Ghana Seed Company in October 1989 and privatization of seed production, beginning with the 1990 season; removal of fertilizer subsidies in 1990 and introduction of spatial variations in ex-depot prices; and the freezing of GFDC storage capacity. Since 1991 the government has moved to implement most if not all of these conditionalities.

What have been the overall effects of these policies? While agricultural performance and prices improved dramatically in 1984 this improvement owed little to the ERP, but was due to favourable weather conditions and the unusually large expansion of small-holdings (in part a reaction to the drought conditions and high prices of 1983) and the availability of agricultural labour made possible by the arrival of the returnees from Nigeria. In any case (or perhaps for this very reason) this improvement was not sustained; the price collapse that followed the bounty harvest of 1984 led to sharp contraction in both acreage and production in 1985, both as farmers tried to curb their losses and marginal cultivators withdrew from the sector in response to the availability of cheap food. For the rest of the decade food agriculture lagged well behind growth in overall GDP, with real growth of about 2.1 percent, and negative growth in two of the six years from 1984 to 1990. Between 1990 and 1993 the overall sector growth rate has improved marginally to 2.9 percent (assuming that the estimates for 1993 are realistic).

Meanwhile the withdrawal of fertilizer subsidies led to rapid rise in prices and consequent fall in consumption. Up to 1980 fertilizer was subsidized by about 80 percent of the price (or about US$5 m. per annum). With its phased withdrawal the size of the subsidy dropped from 66 percent in 1986 to 30 percent in 1988 and 15 percent in 1989. Subsidies were eliminated altogether in 1990. The result of the withdrawal of subsidy, added to the effects of devaluation, has been a steep rise in nominal prices. The price of a 50 kg bag of fertilizer rose by some 900 percent between 1984 and 1990 (from C 450 to C 4200) (Asenso-Okyere, 1991: 82). Privatization of the distribution system was completed and a free market system put in place by the end of 1991. However, fertilizer distribution failed to stimulate much private sector interest. In 1989 only 14 of 351 registered distributors bothered to withdraw any fertilizer from government stores, and in 1990 only 49 out of 656. Only 285 tonnes were distributed by private retailers in 1989 and 4513 tonnes in 1990 (*ibid.*: 81). The reasons for this included low margins and pan-territorial pricing imposed by government (which promised returns well below the prevailing interest rate of 30 percent), the glut of fertilizer stocks in the warehouses of the Ministry of Agriculture which threatened to depress prices, the continued competition from the public sector in the fertilizer market, lack of credit at all levels and high lending rates. But a major consideration was that with the drop in fertilizer consumption the trade no longer commanded the volumes required to attract investors. Total sales of fertilizer fell from 29,000 tonnes in 1989 to 8,400 tonnes in 1990 and fertilizer use reportedly declined from about 7.7 kg per hectare in 1983-84 to about 3.8 kg in 1990 (Jebuni and Seini, 1992).[9]

The available figures suggest two clear developments in the food-crop sector since 1988. One is a large (26 percent, 1988-93) ongoing expansion in the planted area with resulting increases in production (this trend was broken in 1990, when poor rains led to a sharp contraction in the area cultivated). However, except for yam, overall yields have virtually been stagnant, consistent with a corresponding stagnation in the use of inputs and the bringing of marginal lands under cultivation; in some cases (such as plantain, cocoyam, maize and rice) there was a sharp decline in yields after 1988 which is only now being reversed. The trend for maize is particularly instructive given the research attention it has commanded, second only to cocoa. There is evidence here of a productivity squeeze - in part precipitated by rising input costs - which is manifesting itself in efforts to increase production through extensification rather than intensification. The expansion in particular in acreage of starchy staples (especially cassava, which expanded in acreage by 50 percent between 1988 and 1992, making it the fastest growing crop) has implications for soil fertility and the environment (especially in the absence of fertilizer application) as well as for nutritional standards. While cassava functions as a 'survival crop' and is favoured because of its relative resistance to drought, it has little nutritional value and accelerates the exhaustion of marginal soils (the kind of soil on which it tends to be favoured). It is clear that Ghana's environment cannot continue to tolerate this level of pressure indefinitely.

In this context all indications point to the importance of input prices and price stability for increasing input applications geared to higher productivity. As Sarris and others have shown, there are substantial cost/investment differences between 'traditional', 'improved' and advanced technologies (in the case of maize in 1987 it was estimated to be in the ratio of 1:4 for improved and 1:8 for advanced over 'traditional' technologies) (Sarris and Shams, 1991: 175). Research also suggests that farmers are extremely sensitive to weather and price trends, and respond to uncertainties by cutting back or delaying the application of fertilizers. Clearly given the substantial fluctuations in seasonal prices farmers need some form of price stabilization if they are to be assured the returns required to invest in expensive inputs, as well as reliable and efficient market outlets and credit. There is also historical evidence that food farmer are facing a circulation squeeze as a growing proportion of their surplus is appropriated by traders through a variety of mechanisms, particularly the extension of seasonal advances. Nyanteng (1978: 13) noted as far back as the 1970s that food farmers were falling 'deeper and deeper into debt and some eventually find themselves producing for traders, practically on the latter's own terms'. Credit is apparently tied to crop deliveries and traders are actively encouraging such indebtedness. Hodson (1983: 39) confirms these observations, remarking that '[most] small farmers depend heavily on the traders and complain bitterly about the discrepancy between the prices they are paid at the farm and the prices at which the same produce is sold in the retail market'. There is no

---

[9] However, the World Bank denies that this is the case. According to the Bank, fertilizer consumption *increased three-fold*, from 11,000 tonnes in 1986 to 32,000 tonnes in 1990 (World Bank, 1992a: 19) 'notwithstanding a three-fold increase in fertiliser prices resulting from subsidy removal and devaluation'. However, this stance was subsequently revised (see World Bank, 1993a, cited below).

reason to believe that these relationships have been eroded under the ERP. Minimum price supports would have helped to weaken, if not break, this stranglehold. Unfortunately the World Bank has, on the contrary, insisted on abolishing rather than strengthening existing agricultural price supports

One area in which adjustment does appear to have had a positive impact is agricultural research. In the mid-1960s Ghana's agricultural research institutes employed about 90 researchers in 10 institutes, and in the 1970s about 200, mostly in the Cocoa Research Institute or the seven agricultural institutes under the CSIR. A sharp fall-off in spending for research, capital projects and staff renumeration, and deterioration in infrastructure occurred during the late 1970s and early 1980s. Scientists and researchers left for other countries or turned to subsistence activities. With the ERP however considerable funding for operation, research and training has been made available, and real research spending went up sharply. There have been substantial increases in pay for scientists as well as donor funding to support research activity, and this in turn has persuaded large numbers of scientists who left the country to return. However:

Although the increase in donor support has the advantage of providing secure funding for a time, it also resulted in a skewing of agricultural research priorities. The agricultural research institutes became increasingly dependent on foreign aid for both development and operating funds. Research institutes successful in securing large sums of donor assistance could rebuild their operations and augment staff salaries. Research activities of low priority for donor agencies, but which may have been of high priority nationally, were neglected due to a lack of sufficient and secure funding (Tabor *et al.*, 1993: 4).

Moreover, increased funding has been made available without reform of the institutional environment for research, and non-wage operating funds have remained tightly compressed throughout the adjustment period. Agricultural research institutes have spent very little on maintenance of buildings, and facilities, libraries, conferences, meetings and communications (*ibid.*: 5).

On the other hand, these increased resources have been allocated to agriculture in a situation where public expenditure on it generally has stagnated at historically low levels. The share of agriculture in total public expenditure declined from 10.4 percent in 1983 to 4.5 percent in 1985; between 1987 and 1993 spending on agriculture averaged between 3.5 and 4 percent of total government expenditure (see Table 4). Expenditures on transport, maintenance and repairs seem to have been particularly badly hit (Sarris and Shams, 1991: 179-80).

Overall the state of agriculture in Ghana as we enter the second decade of adjustment has been well summed up in the World Bank's own publication *Ghana 2000 and Beyond*, in terms of: deteriorating terms of trade for the sector (p.30); exacerbation of rural income differentials (p.31); reduced fertilizer use (p.32); fragmentation of holdings (p.33); lack of growth in crop yields (p.38); massive encroachment on forests in the Western Region (p.39), and *increasing* imports of certain agricultural raw materials capable of being locally produced. A note of defeatism pervades official discussions of the future of agriculture. The AGS for instance notes that 'it will be a formidable task to raise agricultural output by 3.7 percent a year', a surprising conclusion given the existence of some consensus that the technology already exists for food sufficiency and even surplus in several areas (maize, rice, and other food crops) once constraints of an institutional and infrastructural nature are removed (World Bank, 1993a: 14; Sarris and Shams, 1991: 204). It is for this reason that industry rather than agriculture is identified as the key to accelerated growth in the medium-term! In the meantime Ghana's agriculture 'continues to operate a very low level of productivity' with current average yields at about 40 percent of achievable ones (Ghana Government, 1993a: 12-13).

Beyond this, agriculture demonstrates the problems arising from the lack of a well integrated sector programme. In spite of the belated arrival at a 'coherent' agricultural programme (six or seven years after the commencement of adjustment), World Bank policy remains piecemeal and self-defeating. This is most clearly the case with fertilizer policy, but other examples seem to point in the same direction, i.e., to a conflict between broad macroeconomic postures and the realities of sector policy, as well as poor coordination and sequencing of the various reforms. Abolition of subsidies reduced fertilizer consumption at the moment when the World Bank itself was advocating intensification, and while price decontrol was probably a condition of private sector interest, it killed off interest by consumers. Price supports were also abolished, and storage construction frozen, at the precise moment that the need for both became most apparent.

Similarly the liberalization of bank credit led to virtual cessation of agricultural lending by some banks and a substantial fall in the overall volume of credit to the sector. As a component of total lending, agricultural credit declined from 23.8 percent in 1987 to an average of 14.6 percent from 1988 to 1991 and declined further to 10.0 percent in 1992 and 1993 (Bank of Ghana; also World Bank, 1993a: 59). Apart from the powerful impression that Bank staff were flying by the seat of their pants, the recommended reforms sometimes appeared to be influenced more by ideological positions than by the situation on the ground.

5. Industry

Extended considerably during the 1960s and 1970s, Ghana's industrial sector (and manufacturing in particular) was characterized by excessive dependence on imported inputs, overcapacity, capital intensity and high levels of protection. During the economic crisis that preceded the ERP industry suffered severe shortages in inputs and depreciation in plant and equipment from the squeeze on foreign exchange. Overall capacity utilization in manufacturing fell from 53 percent in 1975 to 25 percent in 1980, while the share of manufacturing in GDP declined from 14 percent in 1975-77 to 10 percent in 1981 (roughly equal to the 1960 figure). The ERP foresaw a three-phase process of industrial recovery and restructuring. The first and most immediate concern was to increase utilization of existing capacity by easing access to imported inputs through Reconstruction Import Credits (RIC) I and II.

The second, medium-term stage was to rehabilitate key industries through increased availability of inputs, spare parts and replacement equipment needed to break bottlenecks within firms, raise productivity and avoid further deterioration of capacity. The third and long-term stage would complete the restructuring process through investment or expansion in industries consistent with Ghana's comparative advantage. The need for industrial restructuring was given added urgency through the recognition under the first Financial Sector Adjustment Credit (FINSAC 1) that one of the reasons for the insolvency of many banks in Ghana was the distressed state of their corporate clients, and that for banking restructuring to be successful on a sustained basis it would have to be accompanied by restructuring of the corporate sector. A study was commissioned under FINSAC 1 to determine the magnitude and causes of corporate distress, targeting 214 enterprises. The study concluded that a significant proportion of the enterprises had good prospects for viability, given appropriate restructuring from a financial, technical and managerial standpoint (World Bank, 1992b: 12).

Table 8   Index of Manufacturing Production, 1987-93 (1977=100)

	Weights	1987	1988	1989	1990	1991	1992	1993[a]
Food products	15.00	50.5	53.6	48.0	57.5	59.3	62.8	63.6
Beverages	8.11	85.2	89.0	98.0	94.0	93.0	112.2	116.4
Tobacco and tobacco products	7.75	54.9	58.0	51.0	57.1	49.6	47.1	49.3
Textiles, wearing apparel, and leather goods	13.71	26.1	28.7	24.0	37.7	39.1	23.7	24.2
Sawmill and wood products	7.22	79.3	98.3	79.9	74.2	133.6	120.2	125.4
Paper products and printing	1.94	59.7	52.8	48.0	53.5	49.3	54.6	57.6
Petroleum products	19.00	62.7	67.7	87.2	70.5	92.2	65.0	87.6
Chemical products other than petroleum	6.56	51.9	67.5	62.9	57.6	44.7	56.7	54.9
Cement and other non-metallic mineral products	2.98	49.7	73.4	100.0	117.3	125.6	177.0	180.1
Iron and steel products	3.25	42.9	18.3	12.0	5.2	---	356.0	402.3
Nonferrous metal basic industries	9.62	90.3	97.3	100.5	103.8	104.6	115.8	116.7
Cutlery and other nonferrous metal products	0.49	51.9	46.2	47.9	55.2	63.2	83.3	83.6
Electrical equipment and appliances	1.34	31.5	47.1	13.5	25.5	40.0	46.3	47.8
Transport equipment and other products	3.03	---	---	---	---	---	11.0	12.2
Overall index	100	56.8	62.1	63.0	63.5	71.3	76.9	79.3
Percentage change in overall index	---	4.8	9.3	1.4	0.8	12.3	7.9	3.1
Average capacity utilization (in percent)[b]	---	35.0	40.0	40.6	---	---	---	---

Source: Ghana government, *Quarterly Digest of Statistics.*
[a]   Provisional.
[b]   For large and medium-scale factories.

Between 1984 and 1988 industrial output grew rapidly (at 8.8 percent per annum between 1986 and 1988 alone). The manufacturing component of this was also about 8.8 percent, slightly better than mining and quarrying (8.2 percent) but well behind water and electricity (12 percent). Since 1989, however, the overall rate of improvement in industrial (and particularly manufacturing) performance has declined markedly. Industrial growth 1989-93 averaged 4.7 percent; the manufacturing production index rose by an annual average of 5.1 percent (see Table 8). As a component of GDP industry rose from 10 percent in 1980 to stabilize at around 14 percent of GDP. Overall capacity utilization rose from 30 percent in 1983 to 40 percent in 1989 and appears to have stagnated around this level.

In any event, as in other areas of the economy the recovery commenced from a very low base, and even by 1993 the index of manufacturing production had recovered to only 79 percent of its 1977 level. Performance has been quite uneven between the various subsectors (see Table 8). Recovery has been strongest in certain sectors which are local-resource-based, such as sawmill and wood products, as well as in cement and non-metallic mineral products, all of which have recovered or exceeded their 1977 production levels. These are also some of the subsectors that have attracted most of the capital (estimated at about US$200 m.) that went into industrial rehabilitation between 1988 and 1992 (Asante and Addo, 1993: 110). Recovery has been particularly weak in tobacco, textiles, wearing apparel and leather products, which came under considerable pressure from cheap imports (particularly used clothing) and transport equipment (mainly vehicle assembly, which had virtually ceased production). The figures for iron and steel simply do not make sense and no comment will be made on them.

It is apparent that the most important factors behind the recovery of manufacturing in the early stages of the ERP were improved access to imported raw materials and other inputs and price decontrol. However, in the short and medium term the restructuring process and competitive ability of the industrial sector has been severely constrained by a number of factors. Devaluation raised sharply the cost of imported inputs and eroded liquidity, and while in principle price liberalization allowed prices to be passed on to consumers, in practice many could not because demand was constrained by stabilization measures and increased competition. Tight credit and high interest rates have squeezed working capital and lack of access to long-term finance has constituted an important constraint on restructuring. Excessively rapid liberalization has led to competition from a flood of imports even before domestic manufacturers have had an opportunity to adjust to the new economic environment. Domestic manufacturers had argued for a phased or selective liberalization which would kick off with inputs and only (after an appropriate period of adjustment) allow the importation of consumerables.

For reasons that are not entirely clear (other than perhaps the effectiveness of World Bank pressure), Ghana did not use the classical route of phased trade liberalization (converting quantitative import restrictions into equivalent tariffs *before* gradually lowering the latter). Instead quantitative restrictions and import licences were dismantled while at the same time the level and range of tariffs were restructured and rates significantly reduced. The result was to hit local industry with a blast of cheap imports while it was still in a fragile recovery. The World Bank admits that 'the transition [to trade liberalization] might have been too abrupt for some industries' (World Bank, 1993a: 49) and recently the government has tried to reintroduce a measure of protection for selected industries through the imposition of a special 10 percent import tax and, for some industries, duty exemptions on imported raw materials.

Assistance for restructuring has been slow to materialize. The Corporate Restructuring Programme which was contemplated as part of FINSAC 1 (involving 214
financially distressed companies which were largely accountable for the non-performing
loans of the private sector) did not materialize until 1994, with the establishment in
August of the Business Assistance Fund of 10 bn Cedis (approximately US$10 m.), a
figure which the Vice-President admitted (with masterful understatement) was
'inadequate in our present circumstances' (*Daily Graphic*, 16 August 1994).

Not surprisingly restructuring remains weak, and a general lack of confidence seems
to be suggested by the fact that there has been no net gain in the number of enterprises
in this sector since the launching of the ERP. Input-output linkages with the rest of the
local economy continue to be limited (from 8 percent in 1968 to only an estimated 12
percent in 1991), and there has been little new technology acquisition.[10] A study by
World Bank staff sums up the Ghanaian experience in the following words:

> The opening up of the Ghanaian economy as well as the ensuing adjustment
> programmes have had important impacts on the industrial sector. While the new
> trade regime offers some incentive for Ghanaian enterprises to enhance their
> technological capabilities and to allocate resources to more competitive activities, the
> evidence suggests that so far the supply response in manufacturing has been weak.
> Relatively few activities have improved their technological performance and raised
> their international competitiveness, while many have closed down or are in serious
> trouble. The activities that have benefited, and in some cases expanded exports, are
> those that already had a resource-based comparative advantage, were specialized in
> market niches (like very simple products for low income consumers) or were
> protected by high transport costs from direct foreign competition (Lall *et al.*, (nd):
> 165).

5.1   The Small-scale Sector

A number of studies by Dawson (1990), the World Bank (1990), Steel and Webster
(1991) and Sowa *et al.* (1993) have given some insights into the behaviour of small-
scale enterprises (SSEs, i.e. enterprises employing less than 10 persons) under
adjustment in Ghana. While there are areas of broad agreement about the impact of
adjustment on this sector, there are also some disagreements springing possibly in part

---

[10] In this area there may well have been a net loss rather than gain under the ERP. The shortage of imported
inputs that preceded the ERP produced notable developments in the indigenous capital goods sector, although
this tended to be small-scale and fragmented, with much of it concentrated in workshops in individual
production units, operating at low levels of capacity and with little benefit of specialization and economies
of scale. Nevertheless a report by the Centre for Scientific and Industrial Research (CSIR) observed a
'potential technological capacity for entry into production of specialized machine tools and general machine
tools at an intermediate level of technological sophistication'. The report went on to argue that 'with the
installation of functional facilities for casting, machining, gear production, heat treatment and testing in ITTUs
[Intermediate Technology Transfer Units] and some private enterprises, the country appears only to lack
production facilities for prime movers in order to boost the endogenous capacity to manufacture machine
tools'. CSIR, 1990). For an account of the ITTUs see Smillie (1986). Trade liberalization effectively destroyed
much of this nascent capital goods industry, with (for example) the domestic producers of machinery and
transport equipment who had been forced to develop local sources of supply once again switching to imports.

from the location and timing of the surveys and from how SSEs were defined. All of these studies suggest that SSEs appear to be adjusting better than many larger enterprises, but they also attest to the strongly differentiated impact of the ERP on this sector. On the other hand, there is a consensus that microenterprises are severely distressed, with many surplus producers flocking into the sector, fierce competition and income-sharing (see also Ninsin, 1991: chapters 4 and 5).

While there has been no net gain in enterprises in the large-scale sector (30 or more workers) under the ERP there has been dynamic growth in enterprise numbers within the small-scale sector, reflecting both retrenchments from other sectors of the economy and a new breed of youthful entrepreneur motivated in part by decreasing employment opportunities in the formal sector and increased opportunities for profit in the private sector. On the whole new (post-ERP) entrants to the sector appear to be better educated than the owners of pre-ERP enterprises, and there also appears to be a significant association between the level of education of the owner and enterprise growth.

In the Sowa survey firms recording the most growth were located at the larger end of the small-scale sector, while most retrenched workers had entered at the lower end, intensifying competition and income-sharing at that end, thus confirming the finding by Steel and Webster that larger small-scale enterprises were much more likely than micro-enterprises to adjust successfully. Location was also an important determinant of growth, with SSEs located in the large cities (Accra, Kumasi, Cape Coast) recording less growth than those in smaller urban centres, presumably because of greater import competition and more retrenchment in the larger urban centres.

Unlike for formal enterprises competition from imports did not seem to be a concern in this sector, with the majority of enterprises reporting most competition from other domestic producers. This competition appeared not to be a barrier to growth, with 90 percent of growth firms reporting competition. Importantly SSEs were also less affected by devaluation (90 percent in the Sowa sample reported that they had no need for foreign exchange) in part because of closer integration with the domestic resource base and the more personalized nature of their clientele, and many firms had adapted to new price incentives by modifying their product mix.

However, there is some disagreement as to whether pre-ERP or post-ERP enterprises have fared better, with the Sowa study claiming that firms established *before* the ERP have recorded more growth while the World Bank study claims the opposite. Also while the Bank and Steel and Webster studies identify lack of demand as one of the key constraints on small enterprises, the majority of the sample in the Sowa survey (60 percent) report *increased* demand for their products (this difference may be a function of the different timing of the surveys). On the other hand, Dawson's study (conducted in 1987-88, and thus preceding all the others) is much more categorical in seeing the overall effect of the ERP on the sector as broadly negative, even though he observes that SSEs have been more than able to hold their own against the large-scale enterprises. Before the ERP SSEs had expanded strongly to occupy the economic space vacated by larger-scale enterprises with less operational and managerial flexibility, manifesting not only quantitative but also qualitative growth, with signs of increasing specialization, division of labour and 'formality' in certain aspects of their operations. The main threat from the ERP - even for the 'successful' enterprises - had come from the retrenched and other unemployed flooding the sector, increasing competition and driving down prices and profit-margins.

However, in spite of differences in market situation and overall performance, for almost all Ghanaian enterprises regardless of size the same conclusion ultimately emerges: while the new macroeconomic environment has facilitated short-term recovery in operations, the medium- and long-term sustainability of this recovery is more in question. All enterprise categories (and SSEs in particular) cited lack of credit as a critical constraint (almost all enterprises in the Steel and Webster survey indicated that credit had actually become *harder* to obtain under the ERP). According to Steel and Webster (1991: 433) even if demand constraints on SSEs were reduced, finance would remain a severe constraint on growth: 'In sum, the incentive side of the side of the adjustment process was working - less efficient firms were being squeezed - but the financial side was not functioning adequately to enable more efficient firms to grow'. On the other hand for micro-enterprises the crucial constraint was that of demand and lack of purchasing power among its lower-income clientele, demonstrating clearly the extent to which the performance of this sector acts as the barometer of poverty. The suggestion is that a *demand-driven* strategy - 'policies that put more money into the hands of the low-income population' - would have been more appropriate for at least this part of the sector (Steel and Webster suggest this antidote, without explaining why the ERP has failed to accomplish it).

6. Mining

As we saw in our earlier analysis, before the ERP the mining sector was characterized by steep across-the-board declines in production due to declining grades of ore in existing workings, lack of prospecting and exploration, failure to modernize and rehabilitate equipment, smuggling (particularly by small-scale miners), and the effects of an overvalued exchange rate and shortages of spare parts and the poor state of the railway system (in the case of bauxite and manganese). On the other hand, a study by the Bank of Ghana determined that for the Ashanti Goldfields Corporation (the richest gold mine, a joint venture between the Ghana Government and Lonrho) production could be brought back to normal at short notice and expanded quickly if mining materials, equipment and spare parts were made available.

The measures adopted under the ERP to revive the sector included immediate improvements in access to critical inputs through export rehabilitation credits, the grant of forex retention accounts ranging from 20 to 45 percent to the mining companies, substantial donor recapitalization for the gold producers, reorganization of the marketing arrangements for diamonds, and regularization of small-scale gold and diamond mining ('*galampsey*'). The mining sector, and gold in particular, has received virtually all the significant foreign investment that has occurred under the ERP. This was no accident, since for both the PNDC (as for the previous government of Limann) the rise in the price of gold stirred images of Ghana as once again the 'Gold Coast'. The first substantial investment was the IFC investment of US$55 m. in the operations of the Ashanti Goldfields Corporation (approved in June 1984). US$22.5 m. of this was to acquire equity by the IFC while another US$22.5 m. was to fund the acquisition of equity by other interested partners. The remaining US$10 m. went toward a rehabilitation loan of US$158 m. to raise production by AGC to 400,000 ounces by 1989-90. Overall investment in the mining sector has since exceeded US$800 m. Following the passage of the new Minerals and Mining Law by the PNDC in 1986 three gold mining companies commenced production in late 1990. These were Bogosu Resources (Canada), Goldenrae Mining (a joint venture between IMT International of Luxembourg, Sikaman Gold Resources of Canada, and the Ghanaian Government) and Teberebie Goldfields Limited. More recent entrants include Goldfields Ghana Ltd., which has acquired the Tarkwa goldmines, and African Star Resources, a subsidiary of Canada's Pacific Comex, which has won a 76 square mile concession at Adansi Asaasi, where there are underground workings developed between 1900 and 1930. In all six new gold ventures have started since 1988 (impressive considering that no new mines have been opened in Ghana since 1940). 66 Ghanaian and 14 foreign companies have been issued with prospecting licences (mainly for gold) and 10 companies have won mining leases.[11]

After declining from 10.6 tonnes in 1981 to 8.9 tonnes in 1986 gold production recovered to 16.5 tonnes in 1990 and then rose rapidly to about 40 tonnes in 1993, an increase of almost 500 percent in production since 1986. In terms of value performance has been even more impressive (see Table 9). Gold production is expected to nearly double again between 1993 and 2000. A large part of this increase has continued to come from Ashanti Goldfields, as well as from reworking of old mines and reprocessing of tailings, but it is expected that a growing proportion of the increased production will come in future from new projects and expansion and rehabilitation projects at other mines.[12] Prospecting plans include a 16,000 sq. km. airborne geological survey, the first high resolution survey ever carried out in Ghana, to cover most of the gold-bearing greenstone belt in south western Ghana. Output of both manganese and bauxite has also more than doubled. On the other hand, diamond production has been erratic, falling from 559,200 carats in 1986 to 171,000 in 1989 and further to 150,400 carats in 1990 before recovering as dramatically to 584,000 carats in 1992. By 1991 mineral production had virtually recovered to 1977 levels though it is only in the case of bauxite and gold that the previous peak production level (in 1970) has been exceeded.

There have also been some limited successes in recapturing the proceeds of small-scale mining production. By 1983 the sale of small-scale mining production through official channels had virtually ceased, (for instance, diamond purchases from small-scale producers fell from 85,000 carats in 1975 to only 400 carats in 1981). Most small-scale gold and diamond production was routinely smuggled. In 1989 the government revised the legal and commercial framework for small-scale mining by passing a Small-Scale Gold Mining Law, a Diamonds Amendment Law, a Precious Minerals Marketing Corporation Law (which established a new marketing corporation of the same name to replace the Diamond Marketing Corporation, for purchasing gold, diamonds and other precious minerals) and the Mercury Law (which regulates the sale, possession and use of mercury by licensed persons). Under the Small-Scale Gold Mining Law selected (and more formalized) small-scale miners may peg claims up to a maximum acreage of 25

---

[11] 'Gold Fever Returns to Ghana', *Financial Times*, 1 June 1994, p. 34.

[12] *Ibid.* Developments in gold producing technology over the last decade and a half have allowed much higher recovery rates from old tailings (waste) to be realized, at comparatively small outlays to producers. Much recent investment in Africa is of this kind rather than in opening new mines. This has created a certain local backlash to talk of a new 'gold rush' in Ghana. For instance the local branch of the mineworkers union alleges that Goldfields Ghana (a South African company which it also accuses of apartheid practices) has invested only US$3 m. and continues to use old mine machinery and infrastructure, *Ghanaian Chronicle*, 17-19 October 1994: 8.

acres, and be exempted from taxation for the first three years of operation, with a liability to a 45 percent rate of taxation thereafter. They may also be granted technical assistance and benefit from an extension service. Gold and diamond prices are set by the Precious Minerals Marketing Corporation (PMMC) based on current prices on the London Metals Market and converted into local currency at the bureau rate. 90 percent of this goes to miners, 3 percent to land reclamation, and 7 percent to the overhead and administrative costs of the PMMC.

Table 9   Mineral Production, 1986-93

	1986	1987	1988	1989	1990	1991	1992	1993[a]
	(In Millions of Cedis)							
Value of output								
Gold	9,343.7	21,840.7	33,298.7	43,838.8	66,576.2	140,626.3	205,786.3	280,072.2
Diamonds	428.3	609.9	502.2	919.3	1,076.1	4,658.3	8,498.0	9,159.6
Manganese	772.5	1,286.5	1,448.4	3,708.6	6,616.3	9,333.5	12,811.0	15,636.7
Bauxite	402.3	689.5	1,337.1	2,286.7	3,366.6	6,050.2	9,000.2	9,695.4
	(In Units Specified)							
Volume								
Gold ('000 kg)	8.9	10.2	11.6	13.2	16.5	26.1	31.4	40.7
Diamonds ('000 carats)	559.2	441.9	215.8	171.1	150.4	419.4	584.5	600.0
Manganese ('000 metric tonnes)	259.3	253.6	230.9	334.2	364.0	415.2	477.7	555.3
Bauxite ('000 metric tonnes)	204.1	195.0	287.3	347.1	382.1	485.1	498.1	523.0

Source: Ghana government and IMF staff estimates.
[a]   Estimates.

These measures have apparently had great success both in increasing more formalized small-scale production and rediverting the proceeds from unofficial to official channels. Between the end of March 1989 and January 1991, 268 licences were issued for small-scale goldmining and 104 for diamond mining to individuals, groups, or cooperatives representing over 15,000 small-scale miners. (World Bank, 1991: 7) Diamond purchases by the Precious Minerals Marketing Corporation went up from only 4444 carats in 1987 to 34,230 carats in 1988, 151,606 in 1989, and 484,876 carats in 1990, valued at US$14.3 m., or three-quarters of total recorded diamond production (*ibid.*).[13]

---

[13] The level of diamond purchases which the World Bank cites cannot be reconciled with those recorded by

Diamonds also improved in quality and in value per carat from US$4.48 in 1988 to US$29.45 in 1990. Gold purchased by the PMMC was nil in 1988, but jumped to 9,272 ounces in 1989, worth US$3.7 m., and 17,233 ounces in 1990 (worth US$6.3 m.) or about 3 percent of total gold exports (*ibid.*). It therefore appears that only a small part of unofficial gold production has been recaptured.

7. Forestry

Like the rest of the export sector before the ERP, the forest sector suffered from transportation bottlenecks, aging equipment and shortage of spare parts, and over-valuation of the cedi, leading to either smuggling or diversion from exports to domestic use. Total production of logs fell from 2.05 million cubic metres in 1975 to 0.48 million cubic metres in 1980. However, exports declined even more rapidly as a percentage of total production as domestic prices became more attractive than export prices; the percentage of exports declined from 40 percent (worth US$130 m.) in 1973 to 9 percent (worth only US$12 m.) in 1982.

However, the decline of the forest sector also reflected serious problems of mismanagement and sustainability of the sector. A study by the Ghana Commercial Bank in 1985 estimated that the high forest zone (HFZ) was being destroyed at the rate of 4.5 percent annually. In 1962 the total HFZ outside the forest reserves was estimated at 9,283 square kilometres; twenty years later (1982) this had been reduced to 3,740 square kilometres. Forest reserves were estimated at less than 19 percent of the HFZ as a whole. According to this report forest management and conservation were non-existent outside the reserves because the staff of the Forestry Department were underpaid and critically overstretched; replanting had been minimal and confined largely to quick-growing species rather than the prime hardwoods which required a much longer period to mature. The method of logging had been very selective and wasteful; marginal operators abandoned large trunks unprocessed after sawing off contract sizes and minor species were often felled and ignored. Serious environmental problems were being created, as fuelwood processors and then slash-and-burn farmers took advantage of logging roads to penetrate the forest (Hutchful, 1989).

The ERP set out to revive the forest sector by renewing access to critical inputs via two IDA Export Rehabilitation Credits (ERC I and II) and less directly via the Reconstruction Import Credits (RIC). Logging companies also benefited from the foreign-exchange retention scheme. Existing restrictions on export of logs were removed (the export of 14 species in log form had been banned in 1979, both as a conservation measure and in order to gain more value from local processing). Meanwhile the Ghana Timber Marketing Board was abolished and replaced by two new agencies, the Timber Export Development Board (to be strictly concerned with exports) and the Forest Products Inspection Bureau. Production and export performance for the forestry sector is shown in Table 10.

---

purchases in 1990, but states that total production was only 150,400 carats. According to this same source, total production rose to 419,000 carats in 1991, of which 280,600 were via PMMC.

Table 10   Production and Exports of Logs and Timber Products, 1988-92

	1984	1985	1986	1987	1988	1989	1990	1991	1992
				(In thousands of cubic meters)					
Logs					1180	996	1290	1229	1318
Exports	123	177	343	352	330	201	155	215	161
Sawn Timber					400	537	632	578	549
Exports	201	353	127	163	170	154	202	183	232
Veneer					60	52	71	---	---
Exports					21	15	17	---	---
Plywood					22	21	29	---	---
Exports					1	1	2	---	---

Source: Ghana Government, *Quarterly Digest of Statistics* and Ministry of Lands and Natural Resources.

The initial approach under the ERP was concerned primarily to restore earnings and maximize returns from the forest industry, even though it was amply evident that forest resource exploitation had already exceeded sustainability. A Bank survey of the industrial sector in 1985 pointed to 'an urgent need for long-range planning to make maximum use of Ghana's forest resources'. Such planning, however, did not appear to have included protection of the remainder of Ghana's rapidly diminishing forests, even though various Bank teams argued about policy details. In reaction to the dwindling forests plans had been put in place by government calling for net allowable removals (after felling losses) to be reduced from 2.9 million cubic metres to only 1.2 cubic metres after 1985. However, a Forestry Project Preparation Mission from the World Bank argued that, in view of substantial undercutting in the past, the allowable cut of industrial wood for the period 1979-2000 could be raised to 2.1 million cubic metres per year. In addition it would be possible in the estimation of the mission to raise the supply of fuelwood and charcoal from 11 million cubic metres roundwood equivalent in 1975 to 17 million cubic metres in 1990. A second Bank report disagreed with this assessment. It noted the existing allowable cut to be 'substantially in excess of the long-term sustainable yield' and urged caution in the way that such figures were applied in the absence of adequate forest inventories. Nevertheless this second report came to similar conclusions in a more roundabout way. It pointed to regional variations in the level of actual cuts and while noting that cuts were exceeded in Eastern, Volta, and Western and Central Regions it argued that in Ashanti, Brong Ahafo and Northern Regions undercutting was the rule and that in these areas 'the cut could be vastly increased' (World Bank, 1983: 23).[14]

Conflicting views of the state of Ghana's forest industry continued to appear in different Bank reports, suggesting the absence of a coherent policy orientation. A Bank

---

[14] ERP projections were that export volumes of wood products would increase from 126,565 cubic metres in 1983-84 to 210,000 cubic metres in 1986-87. It seems that the first of these figures was a considerable underestimate, while the latter was easily exceeded (see Table 10).

staff appraisal of the sector in 1988 noted that actual cuts were far above the allowable cut 'by approximately 1.6 to 2.5 times the current allowable cut' (1.8 to 2.7 million m^3 as opposed to 1.1 million m^3) (World Bank, 1988b, quoted in Hogg, 1993: 107) On the other hand, another Bank report two years later was claiming that Ghana 'has plentiful forestry resources and its timber types are eagerly sought in European markets...With technical know-how and improvements in quality, Ghana could expand exports of wood products substantially' (World Bank, 1990: Annex 2.1).

In 1988 the Bank was itself to admit that 'in spite of the importance of Ghana's forest resources...no up to date and comprehensive policy' existed for the sector (World Bank, 1988b, quoted in Hogg, 1993: 108). The Bank staff appraisal report noted the existence of serious weaknesses among the institutions charged with regulating and promoting various aspects of the forest sector (the Ministry of Land and Mineral Resources, the Forestry Commission, the Forestry Department, the Lands Department and the Game and Wildlife Department) tracing the problems to understaffing and lack of training, shortages of equipment and transportation, and inadequate incentives. This survey of the sector led to the initiation of the Forest Resources Management Project (the National Forestry Action Plan) supported by the IDA. The purpose of the FRMP was to strengthen forestry institutions and to maximize earnings from the industry consistent with the principle of sustainable yield. A new forest revenue system, which includes higher royalty fees and a new concession allocation procedure, has been introduced, with the stated intention of improving the efficiency and productivity of the forestry industry and to secure its viability in the long term. However, some authors have questioned the apparent discrepancy between the diagnosis and the prescriptions in the FRMP, pointing out that the Bank's own export projections seem to assume continued overcutting well in excess of the sustainable yield (Hogg, 1993: 110).

Table 10 shows a rapid rise in log and sawn timber exports in this period immediately after adjustment, in apparent response to the combination of improvements in inputs and incentives and a policy vacuum. Exports have subsequently stabilized at a slightly lower level but the overall cuts seems to have gone on increasing beyond the levels declared unsustainable at the end of the 1980s. The result has been to bring Ghana's traditional export species further to the point of extinction. The stock life of popular species like odum, sapele, mahogany, utile and edinam has been reduced to between 10 and 25 years: the afromosia species is commercially extinct. The government has responded by extending the ban on commercial exploitation to include four more species (to make a total of 18) but it is clear that most of the damage to Ghana's forests has already been done. Both the statistics and the frequency with which local authorities complain about illegal felling and threat of deforestation suggest that existing regulatory structures are still far from effective. Deregulation of the sector has also led to several instances of fraud and malpractice by enterprises involved in the sector, some funded by donor dollars (Friends of the Earth, 1992).

8. Public Sector Reform

8.1 Financial Sector Reform

By the beginning of ERP in 1983 most of Ghana's banking system was virtually bankrupt from a combination of internal problems, such as poor lending decisions, inadequate provision for portfolio losses, artificially inflated profits, high operational costs, weak internal management, and inappropriate monetary and financial policies. High inflation, excessive bank charges and further loss of confidence in the banking system with the confiscation of bank accounts by the PNDC in 1982 led to financial disintermediation. The large adjustments in the external value of the Cedi worsened the situation of the banks, directly by raising their external liabilities and indirectly through deterioration in the financial condition of many corporate clients. Many banks found themselves saddled with huge non-performing loan portfolios. The banking system was therefore unable to undertake the financial functions required to support the ERP, particularly in terms of the provision of credit.

A number of initial measures were taken to improve the operational environment of the banking system. From 1985 interest-rate determination was liberalized in order to allow banks to restore interest rates to positive levels. From 1988 all sectoral credit ceilings were removed, with the last of these - the mandatory 20 percent lending to agriculture - being removed in early 1991. Preferential interest rates to different economic sectors (which subsidized lending to agriculture and other priority sectors, namely manufacturing and exports), were in effect abolished at the same time. Reform of the banking sector commenced with the Financial Sector Adjustment Programme (FINSAC), the first phase (1988-91) of which was funded by an IDA credit of US$100 m. The objectives of FINSAC I were to restructure financially distressed banks, enhance the soundness of banking institutions generally by improving the regulatory framework and strengthening bank supervision by the Bank of Ghana, and through these means improve resource mobilization and increase the efficiency of credit allocation by the banking system. Restructuring of the distressed banks was effected through the government taking over from the banks' portfolios all non-performing loans and other government-guaranteed obligations of state-owned enterprises (a total of 31.4 bn Cedis at the end of 1989), while the non-performing loans of the private sector (amounting to 21.9bn Cedis) were redeemed through offsets and the issuance of government bonds. These assets were then transferred to a Non-Performing Assets Recovery Trust (NPART), which was entrusted with recovering these assets to the extent possible within a six-year time frame, with the help of a special judicial tribunal. Recapitalization of the banks allowed them to meet capital adequacy requirements by the end of 1990. The second objective (improving the regulatory framework) was achieved with the passage of the Amended Banking Law of August 1989 to replace the Banking Act of 1970 as well as the Banking and Financial Institutions Decree of 1979, thus strengthening the ability of the Bank of Ghana to manage and monitor the operations of banks. Under the new regulations banks were required to maintain a minimum capital base equivalent to 6 percent of net assets (adjusted for risk assets), and to limit secondary capital.

A second phase of financial sector reform (FINSAC II) ran from 1992 to 1994 and aimed at deepening the earlier reforms and further diversifying and strengthening the financial sector. FINSAC II had ten major targets, but the most noteworthy were divestiture of the government's interest in the banking system, reduction of bank taxation, reorganization of the structure, procedures and financial condition of the central bank, and enhancement of the effectiveness of non-bank financial institutions.

A new feature of the financial scene in Ghana is the development of a money market through the establishment of two discount houses and a stock exchange (which started operating at the end of 1990). The Consolidated Discount House (CDH), owned by 8 banks and 6 insurance companies, was established in November 1987 to act as an interbank agent dealing in treasury bills, short-term government securities, bankers acceptances, cocoa bills, commercial paper, and so on. A second discount house, Securities Discount House, has been established with IFC assistance.

Judged by some of its key objectives FINSAC has not been entirely successful. As Tsikata and Amuzu (1991: 40) observe: 'Given the considerable reforms which have taken place within the financial system, it is perhaps quite surprising to find that savings mobilization remains quite low'. Total credit extended by the banking system rose from 6.4 percent of GDP in 1984 to 11.6 percent in 1986 and then declined progressively to just over 7 percent of GDP in 1989 and 1990 (World Bank, 1993a: 59). Overall lending contracted further in 1991 but then jumped in 1992 (owing to financing of the government deficit and lending to COCOBOD and the private sector) before being reined back in 1993. Except for the unusual credit picture in 1992 scarcity of credit remains a serious constraint on the activities of the productive sectors; correspondingly, banks continue to be excessively liquid. Interest paid on deposits also remains low, in part necessitated by high reserve requirements, which until recently attracted no interest (a rate of 3 percent is now paid on commercial bank reserves). In addition the liberalization of credit and interest rates had two other undesirable effects. One was an increase in spread between lending and deposit rates. The other was the flow of credit *away* from the productive sectors (as we have already seen from our discussion of the agricultural sector) and into commerce which accounted for almost 30 percent of all lending in 1992, as against 19 percent in 1987.[15] Ghanaian policy-makers had anticipated these consequences and objected in particular to the liberalization of interest rates but were ignored by the Bank (Abbey, 1991: 523).

Broader macroeconomic and structural factors, as well as the slow pace of financial reform, have contributed to the persistent problems with the banking system. High interest rates have made borrowing costs prohibitive. Weak recovery in the industrial sector has further constrained the ability to borrow. Banks continue to be conservative and inefficient in their management and lending practices.[16] The need of government to offset the effect on inflation of a strong inflow of foreign exchange by limiting the growth of domestic credit has necessitated still lower credit ceilings and high reserve requirements, which in turn continue to discourage competition among the banks and the mobilization of deposits. Nevertheless there was some evidence of financial deepening, with a decline in the currency/deposit ratio from 57 percent in 1986 to 36 percent by the end of 1991 and 29 percent by mid-1992. In January 1992 the Bank of Ghana moved to address some of these difficulties by introducing an indirect system of monetary control to shift the instruments of monetary policy and management away from credit ceilings on individual banks to reliance on open market operations. Under this arrangement money market financial instruments or securities are traded in a weekly auction system held at the Bank of Ghana, with discount rates being established

---

[15] The significance of this point should probably not be overemphasized, since throughout the period when the ceilings were applied the banks consistently failed to comply with them. Actual bank lending to the priority sectors was often below the recommended ceilings while those for non-priority sectors were exceeded. In 1983, for example, while credit to commerce and finance (both non-priority sectors) exceeded the ceiling by 94 percent, in none of the priority sectors were the recommended ceilings reached. Tsikata and Amuzu (1993: 34).

[16] See the criticism of banking practices by the Vice-President of Ghana in the *Daily Graphic*, 10 August 1994.

through this auction. With the deterioration of monetary conditions in the second half of 1992, and the large increase in money supply (by 38 percent between June and December and 53 percent for the year as a whole) the currency/deposit ratio shot up once again to 55 percent (a level comparable with the mid-1980s) by the end of the year, forcing the central bank to resort once again to extraordinary measures to restrain credit. Currently in spite of the reforms financial intermediation remains low, with the financial assets of banks and non-bank financial institutions remaining quite small as suggested by the ratio of broad money to GDP, which is less than 15 percent (IMF 1993: 25-26). While broad monetary and economic conditions have contributed to the ongoing difficulties of the banks (in part because the impact of these factors were not taken adequately into account in designing the sector reforms), at the same time the World Bank's efforts at financial sector reform have in general been somewhat experimental (a hint of this may be gathered from the admission that FINSAC was a 'reform programme of considerable complexity, *novelty* and comprehensiveness' (World Bank, 1992b: ii, emphasis added) and the results generally unimpressive (see in particular Gelb and Honohan, 1991).

8.2   State Enterprise Divestiture and Reform

At the beginning of the ERP in 1983 Ghana had a total of 235 state enterprises (SEs), consisting of 181 enterprises in which the state exercised sole or majority ownership and a further 54 with minority shareholding. The acquisition of these enterprises occurred over three distinct phases and reflected a combination of accident and design. The first set of enterprises were those established during the Nkrumah regime in the 1960s. The second phase involved the establishment of new enterprises and partial and complete nationalization of a number of private concerns during the Acheampong era. The third phase of acquisitions took place through the confiscations of the first Rawlings government. The result was a grab-bag of enterprises rather than the expression of a long-range vision of state involvement in the industrial sector. Most of these enterprises had been allowed to deteriorate through mismanagement, political interference in their operations, unrealistic price controls (in part to facilitate the collection of rent by political favourites), shortages of inputs, and lack of maintenance. After the failure of an attempt to divest several state enterprises in the mid-1960s the SEs fell into a policy limbo. Between 1969 and 1981 no divestiture was contemplated, yet the state clearly lacked the resources to either rehabilitate or manage the enterprises properly.

SEs provided about 4.5 percent of 1984 census employment and 27.6 percent of employment in the modern sector, generating between 7.5 and 9.5 percent of total domestic industrial product (Davis, 1991: 989). In the medium and large-scale manufacturing sector they accounted for 45 percent of value added and 40 percent of employment in 1986. Nevertheless state enterprises as a whole piled up considerable losses and hence made little contribution to state revenue, either in terms of profits or repayments of interest or principal on loans. Government subventions to SEs increased from 1.1 bn Cedis in 1982 to 7.35 bn in 1986. A 1987 study of 18 SEs showed that by June 1987 they owed 40 bn Cedis to the government and 5 bn Cedis to each other (Boakye-Danquah, 1990: 90).

PNDC policy on SEs unfolded gradually. An early World Bank document discussing the government's position made no mention of divestiture as one of the options being considered (although the Bank itself obviously considered it to be the most desirable course of action), indicating merely that the Government was 'interested in exploring a formula under which individual state enterprises would be made subject to the discipline of the market, with independent boards-of-directors accountable to the nation for financial and economic performance' (World Bank, 1983: 39).

State enterprise reform did not commence in earnest until 1987. ERP II proposed a two-year plan with three key elements: a) an overall policy framework for dealing with the problems of the sector; b) a divestiture programme; and c) strengthening of state enterprise management, as well as of the Government's ability to monitor enterprise performance. The State Enterprises Commission (SEC) was restructured to improve its monitoring and supervisory capability. Conditionalities relating to SEs included the imposition of financial discipline and restrictions on access to credit and the progressive reduction of their access to government resources (including foreign exchange); and a freeze on new hiring and staff reduction of 5 percent per year for 1987-88, pending a comprehensive plan for labour redeployment. Three-year corporate plans were to be prepared by individual enterprises, and performance contracts concluded with the government. Enterprises remaining in the public sector were to be opened to increased competition and market discipline, including competition from foreign firms through trade liberalization where no domestic competitors existed. Initial focus was placed on 14 large enterprises with a major impact on the government's budget.

For policy purposes these and other SEs were classified into three broad groups, ranging from fully government-owned enterprises to be maintained and managed within the public sector, or placed under management contracts; those to be converted into joint ventures with foreign or local partners; and enterprises (including joint ventures) to be sold off, liquidated, merged or amalgamated. There was to be progressive reduction to only a core of 22 enterprises by 1989 (Boakye-Danquah, 1990: 89).[17]

A preliminary list of 32 SEs to be divested was published in May 1988. This was later expanded to include a further 46 enterprises, including profit-making ones (however, unlike the first list these were not advertised but were to be made available for divestiture if investors expressed interest). However, the pace of both enterprise reform and divestiture was slow and fell well behind the agreed schedule with the World Bank. Between 1987 and the end of 1991 only 49 enterprises were divested, most of them through liquidations (Tangri, 1991: 110; Gyimah-Boadi, 1992). There was lack of coordination among the agencies involved in the exercise. Progress was also slowed by a shortage of Ghanaian technical expertise to undertake the background work required to prepare the enterprises for divestiture. In most enterprises accounts were several years behind, there was no standardized accounting system for SEs as a whole, and in many cases there were no up-to-date statements of assets and liabilities. There was also a lack of agreed criteria for evaluating the enterprises to be offered for sale, and the absence of a stock exchange precluded leaving the issue to market forces. A scandal from earlier failed attempts to divest state enterprises to foreign concerns in the mid-1960s (at what were perceived to be 'give-away' prices) made both the issue of valuation and that of sale to foreigners sensitive ones, particularly given the wide

---

[17] This was later modified in a statement by the State Enterprises Commission to include 17 'core enterprises' (in such areas as transportation, posts and telecommunications, energy, cocoa marketing, and water) plus an extended core of another 21 enterprises which would serve important policy purposes (Tangri, 1992: 110).

divergence between the book and market values of most of the enterprises in question. To further complicate matters the legal status of some of the confiscated enterprises was in doubt since the confiscations were not in many cases supported by the appropriate legal documentation, asset identification, or transfer of ownership.

Most of the enterprises were also saddled with unfunded liabilities from generous retirement benefits negotiated under past collective agreements that in many cases exceeded the net worth of the enterprises, as well as provisions for pay, allowances and benefits under current collective agreements with the public sector unions that were more generous than anything available in the private sector. Prospective private purchasers were unlikely to assume these liabilities unless they were first cleared (Davis, 1991). Davis has argued that it was the existence of such institutional impediments, rather than simply the 'absence of market discipline' that inhibited the possibility of improving enterprise performance through either enterprise reform or divestiture.

Obtaining political consensus and legitimacy for divestiture was the most serious problem, both within the government and among the broader public. There was public opposition in particular to divesting profitable enterprises, and fears of retrenchment from the unions. Many Ghanaians remained unconvinced of the case against public enterprise, particularly where the only viable alternative was foreign control; to many it was even less clear, given the supposedly superior entrepreneurial abilities of foreign enterprise, why already *profitable* enterprises, as opposed to distressed ones, should be turned over to foreign capital. Among Ghanaians the typical reasoning went as follows:

> In face of slow revenue growth, it will be fiscally imprudent to do away with highly profitable enterprises which are major contributors to government revenue. As competition increases, the marginal enterprises will, however, become more vulnerable. It is these potential loss makers that should be included in the basket of enterprises for sale (Tsikata and Amuzu, 1991: 13).

This paper came not from the trade unions or the private or government-owned media (where one encounters such views with regularity) but was co-authored by an official of the Ministry of Finance and Economic Planning. In particular there has been a good deal of public opposition to the sale of government shares in Ashanti Goldfields.[18] On the other hand the conventional rationale for divestiture in the North is that it is precisely the successful enterprises that should be offloaded, since they are likely to fetch the most attractive price. In the view of the World Bank the sale of Ashanti, the most attractive plum in the portfolio of the Ghana Government, would also send an unmistakable signal of Government 'resolve' to investors.

There was little domestic pressure for divestiture, and few political points to be scored. As Gyimah-Boadi rightly argues, 'While the programme poses an immediate threat to many established interests (labour, SOE managers and professionals, private suppliers and contractors, etc.) its potential benefits are indefinite and amorphous' (Gyimah-Boadi, 1992: 204).

There was also less than complete unanimity within either the government or even the Divestiture Implementation Committee (DIC) which was charged with the task of

---

[18] See the results of the opinion survey, 'Many Oppose Sale to Foreigners', *Business and Financial Times*, 21 October - 3 November 1993: 1.

preparing the enterprises for sale, and signals from the relevant government officials to the DIC were not always unambiguous. In order to create the necessary consensus the membership of the DIC itself was drawn from interests with divergent ideological perspectives and attitudes toward divestiture (for instance three of the 10 members were drawn from the trade unions). The workers' defence committees had been particularly strong in the SEs: and this made it difficult on the one hand to secure agreement on divestiture from the workers' organizations and on the other to attract investor interest. Surprisingly the domestic private sector was not represented on the DIC or involved in the decision-making process in any significant way (*ibid.*; Tangri, 1991: 534) and felt discriminated against in the implicit (and sometimes explicit) preference expressed by the authorities for foreign enterprises with access to international capital, technology and markets. The reconstitution of the DIC in late 1989 and early 1990 disrupted the work of the Committee and led to the departure of several officials with valuable accumulated experience in divestiture (Gyimah-Boadi, 1992: 205).

Since 1992, however, the pace of divestiture has accelerated with a number of large enterprises and state banks being offered or prepared for sale. In 1993 and 1994 the government completed the sale of the first and second tranches of its shares in Ashanti Goldfields as well as a minority stake in seven other companies. While there was no question of the desire of the PNDC (within its limited means) to reform the state enterprise sector, and while the increasing flexibility of the PNDC on the question of divestiture was a recognition of the financial constraints to a version of this process which would preserve its basic shape, some measure of arm-twisting by the World Bank was also involved. The Bank sought to pin the blame for the increasingly embarrassing failure of private investment to materialize on the reluctance of government to divest the SEs. According to a key Bank report on the private sector the very existence of the SEs 'has been a major constraint to creating a favourable business environment and healthy competition'. In this light the 'effective implementation of the divestiture programme could become a powerful stimulus to private sector investment in Ghana' (World Bank, 1990: 24-25). However, part of the recent impetus for divestiture has also come from the need to find alternative sources of budgetary support for the large expenditure overruns that have been at the basis of the government's recent fiscal difficulties. While expected revenue from divestiture for 1994 was estimated at US$110 m., by April 1994 receipts had reached US$270 m. (net of US$100 m. in advance payments for Ashanti shares in 1993).

Determining the pace and success of reforms in the enterprises left in the state sector is not easy since comprehensive consolidated accounts for the SEs as a whole is not available. Under the new restructuring plan of the SEC, managements of the SEs have been granted full power to hire and fire employees and determine wage and salary levels, as well as prices for products and services (in the case of non-utilities). The corporate strategy plan for the 14 core enterprises includes performance contracts covering a number of indicators, including producing financial statements, assessing the market value of the enterprise assets, and developing programmes for the payment of taxes and dividends. A major thrust of the restructuring programme is to separate non-commercial operations from purely commercial ones and profitable from loss-making operations, 'downsizing' or terminating the operations of the latter. The SEC can decide to liquidate an enterprise if it makes losses for three consecutive years. These reforms seem to have had some positive impact on the operation of some enterprises, as can be gleaned from the financial performance of some 12-14 key enterprises whose summary accounts are published on a regular basis by the SEC. The enterprises contribute the bulk of the value added and employment in the manufacturing and service sectors in the country. In 1992 the total revenue and costs of these 12 SEs amounted to 401 bn Cedis (13 percent of GDP) and 302 bn Cedis (10 percent of GDP) respectively with aggregate pretax profit amounting to about 99 bn Cedis (three percent of GDP).

Table 11   Summary of Financial Operations of Selected Major State Public Enterprises, 1987-92[a] (in millions of current Cedis)

	1987	1988	1989	1990	1991	1992
Revenues	105,270	142,317	187,329	257,517	297,446	401,281
Costs	89,689	122,619	157,167	206,462	248,739	302,249
Profits	15,580	19,697	30,162	51,055	48,706	99,032
Tax	680	377	302	533	1,029	2,085
Dividend payments	39	62	331	553	5,425	5,425
Subvention receipts	969	271	214	4,767	6,204	6,204
Net lending receipts	90	---	---	---	---	---
Investment	19,006	22,357	57,771	5,924	242,339	234,356
Foreign financing of investment	17,841	16,479	23,137	---	---	---

Source: IMF.
[a]   These are: Volta River Authority (VRA), State Shipping Corporation, Ghana Water and Sewerage Corporation, Ghana Supply Commission, Ghana Railway Corporation, Ghana Post and Telecommunication Corp., Ghana Ports and Harbours Authority, Ghana Oil Company Ltd., Tema Oil Refinery, Electricity Corporation of Ghana, Ghana Airways Corporation, and Ghana Cocoa Board.

Overall the profitability situation has improved over the years. Profits as a proportion of total revenue increased from about 13 percent in the mid-1980s to nearly 25 percent in 1992 (IMF, 1993). Net lending by government to these enterprises has virtually ceased, although there were large subventions to Ghana Water and Sewerage in 1990, 1991, and 1992 amounting to a total of 17.2 bn Cedis (see Table 11). However, the trends in profitability conceal significant inter-enterprise differences in performance.

In recent years most of the profit has been earned by a few large enterprises: the Volta River Authority (VRA), Ghana Water and Sewerage Corporation, Ghana Post and Telecommunication Corporation, Ghana Oil Company and COCOBOD. In addition payment of both taxes and dividends remain low, in part because the four large state enterprises (VRA, ECG, COCOBOD, and Ghana Water and Sewerage Corporation) are legally exempt from payment of taxes, and in part because even those enterprises not legally exempt rarely pay them. In relation to dividends, however, the situation improved markedly in 1991 and 1992 when the government received dividend payments amounting to 5.4 bn Cedis, most of which came from the VRA. Most state enterprises do not pay dividends on the equity investment made by government irrespective of whether they make profits or not. A major reason for the poor tax compliance and low dividend payments is said to be the weak capital base of the public enterprises (*ibid.*: 17-18).

Even so these enterprises, which have absorbed much of the reform efforts should not be seen as necessarily representative. The 1994 Budget Statement gives a bleak picture of the performance of SEs generally. According to the Minister of Finance: (a) of over 220[19] enterprises in which the government still had a stake, only 27 were up to date in their accounts (presumably 13 if we exclude the enterprises discussed above): (b) total dividends for 1994 amounted to C 7.8 bn plus payments arrears of C 3.4 bn. In the view of the government a 'much higher level of dividends could have been realized': (c) SEs were not forwarding dividends to government but retaining them for inordinate periods of time, sometimes investing them in treasury bills, leading the government to pay interest on moneys due to it in the first place: (d) SEs nevertheless continued to make demands on government for capital renewal instead of relying on their own resources; (e) where the government had guaranteed foreign credits to SEs the 'record of repayments has been most disappointing'. 'The impression that evidently has been created is that funds received from government are not meant to be repaid'.[20] This indictment seems to give an impression of very little progress, and would seem to offer one reason as to why the government is much more willing to consider large-scale divestiture.

8.3   Civil Service Reform

Ghana initiated adjustment with a gravely weakened public service system incapable of managing economic reforms of the scope required. This became increasingly evident as the ERP proceeded. As the Policy Framework Paper (June 1987 - July 1990: 14) noted:

> Weaknesses in public sector management and implementation have emerged as serious obstacles to the full success of economic and financial policies. Key economic and financial management institutions are understaffed and suffer from severe shortcomings in organization and equipment. In particular, policy analysis and the planning process, budgetary control, and aid coordination, and debt management needs to be strengthened.

An Institutional Support Programme (with a credit of US$10.8 m.) was approved by the IDA in 1987 to provide training, equipment and materials to strengthen the analytical and management capabilities of the Ministry of Finance and Economic Planning, the National Revenue Secretariat, and the Accountant-General's Department; improve the economic co-ordination functions of the PNDC; attract and retain skilled Ghanaians in the public service; promote civil service reform through the Office of the Head of the Civil Service; and assist in the implementation of labour rationalization. In this section we will address only the civil service reforms. The contract for the Civil Service Reform Programme (CSRP) has been handled since mid-1987 by the Royal Institute for Public Administration International Services, in collaboration with the management

---

[19] The Minister's figure puts into question the total of 49 divestments 1987-91 cited above.

[20] Ghana Government (1994).

consulting firm Coopers and Lybrand Deloitte, funded by the ODA. The main focus of the work has been on strengthening the key central functions of personnel management, management training and services.

The reforms were intended to deal with a number of problems. First, salary levels had deteriorated to an extent where they were having serious effects on morale and productivity, making it difficult to attract or retain senior staff of the appropriate calibre. Inadequate staffing at the senior professional, technical and managerial levels was said to be combined at the same time with major overstaffing and underemployment at the junior levels of the service. Over the previous decade staffing at the lowest grades of the civil service had grown by some 14 percent a year. The central management system (Office of the Head of the Civil Service) had broken down and the management services function in general required revitalizing. Staff development and job-related training had been neglected and key aspects of personnel management were lacking, particularly in the areas of establishment control, accurate personnel records, and staff appraisal systems (Marshall, 1990: 7). Planning in most ministries was almost non-existent and none of the ministries had data storage facilities or proper records management system (Asante, 1991: 3) 90 percent of the civil service budget was going on recurrent expenditure, and only 10 percent on capital expenditure. A large percentage of the overall budget was being spent on salaries and little on the means of delivery of public services.

The reforms have been headed by an Oversight Committee which is chaired by the Head of the Service and is responsible for overall coordination and direction. Below the Oversight Committee are four sub-committees: Incomes Policy and Salary Administration; Management Services; Training and Manpower Development; and Personnel Policy and Management. The work of these four agencies is backed by a Consultancy and Technical Support scheme.

The first task of the reform programme was to gain an accurate idea of the actual size of the civil service and to set the stage for redeployment. This was followed by a redeployment exercise in which the objective was initially to reduce the size of the public service by 15 percent for each of the first three years from 1987 to 1989 and by specified targets in the years following. Redeployment was carried out by the Redeployment Management Committee (RMC) under the office of the Secretary for Mobilization and Social Welfare (chair). Initially identifying the redeployees was carried out by Workplace Staff Appraisal Committees that were decentralized to the Ministry or Department level and consisted of the department or ministry head, middle management, and workers' representatives and were designed to remove the central government from the process and avoid any appearance of victimization. Later, however, redeployment was based on job inspections carried out by the Management Services Division (MSD) and retitled the Labour Rationalization Exercise.

Redeployment affected almost exclusively the lowest ranks of the civil service and also affected disproportionately the youngest and least experienced civil servants,[21] and while this was perhaps inevitable it did not improve perceptions of equity in the exercise. Administrative grade personnel constituted only 0.21 percent of redeployed, even though many of the problems of the service were perceived as stemming from weak performance at this level. By all indications job counselling and retraining, though part of the redeployment package, were never put into effect.

---

[21] ODA (1989: 1).

According to data from the Management Services Division (MSD), which oversees the personnel aspects of the reforms, the size of the civil service was reduced by 30 percent between 1986 and April 1993, but since it is not clear whether this is gross or net of new hirings in the public services the actual scale of attrition is difficult to determine with certainty (ODA, 1993). Personnel and payroll data are being computerized. Both salary scales and pay differentials have been increased and a simplified grading structure has been introduced. With the rebuilding of the MSD the ability of the Office of the Head of the Civil Service (OHCS) to monitor ministerial performance has improved. The implementation of management reviews and job inspections (with job inspection units established in the key sector ministries) and staff retraining is said to have led to some improvement in productivity; manpower budget hearings were reintroduced in 1991, allowing the setting of manpower ceilings for government agencies and thus tightening controls over recruitment. The most visible input facilitated by the Structural Adjustment Institutional Support Project (SAIS) and other forms of donor support has been in the area of office infrastructure and logistics -personal computers and other forms of office equipment, vehicles, etc. Training in computer skills for junior and middle-level (though not apparently senior) civil servants was probably the most popular and successful aspect of the SAIS and on the whole the project proved to be a bonanza for local computer firms and consultants.

However, actual 'institutional reform' seems to have fallen well behind progress in redeployment. While a number of government agencies such as the OHCS, the National Revenue Service (NRS) and the Treasury benefited in terms of institutional capacity, these improvements were not generalized to other government departments (World Bank, 1993b: 9; ODA, 1993; Aryee, 1991). Resentment toward Ghanaian recruits from abroad (at higher salaries than the remainder of the civil service) led to very few being recruited. Several of the key institutional novelties contemplated under the SAIS failed to take off; an example is the lack of progress on a key innovation suggested by the Public Administration Restructuring and Decentralization Implementation Committee (PARDIC) in 1983. This involved the introduction into each ministry of a Policy Planning, Budgeting, Monitoring and Evaluation Department (PPBMED). A survey of PPBMED carried out in 1991-92 in the three key ministries of Agriculture, Education and Health found serious teething problems, but also significant variations in their establishment and performance (Boateng and Asante, 1992). The PPBMEDs were seriously understaffed (that in Agriculture, the best resourced, had only about 23 percent of the required professional staff in post), had weak linkages to other departments (including those in their own units) and lacked the vehicles and equipment required for minimum functioning. It must be remembered that these ministries were responsible for key elements of the adjustment programme, then almost ten years old.

While the various inputs from SAIS and other sources have helped to upgrade the productive capacity of the public sector they have often been injected without necessarily transforming the organizational contexts and relationships within which this technology is to be deployed, and with little concern for standardization and the development of maintenance facilities. One also of course wonders what will happen when these technical inputs begin to depreciate, and about the overall implications that this might carry for sustainability of the reforms. A review of the SAIS observes that: 'useful improvements in capacity occurred in respect of public investment programming, external debt management, tax administration and civil service reforms, as well as in the capacity to track the effect of the ERP on the poor'. However, '(a)lthough many people were able to use their training effectively in more responsible jobs, in general, the technical and managerial capacity of the relevant units did not show sustained improvement' (World Bank, 1993b: 10).

There are many reasons for this lack of progress. At least until the award of large salary increases to the civil service in 1992 unattractive service conditions had made it difficult to attract qualified new personnel, or to retain those who were hired, especially at the middle management level. Restructuring was followed by significant improvements in wages for the smaller civil service that remained, but even with these increases the level of real wages in the civil service lagged behind those prevailing in the private sector, particularly for middle management. Trainees were sometimes not effectively utilized.

MSD, the very agency that was supposed to lead the reforms for efficiency, was demoralized by across-the-board budget cuts like other agencies. As in the rest of the ministries, absence of assured budgetary levels made planning in the MSD difficult. Another source of demoralization was the perceived lack of responsiveness of much of the public sector to reform initiatives. Some of this was attributed to inertia and even deliberate resistance to reform from the very top of the civil service,[22] facilitated in part by the lack of performance appraisal for senior staff and the absence of adequate performance targets (say in the budget review process) and sanctions for failure to perform.

Clearly statements by senior government officials and particularly by the Head of State himself suggest strong concern about the poor performance of top and middle-level bureaucrats. However, my impression is that the key reformers, who, like Rawlings himself have been drawn from outside the bureaucracy, have preferred to ignore or circumvent the civil service and rely on outside consultants (including Bank and Fund staff) whenever necessary. The extensive dependence of the Ghana programme on such consultants (many directly appointed and paid for by donors) is both effect and cause of the weakness of public sector capacity in Ghana. Be this as it may, the limited success in civil service reform lies at the core of many of the implementational problems that characterize almost every aspect of reform in Ghana, and seems to justify the frequent complaints that the changes in macroeconomic climate are not adequately reflected in the attitudes and modus operandi of the public service, particularly at the level of the middle management.

9.   Poverty, Wages and Employment

9.1   The Living Standards Survey

Poverty issues were not formally placed on the agenda of the ERP until 1987, with the introduction of the Programme of Actions to Mitigate the Social Dimensions of Adjustment (PAMSCAD) and the unveiling of a Ghana National Living Standards Survey (GLSS). While the PAMSCAD provided the action framework for attacking the problems of vulnerable groups, the GLSS on the other hand sought to provide some clues as to the geographical, ecological, occupational, and gender distribution of poverty

---

[22] Interview with MSD officials, Accra, 6 May 1993.

in Ghana (Ghana Statistical Service, 1989; Oti-Boateng *et al.*, 1990; Glewwe and Twum-Baah, 1991). The main findings of the GLSS were that 36 percent of all Ghanaians lived below the poverty line (C 32,981 per annum, or approximately half of per capita income, at 1987-88 Accra prices) and around 7 percent were below the hard-core poverty line of C 16,491. The poorest 40 percent of Ghanaians accounted for 19 percent of all consumption while the wealthiest 20 percent accounted for 42 percent. Over 80 percent of the incidence of poverty (and 83.3 percent in the poorest quintile) in Ghana was accounted for by rural poverty. In terms of distribution over 43 percent of rural inhabitants fell below the poverty line - 27 percent of non-Accra residents, but only four percent of Accra residents. At the same time however the GLSS revealed considerable inter- and intra-rural differentiation. 40.9 percent of the wealthiest quintile and 45.5 percent of the two wealthiest quintiles lived in the rural areas, compared with 54.4 percent of the wealthiest quintile in the urban areas. The data suggested that the highest levels of inequality existed in the rural areas followed by the urban areas and the semi-urban areas; in terms of ecological zones, the highest level of inequality was identified in the savannah zone (in terms of overall consumption the 'poorest' zone of the country), followed by the forest zone and the coastal areas (Baffoe, 1992: 26).

In *occupational terms* government and private sector workers were overrepresented among the two wealthiest quintiles (55.5 percent and 61.5 percent respectively) while farmers and self-employed were overrepresented in the poorest two quintiles. In fact one of the most disturbing messages of the GLSS is the strong correlation between poverty and employment in *productive* activity (in particular, productive self-employment), suggesting perhaps both low levels of productivity and strong but regressive official redistributive mechanisms. A second line of stratification was between cocoa and non-cocoa households. While cocoa farmers were fairly evenly spread across all quintiles, non-cocoa farming households were skewed toward the poorest quintiles; while 43 percent of cocoa farming households were in the two poorest quintiles and 35 percent in the two wealthiest, 54 percent of non-cocoa households were in the two poorest quintiles, with only 28.5 percent in the two wealthiest. The difference in living standards between cocoa producing households and non-cocoa producing ones has been picked by other surveys too (ILO/JASPA, 1989: 21). This may be another way of saying that the supposed reversal in 'rural-urban terms of trade' usually credited to structural adjustment programmes is in fact specific to the (larger-scale) producers of export crops (*ibid.*: 16; Sarris and Shams, 1991). As the World Bank (1993a: 31) concedes, 'the benefits of growth accompanying [the] ERP may not have been enjoyed by many outside of cocoa production'. At the same time it is precisely in the depressed wage sectors of agriculture and commerce that employment growth has been strongest. There is strong evidence from other sources that adjustment is not leading to general improvement in rural incomes and conditions of life. A large proportion of rural dwellers interviewed in 1992-93 for the GLSS second round of the (Ghana Statistical Services, 1993) felt that they had not benefited from the ERP, and that in their view rural conditions had actually deteriorated since 1981 (this response was irrespective of the ecological environment). In addition to the impact of natural factors (principally drought) interviewees mentioned the effect of government policies (as indeed did those who mentioned an improvement in their circumstances). One set of respondents (members of a coastal community of 800 inhabitants) were categorical in this respect, citing the 'high cost of living, job retrenchment, lack of adequate rainfall and increase in population leading to pressures on food and social amenities like shelter'. These reasons were echoed by interviewees in a forest community (in Ashanti) which had a far larger population (8000) and thus much better social services and infrastructure, and unlike the coastal community listed cocoa among its products. On the other hand, a savannah community (population 200) surveyed did not mention government policies among its causes of misery. While the scope of the survey excludes any definitive conclusions, the responses do suggest that the recovery has either failed to penetrate the rural areas, has lacked sustainability, or has been highly differentiated in its impact on rural social groups, or possibly all of these at the same time. Certainly these negative responses may be contrasted with the much more optimistic view of their situation recorded by Hodson in interviews with villagers in 1980 (Hodson, 1983: 3).

The Living Standard Survey also showed marked gender differences in employment: while among males employees made up 27 percent of the labour force and self-employed 71 percent, among women employees made up only 7.8 percent and self-employed 91.2 percent. On the other hand, the GLSS found that the 25 percent of the population sample living in female-headed households were actually better-off (by 7 percent) than the average for male-headed households. In part this was because female-headed households were concentrated in the two wealthier parts of the country (the south and the forest zone) and relatively rare in the poorer north and savanna zones. Finally food was by far the dominant item in all household budgets irrespective of quintile, accounting for about two-thirds of total household expenditures, even though there were significant differences in how that food was procured.

The GLSS, however, did not provide any evidence of the connection between adjustment and poverty, nor did it provide the (longitudinal) data with which to make such a connection. The methodology and conclusions of the GLSS were also open to several other criticisms. The definition of 'poverty' and 'poverty-line' in the GLSS was rather arbitrary, making no reference to actual ability to earn a living wage. The study measures consumption-income but not assets (Gayi, 1994) and fails to take account of local *cultural perceptions* of poverty, which seem to differ substantially from those used by the GLSS (Norton *et al.*, n.d.). And while the study focuses attention on horizontal differentiation (between rural and urban areas and ecological zones) the significance of *vertical* differentiation within units is hardly acknowledged, although it seems to account for the majority of the inequality observed in the study (Baffoe, 1992: 26). In themselves these methodological weaknesses may be perceived as an indication of the ambivalent way in which World Bank texts approach the issue of poverty (Hutchful, 1994).

9.2   Wages and Employment

Calculating real wage trends in Ghana under adjustment is no easy matter. There are significant disparities between some of the wage data from different official sources (the Ghana Government, the IMF and the World Bank). The World Bank even offers two contradictory scenarios of trends in the real minimum wage, one (World Bank, 1991) of which shows the wage moving steadily upward (from 35 percent of the 1977 index in 1983 to 66 percent in 1986 and 114 percent in 1990) while the other shows the real minimum wage index falling back after 1987 to barely half the level attained in 1977 (World Bank, 1993a: 55). According to the latest data cited by the IMF (IMF, 1994:

14) and deflated by the consumer price index, the minimum wage stood at 59 percent of its 1977 value in 1987 and 82 percent in 1992. Though this was an improvement, it remained only just over one-third of what the Trade Union Congress (basing its calculations on the GLSS) considered to be the minimum viable household expenditure.

Table 12 Index of Real Wages (1977=100)

	Private Sector			Public Sector		
	1984	1987	1990	1984	1987	1990
All sectors	---	104	118	69	69	92
Agriculture	59	90	105	43	84	93
Mining and Quarrying	81	88	124	34	92	92
Manufacturing	57	120	171	73	83	53
Minimum Wage	---	59	82	---	59	82

Source: Computed from IMF, 1994 and using the national consumer price index as the deflator.

There is also some consensus that the distribution of wage and income gains has been uneven, and that on the whole income differentials have widened between the lower and higher income groups in recent years (ILO/JASPA, 1989; Sarris, 1993). In sector terms, the highest average wage earnings in 1990 (the latest year for which figures are available) were in manufacturing, followed by mining and quarrying, finance and insurance, and transportation, while the lowest average earnings were in construction, agriculture and commerce, in that order (see Table 13, derived from IMF data).

As the figures in Table 12 suggest, overall real wage growth was much stronger in the private than the public sector, particularly after 1987; while average wages in the public and private sectors were virtually identical in 1987, by 1990 recorded wages in the private sector were almost two and a half times those obtaining in the public sector. This differentiation in real wage gains was particularly apparent in the manufacturing sector, with real wages tripling in the private manufacturing sector between 1984 and 1990 (remarkable given the steep fall in the growth rate of the sector after 1988), while in the public manufacturing sector there were significant real wage gains until 1987, followed thereafter by steep declines (from 83 percent of the 1977 index in 1987 to only 53 percent in 1990). In the private sector wage gains were highest in the financial and insurance sector.

While agricultural wages recovered strongly from 29 percent of the 1977 index in 1984 to 90 percent in 1987 and 105 percent in 1990, nevertheless in relative terms wages in the sector lost ground. The figures in Table 13 suggest that whereas in 1984 average agricultural wages were marginally above the average monthly wages for all sectors (C 2984 compared with C 2284) by 1990 average agricultural wages had slipped *below* the average for all sectors by about 30 percent (C 20,948 versus C 30,056). This may reflect the flow of labour from other sectors of the economy into agriculture as a result of retrenchment and lack of employment openings in the urban formal sector, thus depressing agricultural wages.

Table 13   Average Monthly Earnings by Sector, 1984-90 (current prices)

	Total Economy		
	1984	1987	1990
All sectors	2,287	10,524	30,056
Agriculture	2,298	7,955	20,946
Mining and Quarrying	3,370	17,017	38,028
Manufacturing	3,441	15,216	45,045
Construction	1,573	6,882	19,183
Commerce	1,843	9,483	25,375
Transport and Communications	2,321	---	25,375
Finance and Insurance	2,567	13,877	33,650

Source: IMF, 1994.

Although wages are still a matter of considerable concern, perhaps the most problematic aspect of the ERP is the failure to increase formal employment, a reality which has negative implications for poverty alleviation and in particular for the insistence of the designers of the programme that poverty alleviation must ultimately occur through economic growth rather than special projects for the poor (Ghana Government, 1987: 10). The World Bank in its 1993 report acknowledged (after earlier denial) that lack of employment growth was indeed a problem, observing that 'In practice,.. in 1991/92 only about 15 percent of approximately 250,000 young people coming out of the school system would find regular paid employment' (World Bank, 1993a: 25). It was suggested that the rest would have to find employment in the rural and urban informal sector. This is an admission that with the continuing weak performance of the *productive sectors* of the economy adjustment had been unable to reverse the long-term processes of in-formalization observed in the Ghana economy. While most new recorded employment has occurred in agriculture and the informal sector (particularly commerce) at least in agriculture the fact that the *increase* in employment has coincided with at best stagnant overall productivity can only suggest growing underemployment and falling real incomes.

On the other hand explicit recognition that small-scale agriculture and the informal sector will have to constitute the 'shock-absorbers' in the crisis of the formal sector has not been matched by policy initiatives on the same scale. While in the agricultural sector policy change has been often belated, sometimes inappropriate, and generally ineffectual, in the case of the informal sector there has been no policy at all (Ninsin, 1991). Secondly there is a lack of any recognition of the many indications of stress on the absorptive capacity of the informal sector. Retrenchment and liberalization have encouraged a rush into commerce, thus driving up competition. There is much anecdotal evidence of sharply eroded profit margins in the sector, both from liberalization and from increased competition. As commerce is traditionally the preserve of women (in contrast to the other high-growth informal sector, transport, which is controlled almost exclusively by men), this squeeze on the sub-sector has mainly hurt women. Most 'growth' in the informal sector has occurred at the margins of the sector, and new entrants are composed mostly of young men and women, a fact manifest in the obvious increase in the number of youth in the urban centres trying to make a living as hawkers at traffic lights and in other marginal occupations. Ghanaian youth continue to migrate from the country in significant numbers under conditions so hazardous that it has become a major source of concern to the government and diplomatic missions abroad.[23] Hence these developments have both gender and generational implications. Lack of demand ('there is no money in the system') is often cited by informal sector producers and providers of services as their biggest constraint. This situation hurts the poor in two ways: first basic needs among the poor in particular (but not exclusively) remain unfulfilled; while on the other hand the sector is denied the economic stimulus required to expand productivity and employment opportunities.

9.3   PAMSCAD

PAMSCAD was the first and most costly 'Social Dimensions of Adjustment' initiative undertaken by the World Bank in Africa, and for a brief period was even touted as a form of 'good practice' which the whole continent might benefit from replicating.

At the outset (1987-88) PAMSCAD identified four poverty-affected target groups: first, small farmers and hired labour; second, poor households with limited access to basic social services such as health, education, water, etc.; third, the unemployed and those with meagre earnings, especially urban youth; and finally households in the northern regions. It is worth mentioning that this identification was carried out completely independently of the GLSS exercise. The problems of these groups were to be addressed through projects of various kinds: community initiative projects; employment generation projects; redeployment; and the provision of basic needs and services (water, sanitation, health, nutrition, shelter) and education infrastructure, all supposedly to be operated largely on the basis of community participation and mobilization, However, in its first phase the programme encountered numerous problems. There were long delays in commencing the programme. Pledges were limited, a long time in arriving and even slower in being spent. Two years into the programme only US$15 m. of donor financing had been disbursed. Funding was spread over many projects and emanated from a multiplicity of donors with sometimes complex individual procedures. Availability of local counterpart funds was also a problem, particularly for the community initiative projects, and more so given the rapid increases in project costs that occurred from inflation and currency depreciation. Other difficulties were related to the inherent defects in the design of PAMSCAD, in particular the large number of unrelated projects (23 in all). Implementation was scattered over several sectors and sector ministries, giving rise to problems of coordination and conflicts over jurisdiction. In spite of the emphasis placed on decentralization and community participation, control over projects (including sometimes project selection) was centralized in the bureaucracy in Accra, with the result that 'the intended main actors - i.e. the District Assemblies and the people, have rather become the supporting cast' (PAMSCAD Secretariat, 1990: 4). The many difficulties encountered by PAMSCAD were rooted in turn in broader problems of conception and motivation. The first of these was 'short-termism': the programme was designed as a set of quick fixes. Second, there was no clear link

---

[23] See the alarming statement by the Ministry of Foreign Affairs in *West Africa*, 27 February - 3 March 1995: 306-307.

between the social impact of *adjustment* and the direction of aid. The emphasis on 'political marketability and currency' as a guideline in project selection (Ghana Government, 1987) meant that projects were chosen more for their demonstration effect than for their ability to effect real changes in the lives of people, and undoubtedly accounted for the fact that the politically volatile 'new poor' (such as retrenched workers) consumed a large portion of the aid made available through PAMSCAD. This political focus encouraged the belief that the programme was meant to shore up public support for the regime. A third factor was the lack of integration of PAMSCAD into the core design of adjustment. Ghanaian technocrats initially resisted the idea of incorporating social concerns into macroeconomic planning, insisting that social programming was 'not amenable to conventional cost-benefit analysis'.[24] It was not until 1991 that social issues were moved, at least rhetorically, to the 'heart of... strategic planning and the mainstream of the resource allocation process' (Ghana Government, 1991: 40). The resultant 'renewed commitment' to SDA was to be embodied in a revised poverty-alleviation strategy stressing four principles: the continuation of 'sound macro-economic and sector economic policy'; an enhanced profile for social objectives; direct social action programmes; and accelerated employment generation. PAMSCAD itself has been extensively reorganized since (at least on paper) with a single secretariat (PAMSEC) based at the Ministry of Local Government, decentralization of the operations of the programme to encourage greater participation by regional and local bodies, and reduction of the 23 projects to 11. Eight of the projects previously under PAMSCAD were transferred to the Public Investment Programme (PIP).[25]

While this revision in the government's conceptual approach to poverty echoed similar changes in the approach of the World Bank (Hutchful, 1994), it is nevertheless possible to discern not one but three different approaches to poverty emerging among the three institutions which collaborated in designing the original poverty programme in 1987: the Ghana Government, the World Bank and UNICEF. These differences became particularly apparent at the Consultative Group meeting in Paris in June 1993. While poverty reduction was placed (at least rhetorically) at the core of the World Bank's strategy document *Ghana 2000 and Beyond* (World Bank, 1993a), the Ghana Government's own document 'From Economic Recovery to Accelerated Growth' was much more tepid in its discussion of poverty issues, exhausting the issue in three bare paragraphs. Both, however, seemed to agree in subordinating poverty reduction to *growth* (in this respect the Ghanaian Government may simply have felt less obliged to make the public relations noises that characterize the Bank). On the other hand in Paris UNICEF proposed an approach that challenged this view, in envisaging poverty reduction *as a basis for* rather than a *product of* growth.

9.4   'Mainstreaming Poverty Issues': Restructuring Public Expenditure: The PIP and the Budget

Apart from PAMSCAD the supposed major avenue for improved attention to the social dimensions of adjustment was the restructuring of public expenditure. The main tools identified by the Secretary for Finance for accomplishing this were the budget and the

---

[24] See Amissah-Arthur (1988: 17).

[25] For a description and progress report on these projects see Ghana Government (1993a, vol. 2).

Public Investment Programme (PIP). However, a preliminary study by the Ministry of Finance and Economic Planning (MFEP) of the PIP in the areas of Agriculture, Education and Health concluded that the poverty impact of the PIP was negligible, and that the PIP had not succeeded in substantially refocusing public expenditure in Ghana (Ghana Government, 1991b). At least in these three sectors spending continued to be focused disproportionately on urban areas and the south of the country rather than the poorer rural areas and the north. The key reason was that the PIP focused primarily on rehabilitation of existing infrastructure rather than the construction of new facilities. In terms of social impact, however, the picture from the budget appears more favourable, although given the fact that the Ghana Government lacks the data and the machinery for proper analysis of public expenditures and therefore for assessing the social impact of such expenditures, there can be little certainty about such judgements. The Expenditure Monitoring Unit (EMU) of MFEP, which was entrusted with this function, has been 'both understaffed and underequipped for its tasks' (*ibid.*: 11) while the mode of disbursement of central government funds by the Controller and Accountant-General's Office through the ministries has traditionally made it difficult if not impossible to disaggregate the regional and district destination of budget expenditures, and therefore assess their potential social impact.

10.   Health and Education

Ghana entered adjustment with falling nutritional standards and severely deteriorating social services. Expenditures on health and education fell in both relative and absolute terms. The share of education and health in the budget declined from 20.7 percent in 1972 to 20.2 percent in 1982 for education and 7.8 percent to 6.1 percent for health. While this decline may appear modest, it has to be recalled that over the same period the overall budget in turn declined from 18.3 percent to 10.1 percent of GNP. Thus real educational expenditures declined by over two-thirds between 1975 and 1982, while for health the drop was almost 80 percent (UNICEF, 1987a: 101). Utilization of medical services dropped sharply: at Korle Bu out-patient attendance dropped from 198,000 in 1979 to 117,000 in 1983, and overall attendance at health units dropped from 7.6 million in 1979 to 4.5 million in 1983 (on the other hand attendance at mission hospitals, which were better equipped, seems to have risen somewhat in the same period). The story in the education sector was very similar, with shortages of basic educational materials and massive loss of trained instructors at all levels. The sector lost 4000 trained teachers in this period; the proportion of trained teachers in elementary schools dropped from 71 percent in 1976-77 to 54 percent in 1980-81. Both admissions and enrolments suffered as a result.

However, in both sectors the problems were not simply budgetary but structural. Ghana inherited from colonialism a system of modern health care that was highly skewed in a number of respects: toward curative care and toward the urban centres and the south. (Twumasi, 1975; Senah, 1989). It was estimated in 1978 that Greater Accra, with about 9.4 percent of the total population, had 47 percent of total government doctors, 34 percent of hospital beds, and 12.2 percent of all hospitals in the country. The existing nine regional hospitals with only 15 percent of the total population had 55.4 percent of all hospitals in Ghana and 51.2 percent of all hospital beds. One-third of the health budget in the 1974-75 fiscal year went to Korle Bu Teaching Hospital and Greater Accra alone. In the distribution of medical officers the south had 526 while the north had only 40. And with respect to health institutions, the south had 451 (84 percent) while the north had only 87 (16 percent). The ratio of hospital beds to population was 847: 1 in the south and 1293:1 in the north (Ewusi, 1978; Senah, 1989). The system was also dualistic (in its exclusion of the traditional from modern health care), concentrated primarily in the public sector, and heavily subsidized. User fees were either abolished or became highly subsidized from the early 1960s. Total revenue from fees and other hospital charges covered only 2-3 percent of total government health expenditure in the 1970s and was probably not much higher in the 1980s. Efforts by successive governments to increase user fees had to be abandoned due to public resistance.

Reforms in the health sector have focused on cost recovery, reorganization of the Ministry of Health (MoH) to facilitate decentralization of the health care system, and reorienting health care to integrate traditional health care systems into the mainstream of health care and, more importantly, by shifting the focus from curative to preventive health care.

There was an initial round of fee increases in 1983 (following on an earlier round of milder increases under the Limann government) with a second and more substantial round of increases in July 1985 and further adjustments since then. Increases in medical fees and charges have outpaced the overall rate of inflation. Fees collected rose to 11 percent of hospital expenditures in 1986 and further to 16 percent in 1987 but had declined to about 7 percent by 1990. There is some evidence that fees have made an even higher contribution to the finances of some hospitals than these figures would suggest. Under the new organizational structure in the health sector the MoH has the roles of overall policy formulation, technical guidance and central procurement, but no longer exercises direct responsibility for managing or delivering health services (Ziken International, 1993). This is now the responsibility of Regional Directors of Health (other than for the Korle Bu and Komfo Anokye Teaching Hospitals in Accra and Kumasi, which are managed by hospital boards). The Regional Directors oversee a decentralized delivery system structured as follows: at the regional level there are ten Regional Health Management Teams responsible for supervising Regional Hospitals and district health services. Below the regions are three levels of health care structures (designated as Levels A, B and C). Level C services are operated by District Health Management Teams (110 in all), with a core group of five health officials, responsible for planning, managing and implementing all government services in the sector, plus some oversight for non-government health services in the district. Level B services consist of Health Posts and Health Centres, and cover areas with populations of 5,000 to 10,000 residents, with a staff complement made up of a medical assistant, community health nurse or midwife, health inspection assistant, and field technicians in charge of communicable disease control. Level A services constitute the base of the system and are staffed by traditional birth assistants, Village Health workers, and community clinic attendants responsible for basic health education and curative measures. These workers are supposed to receive simple medications and other basic support from the MoH but are expected to receive some form of compensation from the community.

However, as Senah and others have shown, efforts to develop rural-based preventive health care have run into numerous difficulties (Senah, 1989: 251-52; Asenso-Okyere *et al.*, 1993: 17, 38-40). Only 10 percent of the original estimated requirements of these cadres have been trained (Ziken International, 1993: 7-8). As we have seen, the PIP, the most important source of capital spending, has made little contribution to reorienting health care toward PHC or (for that matter) from its traditional urban and southern bias to a rural and northern focus. Consequently the health system continues to manifest the deeply biased structures noted earlier (Ziken International, 1993).

Decentralizing and otherwise reforming the health care system do not in themselves appear to improve modern health care availability to the poor. There has been a continuing decline in utilization of out-patient services at government hospitals, with gross attendance falling from 10.7 million in 1971 to 4.7 million in 1983 and 1.57 million in 1991. On the other hand for some unexplained reason admissions have gone up significantly at the same time, doubling between 1984 and 1991 (Ziken International, 1993: 14-15). But falling attendance at government medical facilities is only one dimension of the overall picture, and may not necessarily suggest that patients have no recourse to medical help. In fact patients have a menu of choices (about 25) ranging from different types of professional consultation (from hospitals to clinics, dispensaries, pharmacies) to traditional healers and self medication. Thus instead of being completely cut off from medical help, patients may be turning to alternative and cheaper forms of health care. Indeed some researchers have claimed that '[i]n response to higher prices, households economize very little in the number of consultations sought, but they are likely to choose less expensive treatment' (Lavy and Quigley, 1993: 26) This is because the price of health services is only one factor (and not necessarily the most important) in determining the utilization of health services; other factors such as the availability and accessibility of treatment, the seriousness of the illness, and household income are at least as important as price in determining the quantity and quality of health care consumption.

Even so there is no escaping the fact that medical care at any level has become a serious burden, particularly for lower-income as well as better-off households. Regardless of the choice of treatment regime, the cost of medicine is a very large fraction of total costs, about 60 percent at all intensities of treatment (access costs are also very high, transportation accounting for 8 to 13 percent of total costs (*ibid.*: 10)). As Lavy and Quigley observe in their survey of low-income Ghanaian households, while 'in absolute terms, the expenditures on medical care are quite small....these are very poor households. On average, one consultation costs 877 Cedis or only about US$3. But average per capita income is only 71,000 cedis a year. Therefore one medical consultation in a four week period consumes roughly 15 percent of monthly income' (*ibid.*). With this kind of burden it is hardly surprising that utilization of government medical facilities has fallen.

Government budgetary allocations to the health sector rose absolutely between 1988 and 1993, while the MoH has retained its share of government spending at roughly the same levels of total government allocations (the figure quoted in the Ziken study is 6 percent and 1.25 percent of GDP, somewhat lower than the estimate in Table 4); on the other hand the Ziken study found that MoH budgetary allocations have little relationship to actual expenditures, which are often considerably higher. Because of population growth per capita spending has increased little, however. Moreover, spending is still below levels necessary for the maintenance of a decent service. According to the Minister of Health the latter would imply expenditure of C 12,000 per capita, compared with a current figure of C 8000. The MoH states that it requires C 225 bn a year for the next 5 years to meet the country's health needs, but the ministerial budget for 1994 was only C 6.3 bn.[26]

Structural problems similar to those of the health sector lay behind the crisis in the educational sector. A historical legacy of collapsing funding has been inherited, while budgetary support has been heavily skewed in favour of the secondary and tertiary sectors.

These and other difficulties were supposed to be addressed through the educational sector adjustment programme commenced in 1987 with IDA support. At the elementary and secondary levels the objectives of the reform were to shorten the excessively long educational system (from 17 years to 12 under the new 6-3-3 system), to make educational output less academic and more practical and oriented toward self-employment, and to improve both access and quality of instruction and the availability of texts and supplies.

A key objective was to restructure the educational spending to direct more funding from tertiary to primary education, on the basis of the argument that primary education had the greatest social returns. At the old elementary level a new set of institutions, Junior Secondary Schools, were created. These had been mooted as far back as 1974 but no action had been taken in the meantime to train teachers to staff them or to provide proper buildings. At the tertiary level there was the need to make education more efficient and cost-effective, to shift the burden of funding from the government to private users and at the same to broaden the funding base from its almost complete reliance on government to include users and the private sector, and to eliminate the contradiction between high investment in tertiary education and high level of reliance on imports of foreign technical skills.

There are surprisingly few systematic assessments of the effects of educational sector adjustment in Africa, Ghana's included. The evidence that does exist seems to be subjected to widely varying interpretations, in part because of the political passions aroused by educational reforms in Ghana. Official data seem to suggest some success in restoring previous levels of educational spending and enrolments. Spending increased from 3.3 percent of GDP in 1987 to 4.5 percent in 1993, and the share of budgeted expenditure was maintained. The share of recurrent expenditure going to primary education is said to have increased by almost half. At the same time gross primary enrolment ratios rose from 68 percent in 1988-89 to 72 percent in 1989-90. Enrolments in the junior grades are also said to have grown at a 'considerably faster rate' in the more deprived regions of the country (World Bank, 1991: 34).

Yet it is not easy to square this official picture of thriving enrolments with the many independent (if anecdotal) reports of declining enrolments and stress in maintaining children enrolled in schools, particularly in the poorer communities (see for instance Dei, 1993, and Ghana Statistical Service, 1993). These pictures may be reconciled by remembering that many children in Ghana attend school only *sporadically* rather than dropping out altogether, staying away for varying periods of time whenever parents are unable to procure school fees, uniforms, or money for books. Overall enrolment figures thus do not tell the whole story. Clearly given the high value placed on education in Ghana many parents continue at least at a formal level to keep their offspring within the educational system but are clearly having difficulty providing them with the substance of an education. Education expenditures, like those of health, are a substantial proportion of household expenditures, particularly for low-income households. For those

---

[26] *West Africa*, 29 August - 4 September 1994: 1516.

in the lowest expenditure quintile, per capita expenditures on education on average amount to 12 percent of total per capita expenditure for children at the primary level, 17 percent for children at the junior secondary school (JSS) level, and 41 percent for children at the senior secondary school (SSS) level (World Bank, 1993a: 22)[27]. Fee increases especially at secondary and tertiary level have dramatically increased the cost of access to education and thereby apparently exacerbated existing rural/urban and gender disparities (Dei, 1992). Nor is this entirely compensated for by improvements in quality. There are many indications that quality problems continue, particularly in connection with the infrastructure of new secondary schools. The burden of building the new JSS schools often fell to communities themselves, many of which were financially ill-prepared, particularly given the austerity and rapid inflation in the cost of building materials, and construction did not always meet the required standards. Sometimes even these modest facilities are not available. At both JSS and SSS levels laboratories are underequipped (where they exist at all) and text books are not always available. The full complement of teachers required for the new system have yet to be trained, and particularly at the SSS level there is less than complete familiarity with the ambitious new syllabus. Teachers continue to be underpaid with occasional late payment of salaries (for instance some 5000 new teachers who were hired in September 1994 had still not been paid by January 1995.) In 1991 and again in 1994 teachers of the Ghana Educational Service declared a strike to press salary demands. Although the education share of the budget has increased absolutely, the reforms have nevertheless been underfunded.

It is interesting that demand for secondary education in Ghana remains a hotter political subject than that of primary education. As already observed, it is the World Bank's contention that social rates of return are greatest at the primary level. Whatever may be the truth of this statement, it is clear that the private economic rates of return to primary education are almost nil. Significant returns do not appear until middle and secondary school (Glewwe, 1991; Lavy, 1992: 25-26) This is not surprising given the very low levels of literacy obtaining at primary level (as demonstrated by low scores on the literacy tests administered in connection with the GLSS), and the fact that students do not in fact begin to learn until middle school. This may be the reason why 'many households decide not to enroll their children in school at all although the direct and indirect costs of schooling in the first few years may be close to zero' (Lavy, 1992: 5). Lavy suggests that 'The post primary-cost of schooling is an important determinant of investment in primary education' and that 'problems of access to middle and

---

[27] According once again to data supplied by the World Bank (1993: 22) in 1992-93 school contributions at primary school levels amounted to Cedis 308 and C 3,522 at the public secondary level in the rural areas, and C 1,102 and C 8,352 respectively in Accra School-related expenses for food, books and other school supplies added another C 2,000 for primary schools and C 7,000 for secondary schools in the rural areas and about C 6,000 and C 15,000 respectively in Accra. As the report admits, 'these are not trivial expenses for the poorer households'.

The costs were the major reason for the sporadic school attendance mentioned above. As a primary school teacher informed a researcher:

> You see, when I visit the parents to find out why their son or daughter has not been in school for a while, they tell me about the economic hardships they are experiencing. They ask me why, under those circumstances, I cannot sympathize with them and understand why these children cannot come to school. They think my questions should be directed to the government, whoever that is... (Dei, 1992: 54).

secondary schools has a substantial and negative effect on primary school enrolment and educational attainment'. Thus in his view 'supply constraints on middle and secondary education are at least as important as the supply of primary schools to hold down enrolment rates and to fuel early drop out of students from the educational system' (*ibid.*: 14). Of course in the long term a revitalized primary system will transform the picture, but in the short and medium term there is also justification for expenditure to be directed at providing more middle and secondary schools (i.e. the levels where personal returns at present are in fact highest). Glewwe (1991: 43) is clearly correct in arguing that the present low returns to primary education justify greater investment aimed at increasing quality and therefore returns at the *primary* school level but it should not be assumed a priori that returns will naturally be highest at that level irrespective of the particular situation.

Table 14   Per Capita Expenditure in the Ghanaian School System, 1970-83 (constant 1983 dollars)

	1970	1975	1980	1983
Primary	66	41	21	16
As % of per capita GNP	13	10	6	5
Secondary	100	131	66	39
As % of per capita GNP	20	31	17	13
Tertiary	--	3638	1195	619
As % of per capita GNP	--	900	300	200

Source: World Bank, 1988a.

Whatever the facts of the case, the argument over the effect of the educational reforms seems for the moment to have been put conclusively to rest by the performance of students who sat the SSS examinations in December 1993. Out of 42,105 students who sat the exams only 1656 (or a mere 3.9 percent) passed. This has precipitated 'widespread condemnation of the new education system'; with results like this it is no wonder that the public has become 'strongly hostile to the new educational system'. The Ministry of Education called a forum on 20 June 1994, where for once students and teachers were allowed to vent their opinions of the educational reforms. The grievances aired by teachers and students represent a microcosm of the feelings of the public. A report in *West Africa* said of the students:

> It was quite evident that they saw themselves as guineas pigs. The recurrent themes were lack of textbooks; inadequate training for teachers of the new system; the non-availability of workshops and science equipment' and the short time within which the broad syllabus had to be completed.[28]

---

[28] 'Students Rip Education Reform Apart', *West Africa*, 4-10 July 1994: 1185.

Products of the new system were perceived as 'second-class'. On the other hand the dreary outcome was attributed by the Minister of Education to poor grasp of English, inadequate preparation and lack of adequate knowledge of the syllabus Yet in whatever language the problem of the educational reforms may be summed up as 'too much spent too fast on too little'.

While the cost of the elementary and (to some extent) secondary levels of the system have traditionally been borne by the users, education at the tertiary/university level has been virtually free. However, at the tertiary level underfunding of the universities (especially in capital spending) was exacerbated by a pattern of erratic disbursements that made forward planning impossible. The limited foreign-exchange component was entirely inadequate for imports of crucial educational materials. The running costs of universities were comparatively high for several reasons. Low levels of utilization of facilities, low student enrolment (none of the three institutions had enrolment exceeding 4000) due to limited boarding space, and unrealistically low staff-student ratios made for high costs per student. The residential structure of the universities necessitated costly municipal and other ancillary services and a large non-teaching staff. For every Cedi spent on teaching activities, the University of Ghana spent C 1.50, the University of Science and Technology C 1.22, and the University of Cape Coast C 3.35 on non-teaching structures and activities. These problems were compounded by low staff morale from unviable salaries, lack of research infrastructure, antiquated and dilapidated classrooms, libraries and equipment, and frequent closures of the universities by the government.

In the case of the tertiary sector a committee - the University Rationalization Committee (URC) - was appointed in 1986-87 to report on possible reforms.[29] The recommendations of the committee included the immediate withdrawal of board and lodging and the conversion of halls of residence to hostels managed as commercial ventures while the universities divested themselves of catering services or contracted them out. Tuition would remain free but students would pay for food, accommodation and recreation, through such avenues as 'work-study' and student loans. In general more of the cost of education was to be shifted from government to students and parents, with increased funding and participation to come from extra-governmental sources. A Student Loan Scheme was put in place, to cover board and lodging, and given legal backing through the Student Loan Scheme Law 1992 (PNDC Law 276 of May 1992).

While it is true that the problems of the universities were partly self-inflicted (the universities themselves had been slow to react to the crisis by cutting costs and initiating the necessary reforms) nevertheless the conduct of the reforms stirred more opposition than need have been the case. First the reforms seemed to be working to very short deadlines (necessitated in turn by the strict deadlines imposed by the IDA, which was funding them). It was suspected that another reason for the haste was the perception of a need to put the reforms firmly in place in order to preempt debate and organized opposition. What was felt to be lack of genuine consultation, and the top-down manner of implementing the reforms, not to mention the cost implications, alienated many who might otherwise have been in support.

The tertiary level reforms were also complicated by the fact that relations between the universities and the government were already strained. The universities feared

---

[29] University Rationalization Committee (URC), *Interim Report* and *Final Report*, both Ministry of Education, January 1988.

designs on their autonomy by the government using the reforms and the expanded power of the Ministry of Education. But the opposition was also built around specific concerns including deboarding, the obligation toward income generation for the universities, and increasing student numbers and labour and capital 'productivity' under conditions of financial stringency.[30] There were also concerns about the implications of the reforms for the quality of instruction as well their impact on financially less well-off students. Finally the reforms were read as an attack on higher education (and coincidentally on that social constituency that was the most vocal critic of adjustment) and an effort to truncate the technological and scientific development of Africans and black people in general[31] - in retrospect a not unreasonable concern given the devastation wrought by structural adjustment on educational, intellectual, and research infrastructure in countries like Russia.

To complicate matters, an appropriate institutional framework to design and direct the reforms did not exist. The policy, planning and administrative structures of the Ministry of Education were, at best, in their infancy and there was legitimate reason to question the extent to which the Ministry could efficiently handle the additional portfolio (see the discussion on Civil Service Reform above). The IDA mission which carried out the preliminary survey in 1991 was critical of the manpower situation in the Higher Education Division of the Ministry of Education and its Project Management Unit, which was charged with administering the tertiary sector, and was initially reluctant to commit the full funding for this reason. Once more this emphasized a reform syndrome which has become all-too familiar in Ghana, in which large-scale reforms were rushed through without careful preparation or consultation and underpinned by fragile or inadequate planning and implementational structures.

11.   Threats to the Environment

There are multiple sources of threat to the environment in Ghana. The beginnings of desertification are evident in parts of the upper North due to a combination of drought and deforestation. There is growing stress on land use, with decreasing fallow periods, increasing utilization of wetlands and other marginal soils, and 'massive encroachment' on the remaining rain forests of the Western region for the establishment of new cocoa and food farms. As in many countries industrialization commenced with little attention to the environmental effects. Industrial effluent and other hazardous wastes are discharged directly into streams and public drains (Akuffo, 1989). Textile mills and breweries are among the leading industrial polluters. Many reports have also testified to the unsatisfactory condition of Ghana's rural and urban sanitation systems and the threat that they pose to public health. In more recent years uncontrolled quarrying to service the construction industry has also become a major environmental threat, particularly in the coastal areas (where beaches have been denuded, causing massive erosion and tidal shifts) and in the vicinity of the capital city.[32] Again this is a long-

---

[30] See page 143 of the Interim Report of the University Rationalization Committee.

[31] See for instance *New African*, January 1989: 18.

[32] Ghana has had the dubious distinction of being twice featured on CNN *World Report* in this regard.

standing problem which has been exacerbated by the building boom accompanying the ERP. The most serious forms of industrial pollution have historically been associated with the goldmining industry with its hazardous wastes (mercury and arsenic) and land, water, and air pollution (particularly visible in the vicinity of the AGC operations in the Obuasi area). Because of its traditionally unregulated character small-scale mining can also lead to serious environmental damage. Diamond mining has created moonscapes in the mining areas.

One reason for the widespread stress on the Ghanaian environment is that the environment has constituted the crucible for both crisis and recovery, the focus on the one hand of survival (social adjustment) strategies by the Ghanaian population - through social forestry practised mostly by women, backyard farming and so on - and on the other hand the recovery strategies of the state. Ghana has chose a path of 'wild capitalism' based on the extensive exploitation of nature rather than on increases in productive investment. If economic stagnation put pressure on the environment, clearly economic recovery through structural adjustment is posing an even greater threat, both in terms of the sustainability of the resource base itself and the reproduction of common property resources (CPR) which, through more sustainable forms of interaction with nature, facilitated the survival of Ghana's rural population. In particular deforestation threatens the traditional dependence of Ghana's village population on the forests for medicines, bushmeat, edible leaves, fruits and nuts, honey and other products, traditionally collected, processed and sold by women. It is only recently that the World Bank has recognized the need to protect the safety net provided by CPRs from rampant exploitation and commercialization (World Bank, 1993a: 15).

In spite of the fact that the Environmental Protection Council (EPC) was established ahead of similar organizations in Africa (it was formed in 1972) the enforcement of even its meagre environmental regulations has been, to say the least, indifferent (Akuffo, 1989). Environmental issues were not added to the agenda of the ERP until 1990, almost seven years into the programme. Policy measures contemplated under the Environmental Action Plan (EAP) include natural resource management, pollution control, and requirements for environmental impact assessments. Project activities proposed include soil and land management; forest conservation and management; measures to control pollution, particularly in the urban, mining and manufacturing sectors; strengthening environmental support services; and environmental education and research. A substantial proportion of the investments, as well as the policy and institutional measures in the EAP, will be incorporated into the existing programmes of the respective sectors. Policy actions that do not lend themselves to integration with existing sector activities would be the responsibility of the EPC.

Given the long-standing disregard for environmental regulation and enforcement in Ghana and the environmental record of the World Bank itself, one has reason to be sceptical that these objectives will be taken seriously. The obvious danger is that in being incorporated at a very late stage into *ongoing* sector SAPs, environmental concerns will receive consideration at best only at the margin, and are unlikely to prompt fundamental rethinking in approaches to adjustment. In addition, from a regulatory standpoint it is hardly reassuring that environmental issues are to be treated as 'sector issues' outside the direct purview of the EPC (with its own indifferent past record). It is also not evident that the funding will be forthcoming to *reverse* much of the already substantial environmental damage, as opposed to ameliorating future environmental impacts. The degree of scepticism even within the Bank was only too well conveyed at the Executive Directors meeting on 10 June 1993, to discuss the Ghana Country Assistance Strategy. Mr. Jean Daniel Gerber, an Executive Director of the Bank, quoting from *Ghana 2000* (the World Bank publication) expressed alarm at the apparent disparity between rhetoric and action in the Ghana Country Strategy in the following words: 'It is particularly alarming to read that increasingly, agricultural production is obtained at the expense of the soils, the forest and the wetlands. The forest, in particular, is just disappearing. Yet, in the country strategy we do not feel that this problem is perceived as an imminent danger calling for immediate action.'[33]

12. Conclusion: From Adjustment to Adjustment-with-Democracy

Ghana has recently capped successful adjustment with a successful return to democracy. What does this suggest about the relationship between democracy and adjustment in Ghana? There have been at least three views in the literature regarding the relationship between adjustment and democracy. One response has been to argue that by promoting markets adjustment will loosen the grip of the state on society and help to foster democratization (Diamond, 1988: 27; World Bank, 1989). A second view, which may be described as libertarian, sees the crisis of the state and the formal economy that preceded adjustment as opening up spaces of freedom for society and strengthening local and community bonds, and worries about the impact that the resuscitation of the state through adjustment may have for these new-found spaces of freedom (Chazan, 1992: 135). A third view has argued that it is the lack of accountability and the repression associated with structural adjustment that have *stimulated* movements for democracy in Africa (Beckman, 1992).

While it was not unusual for the PNDC (and some of its supporters) to claim that the design of adjustment and democratic institutions went together, beginning with elections to the District Assemblies in 1988, curiously neither Rawlings himself nor his supporters took the view that market liberalization implied political pluralism. In the debates preceding the onset of democratization Rawlings advocated a form of democracy which would discard political parties and organized political competition.[34] On the contrary in Ghana the forces that pushed for democracy were primarily the urban middle-class, professional and working-class ones who were broadly identified with opposition both to the PNDC and to the ERP. The social forces that propelled democratization were thus different from those that drove liberalization.

Nevertheless to some degree democratization reflected a response to the limits of current adjustment strategy. The management of adjustment in Ghana was notable both for its dirigisme and for its narrow institutional and social base. Programme management centred around a small macroeconomic team based in the MFEP, the Bank of Ghana, several key ministries and the committee of secretaries. The modus operandi of this team minimized information, consultation and accountability. Throughout most of the period of adjustment the regime concentrated on enlarging its autonomy from, rather

---

[33] Statement by Mr. Gerber, Executive Directors Meeting, Ghana: Country Assistance Strategy, 10 June 1993.

[34] For the changing nature of Rawlings' concepts of democracy, see Hutchful (1991).

than its links to, social groups and institutional forces. This strategy was facilitated by the tension between the 'popular' political base of the regime, a bloc which was put together *before* adjustment, and the thrust of its economic policies, which (at least on the face of it) favoured business. Yet while the 'popular forces' were deliberately distanced from policy-making, business also found that it had little voice either on macroeconomic issues or on matters that directly affected its interests. Not only was Ghanaian business silent in the policy debates that shaped adjustment policy in 1982-83; unlike domestic business in Nigeria or Zimbabwe Ghanaian business never developed a public voice on most adjustment issues, preferring as far as possible to seek consultations in private.[35] Economic policy was shaped by technocrats and former militants, not by business.

This strategy of 'autonomization' was both effective and even appropriate in two senses: first it allowed the PNDC to carry through a drastic reordering of the relative positions of important and powerful social groups with respect to resources, and in the process to defuse and disperse opposition; and second, the suspension of participatory politics and the suppression of policy debate proved positive in the short term for technocratic rationality, rapid decision-making and policy consistency.

Nevertheless this strategy became increasingly dysfunctional as adjustment deepened beyond the early stages of administrative commandism to more complex stages that called for institutionalization and broader social commitment. The limitations of this strategy became increasingly clear, in terms both of adjustment's shallow social roots and of the limited response to and institutional involvement in it on the part of business. Most glaringly the regime has apparently failed, refused or been unable to create the political coalitions required to support the programme into the future.

Furthermore, the demands for democratization came at an awkward time for the regime and for the ERP. Partly, this was because previous political 'reforms' were meant to evade and not facilitate the issue of democracy. The so-called decentralization and reshaping of the state apparatus with the establishment of the District Assemblies was constructed carefully to promote participation and limited self-reliance at the *margins* of the state system, while at the same time outflanking those social and political groups demanding genuine democratization. Therefore the timing of the democratic transition had a number of specific implications for the continuity of adjustment. First, because of the suppression of political debate and freedom of speech support for the ERP within Ghanaian society remained untested, particularly among the political class, and there was no guarantee that a successor regime would be committed to the programme. Secondly, within the civil service the economic team had not laid down the institutional structures that would ensure that the management of the ERP could be carried on in the event of a change of regime. Literally the entire programme could have ground to a halt with the departure of the individuals who had directed it.[36] Thirdly, many of the crucial institutional reforms, such as those in the civil service and in the military, were yet to take root (assuming that time was the issue). Finally and most importantly there was the growing ambivalence and indeed immobilism of the PNDC in regard to the

---

[35] See World Bank (1990) on the lack of influence of the private sector in the regime. This was the main reason for the formation in 1991 of the Private Sector Advisory Group, which has continued to work in a low-key manner.

[36] Interviews with members of the macroeconomic team, Accra, July 1992.

project of democratization which it had set itself at the beginning of the regime.

The PNDC may well have won the elections because of the perceived success of the ERP. However, other factors - such as the tight control exercised by the regime over the transition process, its exploitation of the advantages of incumbency, in particular its ability to mobilize support through control over the state-owned media and the so-called revolutionary organs (the committees for the defence of the revolution, the 31st December Women's Movement, and the civil defence organizations), and the fact that well before the ban on political activity was lifted the future cadres of the regime were organizing underground (the Eagle Party, one of the parties that emerged to form the PNDC, was busy shaking down pro-PNDC businesses for contributions to its war chest) - were at least as important in explaining the victory of the PNDC. What was significant, on the other hand, was the acceptance (with few exceptions) of macroeconomic stability as the guiding philosophy of policy by all the major parties. Although the leading opposition party, the NPP, continued to attack the deprivations of Ghanaians under the ERP, it only promised marginal changes to the adjustment programme to offer greater relief.

The elections also exposed the dilemma faced by the donors when confronted by a possible choice between democratic political change and continued economic reform. Donors were caught between the rhetoric of democracy and a desire to see continuation of adjustment under the existing regime. Indeed, in spite of the sweeping sentiments for democratization, the PNDC was actually subjected to little pressure for democratization by external donors. Many donors responded to domestic pressures for democratization with a 'wait-and-see' attitude. Thus, according to the *Financial Times*, 'Western donors feel that at the very least a defeat of Flt-Lt. Rawlings would cause a period of economic policy instability and that a democratically elected president would be more inclined to pander to populist sentiments and opinion'.[37]

Indeed even under the PNDC the transition to electoral politics implied steps that worried external donors. The most important of these was when civil service salaries were raised by about 70 percent in 1992, with consequences that we have already discussed. Disbursements were held up until a stringent new budget in February 1993 restored the fiscal balance.

Following the (disputed) victory of Rawlings in the presidential elections in October 1992 the opposition parties boycotted the National Assembly elections, ensuring the PNDC (now reincarnated as the NDC) and its allies a sweep of the legislature and the emergence of a one-party Assembly. What emerged consequently was a 'thin' democracy in which the powers of the reformers were actually strengthened in some respects. In relation to adjustment democratization has subsequently had little effect on the management style of the government, the presence of Parliament notwithstanding (the introduction of the crucial 1993 budget in February without waiting for the approval of the new Parliament was a good indication of business as usual). There are strong continuities between the old order and the new, particularly in terms of the Cabinet. To all intents and purposes the President's Office is a reconstituted PNDC and the centre of politics and adjustment-related policy-making. In any case political liberalization was partial and either left key repressive decrees in place or created new ones to replace those abolished under the pressure for political accountability and

---

[37] Quoted in *West Africa*, 16-22 November 1992: 1954.

freedom of self-expression.[38] Third, although the so-called 'revolutionary organs' have been declared 'non-governmental organizations' under the new constitutional order and indeed designate themselves as such, there are many indications that they continue to regard themselves and to act as quasi-state institutions.[39] However, as far as adjustment is concerned the thin democracy is embodied in a palpably weak Parliament, clearly unwilling to challenge the President and his government on macroeconomic issues. Even so, Rawlings continues to complain about 'constitutional anarchy' and to wonder aloud about the appropriateness of democracy under Ghana's present circumstances.[40]

Ghana has played a pioneering role in African adjustment, with not only the most rigorous and sustained macroeconomic programme to date but also the first civil service, educational, financial and social sector adjustment programmes to be executed in Africa. While the overall sustainability (at least in political terms) of the programme has been impressive, as this evaluation would suggest clearly not all the lessons to be learned from Ghana about adjustment are favourable. First, in spite of the sense of confidence imparted by many World Bank publications and country memoranda it is clear that many of the reforms have been somewhat experimental in nature, and that the World Bank itself has been ill-equipped to deal with some of the policy issues that have arisen during the course of adjustment (Hutchful, 1995a). Second, while macroeconomic reform has been rigorous and largely successful, institutional and sector reforms have been slow and the outcomes uneven. In addition, while some form or degree of macroeconomic stability is necessary for supply response the logics of the broad macroeconomic programme and of the sector reforms have not always been consistent (examples are the withdrawal of fertilizer subsidies and price stabilization in agriculture and the effects of credit and trade liberalization policies on the industrial sector). Beyond this the persistent inadequacy of the supply response to the ERP poses the question of whether we have not gone simply from a case of 'government failure' to one of 'market failure'. While it is obvious that the World Bank has been reformulating its conception of the appropriate demarcation and linkage between state and market in the context of practical experience (with inevitable mistakes along the way) - as opposed to the previous headlong rush to 'roll back' the state - this issue is still not being addressed as explicitly as one might wish. Shortfalls in the ERP continue to be seen either as purely fortuitous or due to absence of faith on the part of government, rather than as issuing from fundamental problems of design.

Finally, institutional and structural reforms introduced under the ERP since 1987 have placed serious stress on the implementational capacity of the Ghanaian public

---

[38] For instance repeal of the obnoxious Protective Custody Law 1982 (PNCDL 4) and Habeas Corpus (Amendment) Law 1984 (PNCDL 91), was replaced by Public Order Law of 1992 (PNCD Law 288), described by critics as potential tool for government intimidation and 'another violation of fundamental human rights'.

[39] The CDR, CDO, DWM Menace', *The Statesman*, October 214, 1993: 1. Also CDRs Creeping Back', *The Standard*, October 17-23, p.1, and 31 December Women Show Power', *The Independent*, October 13-19, 1993. The incidents to which the media were referring to were the seizure of control over public toilets in a suburb of Accra by the Kaneshie Zone Three branch of the Association of CDRs and a similar action by the 31 December Women's Movement with respect to market stalls and a nursery built with public funds at Dansoman, another suburb of Accra.

[40] See the interview with Barbara Holecek, 'Paying the Piper', *Transition*, 1993 (Issue 62): 17.

sector, with the result that while reform has been extensive it has not necessarily been *intensive*. It is not at all clear that Ghanaians are assimilating a *culture* (or indeed politics) of reform. The implicit assumption in the approach to reform is a 'framework' one (in other words, given a particular framework of incentives certain behavioural patterns or outcomes can be elicited), not one that engages fundamental cultural perceptions. The pace of reform, particularly given the institutional weaknesses of the Ghanaian public sector, has eroded both the sense of programme ownership on the part of the Ghana Government and the ability of the Ghanaian public to perceive itself as a participant rather than a victim, and a subject rather than an object, of reform.

References

Abbey, J. 1991. 'Comments' in Thomas, V., A. Chhibber, M. Dailami, & J. de Melo, *Restructuring Economies in Distress: Policy Reform and the World Bank*. New York: Oxford University Press for the World Bank.

Abbey, J. 1989. *On Promoting Successful Adjustment: Lessons from Ghana*. Per Jacobsson Lecture. Washington, DC: International Monetary Fund.

Akuffo, S.B. 1989. *Pollution Control in a Developing Country: the Case of Ghana*. Accra: Ghana Universities Press.

Alderman, H. 1991. 'Downturn and Economic Recovery in Ghana: Impacts on the Poor'. Ithaca, NY: Cornell Food and Nutrition Policy Institute, March.

Amissah-Arthur, K. 1988. *Statement in Target Programmes for the Poor During Structural Adjustment*. Report of Proceedings of Symposium on Poverty and Adjustment. Washington, DC. April.

Aryee, J. 1991. 'Civil Service Reform Under the Provisional National Defence Council', *Journal of Management Studies*, Vol. 7, Jan-Dec.

Asante, S. 1991. 'Poverty Alleviation: Focus on Public Expenditure (Analysis of the Availability and Viability of Public Expenditure Data)'. Accra: Ministry of Finance and Economic Planning: SDA desk, October.

Asante, Y. and E.S. Addo. 1993. 'Industrial Development Policies and Options', in V.K. Nyanteng (ed.), *Policies and Options for Ghanaian Economic Development*. Legon: ISSER.

Asenso-Okyere, K. 1991. 'Fertiliser Pricing and Distribution Policy in Ghana', in C. Doss & C. Olson (eds), *Issues in African Rural Development*. Arlington, VA.: Winrock International Institute for Agricultural Development.

Asenso-Okyere, K. *et al.* 1993. *Policies and Strategies for Rural Poverty Alleviation in Ghana*. University of Ghana: ISSER, Technical Publication No. 57.

Baffoe, J. K. 1992. 'Income Distribution and Poverty Profile in Ghana 1987-1988', *African Development Review*, Vol. 4, No. 1.

Baffour, O. & Y. Asante. (no date). 'Review of Social Policy in Ghana'. Accra: Policy Analysis Division, Ministry of Finance and Economic Planning: SDA Desk.

Beckman, B. 1992. 'Empowerment or Repression: the World Bank and the Politics of African Adjustment' in P. Gibbon *et al.*, *Authoritarianism, Democracy and Adjustment: The Politics of Economic Reform in Africa*. Uppsala: Scandinavian Institute of African Studies.

Boakye-Danquah, Y. 1990. 'Structural Adjustment, Divestiture and the Future of State-Owned Enterprises in Ghana', *Journal of Management Studies*, Vol. 6, Jan-Dec.

Boateng, M.Y & E.O. Asante. 1992. 'Administrative Aspects of Implementing Economic Policies: the Case of Public Sector PPBMED with Special Emphasis on the PPMED of the Ministry of Agriculture (MoA)'. Accra: Ministry of Finance and Economic Planning, SDA Desk.

Business and Financial Times. (Accra), various.

Chazan, N. 1992. 'Liberalisation, Governance and Political Space in Ghana', in M. Bratton & G. Hyden (eds.), *Governance and Politics in Africa*. Boulder, Co.: Lynne Rienner.

Council for Industrial and Scientific Research. 1990. *Report on Capital Goods Sector Study*. Accra: Technology Transfer Centre.

Daily Graphic. (Accra), various.

Davis, T. 1991. 'Institutional Impediments to Workforce Retrenchment and Restructuring in Ghana's State Enterprises', *World Development*, Vol. 19, No. 8.

Dawson, J. 1990. 'The Wider Context: The Importance of the Macroeconomic Environment for Small Enterprise Development, *Small Enterprise Development*, Vol. 1, No. 3.

Dei, G.S. 1993. 'Learning in the Time of Structural Adjustment: the Ghanaian Experience', *Canadian and International Education*, Vol. 22, No. 1.

Desai, S. 1992. 'Children at Risk: The Role of Family Structure in Latin America and West Africa', *Population and Development Review*, Vol. 18, No. 4 (December).

Diamond, L. 1988. 'Introduction', in L. Diamond, J. Linz, & S. M. Lipset, *Democracy in Developing Countries: Vol. 2: Africa*. Boulder, CO.: Lynne Rienner.

Ewusi, K. 1978 *Planning for the Neglected Rural Poor in Ghana*. Accra: New Times Corporation.

Financial Times. (London), various.

Fishlow, A. et. al. 1994. *Miracle of Design? Lessons from the East Asian Experience*. Washington, DC: Overseas Development Council.

Friends of the Earth. 1992. *Plunder in Ghana's Rainforest for Illegal Profit: An Expose of Corruption, Fraud and other Malpractices in the International Timber Trade*. London: Friends of the Earth.

Gayi, S. 1994. 'Adjusting to the Social Costs of Adjustment in Ghana: Problems and Prospects' Draft Paper Prepared for the Economic Restructuring and New Social Policies Programme. Geneva: UNRISD (mimeo).

Gelb, A. & P. Honohan. 1991. 'Financial Sector Reform', in V. Thomas, A. Chhibber, M. Dailami, & J. de Melo, *Restructuring Economies in Distress: Policy Reform and the World Bank*. New York: Oxford University Press for the World Bank.

Ghana Government. 1987. *Programme of Actions to Mitigate the Social Costs of Adjustment*. (PAMSCAD), Accra, July.

Ghana Government. 1991a. *Enhancing the Human Impact of the Adjustment Programme*, Report Prepared by the Government of Ghana for the Sixth Meeting of the Consultative Group for Ghana, Paris, 14-15 May.

Ghana Government. 1991b. 'Some Aspects of the Poverty Alleviation Focus of Public Expenditure (PIP)'. Accra: Ministry of Finance and Economic Planning. May.

Ghana Government. 1993a. *From Economic Recovery to Accelerated Growth*, Report Prepared by the Government of Ghana for the Seventh Meeting of the Consultative Group for Ghana, Paris, 24-25 June.

Ghana Government. 1993b. 'Public Investment Programme 1993-95'. Accra: Ministry of Finance and Economic Planning. June.

Ghana Government. 1994. 'Budget Statement', 14 January.

Ghana Statistical Service. 1989. *Ghana Living Standards Survey: First Year Report (September 1987-August 1988)*, Accra, August.

Ghana Statistical Service. 1993. 'Rural Communities in Ghana: Report of a National Rurtal Community Survey'. Accra: Ghana Statistical Service, October (mimeo).

Ghanaian Chronicle. (Accra), various.

Gibbon P. et al. 1993. *Blighted Harvest: The World Bank and African Agriculture in the 1980s*. London: James Currey.

Glewwe, P. 1991. *Schooling, Skills, and the Returns to Government Investment in Education: An Exploration Using Data From Ghana*, Living Standards Measurement Study, Working Paper No. 76. Washington, DC: World Bank, March.

Glewwe P. & K. Twum-Baah. 1991. *The Distribution of Welfare in Ghana 1987-88*, Living Standards Measurement Study, Working Paper No. 75. Washington, DC: World Bank.

Gyimah-Boadi, E. 1992. 'State Enterprise Divestiture: Recent Ghanaian Experience', in D. Rothchild (ed.), *Ghana: The Political Economy of Recovery*. Boulder, CO.: Lynne Rienner.

Hodson, D. 1983. *The General Agricultural Workers Union of the TUC (Ghana)*. Geneva: ILO.

Hogg, D. 1993. *The SAP in the Forest: The Environmental and Social Impacts of Structural Adjustment Programmes in the Philippines, Ghana and Guyana*. London: Friends of the Earth.

Hutchful, E. 1989. 'From 'Revolution' to Monetarism: The Politics and Economics of the Structural Adjustment Programme in Ghana', in J. Loxley & Bonnie Campbell (eds), *Structural Adjustment in Africa*. London: Macmillan

Hutchful, E. 1991. 'Shades of Meaning: The Struggle for Democracy in Ghana', unpublished paper, Department of African Studies, Wayne State University, September.

Hutchful, E. 1994. 'Smoke and Mirrors: the World Bank's Social Dimensions of Adjustment (SDA) Programme', *Review of African Political Economy*, Vol. 21, No. 62, December.

Hutchful, E. 1995a. 'Fifty Years of the Bretton Woods Institutions and Adjustment in Africa: Consolidation or Change?', *Canadian Journal of Development Studies*, forthcoming.

Hutchful, E. 1995b. 'Why Regimes (Do Not) Adjust: The Bank Puzzles Out Its 'Star Pupil'', *Canadian Journal of African Studies*, forthcoming.

International Labour Office (ILO)/Jobs and Skills Programme for Africa (JASPA). 1989. *From Redeployment to Sustained Employment Generation: Challenges for Ghana's Economic Recovery Programme*, Addis Ababa: Job and Skills Programme for Africa.

International Monetary Fund (IMF). 1993. *Ghana: Recent Economic Developments.* Washington, DC: IMF, African Department, 29 June.

International Monetary Fund (IMF). 1994. *Ghana: Statistical Annex*, Washington, DC: IMF, 2 June.

Jebuni, C.D. & W. Seini. 1992. *Agricultural Input Policies Under Structural Adjustment: Their Distributional Implications*, Cornell Food and Nutrition Policy Program, Working Paper 31. Ithaca, NY: Cornell Food and Nutrition Policy Institute.

Kapur, I., M.T. Hadjimichael, P. Hilbers, J. Schiff, & P. Szymczak. 1991. *Ghana: Adjustment and Growth. 1983-1991.* Washington, DC: International Monetary Fund, Occasional Paper No. 86, September.

Killick, T. 1978. *Development Economics in Action*, London: Heinemann.

Kofi, T.A. 1992. 'Implementing World Bank's Structural Adjustment Programmes in Africa Under Uncertainty In Commodity Price Trends: Policy Performance Review: The Case of Ghana'. Helsinki: UNU/WIDER, March (mimeo).

Lall, S., G.B. Navaretti, S. Teitel & G. Wignaraja. (no date). *Technology and Enterprise Development: Ghana Under Structural Adjustment.*, Washington, DC: World Bank: Regional Program on Enterprise Development.

Lavy, V. 1992. *Investment in Human Capital: Schooling Supply Constraints in Rural Ghana*, Living Standards Measurement Study, Working Paper No. 93. Washington, DC: World Bank.

Lavy, V. & J.M. Quigley. 1993. *Willingness to Pay for the Quality and Intensity of Medical Care: Low Income Households in Ghana*, Living Standards Measurement Study, Working Paper No. 94. Washington, DC: World Bank.

Marshall, H. 1990. 'Civil Service Reform in Ghana', *RIPA Report*, Vol. 11, No. 1 (Spring).

Martin, M. 1992. 'Negotiating Adjustment and External Finance: Ghana and the International Community, 1982-1989', in Donald Rothchild (ed.), *Ghana: The Political Economy of Recovery.* Boulder CO.: Lynne Rienner.

May, E. 1985. *Exchange Controls and Parallel Market Economies In Sub-Saharan Africa: Focus on Ghana.* Washington, DC: World Bank Staff Working Papers No. 711.

New African, various.

Ninsin, K. 1991. *The Informal Sector In Ghana's Political Economy.* Accra: Freedom Publications.

Norton, A. *et al.* N.d. (1993?). 'Consolidated Report on Poverty Assessment in Ghana Using Quantitative and Participatory Research Methods (Draft Report)'. London: ODA.

Nyanteng, V.K. 1978. 'Farmer-Trader Relationship: Is There Exploitation?', ISSER (Institute for Social, Statistical and Economic Research, University of Ghana) Discussion Paper No. 3, February.

Oti-Boateng, E., K. Ewusi, R. Kanbur, & A. McKay. 1990. *A Poverty Profile for Ghana 1987-88.* SDA Working Paper No. 5. Washington, DC: World Bank.

Overseas Development Administration (ODA). 1989. 'Civil Service Reform Programme, Ghana. 1988 Data Collection Exercise. Evaluation Report'. London: ODA, March.

Overseas Development Administration (ODA). 1993. *Evaluation of ODA Project in Support of the Ghana Civil Service Reform Programme* (2 Vols.). London: HMSO, September.

Pamscad Secretariat. 1990. 'Proposed Review of Pamscad'. Accra: Ministry of Local Government, Pamscad Secretariat. (mimeo).

Roe, A. & H. Schneider. 1992. *Adjustment and Equity in Ghana.* Paris: OECD.

Sarris, A. & H. Shams. 1991. *Ghana Under Structural Adjustment: the Impact on Agriculture and the Rural Poor*, New York: New York University Press for IFAD.

Sarris, A.H. 1993. 'Household Welfare During Crisis and Adjustment in Ghana', *Journal of African Economies*, Vol. 2, No. 2.

Senah, K. 1989. 'Problems of the Health Care Delivery System', in E. Hansen & K. Ninsin (eds), *The State, Development and Politics in Ghana.* Dakar: Codesria.

Smillie, I. 1986. *No Condition Permanent: Pump-priming Ghana's Industrial Revolution.* London: Intermediate Technology Publications.

Sowa, N.K. *et al.* 1992. *Small Enterprises and Adjustment: The Impact of Ghana's Economic Recovery Programme on Small-Scale Industrial Enterprises.* London: Overseas Development Institute.

The Standard. Accra, various.

The Statesman. Accra, various.

Steel, W. & L. Webster. 1993. 'How Small Enterprises in Ghana have Responded to Adjustment', *World*

Bank Economic Review, Vol. 6, No. 3, September.

Tabor, S., H.K. Quartey-Papafio, & K.A. Haizel. 1993. *Structural Adjustment and Its Impact on Agricultural Research*, International Service for National Agricultural Research, Briefing Paper No. 3, March.

Tangri, R. 1991. 'The Politics of State Divestiture in Ghana', *African Affairs* 90.

Tangri, R. 1992. 'The Politics of Government-Business Relations in Ghana', *Journal of Modern African Studies*, Vol. 30, No. 1.

Toye, J. 1991. 'Ghana', in P. Mosley, J. Harrigan & J. Toye, *Aid and Power: the World Bank and Policy-Based Lending*. London: Routledge.

Transition, various.

Tsikata G.K., & G.K. Amuzu. 1993. 'Fiscal Development Policies and Options', in V.K. Yanteng (ed.), *Policies and Options for Ghanaian Economic Development*. University of Ghana: ISSER.

Twumasi, P.A. 1975. *Medical Systems in Ghana: A Study in Medical Sociology*. Accra-Tema: Ghana Publishing Corporation.

UNICEF. 1987a. 'Adjustment Policies and Programmes to Protect Children and Other Vulnerable Groups in Ghana', in G.A. Cornia, R. Jolly, & F. Stewart, *Adjustment with a Human Face: Protecting the Vulnerable and Promoting Growth*. Oxford: Clarendon Press.

UNICEF. 1987b. 'Ghana', in G.A. Cornia, R. Jolly and F. Stewart, *Adjustment with a Human Face*. Oxford: Clarendon Press.

West Africa, various.

World Bank. 1983. *The Manufacturing Sector*, Background Paper Prepared for 'Ghana: Policies and Programs for Adjustment', Report No. 4702-GH. Washington, DC: Western Africa Department, World Bank, 3 October.

World Bank. 1988a. *Education in Sub-Saharan Africa: Policies for Adjustment, Revitalization and Expansion*, Washington, DC: World Bank.

World Bank. 1988b. *Staff Appraisal Report: Ghana Forest Resource Management*. Washington, DC: Western Africa Department, Agricultural Operations Division, World Bank, 2 May.

World Bank. 1989. *Sub-Saharan Africa: From Crisis to Sustainable Growth: A Long-Term Perspective Study*, Washinton D.C.: The World Bank, November.

World Bank. 1990. *Ghana: Moving Toward Sustainable Private Sector Led Growth*. Washington, DC: Western African Department, World Bank, July.

World Bank. 1991. *Ghana: Progress on Adjustment*, Washington, DC: World Bank, 16 April.

World Bank. 1992a. Report and Recommendation of the President of the International Development Association to the Executive Directors on a Proposed Credit...to the Republic of Ghana for an Agricultural Sector Adjustment Credit (Report No. P-5523-GH). Washington, DC: World Bank, 27 February.

World Bank. 1992b. Report and Recommendation of the President of the International Development Association to the Executive Directors on a Proposed Credit of SDR 74.0 million to the Republic of Ghana for a Second Financial Sector Adjustment Programme, (Report No. P-5659-GH). Washington, DC: World Bank, 15 November.

World Bank. 1993a. *Ghana 2000 and Beyond: Setting the Stage for Accelerated Growth and Poverty Reduction*. Washington, DC: Africa Regional Office, World Bank, February.

World Bank. 1993b. Project Completion Report: Republic of Ghana, Structural Adjustment Institutional Support Project (Credit 1778-GH). Washington, DC: Country Operations Division, Western Africa Department, World Bank, 15 November.

World Bank. 1993c. *The East Asian Miracle. Economic Growth and Public Policy*. New York: Oxford University Press.

Younger, S.D. 1992. 'Aid and the Dutch Disease: Macroeconomic Management When Everybody Loves You', *World Development*, Vol. 20, No. 11.

Ziken International. 1993. *Ghana: Health Sector Consultancy*, Report Prepared for the European Community (mimeo), February.

Tanzania
1986-94

Phil Raikes & Peter Gibbon

Centre for Development Research

Introduction

In the mid-1980s, under strong pressure from the IMF and the World Bank, Tanzania made a series of shifts from socialism and state control, towards a more market-oriented path, involving extensive liberalization of foreign-exchange allocation and internal marketing and general cuts in the extent of state expenditure and economic activity. First in this process came Tanzania's own 'Structural Adjustment Programme' initiated in 1984, which started the process of change but failed to unlock the cupboard of donor funds. This had to await the IMF/World Bank 'Economic Reform Programme' of 1986, and its successor, the Enhanced Structural Adjustment Programme (ESAP, sometimes known as ERP II) from 1989.

The agreement of 1986 ended a four-year 'lending hiatus' imposed by the IFIs,[1] which also involved reduced aid flows from other donors, to pressure Tanzania into changing its policy. This took place at a time when sharply rising interest rates had multiplied Tanzania's debt obligations, and declining terms of trade reduced foreign-exchange earnings, in an economy already facing serious problems. The result was a goods famine of serious proportions, with import compression seriously reducing the output of local industry. Some steps to solve this problem had already been taken in the 1984 programme, but the 1986 agreement unleashed a new burst of donor aid, though significantly smaller in real terms than the 'first aid boom' of the late 1970s, which had done so much to generate the problems of the early 1980s.[2]

Import decompression and liberalization of markets have helped to increase national production since the mid-1980s, and the improved availability of goods seems to be welcomed by almost all, even the large number who cannot afford to buy them. Whatever the Tanzanian people want, it does not seem to be a return to the later Nyerere years; the shortages, the rationing, the waiting and the intrusion of officialdom into personal space and time.[3]

Whether the underlying structure of the Tanzania economy has been strengthened is far more in doubt. Exports have stagnated, and cover less of imports than in 1985, so that indebtedness and dependence on donor aid have continued to grow. The government deficit was reduced for some years - through austerity and increasing donor support - but has risen again in the past two years. Donor aid seems largely to have substituted for local savings, which have fallen sharply to very low, even negative levels. GDP growth has been higher than in the early 1980s, but hardly dramatic, given the increase in investment and the better weather, and is as easily datable from 1984 as 1986. The improvements which have occurred are highly vulnerable to a reduction in donor aid, since the capacity to import from export proceeds has declined almost without break since the mid-1970s.

Before 1986 Tanzania was committed, perhaps too rigidly, to a vision of socialism and to state-directed policies to ameliorate the structural imbalances of the economy. This has all gone, and the current emphasis is solely on market criteria. Concern for

---

[1] International financial institutions, i.e the World Bank and IMF.

[2] See Doriye *et al.*, 1993 for a discussion of this. Also below.

[3] As in mass villagization, followed by masses of arbitrary 'directives' and forced 'self-reliance' or 'nation-building' tasks. .

structural factors or any long-term vision at all is largely absent, as is even a consistent implementation of adjustment. But circumstances (and perhaps statisticians) have conspired to give Tanzania one of the highest growth rates recorded for adjusting countries in Africa. There is thus a tendency on the part of the IFIs to claim it as an adjustment 'success story'. The title of a recent World Bank paper (Mans, 1993) refers to Tanzania's 'resolute action' in relation to structural adjustment policy. This seems glaringly inappropriate. Most observers see weakness, vacillation, lack of perspective, and questionable honesty as the main characteristics of the country's current political leadership, and its main concern as keeping the donors happy and the funds flowing.

Tanzania's dependence goes far beyond the purely economic. Many state agencies function only when donor funds and assistance are channelled through them. Many civil servants survive on the perquisites which they receive via donor agencies - and undertake activities to maximize them, like training courses and seminars, with generous travel and living allowances, whatever the topic. Over the past twenty or thirty years, but especially since the mid-1980s, so much donor orientation has seeped into Tanzanian state decision-making processes, that talk of local 'ownership' of structural adjustment policies is little more than a bad joke.[4] There are many whose interests coincide with one or other aspect of structural adjustment, and a market economy is the general terrain within which any realistic discussion must be held. But there is little sign of the emergence of a private sector capable of or interested in developing Tanzania's productive capacity; rather a speculative 'wild capital' working the angles of state and donor policies and funds.

1. Structural Development Issues in Tanzania prior to Adjustment

Tanzania's economic troubles up to the mid-1980s have been widely attributed to heavy state control of the economy. While there is certainly some truth in this, there is also some misleading over-simplification. Still more misleading is the assumption that this arose solely from the 'rent-seeking' predilections of the élite controlling an 'anti-developmental state'. Certainly Tanzania was responsible for its pre-1986 policies. But they also fitted well with the assumptions of aid donors, were rewarded by them (with increased aid flows) and in some cases actually introduced at their behest. This is particularly true of what is arguably the most disastrous phase of Tanzania policy during the 1970s, when many of the state controls were imposed. So far from donors exerting a moderating influence, this was encouraged, and its negative effects aggravated, by an aid boom arising in part from international events quite unconnected with Tanzania (petro-dollar recycling after the 1973 OPEC oil price rise), but also in part from the enthusiasm of donors (including the World Bank) for policies now seen to have been disastrous.

For six years after independence in 1961, Tanzania followed a standard post-colonial development strategy, aiming to modernize agriculture, to increase exports of primary

---

[4] One pro-adjustment commentary discusses the effectiveness of the 'lending hiatus' of 1980-86 in bringing the Tanzanian government to heel, in tones which border on gloating. It then turns, with no more than an intervening full-stop, to a sententious discussion of how 'ownership' can be introduced - but with the lending-stop option maintained, 'in case'.

agricultural products, to attract foreign funds for industrial and infrastructural investment, to accelerate the training of Africans to take over posts in the state and private industry, to improve and expand provision of health services and clean water, and to weld a colonial territory into a nation. This produced an average growth rate of around 7 percent in GDP and about 7.5 percent in agriculture,[5] which seems high now, but not at the time. In 1964, the market for sisal, then the major export crop, collapsed. A plan to 'transform' peasant agriculture through 'village settlement schemes' was an almost total failure. Agricultural 'improvement' by channelling inputs and credit to small farmers through cooperatives was more successful in increasing output, but involved non-repaid loans which increased marketing costs substantially.

Efforts to attract foreign investors proved unsuccessful, while popular dissatisfaction was increasing over the concentration of the benefits of independence in the hands of Asians and a few politically powerful Africans. In early 1967 President Nyerere issued the Arusha Declaration, signalling a move towards 'socialism and self-reliance'. This was accompanied by nationalization of the small 'commanding heights' of the economy (banks, insurance and trading companies, some agricultural processing and most sisal estates). After this, foreign equity investment ceased, but loans, backed by the Tanzanian and donor states, multiplied rapidly.[6] State policy also involved setting up and expanding parastatal, regional and cooperative entities, and the 'confinement' to them of marketing and productive activities, until they controlled a huge proportion of all economic activity, other than peasant agriculture, which was also entirely surrounded by parastatals for produce marketing and for supply of inputs and credit.

This was only part of a process by which peasant agriculture was squeezed from all sides. *Ujamaa vijijini* (socialism in the villages) was first proposed in 1967, and was to be voluntary. But it became government policy in 1969, to be 'implemented' by state officials, whose achievements in implementation were then assessed - in terms of the number of villages formed and numbers living in them. This criterion then became subject to a process of competitive expansion, as Regional Commissioners outbid each other over the numbers of villages formed until, in 1973, it was decreed that the whole rural population should be in villages within three years. Campaigns and operations to achieve this led to the destruction of thousands of houses (to ensure that peasants did not leave the villages and return to them when the fuss had died down) and enormous disruption to life and production.

Increasing deficits on the state budget and balance of payments should have acted as a brake on this process, especially when a threefold increase in oil prices in 1973 coincided with a serious food shortage and a major increase in imported food prices, necessitating a loan from the IMF. That it did not,nwas due to the flush of easy money from petro-dollar recycling after the oil price increase. This was reflected in a burst of aid inflows, sometimes called 'the first aid boom', which accelerated industrial investment to a point where it far outstretched local capacity to run or maintain the investments. Agriculture was beset by a disastrous combination of forced villagization, accelerated agricultural modernization and 'directives', which significantly reduced agricultural exports and led to major food shortages.

---

[5] 1960/2-1966, constant prices (URT 1967, Table 3).

[6] In this way, foreign firms were able to expand their sales of equipment and management services at no risk to themselves.

Tanzania's unimpressive agricultural performance since the early 1970s is widely attributed to the price effects of state monopoly control of agricultural marketing, with *ujamaa* relegated to a footnote. But the decline in agricultural production had everything to do with the disruption involved in forced villagization and its aftermath. Concentrated in villages, rural people were subjected to decrees and regulations concerning everything from planting famine crops and weeding maize, to not drinking local beer, and to forced labour in 'self-reliance' road-building, trench-digging and 'communal' farm work.

But monopolistic marketing institutions certainly did have a negative impact on agricultural production and exports. Within a few years of Independence, marketing margins for primary agricultural sales began to rise, largely as a result of programmes to spread the use of modern agricultural inputs on credit and/or at subsidized prices. This was (and to some extent still is) standard policy for 'modernizing' agriculture. The costs of distributing inputs to small peasant producers tend to be high, as are those of providing credit. They become still higher if subsidies are given, or if loan repayments are poor - as is often the case. From the mid-1960s cost increases accelerated, as marketing cooperatives were increasingly pressed into 'helping' *ujamaa* villages with grants or uncollectable loans, and had loaded upon them the distribution of consumer goods, 'confined' from private traders. The number and size of agricultural modernization projects grew rapidly in the mid-1970s with easy money and donor enthusiasm for *ujamaa*, and the number and scope of agricultural parastatal corporations grew with them. Administrative overloading increased levels of corruption and misappropriation, reducing effectiveness to very low levels.

It is widely claimed that spending on agriculture declined during the 1970s, leading to declining production. In fact World Bank figures (1994a: 58) show that real government spending on agriculture was higher during 1975-79 than ever before or since. The problem was not lack of spending, but excessive inappropriate spending. Donor projects spearheaded a simultaneous rapid increase in industrial investment, which grew from 10-15 percent of the total in the early 1970s to 35-40 percent in the latter half of the decade (Svendsen, 1986: 66), but generated little corresponding increase in output. Indeed, there was a general decline in the output of productive sectors at the end of the 1970s, with all recorded growth concentrated in the state-dominated tertiary sector.

The investment boom was also self-destructive in macroeconomic terms. Its rapidly rising needs for imports of intermediate and capital goods crowded out consumer imports (under a state foreign-exchange allocation policy), while its multiplier effects were increasing consumer demand at a time when agricultural exports and foreign-exchange receipts were declining. To make things worse, food production was being increasingly diverted away from official cooperative markets, forcing the state-controlled grain supply system to depend on imports. Aggravated by the Uganda War and the second oil shock of 1979, this was already leading to severe foreign-exchange shortage by the end of the 1970s, leaving Tanzania in a weak position to face the major shift in world monetary conditions and economic policy in 1979-81.

In an attempt to increase its external resource flows, Tanzania agreed a standby credit with the IMF in 1979. But the government failed to observe the agreed budget ceilings and the agreement was cancelled. During discussion about the release of its second tranche, the IMF's representative was declared persona non grata and the Minister of Finance, Edwin Mtei, who was perceived by Nyerere as being too close to the IFIs, was dismissed. Shortly after this, Nyerere made a speech in which the IMF was condemned for attempting to set itself up as an 'International Ministry of Finance'. Tanzania then turned to the World Bank, with which intimate relations had been maintained throughout the 1970s (McNamara was on first-name terms with Nyerere and had even attended cabinet meetings). It was surprised to find itself rebuffed, for just at this point the Bank was undergoing its own internal political adjustment in the face of a more hostile US domestic political climate. A part of this adjustment was its (temporary) subordination to the IMF, which now sought to make an example of Tanzania.

There was little further communication between the Tanzania Government and the IFIs until 1981, when the Bank indicated that quick-disbursing aid would be available if certain policy changes were implemented and agreement reached with the IMF on this basis. The latter was now demanding a 50-60 percent devaluation, a major reduction in the budget deficit, removal of most consumer and producer subsidies and a slashing of others, positive real bank interest rates, major increases in agricultural producer prices and steps toward import liberalization.

This was the context in which Tanzania embarked on the National Economic Survival Plan, described in Section 2. While the IMF saw this as a further act of war, neither the World Bank nor the major bilateral donors found it convincing. But they were reluctant to see relations with Tanzania broken completely and, together with the Tanzania Government, sponsored a Technical Advisory Group of eminent economists with the brief of drawing up a compromise package. This included a devaluation, though not of the order proposed by the IMF, but otherwise preservation of most existing government policies. This was rejected by the Tanzania Government, mostly over the issue of devaluation. Had it not been, it is likely that the World Bank would have rejected the proposals for excessive 'softness'. Tanzania then turned to the Nordic bilaterals, to get them to increase their aid to fill the gap left by the IFIs. But by this time Norway and Sweden had themselves been converted to the need for adjustment and rejected the advance. From 1981 to 1985 the overall flow of external assistance fell from US$702 m. to US$487 m.

Tanzania depended heavily on imports of fuel, raw materials, intermediate goods and spares to keep its industrial and agro-industrial investments going. Allocation of foreign exchange for this purpose, combined with a rigid import-licensing system and the aid embargo, further crowded out imports of consumer goods. Combined with a similarly rigid rationing and price control system, this ensured that most basic consumer goods disappeared from the shops by 1981, and stayed that way for the next three or four years.

In some ways, macroeconomic indicators underestimate the disruptive effects. They hide (except as low productivity) the loss of routine and waste of time which result when normal markets disappear underground, especially when state austerity policies are reducing real wages by holding increases below inflation. Efficiency falls as workers use time searching (or queuing) for essential commodities - and in extra-curricular activities to earn the money to buy them with, including corruption and misappropriation. In other ways, official figures may overestimate the extent of the crisis. Recent estimates put the size of the informal economy at upwards of one-third of the formal economy, with most of its growth having occurred during the 1970s and early 1980s (see below section 6).

From 1981 to 1983, the government tried to tighten existing policies, with counterproductive effects. A series of campaigns against corruption and against 'loitering' in towns did not reduce corruption, but did further reduce the supply of goods. By 1984, the shortages were becoming so severe that the government made an important change of course. It 'provisionally' allowed owners of 'own' foreign exchange (money from smuggling or mis-invoicing) to import consumer goods, 'with no questions asked'. It also devalued the currency and increased producer prices for most controlled crops by about 30 percent for 1984-85. Exporters of items not controlled by the major marketing boards were allowed to retain a proportion of their foreign-exchange receipts. User charges for health services were introduced in the same budget. These measures involved a major policy change and brought the beginnings of an upturn before agreement with the IFIs was reached.

2.   Structural Adjustment in Tanzania: History and Objectives

2.1   Evolution of the Dialogue, 1979-86

Prior to the change of course in 1984, the Tanzanian Government tried to resolve the crisis by putting a more liberal face on what was essentially a tightening of existing policies. These efforts were rebuffed by the donors for their failure to agree on the extent of devaluation needed, or to relax the 'confinement' of goods to state-directed agencies, and for their side-stepping of the general issue of liberalization.

The first local plan, the *National Economic Survival Plan* (NESP), 1981-82, was initiated before a renewed application to the IMF, and seen as part of that application. Its focus was to increase export income and to eliminate food shortage through village irrigation schemes and cultivation of drought-resistant crops and to reduce public expenditure through strict control (Wagao, 1990). This depended on tightening up the state-controlled system and increasing capacity in its productive parts. But with capacity utilization already very low, and with wages well under the minimum required to live on, this was a non-starter, as was trying to increase export earnings in a depressed world economy without incentives to offer. In retrospect, the NESP never offered a solution. Made in haste, with too little discussion, its targets were neither realistic nor linked to means for their achievement. NESP was also a non-starter with the IFIs. Any attempt to normalize relations would require something else.

The Structural Adjustment Programme (1982-86) was a more serious attempt to do this. Its approach was to look in some detail at the structure of the economy, and see what needed adjusting. Despite the similarity in names, this is not what is generally referred to as 'structural adjustment'. This latter identifies a number of general 'structural' issues like market distortion as the main (only) effect of state intervention in the economy, and state intervention in the economy as the main (only) cause of market distortions. The former method is concerned to define policy parameters, and fine-tune state intervention for optimal effect. The latter is primarily concerned to minimize state intervention.

The SAP focused on increasing agricultural and especially export production. Devaluations of 20 percent and 40 percent were aimed primarily at neighbouring countries and cross-border smuggling. They were insufficient to close the wide gap to prevailing market rates, and failed to impress or move the IFIs, though they did increase agricultural sales and exports. The industrial component planned to improve capacity utilization by targeted use of foreign exchange. Fiscal and monetary controls were to be further tightened to reduce inflation. Later, as it became clear that these measures were having little effect, the 'own foreign exchange' and other policies mentioned above were introduced. This began a modest process of improvement in the supply of goods (starting at the top with luxuries but moving gradually down), and can now be seen as the start of the upturn in agricultural production, but it did not satisfy the IFIs or unlock the funds.

It did, however, give support to the growing local criticism of state policies. The official line was that, although mistakes had been made, the basic causes of Tanzania's troubles were external; the cost of the war in Uganda,[7] the second oil price increase in 1979 and the deflationary policies in the north, which turned debt into debt-crisis. But major shortages of consumer goods had preceded all of these events, and the gridlock imposed on trade by 'confinement' was increasingly obvious, so the volume of (private) complaint began to swell, despite the efforts of the security police to limit it. Anti-corruption campaigns aroused much populist enthusiasm, which turned to bitterness as they aggravated the supply situation, as most 'high-ups' escaped the net and especially when even the few caught in it were set free.

Public complaint about the content of government policies, as opposed to the corruption with which they were increasingly associated, remained generally limited for most of the early 1980s. Popular opposition largely took the form of avoidance rather than protest. The only source of explicit opposition to the policies came from a group of economics lecturers at the University of Dar es Salaam, who from 1984 onward began holding public annual meetings at which liberalization measures were advocated. This risked official disapproval, but should not be taken as a wholly independent trend. The meetings were sponsored by those sections of the Tanzania state apparatus closest to the IFIs.

President Nyerere strongly disagreed with the changes of 1985, which he saw as both rewarding dishonesty and reversing the policies for which he stood. But he resigned (as the constitution required) in 1985, allowing a new president to take policy directions with which he strongly disagreed. The ruling party, CCM, never explicitly ack-nowledged a change in economic direction - except as a temporary detour necessary to set the socialist project back on course. But those within CCM who wished to impose limits on liberalization and upon the few ministers openly associated with it[8], were isolated. An informal modus vivendi evolved in which private capitalists, old and new, could go about their business increasingly unhindered, while the state bourgeoisie continued to operate 'its' sector (the civil service and parastatals) and to set the political agenda much as before (see Kiondo, forthcoming).

2.2   Formal Objectives of SAPs

In 1986, Tanzania reached agreement with the IMF and not long afterwards made the

---

[7] Undertaken with widespread international approval and on the (incorrect) assumption that donors would foot some of the bill.

[8] Cleopa Msuya, many times Finance Minister and now Prime Minister.

first agreement with the World Bank, thus embarking on 'structural adjustment' in the now official sense of the term. The agreement was entitled *The Economic Recovery Plan* (ERP, 1986-89), which was followed by the *Enhanced Structural Adjustment Programme* (ESAP, also referred to sometimes as ERP II) from 1989 to 1992. Broadly speaking, the ERP focused around a series of specified targets and means for their achievement. Since then, ESAP conditionality has focused more on 'institutional reform', mainly defined as privatization.

The targets of the ERP included:

a. to increase output of food and export crops through appropriate pricing strategies.
b. to increase capacity utilization in industry from 20-30 percent up to 60-70 percent.
c. to restore internal and external macroeconomic balance through 'prudent' monetary, fiscal and trade policies.
d. to reduce inflation from 30 percent to 15-20 percent.
e. to increase forex earnings from exports from US$400 m. to US$630 m. by 1989.
f. to rehabilitate and maintain basic social services.

The policy instruments chosen to achieve these aims included:

1. Raising agricultural producer prices by 5 percent per annum or to 60-70 percent of the world market price, and reducing the incidence of price control.
2. Exchange rates - devalue sufficiently to eliminate exchange-rate over-valuation by mid-1988 and subsequently move to market-based allocation of forex.
3. Trade policy - deconfinement of both imports and local trade.
4. Public expenditure control - continue the austerity measures started in 1984-85, limit government recurrent expenditure and reduce deficit financing from the banking system. Rationalize and reduce parastatal activities and subsidies to them.
5. Tight monetary policy, raise interest rates until positive in real terms, adopt tight credit ceilings and limit the growth of money supply to 15-20 percent per annum.
6. Revenue collection - close monitoring and looking for ways to increase efficiency and/or broaden the tax-base.
7. Non-price measures to increase agricultural production; improving access to consumer goods, distribution of agricultural inputs and transport infrastructure. General freeing of consumer goods markets.

Formally, the ERP and ESAP were divided into six different adjustment programmes focusing in sequence on different areas of the economy, starting with multi-sector rehabilitation, and then going through industrial and agricultural rehabilitation, parastatal adjustment, civil service reform and general structural adjustment. Each was to be achieved under a specific loan programme, not necessarily so tightly bound to a specific end-use as the title might imply.

The Multi-sector Rehabilitation Credit was agreed in 1986. Its main conditions concerned prices, fiscal management and exchange-rate adjustment. Its main aim was to increase agricultural production, especially export crops, via devaluation, marketing improvement and improved transport. It was funded with US$300 m., half from the IDA, and half from other donors. Allocation of the funds was left to the Tanzania Government, subject to compliance with the macro-conditions, imposed through disbursement in tranches. The last of these was to be fed through an Open General Licence, a supposedly more market-oriented means of allocating forex, which did not exist until 1988.

An internal evaluation found the MRC to have been a success in having secured a major change in policy direction although its 'sustainability, taken in isolation, was probably low'. The MRC did indeed involve sweeping reforms: a major devaluation, limits on budget and balance-of-payments deficits and limits on domestic credit. But the evaluation found its approach to adjustment to have been patchy and too slow. The 'lending hiatus' was found to have been a useful means for securing agreement to ERP/MRC, but it was noted, apparently without irony, that Tanzanian 'ownership' of the programme was low. It was thus recommended that both the external pressure for adjustment and the level of Tanzanian 'ownership' be increased!

The Industrial Rehabilitation and Trade Adjustment Credit (IRTAC) was approved in December 1988, for a total US$242 m., of which US$182 m. was from the IDA. Its major focus was on trade liberalization, tariff and sales tax reforms, and industrial restructuring in the areas of textiles, leather and agricultural processing. Funds were channelled only through the OGL system, which was expanded thereby and the list of items eligible for import under it extended. Otherwise it was, to all intents and purposes, a continuation of MRC.

The Tanzania Agricultural Adjustment Credit (TANAA) started in 1990, for a total US$385 m. of which US$200 m. was from the IDA. It focused on liberalization of marketing for agricultural products and inputs. As with IRTAC, the funds were channelled through the OGL and the list of eligible items was replaced by a short 'negative list' of what could not be funded through it. Thus, despite the name, the funds did not have to be used for agricultural supplies.

The Financial Sector Adjustment Programme was signed in 1991 with US$275 m., of which US$200 m. was from the IDA. It focused on the banking sector, with privatization and allowing forex bureaux and foreign private banks to enter the Tanzanian market.

The Structural Adjustment Credit focuses upon parastatal restructuring and privatization, civil service reform and more restructuring of markets for traditional agricultural exports.

The last three were in effect part of the *Economic and Structural Adjustment Programme* (ESAP), which continued where the ERP left off in 1989 and included liberalization of foreign investment regulations. As mentioned above, the notion of an overall combined programme has lost some of its meaning with the shift from specified numerical targets and means for achievement (by state and parastatal organs) to privatization which reduces the capacity of the state for direct intervention. While the overall programme since 1992 (when ESAP finished) may have a name, it is not used in IFI and CG documents, which refer to specific loans or to the two-year Policy Framework Papers prepared under IFI supervision by Tanzania, or their more detailed specification in the Rolling Plans and Forward Budgets, which have replaced Five-Year Plans as the only means for considering the medium term. The principal focus of these plans and budgets has been in the area of civil service and parastatal reform.

There have been a number of internal or IFI-sponsored assessments of the ERP and economic reform, more generally. Most have been quite enthusiastic about the extent of policy change achieved, and see the need for more reform on the same lines. But, as will be shown below, the results in terms of concrete achievements are hardly impressive. In terms of the explicit targets of the ERP, by 1989 the following was roughly the position:

- Growth in agriculture was confined to food crops, that of export crops stagnated. Far from increasing from US$400 m. to US$630 m., export revenues only reached US$430 m.
- Industrial capacity utilization had increased, but only to about 35 percent.
- The foreign-exchange gap had thus increased (and been filled with donor aid), the direct state budget deficit had been reduced but by means which included shifting expenses to parastatals (and their deficits). Investment seemed to be paid for exclusively by foreign aid with local saving low or even negative.
- The pre-existing decline in social service spending is said to have been checked, but there is no evidence of any improvement in services.

By early 1995, the only improvement over the above has been a slight increase in export-crop production and revenue, but even with the assistance of a sharp (and temporary) increase in coffee prices, to only about US$523 m. Macroeconomic balances have deteriorated significantly since 1989, with social service expenditure now apparently in sharp decline.

2.3   Aid Relations

There has been a rapid increase in aid flows since 1986 and a shift towards import support, though project aid still dominates, with about two-thirds of the total. After the fall in disposable aid receipts of the early 1980s, this has made a large difference, and is sometimes termed the 'second aid boom', though in real terms, the amounts involved are smaller than those of the 1970s and do not even fully compensate for terms-of-trade losses since then. This raises two important general questions; firstly regarding the degree to which the achievements of adjustment (such as they are) derive from import decompression arising from increased grant inflows; secondly, is whether a large increase in grant flows may not conflict with other aspects of adjustment by 'softening' budget constraints.

The increased prominence of macro-conditionality with the shift from project to programme aid requires greater coordination between donors for its imposition. This means coordination through one or both of the IFIs, whose influence over the disposal of aid funds has enormously increased during the period of structural adjustment. But there are differences between the stated policies of the World Bank and IMF and those of some bilateral donors both as regards satisfaction or otherwise with Tanzania's progress and with regard to willingness to take 'hard' actions like cutting off funds.

Very briefly, the trajectory of donor attitudes seems to have been somewhat as follows. By 1986, most of the residual sympathy for Tanzania's socialist aims had been replaced by cynicism and concern for change. During the ERP period, 1986-89, there was considerable suspicion on the part of donors over whether Tanzania had really changed course, combined with higher hopes for the success of adjustment elsewhere in Africa. During the period 1989-93, largely as a result of glowing IFI reports on Tanzania's progress and much less glowing results elsewhere, this changed radically. Tanzania now came to be seen as a much better prospect than most neighbours (notably

Kenya, previously held up as a shining example of market-orientation). This involved talking the achievements up and the problems down, with much reference to 'resolute action' and 'vibrancy'. By 1993-95, the lack of direction, enhanced dependence and corruption of the new system were becoming increasingly hard for donors to ignore - except for the IFIs, which had invested too much prestige in Tanzania and its success (the money is comparatively small in international terms) for this to be admissible. What makes this situation especially dangerous for Tanzania is that if and when the problems are recognized, the blame for both the situation and the donors' misreading of it will certainly be piled on Tanzania, laying the 'moral' basis for a new 'lending hiatus'.

Given that Tanzania depends for well over half of its official foreign exchange on aid funds this is no small danger, either as a consequence of hard conditionality or, more gradually, as a result of 'donor fatigue'. In November 1994, the Nordic donors other than Denmark suspended aid payments over the issue of tax exemptions to politically favoured persons (see Section 6 for details). Among other things tax-exempt imports were (are) competing unfairly with (taxed) local products and reducing government revenues significantly. By early December, the government response had been to promise a thoroughgoing investigation and (after some weeks of doing nothing) to make the minimum cabinet reshuffle necessary to get the aid tap turned on again. 'Resolute action' was not much in evidence. By the CG meeting of February 1995 the investigation was still uncompleted and no formal decision had been taken by donors on the resumption of aid. Responsibility for resolving the issue was delegated to the IMF, now ironically one of the donors most sympathetic to the Tanzania Government.

2.4   Public Debate

Since the adoption of adjustment in 1986, some of the economists who had earlier criticized government policies have been absorbed into the government. In the following years, adjustment moved from being the proposal of a small minority to an accepted fact of life. In external relations it became an official discourse. It did not figure much in internal politics at all under the modus vivendi described above.

Until the early 1990s internal debate about the policies was confined largely to complaints about the run-down condition of social services which, with devaluation-related inflation, was seen as the Achilles' heel of adjustment. Participants in the social services debate tended to underestimate non-adjustment factors in the decline and to cite figures which excluded local government spending. By contrast, deconfinement seems to have met with widespread public approval. Public opposition to government revolved more around lack of political democracy than structural adjustment, this being reflected in the broadly pro-adjustment stances of most opposition parties after political liberalization in 1991-92.

The early 1990s witnessed some changes in this situation. One important trend was the emergence of popular struggles explicitly directed against particular adjustment policies. In 1992 there were major upheavals at the two universities over the attempted imposition of cost-sharing, required as a condition of a World Bank Higher Education Credit. Small-scale miners in Arusha region organized with partial success to resist the alienation of their mining rights to new companies (some foreign) under the new investment regulations. Secondly, political liberalization and the growth of an independent press (from 1988, accelerating after 1991) allowed the articulation of certain previously repressed political issues. These included religion, the union between Tanganyika and Zanzibar and questions of corruption/'leadership'.

These issues are indirectly linked to each other, and through that of corruption/'leadership' to adjustment. Especially since the abolition of the 'leadership code' in 1992, a loosely structured but clearly identifiable group of civil servants, politicians and private importers has emerged, profiting from the new business climate in ways which include increasingly flagrant rule-bending. Some of the politicians have previously been associated with opposition to adjustment, and the development is part of a more general shift away from the modus vivendi of the late 1980s (see Kiondo, forthcoming). The independent newspapers at the forefront of exposing rule-bending by this new 'public-private' bourgeoisie generally saw it as the product of too little rather than too much adjustment, and gave the main donors a platform to develop this argument at length.

The issue most likely to subvert this interpretation of the relationship between corruption and adjustment, and which links them both to religion, ethnicity and 'Union', is privatization. Private sector interest in purchasing Tanzanian public companies has come mainly from East African Asian and South African European capital (see below, section 9). So responses to their acquisitions of Tanzanian parastatals have combined questions about the procedures and deals involved with concerns about 'recolonization', and have activated latent and not-so-latent popular racial stereotypes about the 'public-private' bourgeoisie. It is highly relevant that this linkage between privatization, adjustment and 'leadership' has been the focus of the first public speeches as an opposition figure by the very popular former Minister of Home Affairs, Augustine Mrema, in March 1995.[9]

2.5   Impact on National Policy

Much of the following section will detail different effects of the SAP on policy-making. In general, however, the structural adjustment process has affected just about every area of policy-making, whether in terms of compliance or evasive action. In many respects, the stated aims of Tanzania's economic policy are the diametric opposite of those before 1986. The notion of economic structure (other than degree of market orientation) has virtually disappeared from the policy discourse, as have most other aspects of long-term thinking (other than 'let the market decide').

But when it comes to specific changes, the degree of compliance is considerably lower and slower than the above would imply. Civil service and parastatal reform/privatization are rather obvious examples, since both vitally concern decision-makers through their effect on jobs - and access to state resources. Both have taken considerably longer than expected. But this is not only a matter of self-interested obstruction, since both do involve rather intractable problems. For civil service reform, the task is to sack enough civil servants for the remainder to receive a sufficient consolidated wage to live on (and at the top to live well on) without expanding the total recurrent budget (most of it already spent on wages).

The extent of the task can be gauged by the fact that pay is said to cover only one quarter of living expenses for most civil servants (with allowances coming to another

---

[9] See section 6, note 3 for the circumstances of his removal from office.

quarter or half). The difficulties are aggravated by the fact that, like every civil service reform, it is being done from the top down, and has favoured and will continue to favour upper-level employees. Given this, the problem changes from intractable to impossible except by simply closing down most ministries. Parastatal privatization is also going more slowly than the IFIs would like, but too quickly and with too little discussion for many Tanzanians.

More generally two further observations can be made about the policy-making process under adjustment. The first is that while adjustment has penetrated policy-making to some degree in most fields, the main result of the transition from *ujamaa* to economic liberalization has been that - with the fairly obvious exception of the banking sector - there is no longer any central policy direction in any field. This includes and is even perhaps most obvious in agriculture, where a series of institutional changes have been introduced in the absence of any strategic long-term priorities. It also goes for the overall distribution of state expenditure between ministries and within ministerial budget headings, which continue to be dominated largely by historical convention. Where other priorities intrude, such as in the curious priority given by the Ministry of Education to the needs of 'specially gifted children', these seem to reflect the whims of unaccountable individual civil servants. There is serious doubt as to whether any capacity still exists for setting and implementing an integrated set of national priorities, or even a non-integrated one. Both (1989 and 1994) Public Expenditure Reviews were apparently carried out with only the most tangential Tanzania Government participation.

The second is that certain of the methods whereby donors and the Tanzania Government have sought to resolve - or, more cynically, postpone resolution of - their differences have led to useful and informed public debate on important policy questions. Presidential Commissions on both the tax system (chaired by E. Mtei) and the land question (chaired by I. Shivji) have served to increase public information on these issues, even if this was not their main intent. The Commission system has also provided an additional public forum, alongside the independent press and the increasingly assertive parliament.

3. Overall and Macroeconomic Effects of Structural Adjustment

3.1 Introduction

This chapter attempts to assess the effects of structural adjustment in general macro-economic terms. This involves a multi-stage argument, starting out by establishing (so far as possible) what did happen and then assessing (again so far as possible) to what extent changes noted, both positive and negative, can be attributed to structural adjustment. But since adjustment consists *both* of a large number of different conditions, imposed with varying severity at different points in time, *and* of the release of foreign funds in return for (or in expectation of) compliance with the conditions, this can rapidly become complicated. This is still more the case, since some aspects may actually work against others. Thus raising real interest rates tends to increase parastatal deficits, when adjustment seeks to reduce them. Large increases in donor grant aid inflows may obstruct the imposition of hard budget constraints, while having other positive effects.[10]

Behind these lie other questions, even more important in the long term since they concern the sustainability of adjustment policies. The question is often asked whether internal or external forces were primarily responsible for Africa's or Tanzania's pre-adjustment problems. We have tried to show in section 2 that interactions between the two are as, or more, important. But behind this is disagreement over the nature of the world economic changes occurring from 1979 to 1981. For neo-liberals, these served primarily to point up the shortcomings of previous development patterns, and the problems they raise are seen to be surmountable with adjustment. Others note that international financial deregulation and advances in communications technology have fundamentally changed the structure of the world economy to the clear disadvantage of Africa. Given the massive decline in terms of trade for Africa's exports during the 1980s and 90s and the accumulation of debt to quite unsustainable levels, adjustment seems a bit like privatizing the deckchairs on the Titanic.

The macroeconomics of adjustment can usefully be discussed in terms of three 'balances' or 'gaps', expressed in the identity

(Investment - Savings) + (Government spending - Revenue) = (Imports - Exports)

That is, if the country invests more than is saved and the government spends more than its tax and other revenue, this involves using more resources than are produced locally and so requires net imports. The identity does not mention the many other complex interactions between these magnitudes, nor how they are funded, but clearly enough imports greater than exports must be funded by loans, grants or remittances from abroad.

The balance between investment and savings depends mainly on the real rate of interest. Increasing it encourages people to save and discourages investment (other things being equal) and vice versa. The real interest rate depends in turn on the nominal interest rate and the rate of inflation. The former can be set directly (or indirectly) by the government via the central bank. Inflation depends, among other things, upon fiscal and monetary policy, the latter of which has mainly to do with credit.[11]

This also relates to the second balance. The 'fiscal gap' between tax revenue and government spending is one of the factors affecting the rate of inflation, via increases in the supply of money. At first sight, it would seem amenable to direct state policy, since the government sets the taxes and produces the budget. In fact it is less simple:

- Actual revenue collection normally depends on the level of economic activity and, if that falls, may be insufficient to cover budgeted expenditure.
- Items like interest payments depend on the rate of interest.
- Parastatal corporations can increase their spending through running up debts which are part of the public expenditure gap (though if this is investment, it should more properly be included under the savings-investment balance).

As will emerge, this latter point is highly relevant to Tanzania. The state (as such) has

---

[10] The obverse of this is that fungible aid-flows may relieve bottlenecks at macro level, even if related to projects whose impact is negative.

[11] Nowadays printing money is not a major factor in the money supply. Major transactions all involve credit and accounting changes, not notes or coin.

sometimes 'complied' with IFI conditions requiring it to reduce expenditures by off-loading these onto parastatal corporations without budgeting payments for them. Since the latter are part of the state, they (and the state banks supplying them with credit) have put policy implementation above keeping within borrowing limits, so that raising interest rates has had the reverse effect from that intended.

The macroeconomic purpose of adjustment is broadly to achieve 'balance' and 'stability' as a means to induce - rather than directly produce - investment and growth, largely from the private sector. This makes for problems in assessing the degree to which any given level of investment or other outcome has been induced by improved balance and stability as opposed to other factors. But neither 'balance' nor 'stability' can be defined objectively - and no-one aims at complete balance, at least for investment/savings and imports/exports. There are rules of thumb which purport to indicate what level of imbalance can be considered 'stable' or 'sustainable', but in reality both refer to what external financiers (that is primarily the IFIs themselves) regard as adequate and are willing to 'sustain'.

Thus, almost by definition, the adoption by a country of an adjustment programme improves both 'balance' and 'stability', whether or not the objective indicators improve. This is certainly the case with Tanzania, which is regarded by the IFIs as having made significant strides towards sustainability, even though its debt and trade gaps have grown in absolute terms and as a proportion of GDP, while other indicators have remained unchanged or improved marginally. The element of circularity is increased if one considers the impact on foreign investment and inflows of funds. With a very few exceptions, foreign capital has shown little interest in buying into Tanzania's run-down parastatal sector, even at the rock-bottom prices for which it is being offered (see section 9). Almost all of the inflow of funds occasioned by adjustment has come from the IFIs and other donors, responding with approval to the fact that Tanzania is adjusting rather than to any positive effects it may have had.

On the other hand, there is a tendency to under-estimate what is probably the most valuable effect of adjustment. From the mid-1970s onwards, increasing state control and confinement of almost all domestic trade tied the country's economy in knots, tightened by the arbitrary allocation of the country's resources and the people's labour time through political directives. Both of these succumbed at a relatively early stage to adjustment conditionality (and the sheer inability of the state to maintain either), to the clear and unambiguous benefit of nearly all concerned. Part of this benefit, being direct (like relief from being messed around), does not appear in economic magnitudes, except to the extent that it generates more output - and much of the latter is likely to occur in non-measured areas of the economy.

Given these and other complications, the approach adopted here will be more or less as follows (though not necessarily in the order outlined):

1. Try to estimate (and where possible measure) trends before and during adjustment, paying special attention to changes in them.
2. Consider relevant aspects of adjustment conditionality, how they might be expected to have affected the trend in question, the degree to which they have been fulfilled in practice and their effects - including indirect and unintended ones.
3. Consider the relative effectiveness of conditionality and aid inflows - and their degree of interdependence.

4. Consider the importance of exogenous factors, ranging from weather and terms of trade[12] to the general state of the world economy and political and related trends in Tanzania. One such issue is the extent of 'donor fatigue', which has both general dimensions - the worldwide trend to reduce aid levels, most sharply evident in the USA, and directly related to neo-liberal thinking - and a dimension which focuses around dis/satisfaction with Tanzania's general development and/or response to adjustment.

Given the inter-related nature of many of these questions, it will often be simpler to present them in a general account of 'what happened', rather than to list 'factors a,b, and c.'. It may also be a bit less boring to read.

The logic of the above might suggest that discussion of changes in GDP should be preceded by discussion of the various factors affecting it. But the basic national income figures are so central to the account that they are introduced first - after a brief discussion of data problems.

Tanzania statistics - There is serious doubt and disagreement about almost every important statistical magnitude in Tanzania, starting with the size of the national income, for which different series and interpretations give very different results. Nor is there any way of resolving the issues, since the basis for estimating a large part of the total is very weak. Agriculture accounts for between 45 and 63 percent of the total GDP, according to different calculations and at different times, and well over 80 percent of the value of agricultural production does not pass through marketing channels, where there is statistical data collection. Thus up to 40 percent of total GDP is 'estimated' by means including plain guesswork and adjusting upwards by estimated population growth.

It is widely thought that GDP estimation misses out a large proportion of 'informal' economic activities, leading to under-estimation of total GDP by 30 percent or even 60-70 percent,[13] and that inclusion of informal exports would increase estimates of total exports by 50, 60 or even 100 percent. This does not affect growth-rate estimates unless the figures are (improperly) revised only for post-adjustment years. It does reduce consumption estimates (since what has been exported could not have been consumed) and so improves an otherwise unimpressive negative rate of savings.[14] It seems clear that some adjustment for informal activities is justified, but some of the above-mentioned calculations seem to exaggerate their extent, and to ignore significant levels of 'informal imports', which would reverse the upward adjustment of savings. But in the context of such huge disparities, there is not much hope of resolving disagreements over

---

[12] As discussed in Part I of this book, terms-of-trade change is only partially exogenous. Its extent has certainly been increased by the success of export-oriented adjustment programmes, albeit mostly in other parts of the world than Africa. Moreover the decline was clearly predictable (and widely predicted) before adjustment started. Failure to take this into account (and refusal to include it in price predictions) could be considered culpably irresponsible advice on the part of the IFIs.

[13] See Maliyamkono and Bagachwa (1990); Sarris and van den Brink (1993).

[14] This adjustment is one of the major points of a World Bank policy research working paper; Agrawal *et al.*, 1993.

whether the 'true' rate of growth is (say) 3.2 percent or 5.1 percent or 7.3 percent.

Investment figures are, if anything, still less reliable. For private investment, estimates of buildings and other works are based on local cement and steel production, while estimates of investment in machinery and equipment come from import data . As Rattsø (1992) points out, it is not clear how closely this even relates to productive investment, since cement is used in house construction and equipment like cars and refrigerators may be consumer goods. In Tanzania's current situation, there are two further complications. Firstly recent donor spending on 'rehabilitation' lies right on the boundary between maintenance (a recurrent cost, classed as consumption) and investment. Rehabilitation may be considered 'capitalized maintenance', in the sense that it involves re-investment because of previous failure to operate and maintain equipment properly. But at least, this involves something like investment. Far more serious are problems of fungibility or 'leakage'. As discussed in section 6, Tanzania's investment promotion measures offer generous tax and duty relief on goods imported for investment, and impose very limited control over what this covers. It thus seems likely that a significant proportion of 'investment' is composed of consumer goods which have been mis-classified as investment goods to take advantage of these 'incentives'.

All of the different macroeconomic figures have serious problems and most have been revised frequently. As Rattsø puts it, 'the numbers presented in this report should be handled with care'. So should those in all other reports, however confidently they are presented.

3.2   National Income

It is generally agreed that national income (Gross Domestic Product) has grown more rapidly since 1985 than during the preceding four years, though there is disagreement about the figures, about how much of an achievement this represents and whether it results primarily from import decompression or from conditionality and policy change. It is asserted by some that per capita income, having declined from 1980 to 1985, has increased (just) thereafter. Other sources show a decline throughout, though slower in the latter period.

In the course of making this study, some 10-15 different sources of national income tables were consulted, most of them claiming to be cited from each other or from basic Tanzania Government data. Despite this, for no single year were there less than three different estimates of inter-annual growth-rates and over the period 1982/93-1991/92, the average disparity between top and bottom estimates was 3.1 percent! In several cases it seemed as if years had been wrongly placed. Up until 1990, one can use a fairly authoritative series from *Tanzania Economic Trends*.[15] Since then, the range of 'factor-cost' figures has been used.

Table 1 shows the growth of Gross Domestic Product since 1980 in Tanzania shillings (Tsh), at 1976 prices and in US$, with per capita figures in 1976 Tsh. The two left-hand columns show GDP in 1976 prices and are based on the series mentioned above to 1990. Thereafter, they show the range of 'factor cost' figures, including an apparently anomalous negative figure for 1991 from Tanzania's most recent *Budget*

---

[15] Produced, after discussion of the problems, by authors who include Tanzania's most experienced national income statistician and the economist who produced the 1969-74 development plan.

Survey.[16] In either case, the general picture is of the growth rate having increased since the early 1980s, though the increase could as easily be dated to 1984 or 1987 as to 1986, when the ERP was agreed.

Table 1   GDP Growth, 1981-93

	1976 constant prices		GDP per capita 1976 constant prices			
	Tsh bn	%	Tsh	%	US$ m.	%
1980/81	23.3	-0.5	1249	..		
1981/82	23.4	0.5	1217	-2.5		
1982/83	22.9	-2.4	1152	-5.3	6328	
1983/84	23.7	3.4	1154	0.1		
1984/85	24.3	2.6	1172	1.6		
1985/86	25.1	3.3	1181	2.3	4883	
1986/87	26.3	5.1	1189	0.7	3409	-30.0
1987/88	27.5	4.2	1203	1.2	3300	-3.2
1988/89	28.4	3.3	1223	1.7	2984	-9.3
1989/90	29.9	4.8	1262	3.2	2774	-7.0
1990/91	28.4 / 31.6	-5 / 5.7	1295	2.6	2728	-8.5
1991/92	29.2 / 32.7	2.6 / 4.2	1305	0.8	2667	-2.6
1992/93	30.4 / 33.9	3.3 / 4.1	1315	0.8	2492	-6.6
1993/94	..	3.5[a]	..	0.8	..	..

Sources: van Arkadie *et al.* (TET) 1991; URT, 1994d; URT, Bureau of Statistics, 1994a; World Bank documents; EIU, 1995/1.

Notes: For 1990/91, the *Budget Survey* shows -5.2%. All other sources show between 3.7 and 5.7%. For 1991/92, one (IFI) source shows negative growth (-3.6%) after adjustment for terms-of-trade change; others positive. Figures in US$ are just one among a wide variety of (significantly varying) sets of estimates.

[a]   Provisional figure from EIU, 1995.

Per capita figures at 1976 prices show similar trends, i.e. negative or minimal growth from 1981 to 1986, followed by positive growth at slightly below 1 percent. Other sources give a less positive picture. A World Bank document gives a variety of different estimates of real per capita incomes, presented in Table 2 as three-year averages.

So, depending on what deflator is used, per capita income either increasess very slightly or falls quite significantly. On the face of it, deflation by the National

---

[16] There seems no reason for downward bias in the *Budget Survey*, but proof-reading is so bad (whole columns missing from some tables) that its data must be treated with extra caution.

Consumer Price Index should at least not overstate real incomes, since it is widely thought to under-estimate the real extent of price increases. The difference between the series based on the NCPI and the Low Income NCPI would imply that items of particular importance to low-income households have risen in price more than others, so reducing the relative real incomes of those households. The agricultural figures are higher, but there is the same disparity, halving the imputed growth rate. With similar rates of growth in cash income for poor and wealthy households, the poor would benefit less because of different rates of price increase.

Table 2   Alternative Estimates of Change in per Capita GDP (Tsh)

	1981-83	1986-89	1990-92
Per capita GDP, 1976 prices	100	100	104
Per capita GDP by 1985 deflator	100	100	104
Per capita GDP by NCPI[a]	100	83	84
Per capita GDP by LI[b]/NCPI[a]	100	88	75
Per capita Agricultural GDP, 1976 prices	100	113	122
Per capita Agricultural GDP, by NCPI[a]	100	106	107

[a]   NCPI = National Consumer Price Index.
[b]   LI = Low Income.

Most of the recent writing on poverty in Tanzania comes from a joint Cornell University - University of Dar es Salaam research project which explicitly rejects national income data as source material. It argues that survey data capture incomes from unrecorded activities better and claims that applying even the low-income deflator to such data shows per capita incomes rising slightly between 1983 and 1991. But this slight overall increase masks increasing differentiation between the better-off and the poor and between urban and rural areas, implying a process of impoverishment at the lower end of the scale (see section 7).

While GDP has grown in constant Tsh terms, in US$ Tanzania's 1993 national income was less than 40 percent of that in 1983 and, at about US$100 per capita, put Tanzania second from bottom in world rankings. In many respects this is an absurd figure, and constant-price Tsh is a more relevant measure of capacity to consume (to the extent that 1976 weights and prices represent the situation today). One would expect a fall in the dollar value of GDP, given the very sharp devaluations the country has been through. But this does mean that Tanzania's foreign debt increases by the extent of devaluation in Tsh terms - and of course the enormous shift in rates affects relative prices in every area of the economy. It also means that there is a 'technical' or automatic component to the increase in Tanzania's foreign aid dependence, since a given amount of aid in dollars increases as a proportion of dollar-GDP, as devaluation reduces its level. The same is true of parastatal debts which have a large external component.

Table 3 shows the sectoral division of GDP, in percentage terms. The most striking feature is the dominance of the agricultural sector, and its higher than average growth rate. Comparing the current and 1976 price figures in Table 3 shows a much larger increase in agriculture's share of total GDP under current prices, indicating that an increase in real prices has been among the components of this growth. Another factor may have been the increasing shilling value of foreign aid involved in agricultural projects, which are included in current price agricultural GDP. All the same, it is unusual for dependence on agriculture to increase so markedly, from under 40 percent in the mid-1970s to over 60 percent in the late 1980s. Two other factors seem relevant. The first concerns stagnation in the industrial sector since the late 1970s. The other involves a tendency to 'upgrade' estimates of agricultural subsistence production at intervals. There are many good reasons to suppose that this has historically been under-estimated, but the improvement of estimates over time does impart an upward bias to growth rates (section 4).

Table 3   Sectoral Division of GDP, 1976-93. Percent of total, current and 1976 prices

	1976	1980	1981-85	1986-89	1990-93
Current Prices					
Agriculture, forestry, fisheries and hunting	42	44	53	61	56
Mining & manufacturing	14	12	9	6	7
Electricity, water, construction	5	5	4	5	8
Wholesale & retail trade, hotels and restaurants	13	13	13	14	15
Transport & communication	8	8	6	6	10
Finance, insurance, real estate & business services	9	10	8	6	5
Public administration	11	11	11	7	7
Imputed bank service charges (i.e. balance item)	-2	-3	-2	-4	-6
1976 prices					
Agriculture, forestry, fisheries and hunging	42	40	43	46	49
Mining & manufacturing	14	12	10	9	9
Electricity, water, construction	5	6	6	6	6
Wholesale % retail trade, hotels and restaurants	13	12	11	12	11
Transport & communication	8	8	7	6	6
Finance, insurance, real estate & business services	9	11	12	13	12
Public administration	11	14	15	12	11
Imputed bank service charges (i.e. balance item).	-2	-2	-3	-3	-4

Source: URT, Bureau of Statistics, 1994a: Tables 3a, 4a.

Of the other sectors, mining and manufacturing have clearly fallen in proportional terms. Manufacturing output grew from the mid-1980s until around 1991, but not enough to reach the 1980 level, and has since fallen back again (see section 5). Mining has also grown rapidly in some areas, but is still too small and mostly too illegal for it to have much impact on the figures. Sectors increasing their proportion of total GDP are construction, water and electricity supply, with significant donor activities in all three. Transport and communications have also increased significantly, reflecting the investments made after the freeing of import restrictions on vehicles and to take advantage of openings in trading.

3.3 Investment

At a very general level, rates of growth and development are linked to levels and rates of investment. But there is nothing automatic about this, and one of the most misleading assumptions sometimes made by development planners is that of the 'fixed capital-output ratio', which implies that each successive dollar invested will increase output and income by the same amount. The falsity of this assumption was shown clearly and disastrously during the 'first aid boom' of the late 1970s.

But the relationship between investment and output seems no clearer today; in some ways still less so. The major increase in aid inflows and investment from 1974 to 1979 did increase production in the short run, despite the fact that much of it was (by intention) long-term investment. The increase in investment since 1986 has been to no small extent focused on rehabilitation, and should thus have had a fairly immediate effect on production, yet, as shown below, its impact seems to have been limited.

Table 4 shows investment in real terms, as a proportion of GDP, and divided by asset type. Investment fell as a proportion of GDP from 1981 to 1984, starting to rise again in 1985 towards the high levels of the present. In fixed price terms, Gross Fixed Capital Formation fell from Tsh 6.4 bn in 1979 to about Tsh 5.5 bn in 1980-85, rising by some 20 percent to Tsh 6.5 bn in 1986-89 and again by over 50 percent to Tsh 9.8 bn in 1990-93. A similar sharp increase shows in percent of GDP, with extremely high figures for the post-1986 period. With 40-50 percent of GDP being invested every year, one might have expected GDP growth rates higher than the 3-5 percent per annum shown above. But a major reason for this is the huge rise in locally denominated costs of imported machinery and equipment as a result of devaluation.

It is thus not surprising to find a similarly sharp shift in the composition of investment, with machinery and equipment rising from about half of the total in the early 1980s to around 70 percent more recently. Within the machinery category, there has been an even more rapid increase in the proportion made up of 'transport equipment' (vehicles of one or other sort), most especially from 1984 to 1988, when own-funds imports and other mechanisms eased the import of vehicles. What proportion is made up of 'dual-purpose' vehicles (i.e pick-up trucks for personal use and trading) is unknown, but it is probably significant.[17] Since the late 1980s there has been some increase in investment in housing and other works. Part of this seems to be donor-funded infrastructural works, part private housing boom. There seems to have been little investment in new productive capacity (see section 5).

---

[17] Apart from being useful to those combining formal sector work and informal trading/transport, there were tax and import-licence savings for importers of these vehicles until recently.

Table 4   Capital Formation in 1976 Tsh as Percent of GDP and by Asset

| | GFCF[a], 1976 Tsh m. prices | GCF[b] as % of current prices GDP | Percent of total investment | | | |
			Buildings	Other works	Equipment	*Of which transport equipt.*
1976	5159	23 - ..	19	31	50	*15*
1980	5615	23 - ..	21	29	49	*13*
1981	5806	25 - 25	23	21	56	*13*
1982	6052	21 - 26	22	28	50	*12*
1983	4042	14 - 18	24	22	54	*13*
1984	5891	15 - 25	19	18	61	*42*
1985	7283	18 - 30	18	16	65	*45*
1986	5194	25 - 21	15	17	68	*49*
1987	5983	50 - 23	9	20	71	*48*
1988	7240	13 - 26	9	21	70	*48*
1989	6805	45 - 24	8	13	79	*33*
1990	8760	43 - 29	8	30	62	*41*
1991	10019	48 - 34	10	16	70	*34*
1992	10431	49 - 34	10	18	72	*29*
1993	9871	51 - 31	9	19	72	*25*

Source: *Ibid.,* (Right-hand figures of col. 1 are from Table 1 above).
[a]   Gross Fixed Capital Formation.
[b]   Gross Capital Formation.

Table 5 shows investment divided between GDP categories. Agriculture may be by far the largest productive sector, but receives a far smaller proportion of investment. Economic infrastructure take by far the greatest proportion of the total. Transport, storage and communications (road, rail, air) take almost a third of total investment, while electricity and water (including hydro-power) have grown from under 10 percent 3 to 17 percent or so in recent years. If one assumes that part of investment in construction is related to this, then it would seem that economic infrastructure accounted for about 35-40 percent of the total before adjustment and has climbed to over half since. The other main investment sector is manufacturing, taking a bit less than one quarter of the total.

There seems to be no clear relation between investment and level of output. Agriculture and mining are among the two sectors to have grown most rapidly, both having seen an apparent decline in their share of total investment, whereas manufacturing has high investment but low output growth. There seem to be several reasons for this lack of correspondence. Where agriculture is concerned, there is always a 'boundary' problem. Investment in roads, for example, is arguably among the forms of expenditure most important for agricultural growth. On the other hand, much direct investment in agricultural production has been made through and contributed to parastatal monopolies, where its net effect can easily be negative.

Table 5   Capital Formation by Sector. (Percent of current price total)

Sector	1976	1979-81	1982-85	1986-89	1990-93
Agriculture	9	8	9	6	5
Mining & quarrying	3	2	1	..	..
Manufacturing	6	23	25	21	24
Electricity & water	7	8	11	25	17
Construction	2	6	10	9	11
Trade, hotels etc.	4	2	3	2	1
Transport, storage & communication	32	25	24	27	32
Finance etc.	7	8	4	3	6
Public administration	13	21	14	6	7

Source: Ibid.

Another factor is the effect of donor import support on the financial position of firms 'assisted'. When aid expanded in 1986, the first priority for many parastatal corporations and donors was to get production moving again by rehabilitating machinery and providing raw materials or intermediate goods. Much of this was provided through import-support grants. But while these were grants to the country, they were either provided as loans to the parastatal corporation concerned, or retrospectively made into loans as pressures to impose market discipline upon parastatals increased. On the other hand, funds and materials were sometimes provided to parastatal corporations whose accounting and administrative structures were in such a state of decay as to nullify their effect.

Here another issue is relevant: a tendency among donors to look with greater favour on investments which they themselves have initiated at some time in the past. Donor project selection may include market criteria and concern over importance to the economy or consistency with other formal goals. But decisions usually take place within a framework defined by past activities, experience and links. Funds and expertise were provided to build a factory; commitments have been made to a ministry, parastatal, or department; in the process, working relationships have been formed. Whatever the reason for getting into a particular project or sector, there are always extra reasons for staying there.

But the main factor relates to how much of the measured 'investment' is really investment at all. Given the incentives to cheat and the lack of control, the proportion made up of mis-labelled consumer goods is probably significant. To that extent it is hardly surprising that its effect on capacity and production is low.

3.4 Foreign Trade and the Balance of Payments

Tanzania has been importing more than was exported since the early 1970s, and by the early 1980s imports were well over double the value of exports. This was (and is) a very important economic imbalance - and that over which the IFIs and the Tanzania Government were most in disagreement before 1986, as to both definition and policy implications.

Prior to 1984, Tanzania held the shilling in a fixed relation to the dollar and attempted to control the level of imports and outflows of forex directly, through a system of import permits and foreign-exchange allocation. Even the devaluations before 1986 were made within this framework. The purpose of adjustment was to get rid of this system of regulations by real devaluation of sufficient scale to make the market the means of both allocating foreign exchange and setting the exchange rate. This also involved a major change in trade policy, shifting away from the existing non-tariff protection afforded by import licences (often held for specific products by the parastatal producing them locally), towards tariffs, to be followed by reducing the latter. It was expected (hoped) that liberalization of both forex and protection systems, combined with devaluation, would permit a sufficient increase in efficiency to allow local firms to hold their market share and increase exports. In retrospect, this can be seen to have been over-optimistic - as many would have predicted from the start.

The ERP in 1986 focused heavily on devaluation which was both to provide the stimulus for increased production of agricultural exports and, by increasing its price, limit the demand for forex. Donor funds were seen as helping this process along. In reality they replaced it, since neither objective was successful up to 1990. As discussed below, the incentive effect of devaluation was reduced by terms-of-trade losses, but far more because parastatal marketing agencies ate up the price increase leaving little or nothing for producers. Nor did devaluation have the intended effect on the demand side. So long as the main institutional users of forex were parastatal corporations, with politically defined goals and government funds to soften budget constraints, the price of foreign exchange was not a decision variable. This was particularly the case with much commodity import support (CIS) which was supplied direct to parastatal (and a few other) firms with (at least in the first instance) limited attention to payment of the 'cash cover', or its addition to parastatal deficits if not paid. The effect was thus to increase these significantly.

The availability of foreign exchange to those outside the state and parastatal sectors did not improve markedly during this period. The pre-ERP permission to use 'own funds' continued, and accounted for about one third of total foreign-exchange availability during the late 1980s, declining to around 20 percent in the 1990s. Export retentions for official exporters of 'non-traditional exports' were introduced and their scope expanded several times during the late 1980s; but though they increased nearly twentyfold between 1986 and 1990, at the end they still accounted for only 1-2 percent of total forex.

As of 1988 an Open General Licence (OGL) system was introduced, financed by the World Bank and increasingly by other donors, who were encouraged to route their import support through it as cash rather than individual CIS grants. Under the OGL donor-supplied forex was allocated on a 'first-come-first-served' basis to parastatal and private firms. At first applications were only accepted for a list of commodities considered essential to the economy. This list was gradually expanded, and then replaced by a 'negative list' of those commodities which could not be imported under the OGL, which was then gradually reduced to a small handful of items. This system was ostensibly market-driven, but the funds were allocated until they ran out at one fixed rate, and with this held down by the supply of donor funds, it constituted a 'non-targeted subsidy' to the beneficiary firms - a mechanism otherwise strongly opposed by the IFIs.[18] Moreover, while failure to pay 'cash-cover' was lower than under CIS, it was still quite substantial, making OGL allocation still less market-based.

By 1993, with the difference between official and market exchange rates almost gone,[19] and after a series of scandals concerning OGL funds (see section 6), a new auction system was set up, with applicants bidding for the available forex every two weeks and the official exchange rate emerging from this process. This is market-driven, but still supplies forex at a below-market rate, since the supply is made up of donor grant funds.

Table 6   Imports, Exports, Trade Balance and Current Account Deficit (US$ million and percent of GDP)

	Imports	Exports	Trade Balance	Current Account Deficit	Deficit as % of GDP
1981	1139	613	-526	-694	10
1982	1098	413	-1211	-538	11
1983	805	379	-426	-281 / -659	4 / 7
1984	863	389	-474	-397 / -412	10
1985	986	286	-700	-785 / -539	11
1986	1030	348	-682	-851 / -782	8 / 16
1987	1153	347	-806	-983 / -785	22 / 20
1988	1150	387	-763	-927 / -973	23 / 26
1989	1288	415	-873	-1037 / -971	26 / 29
1990	1166	408	-758	-949	30 / 32
1991	1155 / 1388	384 / 360	-771 / -1028	-1246	36
1992	1428 / 1799	442 / 437	-986 / -1362	-1458	31
1993	1304 / ..	454 / ..	-850 / ..	..	..

Sources: Wagao, 1990; EIU, 1995 and various WB/IDA reports.

To consider the effects of this, one can start by looking at the balance of trade, as shown in Table 6. The precise figures differ between sources, but the picture is fairly clear. Import compression from 1982 to 1985 reduced imports faster than exports, so reducing the trade balance deficit, until the introduction of 'own forex' in 1985. But despite decompression after 1986, import levels *seem* to have grown slowly from 1986 until the early 1990s. But, given the large increase ·in foreign transfers (Table 6), it seems more likely that this reflects under-accounting of CIS imports, so that much of

---

[18] It is curious that almost all sources refer to this as 'market-driven' when 'first-come-first-served', otherwise known as queuing, is the classic *non-market* form of allocation.

[19] Devaluation to align official and real exchange rates is always a multi-stage process, since each nominal devaluation tends to shift the real rate.

the sharp increase in 1991 and 1992 reflects improved accounting of donor grants. The figures also refer only to official imports and exports.[20] Another part of the 25-3 percent increase in 1992 seems to have arisen from poor sequencing of reforms, which aimed to lower tariff levels and simplify the system. This was to be paid for by an elimination of tax exemptions which failed to occur, reducing both import-duty and sales-tax revenue.

Exports have not grown much since the mid-1980s. By far the most exports are of agricultural products, so this is considered in section 4. Export volumes of 'traditional export crops' have stagnated, and terms of trade deteriorated. The value of 'non-traditional exports' doubled between 1985 and 1990, but still reached no more than 80 percent of their 1980 level, and have not grown since (UNCTAD, 1994: 14). Some sources claim rapid expansion of crop exports in 1993 and 1994, but this is not confirmed by the most recent figures (early 1995). It is widely agreed that official figures understate the real extent of exports, since the origin of 'own foreign exchange' is referred to in balance-of-payments figures as 'private transfers', whereas it really refers, at least in part, to unofficial exports or unofficial payments in respect of traded goods; that is, goods smuggled out, under-invoiced exports and over-invoiced imports. The first can be seen with some plausibility as 'unofficial exports', though not necessarily a net addition thereto. The rest cannot. In any case, while highly profitable for the individuals involved, illegal exports (especially of gemstones and elephants' tusks) are a very expensive and inefficient way for Tanzania to earn forex. Unofficial trade in agricultural products seems to be balanced with earnings from smuggled exports turned into goods which are smuggled back in.

For reasons which are discussed in section 6 below, there is little reason to suppose that unofficial exports have historically been higher than unofficial imports. Indeed, despite the circumstantial evidence for an 'unofficial export boom' in the late 1980s, the trend seems to be in the other direction, with unofficial imports increasingly outweighing exports. Given that both 'exempted' and smuggled imports evade taxes to which local produce is liable, this adds 'negative protection' to the many problems facing Tanzania's manufacturing sector.

The trade deficit has grown by over 11 percent per annum since 1986, and from under 10 percent to around one-third of GDP. This has been largely paid for by donor loans and grants. Table 7 shows different estimates of aid inflows.

As can be seen, Tanzanian official figures, and those presented in World Bank reports, under-estimate aid inflows significantly. That is, 'large amounts of grants circumvent the government budget or any other official registration by being channelled directly to specific projects or to NGOs', while large amounts of donor grant aid (including all import support) are incorrectly booked as capital inflows rather than transfers (Bhaduri *et al.*, 1993: 120). But under any estimation, the value of foreign aid inflows exceeds that of exports considerably. Using the higher estimates, it has climbed from about twice the value of exports in the mid-1980s to about two and a half times in the early 1990s. Another calculation (based on the lower Netherlands figures) shows

---

[20] Exports are considered below. Casual evidence suggests extensive unofficial imports. The shops and street-kiosks of Dar es Salaam are full of goods whose prices make clear that no tax has been paid on them. It is hard to draw a line, though, between smuggled goods and those imported under tax and duty exemptions - for 'investment goods'.

ODA[21] increasing as a proportion of GDP from about 12 percent in 1975 to nearly 43 percent in 1990 and from 39 percent to 85 percent of imports over the same period. This gives a sobering indication of what heavy devaluation can mean, and of the effects if donors should suffer 'fatigue' or otherwise decide to withdraw their support. Of course there is no realistic sense in which the sum of donor inflows, large as it is, can be 'worth' 43 percent of the sum total of labour, production and transactions in the Tanzania economy. But the figures do indicate what a hole withdrawal might leave.

Table 7   Aid Inflows, Various Estimates. US$ million

	Adam *et al.* 1994	Netherlands 1994	WB 1994	WB 1991
1960-64	24	..	..	..
1966-73	52	..	..	..
1974-80	386	..	..	..
1980	650	..	..	..
1981	657	..	..	..
1982	673	..	..	..
1983	579	..	..	..
1984	549	..	..	288
1985	477	384	..	357
1986	675	410	622	388
1987	882	760	679	551
1988	1012	863	719	653
1989	917	872	799	741
1990	1171	843	817	748
1991	1081	910	840	..
1992	..	..	826	..

Sources: Col. 1, OECD Geographical Distribution of Financial Flows, various. Cited from Adam *et al.*, 1994. For 1960-91, from Bagachwa *et al.*. For 1992, forthcoming. Col. 2, Netherlands Development Corporation, 1994, table 22. Col. 3, Calculated by setting together grants from World Bank, 1994c, Documentation for planned CG meeting, November 1994, and figures for loans from various IFI sources. Col. 4, World Bank, 1991.

Donor grants have filled much of the trade gap, but not enough to prevent total indebtedness increasing significantly in dollar terms, and much more as a proportion of GDP (1976 prices), reflecting the impact of devaluation.[22] This is shown in Table 8.

---

[21] ODA = overseas development assistance, the OECD term for aid.

[22] There is some overlap here since the aid figures include loans (mainly from the IFIs) which are a major component of the increase in debt.

Table 8   Tanzania, Debt and Debt-Service. US$ million and percent

Year	Total Debt US$ m.	Total Debt as % of GDP	Debt-Service US$ m.	Debt-Service % of Export[a]
1970	265	17	..	..
1975	945	25	..	..
1980	2476	54	151 / 199	20 / 29 / ..
1985	3752	61	168 / ..	37 / .. / 21
1986	4291	103	130 / 203	29 / 41 / ..
1987	5876	175	129 / 218	32 / 41 / 14.5
1988	6112	194	125 / 227	25 / 42 / 12.9
1989	6042	229	119 / 213	22 / 34 / 12.4
1990	6880	289	148 / 234	27 / 38 / 15.0
1991	7175	240	132 / 220	25 / 36 / 16.0
1992	7304	285	.. / 304	.. / 46 / 17.2
1993	7522	..	.. / 155	.. / 25 / 11.9

Sources: Columns 1 & 2: World Bank, World Debt Tables (WDT) 1994-95: 466-69. Column 3 left: WDT 93-94: 442; right: WDT 94-95: 466. Column 4 left: WDT 93-94: 442; middle: WDT 94-95: 466; right: debt-service actually paid (after rescheduling), various World Bank, Tanzania documents.
[a]   Including net private transfers (i.e. estimated informal exports).

Table 9   Paris Club Rescheduling and Cancellation of Tanzania's Debt

Paris Club No. and Date	Rescheculing US$ m.	Rescheduling % of Debt	Cancellation US$ m.	Cancellation % of Debt
I - 1986	863	20.0	0	0.0
II - 1988	242	4.5	21	0.4
III - 1990	204	3.3	19	0.3
IV - 1992	328	4.5	112	1.5

Source: Bagachwa *et al.*, forthcoming, citing Lipumba *et al.*, 1993.

Total debt figures change significantly between different versions of the World Bank *World Debt Tables*, the most recent being shown here. The disparity is still greater for debt-service, for which 1992/93 and 1994/95 versions are compared. The right-hand column shows 1992/93 and 1994/95 estimates of the debt-service ratio (the proportion of exports going to debt-service) before rescheduling, while the right-hand figure shows what was paid after it. Again Tanzania's dependence on the goodwill of donors comes over strikingly. So long as Tanzania can meet the Paris Club regulations, rescheduling keeps the debt-service ratio down to reasonable proportions. Without that, it would quickly double, and aid inflows would fall as rapidly, leaving the country in a desperate situation.

Debt rescheduling certainly helps in the short run, by reducing the annual debt-service payments to well under half what they would otherwise be. But it only defers their payment in full. Table 9 shows rescheduling and debt cancellations under the four Paris Club Agreements. Cancellation is clearly proceeding very slowly, and the total debt is increasing, not only with new loans but with capitalized arrears and re-scheduling.

3.5 Public Finance, Fiscal and Monetary Policy

Another main area in which adjustment aims to affect government policy concerns the size of the government (and parastatal) budget, the means of financing it and changes in the supply of money and credit, which in turn affect the rate of inflation. Broadly speaking, the purpose of adjustment conditionality has been to reduce the size of the government deficit and particularly to shift its funding away from bank borrowing - and back to taxation. This, together with increases in interest rates, has had the macro-economic purposes of reducing the rate of inflation, but is also aimed to improve the supply of credit to the private sector, which is assumed to have been 'crowded out' by government borrowing. The means chosen to achieve this under the ERP was primarily budgetary austerity and interest-rate increases. In the event this led to high budgetary costs without hard budget constraints on parastatals, increasing rather than reducing their deficits, thus generating a policy shift towards privatization under ESAP.[23]

Government budgets are conventionally divided into recurrent expenditures, classed as government 'consumption', composed of wages, operating costs and similar items, which are supposed to be paid out of recurrent revenues: - taxes, licences, tariffs and non-tax items like rents on government property. 'Development expenditure' is considered to be investment, and intendedly funded from borrowing or donor grants. But a large proportion of 'development spending' (and donor grants) in the 1980s has been for rehabilitation, which as 'capitalized maintenance' falls on the boundary between the two, which is also far from watertight in other respects, including revenue transfers. Tanzania's budget has been in deficit since the late 1960s, though there was a surplus of revenue over recurrent spending until the mid-1970s. Since then, there has been a recurrent deficit, to be filled by borrowing or by transfer of donor grants from 'development revenue' to the recurrent budget. During recent years, the recurrent deficit has exceeded the whole development budget, implying that a larger proportion of donor (development) grants are used for the recurrent budget than for development.

The line between state and parastatal finances is also complex. A standard feature of Tanzanian development strategy in the 1970s was for the state to initiate an activity, and then hand it over to a parastatal corporation, usually with a series of subventions and subsidies to cover loss-making activities, like unsecured input-credits to villages,

---

[23] One might wonder how institutions employing so many economists as the IFIs could have failed to figure this out - or alternatively wonder just how disingenuous is the 'shock' expressed over rising parastatal deficits.

transport equalization subsidies, or delivery of goods at prices fixed below full costs. Since the corporations also paid taxes and dividends to the state, and since subventions were not infrequently made retrospectively (i.e after the activity had led to large deficits), the balance was complex.

Table 10   Government Revenue, Expenditure, Deficit and Rate of Inflation (percent)

	Revenue as % of GDP	Expenditures as % of GDP	Deficit as % of GDP	Rate of Inflation	Aid as % of Total Expenditures
1980	16.9	29.4	-12.5	30.1	13
1981	18.5	32.7	-14.2	25.7	16
1982	19.8	28.2	-8.4	28.9	19
1985	16.8	25.4	-8.6	33.3	10
1986	14.9	23.1	-8.2	32.5	27
1987	16.1	24.6	-8.5	30.0	24
1988	16.7	26.3	-9.6	31.3	27
1989	19.5	25.5	-6.0	25.8	30
1990	21.0	28.0	-7.0	19.7	30
1991	22.1	25.2	-3.1	22.2	..
1992	23.3	26.2	-2.9	22.1	..
1993	17.5	32.1	-14.6	26.7	..
1994[a]	21.0	32.2	-11.1	35.0	..

Source: Inflation: 1980-92: URT, 1994. *Deficit:* Adam *et al.,* 1994.
Adam *et al.* (1994: 91) show a different pattern, with the deficit falling from about 18 percent of GDP in 1980 to a low point of 7 percent in 1985/96, rising to some 12 percent until 1993 when it seems to be around 17-20 percent.
[a]   Budget figures targets. So actual results will probably be less favourable.

As Table 10 shows, the aim of the ERP to reduce the deficit appears to have succeeded up to 1992, but to have slipped badly thereafter. The table shows government revenue, expenditure and deficit, all as proportions of GDP. In 1980/81, the deficit grew to well over 10 percent of GDP. This was reduced in the following years, and especially after 1986, with large quantities of foreign (counterpart) funds filling some of the gaps.[24] But in the early 1990s financial management seems to have slipped and pushed the deficit back up over 10 percent of GDP. Alternative figures show the gap as larger, but following the same trend and rising to 22 percent of GDP in 1993.

It would be a mistake to see this reversal simply as 'backsliding'. For while general austerity was certainly one means to cut government spending, another was to cut subventions to parastatal corporations, or to transfer costs to them without subvention.

---

[24] Donors give a forex grant via the Tanzania Treasury (or a grant in kind) for (say) machinery for a factory or fertilizer for an extension programme. When (or if) the parastatal in questions pays the shilling value of this, the money (the counterpart funds) become a shilling grant to the Treasury, thus reducing the deficit. .

This 'worked', at least for some years, for a number of reasons. Increased CIS after 1986 was primarily aimed at parastatal corporations. Not only did the equipment and materials help to assure physical operation and output, but the significant proportion which was not reported to the Treasury (seemingly between US$200 m. and US$500 m. from Table 6) was not (at least initially) subject to 'cash-cover' in local currency, and thus became effectively a grant to the parastatal. Even where CIS was reported, major arrears in the credit which paid for 'cash-cover' are reported by all sources (40 percent of the total according to Mans (1994: 366), see also section 6). In addition, any investment project (especially in its 'start-up' phase) involves a number of payments which can be used to 'roll-over' previous deficits and hide them a bit longer.

This seems especially to have affected agricultural marketing parastatals, which accumulated some of the largest debts. A number of subsidies were taken out of the state budget and allowed to accumulate as parastatal debts, notably transport for NMC and fertilizers for TFC. The Cooperative & Rural Development Bank (CRDB) continued to be ordered to make unrecoverable loans, without state provision to cover them. On the other hand, apart from fertilizer, most import support went to industry and infrastructure, and increasingly so after the introduction of the OGL. Fewer new projects were started in agriculture, and those there were tended to be more modest and to have a lower input or equipment content. All this reduced fungibility and options for rolling-over expenditures, except for export-crop marketing agencies, which were able to take the devaluation-induced price increase intended to incentivize producers.

As the easier options were blocked off in the late 1980s, the deficit grew more rapidly, especially since interest rates had been increased sharply. By 1989-90, parastatal indebtedness was sufficient to add several points to the inflation rate and had become one of the major concerns of the IFIs. From 1991, with much harder conditionality being imposed under ESAP over limits on loans to parastatals, some of these debts returned to the central state budget, producing some, but not all, of the much enlarged deficits shown in Table 10. Another factor increasing the public expenditure deficit was failure to implement an agreement between the IFIs and Tanzania Government in 1993. This proposed a reduction and simplification of the tariff structure, to be paid for by improved collection and a reduction in tax exemptions. In the event there was no reduction in exemptions (see section 6 below). After some months the higher tariffs had to be restored, but in the interim the deficit, and need for state bank borrowing, increased.

As of late 1994 and early 1995, further evidence of slippage could be observed. In response to evidence that exemptions were still increasing rather than decreasing, and of a general increase in tax evasion (section 6), certain donors delayed release of funds until action had been taken. The action finally taken was the minimal cabinet shift which could get the funds moving, but in the interim bank borrowing again increased to fill the gap. Reports as of January 1995 indicate a possible increase in the rate of inflation to 35-40 percent, above the levels of the 1981-85 'crisis' period.

3.6 State Expenditure

Overall government expenditure appears to have risen or remained stable as a proportion of GDP, and so to have increased (slightly) in real terms. Yet deterioration in government social services is a much remarked phenomenon and has been since the late 1970s. There are several reasons for this apparent disparity. In the first place, the deterioration from the mid-1970s was so large and the increase in funding from 1986 so small that it led to no significant improvement from already abysmal levels. Apart from this, an increasing proportion of total government expenditure has to be set aside for servicing debt. Moreover the population has increased, so that per capita spending on most budget headings will have fallen, even if absolute spending has increased. Table 11 shows these adjustments.

**Table 11   Real Total Government Expenditure per Capita
Tsh million deflated by NCPI; Index 1982/83 = 100**

Year	Real total expenditure	% spent on debt service	Total less debt service	1982/83 = 100	Per capita index
1975-76	6125	7.3	5678	116	123
1982-83	6159	20.2	4915	100	100
1986-87	5571	25.0	4178	85	76
1987-88	5947	31.3	4086	83	72
1988-89	6395	30.5	4438	90	76
1989-90	6368	25.6	4738	96	79
1990-91	6556	29.8	4602	94	75
1991-92[a]	6281	23.9	4780	97	76
1992-93[b]	8840	31.3	6074	124	94

Source: M. Bagachwa, 1992.
[a]   Expected.
[b]   Estimates.

As can be seen, there was little or no increase even in aggregate terms before 1992, while the per capita index is well below the 1982/83 level (that is, the middle of the 'crisis'), even for 1992/93, when an expenditure increase of 6 percent of GDP was responsible for half of the rise in the deficit (Table 10). In general, since 1986, the real per capita value of expenditure has been only about three-quarters of the 1982/83 level and about 60 percent of the mid-1970s level. The proportion of total expenditure allocated to health and education in the central budget also fell significantly between the early 1980s and early 1990s, but this is because most expenditures on primary health and education were transferred to local government budgets in 1984. In the aggregate, they are found by Semboja and Therkildsen (1995) to have increased in real terms up to 1991.

Recurrent and development expenditure. Foreign grant funds pay for almost all of the development budget and significant proportions of recurrent spending as well. In recent years, the recurrent deficit has been greater than total development expenditure, which means that more of the grants and loans which pay for the development budget are spent on recurrent costs than on development.

There is nothing wrong with this, as such. Indeed in the past, the Tanzania Government has been criticized for over-spending on development without sufficient attention to maintenance and other recurrent costs. Unfortunately, the transfer of 'development funds' to recurrent use does not mean improved maintenance (much of which actually comes under 'development', as donor-financed rehabilitation). Given the steady expansion of the state-employed labour force (not just 'civil servants' but primary school teachers, dispensary attendants, etc. - see sections 8 and 9 below), wages and allowances pre-empt a very large proportion of the total recurrent budget, despite their very low levels. Much of the rest goes on transport for officers, even though a large proportion are 'grounded' for much of the time unless a donor is running a project through which petrol, spares and allowances can be funded. This in turn implies a further leverage by which Tanzanian funds adjust themselves to donor priorities rather than the other way round.

Table 12   Sectoral Allocation of Central Government Expenditure

	GPS[a]	Defence	Education	Health	Economic services	Public debt	Other
1970/71	20	7	14	6	38	7	8
1975/76	16	12	11	7	37	7	3
1980/81	19	11	12	5	37	12	4
1985/86	30	15	7	5	19	20	4
1986/87	27	15	6	5	19	25	4
1987/88	28	10	5	4	16	31	4
1988/89	27	9	6	5	17	31	7
1989/90	31	9	7	5	16	26	7
1990/91	23	6	7	5	22	30	7
1991/92	33	9	7	5	17	24	6
1992/93	19	7	9	6	25	32	4

Source: M. Bagachwa, 1992.
[a]   GPS = General Public Service; includes administration, foreign affairs and security.

Sectoral division. Table 12 shows how central government expenditure is divided between different sectors. The most obvious trend is the growth in public debt, which now accounts for about one-third of the total. The largest decline is in economic services (mainly infrastructure) where allocation has declined to not much more than half the proportion of the 1970s.

Proportions to education and health have both declined since the 1970s, and though the inclusion of district spending would show increased real spending in both categories since 1986, this would in no way bring levels back to those of the 1970s. On the more optimistic side, military spending also seems to have fallen, but despite claims there is little evidence of a downward trend in the main administrative category 'GPS'.

Banking and monetary policy under the ERP has had most of the same aims as fiscal policy. In macroeconomic terms it aimed to reduce state borrowing from domestic banks, limiting growth in the money supply to below 20 percent and curbing inflation, in micro-terms to direct credit to the private sector, thought to have been 'crowded out'. But where fiscal policy aims to achieve this directly through budgetary austerity and (to a lesser extent) through increased taxation, monetary policy focuses on trying to restrict the expansion of credit and thus the money supply and inflation, by means which emphasize interest-rate changes. The idea is that increasing the cost of borrowing and the return to lending will discourage borrowing and encourage saving. The problem is that this does not work very well when both lenders and borrowers are state institutions. Commercial banks in Tanzania were nationalized in 1967 and formed into the National Bank of Commerce (NBC) whose lending was then directed mainly towards the state and parastatal sectors. Input credit to peasant farmers was organized through input-supply programmes, channelled through the parastatal CRDB and through marketing boards and cooperative unions, which undertook the administration and were responsible for arranging repayment out of crop sale proceeds. Despite some attempts on the part of bank managements to operate commercially, political directives, from the early 1970s onwards, made it increasingly impossible for NBC or CRDB to avoid lending to parastatals or villages which had failed to repay all previous loans or otherwise shown themselves to be poor risks. In this situation, the interest rate played no role in decision-making, so there was a certain logic in keeping it under the market rate and negative in real terms.

By the same token increasing interest rates without changing the system could be expected to raise the costs of borrowing without reducing its extent. By the early 1990s, government bank borrowing had been reduced, through IFI-imposed austerity and increased donor grants (not increased interest rates). But parastatal borrowing continued to increase, and here it seems likely that raising interest rates had the reverse effect from that intended. For state corporations, with a statutory obligation to perform given services and with the state ready to underwrite debts (or unable to avoid doing so), increased interest rates affect not the level of borrowing but its cost - and further increase it because of increased debt-service.

Nor is there any sign that increasing real interest rates has had any positive effect on the rate of saving. As mentioned above, official figures show this to be significantly and increasingly negative. One recent source shows that, as a proportion of GDP, savings have fallen from plus 9 percent in 1986 to minus 20 percent in 1993 (DANIDA, 1994: 63). As noted there, even if the correction mentioned above was made (in respect of informal exports and adding nearly 15% to the estimated savings rate), this would not alter the sharply falling trend and the 1993 figure would still be negative.

Under the ESAP the focus has shifted towards privatization of banking, and reducing parastatal debts by imposing hard budget constraints including a lending-stop, forbidding either NBC or CRDB from lending more than minimal amounts. This has already bankrupted some parastatals, and seems likely to affect more, though another aspect of the policy is the shifting of bad debts away from the state-owned commercial banks to a special 'loss-carrying' parastatal the Loans and Realization Trust (LART), allowing the balance sheets of the former to be fattened up for sale. NBC and CRDB are to be part-privatized and run on commercial lines. Banking laws have been changed to allow the entry of foreign private banks, and by early 1995 two had started business in Tanzania, with a third reputedly about to.

Crowding out? - Among the reasons given for bank privatization is that state and parastatal borrowing have 'crowded out' potential private sector borrowers with viable projects, and that private banks will cater to these needs. Neither part of the proposition is very convincing. It is certainly true that lending was largely restricted to parastatals or peasants involved in input loan schemes before 1986, partly because state policy had largely eliminated any private sector worth lending to. In the period after 1986, an increasing number of loan, grant and guarantee programmes from donors were specifically aimed at encouraging the private sector.[25] It seems at least as likely that the limited response of the private sector to opportunities in productive investment reflects less a shortage of funds than a surfeit of higher-return activities like importing goods for sale tax-exempt as 'investment' or making 200-280 percent on purchasing debts. With returns of this sort in prospect, humdrum activities like hauling maize may not attract much interest from those qualified to borrow.

But nor are the new commercial banks likely to make large amounts of cheap credit available in Tanzania. The two foreign banks have so far confined themselves entirely to foreign-exchange transactions. One of them has just gone broke and been shown up as a swindle operation from the start, more likely to take funds out of Tanzania than put them in. At present, the IFI loan-stop places far more effective limits on the private lending of NBC and CRDB than the Tanzania Government ever did. But when they are fully sanitized and commercialized, the most likely result is a severe curtailing of activities, rather than increased service to the private sector, especially outside of the main towns, where bank branches seem most unlikely to survive requirements to make a profit. As discussed in section 4, the curtailment of lending by CRDB and its focusing upon a few rich farmers seem likely to be even more drastic, prompting questions about how this fits with the poverty orientation of DANIDA, its main foreign shareholder.

4.   Agriculture

Agriculture is the most important economic sector in Tanzania, accounting for about half of GDP, providing the major source of income for 80 percent of the population and contributing over 60 percent of exports. It is also the sector whose growth since 1986 is claimed to demonstrate the success of structural adjustment. It thus poses a number of important questions. How rapid has the growth in agriculture been, and where has it occurred? To what extent can this be attributed to structural adjustment, and to what extent have the specific aims of SA been met? Behind this lie other questions, about the relative weight of local and external factors or (more relevantly) the inter-relations between them, which in turn lead to more strategic questions about whether even the best adjustment policies can solve the enormous problems posed by deteriorating terms of trade and massive debt. These questions cannot be answered without some background discussion of Tanzania agriculture.

Tanzanian agriculture is overwhelmingly based on small peasant production. Large farms and ranches account for less than 10 percent of the cultivated area and 15-20 percent of production and exports. Some 40 percent of peasant farms are less than half

---

[25] It is also worth noting that CRDB's deficits bulge with non-viable loans to the private sector.

a hectare in size, and over 60 percent are less than one hectare (World Bank, 1994b, Stat. App.: 24-25). Over the past century or so, most African agriculture has changed out of all recognition from a basis in long fallows and shifting cultivation, through progressive shortening of fallows towards permanent cultivation, often using purchased inputs, though usually at quite low levels.

For most of the colonial period, policy towards African agriculture was highly differentiated, ranging from enforcement of cotton production and encouragement of coffee in some areas, to the outright banning of African production of high-value crops, like tea, pyrethrum, tobacco and sometimes coffee, to limit competition with white settlers for markets and labour. Where African export-crop production was encouraged, this was done by the state extension service, and the produce handled by state marketing boards, with licensed private or cooperative monopolies at local level.[26]

As policy shifted towards encouraging African peasant export production, with the approach of independence, this was seen to require the expansion and coordination of state activities and institutions. Prevailing notions of development focused on agricultural modernization - the replacement of 'traditional' agricultural methods (assumed to be non-rational and unchanging) by methods based on modern science, in the form of purchased inputs, brought from the outside by 'change-agents' and diffused among or imposed upon 'traditional cultivators' who were assumed to be 'resistant to change'. While coercion through bye-laws ('plant one acre cotton, or risk x days forced labour or y shillings fine') was considered suitable where extra labour was the main or only input, this was less suited to the encouragement of fertilizer or chemical use. Here attention focused on getting materials out to peasants at reasonable prices (normally involving subsidy) and providing credit for their purchase (also usually subsidized). The credit could not be based on collateral, since land under 'customary tenure' could not be pledged, but since most crop sales were monopolized, this was not seen to present major problems. Purchasing agencies could (in theory) 'deduct-at-source' - and cheapen the price of inputs by cross-subsidizing from deductions from the prices paid to producers for their crops.

In short, the kernel of the system grew to encompass massive nationwide parastatals - and their equally massive deficits. Another innovation of the time was the settlement scheme, in which peasant farmers were introduced to export-crop production under more controlled (and costly) institutional surroundings, with a manager to direct cultivation methods and rules to instil modernity (for example, all houses to be similar and arranged in straight lines, with untidy things like trees removed). This was seen as particularly suitable to the previously banned high-value crops, which could bear the considerable expenses involved. It also prevented too rapid growth of African production in competition with settlers.

After independence these (as all other) aspects of state policy were pushed with greater energy and enthusiasm, and the expansion of cooperatives, cooperative unions and marketing boards to implement them accelerated. This led by the mid-1960s to major cost increases, arising especially from peasant evasion of loan repayment by selling outside the official channels, so reducing producer prices within the official markets. Concern over this was swamped by the shift in pace and direction which

---

[26] The private traders were almost all Asian. Africans were excluded directly and through the Credit to Natives (Restriction) Act, which performed its function by making debts to Africans legally uncollectable.

accompanied the Arusha Declaration in 1967. Monopoly control over primary agricultural marketing was extended and tightened, trade in a number of basic consumer goods was 'confined' to state, regional or cooperative monopolies, the size and scope of credit and input programmes increased, and an increasing proportion was directed to the new villages, where the distinction between loans and grants all but disappeared (except in the accounts of the credit agency).

The foreign-exchange constraints which should have slowed this process were swept away by increased aid inflows after 1973, just as *ujamaa* moved into overdrive, with compulsory villagization and the re-introduction of colonial-type coercion through directives imposed on villagers. A burst of donor projects, accelerated the size, scope, costs and corruption of marketing boards (often renamed 'crop authorities'). There had been corruption under colonial monopoly marketing, and its scale increased with the post-independence expansion of credit programmes and the ease of evading repayment. But its acceleration from the mid-1970s was on a completely new scale.

It is widely asserted that the downturn in growth of agricultural production in Tanzania from the mid-1970s arose from state neglect of the sector, though the same critics often also blame the size and inefficiency of agricultural parastatals. In fact, real state spending on agriculture reached heights during the late 1970s which have never been equalled before or since,[27] and, as a result of both Tanzanian and donor assumptions, by far the most of this was fed through agricultural parastatals, with the disastrous results on which all observers are now agreed. It is worth emphasizing that the donor agency most heavily involved in this was the World Bank, with large-scale projects involving parastatals (and huge losses) in maize, tea, tobacco, cashewnuts, pyrethrum, beef and dairy ranching, not to mention 'regional integrated planning'. The situation to which the World Bank reacted in the early 1980s was not just 'state monopoly marketing', but an extreme form of it, and one to no small extent of its own making.

In the early 1980s came a limited reduction in donor project spending, a savage 'lending hiatus' for non-project aid flows, and pressures both to increase spending on agriculture and reduce it on parastatals. These were mutually inconsistent under the existing paradigm of modernization through (state) change-agents. With pressures to cut the state budget, there was some tendency to cut state subventions to parastatals but little control over political directives to them to fund village activities, operate subsidy schemes, equalize transport costs and generally continue the high-spending ways of the 1970s. A number of policy changes embodied this contradiction between efforts to reduce costs and the concern of the Party and its regional leaders to maintain their authority and capacity to implement policy with parastatal funds. This particularly concerned the re-introduction of marketing cooperatives (replaced by marketing boards in the early 1970s). The donors who encouraged this saw cooperatives as at least partly 'private sector'. CCM saw them as (its) agents of rural change.

The ERP from 1986 increased the pressures, notably on parastatal deficits, which had grown rapidly since 1980. The focus of the ERP was export crops, where devaluation and increasing the producer price to 70 percent of the export price were intended to shift producers back from food-crop production and expand export production and proceeds. It was also proposed that investment in agriculture should increase, facing donors with the question of how this should be channelled, if not through parastatals,

---

[27] World Bank, 1994 (Agric Sector Memo).

most especially since channelling donor funds through private firms, cooperatives or NGOs, tends to 'parastatalize' them.

The burst of Commodity Import Support (CIS) grants which followed the ERP was a distinctly mixed blessing. They provided the country as a whole with foreign exchange (or goods costing it) on a grant basis. But to the parastatals receiving the funds they were not grants, so though many failed to pay the counterpart funds, this merely increased their debit balances (and the deficits of the parastatal banks from which they borrowed the funds). Moreover devaluation and increased interest rates accelerated the build-up of deficits.

4.1   Trends in Tanzanian Agricultural Production

Over 80 percent of Tanzania's crop production is sold through markets beyond the reach of any form of statistical data gathering, so that output estimation is little more than informed guesswork. This might start in a given year, with estimates of what might be a 'reasonable' level of production and proceed by adding to, or subtracting from, that figure in subsequent years for population increase, the state of the harvest and whether the area planted was thought to have increased or fallen. For crops accounting for about one-third of total value, the annual increase is taken to be the population growth rate.[28]

Even for maize, Tanzania's major staple food crop, the Ministry of Agriculture puts out two separate sets of production figures. As Table 13 shows, it is hard to believe that these estimate the same things. Even the direction of change - whether production increased or decreased from one year to the next - is different in three out of five cases! There is also evidence from the figures of periodic revision upwards - a series cited by a World Bank publication shows breaks in 1973/74-1974/75 and 1982/83-1983/84. There is probably good reason for upward revision of figures concerning 'subsistence', but this does impart an upward bias to time series data.

One can conclude that Tanzanian agricultural production figures must be used with the greatest caution and seldom to draw conclusions which lack independent backing.

With these cautions, Table 14 shows the growth of agricultural production since 1980, at 1976 prices, and as a proportion of total GDP, at current and 1976 prices. The rate of growth increases significantly from 1984 onwards, from around 2 percent per annum for 1980-84 up to over 4 percent for 1985-89. This leads to a 5 percent increase in the measured contribution of agriculture to total GDP in 1976 prices, or about 15 percent in current prices, indicating a significant shift in the rural-urban terms of trade in favour of agriculture. This growth came almost without exception from the non-measured (food-crop) sub-sector, since export-crop production, the main focus of ERP policies, scarcely increased at all. Devaluation led to a large increase in the border price of Tanzania's exports, albeit offset to some extent by terms-of-trade decline. But since marketing remained monopolized by parastatals, and since adjustment-oriented macro-economic policies imposed extra costs on them, producers saw little of this. Their share of the international price fell from 72.5 percent in 1981-85 to 59 percent in 1986-91 (Mans, 1994: Table 23), which also meant a fall in real producer prices and a larger fall in net revenues (less devaluation-increased input costs).

---

[28] This is at least superior to the method often used by FAO statisticians, which is to copy last year's figures without allowing for population increase. .

Table 13 Alternative Estimates of Maize Production ('000 tonnes)

Year	A	B	A - B
1985/86	2671	2211	+460
1986/87	2244	2359	-115
1987/88	2423	2339	+84
1988/89	2528	3128	-600
1989/90	2227	2445	-218
1990/91	2332	2331	+1

Source: Bhaduri *et al.*, 1993.

Table 14 Agricultural GDP, 1980-93

	Agricultural GDP, 1976 Tsh bn	Inter-annual growth	Agriculture as % of GDP, current prices	Agriculture as % of GDP, 1976 prices
1980	9.4		44	40
1981	9.5	1.0	46	41
1982	9.6	1.3	50	41
1983	9.9	2.8	52	43
1984	10.3	4.0	53	44
1985	10.9	6.0	57	45
1986	11.6	5.7	59	46
1987	12.1	4.4	59	46
1988	12.6	4.5	63	46
1989	13.2	4.6	62	46
1990	14.1	6.6	57	47
1991	14.6	4.0	61	47
1992	15.3	4.4	61	47

Sources: 1976 price GDP and growth-rates from URT, Bureau of Statistics, 1994a. Agriculture as percent of GDP from World Bank, 1994b, Stat. Appendix: 2-4.

Even for major food crops, *official* producer prices declined in real terms from 1985/86 onwards, as shown in Table 15.

But since marketing was liberalized and state monopolies had never controlled much of food markets, it is highly likely that the asserted increase in growth (or some of it) did occur.

Some World Bank reports claim increasing food-crop production as a success. Others attribute the failure to expand export-crop production to parastatal obstruction and inefficiency, apparently unaware that critics had made this argument against a 'single-string' price policy from the early 1980s. That is, simply increasing prices would not necessarily increase production since the price increase might well not reach the producers and physical bottlenecks in the marketing/transport/processing chain could well obstruct increased exports, even if more was produced and offered for sale. This latter was indeed an issue for cotton, where increased production often encountered stores full with the produce of previous years because ginneries were not operating (Netherlands, 1994).

Table 15 Official Producer Prices of Food Crops. (1977 prices, index 1984/85=100)

Crop	1984/85	1989/90 - 1991/92
Maize	100	70
Paddy	100	89
Wheat	100	126
Sorghum and Millet	100	60
Cassava	100	68
Beans	100	94

Source: URT, Bureau of Statistics, 1994: Table 24.

Figures for more recent years differ widely between sources, as shown in Table 16.

Table 16 Different Estimates of Agricultural GDP Growth, 1990/91 to 1993/94

	1990-91	1991-92	1992-93	1993-94
National Accounts of Tanzania 1993	9.5	3.5	5.7	..
Budget Survey 1993	-16.0	2.3	7.3	..
URT 11/94 (for Central Government Meeting)	0.0	2.2	7.3	2.7[a]
WB Agricultural Sector Memo 1993	4.0	4.4	..	..
EIU 95/1, Table p. 5	..	3.5	5.7	3.5
EIU 95/1, diagram p. 19	-2.0	-4.0	-1.3	..
FAO Productionn Yearbook 1993	-2.0	-4.3	-1.1	..

[a] Provisional

Despite the negative figures, it seems likely that growth has continued at about 4-5 percent, and with some growth of exports. But claims of 25 percent export-crop growth in 1994, on account of liberalization and increased coffee prices, seem far-fetched. In early 1995, the Economist Intelligence Unit estimated 4.0 percent growth for total agriculture, and no-one met in Tanzania in November 1994 mentioned an export boom.

To get more idea of where growth has occurred, one can turn to a recent World Bank study (*Agricultural Sector Memorandum*, 1994), which provides estimates of value added (value of production, less purchased inputs and services) by crop or group of crops (33 different categories), at fixed 1990 prices. Table 17 presents this in percentage terms for broad crop categories from 1976 to 1991.

Table 17   Contribution to Total Value Added. Percent, 1990 prices

	A	B	C	D	E	F	G
	Starchy staples	Beans & pulses	Oil-seeds	Fruit & vegetables	Total food crops	Sugar	'Traditional' export crop
1976	48	9	9	9	75	1	25
1977	49	7	9	9	75	1	25
1978	51	8	9	9	78	1	21
1979	52	8	10	10	79	1	20
1980	51	10	9	9	80	1	19
1981	51	9	10	9	80	1	19
1982	54	10	9	10	83	1	16
1983	56	10	10	10	85	1	14
1984	53	15	9	9	86	1	13
1985	57	13	9	10	88	1	11
1986	60	10	9	10	89	1	10
1987	58	13	9	10	89	1	10
1988	57	12	9	10	88	1	11
1989	58	13	10	9	90	1	10
1990	57	12	11	10	90	1	9
1991	55	13	11	10	88	1	11

Source: World Bank, 1994b: Unnumbered Appendix Table, p. 30.
Notes: A = Starchy staples, B = beans & pulses, C = oil-seeds, D = fruit & vegetables, E = total food crops, F = sugar, G = 'traditional' export crops.

The most obvious trend to show is the steady decline, up to 1991, in the proportion contributed by the major export crops, starting at about 25 percent of the total in 1976 and declining to little more than 10 percent now, without taking terms-of-trade losses into account, since this is an index from which price change has been excluded. Growth over the period came entirely from food crops. Taking the years 1976-78 as 100, the overall index for 1989-91 is 133, giving an average growth rate of about 2 percent per annum. For food crops the index was 163, giving average growth of about 3.5 percent. For export crops the index for 1989-91 was just 57, a decline of over 40 percent during the period 1976-78 to 1989-91.

Table 18 shows the same thing in fixed price (1990) Tanzania shillings. What emerges is a halving of export-crop production between 1976 and 1985, with stagnation since then. The obverse of this has been increase in the proportion represented by basic starchy staple crops (grains and starchy roots) and by beans and pulses, while oilseeds and fruits and vegetables held their position without increase or decrease. Sugar, whose production has stagnated, is listed separately from other food crops, since it is produced entirely on plantation scale.[29]

Table 18   Value Added by Different Crops and Crop Groups. Tsh bn 1990 prices

	A	B	C	D	E	F	G	H
	Starchy staples	Beans & pulses	Oil-seeds	Fruit & vegetables	Total food crops	Sugar	'Traditional' export crop	Total
1976	49.4	9.2	9.0	9.3	68.8	1.0	25.3	103.1
1977	52.3	7.9	9.6	9.6	79.4	1.0	26.1	106.3
1978	53.8	8.3	9.6	9.8	81.5	1.0	22.5	105.0
1979	55.2	9.0	10.2	10.1	84.5	1.0	20.9	106.3
1980	56.1	11.4	10.3	10.3	88.1	1.0	20.6	109.7
1981	57.4	10.6	10.7	10.6	89.3	1.0	21.8	112.1
1982	59.9	11.4	10.0	10.8	92.1	1.0	17.7	110.8
1983	62.2	11.2	10.8	11.0	95.2	0.9	15.5	111.7
1984	64.4	17.6	10.5	11.2	103.7	1.1	15.9	120.6
1985	69.1	15.3	11.5	11.7	107.6	1.0	13.7	122.3
1986	73.6	12.6	10.7	12.0	108.9	0.9	12.3	122.0
1987	74.3	16.0	11.2	12.2	113.7	0.8	13.3	127.8
1988	74.3	15.9	11.5	12.9	114.6	1.0	14.7	130.3
1989	85.0	18.9	14.2	13.3	131.4	1.0	14.3	146.7
1990	76.3	16.3	14.9	13.4	120.9	1.3	12.7	134.4
1991	75.9	17.5	15.0	13.9	122.3	0.9	15.1	138.3

Source: As for Table 15.
Notes: A = starchy staples (cereals & roots), B = beans & pulses, C = oilseeds, D= fruits & vegetables, E = total food crops, F = sugar, G = traditional exports, H = total.

---

[29] Strictly speaking, one should also exclude wheat, almost all of which is produced under large-scale (parastatal) conditions.

When figures for the actual value added of specific crops are examined, a rather different pattern shows up. Comparing 1986-91 with 1980-85, overall growth in the latter period is slightly higher, that for export crops and for pulses, oilseeds and vegetables is much higher, while the rate of growth for staple food crops actually falls. What do not show from the table are the severe problems with most of these figures and estimation procedures. One needs more than figures to understand the trends.

4.2   Food-crop Production, Sales, Imports and Security

Tanzania's major marketed food crop is maize. Cassava and other roots, plantains (cooking bananas) and other cereals, like millet and sorghum, are also important staples, but far less of total production comes onto markets, especially official ones. Rice is the second most important officially marketed cereal (about half the value of maize). Wheat production is much smaller, comes mostly from one donor-funded state-farm, is mostly sold and accounts for about half of local consumption. Beans and various pulses and oilseeds are important components of the diet in much of Tanzania, and sold in large (but unofficial and uncounted) quantities. In addition, the diet includes a wide variety of minor crops and collected wild vegetation,[30] including fruits, which make a valuable addition to the diet, especially of children, but which fall outside almost every system of measurement or estimation.

Food security, and its changes over time, is very difficult to estimate. In rural areas it depends in part on own produce consumed and in part, especially for those with insufficient resources to produce their own subsistence, on the price and availability of food to purchase. It also depends on factors having little to with physical food production, like income levels, social networks to help out with loans or gifts in time of need, or movements of cereals by state agencies to hold prices down or provide for emergency. For the urban population, the food price is a much more direct determinant, as are wage-levels, state rations or subsidy policies and social networks. At present it is fashionable to deride any activity by state agencies as inevitably corrupt, inefficient and counter-productive. The record is certainly not good, but rather more complex. Rationing systems have tended to favour civil servants, but emergency actions during famines have sometimes been effective in saving lives and relieving hardship.

There is a tendency to link food security to the price and availability of food to buy, and to equate food insecurity with imports. But food security is not just a matter of physical availability. It is crucially a matter of access or entitlement - the wherewithal to buy it, the work with which to earn it, or the networks through which to beg or borrow it. Discussions of national trends in food availability touch upon the above only at certain points. It is impossible to assess what proportion of Tanzania's food-crop production is aimed at household subsistence production and how much for the market. In all probability, there is a large quantity whose end-use is not decided before the household finds out how large the harvest was, and what are the relative scarcities and prices of a variety of consumer and household necessities. The notion that households produce rigidly for subsistence is one of the more misleading myths about African agriculture. Households have been making decisions across this boundary for many

---

[30] One of the most common sauces eaten with ugali (maize porridge) is based on *mchicha* (spinach) a common term for several wild and cultivated plants. .

decades.

Until its functions were drastically reduced from the late 1980s, the National Milling Corporation (NMC) was the sole official buyer of maize, and purchased between 5 percent and 15 percent of the total crop, according to the harvest (and the crop estimate). It is conventionally asserted that 50 percent of the total crop is self-consumed, an estimate based on little more than that one half is a convenient divider. The remainder is sold in local markets and to traders who move it to deficit areas - in and outside Tanzania. One intractable problem facing any assessment of Tanzania's food production and security, is the large but uncounted portion which is smuggled out of the country in almost all directions.

Trends in maize production. During the colonial period, official emphasis focused on white estate producers. African production was controlled by a marketing board whose main purpose was to prevent competition with the whites. This system was dismantled during the 1950s, stimulating a major increase in marketed output from African producers.[31] This continued during the 1960s, though at a somewhat slower pace. The government introduced monopoly purchase by cooperatives and resuscitated the marketing board, to organize programmes to intensify production through increased input use. Subsidized input distribution and credit had already increased marketing margins significantly by the mid-1960s, but production continued to rise, despite increasing diversions onto informal markets. By 1970 discussions were under way, about reducing the maize price to reduce the surplus which had to be exported at a loss to the treasury. Soon afterwards, this problem disappeared for the next decade and a half. With an increasingly cumbersome marketing system, and a serious harvest shortfall in 1974, partly due to villagization, NMC was unable to purchase enough for local needs and was forced to import maize, which it then did in most years until the late 1980s. The government and donors spent these years trying expensively to increase food production, assuming that falling availability arose from falling production, rather than (as seems more likely) its increasing diversion from official markets.

In 1973-5, a number of programmes to increase food production were set in motion. Most involved increases in fertilizer use and credit for this purpose. Thus they depended heavily on the monopoly institutional structure mentioned above. The parastatal National Milling Corporation (NMC) took over the primary maize purchase from the cooperatives which had previously bought on its behalf, the area within which maize was purchased officially was expanded very significantly, and an already partly existing system of 'pan-territorial pricing' extended.[32] This increased production (or official sales) of maize, but enormously overloaded the limited capacity of NMC. Apart from increases in costs and so reductions in official producer prices, this meant long delays in collecting produce and longer ones in paying for it, virtually forcing production onto parallel markets. All this happened at a time when the 'first donor aid boom' was increasing investment levels and with them urban incomes and demand for food. With low fixed official retail prices and shortages, increasing amounts of food were bid away from official markets, increasing the official shortages and (at least in the short term)

---

[31] Much of it unfortunately produced by cheap but destructive methods of 'mechanized shifting cultivation' which ruined the fertility of Ismani in Iringa Region.

[32] The same price all over the country, regardless of transport costs.

expanding the price difference between the two, to bid yet more produce away. Over-valuation of the exchange rate meant that increasing quantities of maize were smuggled out to Kenya, but ironically also encouraged increased official imports.

The maize shortfall was generally assumed by policy-makers to result from low production rather than its diversion onto parallel markets. Technical agriculturalists have a tendency to see problems in production terms (and to recommend fertilizer use or husbandry improvement as solution). The topic of parallel marketing was embarrassing to officials, since it was illegal and reflected policy failure. And much of the imported grain which filled the gap was food aid, applications for which must refer to 'genuine shortage', not just failure to purchase what is there. Both sides had a further interest here. Food aid allows donors to off-load surpluses at little cost, but higher valuation, to bump up the aid figures. For the NMC, experiencing huge problems in collecting produce from scattered peasant farmers, the arrival of grain in Dar es Salaam by the ship-load was a boon. And the heavy (food aid) subsidy and exchange-rate over-valuation, together with high internal transport costs, combined to make this a cheaper and more convenient solution.

Pan-territorial pricing (PTP) was successful in increasing official maize sales, especially from the areas furthest from Dar es Salaam and most costly to collect from, mainly in the southern highlands. This was supported by successive World Bank and IFAD maize/fertilizer/credit programmes despite the otherwise vehement opposition of the World Bank to PTP. Support for the southward shift was ostensibly based on its more reliable rainfall. But the real reason for unreliability in northern deliveries was the proximity of the Kenya border, and behind it all the commodities which were unavailable in Tanzania, plus Kenya's own variations in crop production. The southern highlands backed onto Zambia, Malawi and Mozambique, none of them expected to compete strongly with NMC, though Zambia did because its maize production campaign sometimes paid higher prices than Tanzania's.

But the soils of the southern highlands are lower in nutrients, especially phosphates, than those of the north, so that growing maize requires more fertilizer. Thus the shift southwards involved a major increase in (imported) input use, further overloading of an already overstretched transport and marketing network *and* a major increase in subsidies, for transport and fertilizer.[33] Two of the 'big four' southern highlands maize-producing regions (Ruvuma and Rukwa, where 90 percent and 70 percent of peasant farmers used fertilizer) are so far from Dar es Salaam, and the nearest railway, that market-determined prices for maize would have been near to zero, and those for fertilizer very high.

Yet under pan-territorial pricing, these regions came to produce over half of the total officially marketed supply because most of what was produced nearer to Dar es Salaam or the northern border was sold informally, for higher prices to private traders. Rukwa and Ruvuma were 'reliable', since only from NMC and under subsidies could they get a reasonable price for their maize and cheap fertilizer.

This system was already being changed prior to adjustment. Cooperatives were re-introduced and purchased maize (for sale to NMC) from 1985. From 1986, under the ERP there were pressures to eliminate consumer subsidies on maize flour, reduce

---

[33] Under Tanzania's period of a myriad directives in 1975, transport had been severely disrupted throughout the country, when the Vice President ordered all trucks to report to Tanga, to move fertilizer from the factory down south.

transport subsidies and eliminate the fertilizer subsidy, and to reduce the role of the NMC to buyer of last resort, while legalizing the already important role of private traders. The course of events is complex and confused (see Bryceson, 1993, Chs 4 & 5), but the fertilizer subsidy still covered 80 percent of cost in 1991, partly because of a large increase in donor grant import-support supplies which had to be used. So were a number of 'unintentional subsidies' arising from miscalculations of costs and inadequate margins set by the government for NMC and the cooperatives. This was especially so in 1986 and 1987, when high prices and good harvests flooded the latter with maize and involved exports at massive losses. Official maize purchases increased rapidly in these years, as the official price was suddenly higher than on the parallel market, but to claim, as Mans (1994: 399) does, that 'foodgrain production doubled' is absurd. Tanzania's official maize purchases have always been extremely volatile from year to year, reflecting the low proportion of the crop sold officially and the fact that official prices are lower than the informal, except after bumper harvests, which often spell financial disaster for the marketing agencies (as in 1987). From 1986 to 1989, pulled in different directions by government directives and IMF conditionality, aggravating its prior problems of inefficiency and corruption, NMC's already massive debts grew further, while its functions were successively transferred to cooperatives (which also accumulated large debts) and the private sector, which was not fully legalized until well into the 1990s. The fertilizer subsidy has now disappeared and all evidence indicates a sharp fall in use (and deliveries from) the southern highlands.

What is astonishing about World Bank accounts of maize marketing is the way in which maize policy tends to be seen as a technical success, entirely ignoring its implications for parastatal costs and inefficiency, while the latter is considered almost entirely without reference to the policies and programmes which made up so much of the costs. It is particularly disconcerting to read that 'returns to extension' are very high, so justifying the introduction of the World Bank's expensive and top-down 'Training and Visit' (T&V) system. The 'return to extension' is measured as the relation between spending on extension and increases in output - (those parts not explained by other factors). When increased production and incomes depend on timely supplies of cheap fertilizer, and when extension personnel can 'facilitate access' in one way or another, it is a fair bet that such a correlation will be found. This says little about whether the content of the extension message is useful, relevant, or even listened to. The chances are, since it refers to using fertilizers, that everyone knows it already but sits through the message for the *nth* time to improve the chances of getting them.

With the dismantling of the state purchasing system and pan-territorial pricing, production has moved back northwards. Official imports have largely ceased, while Tanzania continues unofficially to export maize to neighbouring countries. There is talk of boosting maize as an (official) export crop, though under private management. This seems dubiously realistic, given the distance of surplus areas from markets, as do the calculations which purport to show maize under intensive management as one of Tanzania's most profitable crops. The fertilizer subsidy seems eventually to have gone, as has the fertilizer factory.[34] Quantities used have, very reasonably, fallen. Ex-producers in southern highlands villages, where growing maize needs cheap fertilizer and selling it requires a transport subsidy, could reasonably feel that they had been led

---

[34] No loss. The factory was hopeless in design, location and economically. Some of the fertilizer subsidy leaked into keeping it alive too long.

on a wild goose chase by the designers and implementers of the various maize, fertilizer and subsidy programmes (the Ministry of Agriculture, the World Bank and sundry other donors). But, like everyone else, they will probably just blame the NMC.

Export crops - Although 'traditional' export crops only account for about 10 percent of the total value added in crop production in the 1990s, their strategic value is rather greater than this, since they comprise by far the major proportion of Tanzania's official merchandise exports.

The major aim of the ERP was to increase real producer prices for export crops, reverse the apparent shift of the 1970s and early 1980s into food crops (for informal sale) and increase production and exports. Devaluation and control of parastatal margins were to be the two poles of this policy. In the event, part of the benefit of devaluation was lost to terms-of-trade decline, the proportion going to parastatals increased rather than decreasing and the shift was, if anything, further towards food crops, at least up to 1992/93. More importantly for the long run, it seems highly questionable whether the international prices of Tanzania's major exports will ever recover to an extent which makes them a viable basis for an open, export-oriented strategy.

Table 19 shows the very different trends for the main export crops.

Table 19 Indices of Volumes Sold of Major Export Crops
(1976=100)

	Coffee	Cotton	Tea	Cashew	Tobacco	Sisal
1951-60	39	48	16	..	15	162
1961-70	72	128	45	97	40	188
1971-75	95	168	89	154	100	134
1976-80	93	130	118	84	121	84
1981-85	102	107	115	52	100	44
1986-91	95	151	117	25	96	29
1986	101	74	99	23	88	27
1987	78	163	103	20	116	29
1988	92	183	106	29	91	29
1989	105	131	124	23	81	29
1990	97	79	135	21	83	30
1991	109	109	106	19	42	..
1992	99	172	145	36	89	..
1993	134	168	170	54	92	..

Sources: 1951-91: URT. Bureau of Statistics, 1994c. From 1991: URT, 1994a.

The following paragraphs consider trends and issues for the major crops.

Sisal is grown only on large-scale plantations, where it is processed into fibre as raw materials for string and cordage. It was the major single export crop for most of the colonial period and a few years after, and the major single user of labour during its period of dominance. This ended abruptly in 1964, when synthetic binder twine was introduced, and the bottom fell out of the market. The crop might have been marginally economic since then under efficient management. Under the Tanzania Sisal Corporation it has generally been sub-economic. Recently many estates have been privatized, but so far this has not halted a steady decline in production, which peaked in 1964 at 234,000 tonnes. In 1993, some 6,000 tonnes were sold, a slight increase on the 4,100 tonnes of 1992. One problem with sisal is that clearing the old stumps is more expensive than clearing bush, so they tend to be left, putting the land out of productive use.

Coffee took over as the major export crop after the sisal price crashed, but was soon afterwards hit by price problems, and by quota limits under the International Coffee Agreement, which aimed to hold prices up by limiting exports onto world markets.[35] At Independence, most coffee was produced on settler estates but most growth in production thereafter came from peasants. During the 1960s, coffee production more or less doubled, but since then it has more or less stagnated, fluctuating between 40,000 and 60,000 tonnes. This may hide an increase in total production, much of it smuggled to Kenya and recently Uganda, though low international prices have led to some uprooting in recent years. Smuggling would account for wide fluctuations in supply during the 1980s. For two decades, international coffee prices have been at rock-bottom levels, except when there is a frost in Brazil, by far the world's major producer. Until 1994, the last major frost was in 1977, with a small one in 1986. The extent of smuggling of Tanzania's crop can be gauged from the fact that the current frost has strengthened the currencies of both Kenya and Uganda considerably, but seems not to have affected the Tanzania shilling. This episode now seems to be over (EIU, 95/1: 14) and the prospect for increased export revenue must be near to zero. Coffee marketing has been privatized, and the export retention increased to 100 percent. Combined with high prices this has attracted a reported 40 or so private buyers and has led to optimistic assessments of exports and their future prospects. Recent EIU figures (95/1), however, put exports for 1993 at about half the Budget Survey figure cited in Table 19, with the 1994 level no higher than that of the late 1960s. However, this could reflect lower reporting with privatization or higher smuggling with high international prices.

Cotton has been produced in Tanzania since the early years of the century. By far the most important growing area is to the south and east of Lake Victoria, where its peasant cultivators include some tractor-scale producers. Production grew rapidly in the 1950s, with high prices, and new planting encouraged by the development of cooperatives under the aegis of a fairly efficient (Lint & Seed) Marketing Board. Growth continued until the late 1960s, though avoidance of repayment of credit for tractors and inputs was already raising marketing margins. Production peaked in 1967 and remained at about the same level until the mid-1970s, after which it started to decline. Relevant factors include villagization, which was highly disruptive (especially to livestock owners) in

---

[35] This makes economic sense if achievable, since demand for coffee is inelastic. But it raises problems of equity as between new and established producers and has been opposed (as market distortion) by GATT and the IFIs, whose policies have consistently ignored it. The ICA quota no longer exists.

the lake area, poorer weather in the early 1970s,[36] and price reduction arising from the inefficiency of the marketing structures, aggravated by large-scale projects aiming to increase production, which were put through them. While the Tanzania Cotton Authority (the renamed LSMB) is usually blamed for this, the previous cooperatives were as inefficient and corrupt and just as vulnerable to state pressures to undertake projects or 'assist' villages.

Production sank to very low levels in the early 1980s, when lack of foreign exchange put a number of ginneries out of commission. But the resumption of aid and a major Dutch-funded programme for ginnery rehabilitation (now terminated) have not so far generated a stable increase in production. With prices for 1985-87 set well *above* the f.o.b. price, production increased rapidly to 1988, when it was only just below the 1967 peak, but in 1990 and 1991 it sank to less than half that level. In 1992 and 1993 it rose again, but fell in 1993/94, with a further decline expected for 1994/95. Much of this has to do with marketing and processing. During the 1980s, failure to privatize was held responsible for the problems of inefficiency which kept ginnery capacity too low to deal with the crop. But privatization does not seem to have had much positive effect so far. The run-down condition and large debts of most ginneries seem to have discouraged private buyers, though there have reportedly been purchases in 1994 and one or more new ginneries have been set up. But neither most private operators nor the cooperative which still run most ginneries have access to loan funds for rehabilitation, given the shifts in credit policy. Should these problems be solved, others loom. While TCMB and the cooperative ran marketing as a monopoly, they provided both certified seed and input credit to producers. Neither of these can be expected under private marketing (UNCTAD, 1994: 43-45).

Cashewnut production, in Tanzania started in the 1950s and grew rapidly until 1973, after which production fell even more rapidly. A variety of technical reasons have been sought for this, but villagization did more than anything else to kill cashewnut production. Prior to villagization, most growers lived within their cashewnut groves, which provided shade, while household convenience provided a reason to clear the soil under the trees, so improving yields. Villagization moved producers up to several kilometres away from their trees and brought a deluge of rules, including orders to weed cashewnut groves, with fines of jail sentences for failure to comply. Since this would mean travelling considerable distances to weed cashew groves which could then not be protected against vermin or thieves, many people just forgot about their cashewnuts. Others retained the trees but took the product as cashew apples for alcoholic drinks rather than as nuts.[37] Production, having increased from 56,000 tonnes in 1960 to 128,000 tonnes in 1972, had fallen to 57,000 tonnes in 1979 and continued on downwards to an average of 43,000 tonnes in 1981-85 and only 21,000 tonnes in 1986-91. Cashewnuts were the first major export crop whose marketing was privatized, in 1992, and production is reported to have risen since then. Some 50 private traders were reported to have handled 85 percent of sales in 1993/94 and to have formed 12 export groups from among themselves. But poor reporting leaves the amounts involved

---

[36] This caught out a number of producers who had penetrated too far south into high-risk dry areas in the Shinyanga area.

[37] Producers have to choose between these options, since the nuts do not ripen until the apple has rotted.

unclear. Tanzania's cashewnuts have traditionally been exported raw to South India, where labour costs are lower and productivity higher. From the mid-1960s, efforts were made to encourage factory processing. In the 1970s, just when production was beginning its catastrophic decline, the World Bank funded construction of eight factories (and failed to stop funding despite the increasingly evident absurdity of the venture). Not one of the factories has ever been used or ever will be, but Tanzania bears the debt from this piece of donor stupidity. At present all local processing seems to be manual.

Tea has been produced in Tanzania since the colonial period, at that time all on settler plantations. From the late 1960s, Tanzania started developing smallholder tea, on a nucleus estate - satellite peasant model based on that of the Kenya Tea Development Authority. The Tanzania Tea Authority (TTA), with World Bank funding, spent more of its funds on developing 'nucleus' estates, and less on smallholders, than KTDA. Moreover, like every other agricultural endeavour in Tanzania, tea production was disrupted by villagization, by the costs of subsidy-based programmes initiated during the 1970s, and by the general malaise and lack of morale induced in parastatal officers by declining real wages and economic overheating. Since tea producers were already spatially allocated by the needs of the crop, they probably suffered less from villagization than most, so production stagnated but did not fall in the late 1970s. It held steady from 1981 to 1985, fell significantly for the next three years but has increased since then to record levels. As for other export crops, purchasing has been de-confined, though for tea, this probably does not mean much as satellite smallholders will hardly find alternative processors for their crops. Given the natural monopsony of a tea factory, it is unclear how privatization will benefit small producers at all. Any private purchaser taking on such an undertaking would probably find it necessary to operate on a similar basis, setting fixed delivery schedules to keep the factory in regular use, providing inputs on credit and deducting from the price, to maintain a regular quality level.[38]

Tobacco was grown during the colonial period by whites alone. Limited production by African smallholders was permitted from the mid-1950s, on the basis of organized settlement schemes, this being felt necessary to ensure the correct husbandry measures to ensure quality. Excessive nitrogen in the soil produces a rank and unsmokeable leaf, so tobacco was mainly introduced in areas of *miombo* forest, where the soils tend to be infertile and the trees provide a cheap source of fuel for curing. This is now recognized as a significant cause of serious deforestation in such areas. Until about 1980, international tobacco prices were high enough to cover high scheme administration and marketing costs and still stimulate growth in production from smallholders and continued production by large-scale commercial farmers. In the short run, even villagization stimulated production, since it resulted in the setting-up of a number of new tobacco villages. But in 1980 Zimbabwe re-entered the international market and the world price of tobacco fell by nearly 50 percent, since when it has stagnated at below that level (in deflated US$, World Bank, 1994b: annex). With the other problems of the economy and increasing costs of the bureaucratic superstructure of the

---

[38] But this tends to be referred to by the IFIs as 'contract farming' which is assumed to be efficient, as opposed to 'parastatal monopoly' which is not.

settlements, growth gave way to stagnation in the early 1980s and then decline, with limited signs of recovery until the present. Recent IMF figures show rapid growth in 1992 and 1993, as do one set of Tanzanian figures but not others. Real producer prices were almost doubled between 1990/91 and 1991/92. Since then marketing has reportedly been privatized, or opened to private competition, but no information is available about its operation.

Non-traditional agricultural exports - As problems with increasing traditional export-crop production emerged, attention turned to 'non-traditional exports', many of them actually very traditional exports from even before the colonial period, like honey, beeswax and hides and skins, or from the early colonial period like groundnuts. The advantage of these crops was that they had never been effectively state-controlled and were decontrolled before 1986 with a more generous export retention than for major export crops.

Taken together, non-traditional agricultural and forest products account for around 30 percent of total non-traditional exports, and like them, after rapid growth between 1985 and 1987, they have not grown much since. This conceals differences between particular crops. Horticultural exports started to grow in the late 1980s, but this faded for lack of credit and difficulties in organizing air transport. Exports of forest products increased to 1990, since when they have declined (or gone informal). Exports of meat products have also risen and then declined. The main sustained growth has been in exports of oilseeds and pulses, most of which is apparently accounted for by exports of haricot beans, organized in the northern highlands by a Belgian company, which can organize its own finance and transport. A recent study of this development finds that lack of state support, and credit, is among the major factors limiting growth of non-traditional exports (UNCTAD, 1994).

Agricultural parastatals and liberalization. In 1980, virtually all agricultural marketing was formally confined to parastatal corporations, which also accounted for a varying proportion of production, almost all wheat and sugar, a minor share of maize and rice, quite a lot of what beef and dairy produce was officially marketed though little of total production.[39] By the early 1980s, this very comprehensive and rigid set of controls was not only reducing producer prices and services to producers, but running up huge deficits at the state-owned banks, partly on account of inefficiency and corruption but also because of the many loss-making activities forced upon the parastatals by the government and party.

Adjustment started with the aim of reducing both the scope of their activities and the costs and deficits involved. But for the first several years the latter actually increased. Some of the state austerity was achieved by shifting costs (but not the subventions to cover them) onto parastatals - as for example the fertilizer subsidy. Similarly directives to supply inputs or credit to non-creditworthy individuals and villages continued. At the same time, devaluation increased the costs of equipment (for rehabilitation) and transport (both equipment and fuel). Though CIS made this grant-based for Tanzania, parastatal corporations were supposed to pay the counterpart funds, which were added

---

[39] As of 1993 the Tanzania Government had decided on privatizing all or most of these and ceased to allocate funds to them. But donor spending on seven large parastatal production units came to about 30 percent of total development spending in agriculture for 1993/94 (World Bank, 1994a: 46-47).

to their bank overdrafts if and when they did not, these being further expanded by rising interest rates. The debts of NMC far outweighed those of other parastatals, coming to some 3 percent of GDP alone. But with de facto liberalization its impact on cereal marketing was limited. Export-crop boards ran up smaller (though large) deficits, but retained their monopolies and charged part of the cost to producers whose prices, in real terms and as proportion of export revenues, fell from 1986 to 1989.

Later, both the IFIs and the Tanzania Government (under pressure) shifted to liberalization of marketing and liquidation or privatization of production activities. 'Minor' or 'non-traditional' crops had never been effectively controlled and were liberalized before 1986. Next came cereals other than maize, followed by maize - in fact, if not in law, since private trade was only fully legalized after the NMC had almost entirely left the scene, contributing to a slow response by private traders (UNCTAD, 1994: 27). Of the major export crops only cashewnuts had been liberalized up to 1993, but during that year all the others reportedly were. However, 'owing to the unsure legal basis for private sector activities and the resulting hesitation of the private sector to fill the void, the marketing boards have in fact been asked by the government to execute many more functions than they are supposed to under the reformed system' (ibid.). It is hard to find information on just how privatized most export-crop marketing is, and what this means.

4.3   Other Aspects of Agricultural Change

Land and land tenure. Most of Tanzania's land is held under 'customary tenure', which descends from colonial transcriptions of 'local custom' as recounted by the appointed chiefs, via a system of local courts and their decisions. Ex-settler and some other land is held under formal right of occupancy, normally a 99-year lease. Though formally equal, the customary tenure system has always been less secure than a formal right of occupancy in that it could more easily be over-ridden for purposes of administrative convenience or 'development'. The customary rights of pastoralists to grazing land have been particularly vulnerable since administrators, both during and since the colonial period, tended to see cropping as a more advanced form of agriculture and so gave preference to settlers proposing arable farming. Thus while most alienation of land for European settlement ceased after the 1920s, transfers for settlement schemes, state farms and ranches continued, and increased after independence.

This accelerated in pace during the early 1970s, with a number of new state, regional and military farms and ranches, but most of all with villagization which de facto simply expunged customary land rights, replacing them with new legislation under the Villages Act, whose implications were and are far from clear. One version, the official one, was that titles within villages would gradually be allocated on the basis of land-use plans, the other was that village authorities should simply take over the role of the 'customary authorities' with regard to allocation and conflict resolution over land. With only about 20 percent of villages having even registered a global title, the latter seems far more common. In reality this means a wide variety of different things since customary land law and authorities differ widely between areas, as do the relations between village and customary authorities. Since 1985, this has generated a number of problems as to the extent of village land and the status of sub-rights to land use within villages. There have also been a number of cases where groups of people (notably pastoralists) have complained about alienations of land for 'development' purposes, both public and private. A major current case concerns a several thousand ha. parastatal/donor wheat farm at Bassotu, taken from Barbaig pastoralists. There are also a number of cases of large-scale alienation of Masai grazing land, also in northern Tanzania.

At various points under adjustment, the suggestion has arisen that private registered property in land should be introduced as soon as possible. It could then be pledged as collateral for loans, the argument goes, so avoiding the problems of low repayment which have plagued small-scale credit schemes in tropical Africa, and notably Tanzania. There are several problems with this. Experience from Kenya and elsewhere shows that, even with registration of title deeds, small parcels of land are not satisfactory collateral for banks. If such a system does work, it does so through mortgage foreclosure, historically the most effective process for dispossessing peasants of their land and concentrating it in larger holdings. Experience from other African countries shows that women lose unwritten, but often quite important rights in land as land held under complex systems of overlapping rights is simply registered as the property of a male household head. Individual property rights are especially unsuitable for pastoralist herding people, where common access to rangeland and water is a necessary condition for continuing the method of production.

IFI support for freehold titling has probably receded somewhat, since the publication of a recent World Bank study (Bruce and Migot-Adholla, 1994) making some of the above points. But locally, World Bank economists may still be pushing it. In Tanzania, all this resonates with local disagreements over the topic, with powerful forces favouring freehold and having down-graded the report of a Land Commission which found against.

Livestock herding is an important component of agriculture in many parts of Tanzania, but one hardly touched on here for lack of space. State and donor policy has been even more modernization-dominated than for crop production, with policies and programmes mainly focused on costly attempts to set up ranches and dairy farms. Most of these collapsed in the 1980s and now exist mainly as bad debts. Given that most of these were grossly uneconomic and pre-empted land better used by local herders, the schemes themselves are no loss. But the costs and additions to Tanzania's debt are substantial.

Credit and input supply to agriculture have until recently been the province of a parastatal agency, which has passed through various forms and names, but provided input credit through cooperatives, and often in kind under standard modernization assumptions. That is, credit was provided for 'packages' found by the experts to be beneficial, not what the borrowers wanted to borrow for. Security, such as it was, rested on a 'crop mortgage', effected through 'deduction at source' through the standard monopoly marketing system, its marketing boards and cooperatives. These organized repayment (or failed to) and undertook most of the not insubstantial administrative burden. From the very start, before independence, this system was subject to systematic abuse by rich peasants, especially cooperative committee members, employees and other local notables, who allocated loans among themselves, sold outside the single channel and left the loans to be repaid, if at all, through a levy on all the members or a reduction of all their producer prices.

Unsurprisingly, the expansion of input-supply schemes increased the extent of misuse and reduced rates of repayment during the 1960s. This already highly problematic system then became enmired in villagization and 1970s project mania, emerging in the

1980s with huge deficits, which grew still more rapidly after 1986, as repayments declined to vanishing point with removal of monopolies, as the debts of other parastatals were loaded onto the Cooperative and Rural Development Bank and as rising interest rates accelerated their growth. CRDB has now been completely restructured and partially privatized and is to run on a commercial basis. One question is simply who it will lend to, since only a minute fraction of Tanzanian farm households have land title and almost all of them are large farmers. Even they may have problems in getting access to credit. According to UNCTAD (1994: 28), banks do not currently accept even formal right-of-occupancy leasehold titles as collateral for loans unless applicants have erected physical structures on the land, whose value then limits the extent of the loans. For the present, however, almost all credit in Tanzania is on hold, due to the lending-stop imposed by the IFIs as part of their campaign to impose hard budget constraints.

From the 1970s, most agricultural input supply was confined to parastatal agencies and often available only for credit through CRDB. This has now gone, as have fertilizer subsidies, and it remains to be seen how large the drop in use is, since this will affect the interest of private traders in handling such items. Access for poor farmers in areas of poor transport seems likely to disappear almost completely. Thus, while no-one doubts that the massive structures and deficits of the 1970s and 1980s were counterproductive, it is far less certain that some more modest system of non-commercial supply might not be useful.

5.   Formal Sector Manufacturing and Mining

5.1   Formal Sector Industry
Between the Arusha Declaration and the adoption of adjustment programmes, Tanzanian industry underwent a curious pattern of development. In the years after the Declaration all large manufacturing companies were nationalized and large numbers of new manufacturing parastatals were created. Subsequently the parastatal sector has continued to account for around 60 percent of manufacturing output, employment and installed capacity, and to occupy a monopoly in some branches (beer, cigarettes, steel, electric cables, etc). Although there was no detailed planning, the process was guided in a very general way by the 'Basic Industrial Strategy' of the period, which aimed at both an expansion of Tanzanian industry generally and a shift in its output away from consumer goods (70.5 percent of value added in 1966) towards intermediate and capital goods, particularly those which could utilize local raw materials and particularly in the form of large-scale enterprises.

At first the Basic Industrial Strategy appeared quite successful: value added grew by 10.5 percent p.a. between 1967 and 1973. Thereafter it began to fall, declining by an average of 3.3 percent per annum in the following decade. Value added per worker declined much faster than this as employment expanded from 63,000 in 1973 to 103,000 in 1982. Employment growth corresponded to growth in investment and in installed capacity rather than to output. As a result capacity utilization levels fell sharply, from around 70 percent in 1970 to less than 30 percent by 1982 (most of this decline occurred after 1978). Skarstein (1986) further shows that of the industrial branches for which information is available and which it is known increased capacity after 1976, over half were already operating at significantly below capacity when the decision was taken to increase it. Even more remarkably, Skarstein also shows that, despite the huge increase in employment, wage costs declined as a share of value added between 1975 and 1982 due to plummeting real wage levels (in 1982 only 32 percent of their 1972 value).

According to a 1989 industrial census there were roughly 1200 enterprises employing more than 10 persons. Of these the largest number were in wood and wood products (30 percent of the total), followed by textiles and leather (18 percent) and food, beverages and tobacco (17 percent). In Dar es Salaam, besides Tanga the main traditional industrial centre, there were 458 enterprises of this size, of which 98 employed more than 100 persons. 42 of the latter were parastatals (all figures from Dutz and Frischtak, 1993).

As elsewhere, it was anticipated that Tanzanian industry would benefit from adjustment largely through forex liberalization and by the higher premium placed on efficiency through internal and external trade liberalization. In addition, several export promotion incentives were introduced and in 1989 a specific World Bank sectoral operation of 'Industrial Rehabilitation and Trade Adjustment' was adopted. This operation reflected World Bank thinking generally on the industrial sector (and specifically the parastatal one). In relation to four sub-sectors selected for their combination of currently low capacity utilization and supposed high (export) potential - textiles, edible oils, leather goods and meat packing - it aimed to formulate agreed programmes for rationalizing production in a smaller number of more competitive firms, which would then be privatized, and - on the basis of offering funds for their rehabilitation - persuade the government to close the remainder. Studies were carried out in each of these sectors except for meat packing. The textiles and leather sub-sector studies came up with the expected recommendations. Initially it appears that the government implemented only a handful of them, but a number of tanneries have subsequently been reconstituted as joint ventures and the Dar es Salaam branch of the textile company Kiltex has been formally closed for three or four years. The edible oils study actually suggested an expansion of capacity but it seems to have been buried by the World Bank and the general extent of restructuring even the sectors selected has been slight.

On the basis of the rather patchy data available, Table 20 provides a broad picture of trends for manufacturing as a whole under adjustment.

Available data indicate that manufacturing initially benefited in a limited way from adjustment, but with these benefits tailing off after 1991. After dropping sharply in the crisis years of 1982-85 output recovered to levels close or identical to those of the pre-crisis years of 1976-80. Value added recovered less markedly, although the latest figures are not available. Exports grew sharply to 1989 but then declined. Output as a share of GDP has been stabilized, but only at the level of the crisis years. Capacity utilization appears to have remained extremely depressed until around 1989, when it recovered marginally, but also seems to have tailed off since 1991. Meanwhile, as employment continued to rise inexorably, labour productivity appears to have actually declined. Figures for the normal indicator of value added/employee show a fall until 1987, followed by a stabilization to 1990. Data for total output/employee show a fall from Tsh 22,400 per worker in 1982 to Tsh 16,187 in 1986, followed by a limited recovery to Tsh 18,596 in 1989 (all constant 1976 prices). Employment in parastatals rose in line with the increase in employment generally according to government figures, although according to the World Bank it fell. Wages continued to fall precipitously, to

Table 20 Industrial Sector Data, 1980-93

	1980	1982	1983	1984	1985	1986	1987	1988	1989	1990	1991	1992	1993
Output: vol index					100					114	117	110	110
Tsh m.[a]	2,683	2,304	2,103	2,159	2,075	1,991	2,081	2,228	2,399	2,338	2,607	2,663	2,719
Rate of growth (%)	-4.9	-3.3	-8.7	2.7	-3.9	-4.1	4.5	7.1	7.7	-2.5	11.1	2.2	2.1
Output/GDP (%)	11.5	9.8	9.2	9.1	8.5	7.9	7.9	8.1	8.4	7.8	8.2	8.1	8.0
Val-add (Tsh m.)[a]	1972	1693	1564	1425	1546	1493	1556	1666	1794	1749			
Exports (US$ m.)				33	53	39	63	73	105	99	63	86	60
Share tot. exports (%)				9	19	11	18	20	25	22	18	21	16
Capacity utilization (%)					33	27	28	29	31	36	37	38	35
Employment (000)	102	103	115	116	121	123	124	125	129	130			
of which parastatal					58	46	52	54	54	58	62	64	65
Value-added per employee (Tsh[a])[b]	19,333	16,436	13,600	12,284	12,776	12,138	12,548	13,328	13,906	13,453			
Real average wage Tsh per year[b]	6,618	4,196	3,746	3,464	3,164	2,334	2,011	1,874	1,593	1,483	1,483	1,483	

Sources: *Tanzania Economic Trends* (various); URT Bureau of Statistics, 1994a; URT, n.d.; Bhaduri *et al.*, 1993; EIU, 1995.
a)   Constant 1976 prices.
b)   Constant 1977 prices.

be almost completely worthless by 1990 in terms of their 1980 level.

The limited data available on the composition of value added since 1986 show consumer goods industries to have increased their share from 40.2 percent in 1986 to 47.7 percent in 1991. The share of total value added contributed by capital goods fell correspondingly, from 28.5 percent to 12.8 percent. Thus the general structure of industry is moving in the opposite direction to that intended under the Basic Industrial Strategy. Physical output figures show rapid expansion since 1985 in production of spirits, cigarettes, tyres and cement. Output in the important textile sub-sector remained very low (averaging only 29.4 percent of capacity 1986-92). Production of fertilizers ceased completely in 1991 when the German junior partner and managing agent, Klöckner, withdrew.Output levels in 1994 fell back almost to their level of the crisis years (index of production (1985=100) = 101, Economist Intelligence Unit, 1/95). An end-of-year review in the local *Business Times* (30 December 1994) stated that very severe power supply problems, water problems, competition from cheap imports, increased input prices and high interest rates had combined to force the at least temporary closure of many important companies - amongst them Mwatex, Mutex, Tabora Spinning Mill, Ubungo Spinning Mill, Sunguratex, Steel Rolling Mills (Tanga), Ubungo Farm Implements, Sabuni Industries, Rubber Industries, Kibo Match Corporation and Southern Paper Mills.

According to Willer and Rosch (1993) this overall picture conceals rather different performances by enterprises under parastatal, Tanzanian Asian and Tanzanian African ownership. In a non-random sample of 174 enterprises in five urban centres covering performance in 1985-91, the 52 African-owned companies identified had marginally higher profit/turnover ratios and levels of capital growth than the 91 Asian-owned companies, and both out-performed the 31 parastatals in the sample by a very high factor. The African companies had almost all been formed since 1980 and 37 percent had been formed since 1986, and they still had on average only a quarter as many employees and fixed assets as the Asian-owned companies. Bhaduri *et al.* (1993) give capacity utilization figures for private and parastatal manufacturing in 1991 and 1992, in which private companies averaged utilization levels of 38.5 percent and parastatals 30.3 percent.

Parastatal industrial performance seems to have dramatically worsened during the adjustment phase. According to Tanzania Audit Commission data[40] analyzed by Ericsson (1993), net profits for manufacturing parastatals were recorded from 1983 to 1986. Throughout this period there were about 30 companies recording losses each year and around 70 recording profits. In 1987 the number of companies recording losses outnumbered those recording profits for the first time. Subsequently net losses grew from Tsh 2,000 m. in 1987 to Tsh 31,000 m. in 1991, with about half of all companies recording losses each year. Recorded losses fell sharply in 1992, but according to Ericsson this was because many loss-makers failed to return audited accounts. For the whole period the worst loss-makers were Mwatex, Kiltex, Tanganyika Dyeing and Weaving Mills, Mbeya Cement, Tanga Cement, Southern Paper Mills and the Tanzania Fertiliser Company. As noted above, some of these companies have subsequently

---

[40] Ericsson (see also Section 8) uses Tanzania Audit Commission data throughout, in preference to the parastatal accounts produced by the Bureau of Statistics (URT, n.d.). The latter show net profits by parastatals in every year from 1967 until the current year. This results from rather curious accounting techniques, which count increases in stock as income.

closed. The poor performance of the textile producers seems to date from the initiation of the 'own funds imports' scheme in 1984. Presumably there were also some substantial profit-makers but no researcher has so far identified which they are.

No reliable data are available on new industrial investment. Of the 300 projects approved by the Investment Promotion Centre (IPC) from its inception in July 1990 to September 1992, 133 were industrial, supposedly corresponding to new investment worth US$80.6 m. However, a 1993 World Bank document stated that not a single one of these projects had yet materialized. An examination of the *Business Times* for 1994-95 indicates that by February 1995 there had still been only a few new industrial start-ups, comprising three or four breweries, a gin distillery (Macholong), a diamond cutter, an aluminium windows and doors producer (Show Max) and a broiler chicken producer (Pollo Italian Tanzania).

The IPC continues to produce apparently impressive figures (534 projects worth US$1.3 bn by mid-1994). It would not be entirely correct to describe these figures as worthless, however, at least for the individuals gaining approval. Until July 1994 such approval meant that, regardless of whether their project was genuine or not, they could then take steps to obtain from the Treasury letters giving them exemption from import duties and sales taxes (see below, Section 6). The local industrial lobby, such as it is (particularly managers of the textile parastatals), has complained that this system, far from leading to foreign investment, is simply leading to subsidized imports, and in the process making more severe the difficulties of companies already experiencing crisis conditions.

5.2   Formal Sector Mining

In the 1950s mining's share of GDP was 10 percent and the industry - mainly comprising gold and precious stones - provided a major source of government revenue. In the 1960s activities wound down, largely because of the stagnation of the gold price (less than 10 percent of its present levels). A number of smaller foreign companies withdrew in 1967-72 leaving Williamson's Diamonds Limited (since before independence a joint venture between the state and De Beers) as the only large-scale operation. The State Mining Company (STAMICO) took over the running of all companies in 1972 (though De Beers remained a minority shareholder in Williamson's). Of the 11 companies taken over or established by STAMICO, only two (Williamson's and Kiwara Coal Mines) were still functioning in 1994. Williamson's remains the only large-scale company and has registered steadily declining production, but official mining production and exports have soared since 1989 on the basis of the partial officialization of a long-established and extremely extensive informal mining industry (see Table 21).

The adjustment period has also seen the emergence of renewed interest in the country by some genuinely large-scale international companies. The only tangible results so far have been De Beers' purchase of a controlling interest in Williamson's, a limited rehabilitation (valued at US$3.5 m.) of the Mwadui mine and a US$13.6 investment in graphite production by Graphtan (a subsidiary of the UK-based junior company, Samax) at the Mererani tanzanite site near Moshi. The large-scale Canadian operations Sutton Resources and Romanex International have been involved in serious exploration of both gold and nickel/copper/cobalt reserves in Kagera region since 1992, and mine development seems likely, though not until 1999. At least one well-known junior gold producer, the Anglo-Zimbabwean Cluff Resources, is seriously considering investment as is a well-known junior diamond producer of similar provenance, Réunion. 55 Prospecting and Reconnaissance Licences were issued in 1993, almost as many as those currently valid at the beginning of the year. Other than in tourism, mining presents the most serious prospect for new direct foreign investment. However, except in base metals this is likely to be at the direct expense of informal producers.

Table 21   Mining Data, 1962-93

	62	70	80	85	89	90	91	92	93
Diamonds									
Official production (kg)	139	142	54	43		14	14	14	7
,000 carats								67.3	42.7
Unofficial production (kg)[a]								1.5	
Gemstones (kg)									
Official production	330	1072	5748	218					3520
Unofficial production[a]								500	
Gold (tonnes)									
Official production	3.1	2.4	0	0.005		1.64	3.85	3.13	3.24/4.49[c]
Unofficial production[a]								1.5	
Minerals									
Official output (Tsh m.)[b]					139	165	236	293	
Official output/GDP (%)					0.5	0.6	0.8	0.9	
Official exports, (US$ m.)					11.9	26.6	45.0	53.2	
of which gold					*1.2*	*13.6*	*29.1*	*40.3*	
Exports, % of total exports					3.1	6.0	10.7	12.3	

Sources: Chachage, 1995; Nanyaro, 1994; World Bank; *Tanzania Economic Trends*, var.; *Business Times*, var.
a)   World Bank estimates.
b)   Constant 1976 prices.
c)   Both figures have appeared in the *Business Times*.

6.   Informal Economic Activities

Under this heading will be discussed two distinct but loosely related sets of economic activities. The first are those of small-scale enterprises (SSEs, normally defined as enterprises with less than 10 employees), whose activities are 'informal' in the sense of not necessarily being registered, not necessarily following formal legal requirements regarding conditions of operation and payment of relevant taxes, and equally not normally being eligible for the benefits of formality - for example, credit. The second are informalized aspects of formal economic activities, or formal political/administrative activities with economic dimensions. These generally imply activities organized on a larger scale than SSEs - not necessarily in terms of numbers of persons who are involved in a specific operation, but in terms of turnover and profit.

6.1   Small-scale Enterprises

Data on informal sector manufacturing, especially on a time series basis, are almost completely absent. The 1989 census reported by Dutz and Frischtak (1993) counted 16,747 manufacturing SSEs in Tanzania, of which almost half were in the textiles and leather branches, followed in terms of numerical significance by food manufacturing and wood and wood products. A slightly different rank order is suggested by Bagachwa *et al.'s* (1993) survey in five urban centres, which, however, was based on a stratified sample and attempted no general head count. The largest group of manufacturing enterprises in the sample were in food manufacturing (bakeries, posho mills, etc.) followed by footwear, furniture, 'iron and metal products' and transport equipment manufacture and repair. The latter three categories made up the bulk of operations described as 'Intermediate and Capital Goods Manufacture', where enterprises appeared to be significantly older than in other sectors and where cash wages were the highest (approx. Tsh 6,000 (US$12)/month, assuming a 54-hour working week). The authors draw no conclusions about the relation between adjustment and changes in the sub-sector, except to point out that since liberalization there has been a major expansion of privately-owned grain processing (posho mills). Earlier regional surveys dating from the pre-adjustment crisis years (e.g., Havnevik, 1993) show already high concentrations of small-scale manufacturing and repair activities even in remote rural areas, supporting the impression that most of such activities are not a new phenomenon. Indeed, it seems likely that prior to trade liberalization, many branches of small-scale manufacturing and repair - specifically those substituting for confined/unavailable consumption goods - probably existed on a larger scale than is the case today, when better quality imported versions of most such goods are now freely available.

If there has been one major internal change in the composition of SSEs before and after adjustment it has almost certainly been in an expansion in retail and wholesale trade and in services. Private activities in these sectors, particularly trade, were restricted by confinement and other policies in much of the 1970s and early 1980s - and via the absence of incentive and investment goods caused major problems for agriculture. There are few or no hard data on the subsequent expansion of trade, except the limited information cited above on trade in agricultural products. A survey of 12 villages carried out by Booth *et al.* in 1992 (Booth *et al.*, 1993) suggested that the lines of retail trade which have expanded fastest in rural areas have been in *mitumba* (second-hand clothing), cycles and ploughs. However, there has undoubtedly also been a vast expansion in the turnover of basic consumer items. In urban areas there also seems to have been a major expansion in small-scale construction activities, although data on this are completely absent. In urban areas demand has not only increased through the removal of previous artificial restrictions, but also probably reflects an overall increase in household incomes. In rural areas the situation is less certain (see below, section 7). Booth *et al.* (1993) report increased rural consumption being funded by a diversification of household activities through the multiplication of minor *miradi* (projects), listing beer, wine and spirit brewing/distilling, selling cooked foodstuffs, mat and basket making, quarrying and sand collection and 'sending children to carry water up the hill' as the most popular activity lines.

Informal sector mining involves somewhere upwards of 300,000 persons (a million including all those living in villages whose main activity is mining, according to Chachage (1995)), on hundreds of sites all over the country. The main minerals involved are gold, rubies and tanzanite in rank order. The industry has a highly organized internal structure but very low levels of technology. The main beneficiaries have traditionally been those owning claims - who collect rent basically as landlords - and gold and gemstone dealers. This branch of mining dates back to the 1930s. However, the adjustment period has seen the emergence of two completely new phenomena.

The first of these has been the official purchase of informally produced minerals - especially gold - by the Bank of Tanzania (in practice by local branches of the National Bank of Commerce and the Cooperative Rural Development Bank) at around 70 percent of the world price. This began in 1990, with the results indicated in Table 21. In 1994 official gold production/exports will undoubtedly show a decline as the prices offered by the Bank of Tanzania (BoT) increasingly diverged from the world price. As it is, the Bank of Tanzania never captured the whole market and some participants in the industry estimated non-recorded production even in 1992 as 6 tonnes. In 1994 stories began to circulate that the IMF had advised the BoT to withdraw from gold purchase and at the end of the year the latter announced that it would do so, albeit only 'in the medium term', 'as gold purchase operations are in conflict with the bank's basic objective of maintaining monetary stability' (*Business Times*, 30 December 1994).

A second major change has been the registration and operation of a layer of new, ostensibly 'large-scale' companies. These companies, some owned by residents but the majority not, have been granted claims after having registered with the Ministry of Energy and/or IPC, in the process thus gaining access to the benefits mentioned in the previous section and explored at greater length below. A few undertake some mining operations of their own, at a technological level only fractionally higher than the small-scale miners, but most simply operate as landlords and/or dealers. As a result the mining areas are probably the only parts of the country where there has been large-scale popular hostility to structural adjustment, locally identified as being responsible for the parasitic insertion of these companies into the existing production process (for a detailed analysis see Chachage, 1995). There is justification for this linkage, since, despite its otherwise general enthusiasm for the informal sector, World Bank policy on informal mining is unremittingly hostile (see World Bank, 1992).[41]

6.2 Informal Aspects of Formal Business

As elsewhere in Africa, throughout the 'modern' period Tanzania has experienced significant levels of smuggling, illicit dealings in hard currency and restricted goods,

---

[41] A recent document describes the Tanzanian government small-scale mining policy as 'to intensify the regulation and monitoring function of the Mineral Resource Department' and to 'allow small-scale miners to sell their mineral rights and claims freely with a view to encouraging the formation of modern formal mining ventures by small and medium-scale Tanzanian investors'.

and systematic fraud of various kinds. The few studies touching on this question tend not to distinguish activities of this kind from the legitimate though equally unrecorded activities of small-scale enterprises. Nonetheless they provide evidence both of a major increase in such activities from around 1978, and significant changes in their content at regular intervals subsequently.

Maliyamkono and Bagachwa (1990) estimate the overall size of the 'second economy' in 1978 at 9.8 percent of GDP. According to them it grew very rapidly from 1978 to 1980, and then steadily up to 1986, when its size reached 31.4 percent of GDP. Other authors, writing in the 1990s, argue that Maliyamkono and Bagachwa were guilty of underestimating its size at this time, and go on to provide estimates of its current size almost double this level. In general it seems to be accepted that both elements of the second economy have continued to expand.

Launching the 'Campaign against Economic Sabotage' in April 1983, the late Edward Sokoine cited the major components of what has here been called 'informal aspects of formal business' as being smuggling (export of agricultural products and gold and import of consumption goods from basic to luxury items), diversion of official imports, illegal dealing in and hoarding of confined goods by private traders, illegal dealing in foreign exchange and under-invoicing of imports (to avoid customs duty) and exports (to allow accumulation overseas of illicit foreign exchange holdings), and abuse of expatriates' import privileges. Another issue identified by Sokoine around the same time was poaching and export of trophies (ivory, hides, skins). Growth in many of these activities can be directly related to the incentive structure provided by contemporary economic conditions and policies, such as the increasing over-valuation of the Tsh (official: parallel market rates moved from 1: 2.6 in 1980 to 1: 5.7 in 1985), declines in manufacturing output (e.g., of cement) and manufactured imports and subsequent shortages of basic consumption items, the NCB grain marketing monopoly, etc. Maliyamkono and Bagachwa suggest that probably the major one of these activities at this time was illegal dealing in and hoarding of confined goods, and that the main 'partners' of the private traders involved in this practice were the personnel of parastatals and Regional Trading Companies.

As already indicated, the subsequent fiasco of the Campaign against Economic Sabotage (and Sokoine's death in circumstances which still have never been satisfactorally explained) were followed by the first 'home-grown' moves toward deregulation, including the 'Own Funds Import Scheme' launched in 1984. Under this scheme, private traders with undeclared overseas forex holdings could obtain licences to import goods of certain kinds on a 'no questions asked' basis. Simultaneously, the first significant devaluations began the slow process of reducing the premium on illicit forex dealings. After IFI-led adjustment followed in 1986, much of internal private trade became deconfined and foreign exchange also became officially fairly freely available, through Commodity Import Support (CIS) and the OGL. There was also a renewed influx of expatriates, growing uncertainty about the long-term fate of parastatals and a general (informal) weakening of controls on acquisition of assets such as land, as state regulative agencies became debilitated through collapsing salary levels. According to Maliyamkono and Bagachwa (1990) these changes eliminated illegal trade in confined mass consumption items and made illegal trading in foreign exchange much rarer but at the same time created incentives and opportunities for new types of illicit activities, including land speculation, building/renting of housing for lease to expatriates in hard currency, theft of public property, and illegal foreign-exchange acquisition and export through the OGL (by over-invoicing imports). The CIS and OGL were also subject to a variety of other abuses, mainly non-payment of counterpart funds. By the end of 1994 Tsh 112 bn (US$5.5 m.) were said to be outstanding on the CIS, of which approximately Tsh 80 bn was owed by parastatals (some of them apparently now under receivership) and Tsh 32 bn by private sector companies. Somewhere between a further Tsh 16 and 26.6 bn was outstanding on the OGL. Moreover, their claimed role of relieving capital and intermediate goods shortages was never really reflected in correspondingly higher levels of industrial capacity utilization or agricultural production.

Bol (1993) argues that despite the own funds import scheme and trade liberalization via the OGL, the period 1986-90 was also characterized by continuing perceived shortages of certain consumption goods, especially luxury items. This meant that internationally very high prices could be obtained for them. As a result of this, and increased incentives in the form of fairly high Export Retention Scheme quotients, a boom in 'non-traditional exports' (NTEs) ensued. Officially recorded NTEs increased from US$86 m. in 1986 to US$202 m. in 1990, before subsiding to US$177 m. in 1992. Besides this there is evidence of a contemporary boom in unrecorded NTEs. Both officially and unofficially the main growth areas apparently involved the plunder of natural resources of various kinds (especially mineral, marine and forest products). Bol relates the subsiding of the NTE boom to a combination of depressed demand and falling prices for luxury goods on the Tanzanian market and increasingly freely available foreign-exchange as the OGL window steadily grew in size and as foreign-exchange bureaux were allowed to function (see section 9).

Since 1992 much donor attention has been focused upon issues of import duty and tax avoidance. As will be seen, this has been a long-standing source of additional income for many enterprises and individuals in Tanzania and in historical terms may actually have declined; the main novelties are that - ostensibly at least - it is the private sector which now seems to be the main beneficiary, and that as other fiscal reforms were implemented its visibility dramatically increased.

According to Ericsson (1993: 29-33) official exemptions for payment of import taxes and duties have been common ever since independence. Besides those statutorily provided for (i.e., for foreign diplomatic missions, religious bodies, NGOs, etc.) between 19 and 225 discretionary exemptions were issued by either the Treasury or the Minister of Finance personally each year from 1961 to 1988. Average numbers in 1985-88 were around a hundred each year. Ericsson estimates their value as between 31 and 57 percent of all imports during 1982-87, although she admits that it is unclear whether or not these values refer to only discretionary or all exemptions. In relation to the value of duties actually collected their value fluctuated between 60 and 147 percent each year. In 1989 their relative value was 122 percent and in 1990 241 percent. Ericsson states that parastatals accounted for most of the exemptions granted, especially after 1986 when devaluation strongly increased their operating costs.

This implicit subsidy to parastatals was of considerable concern to donors in the late 1980s and was one of the main concerns behind pressure on the Tanzanian Government to review the entire taxation system. A comprehensive tax reform was eventually introduced in 1992 under the incoming Minister of Finance, Kighoma Malima, and included legislation abolishing all exemptions currently granted to government organs.

Despite the apparent increasing level of exemption values during the period to 1992, total tax revenue as a share of GDP increased from 17.1 percent in 1988-89 to 19.6 percent in 1990-91 and further to 20.7 percent in 1991-92. However, it then fell sharply to only 15 percent in 1992-93. At the time the IMF attributed this to lack of administrative capacity to implement the tax reform agenda. By 1994, however, a different view had emerged. The non-termination of many existing exemptions, the issuing of many new ones, and non-collection of duty/taxes on non-exempted imports were identified as central problems. According to IMF figures, in the first half-year after the tax reform exemption values declined to 4.5 percent of total dutiable values; in the first three quarters of 1994 they ran at 35.3 percent. The ratio of exemption values to taxes collected did not dramatically change from the late 1980s, being 132 percent for the second half of 1993 and 161 percent for the first three quarters of 1994. All the latter figures, however, refer to what the IMF describes as 'Tax Assessment Notice Programme' imports, which account for only US$1250 m. worth of the annual overall official import volumes of roughly US$1500 m., and their method of calculation may not be precisely comparable with Ericsson's.

One of the main 1992 changes in the import duty regime was to end exemptions on the import of raw materials, then identified as the main form of subsidy which the system was providing to parastatals. Their actual share of exemption values prior to 1993 is not known, but between the second half of 1993 and the first quarter of 1994 this fell from 51 percent of values to 17 percent. There was a steep rise instead in exemptions granted as a result of project registration with IPC, from 38 percent to 60 percent. The significance of the latter is that IPC registrations are exclusively private sector or joint ventures, and wholly state-owned parastatals are excluded. Of a total of Tsh 70 bn in exemptions and uncollected taxes in the first three quarters of 1993, Tsh 15.4 bn could be attributed to 20 companies, including Tsh 10 bn to one alone (Merchant Vintners Ltd.).

The overall revenue situation began to improve again after 1993, but it is clear that this is largely the result of increases in revenue from petrol, road tolls and sales tax levied on locally produced goods and services. Not only has the value of import duty exemptions rebounded but levels of collected tax on non-exempted imports fell from 77 percent in the first half of 1993 to 35 percent in the first three quarters of 1994. This is despite the contracting out to private agencies of an increasing number of the functions of the customs and excise department (see below, section 9). Interestingly, this increased contracting out was undertaken mainly in order to combat the reappearance of the problem of import *under*-invoicing - a phenomenon whose recurrence seems to be related mainly to attempts to annul the effects of various elements of the 1992 tax reform package.Towards the end of 1994 donor pressure led to the removal of Kighoma Malima from the Ministry of Finance, only for him to metamorphose as Minister of Industry and Commerce. He was replaced by the minister previously responsible for minerals (!). It also led to a public act of contrition by the Head of State, and promises of a thorough-going investigation and collection of at least Tsh 20 bn in outstanding taxes prior to the consultative group (CG) meeting at the end of February 1995. A few weeks later, on 20 January 1995, the *Business Times* carried a letter claiming that one private company at the centre of controversy on this and other issues, Mohamed Enterprises, had already received fresh exemptions; a month later, to coincide with the CG meeting, it carried a story stating that only Tsh 2.8 bn of the Tsh 20 bn target had actually been recovered and that the investigation had not been completed (*Business Times*, 25 February 1995).

An aspect of the problem of import duty/tax evasion has been the proliferation of unsupervised bonded warehouses, mostly on the premises of importers. 177 such installations were identified in June 1994. After donor pressure the Tanzania Government undertook to reduce the number to 65 by June 1995. A separate but related issue is tax and sales exemptions granted on goods landed in Zanzibar or Tanzania mainland and declared to be in transit either to each other or to beyond Tanzanian frontiers, but which in fact never leave their original destination. No estimates are available of the magnitude of this practice, but it is said to have become widespread during the 1990s.

Besides the OGL and the tax exemptions, a third area recently identified as a major locus of corruption has been the Debt Conversion Programme. Billions of Tanzania shillings are said to be unaccounted for through this programme, whose beneficiaries are private sector entrepreneurs undertaking new investments. One beneficiary was charged with illegally repatriating US$1.25 m. fraudulently received as part of the programme but before he was brought to trial was declared persona non grata and thereby subject only to deportation. The former Minister of Home Affairs, Augustine Mrema, threatened to resign his current job (Minister of Labour) in protest, but was pre-emptively sacked before he could do so (*East African*, 26 February 1995).[42]

There has also been a notable increase in Tanzanian involvement in the international drug trade. The country appears to be part of triangular trades involving export of gold and gemstones to Asia and purchase of opium/heroin (mainly destined for Europe) or mandrax (mainly destined for South Africa) with the proceeds. In January 1994 a consignment of mandrax said to be worth Tsh 4.7 bn (US$9.4 m.) was seized in Dar es Salaam (*Uhuru*, 7 January 1994).

Throughout the periods both of pre-adjustment crisis and of adjustment itself it is evident that most of the major money-making niches in Tanzanian society have been located at the intersection of the public and private sectors. Adjustment has largely involved shifting their specific locations, but not this aspect of their character. However, ostensibly at least the centre of gravity of the public-private straddling involved has increasingly shifted to the private sector, although some of it involves public programmes to assist the latter. In any case, according to local 'street wisdom' many private sector 'entrepreneurs' are simply fronting for the interests of individuals who remain firmly embedded in the state apparatus.

7. Poverty

Unlike most neighbouring countries, Tanzania has witnessed a relative surfeit of survey-based studies attempting to measure household incomes and expenditures. The first (1976-77) was a large-scale Household Budget Survey (HBS) carried out by the Government of Tanzania Bureau of Statistics. Following this, two smaller surveys based on the same sample were carried out in 1980 and 1983 by teams led by British academics (Collier *et al.*, 1986; Bevan *et al.* 1988). Finally in 1990-93 no less than four studies were produced, one based on a new sample by a team from Cornell University and the Economic Research Bureau, University of Dar es Salaam (Tinios *et al.*, 1993;

---

[42] The businessman involved also mysteriously received Tsh 78 million in compensation from TANESCO for the construction of electricity lines across the sisal estates, which he had purchased from government for less than 10 million.

Ferreira, 1993; Sarris and Tinios, 1994a), and three by different Government of Tanzania departments. The Bureau of Statistics produced a further round of the large-scale Household Budget Survey (HBS) (URT, Bureau of Statistics, 1994c), while other departments produced a Labour Force Survey (LFS) (URT, 1993) and a Human Resource Development Survey (HRDS) (URT, 1994a), respectively.

The four studies carried out in 1990-93 all came up with measures of household income or consumption/expenditure (see Table 22).

Table 22   Household Surveys, 1990-92. Tsh, current prices

	ERB/Cornell 1991	HBS 1991/92	HRDS 1993	LFS 190/91
Sample size[a]	1,046	5,328	n.s.	7,762[b]
Average household consumption[c]	225,382	262,934		
including subsistence	*(61,94)*	*(67,267)*		
Average p.c. expenditure	36,988		113,480[d]	
Average household monetary income				167,280

[a]	Number of households sampled.
[b]	Urban.
[c]	Value of average household consumption (monetary and non-monetary).
[d]	See text below.

As can be seen, the figures in two of the studies appear fairly consistent. The HBS of 1991-92 gives an average household consumption figure 16.7 percent higher than the ERB/Cornell study, but was carried out some months later in a year in which the NCPI rose by 22 percent. At first sight the figure from the LFS survey of 1990-91 also appears broadly consistent with these two others, but the LFS covered only urban areas where, according to the ERB/Cornell and HBS studies, consumption was respectively 67.9 percent and 23 percent higher than for the country as a whole. However, allowing for the fact that it was carried out over a year before the HBS and some months before the ERB/Cornell one, this apparent inconsistency is reduced. The only really 'rogue' result is that of the HRDS, which gives an apparently staggeringly high figure of Tsh 113,480 for per capita expenditure. However, this is found in a table which apparently describes *household* expenditure and in fact probably refers to monetary expenditure by the latter. If so, this represents a figure 22.2 percent lower than the average household monetary consumption figure of the ERB/Cornell study, for a period two years later. The overall impression generated is therefore of a band of figures which, when interpreted, are in a range which has some underlying consistency but also fairly sharp differences. The HRDS is at the bottom of the range and the HBS at the top. The ERB/Cornell figures are toward the top, and the LFS toward the bottom. Although the following discussion treats data from most of these surveys as meaningful, it should be stated that some of the findings cast doubt on both sampling methods and data quality. The HBS suggests that no less than 6 percent of households in mainland Tanzania own a motor vehicle, for example.

Recent discussion of the extent of poverty in contemporary Tanzania has been based exclusively on the ERB/Cornell study, since the others listed above have not been as widely available. Using data from the ERB/Cornell study different authors have tried to draw poverty lines and estimate the proportion of the population below them. Tinios *et al.* (1993) argue for a nutritionally-based poverty line and use the survey's data to show that the daily calorific intake of 1900k calories/person needed to sustain the average person in a minimally healthy state would require annual per capita expenditure of Tsh 51,000 in Dar es Salaam, Tsh 29,000 in urban areas other than Dar, and Tsh 25,000 in rural areas. On this basis 43.6 percent of the whole population would not be sustaining themselves. 12 percent would be consuming less than 1200k calories per person, i.e., would be severely under-nourished. If the cut-off point is raised to 2100k calories/person, 51.4 percent of the population would have to be considered poor.

A more arbitrary poverty line has been specified by Ferreira, who takes an adult equivalent per capita income of Tsh 15,030 per annum (1991 prices), and also suggests a 'hard-core poverty line' of Tsh 11,171 per annum. These lines are supposed to be based upon the current local Purchasing Power Parity equivalents of US$1/day and US$0.75/day respectively, apparently assuming an exchange rate of only Tsh 40: US$1, as opposed to the actual 1991 rate of Tsh 230: US$1.[43] According to these lines, in 1991 51 percent of total households were poor and 42 percent hard-core poor; if actual as opposed to imputed exchange rates had been used, four-fifths of the population would have had to have been counted as hard-core poor.

A limited amount of distributional data is also available from the surveys, although this has generated less discussion. All the studies, however, appear to point to a considerable polarization of consumption/expenditure and incomes. It is interesting to note, for example, that only 18 percent of households in the study carried out by ERB/Cornell had incomes at or above the average level of consumption that they calculate. Despite the much higher average consumption level figure given, the HBS survey comes to an identical conclusion. The same survey states that the members of 68 percent of all households had per capita incomes of below Tsh 12,857/year and that no less than 28 percent of all households had *total household income* of below Tsh 12,000/year.

Both Sarris and Tinios (1994) and Ferreira (1994) have tried to make comparisons between the results of the ERB/Cornell survey and earlier surveys, and on this basis draw conclusions about the effects (or non-effects) of structural adjustment. However, these exercises are sometimes not rigorously conducted, or the conclusions drawn from them are not really warranted. Sarris and Tinios make their comparison with the 1976-7 HBS data. It should be recalled in this context that 1976-7 was a good year in terms of agricultural incomes and was definitely prior to the onset of the economic crisis. The comparison nevertheless apparently shows extremely impressive increases in real consumption expenditure. These range from 35 percent/person in rural areas to 125 percent/person in urban ones. On this basis the authors declare that 'the results explored

---

[43] However derived, this calculation assumes that in 1991 Tsh 40 had a purchasing power parity (PPP) equivalent to the international purchasing power of US$1. At the time, the exchange rate was Tsh 230: US$1, making an ironic comment on the realism of prevailing exchange rates. They are, at best, dubiously 'market' determined, given that they derive almost exclusively from forex obtained outside of international trade. The large discrepancy between the exchange rate and the PPP underlines the fact that, apart from donor balance-of-payments support, the major factor determining the exchange rate is the price local economic operators are prepared to pay to engage in capital flight.

in this paper should help quiet the critics of stabilisation and adjustment programmes in Tanzania who claim that they have a detrimental effect on the poor' (1994: 35). However, elsewhere in the same text the authors point out that these apparent increases should be weighted against an in-depth consideration of how to calculate the increase in living costs. Using a Laspeyres-type Base Weight deflator instead of the national consumer price index (NCPI) to take account of these, the authors generate a second set of figures showing that average household per capita monetary consumption in rural areas actually fell slightly, although in urban areas it still increased by 67.3 percent. Moreover, even if their first set of figures is accepted what is basically shown is a movement of considerable numbers of (largely urban) households out of the 'poor' category, rather than any improvement in the position of those who have remained poor (see below).

Ferreira meanwhile compares the same 1991 data with those from Bevan *et al.'s* 1983 study. 1983 was a year of extremely poor economic performance and in most respects represented the nadir of the crisis. In any event, using 'the deflator implicit in the GDP' on the income side, a fall is said to have been recorded from 65 percent to 51 percent of households in poverty and from 54 percent to 42 percent of households in hard-core poverty. Probably the most favourable description which could be applied to these procedures is that they are methodologically sketchy. Leaving aside the issue of the non-transparency of the poverty criterion employed, using what amounts to the NCPI as the sole income deflator generates only one set of figures within a broader range which should have been considered.

Another problem with both Sarris and Tinios' and Ferreira's use of the ERB/Cornell data is that it focuses almost exclusively on the consumption side. In the process there is a general neglect of questions of individual incomes and the numbers and statuses of individuals within the household contributing to the overall household income. It is clear that real formal sector incomes have fallen consistently throughout the period and while little is known about changing levels of real informal incomes it is widely acknowledged that there are now more household members contributing to the aggregate household budget than in earlier periods. Increasing amounts of work for appallingly low returns by household members who in an earlier period may either have been at school, or retired, is therefore an aspect of poverty which should be taken account of with the same seriousness as overall levels of household expenditure, but about which little is known.

Despite suggesting an overall reduction in the proportion of the population who are poor, both Sarris and Tinios and Ferreira conclude that the gap between the better-off and those who have remained poor has widened considerably during the adjustment period. Ferreira for example calculates that while the average real per capita income of the 'better-off' increased from Tsh 27,100/year to Tsh 70,069/year (1991 prices) between 1983 and 1991, the average real per capita income of the bottom half of the population fell from Tsh 4053/year to Tsh 3295 and of the lowest 40 percent from Tsh 3326 to Tsh 2366. In the process the ratio of the average income of the better-off to the hard-core poor rose from 8.1:1 to 29.6:1.

On the basis of the data from the ERB/Cornell survey, the widening gap between rich and those who have remained poor appears to substantially overlap with what appears to be a widening urban-rural gap. The HSB survey confirms such a gap, but one rather smaller than that suggested by the other survey (its figures for urban consumption/expenditure are considerably below the ERB/Cornell ones while its figures for rural consumption/expenditure are considerably above).

All those working from the ERB/Cornell study also note an apparent increase in differentiation in rural areas, although the degree of significance they attach to this varies. Ferreira in particular notes a polarization in land ownership, a finding supported by case-study research such as Loiske (1994) and by the Presidential Commission of Inquiry into Land Matters (United Republic of Tanzania, 1994b). Loiske surveyed 600 peasant households in Babati in 1991, finding that 50 were landless while another five were accumulating extensive tracts of land both in their own villages and neighbouring ones. Meanwhile the Land Commission found evidence of very extensive land alienation in Morogoro, Arusha, Tanga, Coast, Lindi, Mtwara and Kilimanjaro regions, often to very small numbers of highly placed officials. The ERB/Cornell study reports a sharp increase in the hiring-in of rural labour (and therefore presumably in its hiring out) but does not link this to the land question.

The official gloss placed on the ERB/Cornell study seems to be that the main sources of poverty and inequality are inter-area differences in environmental and infrastructural advantage and inter-household ones in 'human capital'. The latter are said to be reflected in low agricultural market involvement and low off-farm incomes. What is therefore required is more growth, a widening of markets and more adjustment. This broadly repeats the conclusions of the British studies of the early 1980s, and is in line with current general thinking about poverty in the World Bank, while implicitly acknowledging of course that adjustment in Tanzania has so far rewarded and penalized almost exactly the opposite groups to those intended. However, it is difficult to reconcile with the growing evidence of structural differentiation in ownership of material assets like land and appears to systematically overlook intra-household differentiation. The latter is examined in the ERB/Cornell study only with reference to literacy, where the gender gap is said to be closing and education, where somewhat paradoxically it is said to be growing. Otherwise gender is examined in either the ERB/Cornell study or the HBS one only through looking at the levels of consumption of male and female-headed households. (The findings of the two studies in this respect are consistent with regard to stating that rural female-headed households are worse-off than male ones, but appear to be inconsistent on this same issue in urban areas.)

No systematic data on formal wage employment and average monthly pay have been available since 1989. According to World Bank documents on the manufacturing sector, wages there held up somewhat better than in most areas of employment. However, the figures cited in Section 5 above indicate that they still fell in value by 78 percent between 1980 and 1990. This compares with a fall of 39 percent between 1970 and 1980, making real wages in 1990 worth only 13 percent of their 1970 level. The sharpest falls were in 1980-82 and 1985-6 but the trend has continued steadily downward in the adjustment period. Wage employment is apparently retained not because of the value of wage incomes but because the latter are at least paid regularly, and because the workplace is a useful source of other benefits (allowances and fringe benefits, employer property and contacts for other economic projects). As elsewhere in Africa, labour has felt the costs of crisis and adjustment in the manufacturing and parastatal sectors in income terms rather than in retrenchments. The finding casts doubt on how an apparently massive improvement in urban living standards such as is reported by Sarris and Tinios could have occurred without almost all household members having substantial incomes from 'business'.

Like most other adjusting countries in Africa, Tanzania acquired a Social Dimensions of Adjustment programme at the end of the 1980s, known in the Tanzanian case as the 'Priority Social Action Programme' (PSAP). Unlike in other adjusting countries, however, there was little or no emphasis on assisting retrenches. The programme contained a number of projects, or ideas for initiatives, in the education, health, water and agricultural sectors, plus a monitoring project. Some of the initiatives outlined were already being undertaken, while others took the form of vague general commitments to increase expenditure or rehabilitate unspecified numbers of 'badly run-down schools' (a description which could be validly applied to almost any school in the country), and the programme lacked any core or - apparently - any coordinated means of implementation. The monitoring project appears to have disappeared without trace.

8.   The Social Sectors

This discussion will deal with developments in education and health. General patterns of outcomes in both cases are obviously affected by developments in the economy as a whole (levels of employment, incomes, subsidies on consumer goods, etc.) as well as by other exogenous factors, for example food security, and by trends within the education and health services themselves. The presentation will deal mainly with trends within the services themselves but acknowledge other factors where relevant.

8.1   Trends in Health and Education Provision

Most figures provided on state expenditure in the health and education sectors appear to show these sectors increasing their share of GDP and per capita expenditure in the first five years of adjustment but then declining quite sharply. Moreover, the downward trend may be sharper than is apparent here. Until the last three years figures have tended to exclude a considerable level of donor expenditure not included in central budgets. As a result of changes in practices, a far higher proportion of the latter has now been recorded as mainstream spending. Since the overall shares described have remained fairly constant this implies a real decline (however, no attempt has been made to quantify this). A further problem is that relative to many other African countries both health and education expenditures (and outcome data) are quite incomplete.

The overall pattern of government health expenditure also seems to have remained fairly consistent during the adjustment period. Curative medicine has accounted for around 80 percent of total expenditure, roughly evenly divided between hospital- and non-hospital-based facilities. Preventive medicine has accounted for only about 14 percent (and a much smaller proportion of the recurrent budget). Had donor spending on immunization programmes been generally 'on' rather than 'off' the books, this figure would presumably be much higher, however.

The adjustment period has seen a considerable rise in the importance of non-governmental providers. One source gives figures for non-governmental ownership of hospital facilities, health centres and dispensaries in 1990 of 44 percent, 96 percent and 74 percent respectively. More recent work in 1993 in nine regions by Kiondo (1995) gives proportions of 57 percent, 76 percent and 63 percent respectively and reports a major growth in non-governmental provision (NGO and commercial) in Dar es Salaam.

Official figures meanwhile also show an increase in government-provided medical facilities during the adjustment period. Health centres rose from 183 in 1979 to 267 in 1992, while dispensaries rose in number from 2,282 to 2,392.

Table 23　Health Expenditure Data 1986-87 to 1993-94

	86-87	87-88	88-89	89-90	90-91	91-92	92-93	93-94	Average 90-94
Share net public expend (%)								12.8	10.1
Share GDP (%)	4.1	4.3	4.8					3.7	
Share recurrent expend (%)									12.8
Share develop expend (%)									3.2
Health expenditure p.c. (constant 1976 Tsh)	10	12	15	18	28	17	14		
of which public health								*0.5*	
of which recurrent (ECU)	*0.8*	*0.9*	*1.1*	*1.3*	*1.1*	*0.9*	*0.8*		
No. of health workers (,000)			32						

Sources: World Bank; Bloom *et al.*, 1992; Semboja and Therkildsen, 1995.

Most observers concur that the central problem of health provision in Tanzania is less that of coverage by health facilities and more the grossly inadequate nature of the services which the latter are able to provide. There are major (but unquantified) shortages of most grades of professionally qualified staff and most facilities are run-down and poorly supplied with basic necessities. Munishi (1995) details the sorry state of the public health sector in Kagera region, the epicentre of the AIDS epidemic in Tanzania, where only 12 percent of rural dispensaries surveyed were headed as recommended by a rural medical aid, only 32 percent had an employee qualified to use a microscope and where only 20 percent of total diagnostic instruments at all dispensaries surveyed were in working order. Despite new and more efficient procedures for distribution of drugs, public health facilities routinely obtain levels of monthly supplies which are exhausted two weeks into the month. Though real funding levels have probably been maintained, they are increasingly unable to support the provision of gradually expanding services to a rapidly expanding population.

A roster of user charges for designated services in public health institutions was introduced during the period 1992-94. However, according to Lawson (1994), at District Hospital level at least, none of the preconditions specified by the designers for their successful implementation had been met in advance. For example in 1994 there was still no system enabling units levying charges to replenish their drug stocks from government stores with the money collected. No data are yet available on collection rates or magnitudes.

Non-governmental health facilities are not necessarily in better condition than public ones, particularly with regard to the presence of qualified staff (Kiondo, 1995).

However, despite the fact that government grant levels to them have remained unchanged since 1986 they appear to be on a better financial footing than state ones. Bloom *et al.* (1992) observe that, contrary to widespread impressions, roughly two-thirds of their income comes from user fees.

Table 24 Education Expenditure Data, 1970-94

	Average 1970-1979	80	90-91	92-93	93-94	94-95	Average 1990-1994
Educational expenditures as percent of:							
public expenditure	16				15.1		17.5
GDP		4.4	4.0		4.5		
recurrent expenditure							21.8
development expenditure							6.0
Educational expenditures per capita (US$)							
primary				16.2	15/16.8[a]	15.2	
secondary					167		
university					3500		
Total (constant 1976 Tsh)		50	30	25	22		

Sources: World Bank; Svantesson, 1994; Semboja and Therkildsen, 1995.
[a]   World Bank Public Expenditure Review document/Svantesson, 1994. Svantesson states that donor assistance to primary education per capita in 1993-94 was US$2.7.

The broad picture of public education closely resembles that of health. After falling sharply in the early 1980s, expenditure recovered in the first five years of adjustment before falling again after 1990. The pattern of expenditure has meanwhile again remained broadly constant, with primary education, secondary and university and other tertiary accounting for about 50, 13 and 19 percent of expenditure respectively, and with teacher remuneration accounting for 81 percent and O & M and materials together only 5 percent of the primary recurrent budget. Again there has been a slight increase in the number of facilities, even under adjustment. Primary schools (almost wholly public), for example, increased from 10,583 in 1992 to 10,892 in 1994 (Wort, 1994). Likewise there has been an increase in both primary and secondary school teachers, with the result that national pupil:teacher ratios in public education have remained fairly stable (see Table 25). Probably from the inauguration of Universal Primary Education, and definitely now, these expenditures are grossly inadequate for the coverage of services offered, however.

Lawson (1994) provides a telling example to illustrate this point. In 1992-3, student welfare costs accounted for 51 percent of the recurrent expenditure for public secondary schools (about 110 schools out of a total of about 330). But this was only half of the overall budget allocation. Meanwhile the budget allocation was itself calculated on the basis of being sufficient only for four months' boarding expenses per pupil. A similar picture emerges concerning teacher remuneration. Although accounting for excessively high levels of expenditure, it is grossly inadequate to attract or retain properly qualified teachers. The vast majority of primary teachers in 1994 earned less than Tsh 120,000 per annum, i.e. about half of average household consumption (monetary and non-monetary) levels. According to a 1991 World Bank study, at least three quarters of all teachers had other occupations. Interviews with teachers at three secondary schools in Dar es Salaam in 1992 indicated that, without exception, teachers regularly undertook paid private tuition (Lugalla, 1993).

Table 25   Teacher Numbers 1985-92

	1985	1989	1990	1992
Primary	92,586	98,392	96,850	101,306
of which: *women teachers (%)*				*42*
properly trained (%)				*30*
pupil:teacher ratio			32:1	35:1
Secondary	3837	5267	7863	5060[a] + 3866[b]
of which graduates (%)		30.3		18.1

Source: World Bank.
[a]   Public.
[b]   Private.

Fees were introduced for public sector schools in the 1984-5 budget and today stand at Tsh 200/pupil/year for primary schools and Tsh 2500/pupil/year for secondary schools. These are very low, but they are only a small part of what parents have to pay in practice. The total current costs (registration fee, levy, materials and uniforms) for public primary education are Tsh 4,000-8,000/pupil/year and for public secondary education up to Tsh 100,000/pupil/year (Lugalla, 1993). According to the recent World Bank-drafted Public Expenditure Review, the government plans to increase expenditure on primary education by Tsh 10 bn in 1994-95, through increasing fees and (except in teacher training institutions) charging parents formally for most elements of provision except teacher salaries and buildings maintenance. At the same time they plan to reduce teacher numbers, on the basis of 'competency testing' (!). The idea of distributing vouchers to parents, presumably floated by 'libertarian' neo-classical consultants, is also mentioned in recent government documents. How the additional Tsh 10 bn is to be spent is not spelt out and it is not clear that the government is even in a position to allocate this amount.

8.2   Health and Education Outcomes
Given the state of both health facilities and the government statistical service it is hardly a surprise that data on health in Tanzania are sketchy in the extreme. This is by

no means a new phenomenon. Even in 1978 available statistics on life expectancy diverged in a range between 44 and 51 years (the commonest estimate for 1991 was also 51). Today the situation makes impossible any firm conclusions about trends. For example, estimates for infant mortality (deaths 0-12 months) in 1988 varied between 107 and 115 per 1,000 and in 1991 (the last year for which estimates are available) between 99 and 115. Similar discrepancies are evident in estimates of the child mortality (deaths 13-60 months) rate. The only apparently unambiguous data are on under-fives malnutrition, from a UNICEF survey of 1991-92, which showed over half of this age group to be suffering from one form of malnutrition or another. The commonest form was height-for-age (47 percent nationally, ranging from 28 percent in Dar es Salaam to 65 percent in Mtwara). 29 percent nationally suffered from weight-for-age malnutrition and 6 percent from weight-for-height. Lindi, Mtwara, Singida and Coast regions had consistently the worst scores for all types. The same survey reported that 80 percent of all pregnant women presenting at UNICEF-run facilities were anaemic. No time series data exist from earlier in the adjustment period, or prior to it, to compare with these.

Table 26   Estimates of Primary School Enrolments, 1978-94. Percent of age group

	1978	1980	1983	1984	1988	1990	1991	1992	1993	1994
Official estimates, gross	95	93			73	74	81			
Lugalla est, gross				83		63		68	69	69
Official est, net						63	59			
Cooksey, net	60				47					
Bevan *et al.*/ERB/Cornell										
net 7-9 y.o.			*31*				*27*			
net 10-13 y.o.			*78*				*65*			

Sources: Svantesson, 1994; Lugalla, 1993: adapted; Cooksey *et al.* (1993); Bevan *et al.*, 1988; Ferreira, 1994.

Note: Gross enrolments: total enrolments as proportion of all 7-13 year olds.
             Net enrolments: proportion of 7-13 year olds attending school.

It seems that infectious diseases, particularly Cholera, are on the increase but again systematic data absent. In any event it is notoriously difficult to attribute changes in health status to changes in economic policies, even where the effects of the latter on incomes are unambiguous.

The same goes for educational outcomes. However, in this case there are at least more data available, particularly on enrolments. Enrolments in secondary schools in Tanzania have for some time been the lowest in eastern and southern Africa and have remained consistently around the 3 to 4 percent of age group level (girls 45 percent of lower grades, 25 percent of upper ones). The main trend in the sector is a growth in non-government-owned schools, most of them run by local development trusts (see below, section 9) and mostly considerably worse-off in resource terms than the public schools.

Although secondary education is not expanding it is at least not in a state of crisis. Unfortunately this is the only way to describe the situation with regard to primary education. Enrolment trends in this sub-sector are described in Table 26.

Since 1990 there has been a significant increase in official enrolments, of a perhaps suspiciously sharp character, but an extension of Lugalla's method of calculation shows that even if they are accepted as genuine they are still considerably below the pre-adjustment level of 1984. The net statistics, extracted by Cooksey *et al.* from census returns, are even more depressing, although the survey material results of 1983 and 1991 seem to suggest somewhat higher levels. This might be an effect of geographical biases in their sampling frame, for Cooksey *et al.* also report a regional spread of 1988 net enrolment rates between 36 percent (Singida) and 64 percent (Kilimanjaro). But whatever series is accepted, a downward trend is clear. Fieldwork by Cooksey *et al.* (1993) presents overwhelming evidence that the decline is based on low parental perceptions of the quality and cost effectiveness of public primary education, which is perceived in a fairly widespread way as a service offered by semi-literates and performed under totally unconducive conditions. As already noted, only a minority of primary teachers have received proper training. Concerning conditions of instruction it is perhaps sufficient to cite data from Coast Region presented by Lugalla (1993) . In 1983 the region boasted 1,884 classrooms and 26,868 desks. By 1992 the number of classrooms had fallen by a third and the number of desks per classroom by a half.

Girls and boys suffer in fairly even measures under these conditions. Recent years have also seen the difference close in the (appallingly low) rates of completion of primary school (Standard 7). In 1991-92 the rate for boys was 9.4 percent of the cohort and for girls 7.6 percent.

Given these trends, literacy rates have predictably fallen. Official estimates of illiteracy in 1986 were 10 percent and in 1992 16 percent. The self-assessed figure provided by the ERB/Cornell survey (1991) was 32 percent. A national figure from the 1988 census is not yet available but figures cited by Kiondo (1995) for some of the regions covered in his survey suggest that even the ERB/Cornell figure is on the optimistic side.

As already implied, the planning and budgeting aspects of social sector provision in Tanzania have never been well-coordinated, particularly in the case of education, and the quality of the services offered have deteriorated extremely sharply as natural population growth and a tendency to add on new projects have continued in the absence of new resources. Structural adjustment has impacted on the social sector mainly via its dampening effect on government deficit financing and its apparently demoralizing effect, via falling real incomes, on workers in the sector. Had structural adjustment not been applied then spending levels would have been higher and sector workers would perhaps have retained a greater level of professionalism. But the basic problems of the sector are likely to have been at least equally intractable.

9.   Public Sector Reforms

9.1   Civil Service Reform

The Tanzanian mainland civil service grew in size from 90,000 employees in 1961 to 139,000 in 1971, 215,000 in 1981 and 299,000 in 1988. The major part of the increase between 1971 and 1981 was accounted for by a growth in primary school teachers. The growth between 1981 and 1988 was mainly in the category of 'other employees', i.e., non-education, -health and -agricultural service personnel.

Already in the phase of 'home-grown' adjustment, two government commissions were set up to investigate a rationalization of civil service functions and employment, and civil service wages were allowed to fall, although not by levels as precipitous as in other sectors. 12,760 central government retrenchments were carried out in 1985 although many of those retrenched appear to have been re-employed as local government staff (Mamuya, 1991). Local government, resurrected in 1983 and broadly responsible for local social service delivery, today employs around half of all those counted as in civil service employment.

World Bank and IMF agendas on civil service reform in Tanzania have been almost identical to those elsewhere in Africa. The civil service is said to be overstaffed, underpaid, poorly equipped, and suffering from poor morale, low motivation, widespread absenteeism and corruption. The World Bank and the IMF have concentrated on trying to reduce numbers (said to be a precondition of any significant wage increase), while the UNDP has been deputed the task of carrying out inventories aimed at rationally adjusting staffing levels to agreed functions.

The first serious attempt to address these issues was via a ghost worker census in 1988. This was poorly designed and concluded that almost a third of all those registered as in civil service employment were ghost workers. Later this number was reduced to 16,000 (or about 5 percent), and these were eliminated from the payroll. A World Bank-produced Public Expenditure Review was conducted the following year, which concluded, on the basis of inexplicit reasoning, that the civil service was overstaffed by 50,000 in relation to its currently agreed functions. UNDP was brought in to identify which posts should be abolished and eventually concluded that the actual level of overstaffing was 27,000.

Here the matter appears to have rested until 1992-93 when the World Bank succeeded in getting the number 50,000 reinstated and a timetable apparently agreed whereby 10,000 would be retrenched in 1992-93 and 20,000 more in each of the following two years. A retrenchment package was also simultaneously agreed. It is unclear how many retrenchments have actually occurred under this agreement. According to the *Daily News* (10 March 1993) 2,123 retrenchments were carried out in 1992-93. Mans (1994) puts the figure at 3,000, but the Tanzania Government Civil Service Reform Programme Action Plan, produced for the 1994 Consultative Group meeting, states that there had been 10,292 retrenchments by mid-1994. Personnel in health and education were exempted from the exercise on the grounds that they were in 'short supply' . In fact, in education at least, their numbers have continued to grow (see Section 8). It also appears that, intentionally or otherwise, local government generally was excluded from the exercise.

The 1989 Public Expenditure Review also drew attention to the current low level of wages in the sector. Pay was said to have fallen between an unspecified date in the 1970s and 1989 by 80 percent in real terms. An increase in the salaries of certain grades was stated to be desirable (it was said that the minimum:maximum pay differential within the service of 1:10 was a performance disincentive to managers and professionals), but no mechanisms were suggested for effecting it.

The 1994 Public Expenditure Review, also carried out with little or no Tanzania Government input, took a still more critical tone than that of 1989. Civil service numbers were said to have actually increased to 355,000. This was blamed on continued hiring of all teaching and health trainees graduating from government institutions each year (in fact this accounts only for about a third of the increase, if an increase on this scale has indeed occurred). The Tanzanian Government therefore had to consider not just the adjustment of its staffing levels to the agreed range of functions but also the immediate pruning of these functions themselves. The Review now stated (again on the basis of inexplicit reasoning) that the 'real feasible' size of the civil service was only 225,000. It was therefore necessary to carry out 40,000 retrenchments per annum for the next three years, and previously exempted grades were to be included in the target groups.

It seems extremely unlikely that much will come of this proposal. Reasons have been found to avoid implementing even the later stages of the 1992-93 to 1994-95 retrenchment plan. A new ghost worker survey was conducted in March 1994, resulting in the removal of a further 14,764 names from the payroll. All but a thousand of these were then deducted from the target of 20,000 retrenchments for 1993-94. Likewise the list of government functions from which the Tanzanian Government has explicitly proposed that it should withdraw (as opposed to consider withdrawing) was still by October 1994 confined to the running of a water depot, three small Ministry of Tourism boat yards, four bee centres and the Central Medical Stores (already under the effective control of DANIDA).

Both the 1994 Public Expenditure Review and the 1994 IMF Background Report focused increasing attention on the issue of civil service pay, where attention has increasingly shifted from inadequate basic levels to the 'non-transparency' of the whole remuneration system. Of course, already in the late 1980s this system had become non-transparent, with most managerial grade employees supplementing their basic pay not merely through official personal allowances and rebates of various kinds but also through frequent safaris, for which per diems could be claimed. Since 1989 the allowance element of total official remuneration has increased considerably, especially for senior grades, where in some cases they contribute 80 percent of remuneration. The introduction of petrol allowances for lecturers at the University of Dar es Salaam in 1992 after the departure for overseas employment of many senior staff led, for example, to the restoration of salary levels comparable with many better-off Third World countries, but a protracted struggle to withdraw them again occurred in 1994. Prior to this there is said to have been a decompression of public sector wages to the extent that the ratio of highest to lowest real official civil service income had reached 50:1. Such allowances are much scarcer in local government, however, where both incomes and services seem to be in an virtual free-fall situation.

Alongside these trends has been a growing tendency of official and unofficial privatization of civil service functions. The most important example of official privatization has been in customs duty collection. Some time prior to adjustment pre-shipment import inspection and tax assessment was contracted out to a Swiss agency, SGS. Early in the 1990s a similar contract was awarded to another (linked) Swiss company, Cotegna, on the basis of a geographical division of labour. In 1993 their contracts were extended to include the issuing of tax notices on these assessments and in July 1994 they were also made responsible for ensuring that tax and duty had been paid on them, by means of reconciliation exercises with the Treasury and Bank of Tanzania (see above). The selection of these companies has been challenged by a number of donors on the grounds that it was non-transparent. A joint donor mission carried out early in 1995 under the auspices of the Special Programme for Africa found that their reporting procedures were not uniform, lacked clarity in some respects and were actually unintelligible in others. A steering committee set up to coordinate their activities with the Treasury, Customs department and BoT had never met and there was little communication between the different agencies.

A second, unofficial, form of privatization was noted by Kiondo in his recent (1995) survey of local development politics in eight regions. Here, alongside the more predictable extension of the role of non-government providers in education and health was found to be the emergence of local elite-rooted organizations providing or aiming to provide a comprehensive set of services across a number of sectors. The most developed of those he encountered were in Hai (Kilimanjaro Region) and Newala (Mtwara Region). In both districts private and apparently unaccountable (explicitly and deliberately unaccountable in the case of Newala) Development Funds were not merely running schools or other services on the basis of voluntary contributions but were levying compulsory cesses and taxes and in the case of Hai had become the actual employer of most local government workers. In the case of Newala they were also carrying on purely commercial activities in partnership with leading members of the business community.

9.2   Parastatal Reform

Even basic data on parastatal enterprises in Tanzania are somewhat vague. In the late 1980s most texts on the subject refer to there being around 400-410 parastatals. In the early 1990s, however, the figure 344 seems to be the most widely used. Equally unclear is the breakdown of this number between commercial and non-commercial organizations. The World Bank in different documents gives figures of 30 to 100 non-commercial parastatals and in its main report on the subject refers in different places to there being 270 and 290 commercial ones. Figures on total employment are correspondingly inconsistent. The World Bank puts the latter at 'around 150,000' while the government's *Analysis of Accounts of Parastatal Enterprises 1983-92* (URT, n.d.) gives figures of 168,000 for 1983, 160,000 for 1986, 185,000 for 1989 and 192,000 for 1992. The same data source suggests that this growth in parastatal employment is largely accounted for by a growth in employment in parastatal manufacturing companies.

An initial, limited parastatal restructuring exercise was carried out in 1987, immediately after the adoption of adjustment. 10 parastatals, almost all involved in agro-processing or marketing, were liquidated and 12 others, all estates owned by the Tanzania Sisal Authority, were sold off. The latter sales were mainly to Asian former owners and attracted accusations of favouritism and underpricing. The exercise was discontinued without explanation in 1988 (Kiondo, forthcoming).

The main feature of parastatal performance generally under adjustment has been a very sharp increase in their losses and debts. While an unduly catastrophic picture has been painted of these by some authors and donor agencies, they are still very serious indeed. Like the problems of the manufacturing parastatals - to which they are closely related - they appear to be a phenomenon which first emerged in a major way in 1984. According to Ericsson (1993) total parastatal losses in the latter year were only Tsh 1,800 m., but since 1989 have never fallen below Tsh 32,000 m. Net losses (these figures minus the surpluses generated by profit-making parastatals) were recorded in 1984 and 1988-91. The largest net losses were Tsh 7,453 m. in 1988 and Tsh 11,176 m. in 1989, corresponding to 2.6 percent and 3.3 percent of GDP respectively.[44] Ericsson goes on to show that agricultural parastatals, especially NMC and the Cotton Marketing Board, accounted for the bulk of losses in 1984-6, and industrial parastatals in 1987-91 (see section 5 above). There are also some heavy loss-makers in other sectors, notably the railway company. This situation has led to recent heavy borrowing (apparently mainly local) and to an accumulation of debt. The World Bank estimated the latter in 1992 as Tsh 1 trillion. How this has been computed is unclear: as will be seen, the total cost of cleaning up the balance sheets of the Bank of Tanzania, National Bank of Commerce and Cooperative Rural Development Bank in 1992-3 was at the most Tsh 240 bn, although of course foreign debts may be high.

Parastatals are also said to be a major beneficiary of subsidies. Ericsson states that these have officially amounted to Tsh 600-7,400 m. per annum over the last decade. The great bulk of the official subsidy turns out to be accounted for by the routing of the fertilizer subsidy to peasants through the account of the Tanzania Fertilizer Company, however. Parastatals have also enjoyed additional subsidy-like 'elasticities', in the form of non-payment of counterpart funds, exemptions from import duties and sales taxes and non-payment of pension fund contributions. Like bad debts, these still appear on their balance sheets as increased deficits, however. And while it is clear that the parastatal sector has enjoyed the bulk of them, the private sector has also apparently systematically avoided its commitments in this respect.

Besides the industrial restructuring operation of 1989-92 described in section 5, and the various reforms to the agricultural parastatals described in section 4, efforts since 1988 at public enterprise reform have been directed mainly at the banking sector. Since 1992-3 there has been a more general public enterprise reform programme also.

Banking sector reform was at the heart of the second adjustment programme and has probably been the most successfully implemented element of any of the different programmes. The reform comprised an effort to open up the sector to private participation and to reconstitute the three main state banks (the Bank of Tanzania (BoT), which is the central bank, the National Bank of Commerce (NBC) and the Cooperative Rural Development Bank (CRDB)) on a viable basis.

As a result of legal changes allowing the establishment of new private banks and forex bureaux, two international banks have started operations in Tanzania and a third will do so in 1995. The international banks which have already started operations are the South African multinational Standard Chartered and Meridien BIAO, a multinational domiciled in Zambia. Both apparently concentrate on forex-related business. The US-owned Citibank and Eurafrican, a subsidiary of Banque belgolaise, will soon join them. Meridien BIAO almost collapsed internationally in February 1995 after becoming unable to meet the Zambian Central Bank's statutory reserve requirements (*Financial Times*, 28 February 1995) and its Tanzanian operation had to be taken over by the Bank of Tanzania shortly afterwards. According to the *Financial Times* (10 April 1995) the bank had lent excessively to a company owned by the Sardanis family, who were also the bank's main shareholders. No data appear to be available on numbers of forex bureaux, but there are visibly large numbers of them in the main towns and their

---

[44] Ericsson and the World Bank give ratios several times larger than this, but these are based on considering loss-making enterprises alone.

officially recorded transactions increased from purchases and sales with a combined value of US$11.8 m./month in May 1992 to US$106.8 m./month in December 1993. According to local critics of adjustment, despite this high overall turnover level many bureaux systematically underdeclare their real level of transactions and are vehicles for continuing capital flight.[45]

Reforms to the BoT, NBC and CRDB have, as already indicated, mainly taken the form of ridding them of the non-performing debts and overdrafts of parastatals (including marketing boards) and cooperatives. During 1992 and 1993 Tsh 24 bn on non-performing loans were transferred from them to a Loans and Advances Realization Trust (LART), which is charged with trying to recoup as much of the debt as possible. A further Tsh 205 bn in overdrafts has been formally replaced by 20-year Treasury bonds at 11 percent and Tsh 8 bn has been injected for recapitalization. The costs of servicing the bonds to the Tanzanian Government was Tsh 13 bn in 1993, while the budget reservation for 1994-5 is Tsh 12 bn (Ericsson, 1993).

According to the IMF, even while this operation was under way, NBC and CRDB continued to make credit available to cooperatives with poor repayment records. There was also a continuation of the expansion of credit to the private sector which began to take off around 1989 (NBC lending to the private sector rose from Tsh 8.103 m. in 1988 to Tsh 24,243 m. in 1990 and Tsh 46,201 m. in 1992 (*ibid.*). In March 1995 Augustine Mrema, now in opposition, claimed that 51 private businessmen accounted for Tsh 90 bn of debt to the CRDB alone (*Business Times*, 24 March 1995)). In any event, CRDB credit was frozen completely in August 1993 and NBC credit was frozen with effect from January 1994. These freezes were still apparently in force at the end of 1994. If enforced, these drastic measures will obviously have major repercussions throughout the economy.

The current objective of the banking reforms is to turn over NBC and CRDB to the private sector. The Boards of both organizations have been restructured and attempts made to call in non-performing loans from former directors and employees. A first instalment of retrenchments has occurred at NBC and at the end of 1994 a partial flotation of CRDB, aimed at small local shareholders, occurred. Apparently DANIDA will also take a major equity stake in CRDB. The BoT has also experienced considerable retrenchments and is said to be being restructured into a 'monetary management and banking supervision role'.

The likely outcome of this development is that, unless it is split up, NBC will become a private monopoly in urban Tanzania with some indirect competition from CRDB in rural areas. Both are likely to contract very sharply because there are so few viable large-scale customers to do business with. The foreign banks which have started business seem unlikely to become involved in mainstream commercial banking. The main result will therefore probably be the bankrupting of most of NBC and CRBD's unviable account holders.

After a number of years of pressure, the Tanzania Government eventually agreed to undertake a comprehensive programme of public enterprise reform in 1992-93. As elsewhere this is supposed to comprise re-allocation of non-commercial parastatals to government departments, commercialization of utilities and the closure or divestment (whole or partial) of all other commercial parastatals, by 1997.

A Parastatal Sector Reform Commission (PSRC) was set up in 1992 under the

---

[45] The method used is to provide informal Tsh premia to customers selling dollars but not requiring receipts.

chairmanship of George Mbowe with a brief to work out a timetable and modalities for this programme, which is supported by a specific World Bank Parastatal and Public Sector Reform Credit.[46] Two timetables have subsequently been published. At the end of 1994 the PSRC stated that 30 parastatals had been sold or leased, 22 had been closed or were under receivership (with LART acting as the receiver) and a further 117 were at 'various stages of preparation for privatization'. However, this figure appears to include a few liquidations and privatizcations occurring prior to 1992 and it is unclear how many have occurred as a result of the efforts of the Commission.

Information has appeared in the press concerning only about a dozen of the sales. The PSRC has supplied information to donors on about 9 others, all except one sisal estates. The different sources suggest a number of trends. Firstly, interest by large transnational companies - despite being courted - is quite limited. Acquisitions in this category are restricted to the purchase by Indol (South African Breweries) of 50 percent of Tanzania Breweries and three subsidiaries, South African Airways' effective purchase of Air Tanzania (and Air Uganda) to form a new regional airline, Alliance,[47] and Asea Brown Boveri's purchase of a majority stake in the electrical engineers TANALEC. BAT is being courted hard to acquire the Tanzania Cigarette Corporation, and this may soon be added to the list. The Commonwealth Development Corporation is purchasing Sao Hill Saw Mill, but while a transnational the latter is a public sector rather than private one and hence this arrangement does not even count as a privatization.

Secondly, most if not all of the remaining private purchasers are of east African Asian origin (Chandaria Group, Nas Hauliers, Rostrom Aziz, Gulled & Co., etc.). Thirdly, deals have tended to be surrounded by controversies about the methods of handling bids, the relation of the agreed price to known valuations and the post-purchase behaviour of the purchaser. Complaints respectively focus on 'sweetheart' deals and on asset stripping/substitution of distribution for production functions.

There are good reasons for thinking that the remainder of the programme's stated objectives will not be fulfilled. The main reason for this is that it has apparently been agreed that individual parastatals will in the first instance be responsible for assessing their own prospects of viability, financial needs for privatization and other requirements. This is likely to slow down the process indefinitely. Secondly, even if parastatals assess themselves as ripe for divestment and preparations are made to this effect, most are unlikely to find buyers or partners, given their generally run-down plant and low net value. Meanwhile it is also important to note that the institutions which hitherto had responsibility for regulating the parastatals, SCOPO and the holding companies, have technically been abolished (although many of the holding companies, notably the National Development Corporation actually continue to exist and in some cases have taken over the viability assessments mentioned above). Except in the case of the utilities for which performance contracts have been agreed - and there is considerable doubt about the likely effectiveness of these too[48] - there is no working system of super-

---

[46] The credit involves hiring six expatriates on contracts of between 3 and 5 years at salaries (presumably tax-free) of US$180-240,000/year. Some will receive over US$1 m. in remuneration in the process.

[47] It might be argued that Air Tanzania had already all but disappeared prior to this development, since it owned only one plane (and rented another). Nevertheless it had a staff of 700 plus including no fewer than 50 pilots.

[48] Effective performance contracts presuppose, amongst other things, long-run underlying enterprise viability

vision. The most probable consequence, as Mans (1994) has pointed out, is that since the now effectively autonomous parastatal managers have no clear future role, they will engage in (or step up) informalized asset-stripping.

10. Environmental Issues

Land shortage, soil fertility and soil erosion. During the past fifty years, under the stimulus of population increase, many or most of Tanzania's rural households have intensified their cultivation enormously. At the end of the last century, most cultivators based their techniques on long fallow shifting cultivation, though there were areas where permanent cultivation and irrigation were already practised. Since then fallow lengths have invariably been sharply reduced, where they have not disappeared entirely. Similar pressures have forced people to move out of the most climatically favoured areas into areas of low and variable rainfall, where their previous cultivation methods may not be adequate and where they may come into conflict with herders who graze the drier areas on a seasonal or rotational basis. In other cases, population and other pressures push people into cultivating on increasingly steep slopes.

Such processes are under way in many parts of Tanzania. As is almost always the case, it takes people time to adjust their cultivation methods to changed circumstances, and this has produced soil deterioration and erosion in a number of areas. This does not relate closely to structural adjustment in either direction. There are those who claim that ending fertilizer subsidies will lead to accelerated soil fertility decline. But since fertilizer has all too often (and especially under heavy subsidy) been used as a substitute for more intensive cultivation and conservation methods, rather than as a complement to them, this is not necessarily true. On the other hand, it may push people into cultivating more steeply sloping and erodible areas. Others see the ending of fertilizer subsidies as environmentally positive, by reducing the pollution of groundwater by nitrates, though this is hardly a serious problem in most of Tanzania given low levels of fertilizer use. The point is that one cannot generalize without taking into account local factors - which will usually turn out to be more important than adjustment.

Deforestation and catchment problems. By no means all erosion either occurs on farms, or has its effect confined there. Given current problems with the hydro-electricity supply, these are of some relevance at present. Other things being equal, reduction of vegetation cover in a river catchment alters the river-flow regime (increasing it during and just after the rains, reducing it later in the year) so putting at risk the electricity at the end of the dry season, especially after a few dry years, as at present, when the reservoirs do not recharge fully. Deforestation is generally seen as one of the main causes of accelerated catchment erosion, though, under certain circumstances, grass cover has been shown to be a better catchment protection than trees, and though there is wide disagreement over whether tree-clearing in the catchments is a significant cause of Tanzania's current hydro-electricity shortage problems.

---

and the respective capacities of the regulator to regulate efficiently and of the management to restructure effectively. It is unclear whether any of these conditions are present.

Reasons for cutting trees or clearing forest include the following:
- Logging is extensively practised, though mostly informally. Most of Tanzania's hardwood stand has already gone. The demand for softwood building timber is increasing, but so is woodlot production.
- Charcoal is a major urban fuel and so demand continues to grow. It can destroy large areas of forest, but the effects vary enormously according to conditions of production.
- Firewood is by far the most important rural fuel. Villagization, by concentrating people, has concentrated the effects of their fuelwood gathering around them, both leaving ever larger areas denuded and involving extra labour and travelling time for the women who cut firewood. Here the development of woodlots is complicated by the fact that most customary tenure systems makes trees male property.
- Clearing for cultivation is a major reason for deforestation, and is cause for particular concern when it occurs on steep slopes and/or in important river catchments. In some cases charcoal burning is wrongly blamed for deforestation, since it merely uses wood which would have been felled for clearing in any case.
- Crop processing - two of the worst crops for deforestation are tea and tobacco, since both use large amounts of timber as fuel in processing the crops. In both Iringa and Tabora, tobacco farmers have denuded much of the land around their farms. In late 1994, and despite assurances to the contrary, the Tanzania Tea Authority was still clearing some of the last rain-forest in highland Iringa, both for plantation establishment and for fuelwood.
- Burning - cultivators, herders, hunters, poachers and miners all have occasion to burn the vegetation off the land, each different type of burn having different effects on the subsequent vegetation. There is much talk of stopping this through bye-laws. But most bye-laws have been on the books for decades now without the slightest effect. When cultivators have no more than hand-tools, it is inevitable that fire will be used to clear new land.

In most cases, the relation of this to structural adjustment is not very clear. In some it is more so. Devaluation increases the cost of imported fossil fuels and so would tend to increase use of firewood or charcoal. Various encouragements to informal exports seem likely to have increased the extent of hardwood logging, which is among the more successful 'non-traditional exports'. In general, the increasing pressure to earn foreign exchange may increase the difficulties in enforcing rules which may limit that goal - though there was not much evidence of effective enforcement before. In any case, current thinking is that plain enforcement achieves little more than to alienate local people, and that efforts to increase their material interest in (say) forest or game reserves are more likely to be effective.

Erosive and non-erosive crops. One argument recently put forward is that adjustment by increasing the returns to 'tradables' (in this context export crops) could lead to a positive shift away from erosive crops, like maize and cotton, towards non-erosive crops like coffee and tea. Apart from the fact that cotton is as much an export crop as coffee, this argument seems to have little to recommend it. Not only is the relation between 'tradable' and non-erosive purely fortuitous, the different groups of crops in question are not feasible substitutes. Most maize, for example, is grown at altitudes and in climates where neither tea nor coffee would survive. In any case, it makes little sense to recommend a general shift away from Africa's most important food crop. It makes far more sense to consider erosive and non-erosive ways of growing crops than crops themselves.

Chemical use. Another issue concerns the negative effects of excessive fertilizer or chemical use, in terms of pollution of soil or water, or of direct poisoning. A variety of studies purport to show that structural adjustment either does or does not favour 'dirty' (chemical-using) crops at the expense of others. Most such studies can point in either direction, according to the prices chosen (or prevailing). It seems highly likely that reduction or elimination of fertilizer subsidies will lead to its lower and more careful use. Whatever the effect of structural adjustment, the problems are more serious for the really poisonous chemicals, like insecticides and herbicides. Few peasant farmers know about the rules for their use and avoidance. Fewer take any notice of them. Pointing out that people's children will suffer from pesticide poisoning twenty years ahead seems to have limited impact, besides which, the instructions are usually in a foreign language and not all farmers are functionally literate anyway.

There is little sign that the authorities are any better informed or more concerned. One of the definite health gains from SA-induced austerity is that most Districts have had to close down their cattle-dipping services. This may (or may not) reduce cattle health but also reduces the amount of deadly poisonous acaricide which seeps into the groundwater or local rivers (many dips are sited far too near running water for safety).

Pollution from industry and mining. Mining is among the most polluting activities, and especially gold-mining as currently carried on in Tanzania. This involves the use of mercury as a catalyst with which gold grains are precipitated from a watery sludge. There are two different ways in which this mercury pollutes its surroundings and puts human beings in danger. The atmosphere of informal mining ventures is not such as to increase concern or care about such factors.

Tanzania's own industrial sector is so small and declining that pollution problems might be assumed to be negligible. That would be too optimistic, for controls are so minimal that industrial production near to human habitation may easily lead to dangers.

To date, there is no evidence of Tanzania importing and 'disposing of' other countries' poisonous or radio-active wastes. But given the country's poverty and foreign dependence, its lack of other foreign-exchange earning opportunities and the general insensitivity of political leaders to such problems, it would seem not unlikely for the future.

Water pollution. Another problem is the pollution of drinking water supplies in Dar es Salaam and a number of other cities. For Dar es Salaam, the city's population has expanded far beyond what the water supply was designed for, so that water passes through the treatment plant too quickly for pollutants to precipitate out. More importantly, low pressure in the pipes (and no water in them at all for much of the time) means that groundwater seeps into the very old pipes. Since much of the groundwater around Dar es Salaam is polluted by leaking septic tanks and other sources of faecal matter, drinking unboiled tapwater is 'a recipe for chronic diarrhoea'. Here the relation to reduced government spending is more direct.

11. Conclusions

There is no doubt that Tanzania's pre-adjustment economy was much constrained and distorted by the effects of a dogmatic state orientation, and that de-confinement of trade was very necessary to unlock resources and skills. In our opinion, the course of adjustment has been marred by a similarly dogmatic attachment to the market and a current stance which can be summarized in the words 'privatize it'. This, together with weaknesses of the current Tanzanian leadership, has led to a situation in which any direction to policy is largely notable for its absence, and in which the major beneficiary seems to be 'wild capital', more concerned with working the donor-driven incentive system in speculation and smuggling than in more mundane and less profitable productive activities.

Overall production (GDP) has grown faster since 1986 than in the preceding years, but once allowance has been made for better weather, high investment rates and import decompression it does not appear particularly impressive. Adding informal production and exports should not increase growth rates, since, if anything, the proportion of such activities should have fallen as adjustment brought activities back into the official economy. It probably has not, but there is no reason to suppose it to have increased.

Other macroeconomic indicators are rather less favourable. The real exchange rate is now 'market-determined' *with* large amounts of donor grant funds, but the system would rapidly collapse without them and most of the effects supposed to follow it have not. The gap between imports and exports has not narrowed, and in consequence, despite large flows of donor aid, the level of indebtedness has continued to increase to quite unsustainable levels. Current levels of debt-service, though quite high, are less than half what they would be without rescheduling, underlining Tanzania's heavy dependence on donors.

While devaluation has had some effects on agricultural exports, these have been limited by structural factors and poor sequencing of adjustment. For industry the impact of lowered protection (but most of all the arbitrary system of exemptions for which adjustment cannot be blamed) seems to have reduced rather than increased competitiveness. A system of lower but coherent tariffs without exemptions would arguably provide better protection and more revenue than the present system, but rapid change cannot be expected under present circumstances.

Similarly, while there was some success in the first few years after 1986 in reducing the public spending gap, this turned out to be less sustainable and more vulnerable than envisaged. Inflation in the current year seems likely to be up to the levels of the early 1980s. Nor is there much evidence that the imposition of hard budget constraints on parastatal corporations has released funds for private investment. This is put out of the question currently by the IFI-imposed loan stop. But even when this finishes, it seems unlikely that many of those in Tanzania who need credit will qualify for it.

Agriculture is where most of the increase in growth since adjustment has taken place, though not in the main export crops which were prioritized. On the one hand, there can be no doubting the benefits of de-confinement in improving access to basic consumer necessities or its positive effects on output levels in the short run. There does remain some doubt whether the uncoordinated sequencing of donor projects and CIS with adjustment conditionality, devaluation and interest-rate increases may not have aggravated the problems and magnified the deficits of parastatals and cooperatives. There are also questions about whether the newly privatized marketing channels will continue to supply inputs to peasant farmers, especially those in the less easily accessible areas. Credit for such purposes seems likely to be a thing of the past, with CRDB confining itself to commercial loans to the small minority of farmers with formal leasehold title (and even then, according to UNCTAD, only those with permanent structures built on their land).

This points to a contradiction between market orientation and many of the basic premises underlying standard agricultural modernization policy. It makes particularly dubious the World Bank's pushing of its T&V extension model, which is both expensive and stuck within the former paradigm. Sustainable agriculture with high (devaluation-increased) input prices, requires considerable imagination and capacity to learn from peasants as well as teach them. With high input prices likely to persist, it is particularly important that efforts to develop peasant agriculture should focus on more effective input use rather than just more input use. This is likely to involve the integration of (for example) fertilizer use and local methods of soil maintenance like inter-cropping. It seems unlikely that T & V could contribute much to this.

Industry seems the sector most negatively affected by adjustment in the long run. Attempts under ERP to increase capacity utilization were not very successful - and some of what was achieved rested on reduced capacity rather than increased utilization. The long-term outlook for Tanzania's run-down parastatal industrial sector is far from bright. It is being sold off with all the haste the IFIs can achieve in the face of considerable, if muted, Tanzanian reluctance. Evidence to date is unclear, but actual and potential buyers seem as, or more, interested in stripping the assets or gaining the markets for imports, as in (re)developing production.

Parastatals are the villain of the piece for the IFIs, and few if any disagree about their inefficiency and corruption, though our understanding differs from that of the IFIs in several respects. Firstly, we see the situation as arising not from general tendencies to rent-seeking by the state and its employees, but from the particular history of the political process in Tanzania, and that of the institution in question. We do not therefore assume that all parastatals are equally bad (while agreeing that in present-day Tanzania all have serious problems), nor that the sole and single answer should always be privatization. We lay considerable stress on the interaction between the Tanzania Government and foreign donors in the prosecution of a series of policies which depended on and contributed to parastatal expansion - not to exculpate the Tanzania Government or political leadership but because it is striking how totally absent this is from IFI and other donor accounts and because this seems to contribute to serious misconceptions. Failure to understand how the system worked, together with lack of consistency between project aid seeking to expand operations and stabilization policies aiming to curb spending, led to sequencing errors which aggravated the problems and indebtedness. In particular, the effects of import support seem to have been highly ambiguous, being grants to Tanzania but loans to the companies involved, and this, with devaluation and interest-rate increases, clearly added to their deficits. But most importantly, there are signs that recent donor support to the private sector is producing some of the same effects previously noted within parastatals. This reflects the fact that simplified notions about separate public and private 'sectors' ignore the complex and shifting set of interfaces between public and private economic activities in Tanzania, and the position of economic power astride them.

Poverty. Most of the more critical writings on adjustment have focused on its effects in impoverishing the already vulnerable, and this would seem to be amply confirmed by the results of the recent and massive Cornell/ERB poverty survey, though this is not the interpretation from its authors. The optimistic view of this is that the survey should quiet the fears of those concerned about the effects of adjustment on poverty in Tanzania. According to these findings, the proportion of the total population below an arbitrarily drawn 'poverty-line' in Tanzania has fallen by 10-15 percent, from 65 percent to about 50 percent between 1983, the worst of the pre-adjustment years, and 1991. Yet as both of these studies make clear, this has been accompanied by a sharp increase in income differentiation, both between urban and rural areas and among households within each. One of them calculates that while the real incomes of the richer half of the population have increased by over three times, that of the bottom half fell by about 20 percent and of the bottom 40 percent by almost a third. When upwards of 10 million of the poorest people in Tanzania have seen their real incomes fall by nearly 30 percent since the worst years of the pre-adjustment period, the finding that 3 or 4 million people from the lower-middle part of the range have moved up out of 'poverty' over the same period will hardly be enough to quiet the critics. Moreover, the Cornell/ERB study, by restricting itself to looking at consumption, missed out on other aspects of poverty, like pressures on school-age children or the old to work and others to extend the working day to exhaustion point to get by.

Women. This sort of issue is particularly relevant to the impact of adjustment on women, but unfortunately there is relatively little information. Sample surveys of urban women agree on the increased participation of women in income-earning activities but disagree on the impact on incomes or explanations, one seeing expanding opportunities, the other 'distress sale' of already overburdened labour-power. Deterioration in social services could be said to hit women harder than men, but, as discussed below, it is unclear whether they have got worse under adjustment or just stayed bad. The costs have two dimensions, money payments and time spent. It is very difficult, in the absence of detailed information, to weigh up the costs and benefits of time spent looking for basic consumer goods or waiting for health services, and the money costs of these and other necessities.

Social services. Another area where critics have attacked adjustment is social service provision, which is widely seen as having deteriorated seriously under adjustment. Some of this criticism seems to rest on an overstatement of social benefits in the pre-adjustment period. A significant proportion of the state spending in rural areas which earned Tanzania so much praise in the 1970s, was spent on compulsorily villagizing the rural population, by means which including burning their houses down. The much-praised policy for Universal Primary Education probably did as much to reduce educational standards as falling expenditure under adjustment, and the earlier 'Education for Self-Reliance', with its accompanying shamba-work and marching/singing political songs, still more so. In the case of primary health care, the negative effects of previous policy may have been less direct, but the decline certainly pre-dated adjustment. It appears that if one takes local government spending into account, total government spending on social services did increase in real terms between 1986 and 1991. But this was certainly not sufficient to improve service levels.

Environment. Many of Tanzania's environmental problems arise out of long-term processes and are highly area-specific, making it hard to generalize about the impact of adjustment. The encouragement to non-traditional exports under adjustment makes yet harder the imposition of controls on the cutting of Tanzania's remaining hardwood forest, but control was largely ineffective before. The same is true of mining pollution. One negative effect of devaluation is to shift consumption patterns in favour of woodfuel - and especially in the processing of tobacco, which has already laid waste many thousand of hectares of *miombo* forest.

General. As a solution to the problems of Tanzania, adjustment has been and is being oversold. With all the supposed refinements added, the focus seems ever more single-mindedly on privatization - and support to a private sector apparently no less skilled in extracting rent from an 'enabling environment' than its predecessor or previous incarnation in the parastatal sector. In this complex and difficult situation, Tanzania deserves better than simplicities about the inevitable superiority of the private sector.

References

Adam, C. *et al.* 1994. *Evaluation of Swedish Development Co-operation with Tanzania.* A Report for the Secretariat for Analysis of Swedish Development Assistance. Göteborg and Oxford (mimeo).

Agrawal N., Z. Ahmed, M. Mered & R. Nord. 1993. *Structural Adjustment, Economic Performance and Aid Dependency in Tanzania.* Policy Research Working Papers. Washington, DC: World Bank

Arkadie, B. van., J. Komba & I. Karamagi. 1991. 'Trends and Cycles in Groww Domestic Product in Tanzania', *Tanzania Economic Trends*, Vol. 4., No. 2. Dar es Salaam, April.

Arkadie, B. van. 1994. *Economic Strategy and Structural Adjustment in Tanzania.* Washington, DC: World Bank, Governance and Successful Adjustment Conference, Private Sector Development Dept.

Bagachwa, M. 1992. 'Comments on the 1992/93 Government Budget'. *Tanzania Economic Trends*, Vol. 5, No. 1&2, Dar es Salaam.

Bagachwa, M. *et al.* 1993. *Small Scale Urban Enterprises in Tanzania: Results from a 1991 Survey.* Ithaca, NY: Cornell Food and Nutrition Policy Program Working Paper No. 44.

Bagachwa, M.D. *et al.* Forthcoming. *Study of the Effectiveness of Danish Aid* (Tables cited from preliminary version).

Bevan, D. *et al.* 1988. 'Incomes in the United Republic of Tanzania during the Nyerere Experiment', in W. van Ginnecken (ed.), *Trends in Employment and Labour Incomes.* Geneva: ILO.

Bhaduri, A. *et al.* 1993. *Evaluation of Macroeconomic Impacts of Import Support to Tanzania.* NORAD Report 4/93. Oslo: NORAD.

Bloom, G. *et al.* 1992. 'Public Expenditure in the Tanzanian Health Sector during Structural Adjustment. Report prepared for the EC'. Brighton: Institute of Development Studies (mimeo).

Bol, D. 1993. 'Non-traditional Exports in Tanzania: Trends and Prospects', *Tanzania Economic Trends*, Vol. 5, No. 3/4.

Booth, D. *et al.* 1993. *Social, Economic and Cultural Change in Contemporary Tanzania: A People-Oriented Focus.* Stockholm: SIDA.

Bruce, J.W. & S. Migot-Adholla (eds.). 1993. *Searching for Land Tenure Security in Africa.* Dubuque, Iowa: Kendall/Hunt for the World Bank.

Bryceson, D.F. 1993. *Liberalizing Tanzania's Food Trade.* London: James Currey.

Chachage, C. 1995. 'The Meek Shall Inherit the Earth but Not the Mining Rights: the Mining Industry and Accumulation in Tanzania', in C. Chachage, A. Kiondo & P. Gibbon, *Liberalised Development in Tanzania.* Uppsala: Scandinavian Institute of African Studies.

Collier, P. *et al.* 1986. *Labour and Poverty in Tanzania.* Oxford: Clarendon Press.

Cooksey, B. *et al.* 1993. *Parents' Attitudes towards Education in Rural Tanzania.* Dar es Salaam: TADREG Report No 5.

DANIDA. 1994. *Evaluation of Danida's Balance of Payments Support, Vol III, Case Studies of Uganda, Tanzania and Mozambique.* Copenhagen: Ministry of Foreign Affairs.

Doriye J., H. White & M. Wuyts. 1993. *Fungibility and Sustainability: Import Support to Tanzania.* Stockholm: SIDA Evaluation Report 1993/5.

Dutz, M. and C. Frischtak. 1993. 'The Entrepreneur as Agent of Industrial Change: Determinants of Successful Adjustment and Remaining Obstacles to Restructuring in Tanzania' (draft). Report prepared for the World Bank.

The East African. Various. Nairobi.

Economist Intelligence Unit (EIU). *Tanzanian Country Reports* (various).

Ericsson, G. 1993. *The Incidence and Pattern of the Soft Budget Constraint in Tanzania.* Stockholm: SIDA Macroeconomic Studies 44/93.

FAO. Annual. *Production Yearbooks.* Rome.

Ferreira, L. 1994. *Poverty and Inequality During Structural Adjustment in Rural Tanzania.* Washington, DC: World Bank Transitional Economics Department Research Paper Series No 8.

Havnevik, K.J. 1993. *Tanzania, the Limites to Development from Above.* Uppsala: Nordic Africa Institute.

Kiondo, A. 1995. 'When the State Withdraws. Local Development, Politics and Liberalisation in Tanzania', in C. Chachage, A. Kiondo & P. Gibbon, *Liberalised Development in Tanzania.* Uppsala: Scandinavian Institute of African Studies.

Kiondo, A. Forthcoming. *The Politics of Economic Liberalisation in Tanzania*. Uppsala: Scandinavian Institute of African Studies.

Lawson, A. 1994. *Underfunding in the Social Sectors in Tanzania: Origins and Possible Responses*. Dar es Salaam: TADREG Working Paper No. 2.

Loiske, V. 1994. 'Social Differentiation, Conflicts and Rural-Urban Interaction in the Babati area, Tanzania', in J. Baker (ed.), *Migration in Africa*. Uppsala: Scandinavian Institute of African Studies.

Lugalla, J. 1993. 'Structural Adjustment Policies and Education in Tanzania', in P. Gibbon (ed.), *Social Change and Economic Reform in Africa*. Uppsala: Scandinavian Institute of African Studies.

Maliyamkono, T. & M. Bagachwa. 1990. *The Second Economy in Tanzania*. London: James Currey.

Mamuya, I. 1991. *Structural Adjustment and Retrenchment in the Civil Service: The Case of Tanzania*. Geneva: ILO World Employment Programme Working Paper No. 50.

Mans, D. 1994. 'Tanzania: Resolute Action', in I. Husein & R. Faruqee (eds), *Adjustment in Africa: Lessons from Country Case Studies*. Washington, DC: World Bank.

Mbelle, A. 1994. 'Sustainable Industrial Development in Tanzania: Can it be Achieved?', in L. Msambichika *et al.* (eds), *Development Challenges and Strategies for Tanzania: An Agenda for the 21st Century*. Dar es Salaam: University of Dar es Salaam Press.

Munishi, S. 1995. 'The Social Sector in Tanzania', in Therkildsen & Semboja.

Nanyaro, J. 1994. 'The Mining Industry of Tanzania: Current Status and Strategies for its Sustainable Development into the 21st Century', in L. Msambichika *et al.* (eds), *Development Challenges and Strategies for Tanzania: An Agenda for the 21st Century*. Dar es Salaam: University of Dar es Salaam Press.

Netherlands Development Co-operation/IOV. 1994. *Evaluation of the Netherlands Development Programme with Tanzania 1970-92*. The Hague: Ministry of Foreign Affairs.

OECD. Annual. *Geographical Distribution of Financial Flows*. Paris.

Rattsø, J. 1992. 'Structural Adjustment in Tanzania' (mimeo).

Sarris, A. & R. van der Brink. 1993. *Economic Policy and Household Welfare during Crisis and Adjustment in Tanzania*. New York & London: New York University Press.

Sarris, A. & P. Tinios. 1994. 'Consumption and Poverty in Tanzania in 1976 and 1991: A Comparison Using Survey Data'. Ithaca, NY: Cornell University Food and Nutrition Policy Program (mimeo).

Semboja, J. and O. Therkildsen. 1995. 'Introduction'. in Therkildsen & Semboja.

Skarstein, R. 1986. 'Growth and Crisis in the Manufacturing Sector', in J. Boesen *et al.* (eds), *Tanzania: Crisis and Struggle for Survival*. Uppsala: Scandinavian Institute of African Studies.

Svantesson, B. 1994. 'Donor and Government Financing of Primary Education in Tanzania'. Copenhagen: DANIDA (mimeo).

Svendsen, K. 1986. 'The Creation of Macroeconomic Imbalances and a Structural Crisis'. in J.B. Boesen *et al.* (eds) *Tanzania, Crisis and Struggle for Survival*. Uppsala: SIAS.

Tanzania Economic Trends (TET). Economic Research Bureau periodical. University of Dar es Salaam.

Therkildsen, O. & J. Semboja (eds). 1995. *Service Provision under Stress; States & Voluntary Organizations in Kenya, Tanzania and Uganda*. London: James Currey.

Tinios, P. *et al.* 1993. 'Households, Consumption and Poverty in Tanzania: Results from a 1991 Household Survey'. Ithaca, NY: Cornell University Food and Nutrition Policy Program (mimeo).

Uhuru (various). Dar es Salaam.

UNCTAD 1994. *Case Study on the National Experience of the United Republic of Tanzania in Horizontal and Vertical Diversification, Including Possibilities for Crop Substitution*. GE.94-5482. Geneva: UNCTAD.

United Republic of Tanzania (URT). 1967. *Background to the Budget; An Economic Survey, 1967-68*. Dar es Salaam: Government Printer.

United Republic of Tanzania (URT). n.d. *Analysis of the Accounts of Parastatal Enterprises, 1983-92*. Dar es Salaam: Government Printer.

United Republic of Tanzania (URT). 1993. *Labour Force Survey 1990-91*. Dar es Salaam: Government Printer.

United Republic of Tanzania (URT). 1994a. 'Social Sector Strategy'. Paper for the Consultative Group Meeting.

United Republic of Tanzania (URT). 1994b. *Report of the Presidential Commission of Inquiry into Land Matters*. Dar es Salaam: Government Printer.

United Republic of Tanzania. 1994c. 'Implementation Status and Progress Report'. Paper for the Consultative Group Meeting for Tanzania, Nov. 1994, Dar es Salaam (mimeo).

United Republic of Tanzania. 1994d. *Hali ya Uchumi wa Taifa katika Mwaka 1993 (Budget Survey 1993)*. Dar es Salaam: Government Printer.

United Republic of Tanzania, Bureau of Statistics. 1994a. *National Accounts of Tanzania 1976-93*. Dar es Salaam: Government Printer, August.

United Republic of Tanzania, Bureau of Statistics. 1994b. 'Household Budget Survey 1991-92, unclassified tables on household consumption' (mimeo).

United Republic of Tanzania, Bureau of Statistics. 1994c. *Selected Statistical Series, 1951-91*. Dar es Salaam: Government Printer.

Wagao, J. 1990. *Adjustment Policies in Tanzania, 1981-89: The Impact on Growth, Structure and Human Welfare*. Florence: Innocenti Occasional Papers, UNICEF.

Wangwe, S.M. 1989. 'Structural Adjustment in Tanzania: Some Recent Experiences'. Copenhagen (mimeo).

World Bank (annual). *World Debt Tables*. Washington, DC: World Bank.

World Bank. 1991. *Tanzania Economic Report - Towards Sustainable Development in the 1990s*. Washington, DC: World Bank.

World Bank. 1992. *Strategy for African Mining*. Washington, DC: Africa Technical Department Series, Technical Paper No. 181, World Bank.

World Bank. 1994a. *Tanzania Role of Government - Public Expenditure Review*. Washington, DC: World Bank.

World Bank. 1994b. *Tanzania - Agricultural Sector Memorandum,* July 1994. Washington, DC: World Bank, July.

Wort, M. 1994. 'Situational Analysis (Tanzanian Education)', draft (mimeo).

Uganda
1987-94

E.A. Brett

London School of Economics

1. Structural Adjustment, Efficiency and Equity in Uganda

Structural adjustment in Africa has given a coalition of donors led by the World Bank and IMF (the IFIs) a decisive say in the decision-making process and produced fundamental changes in economic policy. This is a highly conflictual process, in which the IFIs use the technical prescriptions of neo-classical theory to override solutions emerging out of the domestic ideological and political debate. The resulting programmes have been criticized for reducing services to the poor, undermining the authority of governments by insisting on market solutions, and reinforcing external dependence and the power of the foreign and local capitalist classes.[1]

Economic performance under these conditions has improved only marginally in some countries, while political and economic crises have intensified dramatically in many others, thus discrediting not only the efforts of the IFIs, but also the role of external donors and of aid in general. Donors are now attempting to respond to some of these criticisms by shifting their focus from macroeconomic stabilization to institutional reform, and increasing their emphasis on poverty alleviation.[2] However, the outcome of these changes has yet to make itself felt in practice, or to modify the generally negative view of structural adjustment which now dominates the policy debate.

This study of structural adjustment will take account of these criticisms, but it will also subject them to close examination. Large and powerful agencies make tempting targets, especially where they are involved in what is an inherently unequal relationship with poor and vulnerable countries. However, adjustment only occurs after major policy errors have been made, local resources have dried up and reductions in consumption have become unavoidable. Reform then usually involves losses for significant social groups which can be blamed on the IFIs, although they would generally have been even greater without the financial support which the latter provide. Reforms threaten the privileges of articulate members of the elite who are in fact responsible for political and economic failures, but can use anti-colonial rhetoric to discredit necessary changes. Further, critics who attribute economic failure to neo-liberal programmes often do so without establishing how effectively they have actually been put into operation. In reality, governments are often able to delay or avoid implementation, so poor performance may actually be the outcome of the failure to act on their policies rather than to the policies themselves.

Thus a fair evaluation of the structural adjustment experience requires a review of current practice and theory which distinguishes between criticisms which stem from the special pleading of groups whose privileges are' threatened by necessary economic reforms, and those which stem from a realistic assessment of weaknesses in the programmes themselves. This must also distinguish between failures which stem from weaknesses in adjustment theory, and those which stem from an inability to persuade governments to take the tough decisions involved in implementing unpopular policies.

---

[1] See, for example, Mamdani (1994).

[2] The UNDP has initiated what is perhaps the most radical review of development strategy in its *Human Development Reports*, but this will not be examined here since its influence on state policy and project implementation in Uganda has not been significant.

This study is an attempt to provide a balanced view of the reform process by reviewing the structural adjustment process in Uganda whose recent experience makes it an extremely important case for those concerned to assess the costs and benefits of structural adjustment, since it is one of the most successful programmes in Africa. Uganda was regarded as a 'basket case' in the 1970s and early 1980s, when it was dominated by political violence, mismanagement and economic decline. Structural adjustment programmes operated between 1982 and 1984, and from 1987 until the present. While the first experiment was undermined by civil war in 1983-84, the second has, after several false starts, produced much more successful results.

This study will attempt to review this experience, by looking at the factors which led to the political and economic collapse in the 1970s and early 1980s, at the nature of the adjustment programmes and the processes involved in their implementation, and at their achievements and failures in terms of growth and equity. It will do so by looking at two aspects of the reform process - the problems associated with macro-economic stabilization (exchange rates, budgetary management, interest rates, etc.), which dominated the early phases of the recovery process; and the deeper-seated issues associated with the restoration of productive capacity and services. It will suggest that considerable success in the first area has been accompanied by relative failure in the second, not least because of problems associated with the orientation and structure of the external agencies themselves.

The review is heavily based on documentation from the IFIs, and relies, to some extent, on official economic data which are, given the nature of the administrative and economic system in Uganda, inherently unreliable.[3] More generally it is based on personal research and consultancy work carried out in Uganda over more than thirty years.[4]

2.   The Development Problem in Uganda

Structural adjustment in Uganda is an attempt to repair the damage inflicted by fifteen years of conflict and mismanagement. Relative prosperity and good public services in 1966 had been devastated by 1986 when the National Resistance Movement (NRM) took over. The post-colonial regime had inherited a centralized and monopolistic administrative and economic system and used it to destroy democratic accountability, and turn the state into an instrument of predatoriness.

The Uganda People's Congress (UPC) government led by Milton Obote which took power in 1962 was unable to contain regional and ethnic conflicts, and, threatened by

---

[3] The official statistical services collapsed soon after the 1971 coup, and have only recently been reconstructed. Further, a substantial proportion of the economic system has operated in the 'black market' during the same period, surviving by evading official controls over borders, foreign exchange and taxation, so official figures certainly greatly underestimate the scale of real transactions. This suggests that real output and transactions are certainly higher than the official figures show, though it may also imply that growth rates may have been exaggerated by recent improvements in statistical services and reductions in economic controls. While this may have influenced the optimistic tone of the interpretation presented here, it seems likely that the general tendency towards under-reporting in the system means that actual economic performance is stronger rather than weaker than the official figures suggest.

[4] For my sources and a general review of the first six years of NRM rule see Brett (1993).

a loss of its majority, suspended the democratic process in 1966 and used the army to eliminate opponents and destroy the autonomy of traditional rulers and democratically elected local governments. In 1971 it was removed by a military coup led by General Idi Amin whose reign of terror and economic mismanagement reduced the country to ruin. Amin was defeated in 1979 by the Tanzanian Army assisted by Ugandan irregulars, and replaced by an interim Uganda National Liberation Front government. Obote and the UPC returned to power in 1981 after an election whose results were widely disputed. The Obote II regime was soon challenged in the south by the National Resistance Army, a rebel movement led by Yoeri Museveni, and by smaller groups in the north-west. These wars destroyed lives and economic resources, disrupting the first structural adjustment programme introduced in 1982. The NRA victory in January 1986 enabled the National Resistance Movement under President Museveni to take power, but his position was soon challenged by rebel groups in the north and north-east. As a result civil war continued in about 25 percent of the country until 1991, leading to further military spending and economic devastation.[5]

The costs of political conflict were compounded by mismanagement and predatoriness encouraged by monopoly controls and administered prices. The economic system in 1962 was highly regulated and racially segregated. The marketing of major export crops was concentrated in monopolistic marketing boards; the state-owned Uganda Development Corporation (UDC) controlled heavy industry; and access to the formal sector was closely regulated through licensing. The private Asian Madhvani and Mehta Corporations controlled sugar production and invested heavily in industry, usually in close association with the state. Most formal sector businesses were owned by Asian or British expatriates, and Africans were only active outside agriculture in processing and marketing cooperatives which also depended on state monopolies and were directly supervised by government.

The new government extended these controls, using them to promote Africans into positions of economic authority in the public sector and to advantage them in the private sector by limiting the rights of Asian entrepreneurs. The World Bank did not object, accepting then fashionable arguments for central planning and Import Substituting Industrialization (ISI). Bilateral donors did so too, in part since they allowed them to justify aid programmes in agriculture and industry which enabled them to subsidize capital-intensive exports from their own firms. A Central Bank was set up which controlled the allocation and price of foreign exchange, and high tariffs and quotas were used to protect local industries. In 1968 most of the major foreign banks and large companies were nationalized or partially nationalized, giving even more power to an increasingly unaccountable state elite. African capitalists were given privileged access to credit, markets and land. The school system which had been controlled by missions was taken over by the state. From 1963 to 1971 GDP grew by 5.8 percent annually because administrative competence survived, world prices were high and there was strong donor support.

The rigidities, distortions and potential for abuse built into this state-led economic system would probably have produced serious economic problems as the international economic situation worsened in the 1970s even without the advent of Amin. Once he came to power, however, they maximized opportunities for irrationality and abuse. Amin replaced key personnel with his own cronies and, in August 1972, expropriated

---

[5] I have reviewed the role of the military in Uganda in Brett (1993).

most of the assets of the dominant Asian business class. Other foreign investors then withdrew, and their assets were also taken over by the state. The largest companies were added to the state's portfolio; many thousands of small businesses and residences were vested in the Departed Asians' Property Custodian Board (DAPCB) and allocated to African tenants. This loss of foreign business and professional skills was immediately followed by the loss of all international credit facilities and capital flows. Foreign exchange and essential goods disappeared, and an era of hyper-inflation and predatory government followed.

State control now dominated the formal sector, with administered prices and direct allocations of essential commodities, but this simply allowed for corrupt transfers to favoured members of the political elite. Military spending and political repression escalated, and the best educated members of the indigenous elite were murdered or fled. Accounting and management systems in the civil service collapsed, the DAPCB, parastatals, marketing boards and cooperatives became instruments of plunder, the grossly overvalued exchange rate suppressed official exports and transferred resources to the parasitic political class and their cronies, tax collection collapsed and the state funded itself by printing money.

Between 1972 and 1981 the price to cotton growers fell almost six-fold and the coffee price four-fold; cotton exports fell from 86,400 tonnes in 1970 to 1,200 tonnes in 1981, coffee exports from 237,000 in 1973 to 123,000 in 1981.[6] Farmers switched from export into food crops sold on domestic or regional markets, while large quantities of coffee were smuggled into neighbouring countries. Most commercial transactions moved into the black or *magendo* economy which by-passed the state's regulative, tax, and foreign-exchange controls, thus criminalizing virtually the whole private enterprise system.[7] This undermined state control by denying the government foreign exchange and revenue so that it could not pay officials a living wage or maintain regulatory structures. Corruption was institutionalized, producing a de facto privatization of most public services, while roads, public utilities, hospitals, schools and public buildings all fell into disrepair. Officially recorded per capita GNP fell by 6.2 percent annually between 1973 and 1980[8] while registered per capita GDP fell by 27.2 percent between 1978 and 1980.[9]

3.   Macroeconomic Policy and Performance

3.1   The First Phase: 1981-84

The Obote II regime soon established an agreement with the Bank and IMF which guaranteed renewed financial support in exchange for the usual package of policy requirements. These included exchange- and interest-rate realignment, higher producer

---

[6] Uganda Government (1987: 18).

[7] Green (1981).

[8] Lateef (1991).

[9] These figures almost certainly overstate the real changes for the reasons set out in fn. 3, although the trend was certainly sharply downward.

prices, reduced price controls, rationalization of the distribution and import licensing system, improved fiscal controls, and the return of expropriated properties.[10] These, together with external assistance which 'exceeded US$1 bn',[11] immediately produced a significant improvement in performance - registered GDP grew by 5.5 percent between 1981 and 1984, and by June 1984 inflation had fallen to about 20 percent and the current account was in surplus.[12]

This stabilization attempt was a success given the circumstances, but progress was halted by the crisis induced by the intensification of the war in the second half of 1984. This diverted resources to the military and undermined fiscal discipline. The government increased spending by printing money and failed to reach a new agreement with the IMF.[13] The exchange rate depreciated sharply and inflation increased to 169 percent by 1986. These problems were compounded by increasing corruption and mis-appropriation in the state apparatus, and yet another campaign of political terror and repression. This reversed earlier gains so that most people remembered the 1981 programme as 'a failure' and virtually nobody 'believed that the new structural adjustment programme would work'.[14] This scepticism about the efficacy of the conventional policy package was compounded by the fact that the key leaders of the NRM all strongly supported state-led economic policies and were deeply suspicious of the IMF.[15]

3.2   Adjustment under the NRM[16]

Given this history and the difficulties encountered by other left-wing regimes like the Sandanistas in Nicaragua, Uganda's prospects looked bleak in 1986. The new regime and its external advisers confronted an economic system in ruins, a demoralized and dishonest civil service, intense ethnic conflict which would soon erupt into civil war, and an untried political leadership wedded to statist policies which had failed in the past and which precluded immediate agreement with the donor community.

The policy process in Uganda has gone through three phases since 1986. The regime attempted to 'go it alone' from 1986 to early 1987, but was then forced to accept an orthodox stabilization programme in May 1987 which was contested by many key figures in the NRM, and only partially implemented until 1992. Key figures in the

---

[10] Ochieng (1991: 44); Edmonds (1988).

[11] This is a World Bank (1988: 1) estimate. It included USD 370 million of high interest loans from the IMF, leaving the balance of payments 'weak and vulnerable' in part because of 'a debt service burden in excess of 50 per cent of export earnings'.

[12] Edmonds (1988: 108).

[13] *Ibid.*

[14] Harvey and Robinson (1994: 4).

[15] Joshua Mugenyi, Secretary of the Bank of Uganda, documents the hostility of the NRM to the IMF in 1986 (Mugenyi, 1991: 64-68).

[16] Brett (1994) is an earlier review written without access to additional official documentation provided by the Centre for Development Research.

regime then fully accepted the new programme, which was actively implemented thereafter. By 1995 many of the problems associated with stabilization and rehabilitation had been solved, though many others, relating to the need to increase productivity, exports and social services and reduce poverty had not. A review of these processes suggests that many critics of adjustment significantly understate its importance in creating the preconditions for economic and political stability, and also the capacity of governments to resist necessary but uncomfortable changes.

3.2.1   Resistance and Economic Failure, 1986-87

In 1986 the NRM, deeply suspicious of markets and a private sector which it saw as little more than a criminal conspiracy, reverted to statist policies involving administered prices and monopoly controls. It fixed the exchange rate at less than a quarter of the parallel market rate and coffee prices at 60 percent below the 1983-84 level; it gave the Produce Marketing Board a monopoly over the export of five key foodstuffs; and attempted to set maximum prices for essential commodities (sugar, salt, soap and beer), which were allocated locally through newly established village Resistance Councils. It allowed credit to government to expand at a yearly rate of 156 percent, and failed to secure increased aid inflows.[17]

The results were disastrous. Inflation measured 147 percent between July and December 1986 and the real effective exchange rate increased by 128 percent during the period.[18] There was also a decline in real GDP of 2 percent 'with major losses in the manufacturing sector, but also with a marked decline in agriculture'.[19] These failures forced the regime to negotiate at the end of 1986. The Ugandans were reluctantly persuaded to accept an orthodox package, because the new government was neither financially nor technically able to resist the demands being made by its advisers and backers.[20] However, this meant that the programme would now have to be introduced against the opposition of many key decision-makers, including the President, Prime Minister and Minister of Finance.

3.2.2   The Economic Recovery Programme: Objectives and Financing

In May 1987 a new Economic Recovery Program (ERP) was launched which offered a considerable increase in financial support in exchange for an orthodox policy package designed to deal with the balance-of-payments and fiscal crises, reduce state controls and restore public services. The policy agenda was formally accepted by government, but administrative inefficiency and political opposition meant that it was only to be implemented slowly and partially, and its results have yet to be fully realized. The basic thrust of the 1987 programme, however, still dominates the policy process.

The initial programme involved a 77 percent devaluation (43 percent in real terms), increases in all export-crop prices, and improvements in export-crop marketing and crop

---

[17] World Bank (1988: 2-4); Ochieng (1991: 49).

[18] World Bank (1988: 3).

[19] *Ibid.*, p. 4.

[20] Mugenyi (1991: 70-1).

finance to increase exports. The budget deficit was to be covered through a one-off 30 percent tax on all cash holdings when a new currency was introduced, higher petrol taxes, increased revenue from coffee export taxes resulting from currency depreciation and improved tax administration, with budgetary discipline to be improved through a shift in access to bank credit from government to private and parastatal enterprises. Central controls were to be reduced through the introduction of an Open General Licensing system for foreign-exchange allocations, a reduction in price controls, privatization of a large number of parastatals, and a long-term commitment to liberalization of the crop marketing system. The performance of government was to be improved through civil service reform, improved tax administration and higher civil service wages.[21]

These policy conditions were backed by substantial aid flows. Uganda was allocated SDR 69.7 million under a Structural Adjustment Facility by the IMF in 1987 and SDR 219 m. under an Extended Structural Adjustment Facility in 1989, of which it had drawn SDR 149 m. by 1993.[22] The World Bank's first Economic Recovery Credit (supplemented by a second in 1991) included an IDA contribution of US$132 m., together with about US$120 m. from other donors mobilized by the IDA (of which DANIDA provided US$6 m.).[23] This money was used to financial imports, especially for the private sector, and was critical to recovery, since it was 'for most of the period the only foreign exchange available for allocation for private imports under official arrangements.'[24] The local currency generated as counterpart funds by these allocations was then used to support the budget. Disbursement took longer to arrange than anticipated, but by 1990 these funds were providing about half of the government's recurrent budget. Once the programme had been set up individual donors supported the development budget on a project-by-project basis, providing more than 80 percent of all resources. In the 1990s total flows, including considerable amounts provided by NGOs, have probably been in the order of US$500 m. p.a. By 1994 Uganda had undoubtedly become a most-favoured-aid-receiving-nation.

By 1994 the direct backing provided to Uganda by the IFIs had included two Economic Recovery Credits, an Agricultural Sector Adjustment Credit, a Structural Adjustment Credit, a Financial Sector Adjustment Credit and several investment credits from IDA; two Structural Adjustment Facility loans and four annual arrangements under the Extended Structural Adjustment Facility had been concluded with the IMF.[25] By the end of 1993 IDA had allocated US$1,883 m. in loans to Uganda of which US$587 m. had been allocated before May 1987 and US$675 m. remained to be disbursed,[26] while US$21.7 m. had been invested in the private sector through the IFC.[27]

---

[21] Details from World Bank (1987).

[22] IMF (1993: 43).

[23] World Bank (1992a: 19).

[24] *Ibid.*, p. 20

[25] Details from the 'Letter of Development Policy' by the Minister of Finance in World Bank (1991 and 1994a).

[26] World Bank (1987: Annex III; 1991; 1994a: Annex IV).

[27] World Bank (1994a: Annex IV).

Between 1987 and 1992 the original policy demands were confirmed and deepened, with continuous pressure to bring the exchange rate into line with the parallel market rate, to reduce inflation principally by controlling the budget deficit, to improve export marketing by eliminating export-crop monopolies, to encourage private and especially foreign investment through a reduction in licensing controls and the restoration of property rights, to privatize parastatals and to improve civil service efficiency by staff reductions, improved salaries and management. A strong donor consensus was maintained on these objectives through regular review meetings held in Kampala and in Paris, which allowed aid flows to continue and cooperation with government to continue despite serious reservations about its failure to implement many key items on schedule.

3.2.3   Implementing the Adjustment Programme

Between 1987 and 1992 growth improved significantly, but most other indicators - inflation, exchange rates, exports, and services - did not, suggesting yet another failure of the neo-liberal paradigm. However, there can be little doubt that many of these were directly attributable to incomplete implementation stemming from the government's ability to resist the terms imposed on it through a variety of stratagems, ranging from foot-dragging to an outright refusal to implement recommendations.

Table 1   Main Macroeconomic Indicators, 1985-94

	85	86	87	88	89	90	91	92	93	94
GDP, market prices (% increase)	0.9	1.2	6.3	7.8	6.8	4.4	4.3	3.4	5.4	
Budget deficit/GDP (excluding grants)	2.6							11.7	4.7	
Balance of payments (US$ m.)					-62	-108	-122	-41	+41	
Exchange rate (Ush:US$)	7	14	43	106	223	429	734	1134	1195	990
Inflation rate (CPI)		161	200	194	60	33	28	52	6	15
Interest (discount) rate			31	45	55	50	46		41	24
Exports f.o.b (US$ m.)		423			217	175	172	157	237	
Imports f.o.b. (US$)		438			591	545	451	533	696	
Trade balance (US$)		-5			-374	-370	-279	-376	-459	
Current Account balance (US$)					-249	-187	-132	-141	-104	

Source: Uganda Government, 1994a; IMF, 1993.

The IFIs were sometimes prepared to make an issue of this and threaten to withdraw support, but were usually forced to accept low levels of compliance because they were unwilling to put the whole programme at risk, given their need to continue to lend and to retain an ability to influence events. In virtually every important policy area weak implementation in the late 1980s was associated with poor economic outcomes, while significant improvements in the 1990s have been followed by much better performance.

Exchange Rates

Exchange-rate over-valuation continued until 1991. This was 700 percent in 1986, while the 77 percent devaluation in 1987 was followed by triple digit inflation, so the premium over the parallel rate was still 650 percent in June 1988. There were then three devaluations in 1988-89 and the adoption of real exchange rule late in 1989 followed by regular small devaluations which narrowed the gap significantly. In 1990, however, the parallel market was legalized (a decision taken without donor pressure[28]) and the official rate progressively reduced until the premium was only 15 percent in September 1991. The official dollar rate rose from 14 in 1986 to 1,037 in 1993, while the parallel rate moved from 100 to 1,172. In November 1993 'all transactions other than a few Government payments were shifted to a unified interbank foreign exchange market' effectively ending direct state controls.[29]

Table 2 Government Revenue and Expenditure (Million Ush)

	1990-91	1991-92	1992-93 annual	1993-94 annual
Tax revenue	133.365	180.328	284.725	382.949
Revenue/GDP (%)			8	9.5
Current expenditure			323.452	408.438
Wages/salaries			62.691	89.000
Non-wage			191.375	248.918
Interest			69.386	70.520
Capital expenditure			393.690	371.225
Expenditure/GDP (%)			19.7	19.2
Total export (US$)			2496	
/exports (%)			907	
service/exports (%)			40.2	

Sources: Uganda Government 1994a; World Bank, *World Development Report 1994.*

These changes eliminated the rents and delays involved in direct official forex allocations, brought the parallel market into the open, and was followed by a market-driven *appreciation* of the shilling. Monthly forex bureau purchases increased from about US$6 m. per month at the end of 1990 to US$22 m. in July 1992 and US$37 m. in April 1994, averaging US$34 m. per month during the previous six-month period.

---

[28] Lamont (1994).

[29] See Malik (1994: 4).

In 1994 the shilling fell to 976 and has remained at that level into 1995, in response to strong forex inflows from coffee exports and private and official flows. This was an outcome no-one would have anticipated even a year earlier and one which is now creating significant problems for exporters.

Budgetary Controls

Effective fiscal discipline was only established in 1992 because of increased expenditure (notably for defence), and shortfalls in revenue. By 1986 the government's capacity to generate revenue had fallen to 9.4 percent of GDP, to which the coffee export tax accounted for two thirds. The collapse in output and prices the following year reduced its contribution to 34.3 percent and revenue to 4.8 percent of GDP.[30] The coffee tax virtually disappeared in 1992,[31] but increases in other taxes (notably on petrol) and improved administration had restored revenue to 9.4 percent of GDP by 1994. The government continued to finance itself through the printing press until 1992 despite pressures from donors. Government claims on the banking system rose by Ush 20 bn in the first two years instead of declining according to the target, while the budget for 89-90 had to be revised 'with the assistance of IDA and Bank staff'. The problem continued into early 1992, with the Ministry of Finance refusing to curtail spending, leading to a resurgence of inflation which increased from 32 percent to 66 percent between 1991 and 1992.

The Minister was then sacked in March 1992 at the behest of the IFIs and the Ministry of Finance was merged with the Ministry of Planning and Economic Development (the key source of internal support for the programme) which became the 'dominant influence' over policy. Tight budgetary controls were introduced and allocations to spending departments tied directly to revenue and released on a monthly basis. In 1991 tax administration was taken out of the Ministry of Finance and given to a new Uganda Revenue Authority, leading to a real increase of 381 percent in collections by 1994. Budgetary pressure was greatly reduced after 1991 by the ending of the civil war and by a successful demobilization of 30-40,000 men in 1993-94. Inflation declined dramatically, and was -2.4 percent in 1993 and 16 percent in 1994.

Financial Sector Management

Generally lax financial management prevailed in the late 1980s with negative interest rates and poor controls over the private banking system dominated by the publicly controlled Uganda Commercial Bank (UCB) and Cooperative Bank. Government allowed private credit to increase by 200 percent in 87-88 and 248 percent in 88-89 alongside an explosive increase in credit to public marketing boards and cooperatives for crop finance. Broad money increased by 356 percent over the first two years compared with a target of 105 percent. State banks were allowed 'huge overdrafts with the central bank', while interest rates were suppressed and remained negative until the second half of 1992. A large number of unviable rural branches were established in the late 1980s, and this, combined with corruption, meant that both public banks were

---

[30] The decline in the public contribution to revenue is not as great as it seems, since it is associated with a significant increase in direct payments for public services, notably in health and education. See Brett (1994).

[31] A temporary tax was reintroduced in 1994 in response to the sudden increase in international prices occasioned by a decline in Brazilian supplies.

technically insolvent by 1990. As a result savings moved out of domestic financial assets into real domestic assets and foreign currency.[32]

In April 1992 a Treasury Bill auction was introduced and interest rates were raised, becoming, with the fall in inflation, strongly positive by the end of 1992 when they were more than 30 percent. Deposits increased from Ush 7.5 bn in 1992 to Ush 13.8 bn in 1994,[33] and interest rates had fallen to 14 percent.

In 1993 the Bank of Uganda (BoU) was given more autonomy from the Ministry of Finance and its supervisory role over the commercial banks was strengthened as part of the Financial Sector Reform Programme. The BoU sets its own lending and rediscount rates, while commercial rates are left to the market. Pressure was exerted to end automatic extensions of 'development' credit to the commercial banks and the management of the UCB was replaced in 1992-93 because it refused to accept this view.[34] The new team includes four expatriates, many branches have since been closed, half the staff have been retrenched, and bad debts have been transferred to a Trust.[35] The Co-op Bank was given Swedish support at the start of the 1990s and its performance improved, it has since continued to improve with support from USAID.

There is no doubt that tightening up credit creation and interest rates was essential to reduce inflation and increase deposits, although it is probably the case that high real rates have discouraged investment, though reduction in inflation and increased inward investment have now brought them down. However, the banking system is still characterized by high levels of centralization and inefficiency. The foreign banks operate exclusively in Kampala, while the UCB and Co-op still provide a very in-efficient service. The result is very low rates of registered savings and investment, with Gross Domestic Investment rising from 10.3 percent of GDP in 1988 to 15.3 percent in 1993, and Gross National Savings from 0.7 percent to 3.4 percent.[36] However, these figures give no real indications of the levels of real savings and investment in a country with grossly inefficient formal sector credit institutions and a predominantly informal sector economy. In the informal sector most savings are held in real assets, while investments take the form of domestic labour inputs, reinvested income or borrowing from families or friends. Given the considerable increases in output which have occurred over the past nine years, it seems probable that both savings and investments have increased significantly in response to improvements in infrastructure, security and incentives. The weakness of the formal banking system nevertheless remains one of the most significant obstacles to the growth of a strong indigenous capitalist class.

Export-Crop Marketing
Real export-crop prices had not been improved by 1990, nor was any serious attempt made to improve the poor performance of the Coffee and Cotton Boards until 1991. The Produce Marketing Board (PMB) was given an export monopoly over five food crops,

---

[32] Brett (1994).

[33] *Ibid.*, p. 20 (figures in constant 1987 Ush).

[34] *Ibid.*, p. 8

[35] Harvey & Robinson (1994: 50).

[36] World Bank (1994a: 69).

and was used by government to organize barter trade deals for essential imports against donor advice. Coffee marketing was fully liberalized only in 1991 and cotton only in 1994, with threats to suspend aid being required to overcome resistance from the Ministry of Marketing and Cooperatives. The PMB was unable to compete with private buyers and therefore failed completely. Its monopoly was removed in 1989, as were price and distribution controls over essential commodities for the domestic market. Barter deals, which were uniformly unsuccessful, were stopped by 1990. The removal of the coffee monopoly greatly increased the efficiency of the marketing system and increased the price to growers (from Ush 75 per kilo in 1990 to Ush 400 in 1993) despite depressed prices.

Public Sector Reform
The adjustment programme was mainly concerned with macroeconomic reform and reconstruction, but its dependence on support from government and its wish to shift from state to market controls have meant that institutional reform has been a critical element in the process. More recently 'good governance' has become a part of structural adjustment packages, but in Uganda this concern was articulated by government itself after 1986 since democratization was a key element in the NRM's 10 Point Programme. Programmes involved here include privatization, civil service reform, decentralization and constitutional reform.

Privatization: In 1986 the government owned more than 150 companies, almost all of which were making heavy losses which were being funded directly or indirectly by government. Divestiture was part of the initial agreement in 1987, but the first companies were only sold in 1994, despite continuing subsidies and losses. The World Bank reached an agreement to finance a privatization secretariat in December 1988, but this only became operational in 1990 and significant progress was delayed until a new agreement in December 1991. The Bank then provided a US$65 m. credit in 1992 to finance the Public Enterprises Reform and Divestiture Board (PERD) to manage the process, employing a large number of very expensive foreign consultants. This was set up before the appropriate legislation had gone through Parliament and was halted by opposition there until the Statute was enacted in August 1993 after a strong Presidential intervention in its favour and a threat that further aid disbursements would be held up. PERD itself operated so badly that it had to be restructured in 1994 with its Chief Adviser and two others being removed.[37] By the end of 1994 nine corporations had been privatized, eight repossessed by former Asian owners, and 16 were up for sale.[38]

The process has taken much longer and been far more costly than was originally envisaged, mainly because of a refusal to accept the need to write off irretrievable debts and a desire to rehabilitate many of the companies and sell them as going concerns rather than to write off their losses and sell them on the open market for whatever they were worth. Here domestic political opposition among key Ministers, MPs, managers and workers and the willingness of the World Bank to fund a wasteful rehabilitation programme clearly contributed to budgetary weakness and inhibited the return to productivity of valuable economic assets.

---

[37] World Bank (1994b).

[38] Details from Ketley (1994).

A more successful element in the privatization process has been the return to their owners of almost all the Asian properties expropriated in 1972, although this, too, only began in 1991. Since then 2,500 properties have been returned. Unclaimed properties are to be sold by competitive tender, and 1,700 owners who have applied for compensation rather than repossession should have their claims met.[39] Many of the larger operators, including the Madhvani and Mehta groups, have returned to rehabilitate and rebuild their businesses, while many more businesses and residences are being sold to Ugandans at relatively low prices. This process, which involved considerable political risks given the opposition engendered amongst Ugandan occupiers forced out by the change, has given real credibility to the regime's claim to be making a serious effort to consolidate the rule of law and guarantee property rights.

In addition the business environment was progressively liberalized through the elimination of export and industrial licensing and price controls, the removal of most import prohibitions, the introduction of an Investment Code and creation of an Investment Authority to expedite registrations and encourage foreign investment.

Civil service reform: A high level Public Service Review and Reorganization Commission (PSRRC) was appointed to review the civil service in 1988 which reported in 1990 recommending significant reductions in staff, increases in wages and Results Oriented Management.[40] However, effective action on the programme was blocked by resistance inside the Ministry of Public Service until 1991.

This changed with the arrival of a full-time Chief Technical Adviser seconded from the World Bank at the end of 1992 who was able to secure high level political support for the programme and to build internal structures in the Ministry which enabled retrenchment to begin. Thereafter progress was rapid, and by mid-1994 66,000 group employees and 14,000 core civil servants had gone, and some 40,000 'ghost workers' had been eliminated. Staff houses and vehicles are now being sold off and all benefits monetized.

These programmes have apparently gone through without significant political opposition, apart from initial resistance in the service itself. This has had to do with the fact that the original proposals were produced by a local Commission, generous redundancy terms funded by donors, the fact that all officials have already been involved in outside business activities, and because the public have little sympathy for an official class that has failed to provide adequate services for many years.[41]

Retrenchment is not intended to reduce public spending, but should be accompanied by higher salaries to achieve a 'living wage', and by improvements in training, management and accountability to improve levels of performance. However, while retrenchment is relatively easy to measure and enforce, creating effective management and accountability systems in a demoralized civil service is far more difficult. The Bank has been attempting to develop a 'Capacity Building Initiative' in conjunction with the Ministry of Planning for more than three years, but has given this low priority. However, a project for US$32.9 m. was recommended in July 1994 and should be implemented

---

[39] World Bank (1994a: 23-24).

[40] Uganda Government (1990).

[41] Details from Harvey & Robinson (1994: 42ff).

Uganda

in 1995.[42] The problem is not only to generate higher levels of managerial skill, but also to establish effective mechanisms for the monitoring and evaluation of performance. This presupposes the need for significant improvements in tertiary education (to be considered below), and a need to keep an effective check on administrative performance through the press and Parliament. Considerable progress has been made here, but more support needs to be given to the relevant institutions.

Decentralization: In 1986 the NRM introduced a highly democratic local government system based on Resistance Councils (RC) which operate at five levels from the Village to the District in rural areas and also operate in urban areas.[43] These councils initially had limited powers and financial resources; in 1991 the government decided to devolve a significant level power to councils, and a Decentralization Statute was passed in 1993. This will allow district councils to take control over central Ministerial staff and ensure that budgetary allocations go direct to councils rather than through Ministries. This latter arrangement became operational in 13 districts in 1994, and progress has apparently been good - local hospitals have made 'a substantial improvement in number of patients ... served, availability of drugs, food to patients, rehabilitation of premises, payment of staff salaries and payment of utility bills'.[44] The success of this programme is critical to the long-term political and economic future of the country. While it has generally been welcomed by donors, it has only received significant support from DANIDA which has been the lead donor in this area, perhaps because the World Bank was concerned about its possibly negative budgetary implications. Now two processes are critical - firstly, effective mechanisms must be put in place to ensure that central funding is sent to districts on a regular basis, and that spending can be audited; secondly that significant amounts of investment are put into the rehabilitation of the administrative and infrastructural systems in the Districts which are still unable to provide effective services or manage their local staff.

Constitutional reform: Constitutional reform has always been a central element in the NRM programme, and it set up a Constitutional Commission in 1989 which conducted extensive public soundings and produced a report and a Draft Constitution at the end of 1992 with DANIDA support. A Constituent Assembly was elected in March 1994, after a long and intensely competitive campaign, and it has been debating the Draft ever since. National elections for the Presidency and Parliament should take place by the end of 1995.

The constitutional debate has been dominated by concerns about the nature of the party system and the possibility of federalism. While the NRM favours a continuation of the present system for the next few years, which allows parties to exist but not to campaign openly, the UPC and some DP members demand an immediate restoration of the party system. The Constituent Assembly elections confirmed the NRM's position, so the next national elections at least will probably be conducted in the same way as the Constituent Assembly elections. The demand for federalism was being strongly

---

[42] World Bank (1944c).

[43] See Brett (1993: Ch.3); World Bank (1992b).

[44] World Bank (1994c: 7).

pressed by delegates from Buganda, the most significant single group in the Assembly, but does not appear to have had a significant degree of support from anyone else, so the final solution will probably consolidate the rights of the district council system without setting up a formal federal structure. This constitution-making process has again taken longer than expected, but been conducted in an exemplary fashion. Provided that all key groups (including the federalists from Buganda and UPC supporters in the north) are prepared to accept the outcome, it could provide the basis for democratic processes which will rule out the possibility of a reversion to the politics of predatoriness and repression which produced such disastrous results in the past.

Disbursement Problems
Finally one should note that the programme was also significantly held back by rigidities in the disbursement processes, partly stemming from donor requirements, partly from the rigidities in the early allocation processes applying in Uganda, especially relating to the allocation of forex to approved importers. However, this problem was virtually eliminated by 1992 as a result of an almost complete liberalization of the import licensing system.

3.2.4 Economic Performance under the ERP
Despite the uneven levels of implementation, there is little doubt that the overall impact of the ERP has been strongly positive, even before effective discipline was restored. Much of this was due to improvements in law and order, heavy investments (especially by the World Bank) in the rehabilitation of infrastructure, and significant aid flows, especially for import support. GDP growth has averaged 5.4 percent, and per capita growth 2.4 percent over the eight fiscal years since 1986-87.[45] This will be much higher in 1994-95 given higher coffee prices, relief food sales for Rwanda and Sudan, and significant inflows of private investment stimulated by recent international recognition of the country's stability and potential. As we have seen, inflation, which was 262 percent in 1988 before policy was tightened up, had fallen to 16 percent in 1994. However, performance has varied significantly in different sectors. Firstly, the ERP has probably led to a significant but very uneven reduction in poverty. Donor support did not lead to cuts in service provision, but made it possible for social services, infrastructure, and development spending to be sustained at a much higher level than would have been possible without them. In fact real government spending increased 'by nearly five times since 1987, and although this has resulted in a budget deficit twice as large as 1987 in real terms, the increased flow of foreign finance ... allowed this to occur' without inflation while the government was repaying the banking system.[46] The most important contribution to growth has been made by small-scale local producers, since economic assets are widely distributed. The demand for labour also appears to have been strong, and the Bank estimates that 'the welfare of the rural and urban poor, in real terms, on a per capita output basis, has improved by between 14 and 16 percent' between 1987 and 1991.[47]

---

[45] Uganda Government (1994a: Table 4).

[46] Harvey & Robinson (1994: 29).

[47] World Bank (1993a: xiv).

Table 3   Monetary GDP at Factor Cost by Sector (billion Ush, constant 1991 prices)

	1986	1987	1988	1989	1990	1991	1992	1993	Av. annual growth 1986-93 (%)
Agriculture	386	407	434	459	474	469	513	522	4.4
Manufacturing	72	84	93	96	102	121	121	139	11.6
Construction	69	84	93	102	110	111	117	126	10.3
Commerce	189	213	230	240	251	264	283	298	7.2
Transport	69	73	77	81	85	87	92	97	5.1
Government Services	230	240	256	275	296	320	241	357	6.9
Non-monetary	567	597	633	663	677	669	726	739	3.5

Source: Uganda Government, 1994a.

However, there are very significant differences in levels of activity as between the most prosperous areas in the south and the rest of the country. Thus the Integrated Household Survey in 1992-93 put average monthly incomes at Ush 75,000 in the Central Region, and 40,000 in the North,[48] while the World Bank suggests that wages were more than twice as high in Mbale as in Kabarole Districts.[49] Further, it is important to recognize that growth has taken place from such low levels that these improvements have hardly begun to address the poverty problem, while recent improvements have also done little for the poorest groups in society - the old, the disabled and the dispossessed.[50]

Secondly, export performance has been poor, with registered exports falling from US$423 m. in 1986 to US$157 m. in 1992 and US$198 m. in 1993, because of a precipitous fall in coffee prices at the end of the 1980s. Non-coffee exports increased from US$29 m. in 1986 to US$62 m. in 1992, although these figures must understate reality, given smuggling and under-reporting.[51] Imports increased from US$438 m. in 1986 to US$696 m. in 1993-94. The trade gap, widened by service and interest charges, was initially covered by official inflows; more recently these have been supplemented by private transfers which increased from US$209 m. in 1992-93 to US$282 m. in 1993-94.

The coffee price has now risen dramatically, and supplies have also responded to market liberalisation, so earnings will be much higher in 1994. Cotton exports have not recovered because of the failure to improve marketing and the availability of more attractive alternative crops. Despite much talk of export promotion programmes, significant improvements will be slow given limitations in skills, financial services, capital, information and infrastructure. These problems will be worsened by the recent rise in

---

[48] Uganda Government (1994b: 4).

[49] World Bank (1993b, 32-33).

[50] See in particular, Institute of Development Studies (1994).

[51] See Meagher (1990).

the value of the shilling. Improving export capacity is now probably the key obstacle to the development of an autonomous capacity for sustained growth in Uganda.

Table 4   Composition of Exports by Principal Commodities, 1986-93 (US$ m.)

	1986	1989	1990	1991	1992	1993
Coffee	394	265	140	177	95	106
Tea	3	3	4	7	8	11
Cotton	5	4	6	12	8	2
Others	21	36	39	36	42	72

Source: Uganda Government, 1994a.

Thirdly, adjustment initially led to a rapid build-up of debt which increased from about US$1.3 bn in 1986 to just under US$2.6 bn in 1991, and then stabilized at slightly above that figure. 60 percent of this was owed to international agencies on concessional terms. Uganda had become a highly indebted country, and was unable to meet its commitments, accumulating arrears of US$583 m. by 1992. In 1992-93 debt was over 122 percent of GDP and service payments were estimated at US$176 m. The debt-service ratio was about 80 percent, not including servicing of arrears. These represented 265 percent of the export of goods and non-factor services.[52] By 1992 Uganda had taken full advantage of cancellations and rescheduling of bilateral debt agreed by the Paris Club, but most of its debt had been incurred too late to benefit from that agreement, and in 1992 the World Bank agreed a debt strategy which included support to buy back small amounts of eligible commercial debt. However, despite general recognition that debt constitutes a long-term threat to stability and redistribution, a problem highlighted in a recent Oxfam campaign,[53] debt relief has only made a marginal impact on the problem.

Oxfam had made a strong case for the revision of the terms agreed by the Paris Club to cover debt incurred since 1981, and to raise the possibility of forgiveness of multilateral debt. In response Bank, Fund and UNDP advisers interviewed in Uganda in 1992 claimed that the burden could decline quite rapidly with anticipated export growth and that the cost of debt payments was in effect being covered indirectly by the balance-of-payments support programme. In fact by 1994 arrears had been cut from US$583 m. to US$294 m., and the actual debt-service ratio had fallen by 12 percent.

In fact the donors do make a significant contribution to limiting the damage created by debt by taking it into account in their calculation of the levels of import support required in annual aid negotiations. Growth and services will only be threatened if the donors refuse to maintain their existing level of support. From their point of view debt keeps Uganda financially dependent, thus guaranteeing them the policy-making leverage

---

[52] World Bank, (1993c: 7).

[53] Oxfam briefing (1994).

which they probably do not want to give up. In the current context where inflows are pushing the exchange rate to unacceptable levels, however, a very strong case can be made for the need to divert some overseas flows into debt repayment in order to reduce the pressure on the shilling.[54]

4.   Rebuilding Productive Capacity

4.1   Agriculture

Uganda is predominantly a country of smallholders, with most families holding enough land for subsistence and some cash-crop production. Significant inequality exists in land holdings, with 32 percent of farmers in a position to hire labour at some time.[55] Population growth has been 2.6-3 percent annually since independence, and most people have had to remain on the land. There is significant population pressure in some areas (the south-west and south-east), leading to out-migration, and surplus land in others. The latter areas on the whole are remote from markets and were particularly disadvantaged by the decline in infrastructure in the 1970s and early 1980s. The AIDS pandemic is expected to result in anything between 820,000 and 3,280,000 deaths in the most productive age group during the 1990s.[56] The dependency ratio is very high, with 50 percent of the population less than 15 years old, and a large number of orphans resulting from the impact of war and AIDS.

Table 5   Procurement of Main Export Cash Crops: 1984-94

Period	Coffee			Tea	Tobacco
	Robusta	*Arabica*	Total		
1984	*136.673*	*9.298*	145.971	5.214	1.969
1985	*133.848*	*10.147*	143.995	5.758	1.613
1986	*151.247*	*8.634*	159.881	3.335	949
1987	*158.002*	*9.065*	167.067	3.511	1.214
1988	*141.718*	*9.439*	151.157	3.512	2.639
1989	*161.154*	*7.888*	169.042	4.658	3.456
1990	*116.607*	*11.940*	128.747	6.704	3.322
1991	*133.456*	*13.903*	147.369	8.877	5.140
1992	*95.174*	*15.119*	110.293	9.504	6.686
1993	*119.258*	*21.818*	141.076	12.320	5.183

Source: Uganda Government, 1994a.

---

[54] Interview, E. Tumusime-Mutibile, Permanent Secretary, Ministry of Finance and Planning, 1994.

[55] Evans (1992).

[56] Barnett & Blaikie (1992).

Almost everyone still uses unimproved seeds and hand-tools, and most of those in the north who had adopted animal traction lost their animals during the civil war. Rural services declined drastically after 1971 and have yet to be restored. Thus rural poverty is deeply entrenched and, despite the existence of numerous donor and NGO development projects, actual access to external resources is the exception rather than the rule. This poverty is closely related to earlier development strategies, which supported large rather than small farmers, and created marketing and processing structures which undermined local entrepreneurs and impoverished growers.

4.1.2 The Farming System

Agricultural policy after independence was based on a 'transformation approach' which assumed that productivity increases required mechanized technology, exotic animals and capitalist farming. This strategy was supported by donors who wished to increase their own exports, and offered large farmers subsidized tractors, exotic animals, and extension services and allowed them to appropriate large amounts of land. The beneficiaries, mainly absentee owners from the political and bureaucratic elite, were high-cost producers who would not have been able to compete with small farmers on equal terms, so the investments did not improve rural productivity.

This strategy also marginalized the small farmers - surplus land which could have absorbed increasing populations was fenced off, animal traction was not extended out of the north-east where it had been adopted before the war, research and extension activities were exclusively devoted to coffee and cotton, and little attention was paid until the 1980s to the potentially profitable development and introduction of improved varieties which were revolutionizing smallholder agriculture throughout Asia at the time. *This failure to improve the productivity of small farmers, despite a highly favourable resource endowment, is the most significant feature of both colonial and post-colonial economic policy in Uganda, and has been a key element in the failure to reduce poverty and establish a sustainable basis for autonomous growth.*

Since 1986 there has been a change in policy orientation, with donors and government finally accepting the need for a low-input development strategy for the small farm sector, but few improvements in output or institutional arrangements. In the late 1980s the Ministry of Agriculture again attempted to interest donors in an expensive tractor programme, and, while the shilling was significantly over-valued, private estate owners could import new machines on a subsidized basis. The tractor programme did not get significant levels of support, and competitive exchange rates soon made tractors unviable. Changes in land legislation are also envisaged to extend private freehold tenure across the whole system, reducing the capacity of government to allocate large units to absentee owners, and encouraging a commercial market which, it was assumed, would shift land to efficient small-scale producers.[57]

By 1990 a consensus had emerged which accepted that agriculture and agro-processing would have to remain the main engine of growth of output and exports, and that this would primarily be secured through improvements in the small farming sector. This was to involve an immediate focus on increased traditional cash-crop exports and 'diversification among the least investment-intensive non-traditional agricultural exports', and longer-term measures to 'diversify exports, improve technology generation and

---

[57] Land relations and policy are reviewed in Makerere Institute of Social Research and Land Tenure Center, University of Wisconsin, (1989).

dissemination, and reduce transaction costs, entry barriers and market failures in the land, labour and capital markets'. The emphasis in this process was no longer on capitalist farms, but on 'prevention of concentration of landownership through judicious management of titling and tenure of public lands', and a commitment to the 'alleviation of rural poverty and the development of sustainable farming systems and participatory production relationships'.[58]

While this represents a commendable shift in orientation, there is little evidence of any significant impact in practice, with the exception of donor-funded input supply projects to be discussed below. USAID has invested large amounts in rehabilitating the existing research stations, while a unified National Agricultural Research Organization has been created to manage research services. However, these stations have always been highly centralized and remote from the needs and conditions of smallholding agriculture, while the breakdown of the extension services means that their findings cannot be effectively disseminated. Institutional failures in both government and donor structures have seriously undermined the productivity of donor projects. The World Bank itself concedes, for example, that key projects

> have had limited success in improving the quality of agricultural services. Implementation has lagged considerably behind schedule. Administrative support from Entebbe has been weak. Government funding allocations have been erratic and low, eroding staff commitment and credibility with farmers. The quality of expatriate technical assistance staff has been mixed, with some teams providing mediocre services.[59]

Farmers have, in fact, benefited from the adjustment programme, though mainly indirectly. Improvements in transport, security and prices have allowed a considerable increase in production and trade for both domestic and regional markets. Some improvements have also taken place in the estate sector. Tea and sugar production have expanded sharply in response to the restoration of expatriate property rights. Milk production has grown rapidly and has fully replaced imports during the wet season at least. Many attempts are being made to develop small-scale cooperative rural credit systems, after the failure of the Rural Farmers' Loan Scheme run by the Uganda Commercial Bank, but it will be some time before their effectiveness can be measured.

4.1.3   Marketing and Processing

Adjustment has also effected marketing controls and prices, though these have been less significant in traditional export crops than the food crops which took their place after 1972. The collapse of state regulatory capacity meant that most rural transactions have taken place in the informal sector, where prices have been set by parallel forex rates and where border controls could easily be evaded. In the late 1980s a thriving border trade existed involving cash- and food-crop exports from Uganda in exchange for gold,

---

[58] World Bank (1993b: xv-xvi).

[59] *Ibid.*, p. 46.

dollars and manufactures from neighbouring countries.[60] The domestic food-crop market had always been private and attempts to allocate monopolies to the Produce Marketing Board in the 1980s could never be enforced, and it could never compete effectively with private traders. The latter have always been highly competitive, and capable of responding rapidly and effectively to changes in prices, as they did in 1990-92 during the period of high sesame seed prices.[61]

However, coffee and cotton were easier to control, so serious inefficiencies persisted. The over-valued exchange rate and marketing monopolies held back improvements until the early 1990s, while the liberalization of coffee marketing described earlier had a dramatic impact on the quality of services and prices. Cotton processing had almost collapsed by 1986 as a result of exchange-rate over-valuation and the monopolies given to the cooperatives and the Lint Marketing Board,[62] while high transport costs reduced the incentive to smuggle. Powerful vested interests, including donors involved in the cooperative sector, substantial amounts of surplus capacity, and large and irrecoverable debts, held back reform until 1993 when the legal basis for liberalization was finally established. This may lead to an increase in output, but previous levels are unlikely to be reached given depressed world prices and cotton's low comparative advantage because of high labour costs and dependence on complex inputs.[63] In tobacco, however, a private monopoly run by the BAT company in conjunction with local cooperatives has proved relatively successful in managing extension, processing and export marketing.[64]

Weaknesses in output marketing are parallelled by even more serious weaknesses in the supply of inputs. According to a key study:

> Virtually no new agricultural methods or technologies have been introduced [in Uganda] since the late 1960s, [and] many ... have fallen into disuse in recent years .... National fertilizer consumption ... has actually fallen from an estimated average of only 1.4 kg/ha in the 1960s to a mere 0.2 kg/ha.... Total annual expenditure on agricultural inputs ... is estimated at only US$10-US$15 per household.[65]

This relates to the poverty of small farmers and institutional arrangements which have marginalized the rural private sector. The sector has always been dominated by donors and government concerned to provide what they thought to be key inputs on a subsidized basis, notably, as we have seen, high technology-produced ones for the large farm sector. In the late 1980s donors provided an average of US$36 m. for imported

---

[60] See in particular Meagher (1990).

[61] I have described the rural private sector in Brett (1993: Ch. 4).

[62] For a review of the Cooperative sector see *ibid.* Ch. 5.

[63] I have dealt with the coffee and cotton monopolies in Brett (1994).

[64] See World Bank (1993b: 47).

[65] R. Laker-Ojok (1992: 3). The analysis here is based entirely on Laker-Ojok's study.

inputs each year. Most were subsidized, and only 18.5 percent were distributed through private suppliers as opposed to government, donors, parastatals, cooperatives or NGOs, creating significant levels of inefficiency and opportunities for corrupt practices.[66] The levels of subsidy also made it impossible for private traders to compete. Most domestic input supplies - fertilizers, improved seed and tools - were produced in grossly inefficient parastatals. More recently the problems associated with these methods have been recognized, but it is too soon to establish whether they have yet been successfully addressed.

In conclusion we can see that a great many key institutional problems have to be solved if sustainable agricultural growth is to be achieved in Uganda. However the relatively egalitarian distribution of assets, the favourable resource endowment and the existence of a wide range of proven innovations which have yet to be implemented does mean that a rapid and equitable growth process could be achieved given rational policies and much better use of external resources.

4.2   Industry

Large-scale industry in Uganda began in the 1950s, managed by the state or large Asian or foreign companies. It collapsed after 1972, 'and by 1986 output was estimated to be little more than a third of ... peak levels achieved in 1970-72'.[67] Most fabrication was then confined to vigorous but technically limited micro-enterprises in the informal sector. Industrial capacity utilization had averaged 20 percent in 1982-86, and there have been regular improvements since then. Using 1987 as a base year of 100, the production index has moved from 86 in 1986 to 214 in 1993. The largest increases have taken place in vehicle accessories, plastics, electrical products, paint, medicines, soap and food processing; leather and footwear and textiles have actually declined. The major textile firms are in the state sector and have been consistently mismanaged. This growth has taken place from a very low base, and manufacturing still contributes barely 5 percent of GDP.

Industrial growth has been inhibited by the failure to restructure and privatize the parastatal sector described earlier, together with the other obstacles to private sector development outlined earlier - high interest rates, an inefficient banking sector, regressive taxation, restrictive licensing and poor communications and information systems. The progress being made in these areas should lead to significant gains over the next five years. Ugandan producers are also hampered by a small domestic market, costly transport systems and competition from much better endowed producers in Kenya.

Although trade liberalization is often a contentious issue in adjustment programmes, it has not been significant in Uganda since 1986. Import tariffs were historically high, but easily evaded, so domestic manufacturers were mainly protected by the high unofficial exchange rate and high transport and transaction costs. The NRM prohibited the import of some commodities (notably beer) which certainly encouraged local production, though this should soon be phased out. There is little discussion in the official documents of the role of tariffs in protection, though manufacturers have often complained of the disadvantage they suffer in having to compete with smuggled imports

---

[66] *Ibid.*, p. 24

[67] Economist Intelligence Unit (1992: 21).

while having to pay high domestic excise duties.[68] The IFIs are unlikely to insist on a reduction in tariffs, largely because of their contribution to revenue.

Table 6   Index of Industrial Production Annual Summary, 1986-93 (1987 = 100)

	Weight	1986	1987	1988	1989	1990	1991	1992	1993
Food processing	20.70	85.3	100.0	128.0	153.7	174.9	227.4	245.6	245.8
Tobacco and beverages	26.10	82.2	100.0	139.6	143.7	155.2	176.1	155.2	170.9
Textiles and clothing	16.30	92.9	100.0	121.8	132.7	116.3	110.9	111.9	93.5
Leather and footwear	2.30	90.0	100.0	62.0	62.9	75.3	60.1	79.5	68.4
Timber, paper and printing	9.00	72.0	100.0	135.1	169.4	183.6	198.2	220.5	237.8
Chemicals, paint and soap	12.30	58.8	100.0	111.2	162.9	183.5	192.9	252.0	339.2
Bricks and cement	4.30	120.6	100.0	94.5	109.0	154.2	162.6	203.1	263.7
Steel and products	5.30	105.9	100.0	87.2	98.9	107.7	149.3	190.7	258.5
Miscellaneous Products	3.70	141.0	100.0	134.0	204.2	183.3	251.2	272.3	371.1
Index all Items	**100.0**	**86.1**	**100.0**	**123.7**	**145.2**	**155.5**	**178.2**	**191.2**	**214.2**
Annual Percentage Change		-5.7	16.1	23.7	17.4	7.1	14.6	7.3	12.0

Source: Uganda Government, 1994a.

There is now some evidence of increased interest in Uganda by foreign investors, especially returning Asian firms and others moving out of increasingly unstable neighbouring countries. They receive generous incentives from the Investment Authority established in 1990. If present stability continues rapid growth is very likely.

4.3   The Informal Sector

Formal sector output is only a small part of total industrial output, given the significance of the informal sector which developed very rapidly after 1972 in response to the collapse of formal sector production.[69] Indeed, the activities which enabled most people to survive over the past twenty years are hardly visible to the policy-makers sitting in Kampala or Washington. Their transactions are too small, their businesses too remote, and their need to avoid restrictive controls and taxes too strong for outsiders to have anything more than a very vague notion about what they do, a situation which is common throughout Africa.[70] Although it is impossible to get an accurate picture

---

[68] Personal interviews, Mr. Karimali of the Mukwano Company.

[69] I have discussed some of the issues involved in Brett (1993).

[70] In a seminal work Janet MacGaffey (1987: 111) notes that 'From official figures on wages, prices and the decline of real income, it would seem to be impossible for the majority of people to stay alive in Zaire. Living there, however, it is soon apparent that people ... not only survive, but that some do very well as they 'fend for themselves' ... in a highly organised system of income-generating activities that are unrecorded in official figures and left out of official reports'.

of what they produce, the totals must be large. For example, the national statistics only measure the output of five formal sector beer and spirit factories. The rural household survey showed that the average rural household spent Sh 106 per month on their products, but Sh 1,283 on locally produced varieties.[71] Alcohol production is mainly carried out by rural women and is one of the most important mechanisms for transferring income from men to women.

Extensive fieldwork would be required to produce a detailed review of the impact of adjustment on the informal sector. However, some information about their operations does exist[72] which allows us to make some speculative points on the impact of economic and policy change on this sector since 1986. It is very probable that the key gains of the past nine years - in security, transport, and growth - will have had a beneficial impact on small producers, although the destruction of key markets in the Sudan, Zaire and Rwanda, will have reduced opportunities in border zones. The decline in formal sector activities and controls after 1972 generated a highly entrepreneurial and flexible small business class which can be relied on to take full advantage of local economic opportunities and improvements in security. What is more problematic, however, is the potential implicit in this class for longer-term development. This raises two issues - the problem of the regulatory regime and of access to skills, capital and markets.

The earlier statist economic system seriously limited their options. The marketing board monopolies excluded them from buying and processing, and licensing legislation often attempted to constrain their freedom.[73] Operating with thin margins, and often trading across borders, they needed to evade the prohibitions and direct and indirect taxes which they would have had to pay had they operated legally. The punitiveness and irrationality of state policy effectively criminalized most of the private sector, since it was impossible to meet all of the demands being made by the state and remain in business. Fortunately the collapse of the state's regulatory capacity allowed this new class, some with access to former Asian assets, to evade these controls and impositions, but this did involve significant transaction costs.

More importantly, the need for invisibility made it difficult for small firms to graduate into viable capitalist enterprises able to take advantage of formal sector credit and enforcement procedures. A recent report emphasized the high 'entry barriers ... and transaction costs' imposed by licensing provisions, and the regressive nature of the tax system which strongly favoured large firms against small ones.[74] The Investment Authority legislation increases the unfairness of the tax system by offering foreign investors tax advantages which threaten to undermine government efforts to increase 'domestic revenue mobilization' and also 'creates a bias against labour and distorts effective rates of protection by providing duty-free access to plant and machinery'.[75] Current reforms are now reducing unnecessary and inequitable controls, thus decrimina-

---

[71] Uganda Government (1991: 1.11-14).

[72] See Meagher (1990); Brett (1993: Ch. 4); Whyte (1987).

[73] On the impact of the marketing system see Brett (1973: Ch. 8); for the constraints confronting the sector in the 1970s see de Coninck (1979).

[74] Uganda Government (1990: v-ix).

[75] World Bank (1994a: 22).

lizing legitimate business activities. This is certainly the right way to approach these problems, but it is also evident that powerful groups in the state apparatus and the formal sector have strong vested interests in policies which will continue to discriminate against a group of producers who have great difficulty in organizing and representing themselves.

Small producers also have to deal with a hostile regulatory environment, and with extreme levels of scarcity and isolation. Demand is low, retail networks are poor, credit is only provided through local kinship networks, and information about technologies and markets only exists in the major urban centres. Regional inequalities are extreme, with most 'modern' activities and markets concentrated in the south. District-level administrative systems cannot provide viable services, apart from some improvement in local roads, and there is little evidence that donor and NGO projects have done more than help a few isolated groups in a sea of deprivation and exclusion. Many donor projects have continued to favour 'cooperative' and 'group'-based projects despite strong evidence which suggests that individual family enterprises operate far more effectively.

While one can understand the reasons for this failure over the past decade, it is clear that developing a regulatory structure and service delivery system which supports rather than suppresses small-scale fabrication and agro-processing activities is as essential to a successful poverty-oriented growth strategy as the development of a comparable strategy for smallholder agriculture.

4.4 Communications

The most important contribution of aid to development in Uganda in the late 1980s involved the rehabilitation of most of the trunk road system, funded by the World Bank and other donors. The Bank had negotiated a Third Highway project worth US$58 m. in 1984, most of which had still to be disbursed in 1986, and this was followed by a Fourth Highway project in 1987 worth US$18 m. With additional support from other donors most of the major trunk roads, virtually impassable in 1986, had been rebuilt by 1992, as had many of the main gravelled roads. A large Rural Feeder Roads project began in 1988-89. The private vehicle fleet increased from 29,000 in 1986 to 40,000 in 1991 and by about another 10,000 by 1993.

Although Uganda Airlines virtually ceased operations in 1991, passenger traffic at Entebbe increased from 96,000 in 1986 to 199,000 in 1993 and freight from 4,367 tonnes in 1986 to 12,834 in 1992. However, railway passenger traffic fell from 195,000 to 59,000, while goods traffic only rose from 71,000 to 130,000 tonnes between 1986 and 1993, partly because of improved road facilities, partly because of inefficiency in the Uganda Railway Corporation. The effects of donor spending on telecommunications and urban water supplies have only been felt very recently, and are almost exclusively concentrated in the major urban centres. Telecommunications in rural areas are almost non-existent, and rural water services are very uneven and generally poor.

4.5 Social Services: Health and Education

Adjustment has often involved public spending cuts and service payments in health and education, with a negative impact on poverty, leading to severe criticisms from those committed to 'adjustment with a human face'. While the resources provided by adjustment have actually enabled the government to avoid cuts which would otherwise have been inevitable, levels of provision are still abysmally low.

In the 1960s health and education were provided by a combination of state, mission and private agencies, on a free or highly subsidized basis. Facilities were well managed, but access was limited and biased towards the provision of high quality facilities for the urban elite. In health Mulago hospital in Kampala allegedly absorbed more than half the MOH budget.[76] In education Makerere University provided high cost, free, residential training to a tiny elite, and recruited most of its students from equally exclusive secondary schools modelled on British public schools. These set standards of excellence which still influence public judgements about appropriate levels of service, and provided the country with a small but well trained leadership whose skills have been critical to the success of the liberation and adjustment processes over the past decade.

The crisis then marginalized salaries, maintenance, supervisory standards and the supply of inputs and materials. Hospitals and schools decayed, teachers and carers were forced to moonlight and accept corrupt payments, and quality plummeted.[77] Little was done about this in the 1980s because of the failure to improve revenue and civil service performance, and the emphasis on defence and economic rehabilitation. However, since 1989 health and education expenditure has increased in absolute and proportional terms (from 21 percent of total budgeted expenditure in 1989-90 to 23 percent in 1992-93), while defence has fallen drastically (from 15 percent in 1991-92 to 9 percent in 1992-93).[78] In 1991-92 the World Bank attempted to impose user fees in the state health sector, but this was rejected by Parliament and never implemented. As a result of external support actual government expenditure rose rather than fell, and its distribution improved when the war ended:

> Not only was the Government able to increase its spending in real terms by a factor of nearly five times between 1987 and 1993, and much faster than the increase in GDP, the *distribution* of government spending shifted in favour of the social sectors and (eventually) away from defense spending.[79]

Thus, while a crisis continues in social service provision in Uganda, this is not the outcome of the adjustment programme. Without it, and many individual donor projects (including US$54 m. one for education from the World Bank), conditions would be much worse than they actually are.

Improvements in service provision will now require fundamental changes in institutional arrangements which take full account of the way in which the crisis affected the formerly state-dominated system.

---

[76] See King (1966).

[77] See Munene (1993); see also the articles by Whyte and Kajubi on health and education respectively in Hansen & Twaddle (1991).

[78] Figures from World Bank (1993d: 10). The figures include total recurrent and project expenditure by government and donors. The relative changes between sectors are much more dramatic in relation to domestically generated expenditure alone.

[79] Harvey & Robinson (1994: 30).

In the 1980s the crisis produced de facto privatization and decentralization in the financing and control of most services. In health the missionary sector, funded through user fees and external grants, expanded while free state provision contracted. 'Under-the-counter payments' became routine for those who used the increasingly inadequate facilities and personnel moved into private practice, using supplies pilfered from official sources.[80] The failure to introduce fees without increasing grants, and the collapse of supervision produced the worst of both worlds. Patients had to pay, but the payments could not be regularized and used to improve the service because they were not part of an accountable bureaucratic system.

Uganda has been attempting to develop an extensive but grossly underfunded primary health care service since the late 1970s, mainly based on voluntary associations with strong support from UNICEF, the missions, and many international NGOs. A national Community Based Health Care Association was set up in 1986, and had 130 registered members by 1991. In some cases these do effective educational and preventative work, but in many the combination of untrained health workers and low remuneration leads to uneven coverage, poor practice and high drop-out rates.[81] The work is of critical importance, but effective services depend on adequate funding, professional skills, high quality referral services, and properly paid and managed staff. While community participation is no doubt important, it cannot be a substitute for adequately funded, universally available and professionally managed programmes.[82]

In education declining grants led Parent-Teacher Associations (PTAs) to introduce supplementary fees at both primary and secondary (though not tertiary) levels. These, together with cash and kind contributions to building funds, have introduced almost full cost user funding into the service which would otherwise have collapsed. They have also improved managerial discipline since PTAs are able to supervise performance and to threaten inefficient headmasters with the withdrawal of support. However, most schools still operate in conditions of extreme scarcity. Classes are large and fees are so high that the poor are excluded from the primary system and all but the rich from the secondary. According to the Household Survey, 17 percent of men and 39.5 percent of women have never attended school, 8 percent of men and only 3.3 percent of women have completed O' levels, and 60 only percent of male and 49 percent of female 5 - 19 year olds are in school.[83] Almost 70 percent of 10 - 14 year olds not in school attributed this to cost.[84]

The failure to introduce fees into tertiary institutions including Makerere University (though three fee-paying private denominational universities have now been set up), and very uneven donor support, have kept the sector in a state of near breakdown with very negative implications for standards. Current populist thinking now emphasizes the need to put most new resources into the primary health and educational sectors, without

---

[80] Whyte (1991).

[81] See Brett (1993: 108ff); Munro (1990).

[82] See for example the trenchant criticisms of the community-based approach made by Stockton, former Oxfam representative in Uganda, in Oxfam Uganda (1994: 25/5).

[83] Uganda Government (1994b, Vol. 2: 7).

[84] *Ibid.* vols. 1 & 2.

recognizing the critical importance of the apex institutions in producing those who will staff lower-level educational institutions and manage key economic, administrative and political structures.

5.   The Politics of the Adjustment Process: Ownership, Dialogue and Consent

External and domestic critics of the adjustment process are deeply concerned about the extent to which it imposes policy choices which have far-reaching social and political consequences, thus marginalizing local interest groups and the autonomy of the state itself. Given the formal status of the IFIs as final arbiters of policy under conditionality, the adjustment process is seen as one where all-powerful donors impose their will on destitute and dependent governments, but this is far from the truth. The details presented earlier suggest that this view underestimates the ability of governments to resist unpopular demands, and the extent to which IFIs depend on support from domestic power brokers if their programmes are to succeed. A brief review of the tensions involved in the implementation process in Uganda provides us with some illuminating insights into the nature of the political dynamic created by this situation.

As we have seen, policy implementation did not evolve smoothly after 1986. Structural adjustment was not a technical programme implemented to order, but a set of objectives which were only partially attained through a long and contested political process which neither donors nor the regime could fully control. Most key objectives had been fully or partially attained by 1994, but the process was slow and uneven, and many of the economic failures associated with it were clearly caused by the inability to implement the original programme effectively.[85]

In 1987 most members of the Ugandan elite, and many key members of the government itself, saw this programme as an external imposition which they accepted, if at all, as the unwanted price which they had to pay for the financial support which came with it. The World Bank's evaluation of the programme accepts this, noting:

> The government's support for the economic recovery program wavered at times and therefore government ownership was weak. There was inadequate follow through of the critical aspects of the programme.... in fact, the government stance varied over time, creating an impression that the government was not committed to the actions.

> An important element in this implementation slowdown was the failure to internalize policy commitments within the government. A narrow circle of ministers and senior officials were directly kept fully abreast of the economic

---

[85] Conflict was most intense between 1987 and 1992. This was reviewed in the World Bank's Completion and Performance Audit Reports, from which most of the following information is taken. World Bank (1992a and 1993c).

recovery program. There was not sufficient effort to foster wider support for the program.[86]

However, there was some support for the programme in government, notably from the Permanent Secretary in the Ministry of Planning, who was able to exploit external demands for discipline and resources provided by the Bank to challenge the prevailing statist orthodoxy. Lamont, a senior policy adviser in the Ministry of Planning, documents the change, emphasizing the openness of the President to argument, and the creation of a number of internal fora where contentious issues could be debated on the basis of technical papers. The main emphasis was on the case for a competitively determined exchange rate, and a major turning point came with a national seminar in December 1989.[87] The parallel market could then be eliminated, while the resources provided by the programme, growing evidence of success, continuing problems with marketing boards and parastatals, and the policy debate, gradually extended support to key local decision-makers, including the President. In early 1992 the hostile Minister of Finance was replaced by supporters of the programme, leading to a widespread consensus and an acceleration of implementation measures. This debate and subsequent change in orientation was then extended more broadly through an open and increasingly informed national press.

During the early years local resistance produced levels of non-compliance which could have been used by donors as justification for withdrawal. Thus the Bank notes that 'Government practically abandoned the stabilization components of the ERP in 1988-89' and made little progress on many other elements of the programme in the early years.[88] However, they continued to lend because they had a strong vested interest in achieving success, they recognized the dire consequences of failure in a country which had been brought so close to ruin by the war, and they believed that the new regime was 'ready to accept its responsibility' for failures and 'work towards a new program'. More especially, it recognised that while it had 'failed in the economic front', it had 'succeeded in tasks that ... posed even greater challenges', notably by maintaining military discipline, incorporating a wide range of political forces, restoring essential services, and establishing law and order.

In a country besieged by political opportunism and mistrust, it achieved a guarded but sincere vote of confidence from key bureaucrats, from a larger segment of the business leadership and, apparently, from the population at large. These accomplishments paved the way for a new, and more decisive round of reforms.[89]

---

[86] World Bank (1993c: 13).

[87] Lamont (1994).

[88] World Bank (1993e: 10ff).

[89] World Bank (1988: 4).

Thus had conditionality been rigorously enforced, cooperation would soon have ended, flows would have dried up and support for the fragile political coalition created by Museveni would have collapsed with disastrous consequences. Thus:

> ... rather than turning their backs on Uganda, IDA and the Fund intensified their dialogue with the Government. It took a great deal of perseverance, over a two-year period, to get the Government to perceive the benefits of a successful stabilization and to focus on this aspect of the program.[90]

Thus, on the positive side, we are forced to recognize that the relationship between the IFIs and the government did not involve a simple process of external imposition, but a complex and ambiguous process of negotiation in which compliance could only be achieved where the former were able to offer real incentives and create effective links with local political and administrative actors. And here it is also clear that the blame for poor performance does not rest with self-interested local actors alone. The Bank itself recognized that its own demands were probably unrealistic in relation to domestic implementation capacity, the availability of critical economic information, and weaknesses in both public and private sector institutional arrangements.[91] We should also note that many of the problems of slippage in programmes, lax administration, poor monitoring and political and bureaucratic resistance were encouraged by the limited amount of time spent by key Bank/Fund officials on the ground.

Key sector personnel are located in Washington, move relatively frequently from one country desk to another, and spend short periods in Kampala on fact-finding or fire-fighting missions, which do not allow them to build up the detailed knowledge of what is happening or to intervene when or (preferably) before problems arise. The advantages of continuous presence on the ground were clearly demonstrated by the impact of the presence of a resident Chief Technical Adviser on the Civil Service Programme after 1992. The critical importance of obtaining local support for policy changes, and ensuring that external advisers have a clear understanding of the real difficulties involved in implementation, suggests the need for greater decentralization in the IFIs whose staff need to move closer to events, and for the development of local structures to facilitate a continuous and inter-active dialogue between donors and governments. Without much greater efforts to secure consensus, local 'ownership' will always be weak and depend on a few sympathetic figures on the local scene.

6.   Conclusions: Efficiency, Equity and Autonomy in Uganda

6.1   Efficiency

This study was intended to demonstrate that the relationship between structural adjustment programmes and economic performance is exceedingly complex, and that

---

[90] World Bank (1993e: 12).

[91] World Bank (1993e: 10).

outcomes depend not only on the nature of the policies themselves, but, even more, on the ability of donors to get them implemented at all. Here the evidence from Uganda offers some important support to those who advocate standard stabilization remedies, while drawing attention to weaknesses in terms of the ability to secure long-term structural improvements. In general it seems clear that the macroeconomic stabilization package, combined with external financial support, produced better results than the local governments could have achieved alone.

First, the changes introduced after 1981 produced significant short-term gains, while the government's failure to maintain discipline and the subsequent political collapse quickly dissipated these advances. Second, the NRM's statist programme, introduced against donor advice and without support in 1986, failed for both financial and technical reasons. Third, the new programme had mixed results in the first four years. Increased external flows plus improved security led to a rapid resumption of growth. However, budget deficits and currency over-valuation continued, while key programmes were not implemented because of weaknesses in political leadership and the civil service, leading to inflation and weak export performance. Had these problems not been brought under control the programme would have gone off track as it had done in 1984. Fourth, the successful resolution of these difficulties in 1991-92, assisted by increased aid flows, allowed growth to continue, but also brought inflation and the exchange rate under control, creating the preconditions for long-term stability.[92] Weaknesses in this recovery can also be attributed to the failure to deal with more intractable elements in the reform agenda - privatization, civil service reform and improvements in tax and agricultural administration.

However, while there seems little doubt that the disciplines involved in the macro-economic stabilization programmes were a necessary precondition for success, the IFIs were much less successful in building the capacity required to develop and manage major projects, whether in agriculture, industry, the financial sector or in public services. This was not only because of weaknesses in Ugandan institutional capacity, but also because of weaknesses associated with the nature of the donors' own structures and the corresponding difficulties encountered in dealing effectively with their local implementing agencies. These weaknesses have yet to be resolved at both the Ugandan and the international levels. Thus, while it is probably true that the first 'stabilization' phase of recovery has been completed in Uganda, the more fundamental reform processes required for long-term growth have manifestly only just begun.

6.2   Equity and Poverty Alleviation

Adjustment programmes are often associated with increased inequality and impoverishment, but it is difficult to claim that this has occurred in Uganda. Here most of the poverty which still exists is clearly the outcome of the mismanagement of the 1970s and 1980s. Overall the growth process since 1987 has been very rapid, there is a relatively favourable distribution of assets, and service provision would have been far worse but for substantial external budgetary support. On the other hand, poverty alleviation was not given high priority in the early stabilization programme. In 1989-90

---

[92] Growth actually declined slightly between 1989 and 1993 as a result of falling coffee prices and intermittent drought; it rebounded very rapidly in 1994.

the Bank did introduce the Programme to Alleviate Poverty and the Social Costs of Adjustment (PAPSCA), as a poverty-focused programme, but this received very little donor support and has only been responsible for a few projects with a very limited impact. Between 1987 and 1992 defence and economic investment were given overwhelming priority, so levels of social service provision hardly improved during the period under review. Thus a social security crisis continues to exist in Uganda with a substantial proportion of the population living in extreme poverty. This problem will certainly intensify over the next decade as deaths from AIDS increase.

At the same time, however, it is likely that improvements in economic management and liberalization have had a positive net impact on poverty. The foreign-exchange, marketing, land allocation and licensing monopolies which dominated earlier policies were systematically used by the elite to expropriate resources from the society as a whole and more usually from its poorest members. Eliminating them has greatly reduced opportunities for predatoriness, while increased competition can only benefit consumers by reducing costs. Growth has sustained the demand for labour in both urban and rural areas and produced rising wages, although these are still very low. Transport and marketing improvements have increased the rate of return to smallholders and opened up opportunities in the rural and urban informal sectors. Political stability and better economic management have created opportunities for foreign investors and larger local entrepreneurs which should increase the demand for labour. Many potential opportunities for further development exist in agro-processing, tourism and small-scale manufacturing, especially given the country's increasingly important economic and political role as a supplier and safe haven in an increasingly disturbed region.

6.3   Political Autonomy

In Uganda the donor presence undoubtedly produced very different policies from those which the NRM would have chosen independently, or that would have emerged from a genuinely democratic debate. However, it is difficult to believe that such a debate could have been effectively managed in the conditions which prevailed in the late 1980s, or that the outcome would have been as successful as it was without the technical and financial resources provided by donors and the leverage which this gave them over local political actors.

This suggests that demands for much greater levels of local autonomy in countries which have been unable to manage their own economic policies successfully should be treated with caution. Consultation and local ownership are important, but programme implementation always involves significant conflicts of interest, not least with local elites whose desire to exploit their monopoly powers is a prime cause of economic failure. The NRM's 1986-87 programme would have been a recipe for disaster even with donor funding since the overvalued exchange rate, underpricing of coffee and cotton, and inflationary budgeting suppressed exports and penalized some of the poorest members of the community. Only a relatively privileged group of civil servants and parastatal managers opposed reform, because it would reduce their privileges, but they were strategically placed and would certainly have been able to block change but for donor pressures. The President was unable to control corrupt Ministers whose political support was essential to his political survival.

Local demands for autonomy are even less credible in countries where democratic accountability is weak, since it may only be donors who can insist on policies which will take real account of the needs of the poor. Thus donors will probably have to exert considerable pressure on governments and, at times, delay funding to secure compliance. This implies some degree of external imposition, though clearly this should be managed in a manner which minimizes conflict and operates on the basis of compromise rather than command.

This view will be contested by many who are deeply concerned by the 'neo-colonial' nature of the relationship between donors and governments in many weak states, and it could certainly be used to justify interventions which had much worse results than those described here. In our view, however, what is actually required is not an unrealistic demand for local autonomy, but better monitoring of the performance of the IFIs and more effective sanctions over their performance. We now live in a world in which global political and economic management is essential, so our concern should not be to reinforce national sovereignties, but to create stronger and more accountable mechanisms for international assistance and control.

Thus the main criticisms of the IFIs which emerge from this study do not relate to the substance of their policy programme, or to their willingness to exert leverage, but to their failure to maintain a constant presence in the country capable of effective monitoring and continuous cooperation with key local actors. They are highly centralized agencies with small local staffs which were greatly over-stretched while real authority was concentrated in Washington. A stronger and more continuous local presence would almost certainly have led to better supervision, less slippage and a more effective dialogue with government and other opinion leaders. It would also have reduced even greater weaknesses associated with their inability to exert effective day-to-day control over the implementation of sectoral programmes and projects.

6.4 Beyond Structural Adjustment

1995 is clearly a transitional moment in Ugandan history, since much of the agenda set out in 1986-87 has been completed or nearly so. Rehabilitation is virtually complete so the problem now is to develop a sustainable long-term development programme which will not only increase output, but do so without producing unacceptable levels of inequality and poverty. We can close by asking how much will have to change if this is to be achieved.

In 1993 the World Bank produced a report intended to unveil a strategy which would combine growth with equity. A recent review criticized it for assuming that poverty could be dealt with by offering 'broad-based agricultural growth plus social services in an adjustment framework; pretty well the strategy already being pursued in the country'.[93] In my view, however, a successful programme on these lines would mean significant improvements for the poor, although perhaps not for the poorest groups identified in the IDS study - the old, the disabled and the dispossessed. At the same time, maintaining a successful programme of this kind will not be easy. It will depend upon the maintenance of existing disciplines and the success of a number of

---

[93] IDS (1994: ii).

programmes which are highly problematic. These include the creation of a land market which does not privilege the already rich; an agricultural development programme based on improved technology for smallholders rather than estate farmers; significant improvements in key rural services - roads, water, education, health, and financial services; a redistributive tax system and institutional arrangements which eliminate corruption and direct oppression. This will require enormous improvements in current administrative and economic capacity, and in the responsiveness and awareness of the donor community.

It will also require continuing donor support at current levels, as well as better levels of consultation and cooperation. While donors could offer a clear programme during the stabilization process, developing a consistent and well prioritized strategy in the next phase will require a greater internal capacity to choose objectives and prioritize (and to coordinate support and spending) than has existed thus far. Given the need to translate support into high productivity services on the ground, the major emphasis has to be on overcoming existing institutional and organizational weaknesses in state, private and voluntary agencies, as well as in the international agencies themselves. The emergency conditions which prevailed in 1986 are now over, but the demands implicit in a successful poverty-oriented programme will be just as exacting over the next decade.

References

Barnett, T. & P. Blaikie. 1992. *AIDS in Africa*. London: Belhaven Press.

Brett, E. 1973. *Colonialism and Underdevelopment in East Africa*. London: Heinemann.

Brett, E. 1993. *Providing for the Rural Poor: Institutional Decay and Transformation in Uganda*. Kampala: Fountain Press.

Brett, E. 1994. 'Rebuilding Organisation Capacity in Uganda Under the National Resistance Movement', *Journal of Modern African Studies*, Vol. 32, No. 1.

de Coninck, J. 1979. 'Artisans and Petty Producers in Uganda' unpublished D.Phil thesis, University of Sussex.

Economist Intelligence Unit. 1992. *Uganda Country Profile 1992-93*. London: Economist Intelligence Unit.

Edmonds, K. 1988. 'Crisis Management: The Lessons for Africa from Obote's Second Term', in Hansen and Twaddle.

Evans, A. 1992. 'A Review of Rural Labour Markets in Uganda' (mimeo).

Green, R. 1981. *'Magendo* in the Political Economy of Uganda'. Brighton: Institute of Development Studies, (mimeo).

Hansen, H. B. & M. Twaddle (eds.). 1988. *Uganda Now*. London: James Currey.

Hansen, H.B. & M. Twaddle (eds.). 1991. *Changing Uganda*. London: James Currey.

Harvey, C. & M. Robinson. 1994. 'The Design of Economic Reforms in the Context of Economic Liberalisation: Uganda Country Study'. Brighton: Institute of Development Studies, (mimeo).

Institute of Development Studies. 1994. *Poverty Assessment and Public Expenditure: A Study for the SPA Working Group on Poverty and Social Policy. Uganda Country Field Study*. Brighton: Institute of Development Studies.

Ketley, R. 1994. 'Issues in Sequencing in Uganda' (mimeo).

King, M. 1966. *Medical Care in Developing Countries*. Nairobi: Oxford University Press.

International Monetary Fund. 1993. Staff Report for the 1993 Article IV Consultation. Washington, D.C.: International Monetary Fund.

Laker-Ojok, R. 1992. 'The Organisation of Input Delivery to Small Farmers in Uganda' (mimeo).

Lamont, T. 1994. 'The Process of Economic Policy Formulation in Uganda' (mimeo).

Lateef, S. 1991. 'Structural Adjustment in Uganda: The Initial Experience', in Hansen and Twaddle.

Makerere Institute of Social Research and Land Tenure Centre, University of Wisconsin. 1989. 'Land Tenure and Agricultural Development in Uganda'. Kampala:Makerere Institute of Social Research.

Malik, M. 1994. 'The Central Bank, the Treasury and Monetary Autonomy: The Experience of Uganda' (mimeo).

Mamdani, M. 1994. 'The Politics of Democratic Reform in Uganda' (mimeo, Kampala).

McGaffey, J. 1987. *Entrepreneurs and Parasites: The Struggle for Indigenous Capitalism in Zaire*. Cambridge: Cambridge University Press.

Meagher, K. 1990. 'The Hidden Economy: Informal and Parallel Trade in North-western Uganda', *Review of African Political Economy*, No. 47.

Mugenyi, J. 1991. 'IMF Conditionality and Structural Adjustment under the National Resistance Movemen', in Hansen and Twaddle.

Muneni, J. 1993. 'Organisational Pathology and Accountability in Health and Education in Rural Uganda' (mimeo).

Munro, L. 1990. *Report on the Uganda Community-based Health Care Fact-finding and Evaluation Exercise*. Kampala: UNICEF.

Ochieng, E. 1991. 'Economic Adjustment Programmes in Uganda', in Hansen and Twaddle.

Oxfam Briefing. 1994. *Multilateral Debt as an Obstacle to Recovery: The Case of Uganda*. Oxford: Oxfam.

Oxfam Uganda. 1994. *Health narrative*. Oxford: Oxfam.

Uganda Government. 1987. 'Ministry of Planning, Agricultural Policy Committee: Final Summary Report'. Kampala: Government Printer.

Uganda Government. 1990. 'Developing the Private Sector through Supporting Markets'. Kampala: Government Printer.

Uganda Government. 1991. *Report on the Uganda National Household Budget Survey, 1989-90.* Entebbe: Government Printer.

Uganda Government. 1994a. *Background to the Budget 1994-95.* Entebbe: Government Printer.

Uganda Government. 1994b. *Report on the Uganda National Integrated Household Survey 1992-93.* Entebbe: Government Printer.

Whyte, M. 1987. 'Crisis and Recentralisation: 'Indigenous Development' in Eastern Uganda'. Copenhagen: University of Copenhagen.

Whyte, M. 1991. 'Medicines and Self-help: The Privatisation of Health Care in Eastern Uganda', in Hansen and Twaddle.

World Bank. 1987. 'Report and Recommendations to the President... on a Proposed Credit... to the Republic of Uganda'. Washington, DC: World Bank.

World Bank. 1988. 'Office Memorandum: Uganda'. CEM Issues Paper. Washington, DC: World Bank, January.

World Bank. 1991. 'Report and Recommendations to the President... on a Proposed Credit ... to the Republic of Uganda'. Washington, DC: World Bank.

World Bank. 1992a. *Project Completion Report, Uganda: First Economic Recovery Credit.* Washington, DC: World Bank, 20 March.

World Bank. 1992b. *Uganda: District Management Study.* Washington, DC: World Bank.

World Bank. 1993a. *Uganda: Growing out of Poverty.* Washington, DC: World Bank.

World Bank. 1993b. *Uganda: Agriculture.* Washington, DC: World Bank.

World Bank. 1993c. 'Report and Recommendations...on a... Debt Reduction Programme'. Washington, DC: World Bank.

World Bank. 1993d. *Uganda: Selected Issues in Public Expenditure Rationalisation.* Washington, DC: World Bank.

World Bank. 1993e. 'Performance Audit Report, Uganda Economic Recovery Credit'. Washington, DC: World Bank, 30 July.

World Bank. 1994a. 'Report and Recommendations to the President... on a Proposed Credit... to the Republic of Uganda'. Washington, DC: World Bank.

World Bank. 1994b. 'Aide Memoire, Enterprise Development Project Supervision Mission'. Washington, DC: World Bank, 2 February.

World Bank. 1994c. *Staff Appraisal Report, Republic of Uganda Institutional Capacity Building Project.* Washington, DC: World Bank.

Zimbabwe
1991-94

Peter Gibbons

Centre for Development Research

1.   Introduction

There are two opposed views of the basic features of Zimbabwean economic performance in the 1980s. One, whose main advocate is Colin Stoneman (e.g., Stoneman, 1993), argues that this performance was a strong one. Real growth is said to have averaged about 4 percent per annum, three times the level in the Republic of South Africa and indeed in Sub-Saharan Africa generally. Exports were increasingly diversified in the direction of manufactured goods, debts were repaid without rescheduling, education and health provision were spectacularly expanded, national savings were at a consistently high level and reasonable food security was established. These achievements can be viewed as outweighing a series of negative tendencies, which Stoneman lists as serious over-borrowing in the early 1980s, a failure to create more jobs, a failure to implement a racial redistribution of assets (especially land), a failure to undertake meaningful economic planning, a failure to properly define government's relation to industry and trade and a failure to respond sufficiently to exogenous shocks.

A more critical view began to be systematically elaborated by the World Bank from around 1986-87. While acknowledging that Zimbabwean economic performance was superior to that of most other African countries during the decade, this argued that the government had failed to properly exploit the economic advantages it had inherited. In particular it had pursued policies favouring stabilization rather than growth. The latter had indeed run at almost 4 percent over the decade, but if the initial post-independence boom years of 1980 and 1981 are discounted the rate was well under 3 percent overall. Exports had increased by just above this level but imports had stagnated as the government restricted forex allocations to allow for debt-servicing. The latter rose to 37 percent/export earnings in 1987 although it declined again after.

The extension to Africans of state education, health and agricultural marketing services occurred on the basis of considerable internal borrowing. This is said to have been responsible for high fiscal deficits (averaging 8.9 percent/GDP 1985-90) and the crowding out of private investors from the local credit market. Inflation was high throughout the decade (averaging around 13 percent). Interest rates were negative in real terms and the high national savings rate was attained only by restrictions on (imported) consumer goods availability. Low formal employment creation was not merely a negative tendency but the country's single most important structural economic problem. Less than 30,000 new jobs were being created each year while over 200,000 secondary school leavers were entering the labour market. Lying at the root of this was said to be very low private investment levels. Between 1985 and 1990 these had averaged only 10 percent/GDP per annum. This was due not to insufficiently rigorous economic planning but to the fiscal deficit/crowding out problem, limited access to forex/imports and what were said to be Zimbabwe's generally high 'transaction costs'.[1]

Although opposed, these views have an interesting common central feature. In neither case was Zimbabwe's macroeconomic stability considered a major issue. Although the World Bank view saw budget deficit levels as problematically high, these

---

[1] The statistics cited here are derived from standard sources including World Bank ones. They have been used in preference to those actually used in World Bank *arguments*, as opposed to tables. The former normally overstate the problems being discussed: for example, the fiscal deficit is described as '10 percent for much of the 1980s', inflation as 'averaging 15 percent' and private investment as having fallen 'below 10 percent in the second half of the 1980s'.

were no more the central concern in this view than in Stoneman's. For both positions the key issue was lack of growth - and more specifically, industrial growth. Stoneman's proposals for promoting growth are not spelt out in much detail, but further resource redistribution and (unspecified) forms of state economic intervention are implied. The World Bank view, on the other hand, is clear: all that was required was for capital to be 'unchained', given greater access to foreign exchange and credit, and freed from regulation and threats of further redistribution.

Rather surprisingly the Zimbabwe Government - or more precisely, the Zimbabwe state - either bought the World Bank arguments wholesale and without qualification, or at least itself had enough confidence in the 'fundamentals' of private industry and agriculture to consider that the substantial concessionary external funding which would accompany the reforms could lift its performance onto a new plane. Structural adjustment was consequently introduced in 1990-91 on the basis of a trade liberalization programme with a five-year life. This programme received broad support from donors and - in its original design - has been implemented fairly systematically since. Indeed, many of the reforms originally slated for completion in late 1995 had already been introduced when this paper was completed (February 1995).

Though the severe drought of 1991-92, whose effects will continue to be felt until after the programme, makes problematic any definitive assessment of the programme, certain conclusions may nonetheless be drawn. Some of the assumptions of the World Bank model for promoting growth were borne out, but most were exposed as naive and there is a good case for further exploration of the suggestions implicit in Stoneman's argument. A local private industrial investment boom occurred, but in the subsequent context of a retreat to restrictive monetary policies served mainly to over-expose company balance-sheets. Absence of strategic state intervention also left industry in a difficult position to cope with adjustment-related intensified foreign competition and drought-related declines in demand.

The combination of drought and lack of supply response conspired to engender a severe economic crisis. In the process Zimbabwean economic management passed from the frail hands of the World Bank to the somewhat steelier grip of the IMF. Following this, the budget deficit and parastatal reform came to occupy prime place on the reform agenda. The adjustment exercise was transformed into an orthodox stabilization one, and most of the long-term goals disappeared from the discussion.

2.   History and Objectives of Zimbabwean Adjustment

2.1   Evolution of Relations with the International Financial Institutions and of Structural Adjustment

Zimbabwe became a member of the World Bank and the IMF shortly after independence. When experiencing budgetary problems in 1983 the Zimbabwe Government obtained an eighteen-month Standby Credit from the IMF, then worth US$390 m. In return, Zimbabwe is said to have agreed to devaluation, restoration of internal and external balances and cuts in development programmes and subsidies (Kadhani, 1986). In early 1984 the Standby was suspended by the IMF. According to Kadhani this was the result of a failure to meet credit targets; for Stoneman and Cliffe (1989: 163) the most important factor was a failure to meet budget reduction targets; for Davies *et al.* (1991: 20) it stemmed from the introduction of tighter import controls in February 1984. Whatever the reason, the break left a residue of ill-feeling and Zimbabwe subsequently avoided dealing with the Fund for the next eight years.

The World Bank's first non-project involvement dated from the mid-1980s when it financed the first of the country's export revolving funds with a US$55 m. loan. The scheme was recognized as successful by both parties and the Zimbabwe Government was anxious to extend it to mining and agriculture, but the Bank argued that in return Zimbabwe should embark on trade liberalization. The government refused and instead borrowed the money from British commercial banks.

In 1986 UNIDO published a report drawing attention to a number of structural problems in Zimbabwe's industrial sector. These included the high levels of vertical and horizontal integration of private capital and the consequent high degree of effective monopoly, but also the lack of significant job creation and the low levels of investment already referred to. Against a background of limited economic recovery but also ongoing stagnation in investment and employment levels, the World Bank sought to get trade liberalization back on the agenda through generating a public debate on these questions, along the lines described in Section 1 above (for an initial statement cf. World Bank, 1987a).

The Confederation of Zimbabwe Industry (CZI), the chief and most influential white-dominated business lobby group, had favoured protectionism throughout the life of the Smith regime and well into the 1980s. However, it had also always resented certain of the controls associated with this, especially those over prices and access to forex. It was also unhappy about the major increases in state expenditure which had been associated with extending social services and agricultural support services to Africans and their implications for tax levels and budgetary financing. Around 1987-88 its concern to increase forex availability led it to begin pressing for trade liberalization, albeit in a slow and planned way and in the context of introducing tariffs in continuation of a broad commitment to import substitution. Other important elements of its agenda were the relaxation of controls on prices, wages, investment and hiring and firing. Despite misgivings the World Bank adapted its approach to the CZI one and its representative at the 1988 CZI congress spoke in favour of gradualism.

Although the Zimbabwean Prime Minister and later President, Robert Mugabe, expressed clear opposition to trade liberalization until quite late in the 1980s (which has since recurred, see below), and although political support for it appeared to be limited to the Minister of Finance, Bernard Chidzero, trade liberalization eventually won the day. Part of the reason for this may lay in the compartmentalization of economic policy-making and the close relation of the latter to the CZI. Despite the government's formal commitment to Marxism and strained government-business relations especially on the question of economic relations with pre-reform South Africa, the CZI had exerted a considerable influence on economic questions throughout the 1980s and was now given representation on a series of committees the government set up in 1989 to recommend concrete trade liberalization measures. Simultaneously a new investment code was promulgated at a London conference sponsored jointly by CZI and the Confederation of British Industry. The code reduced the number of companies which could be described as foreign, established an Investment Centre with authority to independently approve projects of up to US$2 m. and embodied a recognition of the two principal international investment guarantee protocols.

Structural adjustment was unveiled in three stages, July and September 1990 and January 1991. The July package was preceded in February 1990 by the announcement of a major easing of price controls and the abolition of statutory wage regulation except for agricultural and domestic workers. The July 1990 version of structural adjustment (Zimbabwe Government, 1990) stated the government's new economic policies in a forthright but not particularly detailed way. Government would 'de-emphasise its expenditure on social services and emphasise investment in the material production sectors such as agriculture, mining and manufacturing' (*ibid.*: 6). Targets were set of 5 percent annual growth in GDP, 20 percent annual nominal investment growth (later revised to 25 percent) and a reduction of the budget deficit by 1994-95 from 10 to 5 percent. The centre-piece of the package was the announcement that the import control/forex allocation system would be replaced by tariffs and an Open General (Import) License (OGIL), to be phased in over five years. There would be further deregulation of prices and labour laws. The next stage of the proposals was unveiled in September 1990 when additional forex retention/export bonus schemes, more generous earnings remittance regulations and an upgrading of the powers of the Investment Centre were announced.

The World Bank welcomed all these proposals but insisted that more concrete information be provided before it recommended financial support. It also indicated that it felt the time frame of five years to be too long and that the issue of parastatal reform had been soft-pedalled. There may also have been a difference of emphasis on the presentation of social sector cuts, for in the third version of the proposals references to cost recovery in education were deleted and a number of compensatory measures added to protect 'vulnerable groups'.[2]

At the end of January 1991 the Zimbabwe Government announced a more detailed version of the package, *Framework for Economic Reform, 1991-95 (FER)* (Zimbabwe Government, 1991). This opened by specifying 'front-loaded' timetables for reducing subsidies to parastatals from Z\$629 m. in 1990-91 to Z\$40 m. in 1994-95 and for reducing non-education civil service employment by 25 percent (about 23,000 persons) over the same period. A commitment to opening up money and financial services markets to new entrants was followed by a timetable for implementing the OGIL. In the latter's first phase, raw materials would be transferred to it with tariff levels of 5 to 10 percent. In the second stage, intermediate and capital goods would be transferred, with similar tariff levels. In the final stage, consumer goods would go onto the scheme with tariffs of 30 percent. For the first time it was announced that this would be accompanied by a phasing out of export promotion/incentive schemes in favour of an extended export retention scheme. A new investment code would be drawn up, with project feasibility rather than forex savings potential as the main criterion. By 1994-95 earnings remittability would rise to 100 percent for all foreign-owned enterprises investing hard currency. *FER* concluded by announcing that goods would become price decontrolled as they entered the OGIL and that licensing and zoning regulations would be relaxed for informal and small-scale enterprises. *FER* also gave Zimbabwean adjustment a name and an acronym - the Economic Structural Adjustment Programme (ESAP).

---

[2] Somewhat paradoxically it has throughout the process been the World Bank rather than the Zimbabwe Government, which has placed greater emphasis on the need to acknowledge adjustment's 'social dimensions'.

Relative to most other structural adjustment programmes in Africa, ESAP was initially notable for the absence of an accompanying agreement with the IMF. It was this which appears to have given the Zimbabwe Government latitude in some areas, notably the programme's five-year duration (three is more normal) and the limitation of parastatal reform to semi-commercialization rather than privatization. A second unusual feature of the *FER* document was that it embodied a long annex entitled 'Assessing and Addressing Social Dimensions of Adjustment'. This contained proposals for a set of compensatory measures for 'vulnerable groups'. These will be examined in detail below (Section 7).

Zimbabwe's first Consultative Group meeting was held in March 1991, at which donors apparently reacted positively to ESAP and were said to have pledged a total of US$700 m. plus,[3] mostly intended to support the OGIL. It seems that none of this was disbursed in 1991 itself. It was not until the end of December 1991 that the World Bank formally approved its own first loan (SAL 1, worth US$175 m.), and not until March 1992 that this loan's first tranche was disbursed. Of course, disbursement normally follows a long way behind aid pledges. But some speculation occurred in the Zimbabwean independent press, as well in the Economist Intelligence Unit country reports, that the World Bank had held back on disbursements until it obtained a tightening of ESAP. Certainly 1992 was a year in which the main emphases of the adjustment process in Zimbabwe came to resemble more closely those of other African countries. Trade liberalization was not downplayed (although its central instrument was to change, see below), but public expenditure and in particular expenditure by public enterprises were to take on ever more central roles.

Import restrictions were lifted on the first items shifted to the OGIL in October 1990. There followed a surge of imports, much of it apparently speculative, which was to continue for most of 1991. Imports rose in value from US$1477 m. in 1989 to US$1850 m. in 1990 and US$1700 m. in 1991, turning a merchandise trade balance of US$203 m. in 1989 into a deficit of US$121 m. in 1990, before a partial recovery to a surplus of US$85m. in 1991. This increase in imports was roughly double that anticipated. Since there were no disbursements to support the OGIL the government was forced into borrowing US$155 m. on a commercial short-term basis in mid-1991 and attempting to depress import demand by introducing a 20 percent tariff surcharge on all OGIL items and new limitations on forex allocations for those items not so far included. Simultaneously the government was obliged to open negotiations for an IMF loan. Presumably as a precondition, a substantial devaluation of the Z$ was undertaken in the second half of 1991 (the average exchange rate in 1990 was US$1: Z$2.45 and US$1: Z$5.2 by 1992).

The deal signed with the IMF was said to be worth US$484 m. over three years. At first Zimbabwe did not gain access to the softer loan terms of the Fund's 'Enhanced Structural Adjustment Facility' (ESAF), but the latter tranches of the loan will be treated as an ESAF for interest repayment purposes. The conditions of the loan were that the 1991-92 budget deficit should be no higher than 7.1 percent; that public enterprise losses in 1991-92 be limited to Z$370 m.; that the level of monetary expansion in 1992

---

[3] In December 1992 the World Bank gave a figure for total pledges (including its own) much nearer the US$400 million level. It is not clear whether this was meant to cover the whole programme period or merely its first phase through, as the World Bank itself was to make another major loan in 1993 and promised a further one for 1995.

should be no more than 20.5 percent; that positive real interest rates should be introduced and upheld and that certain price controls should be removed.

It seems that these were the preconditions which the World Bank was also seeking for the release of the first tranche of SAL 1. In accepting the latter, the Zimbabwe Government meanwhile agreed to comply with four further conditions before July 1992. These were the expansion of the OGIL to cover 15 percent of all STIC items; an increase to 25 percent in the level of forex retention permitted to exporters under the Export Retention Scheme; an implementation of the 1991-92 Public Sector Investment Plan and adoption of one for 1992-93 after consultation with itself; a reduction of 5,000 authorised civil service posts and an increase in electricity and post and telecommunications charges to specific levels agreed with itself. The World Bank set the same public enterprise operational deficit target as the IMF as a further condition, along with a slightly looser target for the 1991-92 budget deficit (8.3 percent).

The loosening of the budget deficit target occurred at the height of an extremely serious drought - according to many observers the worst of the century - whose effects were exacerbated by the World Bank's earlier advice that Zimbabwe should sell off its grain reserves (see below, Section 4). The Zimbabwe Government had responded to it with a comprehensive package of relief measures. Maize was dispatched to the more severely hit areas, supplementary child feeding programmes were introduced, free seeds and other inputs were supplied to peasants for the 1992-93 season and various recipients of agricultural credit had their interest payments written off or refinanced. The Policy Framework Paper for 1992-95 estimated that drought-related imports would cost US$554 m. in 1992 and US$307 m. in 1993 and that there would be export losses of US$223 m. in 1992, US$200 m. in 1993 and US$164 m. in 1994. The total balance-of-payments impact in 1992 was likely to amount to 16 percent of GDP and 9 percent in 1993, while drought-related government expenditure was likely to be around US$150 m. in 1991-92 and US$400 m. in 1992-93, pushing the budget deficit well above the agreed targets.

Coming on the heels of an initial tightening of ESAP, it might be thought that the drought would be used by the Zimbabwe Government as a reason to reintroduce some slack to it. Somewhat to the surprise of the international financial institutions there were few signs of this. The major emphasis of PFP 1992-95 was that the drought should be used to speed up rather than slow down cuts in those aspects of government expenditure not directly related to drought relief, in order to contribute to the funding of the latter. In particular there would be cuts in subsidies and loans to non-agricultural public enterprises and postponement of government capital projects. It also unveiled proposals for deregulation of the financial sector and further deregulation of foreign investment restrictions (extension from December 1992 of full external remittability of profits and dividends for new foreign investments and shifting of the Zimbabwe Investment Centre from a sanctioning to a promotional role). On this basis, and since some of its other conditions had been fulfilled ahead of schedule, the World Bank showed little hesitation in agreeing to waive its 1991-92 budget and public-enterprise deficit targets. Approval for the disbursement of SAL 1's Second Tranche occurred in October 1992.

Zimbabwe's adjustment programme became formally subject to a more orthodox definition in negotiations leading to a second World Bank Structural Adjustment Credit of US$125 m. (SAC 2) in mid-1993. The Zimbabwe Government had to fulfil four conditions prior to this loan becoming effective.The first three of these concerned reducing the budget deficit for 1993-94 to 6 percent or less of GDP, putting in place an operational framework and performance contract between itself and the electricity supply authority, ZESA, and giving more detail on a promised series of steps toward deregulation of agricultural marketing. The first of these was intended to underline a determination to revert to the original *FER* framework, but the second and third demonstrated the new centrality enjoyed by public sector reform.

In the period 1991-92 both the World Bank and the Zimbabwe Government had approached the issue of public sector reform very much from the angle of budget deficit reduction. Indeed, in putting the case for the waiving of unfulfilled conditions of SAL 1 Bank officials had proudly listed the very steep rises in the tariffs levied by ZESA and the posts and telecommunications authority, PTC. As will be seen, by 1993 the level of these tariffs had become an issue threatening local capital's continued support for structural adjustment. In this context the World Bank began to complain that the Zimbabwe Government had done too little to improve the efficiency of the parastatal utilities and performance contracts to ensure this were suggested instead. Not unrelatedly, the Zimbabwe Government was requested to draw up a plan for comprehensive agricultural sector reform. Four of the nine conditions attached to the release of the second tranche of SAC 2 (during 1994) covered meeting deregulation targets in the markets for grain, cotton, dairy products and beef (see Section 4 for details). Three of the others related to non-agricultural public enterprises (see Section 9 for details).

The remaining conditions attached to both approving SAC 2 and releasing its second tranche concerned trade liberalization. For reasons which will be explained, by early 1993 the Zimbabwe Government apparently took a decision to replace the OGIL system by an enhanced Export Retention Scheme (ERS) as the main instrument of this policy. By then the OGIL had been expanded to include 20 percent of STIC items.The ERS forex retention quota had meanwhile been increased from less than 5 percent of export earnings to 30 percent and trading in ERS entitlements was apparently occurring. Before approval of SAC 2 was granted the Zimbabwe Government was asked to institutionalize this market in forex by allowing prospective importers to hold ERS entitlements in passbooks. For SAC 2's second tranche release, the retention quota would have to be raised to 50 percent by April 1993 and 60 percent by January 1994. From January 1994 the OGIL would be discontinued. It is worth noting in passing that the shift from OGIL to ERS involved an implicit tax on production for the home market and thus on most smaller-scale companies for whom this is a main activity.

In January 1994 the Zimbabwe Government published a second Policy Framework Paper covering the period 1994-96. This listed a series of further additions to the original ESAP agenda again mainly focusing on public enterprises. These aimed to separate the commercial and development functions of parastatals which straddled these roles and fully commercialize both the former and all other operations of those parastatals deemed to be performing wholly commercial activities, as well as bringing producers, processors and private traders onto the boards of the agricultural marketing agencies. One parastatal, the passenger transport company ZUPCO, was to have its 'franchise' terminated.[4] The PFP further disclosed the intention to revert to the aim of shifting the national tax burden from direct to indirect taxes, originally announced in 1991 but suspended because of the drought.

---

[4] The expression 'franchise' is the World Bank's. Since ZUPCO was not franchised but simply allowed a monopoly this was presumably a polite way of saying that it would be abolished.

In its September 1994 background report on the Zimbabwe economy the IMF expressed general satisfaction with the nature and pace of the reform process in the country. The central plank of ESAP, trade liberalization through free access to forex, had even been crossed a year ahead of the original target as, apparently without formal conditionalities having to be applied, the ERS retention rate was raised to 100 percent in July 1994, all limits (in magnitude and time) on forex holdings were removed, and the official exchange rate abolished. All subsidies and price controls and most restrictions on remittances from foreign investment and foreign ownership of Zimbabwe-based companies had also been dismantled. The only major areas of 'slippage' identified were in the continuing high level of deficits of certain loss-making public enterprises and in the tariff regime, which was said to have remained over-complex and high. The report indicated that IMF conditionality was continuing to apply to the first of these.

2.2   The Politics of ESAP in Zimbabwe

Evidence concerning the nature of the policy dialogue between the Zimbabwe government and the international financial institutions is scanty, but given the speed with which the central reforms have been undertaken it seems likely to have been cordial. Many politicians, often at high levels and especially those involved in the sector ministries, have expressed reservations or scepticism about structural adjustment but these have never apparently coalesced into anything amounting to opposition or even systematic criticism. Publications by very senior officials in the key economic ministries (e.g., Matshangala *et al.*, 1994) suggest that the agenda of the international financial institutions is now shared at this level of these departments at least, and that in this regard the World Bank and IMF have been pushing on an open door. On the other hand, the details of the design and implementation of many of the reforms, particularly concerning public enterprises, appears to be in the hands of consultants attached to a Monitoring and Implementation Unit set up in the Ministry of Finance. A UNDP study at the end of 1992 observed that in the process the main existing planning and coordinative mechanisms (already located within the Ministry of Finance) were sidelined. According to the UNDP they could and should have been utilized for the design and implementation of ESAP. The implication is that below the most senior level there is little direct local input to (or ownership of) ESAP in the public service.

Given the state of the Zimbabwean economy at the time, in mid-1992 there was much speculation that the programme would have to be extended for a couple of years or even abandoned completely, and that pressures for this to occur would increase as the 1995 general election approached. But insofar as the Zimbabwean political leadership have in fact reflected on the relation between ESAP and the election, the thinking appears to have been consistent throughout. This appears to have been that ESAP was likely on balance to generate positive results, and that they should be given as much assistance as possible to work their way through before the election takes place. On the other hand, this has not prevented very senior politicians, including the President, being scathing about both the pace and certain aspects of ESAP, especially its impact on national sovereignty and on the poor. At the beginning of February 1995 President Mugabe went as far as describing the reforms as 'disastrous', adding 'we are wiser than we were three years ago and we will not listen willy-nilly to what the international institutions tell us do' (*Financial Times*, 3 February 1995).

Although the Zimbabwe Government has in practice proved a generally compliant reformer, it has, fairly understandably, not been particularly anxious to be publicly identified with explicit 'ownership' of the reforms. After an initial phase in which efforts were made to explain the benefits of the programme through the state-controlled media the subsequent approach largely appears to be one of presenting adjustment as a fact of economic life, perhaps similar to drought - regrettable but over whose inevitability neither the government nor anyone else could exercise much control.

Little public debate for and against ESAP was evident in Zimbabwe prior to the programme's adoption, except in professional social science circles. One important political constituency, the trade unions, were not included in official discussions - presumably because it was believed that they would oppose the programme in principle. After all, the unions had come out strongly against the new investment code announced in 1989. In fact it is unclear whether the trade unions would have been wholly opposed to ESAP. At least some of its provisions (e.g. the deregulation of wage bargaining) corresponded to what they had been demanding for some time. In any event, excluding trade unions from discussions confirmed their probable existing tendency of opposition to the programme. Trade unions have subsequently attempted to organize against the ESAP. The state has tried to reduce the effectiveness of their efforts in draconian ways including brief detentions without trial of leaders and banning of rallies and demonstrations. It should be pointed out, however, that the position of the unions has been broadly anti-government and that the state has been reacting to this as well as to opposition to the ESAP itself.

Possibly surprisingly these bodies have been unable to generate much in the way of organized mass opposition to ESAP. A recent survey by Sachikonye (1995) suggests that this is largely a function of the fact that while the ESAP is widely unpopular, the government has indeed succeeded in conveying the idea that it is inevitable. This in turn has been assisted by the trade unions' inability to suggest any convincing alternative. Meanwhile, at plant level, many employers have blunted antagonisms by introducing or reinforcing paternalistic measures of various kinds.

There is some evidence of a long-term government-inspired strategy to weaken the power of trade unions in the public sector, although this is part of a general deregulative strategy aimed at damaging the Zimbabwe Congress of Trade Unions (ZCTU), a thorn in the government's side even before adjustment. In mid-1991 the Ministry of Labour announced its intention do away with the 'one industry, one union' policy which underlay the monopoly representation of ZCTU and its constituent unions, and which the government had itself supported a decade before when strengthening ZCTU was perceived as in its interest. At the same time management in the National Railways of Zimbabwe (NRZ) assisted artisans and enginemen to form a splinter railway union, in what was widely seen as an effort to break the best organized and financed trade union in the country (ZARU). Efforts by management to promote a similar artisanal union also occurred in PTC, though with little effect (for further details see Tengende, 1994: 427-38).

Besides continuing opposition from ZCTU, the main source of public criticism of ESAP has been from students and from groups within the churches, particularly the Catholic church. The latter have provided a steady stream of critical pamphlets, mainly highlighting the adverse social consequences of ESAP. Their arguments have also been taken up by some international NGOs with a presence in Zimbabwe. Christian Aid, Save the Children Fund and Oxfam have all published highly critical discussions of the

ESAP. A recent Oxfam publication on health and ESAP (Lennock, 1994) led to threats from the Minister of Health to expel Oxfam from the country.

Trade unions, students and the churches were all to one degree or another important political partners of ZANU-PF during its more radical phase and before the personal interests of the latter's leaders began to change, and ZANU-PF's estrangement from them in the context of its apparent embrace of white capital (local and international) has led to it searching for new political allies consonant with both the maintenance of a nationalist stance and the pursuit of economic liberalization. The main fruit of this search appears to be a considerable political and financial investment in the Indigenous Business Development Centre (IBDC), an organization of the more successful African entrepreneurs founded with government assistance in December 1990 to enhance African participation in the national economy. By 1994 the IBDC had become easily the most important conduit for assistance to African businesses and had attracted a membership of over 4,000. However, it was already plagued by leadership wrangles and a breakaway organization, the Affirmative Action Group, had been formed by mid-1994 (*Financial Gazette*, 18 August 1994).

3.   Macroeconomic Developments

3.1   The Macroeconomy

Table 1 summarizes the main macroeconomic developments since 1991, and in relation to economic performance in the previous few years. Very crudely it indicates that up to the end of 1994 ESAP had been accompanied by a small (3.2 percent) cumulative growth in GDP (and a very substantial contraction in GDP per capita, as population continued to grow by about 2.8 percent per annum), a very steep increase in inflation, a sharp drop in exports, a sharp rise in imports which, however, shows signs of tailing off, and no real improvement in the underlying investment situation. On the other hand, within the overall investment situation there has been a sharp fall in public and a significant rise in private investment - albeit from an extremely low base.

Corresponding to the fall in public investment there has been a marginal fall in the budget deficit, but one which was delayed by substantial spending on drought relief in 1992 and only eventually achieved by a combination of shifting parastatal deficits/borrowings off-budget (see below, Section 9) and introducing new taxes. If parastatal deficits and borrowings are included, the budget deficit has undoubtedly grown during the programme's life. Even with these parastatal deficits/borrowings transferred to the banking system, a 'drought surcharge' of no less than Z$1.5 bn (11.5 percent of projected revenue) had to be introduced in February 1995 to keep the budget deficit within levels acceptable to the IFIs. This move was part of a general pattern whereby tax reduction measures promised at the outset of the programme have been postponed, or implemented and then reversed, as the budget deficit problem has demonstrated its intractability.

The drought and measures to deal with it also must have had some impact on the current account balance and on the overall balance of payments. However, the great bulk of the deterioration in both the latter occurred during 1991, before most drought-related imports would have shown up. On the other hand, this continued a trend which seems to have begun prior to the adjustment period, in 1989 and 1990.

There is considerable evidence that there were serious flaws in the Zimbabwean adjustment programme even before the advent of the 1991-92 drought. As already indicated, the basic premise of at least its first stage was that adjustment could be brought about by a gradual OGIL-based trade liberalization. As also noted, unlike most African countries Zimbabwe was considered to have suffered from too much rather than too little stabilization and although there was some attention paid to the budget deficit neither the other major balances nor inflation or the exchange rate were special features of concern. On the other hand, as soon as problems in these areas arising from the combination of OGIL implementation, exchange-rate non-management and non-disbursement of aid began to surface, harsh stabilization measures were suddenly resorted to which killed off prospects of rapid economic growth. Their negative effects were reinforced in 1992 by the nature of the major instruments chosen to replace the OGIL and to bring down the budget deficit.

Table 1   Main Macroeconomic Indicators 1985-94

	1985	1986	1987	1988	1989	1990	1991	1992	1993	1994
GDP market prices (% increase)	6.9	2.6	-0.8	8.9	6.3	2.1	4.9	-7.7	2.0	4.0[a]
Govt deficit/GDP (%)	7.3	7.3	11.6	9.2	8.2	8.3	8.4	11.2	7.7	6.9[a]
Bal. payments (US$ m.)	164	47	141	109	-73	-19	-125	-127[a]	174[a]	
Exch. rate (Z$:US$)	1.24	1.61	1.66	1.89	2.23	2.53	4.95	5.20	6.47	8.20
Inflation rate (CPI)	10.0	14.6	12.3	7.2	12.8	17.4	23.3	42.1	27.6	25.0
Interest (discount) rate				9.0	8.0	10.0	27.0	31.0	32.5	28.0
Exports fob (US$ m.)	1120	1323	1452	1665	1693	1748	1694	1528	1609	
Imports fob (US$ m.)	919	1021	1071	1164	1319	1518	1646	1782	1487	
Trade balance (US$ m.)	201	302	381	501	374	230	48	-254	122	
Curr Acct bal (US$ m.)	-76	7	48	117	9	-147	-459	-605	-116	
Public investment/GDP					10.5	10.3	4.3	4.3	4.3	
Priv investment/GDP	12.0	11.6	8.0	10.0	9.3	10.7	17.7	15.7	16.2	

Sources: IMF, World Bank, Economist Intelligence Unit, Zimbabwe Government, *Quarterly Digest of Statistics.*
[a]   Estimates.

The basic assumption of the OGIL-based strategy was that there were bottlenecks in the export sector which could be removed by allowing companies to import what they needed, over a phased period which also allowed them time to re-equip and become more efficient and therefore competitive. It was also assumed that, prior to exports 'taking off', this would be financed by new grants and loans (an official estimate was that US$218 m. per annum in new money was required for this purpose for the life of the programme (Matshangala *et al.*, 1994)).

Certainly there were really substantial re-equipment needs. But as Durevall and Mlambo (1994) have pointed out, a precondition for OGIL-based imports to be driven by these alone was that a devaluation of the Z$ should have preceded the system's inauguration. Although widely anticipated, this did not occur: in fact the real exchange rate appreciated from (1985=100) 62.1 in 1990 to 64.8 in 1992 (Matshangala *et al.*, 1994). This gave rise to considerable speculative over-importation. Imports increased in value by US$199 m. in 1990 and US$128 m. in 1991, roughly double the level anticipated at this stage. As evidence of the speculative nature of much of this importing Durevall and Mlambo (1994: 41) cite cases of companies applying to re-export goods imported under the OGIL. On the other hand, it seems that most of these imports were in the form of machinery and transport equipment, rather than consumer goods, and must be understood in the context of the very restrictive import conditions which had previously prevailed (see Table 2b).

Table 2a   Composition of Exports by Commodities worth US$100 million + p.a. during period, 1988-94 (in million US$)

	1988	1989	1990	1991	1992[a]	1993[a]	1994
Total agricultural	480	436	580	700	532	491	
Tobacco	279	309	395	532	450	366	303
Total mineral	512	455	455	438	353	391	
Gold	212	180	239	225	164	233	
Total manufactures	602	739	648	590	581	635	
Ferroalloys	191	232	150	155	116	142	
Textiles/clothing	61	68	81	92	109	122	

Source: IMF.
[a]   Estimates.

Table 2b   Composition of Imports by Principal Commodities, 1988-92 (million US$)

	1988	1989	1990[a]	1991[a]	1992[a]
Food	26	n.a	42	20	318
Crude Materials[b]	102	..	69	97	107
Petroleum products	144	..	275	n.a.	251
Chemicals	216	..	286	351	259
Machinery & Transport Equip.	360	..	690	882	808

Source: IMF.
[a]   CIF.
[b]   Natural rubber, synthetic rubber, crude vegetable materials, wood pulp, synthetic fibres, crude sulphur, common salt and manganese ores.

In any event these imports could not be covered. In the same two years cumulative exports remained static while the net increase in foreign aid (none of it specifically targeted at the OGIL at this stage) was only US$105 m. and US$26 m. (Table 4). The result was the opening of a major current account deficit (Table 1), a resort by government to commercial borrowing, and the agreement with the IMF in mid-1991 which the Zimbabwe Government had striven to avoid.

Table 3   Government Revenues and Expenditure 1989-90 to 1994-95 (percentage of GDP)

	1989-90 actual	1990-91 actual	1991-92 actual	1992-93 actual	1993-94 actual	1994-95 budget
Tax revenue	30.4	30.3	32.4	27.4	26.8	25.0
Total revenue	34.1	34.5	35.1	31.0	30.6	28.0
Current Expenditure	34.5	35.0	34.0	35.9	31.2	28.6
Wages/Salaries	14.0	14.9	13.2	12.6	11.2	12.0
Non-wage	7.4	6.1	6.4	7.9	7.6	5.3
Interest	6.2	5.8	6.1	7.1	7.2	6.2
Subsidies	2.0	5.8	4.3	3.4	0.9	1.1
Capital Expenditure	4.0	4.4	4.7	4.4	4.1	3.4
Total Expenditure	42.3	42.8	43.5	42.2	38.3	32.7

Source: IMF.

Table 4   Some Crude Resource Balance Indicators, 1988-93 (million US$)

	1988	1989	1990	1991	1992	1993
GDP market prices	6349	6529	6776	6330	5640	5483
Total expenditure	n.a.	2686	2794	2753	2380	2099
Total tax revenue	n.a.	1930	2053	2050	1545	1469
Gross Official Development Assistance[a]	285	280	385	411	n.a	n.a
of which grants	66	78	108	141	..	..
Net foreign investment	4	-10	-12	3		
Outstanding debt	2601	2506	2649	3404	3920	4221
Debt service ratio (%)[b]	28.5	22.4	23.5	27.6	28.3	31.4

Sources: IMF, World Bank, Economist Intelligence Unit Country Reports.
[a]   OECD definition.
[b]   Total debt service/exports.

The combination of domestic and IMF efforts to reintroduce stability in effect meant that a classic stabilization programme was imposed on the trade liberalization one. A substantial devaluation was accompanied by the introduction of surcharges and surtaxes on OGIL imports and interventions by the Reserve Bank to increase interest rates to positive levels (Table 1), while also dampening lending on the supply side through increasing the legal reserve requirement ratios of commercial banks. Positive interest rates were to be a major burden for local companies, whose credit with the banks had risen from Z$1,200 m. in 1990 to Z$1800 m. in 1991, under the influence of negative ones and the stimulus of the OGIL. These measures combined to induce severe financial crises in many companies, while depressing demand. They did not, however, serve to lower inflation, which was driven to higher rates in 1992 both by devaluation and by the withdrawal of price controls and subsidies (see below).

Shortly after these measures were taken the decision was apparently made to abandon the OGIL in favour of the ERS as the main instrument of trade liberalization. Officially this was because the ERS provided strong incentives to the export sector by supplying with forex those most in 'need' of it, as well as having a stronger 'market orientation' (see below). A more pressing concern was to employ a method of trade liberalization which was self-financing. As already noted, the ERS retention quota was increased from less than 10 percent in 1990 to 100 percent by July 1994. Simultaneously free trading in ERS entitlements was gradually formalized. Initially these commanded a premium of 100 percent, creating a strong disincentive to net importers (mainly medium- and smaller-scale companies).

Unlike the gradualist OGIL scheme, the generalization of ERS implied an immediate and general trade liberalization in those sectors which exported, that is, an unanticipated opening up of all domestic producers of internationally traded goods to international competition. This would be implicitly delayed while there was still a substantial premium on ERS transactions but disappear as the latter declined. In fact this happened rather rapidly; by the end of 1993 the premium on traded ERS entitlements had fallen to 20 percent.

Behind the falling demand for ERS retentions lay the generally depressed state of Zimbabwean production. Even before relatively cheap competing imports were to appear on the scene industry was beset by ongoing low domestic demand, new major costs in the form of higher utility tariffs and further increasing interest rates. In order to meet its budget deficit conditionalities, the Zimbabwe Government had been encouraged by the international financial institutions to raise utility tariffs to 'economic' levels. In practice this meant levels which would make a major dent in these utilities' deficits. Power tariffs were hence raised on average by 65 percent in real terms in 1992 (for some grades of user the increase was much higher); rail and telecommunications charge increases were also very high. Meanwhile, while positive interest rates were also strongly pressed for by the donors, the oligopolistic nature of the local banking system appears to have allowed the banks to force these up to 15 percent in real terms in 1993 and between 5 and 10 percent in 1994.

Together with the substantial increase in forex supply available to exporting companies through the huge increase in the retention quota, this meant that supply of forex now easily exceeded demand. By mid-1994 Zimbabwe had accumulated 5 months' import cover, its highest level on record. This was greeted jubilantly as a sign of the success of ESAP by certain Zimbabwean politicians but rather signals its fundamental problems. Moreover it also signals that these problems are not likely to improve, for with the ERS premium at its present depressed level there is no disincentive to importers to intensify the competition from foreign goods faced by domestic producers.

Structural change in the economy, the ultimate objective of ESAP, appears to be at best slight. Taking Tables 1, 2a and 5 together, it is clear that there has been little shift in the basic structure of the economy in the desired direction - or any other. While there has been a significant growth in agriculture, despite the disastrous 1991-92 crop season, the remaining three of the four sectors exhibiting any dynamism were all in non-tradeables: construction, transport and 'other services'. Mining and manufacturing have hardly expanded at all, except that a substantial growth in the importance of textiles and clothing was cancelled out by the weak performance of ferroalloys. Overall the economy's shape after three years of adjustment very closely resembled that before the process began.

Table 5   GDP at Factor Cost by Sector (million Z$, constant 1980 prices)

	1988	1989	1990	1991	1992	1993	Av. growth 1988-93 (%)
Agriculture & forestry	592	587	548	565	427	634	3.3
Mining & quarrying	295	307	310	327	309	315	0.9
Manufacturing	996	1055	1119	1150	1041	955	0.3
Electricity & water	127	150	146	135	132	114	-0.8
Construction	61	63	57	59	75	95	8.2
Finance & insurance	211	231	237	243	250	254	4.1
Real estate	46	47	47	47	47	50	1.8
Distribution & hotels	451	483	512	529	481	419	0.0
Transport and Comms	248	254	260	287	317	350	7.0
Public admin & defence	409	423	425	442	382	363	-0.8
Education	389	400	401	397	405	413	1.2
Health	107	110	116	124	123	121	2.8
Domestic service	61	62	62	61	61	70	2.5
Other services	150	160	186	249	277	265	16.3
Total	4143	4332	4426	4615	4327	4418	2.4

Source: IMF, except figures for agriculture and forestry (recalculated due to gross error in figures supplied by IMF).

3.2   State Budgets

The general issue of the budget deficit has been touched on already. This section will discuss the changing pattern of state expenditure between the main budget headings.

Table 3 shows total expenditure and total revenue to have both fallen considerably between 1989-90 and 1993-94, revenue slightly more than expenditure. The revenue reduction has occurred through a planned programme of reductions in taxation, or at least personal taxation, which the World Bank believes to have been at levels which have created disincentives. Only briefly during the drought was there any attempt to correct the budget deficit on the revenue side. Expenditure cuts have fallen primarily on the side of wages and salaries. Non-wage current expenditure seems to have been relatively stable, while interest charges have actually risen. Capital expenditure also appears to have been stable, although this must be doubted given the figures provided earlier showing a halving of public investments (see Table 1). Subsidies have been more than halved, officially at least (see below, Section 9).

Table 6   Actual Expenditure[a] by Budget Appropriation Head, 1990-91 to 1993-94

Appropriation head	1990-91		1991-92		1992-93		1993-94	
	Z$ m.	%	Z$ m.	%	Z$ m.	%	Z$ m.	%
Education	1673	24	1972	22	2487	23	3111	26
Defence	1037	15	1194	13	1342	13	1534	13
Health	557	8	631	7	803	8	1083	9
Agriculture/water	600	9	1190	13	1866	17	1018	8
Transport/energy[b]	672	10	816	9	718	7	888	7
Home Affairs	353	5	471	5	529	5	825	7
Construction/housing	581	8	746	8	732	7	930	8
Other	1437	21	1870	22	2284	21	2688	22
Total	**6919**	**100**	**8890**	**100**	**10761**	**100**	**12078**	**100**

Source: Zimbabwe Government *Financial Statements*, various years.
[a]   Excludes debt service and statutory appropriations.
[b]   Includes national supplies.

Table 6 shows a high level of consistency in actual expenditure by budget appropriation head during the adjustment period, except for a sharp rise in expenditure on agriculture/water during the drought years. Home Affairs and Defence continue to account for a very high 20 percent of all expenditure. There has been a consistent decline in expenditure under the transport and energy heading. The figures provided here seem to suggest that education and health spending has been protected, at least in relative terms. But recent World Bank data which will be cited below (Section 8) give both consistently lower shares to the social sectors than are suggested here and also show substantial real declines during the ESAP period.

4.   Agriculture

Certain important continuities and other important differences distinguished Zimbabwean agriculture in 1990 from its character in 1980. On the one hand, the basically dualistic structure of the sector persisted without great change. In 1990 there were about 4,500-4,600 large-scale commercial farms (LSCFs) and corporately- and state-owned estates, averaging 2,400 hectares in size, between them employing around 300,000 workers (far more than manufacturing) and occupying almost 30 percent of the total land area. There has been some reduction in the number of farms in this sub-sector since 1980, basically as a result of the resettlement policies of the early 1980s. Some farms have also been bought by Africans. According to *Africa Confidential* (7 October 1994), Africans now own around 600 of them. There is a sector of about 8,500 officially designated African-owned small commercial farms (SSCFs) but the overwhelming majority of African agriculturalists farm on about 800,000 semi- or non-commercialized plots in the communal areas. SSCFs and resettlement schemes together account for 11 percent of the total land area, and communal area farms 42 percent.

On the other hand, the major development of the 1980s was the incorporation of a significant minority of this last category of farmers into the state-organized marketing system. This occurred through establishing marketing depots, crop collection points and extension services in the communal areas and making modern crop development packages available through Agritex. By 1988-90 farmers in the communal areas were producing roughly half Zimbabwe's marketed maize, a large majority of its marketed cotton, and an important share of certain other commercial crops. The LSCF sector continued to reduce its involvement in maize (and beef) in favour of tobacco, wheat, horticulture/floriculture and game farming. The most important commercial crop by value, tobacco, was grown almost exclusively on LSCFs, and 30-40 percent of households in the communal areas remained net purchasers of maize.

As already noted, agriculture initially featured in ESAP proposals only in terms of the contribution to the overall budget deficit of the losses of the main agricultural parastatal, the Grain Marketing Board (GMB). In the four years 1986-87 to 1989-90 the GMB accounted for Z$740 m. of the total losses of Z$1856 m. by major public enterprises. Maize marketing is said to have accounted for 67 percent of this loss. Unlike in other African countries there has been little or no discussion of how to increase the overall share of the export sector or how to increase peasant involvement in it. There appears to be an understanding that export agriculture can safely be allowed to shape its own future, provided that regular and competitive currency devaluations are carried out.

A long agricultural sector memorandum produced by the World Bank in mid-1991 basically concentrated on maize, arguing that GMB services to farmers in communal areas, and the controls associated with them, were uneconomic and counter-productive. The GMB had increased its number of depots from 38 (1980) to 78 (1990), as well as in 1985 establishing an additional 121 crop buying points (reduced to 50 to 60 by the time of the World Bank study), all in the communal areas. Their overheads were said to have contributed substantially to GMB deficits, although it was admitted that 'in practice it is difficult to separate a specific set of depots which are non-economic' and, moreover, that 'some of the depots opened in the communal areas...are equally or more economic than in the (LSCF) areas'. There were also said to be large diseconomies involved in maintaining the strategic grain reserve and disposing of excess stocks in boom years and in maintaining the centralized system for shipping maize from the remoter depots to a small number of urban-based mills, before shipping it back to these same remote areas in the form of meal. On the basis of a somewhat convoluted argument this system was said simultaneously to introduce national food insecurity (by unduly relying on peasant as opposed to LSCF production), threaten local food security (by draining supplies from the local market, thus exerting upward pressure on local prices) and block the prospects for diversification of smallholder production (by encouraging local farmers to give maize self-sufficiency their first priority) (World Bank, 1991: 108, 88-89).

While the Memorandum spent a lot of time on the marketing network, it spent very little on what might have been considered the at least equally pressing issue of the maize price. While inconsistent from year to year, producer prices were said to have been subsidized by an average of 34 percent between 1981 and 1989. It is not clear what this really means; the guaranteed domestic price of white maize was on average 12 percent higher than the world market price for yellow maize (white maize is little traded internationally), but the world price was itself distorted by subsidized exports from Europe and the US. The Memorandum also reported that the consumer price had been subsidized by an average of 41 percent over the same period. No conclusions regarding appropriate domestic price levels were drawn from this analysis. A discussion of pan-territorial pricing, which suggested that the main winners were bulk producers in the less remote communal areas and the main losers urban consumers, was also inconclusive.

**Table 7   Maize Crop Flows through GMB, 1990-91 to 1994-95
(April 1 to March 31) (million tonnes)**

	Stocks at year start	Purchases	Imports	Total stocks	Domestic sales	Exports	Carried forward
1990-91	1.1	0.7	-	1.8	0.9	0.4	0.5
1991-92	0.5	0.4	0.4	1.3	0.9	0.2	0.2
1992-93	0.2	0.01	1.5	1.7	1.5	-	0.2
1993-94	0.2	1.2	0.4	1.8	0.9	0.1	0.9
1994-95	1.3	n.a	n.a	1.7	n.a	0.7[a]	n.a.

Source: Calculated from Economist Intelligence Unit Country Reports, various.
[a]   Projected.

Concrete agricultural adjustment measures have fallen into two categories. The first concerns changes in the GMB itself. Regarding the coverage of its services there were cuts in the period 1990-92 along the lines broadly suggested in the World Bank Memorandum. The number of GMB crop collection points was reduced from the World Bank Memorandum figure of 50-60 to 9 by the end of 1991, and in 1992 it was announced that 57 of the remaining 74 depots (four of these also seem to have been closed in the interim) would be shut for at least part of each year. The latter measure was related not merely to a desire to cut staff costs but to the simultaneous effort to reduce GMB stock levels. The latter began before adjustment but appears to have intensified under its impetus. This reduction was reflected in a freeze on an EU-funded silo-building programme and the promotion of substantial export levels. Table 7 considers some of the implications of this last tactic through an examination of maize crop flows through the GMB in 1990-94.

Available statistics for both volumes and costs of maize exports and imports are wildly inconsistent between sources, but those given in the EIU Country Reports (based on SADEC Early Warning System data) - unlike some other sets - at least tally with what is known about levels of domestic purchases and sales. It is important to note that exports in 1990-91 were only half of those actually planned due to transport problems. Because domestic producer prices were about Z$200/tonne above export parity prices the savings on reduced storage costs were more than offset by losses incurred on export sales. The main result of the sales policy, however, was that because of crop failure during the 1991-92 crop season it obliged the GMB to undertake massive imports in the 1992-93 marketing season, most of which are known to have been on a commercial basis. (Marketing season dates in Zimbabwe always refer to the previous year's crop season. This frequently gives rise to considerable confusion, and should be borne in mind in reading the tables below, particularly Table 9.)

In 1993 the Zimbabwe Government decided that stocks should be rebuilt to prevent a repetition of the 1992-93 marketing season situation and further imports were undertaken for this purpose. These were predictably opposed by the World Bank, who pointed out that they were costing Z$1600/tonne as opposed to a local selling price to millers of Z$1048/tonne. Meanwhile little effort has gone into clarifying the net costs of the much larger imports of the 1992-93 marketing season, presumably since their scale could be interpreted as having been made necessary by the GMB following World Bank advice on export sales. The difference between the export price in 1990-91 and 1991-92 and the 1992-93 import price probably varied between Z$400 and 1200/tonne. It is not clear what share of this difference was borne by the GMB and what share directly by government and/or donors, but a reasonable estimate of total advice-related losses (loss on exports of 0.6 million tonnes which would not have been undertaken plus losses on re-importation of this amount) is Z$800 m., less storage costs that would have been incurred.

This is the background against which the enormous rise in GMB losses in the 1992-93 and 1993-94 marketing seasons has to be set. Further elements of this background include the fact that before the price rises of 1993, imports being imported at up to Z$1600/tonne were being sold to the large-scale millers at Z$690/tonne, *not including* the further subsidy to the millers of Z$390/tonne abolished in mid-1993. In 1993-94 GMB no longer had to supply this subsidy to the millers, but it had to finance the purchase of a very large domestic maize crop in the context of a reduction in its overhead margins (the difference between the local buying price and the selling price to millers) from 20.3 percent of the buying price to 14.1 percent.

Table 8   GMB Losses and Subsidies 1986-87 to 1993-94 (million Z$)

	1986-87	87-88	88-89	89-90	90-91	91-92	92-93	93-94[a]
Losses	215	193	163	169	186	497	852	1396
Subsidies	210	156	161	185	263	747	786	165

Source: IMF.
[a]   Estimates.

The second category of agricultural adjustment measures concerned market deregulation. During 1991 measures were undertaken to decontrol trading in yellow maize (a crop traditionally used mainly for livestock feed and produced mostly by the LSCF subsector), partly decontrol it in red sorghum, rapoko and groundnuts, and to remove some of the restrictions on movement of ordinary (white) maize. The objective of these reforms was to allow trade in the communal areas to take place directly between producers and processors, except in the case of white maize where it was intended to expand the role of private intermediary traders.

Once the drought had ended in 1992, these measures were followed by two sets of further changes. The first set was intended to eliminate all controls and restrictions in the trade in beef, dairy products, cotton, oil seeds and yellow maize, in the process relegating the role of the responsible marketing boards to one private trader/processor amongst others. The second set was intended to create free trade in wheat and near-free trade in maize, but alongside a preservation of the role of the GMB as a setter and defender of a floor price. The restriction imposed on free trade in maize was that for a certain period in all of the country, and for a longer period (still continuing at the time of writing) in the Harare area, large-scale millers could only purchase direct from the GMB. This was because of the oligopolistic character of the milling trade. (There are seven large-scale millers in the whole country. These accounted for about 80 percent of all GMB sales in the 1980s and one of them alone accounted for over half of all sales.)

Because of the drought and the recent character of most of the reforms it is difficult if not impossible to draw any conclusions concerning their effects from data on hectarages or marketed output trends, etc. Nevertheless these are presented in Table 9 for the main crops and products, along with price trends. The tobacco price has throughout been a market-determined one. Theoretically, for the last two years that of cotton also has been decontrolled. Discussion will be mostly confined to the most important peasant crops, maize and cotton.

Commercial sector maize hectarage and production had been in decline since the mid-1980s, with the planted area now 25-30 percent lower than it was a decade ago. This apparently mainly reflects the crop's returns vis-à-vis tobacco. Although the maize price has remained good (at above the world price), with the exception of the 1991-92 and 1992-93 marketing seasons tobacco prices have been on a continuously rising curve even in US$ terms. It is therefore hardly a surprise that during the adjustment period the number of registered large-scale tobacco growers increased from 1475 (31 percent of all large-scale commercial farmers) in 1991 to 3687 (79 percent) in 1993. An increase in the LSCF maize planted area occurred in 1993-94, however, presumably on more marginal land and in relation to the real price improvement.

The planted maize area on farms in the communal areas was around 0.9 to 1.1 million hectares for most of the 1980s and remains at this level. Marketed production fell badly in the 1990s, obviously largely as a result of the weather, and while recovering sharply in 1993-94 was still perhaps below expectations. Since the late 1980s not only have many crop collection points been closed but up to 1991-92 fertilizer consumption also fell sharply. The communal area share of fertilizer consumption had risen from 8 percent of the national level at independence to 34 percent in 1985-86 but fell to 26 percent by the end of the decade and collapsed during the 1991-92 drought. Consumption seems to have increased substantially during the 1992-93 crop season, however, partly as a result of the free supply of one bag to each household and according to interviews conducted by Pedersen (1994) remained high in the 1993-94 crop season, as a result of the fact that the same maize output could now purchase roughly double the previous amount of fertilizer. There was also a second round of free seed and fertilizer distribution at the outset of the 1994-95 season, said by critics to be for electoral purposes.

Little hard evidence is available on what is happening on the ground regarding grain marketing, but there are suggestions that the LSCF sector is remaining with the GMB rather than selling to the millers, while a much higher than normal share of the communal area crop has passed through the hands of small private traders. It seems that the LSCF sector is extremely wary of the millers. In 1993-94 the commercial wheat farmers' association successfully lobbied the government to be allowed to continue to sell exclusively through the GMB as it was feared that the millers would use their potentially oligopolistic position to force down prices.

While the LSCF sub-sector retains the influence to be able to ensure this, peasants in communal areas do not. As marketing through the GMB became more physically difficult for them more and more turned as anticipated to small-scale private traders (where it is uneconomic for the GMB to buy direct from peasants it is almost certainly equally uneconomic for the millers to do so). Private traders have never been popular with peasants, largely because they have evaded officially allowed margins in farm-gate purchases, while also having a reputation for engaging in cheating. They seem to have become much more unpopular since, with newspaper stories appearing of peasants complaining that the GMB had 'abandoned them to the exploiters', leaving them only with the option of selling to private traders at 60 percent of the floor price. How much this represents a fundamental change from the previously prevailing situation is open to question, and in any case present commercial maize growing in the communal areas may still be economic even at this level. But the impact of these changes on the long-term grain supply situation remains highly uncertain.

The GMB subsidy of Z$562/tonne on white maize to (large-scale) roller millers was removed on 1 June 1993. This was fully - but not more than fully - passed onto consumers and there was an immediate increase of 50 percent in the roller maize retail price. Three months earlier the removal of the subsidy on wheat meal had been followed by a rise in the bread price by 120 percent. This had led to a collapse of demand for bread and presumably more cautious behaviour on the part of the millers.

Cotton production reached a post-independence high in 1988 under the impact of apparently favourable weather and price conditions. From 1989-90 to 1991-92 marketing seasons the price seems to have deteriorated in real terms and production fell, although the planted area remained relatively stable. The reason for this paradox was the replacement of growers from the LSCF sector (whose planted area fell from 75,000 hectares in 1988 to 40,000 in 1991), for whom the price was unattractive, by peasants for whom it was still attractive.

Since the ESAP began the Cotton Marketing Board (CMB) has demonstrated itself to be one of the most market-oriented of Zimbabawe's public enterprises. It has apparently systematically striven to make a profit while offering market-based incentives to producers. In regard to the latter, although the government set a floor price for cotton for the 1992-93 and 1993-94 marketing seasons, the actual price paid by the CMB has been much higher and reflects a real rise similar to that in tobacco and maize. Moreover the CMB also offered its own post-drought crop input package to peasants (farm group members), paralleling that provided by central government to maize growers. The response to these incentives seems to have been disappointing, however. The 1992-93 figures were clearly drought-affected, but relative to 1991-92 both the planted area and production showed little sign of improvement in the 1993-94 marketing season. The uptake of the input package was also lower than expected. Peasants were deterred by the 31 percent interest rate (plus handling charges) attached to the package and the latter had to be reduced to the negative rate of 21 percent in order to clear stocks.

Table 9   Hectarage, Marketed Output and Prices of Major Crops, 1988-89 to 1993-94 Marketing Seasons (thousand hectares and thousand tonnes)

	1988-89	1989-90	1990-91	1991-92	1992-93	1993-94[c]
Maize						
hectares Cfs[a]	151	154	} 1101	100	123	143
hectares CAs	1036	920		781	1115	1258
marketed prod Cfs[a]	682	746	} 779	500	12	550
marketed prod CAs	514	154		140	0	617
producer price (Z$/t)	195	215	225	270	550	900
Wheat						
hectares	51	55	44	49	12	n.a
marketed prod	256	284	320	280	57	250
producer price (Z$/t)	365	400	460	520	995	1450
Cotton						
hectares	248	228	272	235	246	218
marketed production	324	264	188	205	60	214
producer price (Z$/t)[b]	850	925	1170	1350	2915	2976
Tobacco						
hectares	63	63	69	89	83	74
marketed production	105	135	140	177	211	169
producer price (Z$/t)	4485	4133	6192	11079	9840	14000

Sources: Zimbabwe Agricultural Marketing Authority, Agricultural Situation and Outlook Report, 1993-94; IMF; World Bank; ZCSO Quarterly Digest of Statistic; Economist Intelligence Unit Country Reports.

[a]   All types of commercial farm.
[b]   To 1991-92 official producer price, since 1992-93 actual price offered by CMB.
[c]   Estimates.

In regard to its more general efforts to be profit-making the CMB has run into some of the central contradictions of the adjustment process in Zimbabwe. Traditionally local spinners have had the first call on output of lint from the CMB's ginneries (the CMB continues to control most ginning capacity). In the early 1980s the world price of lint rose and the CMB was instructed to provide lint to local spinners at Z$0.10/kg cheaper than the export price. This implicit subsidy has remained ever since, increasing both in nominal and in real terms, and the CMB's efforts at commercialization have since 1990-91 revolved around attempting to reduce its effects in various ways.

Some reduction in the effects of the subsidy was apparently attained in 1990-91, allowing the CMB to make a profit for the first time in its history. It seems that the CMB had simply increased its exports, on which it could make roughly Z$1/kg, rather than supplying local spinners. This apparently occurred again in 1991-92. The CMB began experiencing real resistance from the spinners and the government in the 1992-93 marketing season when it was directed to stop exports and instead import (at Z$6/kg) 70,000 tonnes of lint for the spinners' needs. (The need for this level of imports - equivalent to about 210,000 tonnes of seed cotton - also casts severe doubt on the IMF figures for locally marketed seed cotton in 1992-93.) Ostensibly in line with its mandate to make a profit, but possibly also because the budgeting of its own dramatic increase in the local seed cotton producer price had been based on continuing to export, the CMB tried to charge the spinners Z$8/kg for the imports. The spinners appealed again to the government, who, anxious about the declining viability of some of the spinners, reduced the price to Z$6. The spinners then managed both to maintain the ban on exports and to underline their domination over the CMB by actually transferring part of the costs of the Z$'s further devaluation to the board. In 1993-94 imports were running at Z$13.20/kg while government was allowing the CMB to charge only Z$10.50/kg. The CMB tried to get around this by levying storage charges on the lint it was holding for local sale, but rapidly ran into a cash-flow crisis. In mid-1994 it announced it had no cash to buy during the 1994-95 marketing season.

The CMB has been depicted as suffering politically inspired penalties for trying to follow a 'market-rational' strategy. But the lesson is rather one about the naivety of purely market solutions and the need for their mediation in pragmatic ways. Had the CMB been given its head, the future of the spinning sub-sector would undoubtedly have been compromised. Production had already been severely cut at Merlin and another firm, Zimbabwe Spinners and Weavers, was having to divest subsidiaries.

5. Industry

5.1 Formal Sector Manufacturing

The formal manufacturing sector in Zimbabwe is amongst Africa's largest. Already by 1939 it accounted for 10 percent of GDP and 7 percent of the paid workforce; by the end of the 1980s this had risen to about 26 percent of GDP and 16 percent of the paid workforce. It furthermore accounted for half of all exports, if ferroalloys and cotton lint production are included in its output. The metals and metal products sub-sector predominated, with the highest number of production units (408 of a total of 1364), the second highest gross output value (foodstuffs was first), and the highest shares of value added, total employees (35,000), capital stock and exports. Taken together with foodstuffs and chemicals, it accounted for over 50 percent of all these indicators.

The main phase of expansion of Zimbabwean manufacturing, in terms of both production and employment, was between 1966 and 1975 and certain structural problems with the sector had become evident by the late 1980s. Amongst these was an apparently secular decline in the exported share of its gross output, from 26 percent in 1966 to 18 percent in the late 1970s and further to only 10 percent by the end of the 1980s.

The conventional explanation for such declines, advanced by the World Bank also for Zimbabwe, is a lack of international competitiveness based on high cost structures originating in protectionism and overvalued exchange rates. The latter not only shield domestic industry from the efficiency gains it would need to make but also prevent it from acquiring internationally competitive technology. The analysis applied to Zimbabwe also highlighted the instability and unpredictability of the forex allocation system and the increasing 'crowding-out' effect of the budget deficit (World Bank, 1987). According to this analysis, decline could only be halted and reversed by greater budgetary discipline coupled with forex allocation, external trade and foreign investment liberalizations - or rather, such liberalizations accompanied by fresh resources for in-dustrial re-equipment. Certainly there would be some casualties in this process, both at enterprise and sub-sector levels, but there were other firms and sub-sectors (particularly textiles and clothing) which could look forward to burgeoning export-led growth.

Table 10   Aspects of Manufacturing Performance, 1988-93

	1988	1989	1990	1991	1992	1993[a]
Mfg prod/GDP[b](%)	24.0	24.3	25.3	24.9	24.1	21.6
Mfg emplymt/total emplymt(%)	16.6	16.7	16.5	16.5	15.9	15.1
Mfg exports/total exports(% value)	36.6	44.4	37.6	33.4	38.7	40.8
Index of mfg prod[c], general	123.9	130.8	138.1	143.0	129.9	119.3
foodstuffs/stockfeed	129.7	131.5	144.1	147.2	150.1	123.2
drink/tobacco	117.3	113.8	129.9	133.8	134.3	126.6
clothing/footwear	120.2	137.7	145.0	148.9	124.5	127.8
textiles/cotton ginning	202.7	208.2	216.6	226.2	176.5	192.5
chemical & petroleum prods	130.8	146.0	158.8	159.4	138.1	129.6
metals & metal prods	100.4	106.2	111.4	113.5	100.6	82.4
Output value (Z$[b]) per employee	5317	5401	5677	5598	5278	5195
Mfg exports (US$) per employee	3213	3785	3287	2872	2943	3455

Source: IMF.
[a]   Provisional.
[b]   Constant 1980 prices.
[c]   1980=100.

Writing in response to this analysis, Riddell (1990) criticized its central assumptions and predicted that following its policy implications would lead to generally adverse con-sequences. The argument was said to have seriously underestimated the overall decline in world demand for manufactured products and in the terms of trade of Zimbabwean exports during the 1980s. In addition it failed to acknowledge various important ways in which pre-adjustment policies benefitted industry. Rising recurrent expenditure by government might make it more difficult for industry to borrow but it did expand certain forms of domestic demand. Moreover, when industry got access to local credit it was at subsidized rates precisely because the state was the main creditor. Thirdly, industry benefitted very substantially from the cheap tariffs levied by the parastatal utilities. Structural adjustment would not only eliminate these advantages but it would also expose local industry both to full-scale international competition and to international economic shocks. In addition, the type of industrial growth likely in the wake of adjustment was not one which would see large-scale increases in formal employment.

Table 10 makes grim reading. During the adjustment period manufacturing has not increased its share of total GDP, has declined in its share of total employment, has not increased its share of total exports, has declined absolutely in output generally and in most key sectors (some dramatically), and has failed to increase in labour productivity either generally or in relation to exports. The only bright spot has been that of private investment, reported in Table 1.

A surge of private investment occurred in 1990 and 1991, particularly in the textiles and clothing sub-sectors where according to the Central Africa Textile Manufacturers' Association there was a total investment of Z$1500 m. (about US$300 m.) in re-equipment. According to Sachikonye (*ibid.*) this investment wave was for most practical purposes confined to companies which were already large-scale and directed primarily toward improving their export competitiveness.

Subsequently manufacturing generally has been afflicted by high interest rates (1991 onwards), difficulties in raising local credit (throughout), reduced local demand (1992 onwards), major increases in utility tariffs (1992), drought-related reductions in the availability of local raw materials and electric power supply (1992-93 onwards) and intense competition from imported goods (1992-93 onwards). Notwithstanding World Bank data to the contrary (see Table 1) most investment/re-equipment programmes were shelved from 1992 onwards and there has been little if any new foreign investment in manufacturing, except in the speculative form of trading in the shares of some bluechip companies registered on the Zimbabwe Stock Exchange. Since the middle of 1992 a large majority of manufacturing firms have been said to be working under capacity; the ZCSO *Business Tendency* report for August 1994 put the figure at 88 percent.

The companies experiencing the greatest crisis appear to have been those which managed to borrow heavily in 1990-91, and were therefore most exposed to the jump in interest rates, and who have been most exposed to the collapse of local demand. These have tended to be those which came to prominence in the 1980s in recent growth sectors like textiles, but which lacked the hidden savings accumulated during UDI by many of the old-established multinational conglomerates. Despite a slight upturn in 1993 textiles alone - described as 'reeling from the effects of competition from second hand clothes, cheap fabrics from the Far East, the price of cotton lint, the removal of export incentives, high interest rates and the protective tariffs introduced by South Africa' - has seen the closure of 87 of the 280 companies in the sector since the turn of the decade (*Financial Gazette*, 6 October 1994), including one very large one (Cone Textiles). Another major casualty has been the heavy industrial sector, with severe difficulties also reported by the pulp and paper manufacturer Hunyani, the chemical company Bayer Zimbabwe, the state-owned steel manufacturer ZISCO and the ferroalloys industry, Zimbabwe's traditionally largest volume exporter. Ferroalloys have been particularly hit by increases in rail and especially electricity tariffs, in a context where international markets are both steadily contracting and increasingly flooded by stocks dumped by the CIS countries. By mid-1994 the overall output index had recovered slightly to 130, but was still 10 percent below its 1991 level.

Over the years a number of studies of the Zimbabwean manufacturing sector have pointed to its high degree of concentration of ownership. A study published in 1993 commissioned by USAID stated that of the approximately 7,000 products manufactured in the country, almost a half were produced by three groups. There is reason to believe that concentration has increased under the ESAP as companies have responded to the prevailing difficult trading conditions by redefinition of core activities, sales or closures of peripheral ones and other forms of restructuring.

Retrenchments are a normal accompaniment of restructuring. In Zimbabwe they are supposed to have been made easier by the ESAP-related amendment of the Labour Relations Act in 1991, which diluted some of the main forms of employment protection which had existed since 1981. These forms of protection applied, however, only to permanent employees, and employers systematically evaded them after 1981 by mainly hiring new employees on a short-term contract basis. Even under the new legislation it remains considerably easier not to renew the contracts of temporary workers than to dismiss permanent ones. Official figures on retrenchment are therefore not particularly meaningful and it is more appropriate to look at levels of total employment in the sector. The IMF figures in Table 10 show a fall from a peak of 165,000 employees in manufacturing in 1990 and 1991 to 151,000 in 1993, or a fall of 14,000 in all. Presumably on the basis of a different definition of 'manufacturing', the ZCSO figures are considerably different. These show a total of 197,100 employees in 1990 rising to 205,400 in 1991 before falling to 184,400 in March 1993. However, by January 1994 this total had risen back to 194,700. By this reckoning, only 2,400 manufacturing jobs have been lost during ESAP. Most estimates by Zimbabwean social scientists suggest a net loss of about 25,000 jobs during adjustment, but these include jobs in sectors other than manufacturing and are based on a cut-off point in mid-1993, before the mild upturn. Not surprisingly, published figures on the distribution of retrenchments of permanent workers show these to be concentrated in the metals sub-sector. It is not possible to give a breakdown of job losses by gender.

According to ZCSO data, real per capita earnings in manufacturing were fairly stable between 1981 and 1990, with an index ranging between 99.1 in 1986 and 108.6 in both 1981 and 1990 (1980=100). Between 1990 and June 1993 they fell drastically, however, to 77.9. In terms of relativities this still left manufacturing workers with a smaller fall in living standards than any other group of workers except those in mining and finance, insurance and real estate (the real incomes of the last of these groups were unique in actually registering an increase).

5.2   Informal Sector Manufacturing

Estimates of the overall coverage of the informal sector in Zimbabwe immediately prior to adjustment ranged from 2.1 percent of the economically active population in one World Bank study to 27 percent in the first GEMINI report (MacPherson, 1991). The GEMINI report was the first attempt to estimate the size of the sector to be based on a comprehensive household survey and is probably the most reliable. A second

GEMINI study was carried out two years after the first, in September 1993 (Daniels, 1994). This found that the sector now accounted for 29 percent of all jobs. Of course, not all these jobs are full-time and many are combined with agricultural activities. Table 11 summarizes the main conclusions.

A net growth occurred in small-scale manufacturing enterprises, but at a far lower pace than in retail trade. This basically reflected an increase in entries by low-profit enterprises, according to the authors supporting 'the hypothesis that firm births are driven primarily by an excess supply of labour rather than demand for sector products' (Daniels: ix). Expansion within existing firms decreased between 1991 and 1993, relative to respondents' reports for the period 1989-91. The numbers and proportion of women in the manufacturing branches of the sector increased over the two-year period, but basically again in low-profit areas like crocheting, grass/cane/bamboo preparation (for basketry) and knitting. The 1993 study concluded that developments in the sector were being driven not by the emergence of new ESAP-related opportunities but by an excess supply of labour produced by low economic growth. It refrained from drawing any conclusions concerning the relations of this to ESAP. No data on incomes were included in the 1991 study making impossible comparison between the two surveys on this variable.

Table 11   The Informal Sector in Zimbabwe, 1991-93

	1991	1993
Total employees (m.)	1.30	1.56
Total enterprises (m.)	0.82	0.94
Sectoral distribution (%)		
Manufacturing, of which:	72.00	65.00
-- *food and beverages*	*7.50*	*4.90*
-- *textiles*	*34.30*	*32.80*
-- *wood and wood products*	*21.10*	*18.10*
Trade, of which	21.10	28.20
-- *retail trade*	*20.40*	*27.50*

Source: MacPherson, 1991; Daniels, 1993.

6.   Mining

6.1   Formal Sector Mining

Mining is Zimbabwe's third most important economic sector, accounting for only about 7 percent of GDP but a quarter of export values. Gold has traditionally been the most important metal mined by value followed by nickel and various industrial minerals. By

African mining standards ownership is relatively dispersed: the most important company, Anglo-American, controls 25 percent of output by value. Mining's post-independence history broadly parallels that of manufacturing, with a brief flurry of investment immediately after independence being followed by several years of stagnation, until the late 1980s when investment interest (at least in exploration) began picking up again.

At least in the period 1981-87 Zimbabwean mining shared some of the general problems of large-scale mining in Africa identified in a recent World Bank sector strategy document (World Bank, 1992), namely a declining share of world production and very low investment in exploration. The World Bank has blamed these phenomena on a lack of recent foreign direct investment in African mining, which is itself said to be the result of an excessive state presence in mining activity, general restrictions on foreign economic activity, and macroeconomic instability. Structural adjustment is considered likely to provide the basis for an upturn in mining investment through its association with economic stabilization, privatization and more welcoming conditions for foreign investment - especially where these are rationalized into a new investor-friendly mining code. Table 12 summarizes some of the relevant trends in the sector during the period under consideration.

Table 12   Aspects of (Formal Sector) Mining Performance, 1980-93

	1980	1988	1990	1991	1992	1993
Share of mining in GDP	8	7.1	7.0	7.1	7.1	7.1
Share of mining in employment	6.6	5.3	4.3	4.1	4.1	3.8
Mining exports/total exports (%)	40	31.1	26.4	24.9	23.6	25.1
Index of production, total	**100**	**103**	**108**	**109**	**107**	**104**
gold	100	n.a.	146	155	159	162
nickel	100	n.a.	76	75	67	79
coal	100	n.a.	175	181	177	169
asbestos	100	n.a.	64	57	60	63
chromite	100	n.a.	104	103	94	46
Output value (Z$[a])/Employee	n.a.	5112	6031	6424	6155	6847
Export value (US$)/Employee	n.a.	8880	8842	8614	7035	8495
Valid EPOs	n.a.	11	37	51	81	108

Source: IMF; Ericsson and Gibbon, 1993; Vallières, 1993.
[a]   Constant 1980 prices.

The performance of mining during the adjustment phase has been generally more stable than that of manufacturing, despite facing some of the same problems. Positive trends in this sector are also clearer. Mining has more or less maintained a steady level of output and its share in GDP. Although its share of exports has fallen, its workforce's export productivity has been broadly maintained and labour productivity seems to have risen. The latter trend has been strongly influenced by the increasing importance of high-value minerals in total production, however. Gold production has witnessed a steady and considerable rise while nickel, asbestos and chromate have all collapsed to different degrees and over different periods. Also increasing have been the number of valid Exclusive Prospecting Orders (EPOs), which roughly indicate foreign exploration interest.

The most obvious reason why minerals have fared better than manufacturing is that they do not rely on local markets (except for coal) and that their local borrowing has been considerably lower than manufacturing companies. Hence they have been insulated from depressed local demand on the one hand and from the escalation in interest rates on the other.

The dependence on international markets has of course a double-edged effect. On the whole the terms of trade of most African-produced minerals have been steadily declining since the 1970s. Gold has been one relative exception and platinum group metals (PGMs) another. Long-term trends in the decline of demand for industrial minerals have been exacerbated in the case of certain minerals which are particularly important in Zimbabwe by health concerns (asbestos) and dumping by the CIS countries (nickel, chromate).

The great bulk of mining investment is not financed by local borrowing but by internal company resources in the case of the older generation large multinationals like Anglo, Lonrho and RTZ or by international borrowing/share issues in the case of the newer and/or junior companies. However, the mining companies have been hard hit by other aspects of the recession in Zimbabwe such as the very sharp increase in power and rail tariffs and the drought-related cuts in power supply in 1992-93.

A series of interviews with Zimbabwean mining companies conducted in 1991 and 1992 (Ericsson and Gibbon, 1993) threw doubt on some central aspects of the World Bank interpretation of the causes of mining investment/disinvestment and highlighted some nuances of the mining houses' relations to structural adjustment. For all the companies the principal determinant of investment was the geology/price nexus, with political stability in the host country another major consideration. Only a certain range of companies, mainly quite small junior enterprises, considered investment codes and the like of much interest. The larger new multinationals were large enough to set their own conditions for investment independent of what the codes stated (see below), while the well-established older ones had evolved working arrangements with host governments which allowed them to circumvent those aspects of the regulatory framework which were viewed as major constraints. In this context structural adjustment was viewed by the larger companies as of some ideological significance but of little practical import.

When the 1991 interviews took place some of the well-established large-scale companies, in particular Anglo, were actively considering substantial new investments in gold and PGMs. Probably because the gold price has not fulfilled expectations these proposals have failed so far to get off the drawing board. However, there is one definite large-scale investment in the pipeline, the Australian-based BHP/Utah and Delta Gold PGM project at Chegutu (Hartley). An agreement was signed in August 1994 under which these companies will invest between US$200 and 250 m. in a mine employing around 2,700 persons and with an annual output value of about Z$300 m. This is not only easily the largest single mining investment in Zimbabwe's post-independence history (total new foreign direct investment in mining 1980-88 was only about US$16 m.) but it exceeds total foreign investment in the economy as a whole since 1980 several times over. The owners have apparently secured government agreement that they can market their own output instead of this being done through the state-owned Minerals Marketing Corporation of Zimbabwe (MMCZ), which markets all other minerals produced in the country. Three other large PGM projects are being considered in the same area as the Hartley mine. Most of these had preliminary exploratory work conducted on them prior to independence but were shelved because of price and political stability considerations. A secular increase in PGM demand (and prices) was established only in the 1980s with growing demand for catalytic convertors.

Gold drove most of the EPO interest in the late 1980s, but since the publication of an aeromagnetic survey most outstanding EPOs have concerned diamonds. It seems that large-scale production activity is unlikely in the short term as relations are at a low ebb between the Zimbabwe Government and De Beers, who exercise an effective world monopoly.

Employment in formal sector mining has fallen steadily since independence, a trend which has speeded up under adjustment. This is due less to the advent of more capital-intensive technology than to the rise of new mining methods, especially in gold, which consume both less capital and less labour. Employment is likely to pick up slightly as the new projects come onstream but will probably never again reach the levels of the UDI period. As in manufacturing, mining wages have held up relatively well. Their index (1980=100) rose to 121.6 in 1990 but has fallen considerably since. In June 1993 it was 91.2.

Not only has MMCZ lost its export marketing monopoly during the period but the state-owned production company, the Zimbabwe Minerals Development Corporation (ZMDC), has had its role fundamentally reduced. The Corporation had been responsible for the operation of a relatively large tin mine (Kamativi), and some smaller copper and gold ones, mostly non-commercial. Losses from support for these ventures forced ZMDC eventually to close Kamativi in 1994 and seek buyers for the other mines. Meanwhile it will concentrate on exploration and advisory services.

6.2   Non-formal Sector Mining

Outside the formal sector are three further layers of mining activity. There are around 40,000 persons working under semi-formalized conditions in the 'official' small-scale branch of the industry, a further 2,000 retrenched chromate miners working in chromate cooperatives (also now experiencing a major crisis), and a minimum of 100,000 alluvial gold panners. The last of these activities was totally illegal until 1991. Since then the Reserve Bank of Zimbabwe and the government-owned Fidelity Printers and Refiners have been buying direct from the panners, whose numbers further dramatically increased during the drought. District councils are meant to regulate their activity but have no capacity to do so. Information on sales through official sources does not appear to be available. Unofficial sales are currently estimated at Z$100-200 m. per annum. Both the large companies and the World Bank are essentially hostile to the activities of the panners but the Zimbabwe Government appears to have no immediate plans to move against them.

7.   Poverty

7.1   Poverty Prior to ESAP

Major pockets of poverty and social inequality were of course present in Zimbabwe prior to the ESAP. In rural Zimbabwe large differences in income and consumption existed not only along racial lines but amongst Africans, between regions and within specific communities. Of 170 designated smallholder areas, 18 accounted for around three quarters of the marketed surplus. Even in these areas over half of sales were accounted for by only about 10 percent of peasants, and up to a quarter of peasant households were net grain purchasers. In some low rainfall areas up to 80 percent of peasant households were net grain purchasers, with many having very large household deficits. 30-40 percent of all peasant households owned no cattle, a basic prerequisite for ploughing and hence generating a maize surplus.

Large-scale commercial farms in the rural areas were still major employers of labour in 1990, accounting for almost a quarter of the entire formally employed population. The incomes of farm labourers at this time averaged only Z$183/month, about a third of what a miner earned and less than a quarter of an urban industrial worker's wage. Even worse-off were households in towns depending on the income of domestic workers. Domestics earned around a fifth of the manufacturing wage, a seventh of an employee in the parastatal sector or a teacher and a twelfth of an employee in the financial sector. Below domestics were found many informal sector employees, particularly women fruit and vegetable traders, as well as the usual population of displaced persons, street children, etc.

7.2   Poverty in 1994

No systematic study of poverty has been made during the ESAP phase. The Zimbabwe Government supports regular household surveys (the 'Sentinel' studies) which are meant to monitor the results of ESAP, but although four had been conducted by mid-1994 these rarely seemed to ask relevant questions, or even the same ones each time the survey was administered. In addition, the sampling frame was changed completely after the second round of interviews, making longitudinal comparisons problematic. Certain of the results will be referred to in Section 8. On the other hand, there is sufficient evidence from other sources to suggest that since the beginning of the ESAP a larger proportion of households are poor and that those already poor have become poorer. The drought has contributed substantially to these phenomena but they were already becoming visible prior to its onset.

By 1994 it had become evident that the main aspect of the situation of working people in Zimbabwe which had changed over the previous four years was not that they had become unemployed in large numbers (although of course almost none of those entering the labour force in this period had found jobs) but that their incomes had fallen in quite drastic ways. Total formal employment in June 1993 actually slightly exceeded that in 1990. But across the whole economy average earnings fell by 24 percent from 1990 to 1992 (no figure is available for 1993 because no calculation has been made of the current real wage in agriculture, but the decline has definitely continued).

This decline has not been an even one. Average earnings figures for different sectors show one group (financial sector employees) improving their real incomes by over 20 percent between 1990 and 1993 while the incomes of others - especially the most vulnerable - fell drastically. Agricultural labourers were actually on lower nominal incomes in 1992 than in 1990 and had experienced a fall of 46 percent in real terms in two years. Domestic servants' incomes had fallen by 54 percent from 1990-93. There were some other interesting changes in relativities. Not surprisingly the ratio of parastatal utility workers' earnings to those of workers in the financial sector halved from 1:1.6 to 1:3.2, but given the assumptions of adjustment it was more worrying to find that the ratio of manufacturing to financial sector incomes had also fallen substantially, from 1:2.5 to 1:3.8.

The purchasing power of incomes of the poor also deteriorated faster than that of other groups, mainly because food comprises a larger part of poor people's expenditure and because the food inflation index increased much faster than the general index did. While from 1990 to May 1994 the general price index rose from 100 to 268.3, the food index increased from 100 to 325. Both the dual upper- and lower income inflation indexes (until they were abolished in 1992) and longitudinal surveys such as that by Kanji and Jazdowska (1993) confirm a picture of the poor becoming worse-off in relative terms (the Kanji and Jazdowska study covers the period 1991-92). A survey by Brand *et al.* (1995) of a particularly vulnerable group (women informal sector traders) shows a drop in even nominal incomes, this time over the period 1992-93. The abolition of the maize price subsidy can only accentuate this trend further even in rural areas, since there is a direct relation between poverty (amongst both peasants and agricultural labourers) and levels of maize purchase. From a poverty viewpoint this reform has clearly regressive effects. On the other hand, the increase in the maize producer price which has accompanied the abolition of the subsidy clearly benefits net maize producers. But this price increase is due to efforts to rebuild national food security, not to the ESAP.

Certain authors, notably Chisvo *et al.* (1994), have reported enthusiastically that the abolition of the maize price subsidy in urban areas has basically led to a switch by the majority of urban consumers from roller meal to *mugayiva* or so-called 'straight-run' meal produced at local small-scale hammer mills. The total cost of the latter was Z$4.70-7.05/5 kg bag (November 1993 prices) as against the new roller meal price of 8.83. Yet the top price range of *mugayiva* still exceeded the price of roller meal earlier in the year before the subsidy was withdrawn, while the gender implications of the switch were simply not considered. Whereas buying roller meal simply involved a visit to the nearest store, buying *mugayiva* involves purchasing unprocessed maize, taking it to a hammer mill and waiting in line for it to be milled.

Other long-term dietary changes have been reported in a number of surveys. Most of these show reductions in consumption of items like bread, meat and milk and a tendency for meals to be increasingly composed of *sadza* (maize porridge) alone. Most also report reductions in numbers of meals taken (Sachikonye, 1995; Brand *et al.*, 1995).

7.3   Social Dimensions of Adjustment

The ESAP was one of the first adjustment programmes in Africa to be accompanied from the outset by an explicit attempt to address what was described as the transitional poverty-inducing effects of economic liberalization. At the outset, and for much of the subsequent period, this has consisted of three main elements. Firstly, there has been an 'employment and training' programme directed at retrenched workers. Secondly, there has been a pledge to support a targeted food subsidy, namely one paid to large-scale millers to keep down the price of roller meal. Despite pledges to the contrary, this was removed in mid-1993. Thirdly, there have been efforts to shield poor households from the impact of the introduction of user charges for education and health. The compensatory measures were originally funded by the Zimbabwe Government with Z$20 m. Initially much criticism was directed at the apparently paltry amount which this represented. Subsequently it has emerged that the bureaucratic hurdles created to disbursing any of it were such that later top-ups to it remain largely unspent.

The employment and training programme involved some retrenches being given a 5-day programme in basic business studies at the end of which they were invited to write business project proposals for evaluation (by an inter-ministerial committee (!)) and possible funding. By early 1994, 3,668 retrenchees are said to have received training, 93 percent of them male. At the end of 1993, 193 project proposals had been approved and Z$9.5 m. released to support them: if successful they will generate less than 1,000 jobs, however. Critics have raised questions concerning not only the efficiency of this exercise but whether it addressed an appropriate target group in the first place. By the end of 1993 the programme appears to have been redefined to include support to public works and small-scale enterprises through NGOs, but no details are available on this.

A multi-tier school fee system was introduced in 1992; fee levels were increased by between 10 and 25 percent in 1993 and now range between Z$75/pupil/term (high density urban primary) and Z$1650/pupil/term (secondary boarder). Rural primary schools are exempted. Fee levels do not take account of pre-existing unofficial fees (called 'levies'), book charges and uniform costs which together average around Z$150/pupil/year for the system as a whole. The exemption system involves headmasters being asked to identify pupils of poor households, and issuing notes for identified parents to take to their nearest Social Welfare Office. There a local social worker is supposed to confirm or disconfirm household eligibility, which is based on an income of Z$400/month or less (the 1992 Poverty Datum Line). The qualifying household receives an exemption certificate and refunds from the 'Social Development Fund' are dispatched direct to schools. In 1992 schools waited on average 6-8 months for refunds, although the backlog of applications is now said to have been cleared. Eligible households have also been able to claim exemption from school examination fees.

Kaseke (1993) reports several flaws in the administration of this system. Firstly, headmasters were often found to be applying their own arbitrary criteria of eligibility, screening out most potential applicants. Secondly, social workers were frequently asking for pupils' school reports to ascertain their 'suitability' as characters. Thirdly, Social Welfare Offices may be a day's journey away in some areas, and those receiving exemptions tended to be clustered in areas accessible to them. Figures given for issued exemptions differ considerably between sources but 'it seems likely that around 100,000 pupils may have received fee exemptions and a further 15,000 exam fee exemptions by mid-1994, at a total cost of Z$15-20 m. This former figure represents about 3 percent of gross enrolments. It is not known what proportion of urban primary and national secondary school enrolments it represents.

A second exemption system was supposed to apply to health service fees. These fees have always existed, although households with incomes below Z$150/month were formally exempt. The fees had mostly long ceased to be collected, however. In December 1991 health providers were instructed to enforce the fee scale. In the meantime it was stated that a new exemption level and exemption system would be introduced. In mid-1992 an exemption level of Z$400/month was announced but no mechanisms existed for implementing it until the end of the year. At this time those seeking exemptions were told to present themselves at local Social Welfare Offices where, upon proof of income, they would be issued with exemption letters. About 30,000 such letters appear to have been issued by the end of 1993. These letters only covered the cost of medicines if the latter were actually in stock in the hospital and not if they had to be obtained from a private pharmacy. Meanwhile, early in 1993 health facilities in rural areas were again told that they should waive all fees. No system was worked out for compensating hospitals and health centres for 'lost' fees until 1994, when it was announced that they would receive additional block grants from the Ministry of Health on the basis of an assessment of social need levels in their catchment areas. In the interim most hospitals had adopted their own systems for levying fees and determining exemptions. In January 1994 a new national fee system was introduced with substantial increases for some forms of treatment.

During 1992 a previously unannounced benefit was introduced to assist very low income families in coping with the drought. Households with incomes of Z$200/month and below became eligible for receiving a food money supplement of Z$4/month/ household member. To qualify applicants had to present their national identity cards, marriage certificates, birth certificates for their children, proof of employment and earnings, and proof of their spouse's income to their local Social Welfare Office and to fill in a 2-page form. Local social workers checked their eligibility, which was then re-checked centrally before payment orders were issued and dispatched. According to Kaseke (1993) most applicants needed to spend at least a full day, not including travel, in order to go through the different procedures necessary to obtain the money. The first payments took around 7 months to reach applicants, although the waiting-time has now been considerably reduced. No clear figures are available about how many households have benefitted. At the end of 1993 the Zimbabwe Government stated that Z$310,000 in 'food money' had been disbursed by October 1993 and claimed that 78,000 households had benefitted in the process. Assuming an average household size of 6 and average payment periods of 6 months per household, the actual number of households benefitting is unlikely to have been higher than 2-3,000, however.

As implied above, the bulk of the SDA programmes in Zimbabwe are administered through the Department of Social Welfare, a section of the Ministry of Labour. The latter received no additional staffing to cope with its new tasks until well into 1993 when donors funded a continuation of the salaries of 39 clerks who had been employed temporarily as part of the drought-relief operations. A SDA Coordinator was not appointed until March 1993 and his own relation to the Department of Social Welfare still seems not to have been clarified.

Given these problems and the almost negligible uptake levels of benefits from the programmes, SDA became a focus for disagreement between those donors most interested in compensatory measures (including the World Bank) and the Zimbabwe Government. Since mid-1993 the Zimbabwe Government has been attempting to devise a revised successor for the measures of 1991-94. The main focus of this seems to be a running down of the existing initiatives on food and 'training', in favour of employment creation through funding to NGOs. The future of the health and education exemption schemes is unclear. Nor does the documentation inspire confidence.[5]

An extensive literature has dealt with popular household coping strategies to deal with declining real incomes in other African countries. In Zimbabwe this literature is in its infancy, but one interesting trend may be observed. Whereas in many other African countries there has been a spectacular mushrooming of informal sector activities, this does not seem to have been the case in Zimbabwe. Although the informal sector continues to expand (see above, Section 5 and 6), demand appears to be so depressed that many lines of activity favoured elsewhere are relatively stagnant in Zimbabwe. Daniels (1994), Kanji and Jazdowska (1993) and Brand *et al.* (1995) all report forms of informal sector *disengagement* amongst sections of the urban poor, perhaps suggesting an overall picture of replacement of resource-poor by better resource-endowed participants. Precisely how households which have disengaged support themselves instead is unclear.

8.   The Social Sectors

This section will deal with developments in education and health. General patterns of outcomes in both cases are obviously affected by developments in the economy as a whole (levels of employment, incomes, subsidies on consumption goods, etc.) as well by other exogenous factors, for example drought, and by trends within the education and health services themselves. The presentation will deal mainly with trends within the services themselves, but will acknowledge other factors where relevant.

8.1   Trends in Health and Education Provision

Zimbabwe Government figures on state expenditure by budget heading during the ESAP period appear to show health and education retaining their overall share of spending (Table 6). Even if these are accepted a decline in real expenditure is evident. Recent World Bank figures for health both show a decline in spending shares and provide more detailed information on the decline in real expenditure levels.

According to the World Bank health expenditure in Zimbabwe is now lower in real terms than at any time since independence. Table 13 shows per capita expenditure to have fallen by over 30 percent during the life of the ESAP. Within these overall declines there are some interesting trends. Higher level services/institutions seem to have been better protected from funding cuts than lower ones. The allocation to primary facilities fell from between 15 and 16 percent in the late 1980s to 12 to 13 percent in 1994. Total numbers of personnel have actually increased, from 23,600 in 1989 and 24,100 in 1990 to 25,800 in June 1993. But real pay was almost halved (from an index

---

[5] Activity supported will be 'rooted in Zimbabwean culture, music, language and anchoring development on a person and secure home background which in turn entails the need to mobilise oneself, stand by oneself, employ oneself and fund raise for oneself'(!) (Zimbabwe Government, 1993b: 22).

of 94.4 (1980=100) in 1990 to only 56.6 in June 1993) and several sources speak of an exodus of the more highly trained personnel. According to UNICEF, the number of trained nurses per 10,000 persons fell from between 9.2 and 9.3 in 1988-90 to 7.9 in 1993. There has also been a severe cut in the real level of the government fund dedicated to supplying drugs to state health facilities. This was frozen at Z$17 m. in 1988-89 and its real value (1988 prices) had by 1992-93 fallen to Z$10.4 m. (Chisvo and Munro, 1994: 6).

Table 13   Health Expenditure Data, 1988-89 to 1993-94

	1988-89	89-90	90-91	91-92	92-93	93-94
Share of budget (%)	5.2	5.9	5.3	4.8	4.6	5.1
Share GDP (%)[a]	2.8	3.0	2.6	2.2	2.1	2.1
Exp. per capita (Z$)[b]	46	49	47	41	33	32

Source: World Bank.
[a]   Not including donor contributions.
[b]   1990 prices.

Little progress has been made in monitoring overall levels of receipts from user charges or how they have been employed. An original ESAP target had been to raise 5 percent of total health expenditure through fees by 1993 and 8 percent by 1995. Hongoro and Chandiwana (1994) report that revenue collected by a sample of 8 hospitals in 1992 ranged from 4 percent to 60 percent of recurrent expenditure, largely reflecting inconsistencies in levying practices. For a municipal clinic also monitored the level was 500 percent.

The World Bank figures in Table 14 show that expenditure on education has also fallen during the ESAP period, as a share of the budget and of GDP. Real per capita expenditure on primary and secondary education has declined by 36 percent and 25 percent respectively since 1990-91, although it has significantly increased at university level. As in health, employment in education has actually risen during the adjustment period (from 108,100 in 1990 to 111,400 in June 1993), although not in line with the increase in enrolment levels. Pupils per teacher in primary schools rose from 34.8 in 1990 to 39.5 in 1993 as the underlying rise in the birthrate reasserted its influence after having been concealed for some years by the progress through the system of pupils from outside the age group who managed to acquire primary education only after independence. The real casualties, however, have been both staff wage levels and non-wage educational expenditure. Staff wages fell by between 26 and 43 percent in real terms between 1990 and 1993 (depending on grade), although staff wages rose as a share of total expenditure (from less than 90 percent in 1984 to 95.5 percent 1990-93). By 1993 there were 5,000 teacher resignations per annum, compared with 6,000 new teachers entering the profession. As in health the exodus appears to be greatest in the highest grades, leading to a reduction in overall levels of qualification.

The Zimbabwe Government has collected information on total user charge income in the case of education, unlike health. Z$67.5 m. was collected in 1992 and Z$97.6 m.

in 1993. This corresponded to 2.7 and 3.5 percent of educational expenditure in the two years respectively. Given the hardships involved, and the fact that the whole system is administratively intensive and costly, its net benefits are questionable.

Table 14 Education Expenditure Data, 1988-89 to 1993-94

	1988-89	89-90	90-91	91-92	92-93	93-94
Share of budget (%)	17.5	17.5	18.2	16.2	16.0	16.7
Share of GDP	9.5	9.0	8.9	8.0	8.0	7.9
Primary/GDP (%)	4.6	4.6	4.7	4.1	4.0	3.9
Primary per pupil (Z$[a])	360	370	390	360	280	250
Secondary/GDP(%)	2.6	2.5	2.5	2.2	2.1	2.0
Secondary per pupil (Z$[a])	600	590	630	600	490	470
University/GDP(%)	0.5	0.6	0.5	0.4	0.8	0.9
University per student (Z$[a])	8000	9500	10500	9200	11700	12000

Source: World Bank.
[a] 1990 prices.

8.2 Health and Education Outcomes

Given the short length of the adjustment period in Zimbabwe, data on health and education outcomes are patchy. In particular, little information is available on changes in health status, although this situation should be remedied by the completion in early 1995 of a large two-year longitudinal study carried out by the University of Zimbabwe Community Medicine Department and sponsored by the Scandinavian Institute of African Studies, SIDA and NORAD.

The most comprehensive currently available health study is that of Hongoro and Chandiwana, based on data from 5 large hospitals over the period January 1990 to December 1992. This shows apparently new patterns both of self-referral and of morbidity. An apparent major fall (of 18 percent) in out-patient attendances is recorded in early 1992, coinciding with the enforcement of user fees. This result was confirmed by data from August 1991 and August 1992 from 21 health facilities, published in the results of the second round of the 'Sentinel' studies (Zimbabwe Government Ministry of Labour, Manpower Planning and Social Welfare, 1993a), which showed a 17.5 percent decline in out-patient attendances. The 'Sentinel' study also compared different parts of the country, finding a decline of fully 63.9 percent in the LSCF areas. The Hongoro and Chandiwara study also shows out-patient attendances picking up again towards the end of 1992, but still not reaching their levels before fees were enforced. Hongoro and Chandiwara further show a significant decline in antenatal clinic attendances over the same period, accompanied, however, by a rise in maternity admissions and unbooked deliveries. The mother-and-child morbidity data meanwhile show major increases in babies born before arrival (BBAs), BBAs who die after admission and in the maternal death rate. Hongoro and Chandiwana (1994: 13) observe that this suggests 'that clients cut down on what they thought were unnecessary services, only to come later with more serious conditions'.

While many of these figures can be related fairly directly to the introduction of user charges, some of those concerning morbidity may also be related to the increased prevalence of AIDS (an estimated 800,000 persons were thought to be HIV-positive in 1993, of a total population of just over 10 m.) and to the effects of the drought. The latter applies even more obviously to figures on malnutrition, the other main morbidity measure for which there is up-to-date data. The 'Sentinel' studies collected two sets of separate data on under 5 year-old children presenting at health facilities with malnutrition. The first set involved a comparison of August 1992 and August 1991 at 30 health centres and showed a 52 percent increase (Zimbabwe Government, Ministry of Labour etc., 1993a). The second were collected from the same health centres in January 1991, January 1992 and January 1993 and showed an increase of 54.5 percent during 1991-92 followed by another of 41.5 percent in 1992-93 (Zimbabwe Government, Ministry of Labour etc., 1993b).

While the impact of AIDS and drought on morbidity must be acknowledged it is of course also important to bear in mind that ESAP has also had an impact on the management of the drought (see above, Section 4) and on the management of AIDS. In January 1993 a charge was introduced for condoms, previously distributed free at government health centres. Whereas the number of condoms distributed free had risen from 37,000 in January 1991 to 51,000 in January 1992, in the month following the new token charge only 32,000 were distributed. Fortunately the charge was withdrawn as soon as this came to light.

The most frequently examined educational indicator regarding the possible influence of user charges is that of enrolment ratios. Unfortunately, only scanty data are available. Gross enrolment in primary schools increased by 8.3 percent in 1991-92 over 1990-91 but by only 0.5 percent in 1992-93 over 1991-92. Population growth generally runs at around 3.1 percent. Secondary school gross enrolments increased by 5.5 percent in 1991-92 over 1990-91 but then fell by 7.5 percent in 1992-93. In neither case does a clear trend appear. Information on net enrolments for certain age groups was gathered in the third and fourth 'Sentinel' studies. In the core primary age group of 9-12 year olds non-enrolment was 2.7 percent net in January 1993 and 6 percent in December 1993 (Government of Zimbabwe, Ministry of Labour, etc., 1993b, 1994). However, calculations from data for 8 out 9 of Zimbabwe's provinces from the (August) 1992 census show net non-enrolment for the same age group to be 5.6 percent (Zimbabwe Government, Central Statistics Office, 1994 a-h). Again, no clear trend emerges. One clear trend regarding enrolment which is detectable, however, is an increase in drop-out rates within academic years, which the second 'Sentinel' study annex showed increased for primary schools from 1.4 percent in 1991 to 3.4 percent in 1992 (Government of Zimbabwe, Ministry of Labour, etc. 1993a). Interestingly the drop-out rate for boys was double the level of that for girls, and as a whole could be explained in both years almost entirely by very high rates in LSCF areas (31 percent in 1992).[6]

Two observations can be made concerning these statistics. Firstly, they are consistent

---

[6] Adjustment does not seem to have seen a change in the gender balance of school enrolment generally in Zimbabwe. Girls remain 48.7 to 49.8 percent of all primary school classes and 43.7 to 45.9 percent of the first three secondary school classes, dropping to 33.5 percent of sixth formers.

with a pattern described in the surveys of Kanji and Jazdowska (1993) and Brand *et al.* (1995), which both report great reluctance by parents to withdraw their children from school, even at the price of considerable sacrifice, but which also report that temporary withdrawal is more common than permanent. Secondly, in LSCF areas they are consistent with findings of Sachikonye (1995), who shows that withdrawal is much more prevalent in these areas than in urban ones, and that there is a clear economic rationale for it. Withdrawing children from school is a meaningful survival strategy for agricultural workers since a large part of their pay takes the form of piece work without questions asked as to how the 'piece' has been completed.

In the first two years of adjustment there was some concern raised about a sharp reduction in the number of candidates sitting for Ordinary level examinations. These had been rising for many years but fell by 14 percent in 1992. In 1993 they fell again very slightly. However a more serious trend may be that of the continuous slight decline in numbers of subjects sat per student, detected by Chisvo and Munro (1994).

9.   Public Sector Reforms

9.1   Civil Service Reform

One of the central features of *FER* was the announcement that there would be 'a reduction of 25 percent of the number of civil servants (excluding education) over the next 4 years and a restrictive wage policy' (Zimbabwe Government, 1991: 6). Why the figure of 25 percent was chosen is a complete mystery and no attempt to justify it has ever been made. Later the announcement was modified in two fundamental ways. Firstly, health sector state employment was also exempted from the cuts. This meant that the 25 percent figure would apply to 'core' civil service total employment of roughly 93,500 (1989 figure, up from 71,100 in 1980). Secondly, instead of applying to civil service numbers, the cuts were said to be being applied to civil service *posts*. However, nobody seems ever to have counted how many civil service posts there were in 1989-90. Again on a completely arbitrary basis it was assumed that there were 92,000 posts at this time. There are reasons to believe that the figure was very much higher. In any event, the object of the exercise now became to reduce the 'number of posts' by 25,000 by 1994-95. Over time this target has been reduced to 23,000. A timetable was produced indicating that 12,000 posts would be eliminated by June 1993, a further 7,000 by June 1994 and 3,000 by June 1995, and UNDP assistance was received to identify the posts in question.

The confusion marking the birth of this exercise has continued throughout its life. In October 1992 the World Bank stated that 8,472 posts had already been abolished. The Consultative Group meeting in early 1993 was given a figure of 7,204. By June 1993 this had climbed to 9,700 in one document, 10,044 in another and 13,000 in a third. Over a year later, towards the end of 1994, a figure of 11,000 was given. What is certain is that the number of civil servants retrenched is considerably below all those cited in this paragraph. According to the January 1994 Policy Framework Paper for 1994-96, there had been 4,896 actual civil service retrenchments at this time. IMF figures on employment in public administration show a fall to 89,600 by June 1993 (equivalent to 3,900 retrenchments).

No information has been made available on the balance of retrenchments between ministries and grades, but anecdote suggests that most cuts have come at local government level. Only in one month (July 1993) was a breakdown of public service retrenchments by gender provided. This showed 277 retrenchments in local government of which 10 percent were women, a slightly smaller proportion than women's overall share of civil service employment.

The question of civil service pay is more straightforward. Average pay for public servants fell faster between 1990 and 1993 than in any other sector. The index of civil service real earnings, taking 1980 as 100, fell rapidly shortly after independence but then stabilized at around 60-65 between 1984 and 1990. By June 1993 it had fallen to 34.6 (!). This also reflected widening differentials with the private sector. Median pay levels in the public sector for a range of 13 occupations were on average 40 percent below those in the private sector in 1990. By 1992 they were on average 47.4 percent below them (calculations based on ILO, 1993: 124). Not all categories of public servants suffered equally. In June 1992 retention allowances of 20 percent and upwards were introduced for professional engineers and some categories of managers.

In July 1994 the Zimbabwe Government announced increases in basic rates ranging from 10 percent for senior staff to 23 percent for some lower grades, presumably in recognition of the impact of falling living standards on the commitment to work of most public servants. In addition the transport allowance was raised by similar levels and a housing allowance introduced for all public sector employees. The IMF claims that, as a result, the overall wage bill will rise by 31 percent. Of course, this still falls far short of restoring the 1990 position. Moreover, the award of these increases appears to be the only policy step taken regarding restoring the capacity of the public service. No significant measures have been announced to enhance civil service professionalism or improve civil service training, for example.

9.2   Public Enterprises (PEs)

The basic objective of PE reform in Zimbabwe, as already noted, has been to reduce the budget deficit. Special attention has been paid to the GMB (see above) and other agricultural parastatals, the steel producer ZISCO, Air Zimbabwe, the railways (NRZ) and the electricity utility ZESA. There has also been considerable attention to the Posts and Telecommunication Corporation which, though highly inefficient in service-delivery terms, has been profitable throughout the period. Sections 2 and 3 above trace the conditionalities attached to these efforts. Successively these have involved pricing/tariff increases, the introduction of measures intended to improve efficiency (performance contracts, etc.), and the restructuring of financial relations between PEs and government. There was less talk from the donor side in 1994 of a generic PE loss or subsidy target than there had been at the outset of the adjustment period, for reasons that will soon become clear. Instead attention was now focused on allocating enterprises between the categories of 'viable strategic' (in effect, utilities in which the private sector would not be interested but which nobody can envisage letting die), 'non-strategic viable' (in effect, those which the private sector might be interested in) and 'non-viable' (those which will be allowed to die). However, it seems unlikely that the Zimbabwe Government shares this aspect of the changing adjustment agenda. Although it is clearly deeply concerned by the present level of losses, apart from the mining corporations already mentioned there are few if any candidates which the government is currently willing to identify for membership of the last category. The government has also spoken of a need to create instruments to establish broad 'popular' forms of share ownership before privatization can be considered.

It is now probably clear that while the very large increase in PE tariffs in 1992 was highly damaging to the industrial sector and to a lesser extent to mining, it did nothing to improve the underlying economic position of the PEs (except probably ZESA). According to the World Bank this was because they failed to institute accompanying improvements in efficiency, but the early benefits of the latter are also difficult to detect. Losses of major parastatals, far from falling during the ESAP, have increased sharply. They rose from Z$634 m. in 1990-91 to over Z$1800 m. in 1993-94. Subsidies reached Z$1249 m. in 1991-92, before falling to Z$1020 m. in 1992-93 and Z$490 m. in 1993-94. But this subsidy reduction has been achieved only by saddling the PEs with unsustainable levels of cumulative losses - amounting in 1993-94 to around Z$2,000 m., three times their level at the beginning of the adjustment period. These losses will obviously lead to increasing levels of debt obligations to the domestic financial system as subsidies are withdrawn further, and thereby almost certainly to even greater future losses, as well as to a greater and greater crowding-out of private sector credit seekers. Efforts to privatize loss-making PEs, when they eventually materialize, are unlikely to succeed unless these cumulative debts are somehow written off, but it is also extremely difficult to see how this can take place without a huge increase in the budget deficit (cumulative losses in 1993-94 were equivalent to 6 percent of GDP, as opposed to 3.7 percent before the reforms began).

The high pre-ESAP levels of parastatal losses were attributed by the World Bank mainly to the not fully transparent subsidies they were expected to cover. Some of these subsidies have been eliminated as a result of tariff increases, but others have steadily increased as certain parastatals have had to carry the costs to the economy as a whole of drought and recession - most obviously in the case of the agricultural parastatals.

Table 15 PE Losses and Subsidies, 1989-90 to 1993-94 (million Z$)

	NRZ	ZESA	GMB	CSC	DMB	CMB	AZim	ZISCO	AFC	Total
1989-90										
Loss	228	2	169	49	59	23	10	70	27	534
Subsidy	100	-	185	31	56	18	15	100	15	384
Cumulative loss	312	2	47	67	86	51	13	40	26	644
1990-91										
Loss	120	65	186	45	54	-	23	159	35	634
Subsidy	255	-	263	30	60	46	9	100	40	640
Cumulative loss	177	67	30[a]	82	81	3	27	99	22	640
1991-92										
Loss	188	n.a.	497	83	1	108	9	111	4	
Subsidy	149	n.a.	747	82	81	3	27	139	21	
Cumulative loss	216	n.a.	280[a]	83	1	108	9	171	5	

	NRZ	ZESA	GMB	CSC	DMB	CMB	AZim	ZISCO	AFC	Total
1992-93										
Loss	128	n.a.	852	125	-	101	41	184	16	
Subsidy	94	n.a.	786	56	10	-	-	100	40	
Cumulative loss	250	n.a.	214[a]	152	9[a]	209	50	255	19[a]	
1993-94 (est)										
Loss	116	n.a.	1396	68	9	39	40	164	13	
Subsidy	40	n.a.	165	65	-	-	-	240	45	
Cumulative loss	326	n.a.	1017	155	-	248	90	179	51[a]	

Source: IMF.
[a]   Surplus.

Many have also been paying the cost of badly thought-through advice by donors and/or government, before and during the adjustment period. This has been most obviously the case in relation to the GMB grain stock fiasco but also refers to organizations like ZESA having to carry high debt-service costs for the World Bank-financed but highly inefficient Hwange thermal power station. Thirdly, the PEs have also suffered indirectly from the slowdown in economic activity. NRZ, for example, has had its earnings reduced not only by having to ferry food relief instead of freight but also because the level of the latter has itself contracted. Fourthly, while some PEs like PTC have been the subject of externally funded modernization programmes during the ESAP, others such as ZISCO have seen their state-funded programmes suspended. Although ZISCO has many other problems, including poor management, corruption and bad coordination of the early phases of its rehabilitation programme, the latter's deceleration from 1990-91 was mainly due at first to tightened government finance and then later to the government's search for a private partner to carry part of the cost. The programme's suspension has meant that during the ESAP ZISCO has rarely been able to produce at more than 14-20 percent of its installed capacity. At this level it cannot be expected to meet its costs, even after substantial retrenchments.

By 1994 there were no new ideas from ESAP's designers on how to resolve the situation of the PEs, which was becoming more difficult by the day.

10.   The Environment

10.1   Woodlands

In 1990 indigenous woodland still covered 11-12 m. hectare (about 32 percent of the total land area) in Zimbabwe although considerable deforestation was said to be occurring in some communal areas due to population pressure and demand for agricultural land. The latter have also contributed to loss of wildlife via habitat destruction/poaching. Loss of woodland has in turn led to localized fuelwood shortages and serious problems of soil erosion.

The major portion of the national stock of woodland is found in areas not available for general use (national parks and forests, game reserves, the LSCF area, etc.). Communal areas contain only 21 percent of woodland but 44 percent of total rural land area and 77 percent of the population. There are major shortages of woodland in certain communal areas, notably around Gutu and Masvingo districts although most of the loss of wood cover here seems to have occurred in the 1950s or before. Since the 1960s loss of wood cover has also begun to affect parts of Natural Regions 4 and 5. In all cases deforestation is most acute in those areas experiencing rapid population growth and in-migration. Collection of fuel wood from living trees is said to be a much less frequent occurrence than clearance for agriculture.

Estimates of woodfuel consumption in rural areas range from 2.7 to 6.5 tonnes/-household/year. Latest estimates of national demand are about 8 million tonnes/year. The least sustainable levels of demand are again in Masvingo province, although there are major discrepancies in estimates of deficits. A small market exists for fuelwood, but one which is fragmented and where prices are very low. Fuelwood in the most depleted communal areas sold at Z$15/tonne immediately prior to the ESAP. Information on current prices is not available.

The urban market for fuelwood has been traditionally relatively small due to cheap electricity, which is widely used. Even in a sample of informal women traders in Harare, a relatively deprived group, one third were found to be using electricity for cooking in 1992 (Brand *et al.*, 1995). Most households either use no fuelwood or very little and average urban demand prior to ESAP was only 0.4 tonne/household/year. The impact of urban fuelwood demand on rural environments had been negligible up to this time. Huge real price rises occurred for electricity in 1992. However, Brand *et al.* state that no significant change had occurred in cooking methods by 1993. In any event the major alternative fuel to electricity for poor urban households was not woodfuel but kerosene. Even in 1993 only about 10 percent of those sampled cooked over open fires.

10.2   Wood for Commercial Uses

About 100,000 hectares of fast-growing pine and eucalyptus plantations were established in the 1960s to feed sawmilling and the pulp/paper industry. This appears to have been renewed. There is no evidence of large-scale logging in any of the forest reserves. In the communal areas an unknown amount of wood is cut each year for construction and for beer brewing. These are both very important rural informal sector activities, the first male-dominated and the second female-dominated. According to the first GEMINI survey (MacPherson, 1991), in 1991 construction accounted for 4.3 percent of all informal enterprises and 'food and beverages' for 7.5 percent. However, both these branches experienced severe downturns during the period 1991-93, with the number of construction enterprises contracting by 10 percent and the number of 'food and beverage' ones by 14 percent. Informal construction obviously suffered from the decline of incomes in the communal areas. More surprisingly, beer brewing was distinguished by having the highest enterprise mortality rate amongst low-profit activities. Possibly this the result of the fact that very few people harvested rapoko during the drought. It is thus unlikely that there has been an increase in depletion of wood for commercial purposes during the ESAP period.

10.3   Soil Erosion

Soil erosion has been a problem for some time in the most densely populated communal areas, particularly Save (Manicaland), Mazoe (Mashonaland Central) and Masvingo again. Besides high population levels, soil erosion is typically associated with the cultivation of crops like cotton, maize and tobacco, with the 'extensification' of production into increasingly marginal areas and with over-grazing.

Adjustment has been claimed by some of its proponents to have a generally beneficial relation to soil erosion since it encourages a general replacement of erosive crops and livestock by export crops, which tend to be tree-based and hence less erosive. Actually, of course, potentially erosive crops can also be grown in non-erosive ways. In Zimbabwe the only tree crop grown is coffee, but in very small quantities (from 1988-89 to 1993-94 only 6-12,000 hectares were cultivated - less than 1 percent of the total cultivated area) and exclusively on large-scale commercial farms. There has tended only to be a movement from one potentially erosive crop (maize) to another (tobacco). But this movement has itself been mainly on large-scale commercial farms, where cultivation methods tend to be less damaging.

As noted above, input consumption by farmers in communal areas increased rapidly until the late 1980s but then began to decline as prices fell. This trend was probably accelerated as state investment in input supply was cut back under adjustment. Subsequently, as producer prices were administratively improved to rebuild post-drought grain stocks, input supply stabilized and even rose. Hence 'extensivization' of production to more marginal areas has probably not occurred; however, given the unlikely situation of real producer prices remaining high this eventuality seems likely only to have been postponed.

Cattle numbers have fallen sharply as a result of the drought. In communal areas they fell from approximately 4.2 million in 1990 to 2.9 million in 1992; in LSCF areas they fell from 2.1 million to 1.6 million. Goat numbers are believed to have fallen to a similar extent. This may allow some recovery in rangelands.

10.4   Wildlife Conservation

Since the mid-1970s private landowners have been encouraged to manage and exploit wildlife on lands under their responsibility. Wildlife ranching took off in the 1982-83 drought when large numbers of cattle were slaughtered, beef prices declined and stockfeed prices rose sharply. By 1990 about 35,000 hectares (10 percent of the LSCF area) was being used for commercial wildlife ranching - sometimes jointly with cattle - with a concentration in the more arid areas. The major returns are from hunting and photographic safaris. Since 1986 District councils have also been encouraged to promote the integration of wildlife management into the local economies of communal areas as a form of sustainable resource use.

During the 1991-92 drought farmers in the LSCF areas were encouraged to expand their wildlife herds. The Department of National Parks and Wildlife (DNPW) supplied LSCF areas with large numbers of certain species for the latter's care and protection. Commercial farmers were asked to return half the animals 'lent' them when the National Parks had recovered from the drought. It is not known how many animals were involved in this subsidy to private game farming.

The ESAP period has been one in which poaching appears to have occurred on a widespread scale. While white rhinos were generally de-horned in 1991-92, black ones were not and the herd is subsequently said to have declined from 2,000 to 250 head. A de-horning policy was eventually adopted for black rhino too.

Although it suspended sales of ivory in 1989, Zimbabwe subsequently defied the UN Convention on International Trade in Endangered Species by setting up an Ivory Marketing Authority with four other southern African countries. Zimbabwe claimed it had an elephant population of 67,000 at this time, 27,000 above supposed carrying capacity. Local conservationists disputed both figures and claimed that lifting the suspension served mainly to provide cover for powerful interests involved in poaching. Actually no culling seems to have taken place until 1992, when it was stated that as a result of the drought 4,000 elephants would be killed. Zimbabwe tried to sell trophies from these animals on the international market in 1993, but apparently without success. Meanwhile there have been an increasing number of scandals concerning poaching and illegal wildlife export. One case links organized poaching interests in government and the army with the death in police custody of two 'whistle-blowing' army officers, one in 1989 and the other in 1991. A second concerned a Member of Parliament convicted in February 1993 of illegal possession of trophies. A third involved the unauthorized export of 206 elephants to Botswana in 1992, during which an irregular payment of Z\$1.2 m. is alleged to have been made to senior officials of the DNPW. A fourth case concerns irregularities in the allocation of VIP hunting quotas, said to have cost the government Z\$4 m. in lost fees. While there is no direct relation between the ESAP and these developments, real reductions in salary levels in various state agencies and a more generally permissive economic policy climate seem likely to have contributed to the plunder described and also to have reduced the capacity of responsible agencies to police it.

11.   Summary and Conclusion

The background to Zimbabwean adjustment is relatively unique, but still somewhat unclear. Neither the Zimbabwean economy nor the state was experiencing a crisis at the time of adjustment, although it was broadly acknowledged that there were signs of stagnation. Given the fact that it was voluntarily introduced and that the Zimbabwean state had the opportunity to be centrally involved in its design, surprisingly little attention was given to issues of structural transformation in general and to the public expenditure role which the state could play in strengthening industry in particular. Simultaneously, surprisingly little attention was given to strengthening or even preserving the social sectors. Instead there seems to have been an exaggerated faith in the capacity of the existing industrial sector and potential foreign investors to respond to improved market signals.

The main mechanism of this trade liberalization programme was an open general import licence. However, the introduction of this was not coordinated with a real devaluation. As a result a much needed process of industrial re-equipment was overtaken by speculative over-importing. Relatedly also, there was little or no immediate export response to pay for the latter. Disbursement of donor funding for the scheme was delayed, in some cases probably deliberately, and a massive current account deficit was run up.

In the short term this led to considerable commercial lending and in the medium term brought the IMF into the Zimbabwean picture for the first time since 1983. Following this involvement came a predictably heavy devaluation, major restrictions on credit, major increases in interest rates (later, under deregulation, further inflated by the oligopolistic banking system) and heightened attention to securing reductions in government expenditure. The latter led, inter alia, to parastatal utilities increasing their prices to 'economic' levels. That is, a classic stabilization programme was superimposed on a growth-oriented adjustment one.

The fortunes of Zimbabwean industry were meanwhile being hit by two other developments of considerable importance. The first was the most serious drought for many decades which impacted on it in a variety of direct and indirect ways (and still continues to do so). In the short term the most important of these was a substantial reduction in domestic demand. Secondly, Zimbabwe's trade liberalization was not reciprocated by other important trading partners, notably South Africa, which actually substantially increased barriers to imports of some Zimbabwean goods.

The industrial sector unsurprisingly underwent its most severe crisis since independence. Between 1991 and 1993 its share of GDP fell from 25.3 to 21.6 percent, its output index fell from 143 to 119 (1980=100) and manufactured exports declined. This crisis was not ameliorated either by injections of state support to certain companies or by the replacement of the open general import licence by an export retention scheme. The latter appears to have increased the price of forex to net importers without providing net exporters with significantly improved incentives. A slight recovery occurred in 1993-94, but the output index in August 1994 was still 10 percent below its 1991 level.

Other than industry subsequent adjustment measures have been targeted on agriculture and public enterprises. Agriculture policies appear to have almost exclusively been focused on reducing the cost to the exchequer of the post-independence extension to Africans of the public maize marketing/input supply system, and the long-established strategic grain reserve. White farmers' former monopoly in commercial agriculture was implicitly restored while the fundamental question of food security has simply been left to market forces.

In fact the consequent run-down of the strategic grain reserve just before the 1991-92 drought gave rise not only to losses on the export of 0.6 million tonnes of maize but also to further huge losses on these (and further) supplies which had to be re-imported at much higher prices during the following crop season. These 'advice-based losses' accounted for at least Z$800 m. (less imputed storage costs) and possibly considerably more, i.e. around half of total public enterprise losses during the adjustment period.

Cut-backs in services to African farmers as yet have had little impact, although this is almost certainly due to the fact that in order to replenish the strategic grain reserve the maize producer price was radically improved, making sales to private traders profitable even well below the floor price. Once the strategic grain reserve has been replenished and prices are allowed to fall the outlook for African peasant farmers appears bleak. Meanwhile full liberalization of cotton and wheat marketing has been blocked by the Zimbabwe Government and white commercial farmers respectively, the former in order to find a way of offering some respite to the crisis-ridden spinning industry and the latter in order to protect their profits against erosion by the owners of the highly concentrated private milling industry.

Public enterprise reform has been highly contested during the programme. Reluctant to include it in the adjustment agenda the Zimbabwe Government first conceded commercialization and eventually divestment of a large number of enterprises. The commercialization episode, apparently forced by the IMF, had disastrous consequences for the cost structure of the industrial sector generally but did not contribute to greater viability of the utilities themselves. Parastatal losses are now three times their pre-adjustment level. The opportunity for a non-orthodox strategic rethink of the role of the sector which a self-designed adjustment presented has meanwhile been lost. Divestment itself is meanwhile likely to present severe problems unless the state writes off the debts of the enterprises concerned - which currently it can hardly afford. Some enterprises have become unviable in the course of the accompanying paralysis concerning investment/rehabilitation decisions.

Neither the specific crisis in manufacturing industry, nor the economic crisis as a whole led to major falls in employment - although they were associated with very severe erosion in real wages, which fell by 24 percent across the economy as a whole in 1990-92. The incomes of some groups fell catastrophically. For the population as a whole evidence meanwhile strongly supports a picture of the poor increasingly becoming relatively worse-off, a situation which will become more marked still as the effects of the essentially regressive removal of the maize subsidy become felt. Despite considerable prodding by donors, the government's Social Dimensions of Adjustment initiative was weakly implemented and almost wholly ineffective.

Real per capita expenditure on education and health has fallen notably during the adjustment period. Personnel in these services have increased but real wages have dropped sharply, leading to declining professionalism. The Zimbabwe Government appears incapable of formulating a strategic approach to tackling the constrained resource situation. User fees have been introduced in both education and health. The effects in education are not yet clear, except in the commercial farming areas where they are regressive, but in health a coherent picture is emerging. Patients are deferring treatment until their conditions become serious. Donors' suggestions concentrate on transferring existing allocations from tertiary to primary levels, which has a certain populist ring to it, but whose overall effect on the quality of service offered at primary level would not be great.

The one positive feature of the programme so far has been an increase in private investment in industry - almost without exception local in origin. Should the regional economy pick up and a reorganization occur in regional protection systems this may provide some seeds of hope, but the overall impression is of a surprisingly unambitious and poorly designed programme falling at the first hurdle. With the subsequent onset of the drought the originally modest problems of the Zimbabwean economy have become quite serious ones.

References

Africa Confidential (various) London.

Brand, V. *et al.* 1995. 'Structural Adjustment, Women and Informal Trade in Zimbabwe'. in P. Gibbon (ed.), *Structural Adjustment and the Working Poor in Zimbabwe*. Uppsala: Scandinavian Institute of African Studies.

Chisvo, M. *et al.* 1994. 'The Impact of the Maize Marketing Liberalisation in Zimbabwe's Urban Areas'. Harare: UNICEF and Ministry of Public Service, Labour and Social Welfare (mimeo).

Chisvo, M. and L. Munro. 1994. 'A Review of Social Dimensions of Adjustment in Zimbabwe'. Harare: UNICEF.

Daniels, L. 1994. *Changes in the Small-Scale Enterprise Sector from 1991 to 1993: Results of a Second Nationwide Survey in Zimbabwe*. Bethesda: GEMINI Technical Report No. 71.

Davies, R.D. Sanders and T. Shaw. 1991. *Zimbabwe's Adjustment without the Fund*. Florence: UNICEF Innocenti Occasional Papers No. 16.

Durevall, D. and K. Mlambo. 1994. *Trade Liberalisation and Foreign Exchange Management: Zimbabwe 1990-93*. Stockholm: SIDA Macroeconomic Studies No. 48/94.

Economist Intelligence Unit: *Zimbabwe Country Reports* (quarterly, various).

Ericsson, M. and P. Gibbon. 1993. 'Mining Investment, Structural Adjustment and State-Mining Capital Relations in Zimbabwe' in C. Chachage, M. Ericsson and P. Gibbon, *Mining and Structural Adjustment: Studies on Zimbabwe and Tanzania*, Research Report No. 92. Uppsala: Scandinavian Institute of African Studies.

Financial Gazette (various) Harare.

Financial Times (various) London.

Hongoro, C. and S. Chandiwana. 1994. *The Effects of User Fees on Health Care Delivery in Zimbabwe*. Harare: Blair Research Institute and Ministry of Health and Child Welfare.

ILO. 1993. 'Structural Change and Adjustment in Zimbabwe'. Geneva: Interdepartmental Project on Structural Adjustment, Occasional Paper No. 16.

Kadhani, X. 1986. 'The Economy: Issues, Problems and Prospects', in I. Mandaza (ed.), *Zimbabwe: the Political Economy of Transition, 1980-86*. Dakar: Codesria.

Kanji, N. and N. Jazdowska. 1993. 'Structural Adjustment and Women in Zimbabwe', *Review of African Political Economy*, No. 56.

Kaseke, E. 1993. 'A Situation Analysis of the Social Development Fund', Harare: UNICEF and Zimbabwe Government, Ministry of Labour, Manpower Planning and Social Welfare (mimeo).

Lennock, J. 1994. *Paying for Health: Poverty and Structural Adjustment in Zimbabwe*. Oxford: Oxfam.

MacPherson, M. 1991. *Micro and Small-Scale Enterprises in Zimbabwe: Results of a Countrywide Survey*. Bethesda: GEMINI Technical Report 25.

Matshangala, O. *et al.* 1994. 'The Impact of Imports on Development: Zimbabwe Country Report', External Finance for Africa Project (mimeo).

Pedersen, P.O. 1994. personal communication.

Riddell, R. 1990. 'Zimbabwe', in R. Riddell (ed.), *Manufacturing Africa: Performance and Prospects of Seven Countries in Sub Saharan Africa*. London: James Currey.

Sachikonye, L. 1995. 'Industrial Restructuring and Labour Relations under ESAP in Zimbabwe'. in P. Gibbon (ed.), *Structural Adjustment and the Working Poor in Zimbabwe*. Uppsala: Scandinavian Institute of African Studies.

Skålnes, T. 1993. 'The State, Interest Groups and Structural Adjustment in Zimbabwe', *Journal of Development Studies*, Vol. 29, No. 3.

Stoneman, C. 1993. 'The World Bank: Some Lessons for South Africa', *Review of African Political Economy*, No. 58.

Stoneman, C. and L. Cliffe. 1989. *Zimbabwe: Politics, Economics and Society*. London: Pinter.

Tengende, N. 1994. 'Workers, Students and Struggles for Democracy: State- Civil Society Relations in Zimbabwe', unpublished PhD thesis, Roskilde University Centre.

Vallières, A. 1993. *Zimbabwe: Mineral Exploration and Investment Guide*. London: Mining Journal Research Services.

World Bank. 1987. *Zimbabwe: an Industrial Sector Memorandum*. Washington, DC: World Bank.

World Bank. 1991. *Zimbabwe Agriculture Sector Memorandum.* Washington, DC: World Bank.
World Bank. 1992. *Strategy for African Mining.* Washington, DC: Technical Paper No. 181, World Bank.
Zimbabwe Government. 1991. *Framework for Economic Reform, 1991-95.* Harare: Government Printer.
Zimbabwe Government. 1993a. 'Poverty Alleviation Action Plan' (mimeo).
Zimbabwe Government. 1993b. 'Social Dimensions of Adjustment: Progress Report and Action Plan' (mimeo).
Zimbabwe Government, Central Statistical Office. Various. *Quarterly Digest of Statistics.*
Zimbabwe Government, Central Statistics Office. 1994 a-h. *Census of Zimbabwe: Provincial Profiles* (all provinces except Mashonaland Central). Harare: Government Printer.
Zimbabwe Government, Ministry of Finance, Economic Planning and Development. 1990. *Economic Policy Statement. Macro-economic Adjustment and Trade Liberalisation including the Budget Statement, 1990.* Harare: Government Printer.
Zimbabwe Government, Ministry of Labour, Manpower Planning and Social Welfare. 1993a. *Findings from the Sentinel Site Surveillance for SDA Monitoring, Second Round, October 1992.* Harare.
Zimbabwe Government, Ministry of Labour, Manpower Planning and Social Welfare. 1993b. *Findings from the Sentinel Site Surveillance for SDA Monitoring, Third Round, January 1993.* Harare.
Zimbabwe Government, Ministry of Labour, Manpower Planning and Social Welfare. 1994. *Findings from the Sentinel Site Surveillance for SDA Monitoring, Fourth Round, December 1993.* Harare.

Overview of the Debate
on Structural Adjustment in Africa

Knud Erik Svendsen
Centre for Development Research

1. Background

From the beginning of the 1980s structural adjustment programmes became the major operation in aid relations to Sub-Saharan Africa, changing aid modalities radically, and introducing far reaching aid conditionalities. The role of external forces in Sub-Saharan Africa's economic and social development - always large - became even stronger and more pervasive. Given the magnitude of this change it is no wonder that structural adjustment was and still is controversial. The operation had high ambitions for Sub-Saharan Africa. It was truly a grand design. As most of the countries in the region are still today caught in low economic growth and deep social problems, it is hardly surprising that structural adjustment is often seen as responsible for this state of affairs.

Many factors led to the creation of structural adjustment. Towards the end of the 1970s there were concerns inside the World Bank about slow disbursement for project aid in support of the Bank's poverty agenda. Quick-disbursing forms of assistance were sought. This was reinforced by the burdens of the second oil price increases, creating balance-of-payments deficits which were difficult to handle, especially for the low-income countries. Their external deficits were pushed higher by the recession in the industrial world in the first years of the 1980s and by the large increase in interest rates. Much of the current debt burden was created in these years.

At the same time there was a growing unease in the international financial institutions (IFIs) and among their major shareholders about the development paradigm of Sub-Saharan Africa in the 1970s. The results of investments and development efforts generally were seen to be much too small. The voices advocating basic reforms in the paradigm grew stronger. This was strengthened by the shift in policy stance in the industrial world, as the neo-liberal school launched its message: the functions and size of the state in the economies of the states in Sub-Saharan Africa should be reduced and cut, while markets should be liberalized and relieved of state regulation in order to strengthen the effects of incentives. Opportunities for the private sector in agriculture, manufacturing industry and trade and transport should be expanded.

This radical reform agenda was combined with high expectations of quick results from its implementation in Sub-Saharan Africa (later expressed as a belief in 'quick fixes'). What was advocated was, in fact, fundamental changes in the socio-economic systems of Sub-Saharan Africa.

The governments in Sub-Saharan Africa were in dire need of finance because of the pressure of external deficits on imports. Private sources for borrowing soon dried up. Bilateral donors were having problems with their projects and came to understand the need for some non-project aid to counteract the effects of the economic crisis on basic facilities of transport, energy and water supplies. But they needed some guidance in order to embark on this new form of assistance.

All these factors gave the IFIs a leading role in the operation. The acute imbalances especially gave the IMF an important task, as its basic mandate is to offer short-term support to members with balance-of-payments difficulties. It is true that the IMF had little previous experience with the effects of its tools in economies with the structural problems found in Africa, but it had a strong belief in the necessity of stabilization and liberalization to stop the economic downturn and to lay a foundation for renewed growth. The experience of the World Bank in stabilizing economies in the short term was limited, so an agreement with the IMF became a precondition for assistance from the Bank and other donors (and for treatment of debt in the Paris Club). Budget deficits should be reduced, and expenditures cut across the board; heavily overvalued currencies should be devalued, market regulations removed and prices set right. External finance should be used to soften the blow (and some said to convince the governments to buy the reforms).

Institutionally and conceptually this meant an (albeit overlapping) distinction between stabilization and structural adjustment. Stabilization came to be seen as 'a necessary, but not sufficient condition' for the implementation of structural reforms, primarily institutional changes in the public sector and the civil service. Stabilization together with structural reforms was with time called 'adjustment'. In some discussions this broad concept is meant to include long-run growth and development, e.g. investment in human and physical infrastructure, while others consider development as something to be added to adjustment, i.e. outside the objectives of adjustment programmes. It is an important part of the picture that traditional aid programmes of investment projects continued alongside the adjustment financing, and in fact remained the largest share of total aid.

Stabilization programmes negotiated with the IMF and structural adjustment programmes negotiated with the World Bank became the order of the day and proliferated up to the mid-1990s. There is now a growing recognition of the lack of clarity of these concepts and the short-term connotation of adjustment in particular. The concept 'adjustment' is on its way out. It is interesting to note that the 1994 Annual Report of the World Bank does not present the information in earlier reports on new adjustment lending agreements; instead it is briefly said that adjustment lending has been declining since 1989 from 29 percent of the total in 1989 to 12 percent in 1994. 'This decline is due to the relative maturity of the reform process in many countries, and to constraints and uncertainties in others.'

The programmes consist of the following core elements: broad objectives with lists of conditions, performance ('output') expected, and magnitudes, forms and phasing of finance to be supplied. The conditions are a mixture of broad policy conditions and more specific institutional changes, including details of their extent and timing. 'Policy-based lending' is a good term expressing the nature of the conditions attached to the resource flows.

2.   Major Controversies

Structural adjustment followed a grand design, inevitably generating disagreement. To understand the policy process over the years it is useful to look first at the broad features of these disagreements and then to review the more specific disputes.

It is usual to speak of a growing degree of consensus, by which is meant that the critics have moved closer to the policies advocated by the IFIs - and vice versa. A process of defining a common agenda, i.e. a list of policy spheres and policy instruments, has clearly unfolded. And this crude agreement on an agenda has been accompanied by a broader common understanding of the direction and magnitude of changes needed. In many cases there is no longer an adversary situation. Some may even fear a softening of the debate.

At least two of the most fundamental disagreements persist, however. The first relates to the distinction between internal and external causes of the economic distress. For African governments it was important right from the beginning to stress the dominant importance of external factors in bringing Africa to its knees. For many outside observers, including influential voices in the IFIs, the main explanations were sought in the policy mistakes of the 1970s. It was also emphasized that the external environment had not been worse for Sub-Saharan Africa than for other regions.

This may be seen as a vain argument as common sense tells us that both internal and external factors were at play - something in the world economy went wrong, and something in the African countries needed to change. With hindsight it must be said that the efforts to correct the internal policies have dominated, while the external conditions have been hard and turned harder in the 1990s. The strong conviction in the IFIs of the need for changes in Africa has contributed to an underestimation of the negative effects of the external factors, e.g. the large losses in foreign trade due to falling terms of trade and the unsustainable debt burden.

Even for those who believe that little can be done about falling commodity prices or debt payments, a comprehension of the weight of these factors might have produced a better understanding of the design and magnitude of the efforts needed to redress the situation. In general, Sub-Saharan Africa's losses due to adverse external factors are not fully compensated by adjustment-related inflows of aid, despite the special efforts to increase assistance to Africa.

The second disagreement centres on the appropriate role of the state in economic development in Sub-Saharan Africa. Most are ready to accept that 'the state' was in crisis. And there are good political explanations from the right as well as the left of how special interests produced an expansion of the state bureaucracy and public enterprises. While some adjustment was needed there is not agreement on how far the pendulum should swing in the other direction. The understanding of the importance of a dynamic private sector in the economy has grown, but with time a greater understanding of the important role of the state in supplying vital services for human development and for physical infrastructure has also emerged. In a way there is a call for a stronger state at a time when the capacity of the public sector has been reduced. There is also an acceptance of the importance of the private sector - combined with some doubts about its capacity under the present circumstances in Sub-Saharan Africa, in particular the constraints on access to finance.

These major themes, together with the more technical questions of programme design, are explored below through a summary of recent reports and research literature. The main points very briefly stated are the following:

In three reviews produced by the World Bank (RAL I-III), 1988-92, the recommendation to maintain the course of macroeconomic policy is combined with a growing emphasis on the complementary nature of private and public investment. A paper distilling the main findings on structural adjustment by the Bank's Operations Evaluation Department in 1993 argues for the use of longer-term lending for development purposes and offers advice on a better sequencing of reforms. It shows particular concern about the low degree of recipient ownership and advocates a stronger interest in political economy issues.

The ambitious World Bank publication *Adjustment in Africa* (1994) concentrates on macroeconomic issues and makes an effort to show that adjustment has worked, while underlining that progress so far has been uneven and remains fragile. It finds that adjustment has been to the advantage of the poor, compared with a situation of no adjustment programmes, 'but more could have been done to reduce poverty'. It warns against pessimism: the turnaround in growth shows that adjustment can put African countries back on the road to development.

Two IMF papers on adjustment in low-income countries argue for adjustment, but point to the problems of falling terms of trade. Examples of fields where the IMF may continue to play a role in the process are laid out.

Turning to recent academic contributions, a very wide range of issues are raised. Several authors (e.g. Mosley, Harrigan and Toye) find that there are more justifications for state intervention than the Bank has been ready to accept. The programmes have shown a preoccupation with the short term. The 'Washington consensus' is criticized by Taylor for its austerity, which runs a grave risk of introducing secular stagnation. An elaborate 'non-Washington consensus' is identified, covering the issue of financial equilibrium together with questions of the sequencing of stabilization and adjustment. The theoretical foundation for the adjustment process is analyzed by Tarp, with especially critical remarks on the IMF model, but it is said that the Fund and Bank are both modifying their theories to respond to experience gained.

In a comprehensive and open-ended multi-author collection of papers published in 1994, Helleiner notes the appearance of some consensus, but also points to continuing conflicts on the role of the state, the import regime, financial liberalization, agricultural development and the size of required external support, just to mention a few. He also raises questions about the continued presence of the IMF in Africa.

In a large number of papers a team at Cornell University, managed by David E. Sahn, have since 1991 examined the impact of adjustment on poverty. The results of this are presented in a recent paper (September 1994), which argues for a more positive view of the favourable effects of economic reform on the poor. At the same time the authors recognize that the gains resulting from reform have been marginal in most cases. They note the failure to incorporate complementary measures to promote economic growth early in the process. Projects and technical assistance may be better aid modalities for such measures.

The most recent contributions to this debate are by Killick and Lipumba. The first finds the record of adjustment 'patchy, at best', because of its neglect of long-term issues, the ineffective explosion in conditionality and underfunding. In Killick's view the IFIs should be more ready to say No to recipients, while being more pragmatic toward other development approaches (like the Asian ones). Lipumba presents a detailed critique of the World Bank's publication *Adjustment in Africa*. His major objection concerns the lack of a coherent linkage between medium-term and long-term measures.

3.   The Major Contributions

3.1   Three Reports on Adjustment Lending by the World Bank

Reports on Adjustment Lending, RAL I, II and III, were published in 1988, 1990 and 1992 respectively covering all developing countries receiving adjustment loans. They share a number of findings and recommendations, but they also show the progress of the learning process associated with the experience gained.

The first two reports showed that countries that received several loans starting in the early 1980s succeeded, on average, in restoring growth and in increasing their exports and saving, but investment typically failed to recover to the levels needed to sustain growth in the longer term. Successful adjustment required policy reforms to assure a stable macroeconomic environment, a rational structure of incentives and sufficient public spending to develop complementary infrastructure and human resources. And it typically required substantial initial external funding, often in the form of debt relief. Some countries fell short in complying with conditions 'often with disastrous consequences'. Despite the great variation in the content of programmes, the Bank found it possible to indicate a number of recommendations on the provision of aid, measures to stimulate private and public investments, strengthening of the public sector to provide infrastructure, basic education and health, and the protection of the poor.

When we turn to RAL III of 1992 the catalogue of findings and recommendations is expanded. Among the major findings are that adjustment lending is associated with a recovery in growth rates, but that this did not solve the low-income countries' long-run development problems. These problems will continue to require substantial external support through project and sectoral investment lending from the international community.

Adjustment policies are found to help most of the poor, but recessions associated with adjustment often cause temporary welfare declines for some of them.

Private investment eventually recovers where policy conditions are good, but it remains a problem in low-income countries. There has been substantial public sector adjustment, but misallocation of public sector resources remains a problem. General spending cuts have often been at the expense of critically important operations and maintenance spending, and sometimes at the expense of necessary public investment.

After its critical review of the findings RAL III offers a list of recommendations: stay the course on macroeconomic and pricing reform, even though these 'core reforms' do not appear to be sufficient in low-income countries for satisfactory growth. The Bank should therefore complement adjustment lending by investment lending. There should also be a broader view of constraints on the private sector and increased attention to 'second-generation' policies to support the business environment, as well as increased attention to the allocation of public sector spending and reinforced efforts to design adjustment policy programmes to promote poverty-reducing growth.

3.2   Selected Findings of the Operations Evaluation Department (OED) of the World Bank

Operations evaluation in the World Bank provides an 'independent' assessment of Bank operations. The department reports directly to the Bank's Board. According to the Bank's Annual Report this constitutional independence 'encourages evaluation staff to report candidly'. Hence one turns to the report *Adjustment in Sub-Saharan Africa. Selected Findings from OED Evaluations* (June 1993), expecting straight language and more critical views than were found in the reports presented in the previous section. These expectations are met. The second OED evaluation (June 1992) reviewed the experience of 40 operations in 18 African countries and found mixed results: 'While progress in macroeconomic policy was evident, the fiscal effort remained weak in most countries and the investment and growth record was generally poor. Progress in public enterprise reform was found to be slow and the external debt overhang clouded the prospects for successful adjustment in a number of countries'.

Of the 68 adjustment operations evaluated by the OED only 57 percent were rated as satisfactory. 'All too often, programs have been poorly implemented or have not generated the desired outcomes.' For programme design and implementation the OED finds that structural reforms are usually not sufficient to generate a strong supply response: 'Successful adjustment programs require macroeconomic stability as a precondition, including sustainable levels of external debt, and complementary measures to develop the private sector (basic infrastructure, business support systems, legal reform) as well as long-term institutional reform'. In the view of the OED these issues are better addressed through longer-term lending instruments.

The policy reform programmes tend to be more successful when the objectives and the time frame for implementation are realistic and conditions are clear and prioritized. The OED also offers some findings concerning the sequencing of structural reforms: export promotion should take precedence over import liberalization, but the two must be closely coordinated to avoid the anti-export bias of protectionist policies. The pace of import liberalization must be manageable. Structural reforms are unlikely to be effective unless accompanied (or preceded) by internal competition policies. 'Real' sector adjustment, to generate productive investment opportunities, should normally precede financial sector liberalization.

There is no doubt that adjustment lending can play a valuable role, but without sustained progress on the policy front the provision of balance-of-payments support can be counterproductive. More attention should be given upfront to developing the institutional capacity and borrower ownership needed to sustain reform. Until this is in place it would be more prudent to accept a lower level of adjustment assistance with more funds targeted to specific sectoral programmes or investment projects.

Borrower ownership stands out as a primary determinant of programme success. The OED introduces a classification scheme where ownership is treated as a four-dimensional variable. On this basis it finds that 36 out of 63 programmes have low ownership. Finally in 1993 the OED states that the Bank needs to strengthen its understanding of political economy issues mainly through a regular assessment of the impact of adjustment on various constituencies, and support to efforts to bring the private sector and other social/political groups into the process.

3.3   A World Bank Policy Research Report: *Adjustment in Africa. Reforms, Results, and the Road Ahead* (1994)

Most recently the World Bank has mobilized much effort and talent to produce a book presenting experiences with adjustment in Africa. This book and its companion volume of country cases aims at publicizing the good examples of 'policies getting better' in order to show that 'better policies pay off'. At the same time 'the road ahead for adjustment' is indicated recognizing that 'policies are not good yet' - to use the headings of the overview chapter summarizing the book. It documents the very uneven progress among the 29 countries in focus with extensive documentation on the enormous differentiation in situation as well as changes in performance inside Sub-Saharan Africa. The discussion is less balanced when it comes to the effects of policies because of a heavy emphasis on macroeconomic policies (in one review called 'macroeconomic fundamentalism'). Sweat and tears have been spent on the invention of new ways of proving through statistics and policy indicators that better policies pay off - a conclusion which RALs I-III were more cautious about.

The opening phrase is indicative of the main purpose of the publication: 'In the African countries that have undertaken sustained major policy reforms, adjustment is working'. The proof is that the six countries (of the 29) with the most improvement in macroeconomic policies between the two periods 1981-86 and 1987-91 enjoyed the strongest resurgence in economic performance.

In fact, the variation among good as well as among bad policy performing countries is so great that the difference between the two groups is not statistically significant. And as the book says, policy reforms have been uneven across sectors and across countries. The countries have in general been more successful in improving their macroeconomic, trade and agricultural policies than in implementing structural reforms. However, all reforms remain incomplete. No African country has achieved a sound macroeconomic policy stance. The report notes that reforms undertaken are fragile and are merely returning Africa to the slow growth path of the 1960s and the 1970s. More progress in macroeconomic reform will be required. Growth with equity will call for 'strong political resolve to tackle money-losing public enterprises and bloated bureaucracies'.

Policy progress is documented for budget deficits, inflation and exchange rates. In trade the number of non-tariff barriers has been reduced, and more automatic allocation of foreign exchange has been introduced. In agriculture two-thirds of the countries are taxing their farmers less, and despite huge declines in real export prices, real producer prices have increased in ten countries, while restrictions on trade in food crops have been scaled down or completely removed. For public enterprises and financial enterprises, however, there have been few policy changes.

The better policies have paid off. External transfers have helped. By using a general model calculation it is shown that these transfers cannot fully explain the differences in performance, but they have been important. In African countries that have undertaken some reforms and achieved some increase in growth, the majority of the poor are probably better-off. It is meanwhile emphasized that the absence of empirical studies makes it difficult to document any clear and specific link between adjustment reforms and environmental changes.

Three principles are offered as a guide to the road ahead: get macroeconomic policies right; encourage competition (through domestic deregulation, trade reform and the privatization of public enterprises); and use scarce institutional capacity wisely, i.e. minimize unnecessary government involvement in markets, privatize public enterprises, and replace import restrictions by tariffs. More adjustment - not less - would help the poor. But the poor will benefit more from an increase in growth if spending programmes to develop human resources are protected during the adjustment process . 'More could have been done, and more should have been done, to reduce poverty in the context of adjustment programs.'

Today's large volume of aid poses dangers: it could soften budget constraints and thus finance the postponement of public sector reforms. Expanded aid flows should therefore be linked to strong reform programmes and better governance. There is a need for rethinking the current debt-relief strategy. Even with transformed policies, higher savings and better investments, Africa will still require exceptional external assistance for at least another decade.

3.4   The IMF on Economic Adjustment (1993 and 1994)

In 1986 the structural adjustment facility (SAF) was set up in the IMF to provide highly concessional loans (different from normal IMF support) to support structural adjustment in low-income countries. SAF was followed by the Enhanced Structural Adjustment

Facility (ESAF) in December 1987. Both innovations were based on two experiences of the IMF. First, adjustment programmes focusing on financial policies alone would not address the roots of the countries' problems. Major reforms in economic structures and institutions were needed. Second, the heavy indebtedness of these countries even precluded borrowing from the IMF on conventional terms. Furthermore the Fund was keen to ensure that its earlier support was paid back. Both SAF and ESAF have been funded from special sources.

In September 1993 the IMF published an occasional paper written by Susan Schadler and others on the experience of ESAFs. The emphasis in the review was on taking stock of the accomplishments and on identifying areas where successor arrangements will need further effort.

In light of the many attempts to measure the impact of adjustment it is interesting to note that this paper emphasizes that clear-cut conclusions for differences in countries' performance have proved difficult to draw, except where these differences are stark. This reflects two characteristics that muddy the assessment of even strong adjustment programmes. First, countries faced diverse circumstances, so it was difficult to disentangle the effects of insufficiently comprehensive policy changes from those of adverse exogenous factors. Second, the strength of policy changes was seldom quantifiable or comparable across countries.

The IMF paper points to the fact that the performance of countries under ESAF must be judged against their extraordinarily weak starting positions. On average there has been a strengthening of macroeconomic indicators, but there have also been disappointments, particularly in the small response of investment ratios and the persistence of low savings ratios. It is noted that the largest improvements occurred in countries which combined the most forceful reforms with the least problems from weakening terms of trade.

These declining terms of trade are also mentioned as one of the influences affecting the forcefulness of reform and adjustment. The others are political commitment, administrative capacity to design and implement reforms, and political instability.

A majority of the countries where terms of trade fell made relatively little progress toward external viability, pointing to two lessons. First, as the terms of trade deteriorate, the strength of adjustment needs to be re-evaluated quickly. Second, financing should be on highly concessional terms.

Experience under the ESAF suggests several areas where the IMF should continue to play a role. Continuing inflation, undermining savings and investment, should be brought under control. Frameworks for coordinating domestic financial policies, structural reform, and external financing continue to be needed. Debt reduction will be necessary, contingent on assurances that domestic adjustment and reform efforts are effective. Finally, well-targeted technical assistance from the IMF will be necessary.

A more recent IMF study *Sub-Saharan Africa: Growth, Savings and Investment, 1986-93* by Michael T. Hadjimichael *et al.* (1994) assesses the experiences of 41 countries in the region, confirming significant performance differences among them. A large part of this discrepancy may, according to the authors, be explained by policy decisions. They suggest that 'stronger growth rates were recorded by countries with less macro imbalances and by sustained adjusters'.

During the period the external position of the countries worsened sharply. This was largely the result of downturns in industrial country markets and the collapse of the Soviet Union. Given their high dependence on commodity exports, the terms of trade of the region worsened sharply. Total export earnings virtually stagnated during 1986-93. This export shortfall has also exacerbated Sub-Saharan Africa's external financing requirements. Despite sizable debt forgiveness provided by various official creditors, the external public debt of virtually all the countries sharply increased relative to GDP.

The study finds that the general impact of foreign assistance on domestic savings is negative, but this negative impact is 'concentrated in those countries with protracted imbalances and negative per capita growth'. As to the relationship between foreign aid and growth the authors contend that there is no correlation between the two. They suggest that the underlying issue lies in the efficiency with which foreign aid is used, not its volume.

Looking ahead the authors advocate the adoption and effective implementation of structural adjustment policies. The key ingredient is a growth-oriented adjustment strategy that encourages 'a substantially stronger expansion in private savings and investment'.

3.5   Recent Contributions to the Debate

A new phase in academic debate about adjustment was ushered in with Paul Mosley, Jane Harrigan and John Toye's two volume study *Aid and Power. The World Bank and Policy-Based Lending* (1991), which includes nine country studies (among them Ghana, Malawi, and Kenya) and a set of recommendations.

The study sought to answer two fundamental questions. First, does the giving of aid confer power on the donor, in particular power to change the recipient's economic policies? Second, has the exercise of such power as exists been of any help to the developing countries? The answer, to both questions, is 'a little, but not as much as the World Bank hoped'.

Their starting point is that policy-based lending was a weapon designed by the Bank to kill two birds with one stone, viz. to provide quick-disbursing finance to deal with the crisis in the early 1980s, and to demolish those policy structures which it blamed for the failure of its projects and for the widening gap in economic performance between the Far East and the rest of the developing world. The exercise was a leap in the dark: in terms of economic theory which gave little guidance; in terms of politics where the Bank found itself at the top of the negotiating table in developing countries without any strategy for disarming the forces opposed to the reforms; and in terms of the Bank's relations to the Fund which suddenly found itself supplying medium- term policy-based loans in the same market as the Bank.

According to the authors there are more justifications for government intervention than the Bank has generally been prepared to accept, and further work to determine the appropriate form and levels of such intervention is now urgent. They also found that avoidance of conditions can be more readily contemplated than was expected by recipients because they are aware of the Bank's reluctance to put its disbursement at risk by too rigorous an insistence on compliance. The case studies reveal how wide has been the variance in compliance with conditions. Implementation was partial; it was more complete in respect of price-based instruments, which could be quickly altered, than in respect of institutional changes which required widespread consent and the support of the legislature.

The authors reach the following conclusions. 1) The implementation of structural adjustment programmes was almost always favourable to export growth and the external account. 2) The influence on aggregate investment is almost everywhere negative. 3) The influence on national income and on financial flows from overseas is, on balance, neutral. These results are bound to appear disappointing. They relate this to the conflicting two objectives of the Bank. The financial imperatives confronting the Bank during the debt crisis of the 1980s required it to erect a safety net under the international financial system, and this hidden benefit must be added to the meagre results. But it has had a hidden cost: the downward pressure on the level of investment.

In the view of the authors the 1980s has been a decade of preoccupation with the short term, where appropriate levels of investment in human and material capital have been submerged by pressure to get the macroeconomic balances right. But it has become clear that the manner in which those balances are got right has implications for the long term. It is in the poorer developing countries that we encounter the kernel of the Bank's adjustment dilemma. Both economic theory and the evidence suggest that the Bank's chosen package of reforms has more relevance to Thailand and Turkey, say, than to Ghana and Guyana. The Bank has still to grasp the point that in very poor countries, privatization and removal of infant-industry protective structures are at best an irrelevance.

The authors offer a mixed bag of policy proposals: shorter lists of 'key conditions'; advice on punishment for slippage in reforms which structural adjustment policies should embrace; policies to expand the economic role of the state in addition to measures to remove harmful state intervention; and a more experimental understanding of policy changes (as their merits are uncertain). The Bank is also recommended to find ways of tapping the considerable local knowledge of bilateral donors; policy-based loans aimed at particular sectors should, where possible, be offered in kind; losers from policy-based reforms should be identified and compensated out of the loan.

In *The Rocky Road to Reform* (1993) published by the World Institute for Development Economics Research (United Nations University) Lance Taylor presents critical views on the approaches to economic reform together with 17 country studies, of which six are on countries in Africa (including Tanzania, Uganda and Zimbabwe). The basic message of Taylor's analysis is that attempts at economic reform must fit the situation at hand. Orthodox packages may well be appropriate in some situations; for practical purposes, policies must substantially vary in others. Much of the discussion is devoted to sketching initial and boundary conditions on feasible policy choices.

In Taylor's opinion 'certified economists from the neoliberal to the radical extremes typically agree on one-half or three-quarters of their policy recommendations. There are only a few instruments available and the arguments center around their unfavourable effects on one or the other of the policy targets. Moreover, there has been a convergence of views over the past 10 to 15 years about initiatives that are likely to self-destruct, as bold programmes of both orthodox and heterodox persuasion have failed spectacularly'.

Nonetheless, Taylor stresses that differences between mainstream and structuralist thought persist, as the so-called Washington consensus exemplifies. This consensus, promoted by the Fund and the Bank, encompasses most or all of the following policy moves: fiscal austerity, that is, reductions in public investment, consumption, and subsidy programmes; increased taxes; the privatization of state enterprises; monetary austerity beyond simple reduction of the public sector borrowing, for example, interest-rate increases and credit restraint; devaluation, unification of multiple exchange rates and so on; trade liberalization, supposed to improve the efficiency of the economy. Both Bretton Woods institutions stress that policy-makers should steer toward a liberal market economy even though social costs may be high. Redistribution of income and wealth is implicit in all the policies mentioned.

After an analysis of selected themes (the role of the state, fiscal and foreign constraints, internal vs. external orientation, etc.) Taylor presents a 'non-Washington synthesis'. In his view there would be fair agreement among progressive economists about the following counterpoints to the Washington consensus. 1) Fiscal equilibrium is desirable, but can be devilishly difficult to attain. External support may be required to improve the fiscal, foreign exchange and savings gaps. 2) Changing real 'macro' prices such as wages, the exchange rate and interest rate is not easy. 3) External liberalization programmes have fared no better than packages based on intelligent use of quotas and controls. 4) Privatization brings no obvious productivity gains, and it can adversely perturb saving, investment and financial flows. 5) Labour market deregulation may slash wage costs in the short run, but it may prove inimical to long-run socio-economic development. 6) Sound macroeconomic policy is always desirable 'like stable family relationships and apple pie'. Whether it is feasible under developing country political and distributional conditions is another question. If 'soundness' means austerity, it runs a grave risk of inducing secular stagnation. 7) An increasingly educated, healthy and well-paid population is necessary for long-run productivity growth. Speeding human capital accumulation is not a sufficient condition for raising output in the short run. 8) Stabilization before (or concurrent with) adjustment sounds sensible but does not always work out. Maybe basic improvements in fiscal and balance-of-payments positions are required before macroeconomic difficulties can be overcome. There are recent examples both ways. 9) Indeed there are examples of successes and failures of both orthodox and heterodox policy initiatives worldwide. The problem is how to invent and sequence policy changes effectively in each country's historical and institutional context.

The purpose of Finn Tarp's monograph *Stabilization and Structural Adjustment* (1993) is to analyze in a critical fashion the 'macroeconomic frameworks for analyzing the crisis in Sub-Saharan Africa' (the subtitle). It is stressed explicitly that no attempt has been made in the book to review the empirical evidence on the impact of stabilization and adjustment programmes in the Sub-Saharan context, which Tarp anyway believes to be a difficult task because it is impossible to establish a counterfactual of what trends would have been without the programmes.

The ambition of the book is to examine 1) whether the basic characteristics of the economies of Sub-Saharan Africa are adequately considered within the various analytical models proposed and in use in practical policy-making, and 2) how the central issues for Africa are approached and analyzed. In other words, what is the nature and quality of the theoretical foundations of the IMF, the World Bank and other actors in adjustment.

Tarp is very critical of the model used by the IMF formulated by J.J. Polak in the late 1950s. Excessive attention has on this basis been paid by the IMF to the money demand and supply processes, rather than to savings, investment and growth. He finds that the widespread perception that too restrictive credit policy has in many cases led to more output contraction than was strictly necessary cannot be discarded easily. And his major conclusion is that the financial programming model of the IMF is not a sufficient and theoretically satisfactory basis for recommending and undertaking complex packages of adjustment policy.

What is needed, he emphasizes, is a growth-oriented adjustment approach and models to serve this. Here the approach developed by the Bank in the early 1970s under the special name of the Revised Minimum Standard Model appears more relevant at first sight. The primary purpose is to show what levels of investment, imports and external borrowing will be required for a targeted real output. Provided the resources necessary to fill the estimated two gaps (between savings and investment on the one hand, and between foreign-exchange earnings and needs, on the other hand) are found, growth is assumed to ensue automatically in accordance with the model. But the extreme simplicity of the approach, and the absolute lack of sophisticated causal relationships and interpretations of the actual operation of the economy must be squarely recognized. The two-gap framework does not provide an adequate basis for formulating structural adjustment programmes. Tarp notes that against this background it is remarkable that the IMF and the World Bank were so self-confident in the early years of the 1980s. 'A sizable measure of faith and ideology must have outweighed the calls for a more phased and considered approach.'

Recent efforts to merge the models of the Fund and the Bank are encouraging, but he is not sure that the models can be integrated in an operationally-worthwhile manner. Tarp reviews alternative approaches in a positive way. The UNICEF analysis published in 1987, *Adjustment with a Human Face*, was a critique of the high social costs of the adjustment process, but it also offered a different theoretical approach, advocating more expansionary macroeconomic fiscal, monetary and wage policies, policies that benefited the poor, sectoral policies aimed at restructuring production, restructuring social expenditures to improve equity, and the introduction of compensatory programmes with targeted support for poor people affected by adjustment.

In Tarp's opinion it is the neo-structuralist school that is most directly challenging the IMF/World Bank models of adjustment. Macro-structuralists such as Taylor have made thought-provoking contributions to the analytical and policy-oriented debate on structural adjustment. The structuralists, partly originating in Latin America in the 1940s and 1950s, are now paying more attention to the importance of short-run macro-economic management and macroeconomic balances. This school maintains strong links between the 'real' and the 'monetary' side of the economy. Account is taken of structural rigidities as well as changes in income distribution - in complete opposition to the approaches used by the IMF and the World Bank. The attraction of the neo-structuralist approach is that it recognizes that the distributional impact of decisions is linked with political processes, which cannot be ignored. Tarp presents a list of problems related to the structuralist approach (including the observation that donors are not convinced of this more heterodox approach).

Finn Tarp's review of different theoretical approaches to macroeconomic adjustment (and their consequences for practical policies) ends on the optimistic tone that the IMF and the World Bank are, albeit slowly, able and willing to modify their positions, when particular circumstances prevail. He even speaks of 'reversed leverage' in the Africa-IFI relationship, indicating that the IFIs are becoming dependent on successes in Sub-Saharan Africa.

From Adjustment to Development in Africa. Conflict, Controversy, Convergence, Consensus? edited by Giovanni Andrea Cornia and Gerald K. Helleiner (1994) is a collection of papers covering a wide range of adjustment-related topics based on the discussions at a conference on structural adjustment arranged by UNICEF in 1992. Its main objective is to present a review of the major dimensions of the adjustment issues with an emphasis on the changes in the discourse over time. In fact it is introduced with the statement that it is time to call a formal end to the decade of 'structural adjustment' in Sub-Saharan Africa, with the argument that the debate over its meaning, its instruments and efficacy no longer serves any useful purpose now that all at last agree that there are no economic 'quick fixes' for Africa and that appropriate change will take much longer than was originally thought.

The book is deliberately open-ended and does not offer final recommendations on the policies to follow. Each contribution presents the debate so far, and the conclusions offered reflect the many diverse positions of the authors.

In a concise and clear introduction G.K. Helleiner shows the emergence of consensus on many central issues, but he stresses that this should not blind us to the important continuing disagreements of the following three major types: 1) disagreements as to the appropriateness and efficacy of the process through which adjustment/development programmes are designed, and thus their perceived 'ownership'; 2) remaining matters of substantive policy disagreement, both in terms of overall presumptions as to the 'correct' policy and in terms of the details of individual country programmes; 3) disagreements as to the degree to which rhetoric accords with reality.

As to the process, Helleiner notes the greater awareness of the issue of programme ownership, but he points to disagreements about the degree to which donor practices will actually change, and in particular their willingness to relinquish or loosen accustomed controls. He asks: Are they ready, even now, to leave Africans to learn from their own mistakes? And: If local ownership involves a programme design that differs significantly from that which these outsiders recommend, will it receive their support?

On policy substance he finds growing consensus, so that earlier alternative approaches (UNICEF, UN/ECA *et al.*) no longer seem quite as alternative as they were. There is a stronger interest in the impact on the poor, but there remains much agreement as to the extent to which agreements in principle have been translated into altered policy practice. Also agreed is the strategy of building, in the first instance, primarily on agriculture, and even, where smallholders already dominate, on smallholder agriculture. There is no longer the same exclusive fixation, in the World Bank or elsewhere, on 'getting prices right' in order to support such agricultural development. The importance of non-price factors - notably rural infrastructure; transport, marketing and input distribution systems; and credit - is fully recognized by all. There is also widespread consensus that there is considerable underutilized potential in the small-scale and informal sectors. Consensus has also been reached on the necessity of increasing exports, and where possible, efficient import substitution. Inward-oriented development strategies are still discussed in some African academic circles, but they now carry little weight with policy-makers.

All now seem to agree on the need for rationalizing public sector activities. Helleiner notes that reform efforts in this area do not always involve the downsizing of government as a whole (in Ghana and Uganda adjustment programmes raised the government shares of GDP). Earlier optimism about the prospects for private savings and investment, once policies were set right, has now dissipated.

He then turns to continuing conflict on the following main issues: 1) the appropriate role of the state in development efforts; the appropriate role for non-African expatriate private enterprise, both resident and truly foreign; and the medium-term potential of African enterprise; 2) the import regime, and, in particular, the appropriate approach to industrial protection; 3) the efficacy of financial liberalization and financial sector reforms; 4) the appropriate objectives and instruments for agricultural development; 5) the size of required external financial support; and the potential for improving, or at least stabilizing, primary commodity prices and the terms of trade; 6) the role of the exchange rate.

At the national level, Helleiner asserts that there is bound to be further disagreement as to the appropriate pace, timing and sequencing of development-oriented policy changes as well as a myriad of details on distributional and participatory matters. For all of the six conflict issues listed he offers detailed comments.

As to the reality of poverty alleviation Helleiner notes the World Bank's intensive efforts to improve data on poverty, but they obviously have no direct impact on poverty. Many including the Bank continue to argue that, in the absence of adjustment, Africa's poverty would have been worse. That may, in many cases, be true; but this argument evades the question as to whether better design of its programmes might have generated much more favourable results.

Other striking observations in the papers include:

Lionel Demery on the achievements of structural adjustment. There are three reasons for the lack of consensus on how successful the structural adjustment efforts have been: first, most programmes have had mixed effects; second, the weaknesses of the assessments so far; third, it is possible that insufficient time has elapsed to display the effects.

Vito Tanzi on long-term and short-term objectives of the IMF. The Fund is continually questioning its modus operandi in order to make it more efficient and responsive to major concerns (e.g. poverty). It recognizes that mistakes have occasionally been made and that there is always scope for improvement. In fact, the changes that occurred throughout the 1980s are strong indications that the Fund is not the rigid institution assumed by its critics.

Frances Stewart. Are short-term policies consistent with long-term development needs in Africa? In some important respects the policies advocated by the Fund and the Bank are pushing African economies away from a desirable long-term structure of development, especially because they are running down African capabilities and are reorienting the economies back to a heavy specialization on export agriculture. It is doubtful that the IMF can play a helpful role in African economies, given the heavy emphasis on credit and expenditure control in its programmes.

T.W. Oshikoya on domestic private investment. Restoring private investors' confidence and raising the level of domestic private investment will depend on a predictable and stable macroeconomic environment, credible adjustment programmes and low perceived probability of policy reversal, increases in complementary public sector investment, financial sector rehabilitation, and adequate external support.

Thandika Mkandawire on political conditionality and democratization. The quest for democracy has not left Africa untouched. Yet, all is not well. In a number of cases concessions to democratic demands have been no more than window-dressing. The new democratic regimes are inheriting crisis-ridden economies. Democratization is taking place when the sovereignty of African states has been gravely compromised. If the process of democratization is to be firmly anchored in African societies then we should insist that the initiative towards democratization remains in the hands of democratic forces. External support that is an expression of solidarity, and not the usual meddlesome condescension, is most welcome. A further problem is the prevalence of a dogma that severely narrows the economic options and unwarrantably ties democratization to one economic practice or model.

David E. Sahn on the impact on incomes, health and nutrition. While the general conclusion is that adjustment has had little to do with causing poverty in Africa it should not be expected to be a panacea either. The reforms are necessary, but are not always a sufficient condition for growth. The measures undertaken to date are also, in general, not sufficient for alleviating poverty and meeting social welfare objectives. State investment in physical and social welfare is a key component of a growth strategy. But such investments need to be designed to encourage complementary investments by the private sector as well as community-based action to improve and protect human resources.

G.K. Helleiner on external resource flows. The 'disappointing' performance of Sub-Saharan African countries engaged in adjustment efforts is *not* the product of insufficient policy reform. It is, above all, the product of initial conditions (low levels of development), and of insufficient external support (net of adverse external shocks). Increased debt relief and expanded official development assistance will be necessary. The need for longer-term perspectives and sustained resource flows suggests a relatively diminished future role for the IMF in Sub-Saharan Africa. Expanded external resource flows must be accompanied by improved mechanisms for policy dialogue, broader participation in it, and the development of local 'ownership' of policies and programmes.

Structural Adjustment and Beyond in Sub-Saharan Africa edited by Rolph van der Hoeven and Fred van der Kraaij (1994) arose from a Netherlands-based seminar on structural adjustment in Sub-Saharan Africa held in 1993. This seminar unavoidably covered much of the same ground as the UNICEF conference reported above. But it had a focus of its own, namely the state of the art with regard to research on the impact of structural adjustment, and how research on structural adjustment could contribute better to policy-making. The papers of the seminar have been published together with an extensive record of the discussion and two literature reports on research on adjustment and on industry in Africa.

In his paper Paul Mosley criticizes examples of attempts to assess the effects of adjustment programmes, based on comparisons of before and after adjustment. In his view it is misleading to treat what he calls 'the amalgam' of policy changes commonly referred to as 'structural adjustment' as a unity. There are enormous variations in the packages prescribed: some are centred on trade liberalization, some on agricultural reform, some on public enterprise reform, some on all of these. In the second place, there was for political reasons tremendous diversity in the implementation of the conditions described. And in comparing adjusting with non-adjusting countries, as the World Bank has done in some of its reviews, it should be remembered that a great deal of adjustment was carried out by 'non-adjusting countries' (i.e. countries without adjustment loans). The latter comment is addressed to Elbadawi, a World Bank paper (1992), which showed that in Sub-Saharan Africa the economic performance of non-adjusting countries has been uniformally higher than for the group of early intensive adjustment lending countries.

Mosley stresses that in Africa where so many of the preconditions for drawing welfare conclusions from economic theory are lacking, any worthwhile evaluation of structural adjustment experience must 'decompose' that experience into its component parts. His own preliminary results of such an approach (notwithstanding what he calls the fragility of the data base) lead to the following conclusions for some of these components. 1) Tariff reduction and reductions in credit and agricultural input subsidies are policy instruments which may have negative effectiveness in the African context. 2) The price-based policy instruments typically recommended can work only if other variables which he describe as 'catalysts' are also present (a competitive real exchange rate, policy stability and a rising tendency to government spending are those which he has examined).

Mosley includes in his presentation a critique of David Sahn's proposition that 'a commitment to major policy reform has had strongly positive distributional implications and is essential to protect the poor in the face of an economic crisis'. Mosley states that this conclusion does not emerge from Sahn's time series on the welfare of African smallholders, but emerges from an a priori argument where many of the linkages have yet to be tested.

As to the second focus of the Netherlands' seminar, i.e. the role of research, the report of the discussions suggests more active and frequent interaction between researchers and policy-makers, while pointing to the limited research capacity in Africa. Furthermore the following research issues were proposed: the need for an improved data base, in particular gender-specific information; more research on the household sector and the informal sector; a third cluster of issues concerning the relation between macroeconomic policies and the functioning of the microeconomy; structural transformation as an important research subject; the role of the state (institutions, expenditures, foreign agencies); the role of external influences and external finance; evaluation of adjustment policies (with a strong advocacy, for methodological reasons, of country case studies).

David E. Sahn is the manager of a large research effort jointly sponsored by Cornell University and USAID to examine the issue of adjustment and poverty in Sub-Saharan Africa. He and his associates have generally had a rather positive view of the impact of economic reform on the poor, while stressing the importance of other measures. His conclusions and recommendations have most recently been summed-up in a paper *Economic Reform in Africa: A Foundation for Poverty Alleviation* written together with Paul Dorosh and Stephen Younger (September 1994). Their analysis suggests that on balance the economic policy reforms have not had a deleterious impact on the poor. 'This is not to say that there are not losers as a result of reform. Likewise losers may include some of the poor and vulnerable... The biggest losers, however, are the urban elite who had access to official markets and prices.' This explains why the pace of reforms has been retarded by these elements of society.

Sahn attempts to explain the divergence of these findings from more commonly held perceptions. First, there is often a failure to distinguish between the recession, brought on by egregious policy distortions and unfavourable external conditions, and the subsequent policy response. Second, there is often a failure to distinguish between the receipt of adjustment loans and actual policy reform. Third, few countries have shown a strong commitment to correcting bad policy. An additional point in explaining the results is their attention to the role of parallel markets and the underground economy, while most research has examined movements in official markets.

At the same time the authors recognize that, for the countries that have adjusted, the resulting economic gains have been marginal in most cases. Adjustment programmes have not generated rapid and sustainable growth, nor have they resulted in a radical redistribution of existing resources in favour of the poor.

The unsatisfactory results of economic reform in part reflect the limited purview and scope of balance-of-payments support and of its related conditions. The weakness in actual design of adjustment lending by the external sponsors undoubtedly contributes to this. So too does the failure to incorporate complementary measures to promote economic growth early enough in the process (human resource development, investments to facilitate the growth of the private sector such as infrastructure and improved legal and regulatory frameworks): 'Investment projects and technical assistance may be better modalities than balance-of-payments support to foster the development of human resources, augment physical capital and improve the efficiency and fairness of markets. Furthermore, projects offer greater opportunity for addressing non-economic social and cultural factors that contribute to poverty and deprivation, such as gender discrimination...'

The authors show great concern for the utilization of balance-of-payments support, where they find arguments for greater donor involvement. But this raises a number of problems (limitations in terms of alternative institutional structures to absorb local currency generated by large foreign capital inflows, and broader issues such as state sovereignty). The lack of recipient commitment to reform is an acute problem. 'Greater policy dialogue and consensus building, incorporating stakeholders from without government in the process, are the types of approaches recognized to promote such ownership. Encouraging government participation and enthusiasm in the reform process is, however, difficult to motivate from the outside...'

A very recent research paper on adjustment by Tony Killick builds upon his many theoretical and empirical contributions to the debate on adjustment, in particular the role of the IMF. Best known is his book *The Adaptive Economy: Adjustment Policies in Low-Income Countries* (1993). The paper was contributed in September 1994 to a conference on the occasion of 'fifty years after Bretton Woods'. His topic was conditionality and the adjustment-development connection.

Killick starts out by stating that the record of the results achieved in developing countries by the structural adjustment programmes of the Bretton Woods institutions is 'patchy, at best'. He justifies this statement by a list of generalizations among the empirical literature on the consequences of adjustment programmes: 1) Programmes have high mortality or interruption rates (statistics presented). 2) Programmes have limited revealed ability to achieve their own objectives. The recent World Bank book on adjustment (1994) shows as many adjusting countries slipping back as those accelerating their growth. One reason is that the programmes are associated with reduced investment levels. 3) While the types of economic policy change favoured by the IFIs are associated with economic performance, there is little evidence of a strong connection between adjustment programmes and implementation of such policy changes. 4) The evidence reveals that the programmes have only modest impact on key policy variables and even less on institutions (again with reference to the Bank publication). 5) Some of the policy changes would have been introduced in any case. 6) The most successfully adjusting group of countries are the East Asian 'miracle countries', but their efforts owe little or nothing to IFI adjustment programmes.

Killick then tries to suggest solutions to the puzzle as to why adjustment programmes have such limited potency. Among the multiple causes he concentrates on two, to argue that programmes would be strengthened if they were based on a more satisfactory appreciation of the linkage between medium-term adjustment and long-run development and that programmes are far too reliant on a mode of achieving change (conditionality) of very limited proven effectiveness.

In Killick's opinion the IFIs view adjustment as a catharsis preliminary to the resumption of growth and development. But adjustment is a continuous adaptation to many types of changes. There is some congruence in the policy implications of these two views. But they also diverge in important ways. Adjustment programmes can be seen as too narrow, neglecting important aspects of the task of raising economies' flexibility (for example, IFI programmes rarely contain much of an industrial policy).

Killick then turns to the issue of conditionality, first by showing the increase in the number of conditions imposed in Bank and Fund programmes. He then notes that bilateral donors have followed this and have moreover broadened the character of conditions (e.g. to include political reforms). In his view external determination of programmes will weaken the sense of ownership. He argues that the 'conditionality explosion' aggravates the already formidable pressures on the cadre of key administrators. Additional constraints on the effectiveness of conditionality are identified. The IFIs suffer from resource problems, the most serious of which is inadequate knowledge. In face of this the danger is that they will fall back on institutional orthodoxies. This knowledge constraint is compounded by problems with staffing (numbers and turnover). Finance is a third resource constraint (too many under-funded programmes).

Killick suggests that the IFIs should recognize that their main contribution to successful adjustment has been through their influence on the contemporary intellectual climate in which policy issues are debated and through persuasion of governments by means of regular contacts. The IFIs need a broader view and a longer time horizon. Above all, they should be willing to say 'No' more often to governments with weak commitment to reform, and should insist that all programmes be prepared by the borrowing gover..ments. This would mean more selectivity in funding, and more technical assistance to enhance local capabilities, and less imposition. The IFIs should be more pragmatic and pluralistic in their assessments of the programmes submitted.

The final contribution to the debate to be reviewed is a fair and critical analysis of the World Bank publication *Adjustment in Africa* written by the Tanzanian economist Nguyuru H.I. Lipumba under the title *Africa Beyond Adjustment* and published by the Washington Overseas Development Council in 1994. Lipumba examines the strengths and weaknesses of the World Bank report in order to reach conclusions of his own on what should be done to strengthen the forces of development in Africa. Before presenting his 'programme for Africa' it may be worthwhile to note his contribution to the methodological discussion about the assessment of the effects of adjustment as offered in the World Bank study.

Lipumba first of all criticizes the Bank for measuring the impact in terms of the change in the growth rate of per capita GDP. No similar measurement is reported by the Bank for the growth of agricultural output, manufacturing value added, exports, saving and investment. In fact some of the tables in the World Bank report show no significant improvement in agricultural or manufacturing output or in saving performance for those countries which had large improvements in macroeconomic policy performance. He also disputes the findings of the Bank on the insignificant impact of external flows, enabling increased imports. 'The econometric results reported can be misleading; a more appropriate econometric analysis of the determinants of economic growth should have taken a longer time frame.'

Such a long-term view is reflected in his identification of the major shortcoming of structural adjustment programmes as a lack of coherent linkage between the short-term structural adjustment programmes as a lack of coherent linkage between the short-term objectives of attaining balance-of-payments equilibrium and improving allocative efficiency and the long-term objective of sustainable development. The World Bank report does not analyze this link. Reforms have focused on policy-induced distortions that discourage efficiency in the use of resources and have ignored the physical bottlenecks that require investment expenditure. The report ignores the role of the state in planning public investment expenditures by anticipating sectors and areas that are likely to be socially and privately profitable, i.e. choosing 'the winners'.

Lipumba also shows with examples how the World Bank has overloaded the weak institutional systems in Africa with too many reforms in an inappropriate sequence. The linchpin for making adjustment policies supportive of a long-term strategy is the establishment of a 'developmental state' - one that respects its budget constraints, raises adequate revenues by imposing taxes that do not excessively distort incentives to save and produce efficiently, mobilizes external assistance, and allocates expenditures in priority areas. Politics as usual - in which the state is used to distribute patronage and extract rents - will condemn Africa to permanent poverty.

He is so insistent on this African determination that he concludes that 'if a country does not have a development program of its own, external assistance should be confined mainly to humanitarian aid to support nongovernmental organizations operating in that country.'

4. Concluding Remarks

It may be said that much of the debate on economic adjustment policies in recent years has been groping for a new foundation for policy formulation in Sub-Saharan Africa. There is no agreement on the impact of economic reforms so far - some defend the achievements, some continue to be highly critical of the basic tenets of the approach. But there is across this divide a common acceptance of the hard fact that results have been disappointingly small and that the reform process is fragile. And most seem to agree that stabilization as well as adjustment efforts have had much too short a time horizon. The time has now come to assert the consequences of these conclusions for Africa's long-term development needs, and to turn these into appropriate policies, with appropriate external support.

The major controversy - also for the long-run vision - relates to the role of the state in economic development. Statements on this topic have become more nuanced, but there is still a great gap in opinion.

The consequences drawn for official bilateral development assistance in these studies are not clear. But it is important that the issues in this area should be more actively discussed: Has aid had a positive impact or has it substituted for domestic efforts? What modalities of aid lead to greater aid effectiveness? How can recipient ownership of reforms be promoted? How can aid dependency be avoided or reduced?

The IMF and the World Bank seem to continue to assert their role as lead agencies when it comes to adjustment programmes. But the disappointing results over such a long period are stimulating a number of bilateral donors to become more articulate with regard to the design of these programmes and the role of bilateral aid in implementing them - and supplementing them with long-term measures. Even if this is not reflected in most of the contributions, this bilateral assertion is understandable, given the fact that the bulk of external financing in many African countries is coming from these sources.

In many contributions to the debate it is suggested that the very term 'adjustment' should be dropped in favour of 'development policy'. And it seems clear that many uses of the term 'adjustment' actually blur an understanding of the broader issues of development. But whatever happens in this respect, external policy influence expressed through a wide set of conditionalities seems to remain a more or less permanent feature of Africa's relation to the world, despite a stagnation in aid flows.

References

Cornia, G.A. & G. Helleiner (eds.). 1994. *From Adjustment to Development in Africa: Conflict, Controversy, Convergence, Consensus?* New York: St. Martin's Press.

Elbadawi, I.A., D. Ghura & G. Uwujaren. 1992. *Why Structural Adjustment Has Not Succeeded in Sub-Saharan Africa.* Washington, DC: World Bank Working Paper WPS 1000.

Hadjimichael, M.T., D. Ghura, M. Mühleisen, R. Nord & E.M. Uçer. 1994. *Sub-Saharan Africa: Growth, Savings and Investment, 1986-93.* Washington, DC: International Monetary Fund, Occasional Paper 118.

Killick, T. 1993. *The Adaptive Economy: Adjustment Policies in Low-income Economies.* Washington, DC and London: World Bank and Overseas Development Institute.

Killick, T. 1993. *Conditionality and the Adjustment-development Connection.* Washington, DC: International Monetary Fund & World Bank. Presentation to conference: Fifty Years after Bretton Woods (Madrid, September).

Lipumba, N.H.I. 1994. *Africa Beyond Adjustment.* Washington, DC: Overseas Development Council, Policy Essay No. 15.

Mosley, P., J. Harrigan & J. Toye. 1991. *Aid and Power: The World Bank and Policy-based Lending.* Vol. 1, *Analysis and Policy Proposals.* Vol. 2, *Case Studies.* London: Routledge.

Sahn, D.E., P. Dorosh & S. Younger. 1994. *Economic Reform in Africa: A Foundation for Policy Reform.* Ithaca, NY: Cornell Food and Nutrition Policy Program.

Schadler, S., F. Rozwadowski, S. Tiwari & D.O. Robinson. 1993. *Economic Adjustment in Low-income Countries. Experience under the Enhanced Structural Adjustment Facility.* Washington, DC: International Monetary Fund, Occasional Paper 106.

Tarp, F. 1993. *Stabilization and Structural Adjustment. Macroeconomic Frameworks for Analyzing the Crisis in Sub-Saharan Africa.* London: Routledge.

Taylor, L. 1993. *The Rocky Road to Reform.* Helsinki: WIDER.

Van der Hoeven, R. & F. van der Kraaj. 1994. *Structural Adjustment and Beyond in Sub-Saharan Africa. Research and Policy Issues.* The Hague and London: Ministry of Foreign Affairs (DGIS) and James Currey.

World Bank. 1988. *Report on Adjustment Lending.* Document R 88-199. Washington, DC: World Bank.

World Bank. 1990. *Report on Adjustment Lending II: Policies for the Recovery of Growth.* Document R 90-99. Washington, DC: World Bank.

World Bank. 1992a. *The Third Report on Adjustment Lending: Private and Public Resources for Growth.* Washington, DC: World Bank.

World Bank. 1992b. *World Bank Structural and Sectoral Adjustment Operations: The Second OED Overview.* Washington, DC: World Bank, Operations Evaluation Department Report, No. 10870.

World Bank. 1993. *Adjustment in Sub-Saharan Africa. Selected Findings from OED Evaluations.* Washington, DC: World Bank, Operations Evaluation Department Report, No. 12155.

World Bank. 1994. *Adjustment in Africa. Reforms, Results, and the Road Ahead.* Oxford: Oxford University Press.

Index